INTRODUCTION TO THE OLD TESTAMENT
AS SCRIPTURE

BREVARD S. CHILDS

INTRODUCTION TO THE OLD TESTAMENT AS SCRIPTURE

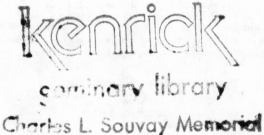

FORTRESS PRESS
PHILADELPHIA

First American Edition by Fortress Press 1979

Third printing 1982

Library of Congress Cataloging in Publication Data

Childs, Brevard S.
    Introduction to the Old Testament as Scripture.

    Includes bibliographies.
    1. Bible. O.T.—Introductions. I. Title.
BS1140.2.C48   221.6   78-14665
ISBN 0-8006-0532-2

9653A82   Printed in the United States of America   1-532

To Ann
whose profound faith
and exuberant love of life
have brought constant joy
and surprise

CONTENTS

PART THREE

THE FORMER PROPHETS

PART SIX

CONCLUSION

PREFACE

Twenty-five years ago, when I returned home from four years of graduate study in Europe, the area within the field of Old Testament which held the least attraction for me was Introduction. I supposed that most of the major problems had already been resolved by the giants of the past. Even allowing for the inevitable process of refinement and modification, could one really expect anything new in this area? I was content to leave the drudgery of writing an Introduction to someone else with more *Sitzfleisch*.

Two decades of teaching have brought many changes in my perspective. Having experienced the demise of the Biblical Theology movement in America, the dissolution of the broad European consensus in which I was trained, and a widespread confusion regarding theological reflection in general, I began to realize that there was something fundamentally wrong with the foundations of the biblical discipline. It was not a question of improving on a source analysis, of discovering some unrecognized new genre, or of bringing a redactional layer into sharper focus. Rather, the crucial issue turned on one's whole concept of the study of the Bible itself. I am now convinced that the relation between the historical critical study of the Bible and its theological use as religious literature within a community of faith and practice needs to be completely rethought. Minor adjustments are not only inadequate, but also conceal the extent of the dry rot.

It is also clear to me that the issues at stake cannot be accurately described with the traditional categories of 'liberal' and 'conservative'. My dissatisfaction has been just as strong with the approach on the 'left' of Wellhausen, Gunkel, and Eissfeldt, as it has been with that on the 'right' of Hengstenberg, Vigouroux, and Cassuto. Nor have the countless mediating positions of Delitzsch, Lagrange, Kaufmann, Engnell, and Albright reached to the heart of the prob-

lem. The basic hermeneutical assumptions are shared by both left
and right within the full spectrum of biblical scholarship. To
determine the degree of a narrative's historicity, whether slightly
more or less, or to fix the age of a composition as somewhat older or
younger, makes little difference in one's total understanding of the
literature. Both left and right work within the parameters established for the discipline by the beginning of the nineteenth century.
Is it possible to break out of this sterile impasse and to enter into a
post-critical era?

This Introduction attempts to offer a different model for the
discipline from that currently represented. It seeks to describe the
form and function of the Hebrew Bible in its role as sacred scripture
for Israel. It argues the case that the biblical literature has not been
correctly understood or interpreted because its role as religious
literature has not been correctly assessed.

The approach which is being proposed is not to be confused with
homiletics, but is descriptive in nature. It is not confessional in the
sense of consciously assuming tenets of Christian theology, but
rather it seeks to describe as objectively as possible the canonical
literature of ancient Israel which is the heritage of both Jew and
Christian. If at times the description becomes theological in its
terminology, it is because the literature itself requires it. The frequent reference to the term 'canonical' is not to suggest that a new
exegetical technique is being developed. Rather, the term denotes a
context from which the literature is being understood. The subject
matter of the Introduction is the received and authoritative writings of ancient Israel which constitute a canon. This analysis is an
attempt to hear the biblical text in the terms compatible with the
collection and transmission of the literature as scripture.

I am acutely aware of the dangers inherent in any proposal
which tries to challenge the critical methodologies which have been
carefully developed over the last two hundred years. The biblical
field has grown weary of hastily-constructed theories which advocate change of direction, and which in most cases have done more
harm than good. Even the serious endeavour to reverse the direction of biblical scholarship which emerged in the twenties and thir-
ties of this century in the aftermath of the First World War, and is
usually associated with the name of Karl Barth, must be judged
unsuccessful in terms of any lasting impact on the study of the
Bible. For this reason I have felt the responsibility of placing my

Old Testament analysis firmly within the context of the present scholarly debate, lest it be too lightly dismissed as ignorant or pious idiosyncrasy.

It would be arrogant and completely untrue to suggest that all the work of generations of critical scholarship has produced little of value. The depth to which my own understanding of the Old Testament has been formed by those who preceded me is everywhere evident. I am much indebted to my own teachers of Old Testament, H. S. Gehman, J. W. Wevers, W. Eichrodt, W. Baumgartner, and G. von Rad, as well as numerous colleagues in America, Britain, Europe and Israel from whom I have learned. Nevertheless, the deep-seated confusion within the discipline remains, and it has often rendered meaningless important observations, gained through years of research, because of the inability to establish a proper context from which to read the literature.

Finally, I would like to express my appreciation for a fellowship from the National Endowment of the Humanities which enabled me to complete my research at Cambridge University. Certain chapters of the book were first offered at Union Theological Seminary, Richmond as the Sprunt Lectures of 1972. I am grateful for the warm hospitality which I experienced on that occasion. I also owe a debt of gratitude to my friend, Gerald T. Sheppard, for much stimulation, insight, and encouragement. The book is dedicated to my wife, Ann, whose enormous contribution at every stage of the enterprise cannot be adequately measured.

ABBREVIATIONS

AB	The Anchor Bible, New York
AcOr	*Acta Orientalia*, Copenhagen
AfO	*Archiv für Orientforschung*, Berlin
AJSL	*American Journal of Semitic Languages*, Chicago
AJT	*American Journal of Theology*, Chicago
AnBib	Analecta Biblica, Rome
ANVAO	Avhandlingar utgitt av Det Norske Videnskaps-Akademi i Oslo
ArOr	*Archiv Orientální*, Prague
ARW	*Archiv für Religionswissenschaft*, Leipzig
ASTI	*Annual of the Swedish Theological Institute in Jerusalem*, Leiden
ATD	Das Alte Testament Deutsch, Göttingen
AThR	*Anglican Theological Review*, Evanston
BA	*Biblical Archaeologist*, New Haven, Missoula
BASOR	*Bulletin of the American Schools of Oriental Research*, New Haven
BAT	Botschaft des Alten Testaments, Stuttgart
BBB	Bonner biblische Beiträge, Bonn
BC	Biblical Commentary, eds. C. F. Keil, F. Delitzsch, Edinburgh
BETL	Bibliotheca Ephemeridum Theologicarum Lovaniensium, Paris, Gembloux
BGBE	Beiträge zur Geschichte der biblischen Exegese, Tübingen
BHH	*Biblisch-historisches Handwörterbuch*, eds. B. Reicke, L. Rost, Göttingen 1962–66
BHT	Beiträge zur historischen Theologie, Tübingen
Bibl	*Biblica*, Rome
BiblRes	*Biblical Research*, Chicago

BiLe	*Bibel und Leben*, Düsseldorf
BJRL	*Bulletin of the John Rylands Library*, Manchester
BK	Biblischer Kommentar, Neukirchen-Vluyn
BOuT	De Boeken van het Oude Testament, Roermond en Masseik
BSt	Biblische Studien, Neukirchen-Vluyn
BTB	*Biblical Theology Bulletin*, Rome
BWA(N)T	Beiträge zur Wissenschaft vom Alten (und Neuen) Testament, Leipzig, Stuttgart
BZ	*Biblische Zeitschrift*, Freiburg, Paderborn
BZAW	Beihefte zur *Zeitschrift für die alttestamentliche Wissenschaft*, Giessen, Berlin
BZNW	Beihefte zur *Zeitschrift für die neutestamentliche Wissenschaft*, Giessen, Berlin
CAH	*Cambridge Ancient History*, 1923–39; [3]1970ff.
Carpzov	J. G. Carpzov, *Introductio ad libros canonicos bibliorum Veteris Testamenti omnes*, Leipzig 1721
CAT	Commentaire de l'Ancien Testament, Neuchâtel
CB	Cambridge Bible for Schools and Colleges, Cambridge
CBQ	*Catholic Biblical Quarterly*, Washington
CeB	Century Bible, London
CNEB	Cambridge Commentary on the New English Bible
COuT	Commentar op het Oude Testament, Kampen
CSS	Cursus Scripturae Sacrae, Paris
CTM	*Concordia Theological Monthly*, St Louis
DACL	*Dictionnaire d'archéologie chrétienne et de liturgie*, Paris, 1907-53
Darling	James Darling, *Cyclopaedia Bibliographia*, London 1854
DB	*A Dictionary of the Bible*, ed. J. Hastings, Edinburgh and New York 1900-4
DBS	*Dictionnaire de la Bible, Supplément*, Paris 1928 ff.
DS	*Dictionnaire de spiritualité*, Paris 1932ff.
Dtr.	Deuteronomistic
DThC	*Dictionnaire de théologie catholique*, Paris 1899-1972
EB	*Encyclopaedia Biblica* (Hebrew), Jerusalem 1950ff.
ÉB	Études bibliques, Paris
EH	Exegetisches Handbuch zum Alten Testament, Münster
EJ	*Encyclopaedia Judaica*, Jerusalem 1971-2
ET	English translation

ETL	*Ephemerides Theologicae Lovanienses*, Louvain
EvQu	*Evangelical Quarterly*, London, Exeter
EvTh	*Evangelische Theologie*, Munich
EVV	English versions
ExB	The Expositor's Bible, London and New York
ExpT	*Expository Times*, Edinburgh
FRLANT	Forschungen zur Religion und Literatur des Alten und Neuen Testaments, Göttingen
FS	*Festschrift*
GSAT	*Gesammelte Schriften des Alten Testaments*
HAT	Handbuch zum Alten Testament, Tübingen
Herm	Hermeneia, Philadelphia
HKAT	Handkommentar zum Alten Testament, Göttingen
HS	Die Heilige Schrift des Alten Testaments, ed. Feldmann, Bonn
HSAT	*Die Heilige Schrift des Alten Testaments*, ed. A. Bertholet, 2 vols., Tübingen ⁴1922–23
HSM	Harvard Semitic Monographs, Cambridge, Mass., Missoula
HTR	*Harvard Theological Review*, Cambridge, Mass.
HUCA	*Hebrew Union College Annual*, Cincinnati
IB	*The Interpreter's Bible*, 12 vols., Nashville 1951–57
ICC	The International Critical Commentary, Edinburgh and New York
IDB	*The Interpreter's Dictionary of the Bible*, Nashville 1962
IDB Suppl	*The Interpreter's Dictionary of the Bible, Supplementary Volume*, Nashville 1976
IEJ	*Israel Exploration Journal*, Jerusalem
Interp	*Interpretation*, Richmond, Va.
JAAR	*Journal of the American Academy of Religion*, Boston
JANE	*Journal of Ancient Near Eastern Studies of Columbia University*, New York
JAOS	*Journal of the American Oriental Society*, New Haven
JB	La Bible de Jerusalem, Paris
JBL	*Journal of Biblical Literature*, Philadelphia, Missoula
JCS	*Journal of Cuneiform Studies*, New Haven
JE	*Jewish Encylopaedia*, New York 1901–06
JJS	*Journal of Jewish Studies*, London
JNES	*Journal of Near Eastern Studies*, Chicago
JPOS	*Journal of Palestine Oriental Society*, Jerusalem
JQR	*Jewish Quarterly Review*, London, Philadelphia
JR	*Journal of Religion*, Chicago

JSOT	*Journal for the Study of the Old Testament*, Sheffield
JSS	*Journal of Semitic Studies*, Manchester
JTS	*Journal of Theological Studies*, Oxford
Jud	*Judaica*, Zürich
KAT	Kommentar zum Alten Testament, Leipzig, Gütersloh
KeH	Kurzgefasstes exegetisches Handbuch zum Alten Testament, Leipzig
KHC	Kurzer Hand-Commentar zum Alten Testament, Tübingen
KS(AT)	*Kleine Schriften (des Alten Testaments)*
KuD	*Kerygma und Dogma*, Göttingen
KV	Korte Verklaring der Heilige Schrift, Kampen
LBC	The Layman's Bible Commentary, Richmond
LCHS	A Commentary on the Holy Scripture, ed. J. P. Lange, Edinburgh and New York
LXX	Septuagint
MGWJ	*Monatschrift für Geschichte und Wissenschaft des Judentums*, Breslau
MPG	J.-P. Migne, Patrologia, Series Graeca, Paris
MPL	J.-P. Migne, Patrologia, Series Latina, Paris
MT	Masoretic Text
NCeB	New Century Bible, London
NEB	New English Bible, Oxford and Cambridge 1970
NedThT	*Nederlands Theologisch Tijdschrift*, Wageningen
NF	Neue Folge
NICOT	The New International Commentary on the Old Testament, Grand Rapids
NKZ	*Neue Kirchliche Zeitschrift*, Erlangen, Leipzig
NS	New series
NTS	*New Testament Studies*, Cambridge
OLZ	*Orientalistische Literaturzeitung*, Berlin
OTL	Old Testament Library, London and Philadelphia
OTS	*Oudtestamentische Studien*, Leiden
OuTWP	*Die Ou Testamentiese Werkgemeenskap in Suid-Afrika*, Pretoria
PAAJR	*Proceedings of the American Academy for Jewish Research*, Philadelphia
PEQ	*Palestine Exploration Quarterly*, London
PJB	*Palästinajahrbuch*, Berlin
POuT	De Prediking van het Oude Testament, Nijkerk
PTR	*Princeton Theological Review*, Princeton

RAC	*Reallexikon für Antike und Christentum*, Stuttgart 1950ff.
RB	*Revue biblique*, Paris
RE	*Realencyklopädie für protestantische Theologie und Kirche*, Leipzig [3]1896ff.
REJ	*Revue des études juives*, Paris
RES	*Revue des études sémitiques*, Paris
RGG	*Die Religion in Geschichte und Gegenwart*, Tübingen [2]1927-31; [3]1957-65
RHE	*Revue d'histoire ecclésiastique*, Louvain
RHPhR	*Revue d'histoire et de philosophie religieuses*, Strasbourg
RHR	*Revue de l'histoire des religions*, Paris
RQ	*Revue de Qumrân*, Paris
RSR	*Recherches de science religieuse*, Paris
RSV	Revised Standard Version of the Bible, London and New York 1952
RThPh	*Revue de théologie et de philosophie*, Lausanne
SAT	*Die Schriften des Alten Testaments*, 3 vols., Göttingen 1920–25
SB	La Sainte Bible, eds. L. Pirot and A. Clamer, Paris
SBL	Society of Biblical Literature, Philadelphia
SBT	Studies in Biblical Theology, London and Nashville
SC	Sources chrétiennes, Paris
ScEc	*Sciences ecclésiastiques*, Montreal
SEA	*Svensk Exegetisk Årsbok*, Lund
SJT	*Scottish Journal of Theology*, Edinburgh, Cambridge
SNVAO	*Skrifter utgitt av Det Norske Videnskaps-Akademi i Oslo*
SoBi	Sources bibliques, Paris
SonB	The Soncino Books of the Bible, Bournemouth
StANT	Studien zum Alten und Neuen Testament, Munich
StTh	*Studia Theologica*, Lund, Aarhus
SVT	*Supplements to Vetus Testamentum*, Leiden
SZ	*Kurzgefasster Kommentar*, eds. H. L. Strack and O. Zöckler, 9 vols., Nördlingen, Munich 1888–94
TB	Torch Bible Commentary, London
TDNT	*Theological Dictionary of the New Testament*, ET, Grand Rapids 1964-1976
ThB	Theologische Bücherei, Munich
TheolEx	Theologische Existenz heute, München
ThQ	*Theologische Quartalschrift*, Tübingen, Stuttgart
ThR	*Theologische Rundschau*, Tübingen
ThRev	*Theologische Revue*, Münster
ThSt	*Theological Studies*, Woodstock, Md.

ThStKr	*Theologische Studien und Kritiken*, Hamburg, Leipzig, Berlin
TLZ	*Theologische Literaturzeitung*, Leipzig
TOTC	Tyndale Old Testament Commentary, London
TU	Texte und Untersuchungen zur Geschichte der altchristlichen Literatur, Berlin
TWNT	*Theologisches Wörterbuch zum Neuen Testament*, ed. G. Kittel, Stuttgart 1932ff.
TZ	*Theologische Zeitschrift*, Basel
UF	*Ugaritforschungen*, Münster
USQR	*Union Seminary Quarterly Review*, New York
VF	*Verkündigung und Forschungen*, Munich
VT	*Vetus Testamentum*, Leiden
WC	Westminster Commentaries, London
WMANT	Wissenschaftliche Monographien zum Alten und Neuen Testament, Neukirchen-Vluyn
WO	*Die Welt Des Orients*, Göttingen
WuD	*Wort und Dienst*, Jahrbuch der theologischen Schule, Bethel
WZ	*Wissenschaftliche Zeitschrift*
ZAW	*Zeitschrift für die alttestamentliche Wissenschaft*, Giessen, Berlin
ZBK	Zürcher Bibelkommentare, Zürich
ZDMG	*Zeitschrift des Deutschen morgenländischen Gesellschaft*, Leipzig, Wiesbaden
ZDPV	*Zeitschrift des Deutschen Palästinavereins*, Wiesbaden
ZNW	*Zeitschrift für die neutestamentliche Wissenschaft*, Giessen, Berlin
ZTK	*Zeitschrift für Theologie und Kirche*, Tübingen
ZWTh	*Zeitschrift für wissenschaftliche Theologie*, Jena, Halle, Leipzig

When authors are referred to by name (or name and page) only, the reference will usually be to the work or works in the bibliography at the head of the chapter.

PART ONE

THE OLD TESTAMENT: INTRODUCTION

I

THE DISCIPLINE OF OLD TESTAMENT INTRODUCTION

Bibliography

B. W. **Anderson**, *Understanding the Old Testament*, Englewood Cliffs [3]1975, = *The Living World of the Old Testament*, London [3]1978; W. **Baumgartner**, 'Alttestamentliche Einleitung und Literaturgeschichte,' *ThR* NF 8, 1936, 179-222; 'Eine alttestamentliche Forschungsgeschichte', *ThR* NF 25, 1959, 93–110; A. **Bentzen**, *Introduction to the Old Testament*, 2 vols., Copenhagen [5]1959; 'Skandinavische Literatur zum Alten Testament 1939–1948', *ThR* NF 17, 1948–9, 273–328; J. **Bewer**, *The Literature of the Old Testament in its Historical Development*, New York 1922; F. **Bleek**, *An Introduction to the Old Testament* I, ET London 1869, 5–28; John **Bright**, 'Modern Study of Old Testament Literature', *The Bible and the Ancient Near East, Essays in Honor of W. F. Albright*, ed. G. E. Wright, Garden City, N.Y. and London 1961, 13–31; J. W. **Brown**, *The Rise of Biblical Criticism in America, 1800–1870*, Middletown, Conn. 1964; M. **Buber** and F. **Rosenzweig**, *Die Schrift und ihre Verdeutschung*, Berlin 1939; K. **Budde**, *Geschichte der althebräischen Literatur*, Leipzig [2]1909; J. **Buxtorf**, *Tiberias, sive commentarius masorethicus triplex*, Basel 1685.

L. **Cappellus**, *Arcanum punctationis revelatum; sive de punctorum vocalium et accentuum apud Hebraeos vera et germana antiquitate libri II*, Leiden 1624; *Critica Sacra, sive de variis quae in sacris Veteris Testamenti libris occurrunt lectionibus libri sex*, Paris 1650; J. G. **Carpzov**, *Introductio ad libros canonicos bibliorum Veteris Testamenti omnes*, Leipzig 1721; Flavius Magnus Aurelius **Cassiodorus**, *De institutione divinarum*, MPL 70; U. **Cassuto**, *The Documentary Hypothesis and the Composition of the Pentateuch*, Jerusalem [3]1959; T. K. **Cheyne**, *Founders of Old Testament Criticism*, London and New York 1893; B. S. **Childs**, 'Sensus Literalis: An Ancient and Modern Problem', *Beiträge zur alttestamentlichen Theologie, FS W. Zimmerli*, Göttingen 1976; R. E. **Clements**, *A Century of Old Testament Study*, London and Philadelphia 1976; R. **Cornely** et A. **Merk**, *Introductionis in S. Scripturae libros compendium*, Paris [12]1940; C. H. **Cornill**, *Einleitung in das Alte Testament*, 1891, ET London and New York 1907.

R. **Davidson** and A. R. C. **Leaney**, *Biblical Criticism, The Pelican Guide to*

Modern Theology, vol. 3, Harmondsworth 1970; Simon **De Vries**, *Bible and Theology in the Netherlands*, Wageningen 1968; F. **Delitzsch**, 'Über Begriff und Methode der sogennanten biblischen und insbesondere alttestamentlichen Einleitung', *Zeitschrift für Protestantismus und Kirche*, NF 28, Erlangen 1854, 133–90; L. **Diestel**, *Geschichte des Alten Testamentes in der christlichen Kirche*, Jena 1869; E. **Dobschütz**, 'The Abandonment of the Canonical Idea', *AJT* 19, 1915, 416ff.; H. **Donner**, 'Das Problem des Alten Testaments in der christlichen Kirche. Überlegungen zu Begriff und Geschichte der alttestamentlichen Einleitung', *Beiträge zur Theorie des neuzeitlichen Christentums, FS W. Trillhaas*, Berlin 1968, 37ff.; S. R. **Driver**, *Introduction to the Literature of the Old Testament*, Edinburgh 1891, ⁹1913; Louis Ellies **Dupin**, *Dissertatio praeliminaris de auctoribus librorum scripturae in Nova Bibliotheca auctorum ecclesiasticorum*, Paris 1688.

   J. G. **Eichhorn**, *Einleitung in das Alte Testament*, 3 vols., Leipzig 1780–3; 5 vols. ⁴1820–24; Otto **Eissfeldt**, *The Old Testament. An Introduction*, ET Oxford and New York 1965; Ivan **Engnell**, *Gamla Testamentet: en traditionshistorisk inledning*, I, Stockholm 1945; Matthias **Flacius** Illyricus, *Clavis Scripturae Sacrae*, Basel 1567; G. **Fohrer**, *Introduction to the Old Testament*, ET Nashville 1968, London 1970; Hans **Frei**, *The Eclipse of Biblical Narrative. A Study in Eighteenth and Nineteenth Century Hermeneutics*, New Haven 1974; J. **Goettsberger**, *Einleitung in das Alte Testament*, Freiburg 1928; N. **Gottwald**, *A Light to the Nations*, New York 1959; E. M. **Gray**, *Old Testament Criticism*, New York and London 1923; G. B. **Gray**, 'Bible, Old Testament Criticism', *The Encyclopaedia Britannica*, vol. 3, ¹¹1910–11, 857–65; W. H. **Green**, *General Introduction to the Old Testament. The Canon*, New York 1905; S. L. **Greenslade** *et al.* eds., *The Cambridge History of the Bible*, 3 vols, Cambridge and New York 1963–70; H. **Gunkel**, 'Die Grundprobleme der israelitischen Literaturgeschichte', *Reden und Aufsätze*, Göttingen 1913, 29–38; ET 'Fundamental Problems of Hebrew Literary History', *What Remains of the Old Testament*, New York and London 1928, 57–68; *Die israelitische Literatur*, Leipzig 1925, Darmstadt 1963.

   Hadrian, *Isagoge ad Sacras Scripturas*, MPG 98, 1273–1312; H. A. C. **Hävernick**, *Handbuch der historische-kritischen Einleitung in das Alte Testament*, 3 Teile, Erlangen 1839–56; parts translated as *A General Historico-Critical Introduction to the Pentateuch and to the Old Testament*, Edinburgh 1850; H. F. **Hahn**, *The Old Testament in Modern Research*, Philadelphia ²1966; R. K. **Harrison**, *Introduction to the Old Testament*, Grand Rapids 1969, London 1970, 3–82; J. H. **Heidegger**, *Enchiridion biblicum*, Zurich 1681, Jena ⁴1723; E. W. **Hengstenberg**, Beiträge zur Einleitung ins Alte Testament, 3 Bände, Berlin 1831–39; J. G. von **Herder**, *The Spirit of Hebrew Poetry*, 2 vols., ET Burlington, Vt. 1833; H. **Höpfl**, *Introductionis in sacros utriusque testamenti libros compendium*, 3 vols., Rome 1921, ⁶1958–63; T. H. **Horne**, *An Introduction to the Critical Study and Knowledge of the Holy Scriptures*, 3 vols. London 1818; ¹⁴1877; G. **Hornig**, *Die Anfänge der historisch-kritischen Theologie*, Göttingen 1961; H. **Hupfeld**, *Über Begriff und Methode der* *sogenannten biblischen Einleitung*, Marburg 1844; Johann **Jahn**, *Einleitung in die göttlichen Bücher des Alten Bundes*, 4 vols., Vienna ²1802; **Junilius** Africanus, *De partibus divinae legis*, MPL 68, 15–42.

Otto **Kaiser**, *Introduction to the Old Testament*, ET Oxford and Minneapolis 1975; **Karlstadt** (Andreas Rudolf Bodenstein), *De canonicis scripturis libellus*, 1520, reprinted in K. A. Credner, *Zur Geschichte des Kanons*, Halle 1847, 291ff.; Y. **Kaufmann**, *The Religion of Israel*, Chicago 1960, London 1961; C. F. **Keil**, *Manual of Historico-Critical Introduction to the Canonical Scriptures of the Old Testament*, 2 vols., ET Edinburgh 1892; W. **Klatt**, *Hermann Gunkel, Zu seiner Theologie der Religionsgeschichte und zur Entstehung der formgeschichtlichen Methode*, FRLANT 100, 1969; D. A. **Knight**, *Rediscovering the Traditions of Israel*, SBL Diss. Series 9, Missoula 1975; K. **Koch**, *The Growth of the Biblical Tradition. The Form-Critical Method*, ET New York and London 1969; H. **Koester**, 'New Testament Introduction. A Critique of a Discipline', *Christianity, Judaism, and other Greco-Roman Cults, Studies for Morton Smith*, Part I, Leiden 1975, 11–20; E. G. **Kraeling**, *The Old Testament since the Reformation*, London 1955, New York 1956; H.-J. **Kraus**, *Geschichte der historisch-kritischen Erforschung des Alten Testaments von der Reformation bis zur Gegenwart*, Neukirchen-Vluyn ²1969; W. G. **Kümmel**, *The New Testament: The History of the Investigation of its Problems*, ET Nashville 1972, London 1973; A. **Kuenen**, *Historisch-kritisch Onderzoek naar het ontstaan en de verzameling van de boeken des Ouden Verbonds*, 3 vols. Leiden 1861–65, ²1885–93; German trans. 1886–94; partial ET London 1865; C. **Kuhl**, 'Bibelwissenschaft des AT', *RGG*³ I, 1227ff.; M. G. **Kyle**, *The Deciding Voice of the Monuments in Biblical Criticism*, Oberlin, Ohio and London 1912, rev. ed. Oberlin 1924.

Jean **Le Clerc(Clericus)**, *Ars Critica*, Amsterdam 1696; A. **Lods**, *Histoire de la littérature hébraïque et juive depuis les origines jusqua'à la ruine de l'état juif (135 après J.-C.)*, Paris 1950; Henri de **Lubac**, *Exégèse Médiévale*, 4 vols., Paris 1959–64; Martin **Luther**, 'Prefaces to the Books of the Bible', *Luther's Works*, vol. 35, Philadelphia 1960, 227ff.; Max L. **Margolis**, *The Hebrew Scriptures in the Making*, Philadelphia 1922; J. D. **Michaelis**, *Einleitung in die göttlichen Schriften des Alten Bundes*, Hamburg 1787; Santes **Pagninus** Lucensis, *Isagogae ad sacras litteras liber unicus*, Lyons 1536; L. **Perlitt**, *Vatke und Wellhausen*, BZAW 94, 1965; R. H. **Pfeiffer**, *Introduction to the Old Testament*, New York 1941; Rolf **Rendtorff**, 'Literarkritik und Traditionsgeschichte', *EvTh* 27, 1967, 138–53; A. **Richardson**, 'The Rise of Modern Biblical Scholarship and the Recent Discussion of the Authority of the Bible', *The Cambridge History of the Bible* 3, Cambridge and New York 1963, 294–338; A. **Rivetus**, *Isagoge, seu introductio generalis, ad scripturam sacram veteris et novi testamenti*, Leiden 1627; A. **Robert** and A. **Feuillet**, *Introduction to the Old Testament*, ET of 2nd ed., New York 1968; Francis **Roberts**, *Clavis Bibliorum. The Key of the Bible*, London 1648; L. **Rost**, *Einleitung in das Alte Testament von D. Dr. Ernst Sellin*, Heidelberg ⁸1950.

S. **Sandmel**, *The Hebrew Scriptures. An Introduction to their Literature and*

Religious Ideas, New York 1963; A. H. **Sayce**, *The 'Higher Criticism' and the Verdict of the Monuments*, London and New York ²1894; F. **Schleiermacher**, *Brief Outline on the Study of Theology*, ET Richmond, Va. 1966; K. **Scholder**, *Ursprünge und Probleme der Bibelkritik im 17. Jahrhundert*, Munich 1966; E. **Sellin**, *Introduction to the Old Testament*, ET London and New York 1923; J. **Semler**, *Abhandlung von freier Untersuchung des Canons*, 4 vols., Halle 1771–76; R. **Simon**, *Histoire critique du vieux testament*, Rotterdam 1685, reprinted Frankfurt 1967; Sixtus **Senensis**, *Bibliotheca sancta*, Venice 1566; R. **Smend**, *Die Entstehung des Alten Testaments*, Stuttgart 1978; W. Robertson **Smith**, *The Old Testament in the Jewish Church*, Edinburgh and New York ²1892; J. A. **Soggin**, *Introduction to the Old Testament*, ET, OTL, 1976; Baruch de **Spinoza**, *Tractatus Theologico-Politicus*, Hamburg 1670, ET London 1887; C. **Steuernagel**, *Lehrbuch der Einleitung in das Alte Testament*, Tübingen 1912; F. **Stummer**, *Die Bedeutung Richard Simons für die Pentateuchkritik*, Münster 1912; M. **Walther**, *Officina biblica*, 1636, Wittenberg ³1703; J. **Weingreen**, G. **Vermes** et al., 'Interpretation, History of', *IDB Suppl.* 436ff.; J. **Wellhausen**, *Die Composition des Hexateuchs und der historischen Bücher des Alten Testament*, Berlin ³1899; *Einleitung in das Alte Testament von Friedrich Bleek*, Berlin ⁴1878; W. M. L. **de Wette**, *Lehrbuch der historisch-kritischen Einleitung in die kanonischen und apokryphischen Bücher des Alten Testamentes*, Berlin 1817, ⁷1852; ET Boston, Mass. 1843; R. D. **Wilson**, *A Scientific Investigation of the Old Testament*, Philadelphia 1926; E. J. **Young**, *An Introduction to the Old Testament*, Grand Rapids 1949.

1. The History of the Discipline

The main lines of the development leading up to the modern Old Testament Introduction are well known. The history has been frequently reviewed in various Introductions (Bleek, Fohrer, Harrison), in several excellent monographs (Hupfeld, Hahn), and in many encyclopaedia articles. Of the surveys of Old Testament scholarship which cover the development of the Introduction, the treatments of L. Diestel and H.-J. Kraus are especially thorough. (Admittedly, the role of British and American scholarship has been consistently underestimated.) In addition, there have appeared within recent years several detailed monographs on many of the key figures in the history (Simon, de Wette, Vatke, Delitzsch, Wellhausen, Kuenen, Gunkel) which have greatly deepened an understanding of the growth of the discipline. *However, the major critical issue is how to interpret this history.* Before addressing this central problem it seems advisable to review, at least briefly, the history of Old Testament Introduction.

The ancient period had no special genre of literature known as Introduction; obviously, however, many of the problems which later were relegated to this discipline within biblical studies were treated, such as textual problems, questions of authorship, and canon. Jerome emerges clearly as the most learned of the church fathers in respect to the Bible – Origen's influence was greatly reduced by the church's censure of him – and because of his knowledge of Hebrew and the Jewish traditions Jerome remained without a close rival for this period. In the introduction to his translation of the Old Testament, in his commentaries, and in his letters there is a wealth of material on introductory problems. In contrast, Augustine's contribution to biblical studies, especially in his *De doctrina christiana*, lay more in the field of hermeneutics than in Introduction. Also Hadrian's *Isagoge*, usually dated in the fifth century AD, focused on various grammatical and rhetorical features of the Old Testament rather than issues which would later be termed introductory. The biblical questions treated by Junilius (sixth century) and Cassiodorus (eighth century) were even more theologically oriented, but are significant for the attention given to the issue of canon, and also for occasional literary and textual observations.

The period of the Middle Ages saw enormous exegetical activity on the part of Jewish scholars, especially in the Talmudic codification of tradition, and in the establishment of the Hebrew text among the various Masoretic schools. Questions of authorship, canon, and text were vigorously pursued, but within a tightly prescribed traditional framework. Occasionally early examples of a historical critical approach to questions of authorship can be found in commentators such as Ibn Ezra and Gersonides, but again not in systematic enough fashion to do more than merely adumbrate the later Introduction. Among Christian medieval scholars Hugh and Andrew of St Victor and Nicholas of Lyra mediated Jewish exegesis based on a study of the Hebrew text, but did not break new ground beyond Jerome when it came to questions of Introduction.

The sixteenth century saw new life infused into the study of the Old Testament, both from the side of the Renaissance and the Reformation. Pagninus' *Isagogae* (1536) collected and passed on much of the traditional ecclesiastical material respecting the Bible which included hermeneutics and theology, but it added a new precision to the study of grammar and text which had arisen from the rebirth of humanistic studies. An even more useful book in

terms of discussing questions of authorship, content, and canonical
status was Sixtus Senensis' *Bibliotheca sancta* (1566). The author
generally followed the traditional perspective of Jewish and Christian interpretation, but he also registered quite objectively differing
opinions on controversial matters, such as the authorship of Deut.
34. Among Roman Catholic interpreters new attention was devoted
to the Hebrew text by such scholars as Cajetan and Vatablus.
However, the major contribution to the discipline of Introduction
was the publication of the Complutensian Polyglot Bible (1514–17)
which dramatized the new philological interest and set the stage for
critical biblical scholarship in the field of Old Testament.

Martin Luther's enormous impact on the study of the Bible cannot be confined to his own publications, but includes the religious
movement which he initiated and which was characterized by its
great seriousness toward the Bible. Luther's attempt to free the
study of the Bible from the restrictions imposed by ecclesiastical
tradition bore immediate fruit. Moreover, his translation of the
Bible into German, his commentaries, sermons, and countless
theological treatises on scripture are without a rival in sheer energy,
insight, and learning. In terms of introductory questions as later
defined, Luther's contribution was slight. In his preface to various
Old Testament books he focused almost entirely on the biblical
content in its relation to broad theological issues, and only in passing commented on the language, text, and order of the laws and
prophecies (cf. Isaiah). Nevertheless, one can sense a new freedom
over against accepted tradition, as, for example, in his remarks on
the book of Esther.

Among Luther's many students and associates there was often
more concern with introductory questions. Karlstadt's early treatise on the canon (1520) not only distinguished various categories of
authority within the Old Testament, but raised critical questions
respecting the authorship of the Pentateuch. However, the poten-
tial impact of Karlstadt's research was lost because of controversy
on other theological issues. Melanchthon's several Old Testament
commentaries showed his humanistic training with close attention
to language and idiom. Literary questions of style and language in
particular were studied by Matthias Flacius as an integral part of
his hermeneutical study. However, one can hardly speak of a break
with the tradition in terms of questions of Introduction. The new
influence came in the change of theological method which only

gradually affected the issues of Old Testament Introduction. The major Lutheran biblical scholars of the sixteenth century continued along the traditional lines when critical issues were involved (e.g. Bugenhagen, Brenz, Strigel).

John Calvin's concern to interpret the biblical text according to its literal sense employed an exegetical method which was very similar to his earlier study of Seneca. It resulted in a more consistent attention to questions of text, authorship, and composition than shown by Luther. Calvin cautiously questioned the authorship of the books of Joshua and Samuel, demonstrating a willingness to leave issues undecided which he considered to be peripheral. He also differed from a later generation of orthodox Protestant scholars in holding the Hebrew vowel points to be of later origin than the consonants. At least for Calvin, such introductory questions in no way compromised his complete insistence on *sola scriptura*. As in the case of Luther, Calvin's impact on a whole generation of biblical scholars – one thinks of W. Musculus, Bucer, Pellican, Mercier, Vermigli – was immediate and remained a major force in shaping the new direction throughout the seventeenth century.

The sixteenth century had seen the rise of a new understanding of the Bible which had emerged from the impetus of the Renaissance and Reformation, but it was left to the seventeenth century, to the second and third generation of post-Reformation scholars, to lay the foundation of the modern Old Testament Introduction. The form developed was the *critica sacra* (it was sometimes called *introductio* or *isagoge*) and it handled questions of text, canon, and hermeneutics in a systematic fashion. However, it developed these topics, at least at first, within the structure of orthodox Protestant dogmatics. A classic example was André Rivetus' *Isagoge* (1627) which bore the subtitle, *Introductio generalis ad scripturam sacram*. Among the Lutherans M. Walther's learned volume, *Officina biblica* (1636), not only discussed the traditional issues, but offered a detailed analysis of each book in a manner which adumbrated the 'special introduction' of the nineteenth century. Among the Reformed wing of Protestantism J. H. Heidegger's *Enchiridion* provided an unusually lucid analysis of the structure and inner movement of each biblical book. In England a similar task was skilfully executed by Francis Roberts in his well-known volume, *Clavis Bibliorum* (1648).

The *critica sacra* continued well into the eighteenth century and included such famous authors as J. Le Clerc and L. Cappellus. By the time it was replaced as a form of Introduction the orthodox confessional framework which it had once supported had been badly damaged, and a very different understanding of the Old Testament had emerged. Increasingly, this type of biblical-theological manual had felt the need to engage in a defensive apologetic to meet the newer questions regarding the Bible which had begun to emerge from all sides. The last great work of this genre which summarized the position of orthodox Lutheranism was J. G. Carpzov's *Introductio ad libros canonicos bibliorum Veteris Testamenti omnes* (1721). In spite of its great erudition and impressive thoroughness, its constant polemic revealed how much the traditional position regarding the Old Testament had been pushed into a defensive, holding action.

The rise of the modern historical study of the Old Testament must be seen in connection with the entire intellectual revolution which occurred during the late sixteenth and early seventeenth centuries, and which issued in a radically different understanding of God, man, and the world (cf. K. Scholder). However, in terms of the development of the discipline of Old Testament Introduction certain key figures played a decisive role in opening up a series of new questions. First, the integrity of the Hebrew text was seriously undermined by Cappellus who was able to demonstrate to the satisfaction of an increasing number of scholars that the Masoretic text had suffered considerable corruption and that its vowel points had originated in medieval times rather than being coterminus with the consonantal text. Secondly, Spinoza's famous book, *Tractatus Theologico-Politicus* (1670) dealt a hard blow to the traditional Jewish theories of biblical composition on which especially orthodox Protestantism had built its theology by rejecting all claims of an authoritative scripture and demanding that all theories be rationally tested. He then proposed historical and psychological explanations of material which had previously been relegated to the supernatural, such as prophecy and miracles. Thirdly, Richard Simon's brilliant book, *Histoire Critique du Vieux Testament* (1685) sought to develop a genuine literature history of the Old Testament which went far beyond the sporadic observations of his predecessors. Above all, he sought to trace the process of growth and change within the literature which no longer treated the Old Testament as a unified and closed body of sacred writings. By extending the history of the literature into the process of collection he also proposed a historical understanding of the development of the Jewish canon. Fourthly, the crucial issue of the canon, first raised in a new way by Simon, was brought to a head in the epoch-making volume of Johann Semler, *Abhandlung von freier Untersuchung des Canons* (1771–76). He succeeded in seriously damaging the central pillar on which Protestant orthodoxy – to a lesser degree Catholicism – had sought to construct its house. Semler argued that the theological interpretation of the Hebrew canon as a unified, accepted body of authoritative Jewish writings rested upon historical misconceptions, and that it should be replaced by a strictly historical definition whose content would be established according to its true historical development.

By the middle of the eighteenth century a variety of new forces had entered the field which not only repudiated the older traditional categories of Christian dogma, but also sought to break out of the older sterile rationalism, still strongly represented in Europe and Britain. In terms of Old Testament Introduction, the influence of J. G. Herder was somewhat indirect, affecting more immediately the areas of hermeneutics and exegesis. Nevertheless, the implications of Herder's recovery of the aesthetic and historical dimensions of Old Testament literature were soon to be felt.

Usually, and with good reason, the credit for structuring the first truly modern, historical critical Introduction to the Old Testament goes to Johann Gottfried Eichhorn, whose massive three-volume *Einleitung* – later expanded to five – began to appear in 1780. In the preceding generation J. D. Michaelis had vainly sought to stretch the traditional ecclesiastical understanding of the Old Testament in such a way as to make room for the newer learning. Eichhorn chose a different path. He exploited aggressively the full insights of the newer learning in the construction of a fresh synthesis which broke decisively with the traditional approach, while at the same time continuing the exhaustive handling of detailed questions which had been characteristic of the older *critica sacra*.

Eichhorn combined the insights of several of his predecessors. He devoted an entire section to an exhaustive investigation of the history of the Hebrew text and versions, in which he fully supported Cappellus against Buxtorf. Again, he followed Herder's lead in classifying his material according to literary genres and, abandoning the older dogmatic categories, he treated prophecy as a special disposition of the human spirit. He approached the Old Testament as an independent record of antiquity, a source from the distant past from which one could reconstruct the early stages in the education of the human race (C. G. Heyne). Moreover, he pursued vigorously the direction initiated by Simon in attempting to trace the development of Israel's literature, and in setting out the source theory of the Pentateuch as it had been analysed by Astruc and others. Finally, the important influence of Semler's study of the canon is everywhere evident. Eichhorn abandoned completely the theological concern with the canon, stating at one point: 'it would have been desirable if one had never even used the term canon' (4th ed., vol. I, p. 106). He replaced the term with a purely historical definition. He was concerned only with the historical process by which the ancient literature was collected. Only occasionally does one see vestiges of the older position. His defence of the 'genuineness of the sources', by which he meant that the literature was not a forgery, was soon to be re-defined in terms of historicity and authorship.

The divisions within Eichhorn's Introduction established a basic structure which has continued ever since in its main lines. It includes a discussion of canon, text, and the development of the literature. Eichhorn also divided his material into general and special introduction. To the former he assigned canon and text; to the latter the treatment of the individual books. The new shape of the critical Introduction can best be appreciated by contrasting it with Carpzov's two volumes, the *Introductio* and the *Critica sacra*. Eichhorn placed the discussion of canon at the beginning, which continued the traditional order, but very shortly among his successors this section was moved to the final chapter of the Introduction where it has generally remained.

The historical critical Introduction continued to develop throughout the nineteenth century and reflected the changes within the discipline of Old Testament studies associated with such significant names as de Wette, Ewald, and Duhm. In the latter half of the nineteenth century interest focused especially on literary critical questions within the section of 'special introduction'. With the hegemony of the critical position associated with Julius Wellhausen, a series of classic literary critical Introductions appeared which were long to dominate the field. Included were Wellhausen's revision of Bleek, Cornill, Sellin and Steuernagel in Germany, Kuenen in Holland, Lods in France, W. Robertson Smith and Driver in Britain, and Bewer and Pfeiffer in America.

Of course, it should not be overlooked that there was a strong conservative reaction which arose immediately in an effort to meet the challenge of the newer critical approach. Shortly after Eichhorn there appeared the lengthy four-volume Introduction of the Catholic scholar, Johann Jahn, who generally followed Eichhorn's division into canon, text, and composition of the individual books, but Jahn continued the older, traditional approach in seeking to tie canon to inspiration and church tradition. Certainly the most aggressive and learned opposition to the newer approach was represented by E. W. Hengstenberg of Berlin. Although he never wrote an Introduction himself, his influence was direct on a host of others who did, including H. A. C. Hävernick, C. F. Keil, Moses Stuart, W. H. Green, and E. J. Young. Moreover, in his numerous writings Hengstenberg established the main lines of the conservative apologetic in most of the crucial areas, namely, Pentateuch, Psalms, Prophets, Wisdom, and Daniel. In the period following Hengstenberg conservatives occasionally attempted to reverse the tide of historical criticism by an appeal to archaeology for a vindication of the traditional position (cf. A. H. Sayce, James Orr, M. G. Kyle, R. K. Harrison). Although W. F. Albright could, in no sense, be classified as a conservative in the Hengstenberg tradition, his work was often cited in support of a less radical position which was empirically grounded. However, no truly fresh formulation of the problems of Old Testament Introduction emerged from the conservative, evangelical wing of Protestantism since Hengstenberg. Rather, with the notable exception of the old Princeton school (W. H. Green, B. B. Warfield, R. D. Wilson, G. Vos) the level of Old Testament scholarship has been in serious decline for the last hundred years. Only very recently has this wing of the church shown signs of new life. Among the Roman Catholics the older traditional position represented by Vigouroux, Cornely, and Höpfl at the turn of the twentieth century has been virtually abandoned in preference to the cautious, but critically oriented formulation of Robert and Feuillet, the *Suppléments* to the *Dictionnaire de la Bible*, and the *Jerome Biblical Commentary*.

The reaction of Jewish scholars to the hegemony of the Wellhausen position was complex and tied to the larger issues of anti-

Semitism and Jewish-Christian relations. It became increasingly clear that the rise of the historical critical study of the Old Testament, had, once and for all, broken the dependence of Christian scholars upon traditional Jewish learning. The hallmark of the new historical method was its approach to the language, history, and literature of the Bible independently of the tradition found in the great medieval interpreters such as Rashi and Kimhi. With the beginning of the Jewish Enlightenment some major Jewish scholars shared the concern to break with tradition. In the early nineteenth century Zunz and Geiger among others made impressive contributions in the area of critical Old Testament Introduction, but there was also strenuous opposition voiced by others who flatly rejected Wellhausen's theory of the Pentateuch (e.g. D. Hoffmann, H. M. Wiener, U. Cassuto). A good barometer of the confusion evoked by the new challenge of historical criticism could be seen in the articles on Bible in the famous *Jewish Encyclopedia* of 1901 which was published in New York. Articles were written on each biblical book which presented both the traditional and the critical positions. The two perspectives were simply juxtaposed without a serious attempt at a resolution of the conflict. In the period following the Second World War, particularly following the establishment of the State of Israel, an effort was made by some to establish a new Jewish position which combined critical and traditional values around the work of Y. Kaufmann. However, it remains a real question as to what extent the establishment of such a school has been successful. The diversity of approach among modern Jewish scholars seems to be almost as wide as among Christians. Perhaps it is fair to conclude that a certain tension, indeed different from that in Christianity, still remains within modern Judaism between the critical and traditional study of the Bible, even in the more liberal circles.

The only major new force on the formulation of the Old Testament Introduction which has not yet been considered was that unleashed by Hermann Gunkel in the beginning of the twentieth century. Gunkel was highly successful in convincing the majority of critical scholars that the history of the oral stage in the development of the biblical literature had not been adequately handled. As a result, it has become an integral part of the critical Introduction to include a form-critical and traditio-critical section. At times this section simply preceded the literary critical discussion, as in Eissfeldt, but at other times the older literary critical method was entirely reworked from the newer perspective (e.g. Bentzen). By and large, Gunkel's influence on questions of Introduction has been regarded by subsequent scholarship as complementary to the literary critical rather than as antithetical. The most notable exception to this generalization was represented by I. Engnell.

Within the last decade there has been increased emphasis on a redaction-critical approach which has often been set forth as a new critical method (cf. Kaiser). In my judgment, redaction criticism does not involve a new methodology, rather it seeks to reassert aspects of an earlier literary criticism which were overshadowed by the enthusiasm for Gunkel's programme. When its results appear to differ from those of the older literary criticism, some of the difference lies in the advantage which the modern critic has in making use of insights from both literary and traditio-critical research.

Finally, it should be noted that there has been a growing dissatisfaction often expressed in recent years with the form which the Old Testament Introduction has now assumed. For some scholars the separation between the form and the content of the Bible called forth an attempt to try a new synthesis by combining Old Testament history, theology, and literary criticism (e.g. B. W. Anderson, N. Gottwald) but the contribution from this effort lay more in its clever packaging than in the substance of the proposal. Most recently, new proposals have been voiced under various rubrics such as structuralism, rhetorical criticism, and socio-traditional criticism, but these suggestions have so far not left any major impact on the structure of the Introduction.

2. A Critique of the Historical Critical Introduction

Although I do not doubt that there are some areas of serious disagreement in my brief survey of the development of the Old Testament Introduction, particularly in matters of detail or emphasis, still I feel that there is a broad consensus among scholars in regard to the general lines of this history. The real point of controversy is how one evaluates this history.

The most common opinion is to view this history in terms of scholarly progress and substantial gain. In a burst of enthusiasm some nineteenth-century scholars portrayed the history as a journey from ignorance and error in which ecclesiastical dogma stifled free research into a era of freedom measured only by critical standards of objective truth. Conversely, some conservative Christians have described this history as a growth in unbelief in which the truth of the Bible has been sacrificed on the altar of human wisdom and pride.

In my judgment, both of these evaluations have missed the mark. On the one hand, it seems to me impossible to deny the enormous gains which have been achieved in many areas of the study of the Old Testament. To compare the church fathers, or the Reformers for that matter, with modern scholarship in terms of philology, textual and literary criticism, or of historical knowledge and exegetical precision should convince any reasonable person of the undeniable achievements of historical critical scholarship in respect to the Old Testament.

On the other hand, there have been serious losses reflected in the victory of the critical Introduction. By this evaluation I do not include the psychological impact of the new knowledge on traditional Jewish and Christian beliefs, which is a subject lying outside the scope of this discussion. Rather in terms of the subject matter, serious reservations can be held regarding the form of the critical Introduction as an adequate approach to the literature it seeks to illuminate.

In the first place, the historical critical Introduction as it has developed since Eichhorn does not have for its goal the analysis of the canonical literature of the synagogue and church, but rather it seeks to describe the history of the development of the Hebrew literature and to trace the earlier and later stages of this history. As a result, there always remains an enormous hiatus between the description of the critically reconstructed literature and the actual canonical text which has been received and used as authoritative scripture by the community.

Secondly, because of the predominantly historical interest, the critical Introduction usually fails to understand the peculiar dynamics of Israel's religious literature, which has been greatly influenced by the process of establishing the scope of the literature, forming its particular shape, and structuring its inner relationships. The whole dimension of resonance within the Bible which issues from a collection with fixed parameters and which affects both the language and its imagery is lost by disregarding the peculiar function of canonical literature.

Thirdly, the usual historical critical Introduction has failed to relate the nature of the literature correctly to the community which treasured it as scripture. It is constitutive of Israel's history that the literature formed the identity of the religious community which in turn shaped the literature. This fundamental dialectic which lies at the heart of the canonical process is lost when the critical Introduction assumes that a historically referential reading of the Old Testament is the key to its interpretation. It assumes the determining force on every biblical text to be political, social, or economic factors which it seeks to establish in disregard of the religious dynamic of the canon. In sum, the issue is not whether or not an Old Testament Introduction should be historical, but the nature of the historical categories being applied.

How does this criticism relate to the history of scholarship leading up to the development of the critical Introduction which we have outlined? It suggests that the friction which characterized the history of the discipline and is still present today between a liberal versus conservative, scientific versus ecclesiastical, objective versus confessional approach to the Old Testament poses a false dichotomy of the problem. Because this issue has been confused throughout its history, the development of critical biblical scholarship has brought both great gains and also serious losses in understanding the Old Testament. In my judgment, the crucial issue which produced the confusion is the problem of the canon, that is to say, how one understands the nature of the Old Testament in relation to its authority for the community of faith and practice which shaped and preserved it.

3. Old Testament Introduction and the Canon

I propose to return to the history of the discipline and review its development from the perspective of the canon in order to support my argument.

The early Christian church inherited the Jewish scriptures along with its understanding of canon. It was simply assumed that these writings functioned authoritatively in the life of the church, even though the extent of the canon and the nature of its authority continued to be debated. In the early church the question was not whether the Jewish scriptures were still canonical, but whether the claims of Jesus Christ could be sustained on the basis of scripture. The first major challenge to the unbroken continuity between the Old Testament and the church was raised when Marcion opposed the traditional view of the canon and sought to introduce a critical principle by which the church could determine its authentic scripture. He argued that the original Christian tradition had been corrupted and needed not only to be cut loose from the Jewish scriptures, but also to be critically recovered by sifting the allegedly authentic sources of the faith. The early church of the second and third centuries through its spokesmen Irenaeus and Tertullian responded to Marcion's challenge by appealing to the 'rule of faith' (*regula fidei*), which set the larger context from which individual portions of scripture were to be understood in relation to the sum of Christian oral tradition. In the writings of Augustine the leads of his predecessors were developed into an impressive canonical hermeneutic within the framework of an analogy of faith in which the goal of all biblical interpretation was to engender the love of God and love of neighbour (*De doct. chr.* I, 36, 40).

There are several impressive strengths to this early Christian understanding of canon. First, it allowed the church to receive these writings as a divine word which claimed an immediate authority for its life rather than regarding them dispassionately as past traditions of Judaism. Secondly, by placing the full Jewish canon within the framework of an analogy of faith, an inclusive principle was followed which allowed, at least in principle, the full diversity of the biblical writings to be maintained. Thirdly, a dynamic relationship, testified to in the church's liturgy, was established between scripture, its author (God), and its addressee (the church).

Conversely, there were some weaknesses in the early church's understanding of canon which ultimately led to its serious erosion. Above all, the early church was not able to hear the Old Testament on its own terms, but increasingly the canonical text was subjected to the dominance of ecclesiastical tradition. The 'plain sense' of the Old Testament text was drowned out by traditional interpretation which assumed that the New Testament had superseded the Old. Jerome's appeal to the Hebrew text rather than to the Greek translation was only a momentary victory for the integrity of the Hebrew Bible. Moreover, the religious and political development of the previous three centuries had effected a bitter alienation between the synagogue and the church and had struck at the heart of a canonical understanding of the scriptures which related the sacred writings of the Jews to a living community of faith.

The breakdown in the concept of the Old Testament as canon became further evident during the medieval period. This complex issue is closely connected to the growth in the concept of the church's teaching *magisterium* and lies beyond the scope of this brief survey. However, in terms of biblical Introduction the recovery of the 'plain sense' of the Old Testament in the eleventh and twelfth centuries, first by Jewish scholars in Northern France, then followed by the Victorines, threatened to shatter the unity of the Christian canon. Some Christians who accepted the Jewish interpretation of the Old Testament as being the plain sense of the text, were forced to argue for a concept of double truth (Lyra) or to sacrifice completely the literal sense in order to defend the church's authority in interpreting the Bible (Jean Gerson).

The impact of the Renaissance and Reformation on the concept of the canon was profound and far-reaching. In the first place, the Protestant Reformers sought to free the Bible from the dominance of ecclesiastical tradition by emphasizing the pre-eminence of word over tradition. The primacy of the literal sense of a biblical passage established once again the canonical distinction between text and commentary. Secondly, the Reformers, in varying degrees of success, sought to recover the unity of scripture by holding together the historical and theological dimensions of the text, its literal and spiritual meanings. Especially in Calvin, an easy bridge was established between the historical community of Israel and the subsequent generations of believers. This basic Reformation understanding contrasted markedly with that of Faber, on the one hand, and Erasmus, on the other. Thirdly, the impetus from the side of the new humanistic learning provided the philological, historical, and literary tools by which to study the Old Testament in its own right and in its original setting.

But again, there were some serious negative features in the sixteenth century's understanding of canon which would prove its dissolution in both Catholic and Protestant camps. First, the problem of the biblical canon became embroiled in heated interconfessional polemics about the issue of the authority of the Bible and church tradition. Many Protestants, especially in Calvinistic circles, sought to reduce the role of the church in the formation of the Bible to an absolute minimum. The effect of the controversy was a narrowing of the early church's understanding of the canon. Rather than a faithful expression of the sum of oral tradition in the *regula fidei*, canon came to be regarded as only one aspect of the written tradition which was now locked into a larger dogmatic framework. Secondly, Calvin's concept of *autopistis (Institutes* I. viii.5) – God alone is sufficient witness – moved in the direction of a doctrine of verbal inspiration which among his successors threatened to separate Bible from church. Thirdly, an arbitrary and individualistic tendency within Luther's exegesis led in the direction of setting up a 'canon within the canon'. A subsequent generation of German scholars would find a warrant in Luther for completely abandoning the church's traditional canon. Finally, the pulling apart of a historical-philological interpretation (*sensus grammaticus*) from a theological-homiletical began to threaten the unity of the canon in the exegesis of Erasmus and his followers.

The rise of the historical critical school of biblical interpretation in the post-Reformation period witnessed the collapse of the traditional concept of canon which had already been severely weakened. As outlined above, the crucial areas in Old Testament scholarship in which the newer methods were developed were in text, canon, and composition. In the area of text, orthodox Protestant scholars had derived from their concept of canonical scripture the theory of a *hebraica veritas* which sought to maintain the absolute veracity of the Masoretic text by even appealing to the divine authorship of the Hebrew vowel points. Cappellus was able to undercut this position and open up the true history of the textual development. In terms of canon, orthodox Protestants and Catholics had defended an unbroken link between the original composition of a biblical book and its official canonical status. The canonical process ended when God ceased to inspire prophets to write, which was sometime after the period of Ezra. However, Semler was able to demonstrate that this theory of the canon rested upon a dogmatic construct rather than a historical basis, and that the actual history of canonization was of a different order. Finally, in terms of composition, orthodox Christians had followed Jewish tradition in assuming that the connection was a simple one between traditional authorship and final composition. The appeal to the canon was used to support this belief in the genuineness and historicity of the Old Testament writings, which were increasingly described as 'sources'. Starting with Richard Simon this description of the history of composition was badly shaken and soon abandoned by the developing school of higher criticism.

By the nineteenth century the traditional forms of the Old Testament discipline had been radically reshaped by the newer methodology. Text criticism had become a discipline devoted to the restoration of a frequently corrupt Masoretic text by the scientific sifting of the versions in search of an earlier and better text tradition. The canon had been defined in strictly historical terms as an external ecclesiastical validation without any real significance for the shaping or interpretation of the biblical literature. Research into the history of composition, which had moved to the centre of the stage, sought to recover the history of each book, distinguishing between its allegedly genuine and non-genuine portions (cf. F. Schleiermacher, *Brief Outline* §§ 110ff.) Conservative scholars – Jewish, Protestant, and Catholic – sought to reverse the tide by appealing in different ways to the traditional views. Occasionally a skirmish was won, but, by and large, this endeavour was deemed unsuccessful by the academic world.

The effect of this history on the concept of the canon was clear. Those scholars who pursued historical criticism of the Old Testament no longer found a significant place for the canon. Conversely, those scholars who sought to retain a concept of the canon were unable to find a significant role for historical criticism. This is the polarity which lies at the centre of the problem of evaluating the nature of Old Testament Introduction.

In my judgment, the crucial task is to rethink the problem of Introduction in such a way as to overcome this long established tension between the canon and criticism. Is it possible to understand the Old Testament as canonical scripture and yet to make full and consistent use of the historical critical tools?

II

THE PROBLEM OF THE CANON

Bibliography

G. C. **Aalders**, *Oud-Testamentische Kanoniek*, Kampen 1952; P. R. **Ackroyd**, 'The Open Canon', *Colloquium, The Australian and New Zealand Theological Review* 3, Auckland 1970, 279–91; G. W. **Anderson**, 'Canonical and Non-Canonical', *The Cambridge History of the Bible* 1, ed. P. R. Ackroyd and C. F. Evans, Cambridge and New York 1970, 113–59; W. R. **Arnold**, 'Observations on the Origin of Holy Scripture', *JBL* 42, 1923, 1–21; J. P. **Audet**, 'A Hebrew-Aramaic List of Books of the Old Testament in Greek Transcription', *JTS*, NS 1, 1950, 135–54; W. **Bacher**, 'Synagogue, the Great', *JE* 11, 640–43; W. J. **Beecher**, 'The Alleged Triple Canon of the Old Testament', *JBL* 15, 1896, 118–28; P. **Billerbeck**, Der Kanon des Alten Testaments und seine Inspiration', *Kommentar zum Neuen Testament aus Talmud und Midrasch* IV 1, Munich 1928, 415–51; L. **Blau**, 'Bible Canon', *JE* 3, 140–50; J. **Blenkinsopp**, *Prophecy and Canon*, Notre Dame, Ind. 1977; J. **Bloch**, 'Outside Books', *Mordecai M. Kaplan Jubilee Volume*, English Section, New York 1953, 87–108; reprinted Leiman, *Canon and Masorah* (see below), 202–23; J. S. **Bloch**, *Studien zur Geschichte der Sammlung der althebräischen Literatur*, Breslau 1876; J. **Bonfrère**, 'In totam scripturam sacram praeloquia', *Commentarii in Pentateuchum*, Antwerp 1625, 1–92; K. **Budde**, *Der Kanon des Alten Testaments*, Giessen 1900; F. **Buhl**, *Canon and Text of the Old Testament*, ET Edinburgh and New York 1892.

H. von **Campenhausen**, *The Formation of the Christian Bible*, ET Philadelphia and London 1972; J. **Carmignac**, 'Les citations de l'Ancien Testament dans "la Guerre des Fils de Lumière contre les Fils de Ténèbres" ', *RB*, 63 1956, 234–60, 375–90; R. E. **Clements**, *Prophecy and Tradition*, Oxford and Philadelphia 1975, 54–7; 'Covenant and Canon in the Old Testament', *Creation, Christ, and Culture. Studies in Honour of T. F. Torrance*, ed. R. W. A. McKinney, Edinburgh 1976, 1–12; Jean **Le Clerc**, *Sentiments de quelques théologiens d'Hollande sur l'Histoire Critique de Vieux Testament*, Amsterdam 1686; R. J. **Coggins**, *Samaritans and Jews. The Origins of Samaritanism Reconsidered*, Oxford and Philadelphia 1975; H. **Corrodi**, *Versuch einer Beleuchtung der Geschichte des jüdischen und christlichen Bibelkanons*, 2 vols. Halle 1792; J. **Cosin**, *A Scholastic History of the Canon of the Holy Scripture*, London 1657, reprinted Oxford 1849; S. **Davidson**, *The Canon of the Bible*, London 1880; L. **Dennefeld**, *Der alttestamentliche Kanon der antiochenischen Schule*, Biblische Studien 14.4, Freiburg 1909; L. **Diestel**, 'Die Kritik des Kanons', *Geschichte des Alten Testamentes in der christlichen Kirche*, Jena 1869, 601–20.

A. **Eberharter**, *Der Kanon des Alten Testaments zur Zeit des Ben Sira*, Münster 1911; O. **Eissfeldt**, *The Old Testament: An Introduction*, Oxford and New York 1965, 560–71; I. H. **Eybers**, 'Some Light on the Canon of the Qumran Sect', *OuTWP* 1962, 1–14, reprinted Leiman, *Canon and Masorah*, 23–36; 'Some Remarks about the Canon of the Old Testament', *Theologia Evangelica* 8, Pretoria 1975, 88–117; L. **Finkelstein**, 'The Maxim of the Anshe Keneset Ha-Gedolah', *JBL* 59, 1940, 455–69; E. **Flesseman-van Leer**, 'Prinzipien der Sammlung und Ausscheidung bei der Bildung des Kanons', *ZTK* 61, 1964, 404–20; D. N. **Freedman**, 'The Law and the Prophets', *SVT* 9, 1962, 250–65, reprinted Leiman, *Canon and Masorah*, 5–20; 'Canon of the Old Testament' *IDB Suppl*, 130–6; J. **Fuerst**, *Der Kanon des Alten Testaments nach den Überlieferungen in Talmud und Midrasch*, Leipzig 1868; A. **Geiger**, 'Warum gehört das Buch Sirach zu den Apokryphen?', *ZDMG* 12, 1858, 536–43; L. **Ginzberg**, 'Some Observations on the Attitude of the Synagogue toward Apocalyptic Writings', *JBL* 41, 1922, 115–36, reprinted Leiman, *Canon and Masorah*, 142–63; H. **Graetz**, 'Der Abschluss des Kanons des Alten Testaments', *MGWJ* 35, 1886, 281–98; W. H. **Green**, *General Introduction to the Old Testament: the Canon*, New York 1905; D. E. **Groh**, 'Hans von Campenhausen on Canon', *Interp* 28, 1974, 331–43; H. A. C. **Hävernick**, *A General Historico-Critical Introduction to the Old Testament*, ET Edinburgh 1852, 17ff.; W. W. **Hallo**, 'New Viewpoints on Cuneiform Literature', *IEJ* 12, 1962, 13–26; M. **Haran**, 'Problems of the Canonization of Scripture' (Hebrew), *Tarbiz* 25, Jerusalem 1955–6, 245–71; G. **Hölscher**, *Kanonisch und Apokryph*, Leipzig 1905.

E. **Jacob**, 'Principe canonique et formation de l'Ancien Testament', *SVT* 28, 1975, 101–22; A. **Jepsen**, 'Kanon und Text des Alten Testaments', *TLZ* 74, 1949, 65–74; 'Zur Kanongeschichte des Alten Testaments', *ZAW* 71, 1959, 114–36; 'Sammlung und Kanonisierung des Alten Testaments', *RGG*[3] 1, 1123–5; A. **Jolles**, *Einfache Formen*, Darmstadt [2]1958, 26–8; P. **Katz**, 'The Old Testament Canon in Palestine and Alexandria', *ZNW* 47, 1956, 191–217, reprinted Leiman, *Canon and Masorah*, 72–98; M. G. **Kline**, *The Structure of Biblical Authority*, Grand Rapids, rev. ed. 1972; E. **Koenig**, *Kanon und Apokryphen*, Gütersloh 1917; J. L. **Koole**, *Het Probleem van de Canonisatie van het Oude Testament*, Kampen 1955; S. **Krauss**, 'The Great Synod', *JQR* 1, 1898, 347–77; A. **Kuenen**, 'Über die Männer der grossen Synagoge', 1876, German tr. *Gesammelte Abhandlungen zur biblischen Wissenschaft von Dr Abraham Kuenen*, Freiburg 1894, 125–69; W. G. **Lambert**, 'Ancestors, Authors and Canonicity', *JCS* 11, 1957, 1–14; J.

C. H. **Lebram**, 'Aspekte der alttestamentlichen Kanonbildung', *VT* 18, 1968, 173–89; Sid Z. **Leiman**, ed., *The Canon and Masorah of the Hebrew Bible*, New York 1974; *The Canonization of Hebrew Scripture*, Hamden, Conn. 1976; J. **Leipoldt**, *Geschichte des neutestamentlichen Kanons*, 2 vols. Leipzig 1907; R. C. **Leonard**, *The Origin of Canonicity in the Old Testament*, Diss. Boston University 1972; Elias **Levita**, *The Massoreth ha-Massoreth*, trans. C. D. Ginsberg, 1867, reprinted New York 1968; J. P. **Lewis**, 'What do we mean by Jabneh?', *Journal of Bible and Religion* 32, Boston, Mass. 1964, 125–32, reprinted Leiman, *Canon and Masorah*, 254–61; A. **Loisy**, *Histoire du canon de l'Ancien Testament*, Paris 1890.

H. **Mantel**, 'The Nature of the Great Synagogue', *HTR* 60, 1967, 75–83; M. **Margolis**, *The Hebrew Scriptures in the Making*, Philadelphia 1922; R. **Meyer**, 'Kanonisch und Apokryph im Judentum', *TWNT* 3, 979–87 = *TDNT* 3, 978–87; F. **Michaéli**, 'À propos du Canon de l'Ancien Testament', *Études Théologiques et Religieuses* 36, Montpellier 1961, 61–81; G. F. **Moore**, 'The Definition of the Jewish Canon and the Repudiation of Christian Scriptures', *C. A. Briggs Testimonial* (*Essays in Modern Theology*), New York 1911, 99–125, reprinted Leiman, *Canon and Masorah*, 115–41; R. E. **Murphy**, A. C. **Sundberg** and S. **Sandmel**, 'A Symposium on the Canon of Scripture', *CBQ* 28, 1966, 189–207; H. **Oppel**, Κανών, *Zur Bedeutungsgeschichte des Wortes und seiner lateinischen Entsprechungen, regula-norma, Philologus*, Supplementband 30.IV, Leipzig 1937; H. M. **Orlinsky**, 'The Canonization of the Bible and the Exclusion of the Apocrypha', *Essays in Biblical Culture and Bible Translation*, New York 1974, 257–86; G. **Östborn**, *Cult and Canon: A Study in the Canonization of the Old Testament*, Uppsala 1950; R. H. **Pfeiffer**, 'The Canon of the Old Testament', *IDB* I, 498–520; J. D. **Purvis**, *The Samaritan Pentateuch and the Origin of the Samaritan Sect*, HSM 2, 1968; E. W. E. **Reuss**, *History of the Canon of the Holy Scriptures in the Christian Church*, ET London and New York ²1891; B. J. **Roberts**, 'The Old Testament Canon: A Suggestion', *BJRL* 46, 1963–64, 164–78; J. **Ruwet**, Les Apocryphes dans l'oeuvre d'Origène', *Bibl* 23, 1942, 18–43; 24, 1943, 18–58; 25, 1944, 143–66; 'Clément d'Alexandrie Canon des Écritures et apocryphes', *Bibl* 29, 1948, 240–71; H. E. **Ryle**, *The Canon of the Old Testament*, London 1892.

J. A. **Sanders**, 'Cave 11 Surprises and the Question of Canon', *McCormick Quarterly* 21, Chicago 1968, 284–98; *Torah and Canon*, Philadelphia 1972; 'Adaptable for Life: The Nature and Function of Canon', *Magnalia Dei. Essays on the Bible and Archaeology in Memory of G. Ernest Wright*, Garden City, N.Y. 1976, 531–60; 'Hermeneutics', *IDB Suppl*, 402–7; N. M. **Sarna**, 'The Order of the Books', *Studies In Jewish Bibliography, History, and Literature in Honor of J. Edward Kiev*, ed. C. Berlin, New York 1971, 407–13; 'Bible: Canon', *EJ* 4, 816–32; C. F. **Schmid**, *Historia antiqua et vindicatio canonis sacri veteris novique testamenti, libris II comprehensa*, Leipzig 1775; I. L. **Seeligmann**, 'Voraussetzungen des Midraschexegese', *SVT* 1, 1953, 150–1; J. S. **Semler**, *Abhandlung von freier Untersuchung des Canon*, 4 vols., Halle 1771–75; L. H. **Silberman**, 'The Making of the Old Testament Canon', in C. M. Laymon, ed., *The Interpreter's One-Volume Commentary on the Bible*, Nashville 1971, 1209–15; Richard **Simon**, *Histoire critique du Vieux Testament*, Rotterdam 1685, reprinted, Frankfurt 1967; Morton **Smith**, *Palestinian Parties and Politics that Shaped the Old Testament*, New York and London 1971; W. Robertson **Smith**, *The Old Testament in the Jewish Church*, 1881, London and New York ²1892; H. L. **Strack**, 'Kanon des Alten Testaments', *RE*³ 9, 741–68; M. **Stuart**, *Critical History and Defence of the Old Testament Canon*, Andover, Mass. 1845, London 1849; A. C. **Sundberg**, *The Old Testament of the Early Church*, Cambridge, Mass. and London 1964; 'The "Old Testament": A Christian Canon', *CBQ* 30, 1968, 143–55; T. N. **Swanson**, *The Closing of the Collection of Holy Scriptures: A Study in the History of the Canonization of the Old Testament*, Diss. Vanderbilt University 1970; H. B. **Swete**, 'Order of the Books in Jewish Lists', *Introduction to the Old Testament in Greek*, Cambridge ²1914, reprinted New York 1968, 200.

G. M. **Tucker**, 'Prophetic Superscriptions and the Growth of a Canon', in *Canon and Authority*, ed. G. W. Coats and B. O. Long, Philadelphia 1977, 56–70; J. C. **Turro** and R. E. **Brown**, 'Canonicity', *The Jerome Biblical Commentary*, Englewood Cliffs, N. J. 1969, II, 515–34; B. F. **Westcott**, *On the Canon of the New Testament*, London ⁷1896; W. M. L. **de Wette**, *A Critical and Historical Introduction to the Canonical Scriptures of the Old Testament*, 2 vols., ET Boston, Mass. 1843; G. **Wildeboer**, *The Origin of the Canon of the Old Testament*, ET London 1895; R. D. **Wilson**, 'The Book of Daniel and the Canon', *PTR* 13, 1915, 352–408, reprinted *Studies in the Book of Daniel*, 2nd series, New York 1938, 9–64; L. B. **Wolfenson**, 'Implications of the Place of the Book of Ruth', *HUCA* 1, 1924, 177f.; T. **Zahn**, 'Zählungen der biblischen Bücher', *Geschichte des neutestamentlichen Kanons* II.1, Erlangen/Leipzig 1890, 318ff.; S. **Zeitlin**, 'An Historical Study of the Canonization of the Hebrew Scriptures', *PAAJR* 3, 1931–2; reprinted Leiman, *Canon and Masorah*, 164–99.

1. Terminology

The initial difficulty in discussing the issue of the canon arises from the ambiguity of the terminology. What is meant by 'the canon'? The philological evidence for the Greek cognates has often been rehearsed (cf. B. F. Westcott, 513ff.; H. W. Beyer, 'κανών', *TWNT* 3, 613–20 = *TDNT* 3, 596–602). The original meaning of the noun in classical Greek is that of 'straight rod' or 'ruler', which also received a metaphorical sense of rule or norm. The word appears in the LXX and in two passages in the New Testament (Gal. 6.16; II Cor. 10.13–16) with a similar range of meaning which extends from a literal to a more metaphorical, abstract connotation. Among the

church fathers the term canon was used in a variety of combinations – 'rule of truth', 'rule of faith' – as a norm of church doctrine
and practice. Although Origen used the term in an adjectival sense
of *scripturae canonicae (De princ.* IV 33), the first application of the
noun to the collection of holy scriptures appears in the last part of
the fourth century and continued in common use from the time of
Jerome.

The use of the term canon to describe the scriptures was of
Christian origin and not applied in classic Jewish literature.
Rather, the rabbis spoke of 'sacred writings' *(kitbê haqqōdeš)* which
were said to 'defile the hands' *(meṭamme'îm 'et-hayyādayim)*.
Nevertheless, the rabbinic concept has enough in common with the
Christian usage for Jews usually not to hesitate to apply the term
canon to their scriptures (cf. Leiman; however, cf. the restrictions of
L. B. Wolfenson, 177f., and my final chapter).

The real problem of defining the term canon is far from settled by
the philological evidence. One needs only a cursory look at the
history of interpretation to see immediately how different have been
the concepts of canon which have been held over the centuries.
Josephus' view of canon (*Contra Apionem* I, 42f.) implies a concept of
divinely inspired writings, fixed in number, originating within a
limited period of time, with an established text. A somewhat similar
definition is reflected in the midrashim (cf. *Bemidbar Rabbah* 14.4),
but it also seems clear that the Talmud allowed for different
categories of canonical books, and that inspiration and canonicity
were carefully distinguished (cf. Leiman, *Canonization*, 127ff.).

Semler argued that such traditional definitions of the canon were
later theological constructions and that originally the canon simply
designated a list of books which were to be read in open assembly.
The term did not imply any particular quality of divine inspiration,
nor was there a fixed number of books agreed upon by a consensus.
Several recent writers (Sundberg, Swanson) have sought to distinguish sharply between scripture and the canon. They argue that the
term scripture designates a body of authoritative writings whereas
the canon involves the essential element of restriction and implies a
closed collection to which nothing more can be added. Finally,
there are those who would project the term canon into the early
stage of the literature's formation and define canonization as any
act of official publication of a document which achieved a normative status (Freedman, Leiman).

In sum, much of the present confusion over the problem of the canon turns on the failure to reach an agreement regarding the terminology. As a result, the points of both consensus and conflict have been frequently obscured within the debate.

2. The Traditional View of the Canon and its Demise

The Old Testament does not address directly the issue of when and how the history of canonization took place, yet various Jewish traditions developed during the Hellenistic period which were accepted by both Jews and Christians at least until the seventeenth century. II Esdras 14.44 (c. AD 100) recounts that Ezra restored in forty days the sacred books which had been destroyed by the Babylonians by his being supernaturally empowered to recall the entire scriptures. The account in II Macc. 2.13 attributes the collection of the sacred writings to Nehemiah. Although the Babylonian Talmud in a famous passage (Baba Bathra 14b–15a) had sought to ascribe authorship to the various books of the Bible, it was Elias Levita who developed the theory of the men of the Great Synagogue under Ezra as having established the canon of the Hebrew Bible and divided it into three parts. This theory was widely accepted by Jews and Christians until the end of the nineteenth century.

In spite of the variations within these traditional viewpoints, they all shared an underlying assumption of an unbroken continuity, even if threatened at times, between the writing and collecting of an authoritative body of scripture. The canon was formed and enlarged as each new book was added. When the last book appeared, the canon was closed. The canon assured an unbroken series of sacred annals which had been preserved from the time of Moses. The establishment of authorship maintained its authenticity, the divine inspiration its truth, the uninterrupted succession its purity.

The collapse of the traditional understanding of the canon was the result of attacks from several directions. First of all, the discovery of a complex historical development of the literature, especially the Pentateuch, seriously damaged the idea of a direct, unbroken link between the original writing and its final stage in which the book's authority had been accepted from its inception. Again, the recognition of a long prehistory raised serious questions respecting the traditional authorship, and thus threatened the canon's authenticity. Then again, the discovery that certain of the biblical books, especially Daniel, probably derived from a period after the alleged closing of the canon under Ezra's leadership did much to question the accuracy of the traditional concept of the canon's history. Kuenen's devastatingly negative judgment regarding the history of the Great Synagogue removed the last foundation block of the older view and wiped the slate clear for a new interpretation.

3. The Nineteenth-century Historical Consensus and its Erosion

The development of a new critical theory of the canon from a strictly historical perspective had been attempted by Eichhorn, Corrodi, de Wette, and others. The varying models suggest that they did not succeed in achieving a wide consensus, chiefly because of the disagreement over the history of the literature. However, with the growing hegemony of Wellhausen's reconstruction of Israel's history and literature, a new consensus began to emerge also regarding the history of the canon. It is reflected in several Introductions (e.g. W. R. Smith, Cornill), in important encyclopaedia articles (Strack), and in the popular handbooks of Wildeboer, Buhl, and Ryle. In spite of some modification the classic literary critical construction of the formation of the canon has continued to be represented in the Introductions of Pfeiffer, Bentzen, and Eissfeldt. The theory agreed on certain main lines of the development.

The Josianic reform of 621 BC, reported in II Kings 22, marked the first step in the process by the canonization of Deuteronomy or some portion of it. At the end of the fifth century in the period of Ezra the Torah had assumed its fixed canonical status with the addition of the Priestly source to the earlier Pentateuchal strands. The dating of the formation of the Pentateuch was established to some extent by the Samaritan schism which marked a *terminus* by which time these books had been set. The prophetic books were next canonized in the third century, and the collection had been firmly closed before the book of Daniel was composed, about 165. The final stage of canonization was assigned to decisions at the Council of Jamnia (c. AD 90) at which time books in use among the Alexandrian Jews were also excluded.

Within the last two decades this classic nineteenth-century reconstruction of the history of the canon has been seriously eroded in several ways. In the first place, most of the fixed historical points upon which the theory had been built seem no longer able to bear the weight placed upon them. For example, recent research into the Samaritan question (Purvis, Coggins) has raised serious doubts whether one can any longer speak of a single event in the fifth or fourth century – the exact date was never settled – which resulted in the Samaritan schism. Nor can the restriction of the Samaritan scriptures to the Pentateuch be used as a *terminus ad quem* for the closing of the first part of the Hebrew canon. Similarly, the argument for the dating of the closing of the final section of the Hebrew Bible by the Council of Jamnia rests on the flimsiest possible evidence. Not only is next to nothing known about this 'council', but what transpired did not relate directly to the closing of the canon. Then again, the research of A. C. Sundberg has successfully destroyed the widespread theory of an Alexandrian canon and seriously damaged the assumption of parallel canons, one narrow and one broad, which were held by different geographical communities within Judaism.

In the second place, the assumption that the Masoretic division of a tripartite canon was the original order reflecting three historical stages in the canon's development, and that the Septuagint's order was a later, secondary adjustment, has been questioned from several sides. Hölscher, Katz and Lebram have demonstrated the antiquity of other non-Masoretic orders. Margolis (70ff.) has argued for the co-existence of Torah, prophecy, and wisdom throughout Israel's literary and religious history. This approach to canon has tended to sustain the older conservative argument (e.g. R. D. Wilson) that Daniel's exclusion from the prophets in the Masoretic order entailed a theological as much as a historical judgment. One cannot assume that one canonical section was tightly closed before another was formed because of the lack of solid evidence from which to draw such a conclusion.

Finally, the recovery of a sense of oral tradition which criticized the older literary critical school for identifying the age of the material within a book with its literary fixation has also had a damaging effect on the classic critical reconstruction of the canon. Even if one could identify the book which was discovered in 621 (II Kings 22) with Deuteronomy, as most scholars do, it does not follow that one can infer that this event constituted the first stage of canonization of Deuteronomy nor that the laws of Moses were without authority up to that point in history. Many of the same assumptions can be questioned regarding the final stage of the Pentateuch's alleged canonization under Ezra resulting from the addition of the Priestly source according to the classic Wellhausen theory. To extrapolate a history of canonization from a highly complex and obscure literary process remains a very fragile and tentative enterprise.

4. The Search for a New Consensus

In the light of this erosion in the classic critical reconstruction, a variety of newer attempts have emerged in recent years in an effort to form a new synthesis. Certain characteristic moves can be sketched without attempting to present an exhaustive review of all the literature.

(i) G. Hölscher argued in *Kanonisch und Apokryph* (1905) for a sharp distinction to be made between the growth of the collection of Hebrew writings and the development of the concept of canon. The former was a literary process, the latter a dogmatic theory. Taking Josephus' understanding of canon as representative of the dogmatic canonical formulation, Hölscher argued against seeing a three-stage historical development of the canon. Neither the collection of the Law nor the Prophets was canonical in the strict sense of the term even by the time of Sirach's grandson (c. 130 BC). Rather, the concept of the canon as a dogmatic theory was a product of rabbinic Pharisaism from the time of Hillel and Shammai, which sought to preserve rabbinic tradition by limiting the canonical scripture to a particular period of the ancient past and thus eliminating the new threat arising from apocalyptic writings. The Alexandrian form, of the canon with twenty-two books, which counted Ruth with Judges and Lamentations with Jeremiah, preserved the older order of the canon, and only later did Palestinian Judaism change the form to adopt the present Hebrew canon, which contains twenty-four books.

In my judgment, Hölscher made an important contribution in challenging the assumption of the nineteenth-century literary critical school that the three-stage division was the key to the historical understanding of the canon. Also his defence of the priority of the tradition of twenty-two books was impressive. However, the application of a very limited interpretation of the term canon prejudiced the discussion from the outset. By adopting a late rabbinic definition of the canon he failed to explain the forces which led to the collection of these writings and their authoritative function which lay behind the final rabbinical form.

(ii) Almost the exact opposite thesis was proposed by David Noel Freedman (*IDB Suppl*) who argued that the Law and the Former Prophets comprised a literary unit and were compiled and published with some form of canonical status by 550 BC. A 'second edition' which included the Latter Prophets appeared some fifty years later. Freedman claimed that these were public documents promulgated by an 'official ecclesiastical group in the Jewish community' (*SVT* 1962, 251). He assumed that any given writing arose as a response to a specific historical circumstance in the life of the people, and could be dated very close to the last event mentioned in the document. Furthermore, he worked on the assumption that to establish the date in which a writing was given a finished form also established the date of canonization, which he understood as an official promulgation of a public document. In my opinion, none of these assumptions can be sustained by historical evidence; in fact I regard them as highly unlikely. By simply identifying the history of the literature's growth with the history of canonization Freedman has closed off any chance of understanding the special history of the book's growth and collection as canonical scripture which is the very issue at stake.

(iii) Sid Z. Leiman begins his history of the formation of the canon with a clear definition of his understanding of the term: 'A canonical book is a book accepted by Jews as authoritative for religious practice and/or doctrine, and whose authority is binding upon the Jewish people for all generations' (*Canonization*, 14). Leiman then distinguishes between uncanonical writings referred to in the Hebrew Bible and canonical writings. Using such verses as Ex. 24.7; I Kings 2.3; II Kings 14.6, Leiman concludes that the biblical text is unequivocal: 'The canonization of the Covenant Code, the Decalogue, Deuteronomy, and perhaps the entire Torah is assumed to have occurred during the lifetime of Moses' (20).

In my judgment, Leiman has made a valuable contribution in showing the early age at which documents, particularly laws, exerted an authoritative role. The history of the canon did not start in 621 BC as if the book of Deuteronomy, which had previously been regarded as among the profane writings, was suddenly deemed authoritative. Also Leiman's discussion of the rabbinic evidence for the closing of the canon is of great value. Nevertheless, there are some problems with Leiman's full proposal, in my opinion. Because he makes no real distinction between a book's authority and its canonicity, the entire Pentateuch is assumed to have been canonized during the period of Moses. But then this portrayal of the canonization process fails to reckon with the very history of the literature's development, the recognition of which caused the collapse of the traditional position. Leiman makes a passing reference to Albright's demonstration that ancient tradition has been preserved in the various sources as evidence against the classic literary critical reconstruction. But he still does not make room for the complex history of the literature's growth. Nor does he adequately deal with a history of accommodating, collecting, and ordering of saga and legends stemming from non-Israelite sources which entered the Pentateuch. In the end, Leiman's reconstruction of the history still seeks to defend an unbroken succession of authoritative, canonical writings from Moses to the close of the canon.

(iv) A similar hypothesis, but considerably more apologetic, has been proposed by M. G. Kline, who attempts to establish an unbroken canonical continuity from the Mosaic period by finding an analogy in the ancient Near Eastern suzerainty treaties. However, Kline's basically dogmatic formulation of the history of the canon in terms of a divine inspiration which assured an inerrant transmission of the Word of God (23) reflects completely the pre-Semler, seventeenth-century understanding which has not even seen the historical problem. These issues are far too complex simply to circumscribe by a strictly theological definition. Therefore, in spite of some excellent insights, the total impact of the book misses its intended goal.

(v) At the other end of the spectrum is the bold attempt of James A. Sanders to reinterpret the history of the canon as an ongoing hermeneutical process extending throughout Israel's entire history. Sanders greatly broadens the definition of the canon to describe the community's attempt to discover its self-identity in the light of its authoritative traditions which it continually reinterprets to meet the changing historical conditions of its existence. According to his model, 'it is the nature of canon to be both stable and adaptable' ('Hermeneutics', 404). It is stable in the sense of having an established structure and content; it is adaptable in addressing the community in each new generation. Although Sanders has not yet worked out the effect of his hermeneutical approach in detail on the entire history of the canonical process, he has drawn some of the broad lines in his book *Torah and Canon*.

In my judgment, Sanders has moved in the right direction in broadening the definition of canon to cover a process extending throughout Israel's history which effected the shaping of the literature itself. However, I am critical of Sanders' existential categories which understand the growth of canon as a search for identity in times of crisis, oscillating between the two poles of stability and adaptability. In my opinion, the historical and theological forces which evoked the formation of the canon were of a very different order from an identity crisis. Nor is the effect of canon on the literature adequately described by Sanders' category of 'monotheistic pluralism', as I shall attempt to demonstrate in the detailed analysis of each biblical book. Finally, I am critical of Sanders' attempt to reconstruct the hermeneutical process within ancient Israel, which appears to be a highly speculative enterprise, especially in the light of the almost total lack of information regarding the history of canonization. He assumes a knowledge of the canonical process from which he extrapolates a hermeneutic without demonstrating, in my opinion, solid evidence for his reconstruction.

To summarize: the task of assessing the role of the canon in understanding the Old Testament has proven to be an enormously difficult problem. Its terminology, history, and function remain highly controversial. In spite of the serious erosion in the classic literary critical reconstruction of the history of canon which emerged at the end of the nineteenth century, no fully satisfactory new interpretation has been able to achieve a consensus.

5. A New Attempt at Understanding Canon

It is necessary at the outset to settle on a definition of the term canon. The difficulty of the subject and its complex historical usage should caution against too quickly claiming the exclusive right for any one definition. It is important that the use of the term does

justice to all the dimensions of the issue without prematurely resolving problems merely by definition. One should also expect a degree
of consistency in the application of the term.

The term canon has both a historical and a theological dimension. The formation of the canon of Hebrew scriptures developed in
a historical process, some lines of which can be accurately
described by the historian. Semler was certainly right in contesting
an exclusively theological definition of canon in which the element
of development was subsumed under the category of divine Providence or *Heilsgeschichte* of some sort. Conversely, the formation of
the canon involved a process of theological reflection within Israel
arising from the impact which certain writings continued to exert
upon the community through their religious use. To seek to explain
the historical process leading toward the formation of the canon
solely through sociological, political, or economic forces prejudices
the investigation from the start.

In recent years there has been a strong insistence from such
scholars as Sundberg and Swanson that a clear distinction be made
between scripture and canon. Accordingly, scripture is defined as
authoritative writings, whereas the canon is restricted to a dogmatic decision through which the limits of scripture are defined and
fixed. There are certain obvious merits in making a sharp distinction between the authority of a writing and its canonization. I have
earlier criticized Leiman's reconstruction for too easily identifying
scriptural authority and canonization, with the result that the complex history of collecting and ordering of a corpus of sacred writings
is inadequately treated.

However, there are also serious problems involved in too sharply
separating the two concepts after the model of Sundberg and Swanson. First of all, to conceive of canon mainly as a dogmatic decision
regarding its scope is to overestimate one feature within the process
which is by no means constitutive of canon. It is still semantically
meaningful to speak of an 'open canon'. Secondly, the sharp distinction obscures some of the most important features in the
development of the canon by limiting the term only to the final
stages of a long and complex process which had already started in
the pre-exilic period. Essential to understanding the growth of the
canon is to see this interaction between a developing corpus of
authoritative literature and the community which treasured it. The
authoritative Word gave the community its form and content in

obedience to the divine imperative, yet conversely the reception of
the authoritative tradition by its hearers gave shape to the same
writings through a historical and theological process of selecting,
collecting, and ordering. The formation of the canon was not a late
extrinsic validation of a corpus of writings, but involved a series of
decisions deeply affecting the shape of the books. Although it is
possible to distinguish different phases within the canonical process
– the term canonization would then be reserved for the final fixing
of the limits of scripture – the earlier decisions were not qualitatively different from the later. When scripture and canon are too
sharply distinguished, the essential element in the process is easily
lost.

Part of the difficulty of defining the canonical process turns on
the model one uses by which to interpret this history. Although
Sanders also understands canon in terms of a dynamic process, we
differ markedly in our descriptions of this history. For Sanders the
heart of the canonical process lay in Israel's search for identity. In
my judgment, this approach turns the canonical process on its head
by couching a basically theological move in anthropological terms.
It thus replaces a theocentric understanding of divine revelation
with an existential history. Indeed, canon involved a response on
Israel's part in receiving the authoritative tradition, but the
response to a continuing experience with God was testified to by a
new understanding of scripture. Israel did not testify to its own
self-understanding, but by means of a canon bore witness to the
divine source of its life. The clearest evidence for this position is
found in the consistent manner in which the identity of the canonical editors has been consciously obscured, and the only signs of an
ongoing history are found in the multi-layered text of scripture
itself. The shape of the canon directs the reader's attention to the
sacred writings rather than to their editors. Israel's own self-
understanding was never accorded a place of autonomy, but was
always interpreted in the light of the authority of scripture. Because
the process of forming the scriptures came to an end, canon marked
off a fixed body of writings as normative for the community rather
than attributing authority to the process itself. When Israel later
reinterpreted its scriptures to address changing needs, it did so in
the form of the targum, that is to say, commentary, which was set
apart sharply from the received sacred text of scripture.

There is one final point to make respecting the nature of the

canonical process. Seeligmann has described a process of interpretation within scripture which he correctly derived from a consciousness of canon *(Kanonbewusstsein)*. This process involved the
skilful use of literary techniques, word-plays, and proto-midrashic
exegesis which emerged during the final stages of the formation of
the canon and continued to be developed and to flower during the
post-biblical period. Although such exegetical activity grew out of a
concept of the canon as an established body of sacred writings, it is
a derivative phenomenon which does not represent the constitutive
force lying behind the actual canonical process. Rather, the decisive
force at work in the formation of the canon emerged in the transmission of a divine word in such a form as to lay authoritative claim
upon the successive generations.

The growth of Israel's canon consciousness can be clearly
detected when the words of a prophet which were directed to a
specific group in a particular historical situation were recognized as
having an authority apart from their original use, and were preserved for their own integrity (cf. Isa. 8.16f.). The heart of the
canonical process lay in transmitting and ordering the authoritative
tradition in a form which was compatible to function as scripture
for a generation which had not participated in the original events of
revelation. The ordering of the tradition for this new function
involved a profoundly hermeneutical activity, the effects of which
are now built into the structure of the canonical text. For this
reason an adequate interpretation of the biblical text, both in terms
of history and theology, depends on taking the canonical shape with
great seriousness. When seen in this light, the usual practice of the
historical-critical Introduction of relegating a treatment of the
canon to the final chapter is entirely misleading and deficient.

6. The Relation between the Literary and Canonical Histories

The recognition of the complex history of the growth of the Old
Testament literature did more than anything else to bring about
the collapse of the older dogmatic understanding of the canon. The
formation of the Hebrew Bible could not be adequately handled
without paying close attention to a history of literary development
which shared many of the features of ancient Near Eastern literature in general. The implications of the discovery of this historical

dimension in the literature's formation were soon drawn in respect to the canon as well. Obviously, the present form of the Hebrew canon was also a product of a historical development. But what is the relation between these two histories, namely, the history of the literature and the history of the canon?

The classic Wellhausen position of Old Testament criticism clearly recognized two distinct historical processes, but sought to relate them closely. Thus, the 'book of the law' discovered in 621 BC during the reign of Josiah was identified as the book of Deuteronomy, which was judged to be a seventh-century platform for the reforming party in Jerusalem. Its acceptance as an authority also marked the first stage of canonization of the Hexateuch according to the theory. As we have seen, the attack on Wellhausen's theory of the literary history of the Old Testament also fell on the reconstruction of the canonical history. In the recent search for a new reconstruction of the literary history of Israel there have been several attempts to identify the two processes, whether by means of a new literary-critical hypothesis (Freedman) or by a return to an older conservative position (Kline). In my judgment, this identification of the literary and the canonical history, whether stemming from the left or right of the theological spectrum, is a step backward and cannot be sustained.

The two processes are not to be identified, but clearly they belong together. Exactly how the two histories relate remains often unclear and much more intensive research will be needed to clarify the problem. Still a few general observations regarding their relationship are in order. First, the development of Hebrew literature involved a much broader history than the history of the canon's development. The former process resulted from innumerable forces such as laws of saga, the use of inherited literary patterns of prose and poetry, the social setting of diverse institutions, the changing scribal techniques etc., whereas the latter process was much more closely defined by those forces which affected the literature's evaluation, transmission, and usage. Although non-religious factors (political, social, and economic) certainly entered into the canonical process, these were subordinated to the religious usage of the literature by its function within the community.

Secondly, there were periods in the history of Israel in which the canonical history was largely subsumed under the history of the literature's development. This fusion of the two processes was especially evident during the early, pre-exilic history, but in the later exilic and post-exilic periods these forces associated with the development of canon increased in importance. There seems to be a direct relationship between the quantity of literature and the interest in its collection and ordering within set parameters.

Thirdly, because of the lack of historical evidence, it is extremely difficult to determine the motivations involved in the canonical process. The Old Testament neither reports directly on this history, nor does it even reflect a tradition of the canonical process. With the one exception of the Deuteronomic tradition of Moses' writing and preservation of the Book of the Law, the Old Testament has no tradition from which one could begin to recover its history. At most we find an occasional isolated event or situation from which some historical information can be inferred. For example, it remains exceedingly difficult to determine to what extent a canonical force was at work in the uniting of the J and E sources of the Pentateuch or how a consciousness of the canon exerted itself in the process. Caution must be exercised not to hypothesize the history of the literature's growth in such a way as to eliminate *a priori* the religious dimensions associated with the function of the canon. One does not have to read far in the standard historical critical Introductions to find hypotheses regarding the literary and canonical histories which rest on untested historiographical assumptions.

7. A Sketch of the Development of the Hebrew Canon

The book of Deuteronomy (31.24ff.) records an act which clearly reflects an early stage in the growth of the canon. Moses wrote the words of the divine law in a book which was deposited by the side of the ark of the covenant for periodical reading before the entire assembly of Israel. Of course, the age of this chapter cannot be unequivocally fixed – many scholars would feel that it is pre-exilic – nor can the scope of the law attributed to Moses be determined with certainty. But from what we know of the history of the literature, it is not to be identified with the whole Pentateuch.

However, there is evidence to show that the Deuteronomic description of Moses' act stands in close continuity with earlier tradition. First, Moses' role as mediator of the divine law is deeply rooted in the Sinai tradition. When Israel was unable to receive the divine law directly, Moses interceded for the people. Moreover, Ex. 24.1–11, which belongs to the earliest strands of the Pentateuch, records Moses' writing the words of the law, reading them in an assembly of the people within a cultic context, and evoking a response of loyalty to their stipulations. But there is a difference between the two passages Deut. 31 and Ex. 24, which already indicates a growth in the history of canon. Both passages speak of an authoritative law written by Moses which was read in the hearing of the people. But in Deut. 31 the written form of the law has received a function far more autonomous than Ex. 24 in relation to its original historical setting. Deuteronomy 31.26 emphasizes the careful preservation of the book commensurate to its sacred quality. The words themselves, apart from Moses, function as an authoritative witness against rebellion. A set period in the future is prescribed for continual reading of the law whose authority is unimpaired by Moses' death.

The discovery of the book of the law in II Kings 22 (cf. II Chron. 34) did not mark the beginning of the canonical process, but provides a further historical confirmation of the already existing authority of the Mosaic law. Of course, many problems remain in establishing the history of the growth of the literature in the seventh century, which relate to the age, circle, and scope of the book of Deuteronomy, but in spite of these uncertainties, the passage does provide historical evidence for the canonical process.

There is further evidence in the canonical development of the Law of Moses to be found in the redactional framework which surrounds the Former Prophets. This sign of editorial activity is usually associated with a Deuteronomistic school in the sixth to fifth centuries. Thus, for example, in the book of Joshua the leadership of the nation is not conceived of as an extension of Moses' office, but is pictured as dependent upon the divine law revealed to Moses and preserved in book form (cf. 1.8; 4.10, etc.). Although the literary history of the late fifth century associated with the role of Ezra is not fully clear, most scholars would agree that the present form of the Pentateuch took its shape at this time. The legal prescriptions recorded in Neh. 8.13–18 reflect the Priestly code. Nevertheless, in terms of the history of the canon, the authority of the Mosaic law is further attested, but the exact extent of the canonical books comprising this law cannot be established from these texts. Nor does it seem possible from the evidence to understand in any detail the process by which the narrative material in the Pentateuch was accorded a similar canonical status to that of the laws.

Another type of evidence in tracing the history of the canon has been deduced from the development of the Hebrew text. Textual history of the Pentateuch can be reconstructed in some measure from the third century BC. One can easily project a history of textual development which had begun considerably earlier. This evidence would seem to confirm that the extent of a canonical corpus had already been settled by then and that the history of establishing the text of the sacred writings had begun. The translation of the Pentateuch into Greek from the middle of the third century is an indication of its authoritative status. The *terminus ad quem* of the canonization of the Pentateuch is provided at the beginning of the second century by Ben Sira whose knowledge and use of all the legal portions can only presuppose the canonical status of the entire Pentateuch (cf. Swanson, 88ff., *contra* Hölscher). Furthermore, there is nothing at Qumran to challenge this conclusion and much indirect evidence to support it.

Not surprisingly in the light of the paucity of evidence, scholarly opinions differ widely regarding the canonical history of the Prophets. The two extremes are marked, on the one hand, by Freedman and Leiman, who argue for a closing of the prophetic canon about 500–450 BC and Swanson, on the other hand, proposing an open collection of prophets well into the Christian era. The major evidence used in support of the first position is that the books themselves refer to no event after c.500, that the Chronicler was too late to be included in this section, and that there was a tradition of the cessation of prophecy after Malachi. In my judgment, none of these arguments carry much historical weight, and they rest on assumptions which have already been criticized. The second position represented by Swanson argues that the designation 'Law and Prophets' included all scripture and that the tripartite division was a late, rabbinic development. In my opinion, Swanson's interpretation cannot be sustained without considerable modification. In spite of his argument, the repeated reference in the prologue of Ben Sira to 'the Law and the Prophets, and the remaining books' cannot be discounted. Moreover, that Ben Sira knows all the prophetic books in a canonical order (46.1–49.13) and even the title of the Book of the Twelve, appears to be strong evidence for a fixed canonical unit of prophets by the beginning of the second century.

However, in spite of fixing a terminus to the history, the more important issues within the canonical process of the prophetic corpus remains still unresolved. There are a few early signs even from the pre-exilic period of a canon consciousness related to the prophetic preaching. In both Isa. 8.16 and Jer. 36.1ff. one sees the transition from the spoken prophetic word to a written form with authority. Later, there is reference in Zech. 1.4ff. to the 'former prophets' whose writings appear to have a form and authoritative status. The exegesis within the Bible itself in the post-exilic period begins to cite earlier oracles *verbatim* as an authoritative text which it seeks to interpret (cf. Isa. 65, 25, which echoes Isa. 1.6ff.). Finally, Dan. 9.2 offers evidence of some sort of fixed collection of prophetic writings.

The basic question of understanding the relation between the Law and the Prophets within the canonical history remains difficult to resolve. Although I do not regard Lebram's theory as correct which sees a series of authoritative prophetic writings preceding the canonical position of the Law, nevertheless, there are signs of mutual influence between the two developing collections. Since Moses was regarded as a prophet, his authority may well have extended to other books written by prophets. The close link between Deuteronomy and the Deuteronomistic editing of the Former Prophets would tend to confirm such an understanding. Certainly Clements (*Prophecy and Tradition*, 55) is right in emphasizing that the canonical process should not be conceived of as a closed section of Law to which the Prophets were joined only secondarily. At an early date the two collections, Law and Prophets, were joined and both experienced expansion. By the first century BC both sections of the canon were regarded as normative scripture (cf. Swanson, 178ff., on the Qumran evidence).

Again, evidence for tracing the canonical history of the final section of the Hebrew Bible, the Writings or Hagiographa, is sparse and highly contested. Sundberg has argued that the Jewish canon by the first century AD consisted of the Law and the Prophets as well as other religious writings which had not been established in a fixed collection. At the Council of Jamnia (c. AD 90) rabbinic Judaism narrowed its canon and excluded many of the religious writings which had been freely circulating up to that time. The forces behind this move have been variously explained as derived from an anti-apocalyptic or anti-Christian concern. From this loosely joined collection of excluded religious writings, the Christian church formed its larger canon.

Against this thesis, Leiman has protested that the extent of the Jewish canon had been settled long before AD 90. He has certainly made a strong case against making Jamnia a key stage in the history of the Jewish canon. The basic text (M. Yadayim 3.5) refers only to a discussion concerning the status of Ecclesiastes and Song of Songs, and not the other books of the Hagiographa. There is good reason to believe that the dispute was a scholastic enterprise (Talmon), turning on the inspired status of the books under consideration, and not canonicity. Moreover, there was no official ruling and debates continued on these same books long after Jamnia (cf. Leiman, *Canonization*, 120ff.).

Several other theories regarding the formation of the Hagiographa have been proposed. Swanson has even argued for the possibility that the bipartite collection of the Hebrew scriptures had been closed and the number of books restricted before the category known as the Writings was formed. In my judgment, Swanson's interpretation of Ben Sira, Josephus, and the New Testament, in which evidence for a tripartite division is usually found, has not been convincing. Still it is quite certain that other canonical arrangements were in competition during the second and first centuries and that the lines between the Prophets and the Writings remained in considerable flux (cf. Katz). Clearly in the case of the book of Daniel, its canonical status was established independently of its location in one of the two canonical collections. Although conclusive evidence for dating the closing of the third section of the Jewish canon is not available, the stabilization of the Hebrew text by the end of the first century AD would further point to a relatively closed Hebrew canon by the beginning of the Christian era.

The problem of the so-called 'apocryphal books' in relation to the Jewish canon has been much discussed in recent years (Sundberg, Leiman, Swanson). There is a consensus that during the Hellenistic period a much wider selection of religious writings were in use than those finally recognized as authoritative within the Jewish canon. Opinions vary on the authority accorded these books. The presence of many non-canonical writings at Qumran brought an additional confirmation to the wide scope of literature in use among Jews of this period. The canonization process within Judaism thus involved a selection of a limited number of books from a much larger resource of available literature. Moreover, this canonical limitation was not confined solely to Palestine, as Sundberg has shown.

The motivation lying behind this narrowing process has also been much debated. Usually, it has been attributed either to a growing conservatism within rabbinic Judaism, or to a fear of apocalyptic literature or to an anti-Christian move. Since the sources are virtually silent, these alleged motivation factors remain in the realm of hypothesis. From indirect evidence of later Jewish writings, the anti-Christian move seems the least likely of the theories. Nevertheless, the effect of the exclusion of the apocryphal and pseudepigraphical books can be clearly recognized in the subsequent history of Judaism. Pharisaic Judaism was increasingly set apart by the scope of its canon from other Jewish and Christian groups which continued to use non-canonical books with varying degrees of authority.

8. Summary and Implications

A brief summary of our conclusions from this history is in order. First of all, it should be incontrovertible that there was a genuine historical development involved in the formation of the canon and that any concept of canon which fails to reckon with this historical dimension is faulty. Secondly, the available historical evidence allows for only a bare skeleton of this development. One searches largely in vain for solid biblical or extra-biblical evidence by which to trace the real causes and motivations behind many of the crucial decisions. How did a writing exert an authority and on whom? What lay behind a particular collection of books at a given historical period? How were the variety of claims of authority related to one another and adjudicated? What groups were involved in the process and how were they affected by their historical milieu?

Certain methodological implications derive from these conclusions. We are faced with an obvious dilemma. Clearly the role of the canon is of fundamental importance in understanding the Hebrew scriptures. Yet the Jewish canon was formed through a complex historical process which is largely inaccessible to critical reconstruction. The history of the canonical process does not seem to be an avenue through which one can greatly illuminate the present canonical text. Not only is the evidence far too skeletal, but the sources seem to conceal the very kind of information which would allow a historian easy access into the material by means of uncovering the process. Is there any way out of this impasse?

III

CANON AND CRITICISM

Bibliography

N. **Appel**, *Kanon und Kirche*, Paderborn 1964; James **Barr**, 'Trends and Prospects in Biblical Theology', *JTS* NS 25, 1974, 265–82; 'Biblical Theology', *IDB Suppl*, 104–11; Karl **Barth**, *Church Dogmatics*, I/1, ET New York 1936, Edinburgh 1938; 2nd ed. Edinburgh and Grand Rapids, Mich. 1975; *Die Schrift in der Kirche*, Zürich 1947; G. **Bornkamm**, 'Die ökumenische Bedeutung der historisch-kritischen Bibelwissenschaft', *Geschichte und Glaube* II, Munich 1971, 11–20; H. **Cazelles**, 'Biblical Criticism, OT', *IDB Suppl*, 98–102; B. S. **Childs**, 'The Old Testament as Scripture of the Church', *CTM* 43, 1972, 709–22; G. W. **Coats** and B. O. **Long**, eds., *Canon and Authority*, Philadelphia 1977; O. **Cullmann**, 'The Tradition', *The Early Church*, ET London and Philadelphia 1956; H. **Diem**, *Das Problem des Schriftkanons*, Zürich 1952; E. **Dobschütz**, 'The Abandonment of the Canonical Idea', *AJT* 19, 1915, 416ff.; P.-G. **Duncker**, 'The Canon of the Old Testament at the Council of Trent', *CBQ* 15, 1953, 277–99; G. **Ebeling**, 'The Significance of the Critical Historical Method for Church and Theology in Protestantism', *Word and Faith*, ET Philadelphia and London 1963, 17–61; ' "Sola scriptura" und das Problem der Tradition', in *Das Neue Testament als Kanon*, ed. E. Käsemann (see below), 282–335; O. C. **Edwards**, Jr., 'Historical Critical Method's Failure of Nerve and a Prescription for a Tonic', *AThR* 59, 1977, 115–34; C. F. **Evans**, *Is Holy Scripture Christian?*, London 1971.

F. V. **Filson**, *Which Books Belong in the Bible? A Study of the Canon*, Philadelphia 1957; I. **Frank**, *Der Sinn Der Kanonbildung*, Freiburg 1971; J. **Gerhard**, *Loci Theologici*, Tübingen 1762, Tom. I, Locus I, chs. I–II, 1–13; H. **Gese**, 'Erwägung zur Einheit der biblischen Theologie', *ZTK* 67, 1970, 417–36, reprinted in *Vom Sinai zum Zion*, Munich 1974, 11–30; B. **Hägglund**, 'Die Bedeutung der "regula fidei" als Grundlage theologischer Aussagen', *StTh* 11, 1957, 1–44; F. **Hahn**, 'Das Problem "Schrift und Tradition" im Urchristentum', *EvTh* 39, 1970, 449–68; H. H. **Howorth**, 'The Origin and Authority of the Biblical Canon according to the Continental Reformers', *JTS* 8, 1906–7, 321–65; 'The Origin and Authority of the Canon among the Later Reformers', *JTS* 10, 1908–9, 183–232; 'The Influence of St Jerome on the Canon of the Western Church, II', *JTS* 11, 1909–10, 321–47; M. **Jugie**, *Histoire du canon de l'Ancien Testment dans l'église grecque et l'église russe*, Paris 1909, reprinted Leipzig 1974; E. **Käsemann**, 'Vom theologischen Recht historisch-kritischer Exegese', *ZTK* 64, 1967, 259–81; ed., *Das Neue Testament als Kanon*, Göttingen 1970; D. H. **Kelsey**, *The Uses of Scripture in Recent Theology*, Philadelphia and London 1975; H.-J. **Kraus**, 'Zur Geschichte des Überlieferungsbegriffs in der alttestamentlichen Wissenschaft', *EvTh* 16, 1956, 371–87, reprinted in *Biblisch-theologische Aufsätze*, Neukirchen-Vluyn 1972, 278–95; E. **Krentz**, *The Historical Critical Method*, Philadelphia 1975; H. **Küng**, 'Der Frühkatholizismus im Neuen Testament also kontroverstheologisches Problem', in *Das Neue Testament als Kanon*, ed. E. Käsemann, 175–204.

  M.-J. **Lagrange**, *La méthode historique*, Paris 1966; A. N. E. **Lane**, 'Scripture, Tradition and Church: An Historical Survey', *Vox Evangelica* 9, London 1975, 37–55; P. **Lengsfeld**, *Überlieferung. Tradition und Schrift in der evangelischen und katholischen Theologie der Gegenwart*, Paderborn 1960; I. **Lönning**, *'Kanon im Kanon'*, Oslo 1972; A. **Maichle**, *Der Kanon der biblischen Bücher und das Konzil von Trent*, Freiburg 1929; G. **Maier**, *Das Ende des historisch-kritischen Methode*, Wuppertal 1974; F. **Mildenberger**, *Gottes Tat im Wort*, Gütersloh 1964; *Die halbe Wahrheit oder die ganze Bibel*, Munich 1967; J. H. **Newman**, 'On the Interpretation of Scripture', *The Nineteenth Century* 15, London 1884, 185–99; D. E. **Nineham**, *The Use and Abuse of the Bible*, London 1976; S. M. **Ogden**, 'The Authority of Scripture for Theology', *Interp* 30, 1976, 242–70; K.-H. **Ohlig**, *Woher nimmt die Bibel ihre Authorität? Zum Verhältnis von Schriftkanon, Kirche und Jesus*, Düsseldorf 1970; *Die theologische Begründung des neutestamentlichen Kanons in der alten Kirche*, Düsseldorf 1972; Eva **Osswald**, 'Zum Problem der hermeneutischen Relevanz des Kanons für die Interpretation alttestamentlicher Texte', *Theologische Versuche* 18, East Berlin 1978; F. **Overbeck**, *Zur Geschichte des Kanons*, 1880, reprinted Darmstadt 1965; P. **Ricoeur**, *La métaphore vive*, Paris 1975; *Conflict of Interpretation*, ET Evanston 1976; J. F. A. **Sawyer**, 'The "Original Meaning of the Text", and other legitimate subjects for semantic description', *BETL* 33, 1974, 63–70; E. **Schlink**, 'Zum Problem der Tradition', *Der kommende Christus und die kirchlichen Tradition*, Göttingen 1961, 196–201; W. **Schrage**, 'Die Frage nach der Mitte und dem Kanon im Kanon des Neuen Testaments in der neueren Diskussion', *Rechtfertigung*, *FS E. Käsemann*, Tübingen 1976, 415–42; S. J. **Schultz**, 'Augustine and the Old Testament Canon', *Bibliotheca Sacra* 113, Dallas 1955, 225–34; E. **Schweizer**, 'Kanon?', *EvTh* 31, 1971, 339–57.

  G. T. **Sheppard**, 'Canon Criticism: The Proposal . . . and an Assessment for Evangelical Hermeneutics', *Studia Biblica et Theologica* 4, Pasadena, Calif. 1974, 3–17; R. **Smend**, 'Nachkritische Schriftauslegung', *Parresia*, *FS Karl Barth*, Zürich 1966, 215–37; W. **Staerk**, 'Der Schrift- und Kanonbegriff der jüdischen Bibel', *Zeitschrift für systematische Theologie* 6,

Berlin 1929, 101–19; P. **Stuhlmacher**, 'Historische Kritik und theologische Schriftauslegung', *Schriftauslegung auf dem Wege zur biblischen Theologie*, Göttingen 1975, 59–127; G. H. **Tavard**, *Holy Writ or Holy Church*, London 1959, New York 1960; E. **Troeltsch**, 'Über historische und dogmatische Methode in der Theologie', reprinted *Theologie als Wissenschaft*, ed. G. Sauter, ThB 43, 1971, 105–27; B. B. **Warfield**, 'Inspiration and Criticism', *The Inspiration and Authority of the Bible*, Philadelphia 1948, London 1951, 419–42; W. **Wink**, *The Bible in Human Transformation*, Philadelphia, 1973; H. W. **Wolff**, 'Zur Hermeneutik des Alten Testaments', 1956, reprinted *GSAT*, Munich 1964, 251–88; G. E. **Wright**, *The Old Testament and Theology*, New York 1969.

The purpose of this chapter is to describe an approach within the discipline of Old Testament Introduction which will attempt to overcome the methodological impasse of the canon which has been described in the previous chapter. Its goal is to take seriously the significance of the canon as a crucial element in understanding the Hebrew scriptures, and yet to understand the canon in its true historical and theological dimensions. It will seek to relate the canonical form of the Old Testament to the complex history of the literature's formation, the discovery of which is the hallmark of the modern historical critical study of the Bible.

Throughout this Introduction I shall be criticizing the failure of the historical critical method, as usually practised, to deal adequately with the canonical literature of the Old Testament. Nevertheless, it is a basic misunderstanding of the canonical approach to describe it as a non-historical reading of the Bible. Nothing could be further from the truth! Rather, the issue at stake is the nature of the Bible's historicality and the search for a historical approach which is commensurate with it. The whole point of emphasizing the canon is to stress the historical nature of the biblical witness. There is no 'revelation' apart from the experience of historical Israel. However, a general hermeneutic is inadequate to deal with the particular medium through which this experience has been registered. The study of the canonical shape of the literature is an attempt to do justice to the nature of Israel's unique history. To take the canon seriously is to stress the special quality of the Old Testament's humanity which is reflected in the form of Israel's sacred scripture.

1. Exegesis in a Canonical Context

At the outset I should like to set certain parameters to the scope of this study. The larger problems for Christian theology of establishing the relation between the two Testaments, as well as of examining the claims of the apocryphal books on the Christian church, lie beyond the scope of this Introduction to the Hebrew scriptures. In my judgment, these important subjects belong to the fields of biblical theology, New Testament, and early church history. However, I will at least express my own conviction regarding the importance of the study of the Hebrew scriptures for Christian theology. It is insufficient that the Christian church seeks to relate itself in some way with the historical events of the Old Testament. Rather, it is essential for a theological relationship to be maintained between the people of the Old Covenant and of the New. Regardless of whatever other writings or traditions were deemed authoritative by each community within a larger canon – for Jews it is the tradition of the sages, for Christians the gospel of Jesus Christ – the common canon of the Hebrew scriptures provides the fundamental basis for any serious relationship. I am well aware that this is a prescriptive statement, and that only seldom has either of the two communities of faith functioned in a way which reflected the common canon of sacred scripture. To seek to trace the development of the Christian canon within the church and to do justice to both the historical and theological problems involved far exceeds the scope of this present enterprise. For this reason the discussion which follows will limit itself, by and large, to the Hebrew scriptures. Only in the final chapter will I return to a reflection on these broader issues of Biblical Theology.

The major task of a canonical analysis of the Hebrew Bible is a descriptive one. It seeks to understand the peculiar shape and special function of these texts which comprise the Hebrew canon. Such an analysis does not assume a particular stance or faith commitment on the part of the reader because the subject of the investigation is the literature of Israel's faith, not that of the reader. However, apart from unintentional bias which is always present to some extent, the religious stance of the modern reader can play a legitimate role after the descriptive task has been accomplished, when the reader chooses whether or not to identify with the perspectives of the canonical texts of Israel which he has studied. Because this literature has had a special history as the religious literature of ancient Israel, its peculiar features must be handled in a way compatible to the material itself. A corpus of religious writings which has been transmitted within a community for over a thousand years cannot properly be compared to inert shreds which have lain in the ground for centuries. This observation is especially in order when one recognizes that Israel's developing religious understanding – the Bible speaks of God's encounter with Israel – left its mark on the literature in a continuing process of reshaping and growth.

Canonical analysis focuses its attention on the final form of the text itself. It seeks neither to use the text merely as a source for other information obtained by means of an oblique reading, nor to reconstruct a history of religious development. Rather, it treats the literature in its own integrity. Its concern is not to establish a history of Hebrew literature in general, but to study the features of this peculiar set of religious texts in relation to their usage within the historical community of ancient Israel. To take the canonical shape of these texts seriously is to seek to do justice to a literature which Israel transmitted as a record of God's revelation to his people along with Israel's response. The canonical approach to the Hebrew Bible does not make any dogmatic claims for the literature apart from the literature itself, as if these texts contained only timeless truths or communicated in a unique idiom, but rather it studies them as historically and theologically conditioned writings which were accorded a normative function in the life of this community. It also acknowledges that the texts served a religious function in closest relationship to the worship and service of God whom Israel confessed to be the source of the sacred word. The witness of the text cannot be separated from the divine reality which Israel testified to have evoked the response.

It is a misunderstanding of the canonical method to characterize it as an attempt to bring extrinsic, dogmatic categories to bear on the biblical text by which to stifle the genuine exegetical endeavour. Rather, the approach seeks to work within that interpretative structure which the biblical text has received from those who formed and used it as sacred scripture. To understand that canonical shape requires the highest degree of exegetical skill in an intensive wrestling with the text. It is to be expected that interpreters will sometimes disagree on the nature of the canonical shaping, but the disagreement will enhance the enterprise if the various interpreters share a common understanding of the nature of the exegetical task.

2. The Canonical Approach Contrasted with Others

Several crucial methodological issues are raised when the canonical approach is described as focusing on the final form of the text. Perhaps these issues can be most sharply profiled by contrasting the approach which I am suggesting with other familiar methods of critical biblical scholarship.

The canonical study of the Old Testament shares an interest in common with several of the newer literary critical methods in its concern to do justice to the integrity of the text itself apart from diachronistic reconstruction. One thinks of the so-called 'newer criticism' of English studies, of various forms of structural analysis, and of rhetorical criticism. Yet the canonical approach differs from a strictly literary approach by interpreting the biblical text in relation to a community of faith and practice for whom it served a particular theological role as possessing divine authority. For theological reasons the biblical texts were often shaped in such a way that the original poetic forms were lost, or a unified narrative badly shattered. The canonical approach is concerned to understand the nature of the theological shape of the text rather than to recover an original literary or aesthetic unity. Moreover, it does not agree with a form of structuralism which seeks to reach a depth structure of meaning lying below the surface of the canonical text.

Then again, the canonical method which is being outlined differs sharply from the so-called 'kerygmatic exegesis' which was popularized by von Rad and his students in the 50s and 60s. Classic examples of this method can be found in the writings of H. W. Wolff, C. Westermann, W. Brueggemann, among others. For several years beginning in 1966 *Interpretation* ran a series of articles under the rubric '*Kerygma* of the Bible'. This method attempted to discover the central intention of a writer, usually by means of formulae or themes, which intention was then linked to a reconstruction of a historical situation which allegedly evoked that given response. Its major concern was to combine historical critical analysis with a type of theological interpretation. A major criticism of the method is the extremely subjective, reductionist method in which the form-critical method has been extended beyond its original function to derive a theological message. Often the assumption that the theological point must be related to an original intention within a reconstructed historical context runs directly in the face of the literature's explicit statement of its function within the final form of the biblical text. The fragile nature of this kind of exegesis is also illustrated by its heavy dependence upon critical theories which bear less and less weight (von Rad's Credo, Noth's amphictyony, etc.).

Again, the canonical study of the Old Testament is to be distinguished from the traditio-critical approach in the way in which it evaluates the history of the text's formation. By assuming the normative status of the final form of the text the canonical approach evokes the strongest opposition from the side of traditio-historical criticism for which the heart of the exegetical task is the recovery of the depth dimension. Form critics raise familiar questions: Why should one stage in the process be accorded a special status? Were not the earlier levels of the text once regarded as canonical as well, and why should they not continue to be so regarded within the exegetical enterprise? Is not the history which one recovers in the growth of a text an important index for studying Israel's development of a self-understanding, and thus the very object of Old Testament theology? Having been trained in the form-critical method, I feel the force of these questions and am aware of the value of the approach. Still I feel strongly that these questions miss the mark and have not fully grasped the methodological issues at stake in the canonical proposal.

3. The Final Form of the Text and its Prehistory

The reason for insisting on the final form of scripture lies in the peculiar relationship between text and people of God which is constitutive of the canon. The shape of the biblical text reflects a history of encounter between God and Israel. The canon serves to describe this peculiar relationship and to define the scope of this history by establishing a beginning and end to the process. It assigns a special quality to this particular segment of human history which became normative for all successive generations of this community of faith. The significance of the final form of the biblical text is that it alone bears witness to the full history of revelation. Within the Old Testament neither the process of the formation of the literature nor the history of its canonization is assigned an independent integrity. This dimension has often been lost or purposely blurred and is therefore dependent on scholarly reconstruction. The fixing of a canon of scripture implies that the witness to Israel's experience with God lies not in recovering such historical processes, but is testified to in the effect on the biblical text itself. Scripture bears witness to God's activity in history on Israel's behalf, but history *per se* is not a medium of revelation which is commensurate with a canon. It is only in the final form of the biblical text in which the normative history has reached an end that the full effect of this revelatory history can be perceived.

It is certainly true that earlier stages in the development of the biblical literature were often regarded as canonical prior to the establishment of the final form. In fact, the final form frequently consists of simply transmitting an earlier, received form of the tradition often unchanged from its original setting. Yet to take the canon seriously is also to take seriously the critical function which it exercises in respect to the earlier stages of the literature's formation. A critical judgment is evidenced in the way in which these earlier stages are handled. At times the material is passed on unchanged; at other times tradents select, rearrange, or expand the received tradition. The purpose of insisting on the authority of the final canonical form is to defend its role of providing this critical norm. To work with the final stage of the text is not to lose the historical dimension, but it is rather to make a critical, theological judgment regarding the process. The depth dimension aids in understanding the interpreted text, and does not function independently of it. To distinguish the Yahwist source from the Priestly in the Pentateuch often allows the interpreter to hear the combined texts with new precision. But it is the full, combined text which has rendered a judgment on the shape of the tradition and which continues to exercise an authority on the community of faith. Of course, it is legitimate and fully necessary for the historian of the ancient Near East to use his written evidence in a different manner, often reading his texts obliquely, but this enterprise is of a different order from the interpretation of sacred scripture which we are seeking to describe.

Then again, the final form of the text performs a crucial hermeneutical function in establishing the peculiar profile of a passage. Its shaping provides an order in highlighting certain elements and subordinating others, in drawing features to the foreground and pushing others into the background. To work from the final form is to resist any method which seeks critically to shift the canonical ordering. Such an exegetical move occurs whenever an overarching category such as *Heilsgeschichte* subordinates the peculiar canonical profile, or a historical critical reconstruction attempts to refocus the picture according to its own standards of aesthetics or historical accuracy.

Although much of my polemical attention up to now has been directed against various forms of historicism which have made the use of the Bible dependent upon a reconstructed form of historical events rather than on the final form of the canonical text, I am also aware that another, very different front has been opened up which is equally incompatible with the canonical approach. In the philosophical hermeneutics of Paul Ricoeur and his followers the Bible is seen as a deposit of metaphors which contain inherent powers by which to interpret and order the present world of experience, regardless of the source of the imagery. The concern is to illuminate what lies 'ahead' (*devant*) of the text, not behind. This approach shows little or no interest in the historical development of the biblical text or even in the historical context of the canonical text. The crucial interpretative context in which the metaphors function is provided by the faith community itself (cf. D. Kelsey). Such an approach fails to take seriously the essential function of the canon in grounding the biblical metaphors within the context of historic Israel. By shaping Israel's traditions into the form of a normative scripture the biblical idiom no longer functions for the community of faith as free-floating metaphor, but as the divine imperative and promise to a historically conditioned people of God whose legacy the Christian church confesses to share.

4. *The Canonical Process and the Shaping of Scripture*

The formation of the canon took place over an extended period of time in close relation to the development of the Hebrew literature. But the canonical process was not simply an external validation of successive stages of literary development, but was an integral part of the literary process. Beginning in the pre-exilic period, but increasing in significance in the post-exilic era, a force was unleashed by Israel's religious use of her traditions which exerted an influence on the shaping of the literature as it was selected, collected and ordered. It is clear from the sketch of the process that particular editors, religious groups, and even political parties were involved. At times one can describe these groups historically or sociologically, such as the reforming Deuteronomic party of Jerusalem, or the editors associated with Hezekiah's court (Prov. 25.1). But basic to the canonical process is that those responsible for the actual editing of the text did their best to obscure their own identity. Thus the actual process by which the text was reworked lies in almost total obscurity. Its presence is detected by the effect on the text. Moreover, increasingly the original sociological and historical differences within the nation of Israel – Northern and Southern Kingdom, pro- and anti-monarchial parties, apocalyptic versus theocratic circles – were lost, and a religious community emerged which found its identity in terms of sacred scripture. Israel defined itself in terms of a book! The canon formed the decisive *Sitz im Leben* for the Jewish community's life, thus blurring the sociological evidence most sought after by the modern historian. When critical exegesis is made to rest on the recovery of these very sociological distinctions which have been obscured, it runs directly in the face of the canon's intention.

The motivations behind the canonical process were diverse and seldom discussed in the biblical text itself. However, the one concern which is expressly mentioned is that a tradition from the past be transmitted in such a way that its authoritative claims be laid upon all successive generations of Israel. Such expressions of intent are found in the promulgation of the law (Deut. 31.9ff.), in the fixing of rituals (Ex. 12.14), and in the provisions for transmitting the sacred story (Ex. 12.26ff.). A study of the biblical text reveals that this concern to pass on the authoritative tradition did not consist in merely passively channelling material from one generation to another, but reflects an involvement which actively shaped both the oral and written traditions. A major hermeneutical move was effected in the process of forming an original law, prophetic oracles, or ancient narrative into a collection of scripture through which every subsequent generation was to be addressed.

It is not clear to what extent the ordering of the oral and written material into a canonical form always involved an intentional decision. At times there is clear evidence for an intentional blurring of the original historical setting (cf. the discussion of 'Second Isaiah'). At other times the canonical shaping depends largely on what appear to be unintentional factors which subsequently were incorporated within a canonical context (e.g. the sequence of the proverbs in Prov. 10ff.). But irrespective of intentionality the effect of the canonical process was to render the tradition accessible to the future generation by means of a 'canonical intentionality', which is coextensive with the meaning of the biblical text.

The implication of this understanding of canon is crucial for one's approach to the problem of the 'actualization' of the biblical text. In the recent hermeneutical debate the term actualization (*Vergegenwärtigung*) denoted that process by which an ancient historical text was rendered accessible to a modern religious usage. An axiom of much redactional criticism is that the layering of a biblical text derives chiefly from a need to 'update' an original tradition. Although this description occasionally applies (Isa. 16.13f.), the chief point to be made by the canonical approach is that actualization is by no means limited to this one model. Rather, it is constitutive of the canon to seek to transmit the tradition in such a way as to prevent its being moored in the past. Actualization derives from a hermeneutical concern which was present during the different stages of the book's canonization. It is built into the structure of the text itself, and reveals an enormous richness of theological interpretation by which to render the text religiously accessible. The modern hermeneutical impasse which has found itself unable successfully to bridge the gap between the past and the present, has arisen in large measure from its disregard of the canonical shaping. The usual critical method of biblical exegesis is, first, to seek to restore an original historical setting by stripping away those very elements which constitute the canonical shape. Little wonder that once the biblical text has been securely anchored in the historical past by 'decanonizing' it, the interpreter has difficulty applying it to the modern religious context. (I am indebted to Gerald T. Sheppard for this formulation of the issue.)

5. Scripture and Tradition

One of the most difficult theological problems of the canonical approach to the Old Testament involves understanding the relationship between the divine initiative in creating Israel's scripture and the human response in receiving and transmitting the authoritative Word. Christian theology has, by and large, continued to describe the Bible in traditional terminology as the 'Word of God' which implies divine authorship in some sense. Nevertheless, few theologians in this post-critical era would wish to deny that the active human participation in the hearing, writing, and transmission of the Bible is an absolutely necessary feature for correctly understanding the text. What then is the relationship between these two dimensions of the Bible?

It is impossible to discuss the problem without being aware of the long and heated controversy within Christian theology which has strongly affected the history of exegesis, and has usually been treated under the rubric of 'Scripture and Tradition'. In the sixteenth century a sharp polarity developed between Protestant insistence on the primacy of the Bible and the Roman Catholic claim of ecclesiastical authority. The Reformers argued that the Bible was authoritative, not because the church made it so, but because of the Word of God which it contained. The Roman Catholic theologians countered that the church had been the human medium through which the Spirit of God had given the scriptures a concrete form and thus tradition could not be set in subordination to Word.

This polemical impasse continued to play an important role throughout the seventeenth century and provided the framework in which much of the historical critical research first emerged (cf. Simon, Le Clerc, Carpzov, etc.). By the middle of the nineteenth century the widespread recognition of the historical dimension in the formation of the Bible had badly damaged the traditional dogmatic positions of both Protestants and Catholics. The older theological issue was lost in the new historical and literary concerns to understand the growth of the literature. Within the dominant critical circles of Liberal Protestantism the role of God in the Bible's formation was relegated to a loosely defined divine purpose lying somewhere behind the evolution of Israel's religion.

The rebirth of confessional theology within Protestantism following World War I brought a renewed emphasis on the primacy of the Word of God, roughly analogous to the position of the sixteenth-century Reformers. However, there was a major difference in the attempt to accommodate orthodox Christian theology to the nineteenth-century historical critical study of the Bible. Several different models were suggested which sought to maintain the full divine initiative, but also to accord theological integrity to the historical process in the formation of the scriptures. Within Roman Catholic theology several imporant theological developments also occurred in this same period, reflected in the papal encyclical of 1943, *Divino afflante spiritu*, and culminating in the theological formulations of Vatican II. First, there was an attempt to offer a more positive view of the results of the historical critical method, which up to that time had been largely negative as a reaction to the earlier Modernist threat. Secondly, in terms of the scripture and tradition problem the new Catholic formulation re-emphasized the active role of the church in the Bible's formation but in a way which did not jeopardize the primacy of the divine Word. Only occasionally was the older Roman position defended. In sum, there has been a remarkable theological rapprochement between Protestants and Catholics regarding the traditional controversy over scripture and tradition. Both camps have returned to a position more akin to that of the early church in which the two elements were closely related, but not fused, in a rule of faith. It is also significant to observe that both the threat and promise arising from the challenge of the historical critical method exerted an important factor in this theological reconciliation.

The major purpose of this brief historical review is to suggest that the canonical method is not tied to one narrowly conceived dogmatic stance respecting the problem of scripture and tradition. The approach seeks to work descriptively within a broad theological framework and is open to a variety of different theological formulations which remains the responsibility of the systematic theologian to develop. I would admit, however, that the canonical method which is here described does run counter to two extreme theological positions. It is incompatible with a position on the far right which would stress the divine initiative in such a way as to rule out any theological significance to the response to the divine Word by the people of God. It is equally incompatible with a position on the far theological left, which would understand the formation of the Bible in purely humanistic terms, such as Israel's search for self-identity, or a process within nature under which God is subsumed.

It is also my sincere hope that Jewish scholars will not feel excluded from the theological enterprise associated with the canon. Even though the language used in the debate tends to stem from Christian circles, the theological issue of Israel's role in the canonical process lies at the heart of Jewish tradition. In my judgment, much of the failure of the usual Jewish-Christian dialogue to achieve a serious theological dimension arises from the loss of a sense of a common Bible which is precisely the issue addressed by the canon.

At the conclusion of each chapter of the descriptive analysis of the Old Testament books, I have added a brief bibliography of the history of exegesis including both Jewish and Christian contributions. Attention to the subsequent history of interpretation of the Bible is absolutely essential for its understanding, but the topic is so immense as to exceed the boundaries suitable for an Introduction. Obviously the purpose of pursuing this history is not to suggest that biblical scholarship needs only to return to the past, but that the future task is sorely impoverished if the great insights of our predecessors are overlooked. Particularly in the search for the canonical shape of a biblical book, pre-critical interpreters often saw dimensions of the text more clearly than those whose perspective was brought into focus by purely historical questions. Conversely, the history of exegesis illustrates some perennial, even ontological, errors in mishearing the text which continue to find new support.

6. Canon and Interpretation

A final word is in order regarding the effect of the canon on the larger exegetical enterprise of interpreting the Old Testament. The approach which I am undertaking has been described by others as 'canonical criticism'. I am unhappy with this term because it implies that the canonical approach is considered another historical critical technique which can take its place alongside of source criticism, form criticism, rhetorical criticism, and similar methods. I do not envision the approach to canon in this light. Rather, the issue at stake in relation to the canon turns on establishing a stance from which the Bible can be read as sacred scripture.

The concern with canon plays both a negative and a positive role in delineating the scope of exegesis. On the one hand, its negative role consists in relativizing the claims to priority of the historical critical method. It strongly resists the assumption that every biblical text has first to be filtered through a set historical critical mesh before one can even start the task of interpretation. On the other hand, its positive role seeks to challenge the interpreter to look closely at the biblical text in its received form and then critically to discern its function for a community of faith. Attention to the canon establishes certain parameters within which the tradition was placed. The canonical shaping serves not so much to establish a given meaning to a particular passage as to chart the boundaries within which the exegetical task is to be carried out.

Attention to these canonical guidelines within this Introduction may seem overly formalistic and too frequently concerned with determining a book's structure or interpretative patterns. However, one should not confuse this one aspect of the canonical approach with the full range of responsibilities comprising the exegetical task. A canonical Introduction is not the end, but only the beginning of exegesis. It prepares the stage for the real performance by clearing away unnecessary distractions and directing one's attention to the main activity which is about to be initiated.

In one sense the canonical method sets limits on the exegetical task by taking seriously the traditional parameters. In another sense the method liberates from the stifling effect of academic scholasticism. By insisting on viewing the exegetical task as constructive as well as descriptive, the interpreter is forced to confront the authoritative text of scripture in a continuing theological reflection. By placing the canonical text within the context of the community of faith and practice a variety of different exegetical models are freed to engage the text, such as the liturgical or the dramatic. In sum, the canon establishes a platform from which exegesis is launched rather than a barrier by which creative activity is restrained.

IV

TEXT AND CANON

Bibliography

P. R. **Ackroyd**, 'Original Text and Canonical Text', *USQR* 32, 1977, 166–73; B. **Albrektson**, 'Reflections on the Emergence of a Standard Text of the Hebrew Bible', *SVT* 29, 1978, 49–65; W. F. **Albright**, 'New Light on Early Recensions of the Hebrew Bible', *BASOR* 140, 1955, 27–33; reprinted F. M. Cross, *Qumran and History* (see below), 140–46; D. R. **Ap-Thomas**, *A Primer of Old Testament Text Criticism*, London 1947; V. **Aptowitzer**, *Das Schriftwort in der rabbinischen Literatur*, 1906, reprinted New York, 1970; W. **Bacher**, 'Targum', *JE* 12, 57–63; J. **Barr**, 'St Jerome's Appreciation of Hebrew', *BJRL* 49, 1966–7, 281–302; *Comparative Philology and the Text of the Old Testament*, Oxford 1968; 'Reading a Script without Vowels', *Writing without Letters*, ed. W. Haas, Manchester 1976, 71–100; D. **Barthélemy**, *Les devanciers d'Aquila*, *SVT* 10, 1963; 'Les Tiqquné Sopherim et la critique textuelle de l'Ancien Testament', *SVT* 9, 1963, 285–304; D. **Barthélemy** et al., *Preliminary and Interim Report on the Hebrew OT Text Project*, London 1973, v–xvii; 'Text, Hebrew, History of', *IDB Suppl*, 878–84; P. **Benoit**, 'L'inspiration des Septante d'après les Pères' in *Mélanges H. de Lubac, Théologie* 56, 1963, 169–87; E. **Bickerman[n]**, 'The Septuagint as a Translation', *PAAJR* 28, 1959, 1–39; J. **Bowman**, 'A Forgotten Controversy', *EvQu* 20, 1948, 46–68; S. P. **Brock**, 'Origen's Aims as a Textual Critic of the Old Testament', *Studia Patristica* 10, TU 107, 1970, 215–18; S. P. **Brock**, C. T. **Fritsch** and S. **Jellicoe**, *A Classified Bibliography of the Septuagint*, Leiden 1973; F. F. **Bruce**, 'Tradition and the Text of Scripture', *Tradition Old and New*, London 1970, 151–62; J. **Buxtorf** (pater), *Tiberias, sive commentarius massorethicus triplex historicus, didacticus, criticus*, Basel 1620, ²1665; J. **Buxtorf** (fil.), *Tractatus de punctorum vocalium, et accentuum in Libris Veteris Testamenti hebraicis, origine, antiquitate et authoritate; oppositus arcano punctationis revelato Ludovici Cappelli*, Basel 1648; *Anticritica seu vindiciae veritatis hebraicae adversus L. Cappelli criticam quam vocant sacram eiusque defensionem*, Basel 1653.

L. **Cappellus**, *Arcanum punctationis revelatum; sive de punctorum vocalium et accentuum apud Hebraeos vera et germana antiquitate libri II*, Leiden 1624; *Critica*

Sacra: sive de variis, quae in sacris Veteris Testamenti libris occurrunt, lectionibus libri sex, Paris 1650, Halle 1775–86; J. G. **Carpzov**, *A Defence of the Hebrew Bible in Answer to the Charge of Corruption*, ET London 1729; F. M. **Cross**, 'The Oldest Manuscripts from Qumran', *JBL* 74, 1955, 147–72; reprinted in *Qumran and History*, 147–76; *The Ancient Library of Qumran*, New York and London 1958, Garden City, N.Y., ²1961; 'The History of the Biblical Text in the Light of Discoveries in the Judaean Desert', *HTR* 57, 1964, 281–99, reprinted in *Qumran and History*, 177–95; 'The Contribution of the Qumrân Discoveries to the Study of the Biblical Text', *IEJ* 16, 1966, 81–95; reprinted in *Qumran and History*, 278–92; 'The Evolution of a Theory of Local Texts', *Qumran and History*, 306–20; F. M. **Cross** and S. **Talmon**, *Qumran and the History of the Biblical Text*, Cambridge, Mass. and London 1975; M. J. **Dahood**, 'The Value of Ugaritic for Textual Criticism', *Bibl* 40, 1959, 160–70; A. **Dotan**, 'Was the Aleppo Codex Actually Vocalized by Aharon ben Asher?' (Hebrew), *Tarbiz* 34, Jerusalem 1964–5, 136–55; 'Masorah', *EJ* 16, 1401–82; G. R. **Driver**, 'Introduction to the Old Testament', *The New English Bible*, Oxford and Cambridge 1970, xv–xviii; S. R. **Driver**, *Notes on the Hebrew Text and the Topography of the Books of Samuel*, Oxford and New York ²1913; D. N. **Freedman**, 'The Massoretic Text and the Qumran Scrolls: A Study in "Orthography"', *Textus* 2, Jerusalem 1962, 87–102; reprinted in *Qumran and History*, 196–211.

H. S. **Gehman**, 'The Hebraic Character of Septuagint Greek', *VT* 1, 1951, 81–90; A. **Geiger**, *Urschrift und Übersetzungen der Bibel in ihrer Abhängigkeit von der innern Entwicklung des Judentums*, Frankfurt ²1928; G. **Gerleman**, *Synoptic Studies in the Old Testament*, Lund 1948; W. **Gesenius**, *De pentateuchi samaritani origine, indole et auctoritate commentatio philologico-critica*, Halle 1815; J. C. L. **Gibson**, 'The Massoretes as Linguists', *Studies in Hebrew Language and Biblical Exegesis*, OTS 19, 1974, 86–96; C. D. **Ginsburg**, *Introduction to the Massoretico-Critical Edition of the Hebrew Bible*, London 1897, reprinted New York 1966; D. W. **Goodwin**, *Text-Restoration Methods in Contemporary USA Scholarship*, Naples 1969; M. **Goshen-Gottstein**, 'The History of the Bible-Text and Comparative Semitics. A Methodological Problem', *VT* 7, 1957, 195–201; 'Prologomena to a Critical Edition of the Peshitta', *Scripta Hierosolymitana* 8, Jerusalem 1960, 26–42; 'Theory and Practice of Textual Criticism', *Textus* 3, Jerusalem 1963, 130–58; 'The Rise of the Tiberian Bible Text', *Biblical and Other Studies*, ed. A. Altmann, Cambridge, Mass. and London 1963, 79–122; reprinted S. Leiman, *Canon and Masorah*, 666–709; *The Book of Isaiah, Sample Edition with Introduction*, Jerusalem 1965; 'The Psalms Scroll (11QPsᵃ). A Problem of Canon and Text', *Textus* 5, 1966, 22–33; 'Hebrew Biblical Manuscripts: Their History and Their Place in the [Hebrew University Bible Project] Edition', *Bibl* 48, 1967, 243–90; reprinted Cross, *Qumran and History*, 42–89; M. **Greenberg**, 'The Stabilization of the Text of the Hebrew Bible, Reviewed in the Light of the Biblical Materials from the Judean Desert', *JAOS* 76, 1956, 157–67; reprinted Leiman, *Canon and Masorah*,

298–319; 'The Use of the Ancient Versions for Interpreting the Hebrew Text', *SVT* 29, 1978, 131–48; P. **Grelot**, 'Sur l'inspiration et la canonicité de la Septante', *ScEc* 16, 1964, 387–418.

W. **Hamm**, *Der Septuagint-Text des Buches Daniel, Kap. 1–2*, Bonn 1969; R. **Hanhart**, 'Die Septuaginta als Problem der Textgeschichte, der Forschungsgeschichte und der Theologie', *SVT* 22, 1972, 185–200; J. G. **Janzen**, *Studies in the Text of Jeremiah*, HSM 6, 1973; S. **Jellicoe**, 'The Hesychian Recension Reconsidered', *JBL* 82, 1963, 409–18; *The Septuagint and Modern Study*, Oxford and New York 1968; *Studies in the Septuagint. Origins, Recensions and Interpretations. Selected Essays with a Prolegomenon*, New York 1974; A. **Jepsen**, 'Von den Aufgaben der alttestamentlichen Textkritik', *VT* 9, 1963, 337–41; P. E. **Kahle**, *Masoreten des Westens*, 2 vols., Stuttgart 1927–30; 'Problems of the Septuagint', *Studia Patristica* 1, TU 63, 1957, 328–38; *The Cairo Geniza*, Oxford ²1959, New York ²1960; 'The Greek Bible Manuscripts Used by Origen', *JBL* 79, 1960, 111–18; P. **Katz**, 'Septuagintal Studies in the Mid-Century', *The Background of the New Testament and its Eschatology, FS C.H. Dodd*, ed. W. D. Davies and D. Daube, Cambridge 1956, 176–208; D. **Kellermann**, 'Bemerkungen zur Neuausgabe der Biblia Hebraica', *ZDMG* Suppl III, 1, 1977, 128–38; B. **Kennicott**, *Vetus Testamentum Hebraicum cum variis lectionibus*, 2 vols., Oxford 1776–1800; R. W. **Klein**, *Textual Criticism of the Old Testament. From the Septuagint to Qumran*, Philadelphia 1974; Elias **Levita**, *The Massoreth Ha-Massoreth*, ed. C. D. Ginsburg, 1867, reprinted New York 1968.

P. **Maas**, *Textual Criticism*, ET Oxford and New York 1958; M. L. **Margolis**, 'Hexapla and Hexaplaric', *AJSL* 32, 1915–16, 126–40; 'Textual Criticism of the Greek Old Testament', *Proceedings of the American Philosophical Society* 67, Philadelphia 1928, 187–97; C. **McCarthy**, 'Emendations of the Scribes', *IDB Suppl*, 263f.; W. **McKane**, 'Benjamin Kennicott: An Eighteenth-Century Researcher', *JTS* 28, 1977, 445–64; B. M. **Metzger**, 'The Lucianic Recension of the Greek Bible', *Chapters in the History of New Testament Textual Criticism*, Leiden 1963, 1–41; J. **Morin**, *Exercitationes ecclesiasticae in utrumque Samaritanorum Pentateuchum*, Paris 1631; H. S. **Nyberg**, *Studien zum Hoseabuche*, Uppsala 1935; K. G. **O'Connell**, *The Theodotionic Revision of the Book of Exodus*, Cambridge, Mass. 1972; 'Greek Versions (Minor)', *IDB Suppl*, 377–81; H. M. **Orlinsky**, 'The Origin of the Kethib-Qere System: A New Approach' *SVT* 7, 1959, 184–92; 'The Textual Criticism of the Old Testament', *The Bible and the Ancient Near East. Essays in Honor of W. F. Albright*, ed. G. E. Wright, London 1960, New York 1961, 113–32; 'The Masoretic Text: Fact or Fiction?', *Prolegomenon* to the KTAV reprint of C. D. Ginsburg, *Introduction to the Massoretico-Critical Edition of the Hebrew Bible*, New York 1966; R. R. **Ottley**, *A Handbook to the Septuagint*, Cambridge and New York 1920; D. F. **Payne**, 'Old Testament Textual Criticism: Its Principles and Practice,' *Tyndale Bulletin* 25, Cambridge 1974, 99–112.

C. **Rabin**, 'The Dead Sea Scrolls and the History of the Old Testament

Text', *JTS* NS 6, 1955, 174–82; 'The Translation Process and the Character of the Septuagint', *Textus* 6, 1968, 1–26; A. **Rahlfs**, 'Lucians Rezension der Königsbücher', *Septuaginta Studien* 3, Göttingen 1911, 361–658; E. J. **Revell**, 'Studies in the Palestinian Vocalization of Hebrew', *Essays in the Ancient Semitic World*, ed. J. W. Wevers and D. B. Redford, Toronto 1970, 51–100; B. J. **Roberts**, 'The Divergencies in the Pre-Tiberian Massoretic Text', *JJS* 1, 1949, 147–55, reprinted Leiman, *Canon and Masorah*, 484–92; *The Old Testament Text and Versions*, Cardiff 1951; J. B. **de Rossi**, *Variae lectiones Veteris Testamenti*, 4 vols., Parma 1784–5; J. A. **Sanders**, 'Pre-Massoretic Psalter Texts', *CBQ* 27, 1965, 114–23; 'Palestinian Manuscripts 1947–1972', *JJS* 4, 1973, 74–83, reprinted Cross, *Qumran and History*, 401–13; M. H. **Segal**, 'The Promulgation of the Authoritative Text of the Hebrew Bible', *JBL* 72, 1953, 35–47, reprinted Leiman, *Canon and Masorah*, 285–97; S. **Segert**, 'The Ugaritic Texts and the Textual Criticism of the Hebrew Bible', *Near Eastern Studies in Honor of W. F. Albright*, ed. Hans Goedicke, Baltimore 1971, 413–20; J. D. **Shenkel**, *Chronology and Recensional Development in the Greek Text of Kings*, HSM 1, 1968; P. **Skehan**, 'A Fragment of the "Song of Moses" (Deut 32) from Qumran', *BASOR* 136, 1954, 12–15; 'Exodus in the Samaritan Recension from Qumran', *JBL* 74, 1955, 182–7; 'The Qumran Manuscripts and Textual Criticism', *SVT* 4, 1957, 148–60, reprinted Cross, *Qumran and History*, 212–25; 'The Biblical Scrolls from Qumran and the Text of the Old Testament', *BA* 28, 1965, 87–100, reprinted Cross, *Qumran and History*, 264–77; 'Texts and Versions', *The Jerome Biblical Commentary*, Englewood Cliffs, N.J. 1968, II, 561–80; A. **Sperber**, 'The Problems of the Septuagint Recensions', *JBL* 54, 1935, 73–92; H. B. **Swete**, *An Introduction to the Old Testament in Greek*, revised by R. R. Ottley, Cambridge [2]1914, reprinted New York 1968.

S. **Talmon**, 'The Samaritan Pentateuch', *JJS* 2, 1951, 144–50; 'Double Readings in the Massoretic Text', *Textus* 1, Jerusalem 1960, 144–84; 'DSIa as a Witness of Ancient Exegesis of the Book of Isaiah', *ASTI* 1, 1962, 62–72; 'The Three Scrolls of the Law that were found in the Temple Court', *Textus* 2, 1962, 14–27; 'Aspects of the Textual Transmission of the Bible in the Light of Qumran Manuscripts', *Textus* 4, 1964, 95–132; 'The Old Testament Text', *The Cambridge History of the Bible* 1, Cambridge and New York 1970, 159–99, reprinted Cross, *Qumran and History*, 1–41; 'The Textual Study of the Bible – A New Outlook', Cross, *Qumran and History*, 321–400; 'Conflate Readings (OT)', *IDB Suppl*, 170–73; H. St John **Thackeray**, 'The Greek Translation of the Four Books of Kings', *JTS* 8, 1906–7, 262–78; *The Septuagint and Jewish Worship: A Study in Origins* (Schweich Lectures 1920), London and New York 1923; D. Winton **Thomas**, 'The Textual Criticism of the Old Testament', *The Old Testament and Modern Study*, ed. H. H. Rowley, Oxford and New York 1951, 238–63; J. A. **Thompson**, 'Textual Criticism, OT', *IDB Suppl*, 886–91; E. **Tov** and R. **Kraft**, 'Septuagint', *IDB Suppl*, 807–15; P. **Walters** and D. W. **Gooding**, *The Text of the Septuagint*, Cambridge and New York 1973; Brian **Walton**,

Prolegomena in Biblia Polyglotta, 1655, reprinted Leipzig 1777; G. E. **Weil**, *Initiation à la Masorah*. *L'Introduction au Sepher Zikranot d'Élie Lévita*, Leiden 1964; 'La Massorah', *REJ* 131, 1972, 5–104; 'Qere-kethibh', *IDB Suppl*, 716–23; J. **Wellhausen**, *Der Text der Bücher Samuelis*, Göttingen 1871; J. W. **Wevers**, 'Septuaginta-Forschungen', *ThR* 22, 1954, 85–138, 171–90; 'Proto-Septuagint Studies', *The Seed of Wisdom, Essays in Honor of T. J. Meek*, ed. W. S. McCullough, Toronto 1964, 58–77; 'Septuaginta Forschungen seit 1954', *ThR* 33, 1968, 18–76; E. **Würthwein**, *The Text of the Old Testament*, ET Oxford and New York 1957; J. **Ziegler**, *Untersuchung zur Septuaginta des Buches Isaias*, Göttingen 1934; 'Die Vorlage der Isaias-Septuaginta (LXX) und die erste Isaias Rolle von Qumran (IQIsᵃ)', *JBL* 78, 1959, 34–59; F. **Zimmermann**, 'The Perpetuation of Variants in the MT', *JQR* 34, 1943–4, 459–74.

1. The Nature of the Problem

The purpose of this chapter is to discuss the problem of text criticism in relation to canon. Few scholars would wish to disparage the importance of the discipline of textual criticism which was one of the first fields to develop a scientific methodology at the beginning of the critical era of biblical scholarship. Within the last three decades the field of text criticism has taken on a new importance, particularly in the light of the Qumran discoveries and the advances in comparative philology, to become one of the most exciting areas of Old Testament studies. However, coupled with the growing interest is the recognition that the methodological problems are far from settled, and that diversity of approach has continued to widen.

The discipline of Old Testament text criticism raises a whole nest of peculiar problems for the canonical approach to scripture which has been outlined in the preceding chapters. The following issues come immediately to mind:

(i) The expression 'final form' has been used to designate the end of the literary development within the canonical process. What about the continuation in the development of a biblical composition in relation to its textual history? Is it also part of the canonical process? What are the similarities and differences between the literary and textual development of a canonical writing?

(ii) What are the goals of textual criticism? If the recovery of the 'original text' (autograph) is defended, even as an unattainable ideal, does not this goal assume a method of historical research sharply opposed to a canonical method which has relativized the importance of recovering an alleged original stage within the literary process? However, if the goal of textual criticism is simply to reconstruct the history of the text's development, does not this goal also run counter to a literary method which focuses on the results of the process rather than the process itself?

(iii) Is it even possible to speak of a canonical Old Testament text in the light of the multiplicity of textual traditions – proto-Masoretic, Old Greek, Samaritan, to name but a few? If the term canon implies a community for which a text is authoritative, which of the various different communities is the one to choose and on what grounds is the choice to be made?

(iv) Why should the Christian church be committed in any way to the authority of the Masoretic text when its development extended long after the inception of the church and was carried on within a rabbinic tradition?

2. History of the Discipline

Before turning to address these problems it is necessary to gain some perspective by briefly reviewing the history of modern Old Testament text criticism. Attention to textual problems extends far back into the ancient period. It includes the work of the rabbis and Masoretes, the contribution of the church fathers, and the various interpretative activities involved in the various translations. However, it has become increasingly clear that these early examples of scholarly activity with the text were of a different order and arose from a different concern from that of the modern discipline of text criticism (cf. Talmon, 'The OT Text', S. Brock, 'Origen's Aim'). The modern critical study of the text of the Old Testament emerged in the sixteenth century and was associated with the publication of the great Polyglot Bibles. The discovery of the Samaritan text of the Pentateuch in 1616 in particular touched off an important critical debate. At first the challenge to the superiority of the Masoretic text was fought along confessional theological lines with Catholics (Morin, Huntley) attacking the MT, and Protestants (Buxtorf, Hottinger) defending it. Closely associated with the issue of the *hebraica veritas* was the controversy over the age and integrity of the

Hebrew vowel points which again lined up Cappellus and the Buxtorfs as antagonists. With the defeat of the old orthodox Protestant
position represented by the Buxtorfs, the issue of text criticism
moved slowly out of the arena of theological polemics toward a
more objectively established critical methodology.

In terms of the Hebrew text the two great collations of biblical
manuscripts published in the last part of the eighteenth century by
Kennicott and de Rossi established definitively the scope of the
variants within the Masoretic consonantal tradition. Then in the
early nineteenth century Gesenius' dissertation brought the controversy over the Samaritan Pentateuch to a generally accepted
resolution.

One of the most creative attempts to open up a new critical
approach to text criticism of the Old Testament was the brilliant
book of Abraham Geiger published in 1857. In his *Urschrift* Geiger
sought to trace the internal history of the Hebrew text and its
ancient translations in order to show that the biblical text had a
history which reflected the changing religious responses within
Judaism. The book caused an enormous controversy among Jews
and Christians, but it did much to undercut the monolithic
interpretation of the Masoretic text as a static entity.

During the last half of the nineteenth century much of the critical
work on the Hebrew text turned on the issue of seeking to recover
an original Hebrew text which lay behind the recensional activity of
the Masoretes. Rosenmüller had propounded the theory that all the
known variants of the MT represented only one recensional source.
Later, Lagarde narrowed the *Urtext* theory even further by deriving
all the variants from one single exemplar (cf. Goshen-Gottstein,
'Hebrew Biblical Manuscripts'). The use of the versions, especially
the Septuagint, seemed to provide the only open avenue by which
to penetrate back to this original. For a time scholars such as
Thenius defended the theory of a general superiority of the Greek
over the Hebrew, but by the end of the century the work of
Wellhausen, Driver and Cornill, among others, had established the
need for a critical evaluation of each individual passage in an effort
to recover the original text without any overarching theory of textual superiority. In some sense, the method of text criticism represented by Kittel's *Biblia Hebraica*, especially the third edition, was
the logical extension of this search for an *Urtext* by means of the
versions and free emendation. In this respect, the new Stuttgart

edition shows some improvement, but still belongs to the same general tradition (cf. Kellermann). Significantly the publication of the two great critical editions of the Septuagint, which demonstrated the complexity of using the Greek, began in the early twentieth century but left little impact on the method reflected in *Biblia Hebraica*.

The discovery of a hoard of new manuscripts from the Cairo Geniza in 1890 produced a fresh impetus for the history of text criticism. In the position of Paul Kahle in particular a major new alternative to Lagarde's hypothesis emerged. Kahle argued that there had never been an *Urtext* and its reconstruction was a futile enterprise. Rather, a great diversity of textual traditions had existed before the establishment of an officially promulgated, standard text which finally formed a confluence from different textual streams. These 'vulgar' texts were never fully discarded, which also accounted for the continuing diversity after the period of stabilization. Although Kahle was able to push his research into the period before stabilization, he agreed with Lagarde in deriving the establishment of the MT from a rather arbitrary set of decisions by the rabbinic academy.

The discovery of the Dead Sea Scrolls broke wide open the field of Old Testament text criticism in the mid-twentieth century and provided scholars with actual manuscript evidence from that long hidden period before the stabilization of the Masoretic text. This characterization is not to suggest that the recovery of the textual history of the Old Testament became a simple enterprise in which consensus immediately reigned. However, the new material has opened up the possibility for major advances in understanding the textual history which has transformed the field within the last several decades.

Space is too limited to describe in detail the important contributions to the field made by Cross, Talmon, Goshen-Gottstein, and Barthélemy, among others. Of particular importance is Cross's elaboration of Albright's local text theory, which has emphasized both the diversity of textual tradition and also the homogeneity within the recensional history of various text types. However, both Talmon and Goshen-Gottstein, in resisting certain aspects of Cross's theory, stress the multiplicity of traditions in a manner which continues to represent some of the important emphases of Kahle. Also Barthélemy, on the basis of the Qumran community itself, emphasizes the ability of divergent textual traditions to co-exist which would caution against too quickly assigning the decisive role in the formation of the text to geographical factors. However, in spite of the ongoing debate regarding the history of the Old Testament text, certain major elements of a consensus have emerged.

Behind the apparently monolithic structure of the MT lay a long history of textual development in which the state of the text was in great fluidity. During several centuries prior to the stabilization of the Hebrew text in the late first century, rival text traditions competed with each other without there emerging any official or authoritative text. The authoritative role of the proto-Masoretic tradition derived from a variety of historical factors many of which remain unknown. However, the authority of the MT did not necessarily entail a textual superiority, in the modern sense, as being the grounds for its selection. Finally, long after the process of stabilization had begun, a considerable amount of textual fluidity continued to be tolerated within Jewish communities (cf. Aptowitzer).

3. The Goals of Old Testament Textual Criticism

There is no better way to illustrate the problematic dimension of modern Old Testament text criticism than to examine the conflicting formulations of the goals of the discipline. At the beginning of the modern critical period it was widely recognized that the MT had suffered some injury, but it was generally assumed that the damage was slight. The task of text criticism was simply to restore the best Hebrew text which was often regarded as only one step removed from the original. Increasingly it has become evident that neither is such a goal attainable nor does it adequately reflect even the nature of the problem. The basic issue at stake is a methodological one. On what level is the Old Testament text to be reconstructed? Is it to be a Masoretic tradition of the Hebrew text from the tenth century AD? Or is it a reconstructed text from the time of stabilization, c. AD 100? Or should it be on the level of the earliest textual evidence from (say) the third century BC? Finally, should it be an attempt to reconstruct the most likely original text as intended by its author by means of comparative philology? All of these options find modern defenders, often in an eclectic, mediating form.

(i) Ralph Klein begins his manual of Old Testament text criticism by accepting the traditional goal: 'Textual criticism is the discipline that tries to recover the original copy (autograph) of a piece of literature by comparing its available copies, all of which inevitably contain mistakes' (vii). But at the conclusion of the book, in the light of his own discussion of the new evidence, and the virtual impossibility of even approximating to the autographs, he qualifies his goal, suggesting that reconstructing the history of the text's growth may be the real contribution of the discipline (84). (For other variations of the 'original text' theory of text criticism see the treatment of Bentzen, *Introduction*, I, 94ff. and R. K. Harrison, *Introduction*, 257ff.).

(ii) Among the major practitioners of the comparative philological method (G. R. Driver, D. Winton Thomas, M. J. Dahood, etc.), the recovery of the original text is also generally assumed to be the goal (cf. Thomas, 258f.). In practice, the method frequently entails disregard of the vocalization, sporadic use of the versions, and a reinterpretation of the consonantal text in the light of comparative Semitics (cf. Driver, xvii). The fragile and speculative nature of much of the practice of this enterprise has been carefully rehearsed by James Barr and needs not be repeated, but the hermeneutical problems of the method still remain largely unexplored. Not surprisingly, Klein also allows for this approach to text criticism without defining its relation to the goals of a recensional history.

(iii) A third approach to the Old Testament text which is represented by Barthélemy, J. A. Thompson, J. A. Sanders, and the other members of the United Bible Project defines its goals in a more consistent, but modest fashion. It limits the task to reconstructing the earliest forms of the text which can be determined by critical analysis of existing textual evidence. This approach recognizes that no one unified form of the text at this stage of reconstruction may appear, and it has as its goal simply to register the degrees of diversity. It also makes no claim as to the relation between its reconstructed level and the original form of the text. However, in spite of the consistency of the goal it remains a serious question whether this proposal is adequate to form the basis of the text of the Old Testament used by modern Jews and Christians as sacred scripture. Why should a level in between the original and the final form of the Hebrew text be deemed normative? Does not this approach imply that the textual development from 300 BC to AD 100 is not part of the canonical process and can be thus disregarded?

(iv) Finally, the confusion regarding the place of the MT is widespread among both Jews and Christians. Orlinsky has polemicized vigorously against the idea that there is any one fixed Masoretic text, and he emphasizes the multiplicity of Masoretic traditions. Yet Goshen-Gottstein has made out a good case that the real variants within the MT are negligible and only variant readings within the one textual family are found. Again, D. F. Payne first warns against treating the MT as sacrosanct, but ends up concluding, at least for Genesis, that the MT seldom 'leads one astray and is to be trusted'. The same ambivalence toward the MT is reflected in Würthwein's manual (cf. 76ff.). Is there still a vestigial assumption of a special place for the MT which continues to resist substituting an eclectic text after the example of Rahlf's Septuagint or Nestle's New Testament?

4. Canon and Text

One of the least satisfactory elements in the text-critical manuals is the failure to relate the text-critical enterprise to the history of the Old Testament canon (cf. Roberts, Würthwein, Klein). Yet the two subjects are closely related. Only when the formation of the literature had reached a final stage of development within the canonical process did concern for the text of the literature emerge (cf. Talmon, 'The OT Text', 159). The textual history of the Old Testament is, therefore, a derivative of the concept of canon.

Although it is evident that the main process of canonization preceded the beginning of the textual history, it has become increasingly clear that the two processes overlapped. The new evidence from Qumran has demonstrated that the Old Testament text history had begun about 300 BC. Most critics would date the final literary form of the book of Daniel more than a hundred years later. Moreover, the strikingly different structure between the Hebrew and Greek forms of such books as Jeremiah would also provide internal evidence to confirm the overlap between the literary and textual formations of the Old Testament books.

In the light of this overlap, it is not surprising to find important elements of similarity between the canonical shaping in its literary development and the canonical shaping in its textual development. In both phases the formation of the literature as sacred scripture involved its ongoing use within a religious community in contrast to a purely scholarly endeavour. Again, both phases involved a process which exerted critical judgments respecting the preservation and transmission of the literature. Nevertheless, there are some equally important elements of difference between the literary and textual phases. The literary process involved major moves affecting the understanding of the literature, such as combining sources, restructuring the material into new patterns, and providing new redactional contexts for interpreting the tradition. By contrast, the textual phase of Old Testament formation was minor in comparison. Differences between the Hebrew and Greek forms of the book of Jeremiah, for example, mark the widest degree of variation within this phase, but generally only slight variations in the meaning are at stake. Again, the literary phase often involved considerable freedom on the part of the tradents in exerting an active, intentional effect. By contrast, the textual phase reflects a far more conservative, passive role with the activity focused on preserving and maintaining traditions rather than creating them.

The relationship between these two phases of the literature has important exegetical implications. Commentaries generally assume that the first task of exegesis is to establish a critical text before one begins the task of interpretation. Clearly such a procedure has some pragmatic advantages which might even support its continuation under certain circumstances. Nevertheless, the interpreter should at least be aware that this exegetical approach has reversed the historical sequence in the canonical formation of the literature. The literary development shaped the major lines of interpretation which the textual development sought to preserve. The danger of misunderstanding is acute when one attempts to establish a text without first understanding its canonical function as a whole. Only recently have Old Testament text critics such as Talmon, Goshen-Gottstein, and Barthélemy demonstrated how many textual decisions reflect a type of midrashic exegetical activity within the Bible itself. By assuming that text criticism is based on a purely objective, scientific methodology by which mechanical errors of transmission are corrected this important dimension of the textual phase is badly misunderstood. The recognition at least of the interdependence of canon and text is an important first step toward correcting this widespread mistake.

5. Goal and Method of a Canonical Approach to Text Criticism

In the face of the widespread confusion regarding the goal of text criticism and the level on which the enterprise operates, the canonical approach to the Old Testament is unequivocal in defining its goal as the recovery and understanding of the canonical text. However, to define what is meant by the canonical text and to describe the method by which this goal is achieved requires a more detailed exposition.

First of all, both the goal and method of procedure stand in an analogy with the previously discussed canonical method which focused its attention on describing the canonical shaping within the literary development of the literature. The method entailed a careful balance between a traditional and a critical perspective. On the one hand, the canonical critic identifies with the historic Jewish community in starting with the received form of the literature which comprised the Hebrew canon. On the other hand, he seeks critically to discern the canonical function of the literature. That is to say, he attempts to analyse how the literature, made up of disparate parts, was constructed to perform a theological role as scripture for a continuing religious community. Thus, the canonical function of a book is neither to be separated from its received form, nor is it to be simply identified with the whole.

The canonical approach to text criticism is broadly analogous to this literary method to the extent that it also entails a traditional and a critical element which are held in a careful balance. The canonical critic also begins with the received textual traditions of the historic Jewish community, thus establishing his point of standing, but at the same time he seeks critically to understand the canonical function of this particular textual tradition. The critical enterprise entails a full description of the history of the text affecting the formation of the received tradition as well as a comparison and critical evaluation of the received text in the light of alternative textual traditions. A basic characteristic of the canonical approach in regard to both its literary and textual level is its concern to describe the literature in terms of its relation to the historic Jewish community rather than seeing its goal to be the reconstruction of the most original literary form of the book, or the most pristine form of a textual tradition. In sum, the methodological issue at stake does not turn on the scope of the task, nor even on the application of the full range of historical critical analysis, but rather on what one understands to be the purpose of the discipline.

In spite of the analogy which has been described between the literary and textual levels within the canonical process, the crucial question still remains: What is meant by the received or canonical text? Which community is doing the receiving? What text is being transmitted, and what period within the history of the biblical text is being discussed? The thesis being proposed is that the Masoretic text of the Hebrew Bible is the *vehicle* both for recovering and for understanding the canonical text of the Old Testament. What is the justification for such a position?

(i) If one takes seriously the development of a canon of Hebrew scriptures, some immediate implications respecting the text of the Hebrew Bible can be drawn. Not only did the literary shape of the tradition receive a fixed form with the establishing of the canon, but the text of the Hebrew Bible also moved out of its earlier stage of fluidity into a stabilized form by the end of the first century AD. This stabilized Hebrew text was clearly a derivative of a fixed canon. Moreover, it was only the Hebrew text that was stabilized. The Greek Old Testament continued to remain fluid and obtained its stability only in its dependence upon the Hebrew. The striking difference in the process of stabilization between the Hebrew text of the Old Testament and the Greek text of the New Testament should not be overlooked. An approach to text criticism which is appropriate to the New Testament does not necessarily apply to the Old Testament. The problems are not identical and critical discernment is called for.

(ii) Constitutive of canon is a religious community for whom this corpus of literature functioned authoritatively. However, there were many different Jewish communities in the Hellenistic period with different authoritative texts. Why should the one community which finally supported the Masoretic text be singled out? The reason is that only this one historic community has continued through history as the living vehicle of the whole canon of Hebrew scripture. The Greek-speaking Jewish community of Egypt died out. Similarly the community of Qumran ceased to exist in the first century. Although the Samaritan community has continued in a very restricted sense, it has retained only a portion of the total Hebrew scriptures, which accounts for its sectarian position within Judaism. Moreover, the relation of canon and text effected an important theological transformation within Judaism. Following the stabilization of the Hebrew text, the various Jewish communities began to establish their identity on the basis of the Masoretic text, thus reversing the historical relationship between text and community. The importance of this move has been largely overlooked by the usual sociological description of the different Hellenistic Jewish communities.

(iii) The stabilized Hebrew text of the Jewish community was only a consonantal text. During the course of its development certain indicators of a few basic long vowel values were introduced in order to aid in the correct reading of the text, but it was not until the sixth or seventh century AD that various systems were developed to designate full vocalization. Moreover, it has become clear that the vowel points served to preserve and register the oral tradition of how the text was to be read and did not function as a critical or innovative grammatical enterprise. Würthwein's discussion is far from the mark when he characterizes the pointing as a 'new beginning' (17). Once again, in terms of the relation of canon and text, only the historic Jewish community whose authoritative text was the Masoretic was the tradent of the oral tradition of the vocalization of the Hebrew Bible. A very different relationship to the oral tradition is represented by the Greek-speaking community of Alexandria and by the Latin-speaking Christians of Jerome's age. (Contrast J. Barr's insightful handling of the textual evidence from Jerome, *Comparative Philology*, 207ff., with the misleading inferences of Bentzen, *Introduction* I, 62f.) In the famous vowel point controversy of the seventeenth century Buxtorf correctly sensed the canonical dependence of the consonantal text upon the proper vocalization – a dimension which escaped Cappellus – but he misunderstood the issue by attempting to draw historical rather than theological implications.

(iv) The increasing authority of the Masoretic text among the Greek-speaking Jews of the Hellenistic period who used a translated form of their Bible is clearly evident in the recensional history of the Septuagint. From the Jewish perspective the Greek Bible never had an independent integrity which could contest the Hebrew. Thus the Greek was continually brought into conformity with the Hebrew and never the reverse.

(v) But was not the relation of canon and text very different for Christians from what it was for Jews? Did not Greek-speaking Jewish Christians continue to use the Septuagint as an authoritative text, as the New Testament and early church fathers appear to demonstrate? Why should decisions within the Jewish community, some of which extended chronologically after the rise of Christianity, be deemed normative in any sense for Christians? It is evident that at the time when the New Testament was being written the vocalization of the Hebrew text was still in a more fluid state than in the period following, and that the New Testament's freedom in the use of textual traditions reflected a practice which was common to that pre-stabilization age. However, the crucial point to be made is that the early Christian community of the New Testament never developed a doctrine of scripture apart from the Jewish. It made no claims of having a better text of scripture, as did, for example, the Samaritans. Rather, the theological concern of Christians with the text of the Old Testament was of a different order. Christians sought to demonstrate the messianic claims of Jesus Christ on the basis of the same scripture held in common as authoritative by both religious communities. Christians at first appeared to lay no emphasis on a given text, but continued to use whatever texts were current among their Jewish contemporaries. By the second century the differences between the Jewish Hebrew Bible and the Christian Greek Bible had become a controversial issue. In time Origen's Hexapla was an attempt to equip Christians with a linguistic tool by which to wage disputation (cf. Brock). With the growing political and religious alienation of Jews and Christians, the church increasingly lost contact with the synagogue and the Hebrew scriptures, but these moves were culturally dictated, rather than being derived from a doctrinal stance. In sum, the church's use of Greek and Latin translations of the Old Testament was valid in its historical context, but theologically provides no grounds for calling into question the ultimate authority of the Hebrew text for church and synagogue.

6. Masoretic Text and Canonical Text

Up to this point the case has been made for describing the Masoretic text as the vehicle for the canonical text of the Old Testament. Now it is in order to pursue more precisely the relationship between the Masoretic text and the canonical text. The term canonical text denotes that official Hebrew text of the Jewish community which had reached a point of stabilization in the first century AD, thus all but ending its long history of fluidity. From that period on, the one form of the Hebrew text of the Bible became the normative and authoritative expression of Israel's sacred scripture. Stabilization marked the point which separated the text's history into two sharply distinguished periods: a pre-stabilization period marked by a wider toleration of divergent text types, and a post-stabilization period characterized by only minor variations of the one official text.

However, the point needs to be emphasized that the Masoretic text is not identical with the canonical text, but is only a vehicle for its recovery. There is no extant canonical text. Rather, what we have is a Hebrew text which has been carefully transmitted and meticulously guarded by a school of scribes through an elaborate Masoretic system. The earliest extant manuscripts of the entire Old Testament stem from about the tenth century AD (the Aleppo Codex is dated to the first half of the tenth century, but has been damaged in part. Codex Leningradensis dates from AD 1008). This means that the canonical text of first-century Judaism is now contained within a post-canonical tradition. Therefore, even though the expressed purpose of the Masoretes was to preserve the canonical text unchanged, in fact, a variety of factors make clear that changes have occurred and that a distinction between the MT and the canonical text must be maintained.

A brief characterization of the MT will serve to illustrate the problem. Orlinsky has made the point convincingly, even if in slightly exaggerated form, that there is not just one Masoretic text, but a variety of different Hebrew texts within the Masoretic tradition. Even after the period of stabilization the Hebrew consonantal text was not fixed absolutely, but a certain small degree of flexibility was maintained. Talmon has demonstrated the role of such devices as double readings in maintaining a diversity of traditions within the one textual family. Similarly such techniques as the *kethib/qere* system and the *seberin* offer the clearest evidence of an attempt to record a diversity in the text's reading. Again, the rabbinic tradition of the *tiqquné sopherim*, the inverted nuns, suspended letters, etc. show a certain degree of freedom in the handling of the text. Finally, that numerous mechanical corruptions within the MT have occurred in spite of the meticulous care in its transmission is evident to anyone who has worked with Kennicott and de Rossi.

If one turns to discuss the vocalization and accentuation of the MT, then the diversity within the textual traditions becomes even greater. This observation is not to suggest that little attention was paid to how the text was read. Rather, exactly the opposite case can be made. However, the differences between the Eastern and Western recensions and between the rival families of Ben Asher and Ben Naphtali affected the orthography as well as the vocalization and accentuation systems.

The first task of the Old Testament text critic is to seek to recover the stabilized canonical text through the vehicle of the Masoretic traditions. This process involves critically establishing the best Masoretic text which is closest to the original text of the first century. It also involves weighing the evidence for the best tradition of vocalization using the familiar historical and logical criteria. It should be noted that in this endeavour the terms 'best' and 'original' text are fully commensurate with a canonical approach. In the post-stabilization period the effort to establish a superior and original text is justified by the canon's concern to distinguish between an established, authoritative text and its subsequent elaboration. A canon implies that text and targum are not to be confused. In actual practice the task of recovering a text close to the first-century Masoretic text is certainly attainable and supported by Qumran manuscripts of the proto-Masoretic text type.

7. The Pre-stabilization Period in Old Testament Textual History

According to the canonical model for doing text criticism the goal of the enterprise is the recovery and the understanding of the canonical text. One begins with the tradition and then seeks critically to understand it. In order to achieve this goal the Old Testament text critic must turn to a study of the Old Testament text before its canonical stabilization and bring to bear upon the investigation the historical dimension of the text's development.

It is of crucial importance to recognize the striking differences in the textual situation which obtain between the pre- and post-stabilization phases. Indeed, the failure to take seriously the difference, which is to say, to take seriously the effect of the canon, lies at the heart of the methodological controversy over Old Testament text criticism. Whereas in the post-stabilization period the differences within the Masoretic traditions are minor in the light of the one dominant, unified tradition, in the pre-stabilization period the multiplicity of textual traditions is the most characteristic feature. Although logically one can posit an original text lying behind the diversity, in terms of textual history the actual forms of the earliest attested traditions are extremely diverse. As a result, the connection between the allegedly original text and the earliest extant manuscripts is highly uncertain. One could even argue that the diversity of texts derives from an oral stage in between the original delivery and textual transmission which would suggest that even the concept of an original text is often misleading. At least in terms of some of the duplicate texts in the Old Testament the extreme diversity would appear to point in this direction.

In terms of the hermeneutical issues involved in establishing a methodology for text criticism, the difference in the analysis of the pre-stabilization period between Cross's local text type theory and Talmon's and Goshen-Gottstein's multiple text family hypothesis is indecisive. Both theories recognize great diversity as well as certain elements of homogeneity within this fluid textual situation. However, Cross's position is useful in delivering the full impact of the recent text-critical evidence on the traditional theories regarding the text. He argues that there is no evidence before the time of Hillel for recensional activity which would eventually lead to stabilization, and thus even the terms 'standard' and 'vulgar' texts are anachronistic during the entire pre-stabilization period. The proto-Masoretic tradition was at best one among many competing traditions with no special claim for authority during an extended period.

Certain important facts affecting the evaluation of the MT emerge from a study of this recensional history. The period of textual fluidity extended from at least 300 BC to AD 100, and can in part be reconstructed, which often provides historical criteria for determining the priority of the different traditions. The present MT developed from an earlier proto-Masoretic text which extended back into the pre-stabilization period. However, the proto-Masoretic text also was comprised of a mixture of different textual families which appears evident in the light of the different text types represented in the parallel passages of Kings and Chronicles. The selection of the MT as the dominant tradition by rabbinic Judaism in the first century AD did not arise from an arbitrary, academic decision, as once postulated, but was rather the culmination of a long recensional history. However, the grounds for selecting this one particular tradition are far from clear, but appear to involve the use of texts within certain religious groups for liturgical and didactic purposes.

The most obvious implication to be drawn from this history of the pre-stabilization period is that the subsequent status accorded the MT did not derive necessarily from its being the best, or the most original, Hebrew text. Its choice as the canonical text was determined often by broad sociological factors and internal religious conflicts (cf. Geiger), and not by scholarly textual judgments. However, this does not imply that the selection was completely haphazard or arbitrary. The MT is frequently a shorter, more pristine tradition showing few signs of later harmonistic expansion. Nevertheless, to characterize the MT as the *hebraica veritas* is to draw an erroneous implication from its canonical status.

8. The Text-critical Task

Up to this point in the discussion an attempt has been made to set out the broad lines of consensus regarding the relation of the MT to the other textual families in the pre-stabilization period without pursuing the many minor differences which continue to exist among scholars. However, the crucial difference in Old Testament text-critical methodology now emerges which separates the canonical approach from the usual practice of the discipline. It is generally assumed that the goal of text criticism is to penetrate as far back as possible in the pre-stabilization period in an effort to recover the earliest or best text possible. At times this attempt at recovery assumes the presence of an *Urtext*, but the practice of text criticism is similar by critics in the school of Kahle who can only reckon with recovering earlier stages from among multiple textual traditions. Several major problems arise from this approach to text criticism. First of all, it is difficult to determine the criteria by which to adjudicate the superiority of a text. Often simple historical criteria are assumed which have customarily been applied to any classical text. The best text is the earliest, pristine form which is closest to the original. But from a canonical perspective this assumption fails to take seriously the peculiar features of the biblical literature. Just as in its literary phase when the literature developed beyond its original stage to reflect a different theological significance in its new canonical shape, so the textual history spanning several generations also shares in the canonical process. By applying the criterion of superiority to the earliest, most pristine text one fails to ascribe integrity to the process leading up to the text's final stabilization. Any subsequent alteration in the text, whether mechanical or intentional, serves to distort the original text and is therefore evaluated negatively.

The canonical approach to text criticism applies a very different methodology in its use of the textual history in the pre-stabilization period. It does not attempt to establish a 'better' text than the Masoretic, but chooses to remain with the canonical text and thus identifies the level of the literature with which it is concerned. Nevertheless, this canonical approach is vitally interested in all the evidence from the recensional history of the pre-stabilization period. It simply uses the evidence in a different manner towards achieving a particular goal, namely, the understanding of the canonical text.

The use of the recensional history of the early period is invaluable in providing a historical perspective by which critically to assess the Masoretic text. The history of the text often enables the interpreter to measure the range of mechanical errors which have entered the Masoretic text. Then again, the nature of the Masoretic text's intentional changes can be better understood when compared with the other textual traditions. One can make judgments as to whether a particular MT has broadened or narrowed a textual tradition, whether a particular reading reflects an ancient stage in the development of the text, or is the result of a later alteration and represented by only one text type. Frequently one can bring into sharper focus the exact contours of the Masoretic interpretation by contrasting it with a rival tradition (cf. Gen. 2.2 in the MT and G).

There is yet another side to the text-critical responsibility within the context of the canon. The usual method of text criticism results in each successive generation of critics offering fresh suggestions regarding the form of the original text. This highly individualistic model seems unaware of the continuing and enduring role of the canonical text, held in common by ongoing religious communities, which serves an authoritative function. The point is not to defend unreflected tradition, but at least to remain in conversation with it. Thus an important part of canonical text criticism is critically to evaluate the effect of a given form of the Hebrew text on its reader within the context of the biblical tradition. For example, in I Sam. 1.24 the peculiar phase w^ehanna'ar nā'ar ('the lad became a lad') appears to have arisen because of a haplography which dropped out a sentence still witnessed to in a Qumran manuscript and in the Greek. The canonical approach to this text would assess the effect of this mechanical error in the MT in relation to its earlier and apparently original reading in the other text families. In addition, it would attempt to assess the range of interpretation possible for this mutilated MT text, both in terms of its syntactical options (cf. Driver, *Samuel*), and its secondary vocalization. Within the fixed parameters of a canonical corpus the method seeks to determine how the meaning of a given passage, even if damaged, was influenced by its relation to other canonical passages. The obvious gain in such an approach is that the continuity with the entire history of exegesis is maintained. Moreover, the means for its critical evaluation is provided rather than arbitrarily setting up an individualistic reading which never had an effect upon any historical community.

Finally, a word is in order respecting the use of the comparative philological method for Old Testament text criticism. Many of the problems of adequately controlling the use of comparative Semitics for interpreting the Hebrew Bible have been discussed by James Barr (*Comparative Philology*) and do not need repeating. For anyone taking seriously the canonical shape of the text, the attempt to recover an original text apart from the tradition raises basic hermeneutical questions. Moreover, the tendency of the philological method to ignore the actual recensional history of the text in the claim that the new linguistic evidence supersedes all previous attempts at interpretation runs completely counter to the method being proposed. Such a method fails utterly to comprehend the nature of the Hebrew scripture which reflects in its very shape the history of its continuing use by a community of faith.

However, the comparative philological method is not to be dismissed out of hand, but can also serve a significant role within the canonical approach, if correctly employed. By determining a range of possible meanings within the context of Semitic languages, the biblical interpreter has an additional tool by which to bring into sharper focus the peculiar effect of the Masoretic interpretation. Or again, when the interpretation of the MT is itself uncertain, as is often the case with *hapax legomena*, the comparative evidence adds additional, extra-biblical evidence for its understanding. Finally, the comparative method can provide an important historical link from which better to comprehend how the text was heard by other diverse textual traditions.

To summarize: This chapter has attempted to outline an understanding of Old Testament text criticism in relation to the canon. The effect of taking the canon seriously is to establish the level of the biblical literature in accordance with its historical stabilization by the Jewish community and to seek to understand this received text in the light of its historical development. The methodological issue at stake is a hermeneutical one, and is of decisive importance in determining how one construes the entire exegetical task.

PART TWO

THE PENTATEUCH

V

INTRODUCTION TO THE PENTATEUCH

Bibliography

W. F. **Albright**, *From the Stone Age to Christianity*, Baltimore ²1957; O. T. **Allis**, *The Five Books of Moses*, Philadelphia ²1949; A. **Alt**, *Essays in Old Testament History and Religion*, ET Oxford and New York 1966; I. **Benzinger**, *Jahwist und Elohist in den Königsbüchern*, Stuttgart 1921; E. C. **Bissell**, *The Pentateuch. Its Origin and Structure*, London and New York 1885 (extensive bibliography of all older literature); J. **Blenkinsopp**, 'The Structure of P', *CBQ* 38, 1976, 275–92; J. **Bright**, 'Modern Study of Old Testament Literature', *The Bible and the Ancient Near East, FS W. F. Albright*, ed. G. E. Wright, Garden City, N.Y. 1961, 13–31; *History of Israel*, London and Philadelphia ²1972; W. **Brueggemann**, 'The Kerygma of the Priestly Writers', *ZAW* 84, 1972, 397–414; 'Questions addressed in the Study of the Pentateuch', *The Vitality of Old Testament Traditions*, Atlanta 1975, 13–28; M. **Buss**, 'The Study of Forms', *Old Testament Form Criticism*, ed. John H. Hayes, San Antonio, Texas 1974, 1–56.

U. **Cassuto**, *The Documentary Hypothesis and the Composition of the Pentateuch*, ET Jerusalem 1961; H. **Cazelles**, 'Positions actuelles dans l'exégèse du Pentateuque', *De Mari à Qumrân. L'Ancien Testament, Hommage à Mgr. J. Coppens*, Gembloux/Paris 1969, 34–57; H. **Cazelles**, and J. P. **Bouhot**, 'Pentateuque', *DBS* 7, 687–858; R. E. **Clements**, 'Covenant and Canon in the Old Testament', *Creation, Christ, and Culture. FS T. F. Torrance*, Edinburgh 1976, 1–12; D. J. A. **Clines**, *The Theme of the Pentateuch, JSOT* Suppl 10, 1978; G. W. **Coats**, *From Canaan to Egypt*, Washington 1976; R. **Cornely**, 'De pentateucho mosaico', *Introductionis in S. Scripturae libros compendium*, Paris ¹¹1934, 303–45; J. F. **Craghan**, 'The Elohist in Recent Literature', *BTB* 7, 1977, 23–35; F. M. **Cross**, *Canaanite Myth and Hebrew Epic*, Cambridge, Mass. and London 1973, esp. 'The Priestly Work', 293–325; F. **Delitzsch**, 'Pentateuch-kritische Studien', *Zeitschrift für kirchliche Wissenschaft und kirchliches Leben* 1, Leipzig 1880 (12 articles); O. **Eissfeldt**, *Hexateuch-Synopse*, Leipzig 1922; K. **Elliger**, 'Sinn und Ursprung der priesterlichen Geschichtserzählung', *ZTK* 49, 1959, 121–43; P. F. **Ellis**, *The Yahwist. The Bible's First Theologian*, Notre Dame, Ind. and London 1968; I.

Engnell, 'The Pentateuch', *A Rigid Scrutiny*, Nashville 1969 (=*Critical Essays on the Old Testament*, London 1970), 50–67; G. **Fohrer**, 'Priesterschrift', *RGG*[3] 5, 568f.; T. E. **Fretheim**, 'Source Criticism, OT', *IDB Suppl*, 838f.

C. H. J. **de Geus**, *The Tribes of Israel. An Investigation into some of the Presuppositions of Martin Noth's Amphictyony Hypothesis*, Assen 1976; C. H. **Gordon**, 'Biblical Customs and the Nuzi Tablets', *BA* 3, 1940, 1–12; N. K. **Gottwald**, *The Tribes of Yahweh*, London (=*Liberated Israel*, Maryknoll, N.Y.) 1979; K. H. **Graf**, 'Die sogenannte Grundschrift des Pentateuchs', *Archiv für wissenschaftliche Erforschung des Alten Testaments* I, Halle 1869, 466–77; W. H. **Green**, *The Higher Criticism of the Pentateuch*, New York 1895; P. **Grelot**, 'La dernière étape de la rédaction sacerdotale', *VT* 6, 1956, 174–89; H. **Gunkel**, 'Die Grundprobleme der israelitischen Literaturgeschichte', *Reden und Aufsätze*, Göttingen 1913, 29–38; H. A. C. **Hävernick**, *An Historico-Critical Introduction to the Pentateuch*, ET Edinburgh 1850; M. **Haran**, 'Shiloh and Jerusalem. The Origin of the Priestly Tradition in the Pentateuch', *JBL* 81, 1962, 14–24; J. H. **Hayes** and J. M. **Miller**, eds., *Israelite and Judaean History*, OTL, 1977; J. **Hempel**, 'Priesterkodex', *Pauly-Wissowa Realencyclopädie der classischen Altertumswissenschaft*, 22, Stuttgart 1954, cols. 1945ff.; E. W. **Hengstenberg**, *Die Authentie des Pentateuchs*, 3 vols, Berlin 1836–39; S. **Herrmann**, *A History of Israel in Old Testament Times*, ET London and Philadelphia 1975; G. **Hölscher**, *Geschichtsschreibung in Israel*, Lund 1952; H. **Holzinger**, *Einleitung in den Hexateuch*, Leipzig 1893; F. **Hommel**, *The Ancient Hebrew Tradition as illustrated by the Monuments*, ET London and New York 1897; A. **Hurwitz**, 'The Evidence of Language in Dating the Priestly Code', *RB* 81, 1974, 24–56; B. **Jacob**, *Der Pentateuch*, Leipzig 1905.

A. S. **Kapelrud**, 'The Date of the Priestly Code (P)', *ASTI* 3, 1964, 58–64; Y. **Kaufmann**, *The Religion of Israel*, ET Chicago 1960, London 1961; R. **Kessler**, *Die Querverweise im Pentateuch. Überlieferungsgeschichtliche Untersuchung der expliziten Querverbindungen innerhalb des vorpriesterlichen Pentateuchs*, Diss. Heidelberg 1972; R. **Knierim**, 'Old Testament Form Criticism Reconsidered', *Interp* 27, 1973, 435–67; H.-J. **Kraus**, *Geschichte der historisch-kritischen Erforschung des Alten Testaments von der Reformation bis zur Gegenwart*, Neukirchen-Vluyn [2]1969; M. G. **Kyle**, *The Deciding Voice of the Monuments in Biblical Criticism*, Oberlin, Ohio [2]1924; M. **Löhr**, *Untersuchungen zum Hexateuchproblem I: Der Priesterkodex in der Genesis*, BZAW 38, 1924; B. **Luther**, 'Die Persönlichkeit des Jahwisten', Appendix to E. Meyer, *Die Israeliten und ihre Nachbarstämme*, Halle 1906; S. E. **McEvenue**, *The Narrative Style of the Priestly Writer*, Rome 1971; G. **Mendenhall**, 'Ancient Oriental and Biblical Law' and 'Covenant Forms in Israelite Tradition', *BA* 17, 1954, 26–46, 50–76=*Law and Covenant in Israel and the Ancient Near East*, Pittsburgh 1955; S. **Mowinckel**, *Erwägungen zur Pentateuch Quellenfrage*, Trondheim 1964; *Tetrateuch-Pentateuch-Hexateuch*, Berlin 1964; C. R. **North**, 'Pentateuchal Criticism', *The Old Testament and Modern*

Study, ed. H. H. Rowley, Oxford and New York 1951, 48–83; M. **Noth**, *Überlieferungsgeschichte des Pentateuch*, Stuttgart 1948; ET *A History of Pentateuchal Traditions*, Englewood Cliffs, N.J. 1972.

E. **Otto**, 'Stehen wir vor einem Umbruch in der Pentateuchkritik?', *VF* 22, 1977, 82–97; L. **Perlitt**, *Vatke und Wellhausen*, BZAW 94, 1965; O. **Plöger**, 'Pentateuch', *RGG*³ 5, 211–17; G. **von Rad**, *Die Priesterschrift im Hexateuch*, BWANT IV 13 (=65), 1934; *Das formgeschichliche Problem des Hexateuchs*, BWANT IV 26 (=78), 1938; ET *The Problem of the Hexateuch and Other Essays*, Edinburgh and New York 1966; R. **Rendtorff**, 'Literaturkritik und Traditionsgeschichte', *EvTh* 27, 1967, 138–53; 'Traditio-historical Method and the Documentary Hypothesis', *Proceedings of the Fifth World Congress of Jewish Studies* (1969), Jerusalem 1971, 5–11; 'Der "Jahwist" als Theologe? Zum Dilemma der Pentateuchkritik', *SVT* 28, 1974, 158–66; *Das überlieferungsgeschichtliche Problem des Pentateuch*, BZAW 147, 1977; W. **Richter**, *Exegese als Literaturwissenschaft*, Göttingen 1971; H. **Ringgren**, 'Literarkritik, Formgeschichte, Überlieferungsgeschichte', *TLZ* 91, 1966, 641–50; L. **Rost**, 'Zum geschichtlichen Ort der Pentateuchquellen', *ZTK* 53, 1956, 1–10; W. **Rudolph**, *Der 'Elohist' von Exodus bis Josua*, BZAW 68, 1938; J. A. **Sanders**, *Torah and Canon*, Philadelphia 1972; A. H. **Sayce**, *The 'Higher Criticism' and the Verdict of the Monuments*, London and New York ²1894; H. H. **Schmid**, *Der sogennante Jahwist: Beobachtungen und Frage zur Pentateuchforschung*, Zürich 1976; K. **Scholder**, *Ursprünge und Probleme der Bibelkritik im 17. Jahrhundert*, Munich 1966; H. **Schulte**, *Die Entstehung der Geschichtsschreibung im Alten Israel*, BZAW 128, 1972; C. A. **Simpson**, *The Early Traditions of Israel*, Oxford and New York 1948; D. C. **Simpson**, *Pentateuchal Criticism*, London and New York 1924; R. **Smend**, *Die Erzählung des Hexateuch auf ihre Quellen untersucht*, Berlin 1912; R. **Smend**, jr., 'Pentateuchforschung', *BHH* 3, 1413–19; J. A. **Soggin**, 'Ancient Biblical Tradition and Modern Archaeological Discoveries', *BA* 23, 1960, 95–100; E. A. **Speiser**, 'The Wife-Sister Motif in the Patriarchal Narratives', *Biblical and Other Studies*, ed. A. Altmann, Cambridge, Mass. 1963, 15–28; W. **Staerk**, 'Zur alttestamentlichen Literarkritik. Grundsätzliches und Methodisches', *ZAW* 42, 1924, 34–74.

R. J. **Thompson**, *Moses and the Law in a Century of Criticism since Graf*, Leiden 1970; J. H. **Tigay**, 'An Empirical Basis for the Documentary Hypothesis', *JBL* 94, 1975, 329–42; J. **Van Seters**, 'Confessional Reformulations in the Exilic Period', *VT* 22, 1972, 448–59; R. **de Vaux**, 'À propos du second centenaire d'Astruc, Réflexions sur l'état actuel de la critique du Pentateuque', *SVT* 1, 1953, 182–98; J. G. **Vink**, 'The Date and Origin of the Priestly Code in the Old Testament', *The Priestly Code and Seven other Studies*, OTS 15, 1969, 1–144; P. **Volz** and W. **Rudolph**, *Der Elohist als Erzähler: Ein Irrweg der Pentateuchkritik*, Berlin 1933; N. **Wagner**, 'Pentateuchal Criticism: No Clear Future', *Canadian Journal of Theology* 13, Toronto 1967, 225–32; H. **Weidmann**, *Die Patriarchen und ihre Religion im Licht der Forschung seit Julius Wellhausen*, FRLANT 94, 1968; A. **Weiser**,

Introduction to the Old Testament, ET London (=*The Old Testament: its Formation and Development*, New York) 1961; J. **Wellhausen**, *Die Composition des Hexateuchs und der historischen Bücher des Alten Testaments*, Berlin ³1899; H. M. **Wiener**, *Essays in Pentateuchal Criticism*, London and Oberlin, Ohio 1910; F. V. **Winnett**, 'Re-Examining the Foundations', *JBL* 84, 1965, 1–19; H. W. **Wolff**, 'The Kerygma of the Yahwist', ET, *Interp* 20, 1966, 131–58=W. Brueggemann and H. W. Wolff, *The Vitality of Old Testament Traditions*, Atlanta 1975, 41–66; 'The Elohistic Fragments in the Pentateuch', ET, *Interpr* 26, 1972, 158–73=*Vitality*, 66–82; G. E. **Wright**, 'Modern Issues in Biblical Studies: History and the Patriarchs', *ExpT* 71, 1960, 292–6; W. **Zimmerli**, 'Sinaibund und Abrahambund', *TZ* 16, 1960, 268–80=*Gottes Offenbarung*, Munich 1963, 205–16.

1. The History of Modern Critical Research

The history of the modern critical study of the Pentateuch has been reviewed many times and is readily available in Old Testament Introductions (Eissfeldt, Fohrer, Kaiser), in encyclopaedia articles (cf. under Pentateuch in *RGG*³, *IDB*, *BHH*, *DBS*), and in several monographs (Hölscher, Kraus). Nevertheless, the importance of this history is such that discussion of it cannot be entirely omitted. First, the basic methodological issues of critical biblical scholarship, which have strongly affected the entire discipline, were hammered out primarily in the study of the Pentateuch. Knowledge of the history is, therefore, indispensable for methodology. Secondly, present research continues to occupy itself with many of the same problems and often returns to the older positions for resolving difficulties. Knowledge of the history is, therefore, crucial for evaluating the continuing debate.

The literary critical method

The traditional Jewish and Christian manner of reading the Pentateuch assumed that the five books had been written by Moses and represented a unified and datable composition which depicted historical events from the creation of the world until the death of Moses. Certain problems with this traditional understanding had been occasionally seen, especially in the seventeenth century (Spinoza, Simon, Le Clerc,) but not until the eighteenth century did a consistent effort emerge which sought to offer a different literary theory regarding the nature and composition of the Pentateuch. The discovery of two different sources in Genesis by Witter (1711) and Astruc (1756) led Eichhorn (1780) to formulate the 'older documentary hypothesis' of two continuing strands of narrative extending throughout Genesis which he designated J and E according to the use of the two divine names. As the complexity of the literary problems increased and critical analysis was extended to the entire Pentateuch, two new theories were formulated. The 'fragment hypothesis' (Geddes, Vater) worked with numerous pieces of documents which were thought not to be continuous. This theory was shortly replaced with a 'supplementary hypothesis' (Ewald, Bleek) which posited one basic source with numerous expansions from other secondary sources. Finally, the 'newer documentary hypothesis' (Hupfeld 1853) returned to the idea of independent sources extending throughout the Pentateuch which could be arranged in a clear historical sequence, namely P(the *Grundschrift*), J, E, and D. The crucial step was taken in establishing the classic literary critical theory of the Pentateuch when Reuss, Graf, Kuenen, and Wellhausen reversed the order of the sources and, placing the Priestly source in the post-exilic period, argued for the sequence of documents JEDP to account for the final form of the Pentateuch.

The great persuasiveness of the newer documentary theory as formulated by Wellhausen was apparent by a sudden halting of new theories and the formation of an impressive critical consensus. In Germany A. Dillmann was the last major figure to oppose Wellhausen's position with any degree of success. In England the ground for its acceptance had been prepared by W. Robertson Smith, but Driver's *Introduction* (1891) shortly secured its virtual hegemony in the English-speaking world. American scholars such as Bewer and Kent popularized the consensus. In France leading scholars such as Lods overwhelmed the last vestige of resistance, except among conservative Roman Catholic circles.

Of course, even at its zenith the literary critical consensus was not absolute. Some learned Protestant, Catholic, and Jewish scholars continued flatly to oppose the theory (W. H. Green, F. Vigouroux, D. Hoffmann, H. M. Wiener). Others attempted to offer important modifications although accepting in principle the presence of literary sources (J. Orr, Lagrange, Kaufmann). Of course, in time the major opposition to source criticism was to develop in

Scandinavia, but this was a much later development.

Of more influence on the history of scholarship was the work of scholars who continued to operate within Wellhausen's general framework but sought further to refine the sources. In the course of the refinement important weaknesses emerged which often unintentionally began to dissolve the reigning consensus. Budde (1883) posited a J^2 source to account for the tension within the J source in Genesis 1–11, and Kuenen (1887) similarly divided E into two strands. On the basis of such further refinements R. Smend (1912) came up with a very different division of sources from that proposed by Wellhausen. In addition, wholly new sources were suggested by Eissfeldt, Pfeiffer and others which began to blur the classic divisions. Another serious problem was opened up by those scholars who sought to extend the pentateuchal sources into the books of Samuel and Kings (Benzinger, Hölscher), an effort which met with a very mixed reception from within the older consensus. Long after the early confidence in the classic documentary theory had disappeared, critical scholars continued to work with Wellhausen's source analysis largely because of the lack of any new consensus by which to replace it. Probably the only major modification which was able to muster wide support was M. Noth's theory of a basic document G underlying both J and E, which seemed to account for the wide areas of overlap in these two sources. But even here, it was the vagueness of the theory – Noth could not decide whether it was an oral or written source – which accounted for much of its attractiveness.

Form-critical and traditio-critical method

Although the literary critical concern with recovering the varying sources of the Pentateuch continued, it is clear with the perspective of hindsight that the dominant force of critical study at the end of the nineteenth century had shifted its focus to the levels of oral tradition lying behind the sources. The major credit for the new direction goes to Hermann Gunkel and his students (Gressmann, Begrich, Baumgartner), although Gunkel did have important predecessors (cf. Buss).

In his famous monograph, *Schöpfung und Chaos* (1895), Gunkel established that the material in Genesis 1, even though set in the post-exilic priestly source, was of great antiquity and had undergone a history of development in its oral stage which could be traced. By means of a form-critical analysis he followed the changes within the stereotyped language of tradition and sought to anchor the material within its original sociological milieu (*Sitz im Leben*). Subsequently, in his Genesis commentary Gunkel tried to isolate individual sagas and trace them back to their earliest forms. Gressmann used a similar method for Exodus. In these early works no sharp distinctions were drawn between the form-critical, traditio-critical, and *religionsgeschichtliche* methods, but Gunkel stressed his concern in his important essay on methodology to maintain the broadest possible relationship between the literature's form and social function.

During Gunkel's lifetime (he died in 1932) and in the period immediately following, many of Gunkel's students worked in areas other than the Pentateuch, especially in the Psalms and Prophets. However, the application of Gunkel's insights to the Pentateuch received a fresh impetus from A. Alt, whose important essays on patriarchal religion (1929) and Israelite law (1934) deeply affected the handling of the Pentateuch. Above all, Alt's influence was crucial in stimulating the research of von Rad and Noth. Clearly von Rad's monograph on the Hexateuch (1938) and Noth's on the Pentateuch (1948) were the two most seminal works in the field during this period and dominated much of the critical discussion for a generation. In his book von Rad sought to expand Gunkel's form-critical method to the whole framework of the Hexateuch and to trace its development from early cultic formulation which he thought to find embedded in skeletal credal forms. Noth continued to build on von Rad's hypothesis, but made important modifications. He also shifted from the classic form-critical method toward developing the traditio-critical method (*Überlieferungsgeschichte*) as a discipline in its own right. It is also important to note that both von Rad and Noth, along with a wide circle of important scholars (Zimmerli, Wolff, Westermann) were interested in showing the relevance of the form-critical method for Old Testament theology, a concern notably missing in Gunkel and the first generation of form critics. During the period of the 50s and 60s a veritable flood of monographs appeared, especially from Germany, which pursued the leads of the traditio-critical method. Of particular importance were the problems of relating the various pentateuchal traditions, such as Exodus and Sinai. The contribution of the American scholar George Mendenhall to the form-critical discussion was significant in the 50s particularly, since he brought to the problem a very different perspective and scholarly tradition in his use of Hittite treaty parallels.

Of course, not all scholars, even within Germany, were in accord with the form-critical direction proposed by von Rad and Noth. Alternative theories were offered by Hölscher, Weiser, Fohrer, and others. But the most critical reaction to German scholarship came from Scandinavia, centring in the work of I. Engnell. He proposed a method of oral criticism which rejected almost completely source-critical analysis and offered a very different approach to the study of the Pentateuch. He envisioned two different circles of oral tradition, a Deuteronomic and a Priestly, which lay behind the present composition. However, Engnell's theory was never worked out in detail, and following his untimely death in 1964 greatly declined in influence.

Archaeological method

Strictly speaking, there is no archaeological method which is comparable to the approaches which have been discussed above. Rather, the rubric is used to include scholars who have consciously distanced themselves from the direction of the critical majority and have sought to find a different model for the study of ancient texts in the science of archaeology.

During much of the nineteenth century recourse to archaeological material as a form of extra-biblical evidence was used by conservative scholars in an effort to resist the predominantly literary emphasis of Old Testament criticism. Hengstenberg's *Egypt and the Books of Moses* (ET 1845) provided an early example of this move. Toward the end of the nineteenth century several British scholars, especially Sayce and Rawlinson, attempted to exploit the new discoveries against the documentary hypothesis. Also in Germany, among critical scholars such as Hommel, Kittel and Sellin, attempts were made to support a more historical understanding of the patriarchs and Moses by recourse to archaeology.

However, in recent years the archaeological method has become largely identified with W. F. Albright and his school. Beginning in the 1920s and continuing through to the 60s Albright brought his enormous philological, historical and literary learning to bear on Old Testament studies, stressing the central role of objective, empirical evidence, an emphasis which he had developed from his archaeological research. Albright's method in reference to the Pentateuch remained highly eclectic. He generally worked with the classic source divisions and welcomed Gunkel's use of extra-biblical evidence to recover Israel's tradition. However, the general focus was very different from the German literary and form criticism. Above all, Albright sought to establish the antiquity and historicity of as much of the Pentateuch as possible which he then interpreted in close analogy with its ancient Near Eastern background. Although his work was often hailed with enthusiam by conservatives, both Christian and Jewish, Albright's work lacked theological motivation and was far more rationalistic in spirit than most of his German counterparts. In the period after World War II, Albright's method of combining archaeology and biblical criticism found additional support from American and Israeli scholars (Speiser, Ginsberg, Mazar) besides, of course, from his own students (Bright, Wright, Mendenhall, Cross and Freedman). Only in very recent times, as we can see from the volume of Hayes and Miller, have some younger American scholars with archaeological interests begun to move outside of the orbit established by Albright and his school.

Postscript to the history of pentateuchal criticism

To trace the history of the rise of the critical study of the Pentateuch in terms of major scholars and their scholarly contributions, as is the custom in an Introduction, does not adequately deal with the broader history of the effect of the academic debate on the ecclesiastical institutions of church and synagogue. Indeed, to study the wider cultural impact of biblical criticism on both church and society would far exceed the reasonable bounds of an Introduction. Nevertheless, it is significant to observe that whereas in the early part of the century opposition to biblical criticism from the side of the established institutions of church and synagogue was almost universal, by the middle of the twentieth century biblical criticism had been very widely accepted, with opposition only represented in conservative fringe groups. Several brief reflections on this striking change of opinion may be in order:

(i) The success of biblical criticism in winning the day, especially regarding the Pentateuch, must be viewed in the light of the radical shift in the whole intellectual climate of the Western world, which was effected by the rise of the natural sciences (cf. Scholder). By setting the traditional view of the Bible in sharp opposition to the developing new scientific disciplines, the traditionalists established a line of resistance which could only spell enormous difficulty for their position.

(ii) The dominant conservative strategy in confronting Old Testament biblical criticism was to defend the truth of the Bible in narrow terms of its historicity while coupling it with a broad philosophical apologetic against rationalism and unbelief. Neither line of the defence was able to withstand the critical assault for long. Conservative scholars, such as Hengstenberg, Keil, and Pusey, were pushed into a defensive position which contented itself with pointing out weaknesses of the literary critical theory (cf. Hoffmann, Orr). Even when competent scholars such as W. H. Green and H. M. Wiener offered significant literary analyses of books within the Pentateuch, these efforts focused on minimizing the history of development lying behind the final composition as a defence of the traditional position. The frequent appeal to archaeology usually resulted in the traditionalists seeking to defend a supernaturalist position by means of rationalistic arguments. In the end, the conservative wing of the Christian church failed to offer any comprehensive new understanding of the Bible in the light of the new evidence, and increasingly lost the ear of the church in the twentieth century.

(iii) Biblical criticism of the Pentateuch was at first associated with theological scepticism in the works of Eichhorn, de Wette, and Kuenen. In Germany, the role of evangelical scholars such as Franz Delitzsch did much to still the fears voiced in the church. Within England churchmen such as S. R. Driver, G. A. Smith, and A. S. Peake performed the same task. Still the theology represented was largely Protestant Liberalism with its strong idealistic flavour. There were some obvious exceptions such as M. Kähler and A. Schlatter. However, only in the era after the First World War did large numbers of Protestant scholars emerge who combined traditionally orthodox Christian theology with aggressive biblical criticism. The same development came in the Roman Church after the Second World War. But perhaps the unintentional effect of the rise and fall of the Biblical Theology movement of the 50s and 60s has been to raise the question once again whether the church's relation to biblical criticism has been fully settled and whether the enthusiastic acceptance of the reigning scholarly consensus has only succeeded in covering over many basic theological problems.

2. The Present State of Critical Debate on the Pentateuch

In describing the present state of the debate it is no longer possible to separate sharply between the various critical disciplines within the field. No one stands uninfluenced by the giants of the past. However, there are some advantages, for the sake of clarity, in treating the subject topically. These categories should not distort the material unduly if not pressed too hard.

The scope of the literary unit

During the height of the literary critical period the term Hexateuch had virtually replaced that of Pentateuch within critical circles (Wellhausen, Kuenen, Smend, Eissfeldt). Hexateuch was still preferred by von Rad in 1938. The picture was radically changed by Noth's theory of the Deuteronomistic historian (1943). Noth not only denied a continuing pentateuchal strand in Joshua, but separated Deuteronomy from the first four books, thus forming a Tetrateuch. In spite of the cogency of many of Noth's arguments, the difficulty of having the Pentateuch left as a torso has not been fully resolved and the debate continues (cf. Mowinckel, *Tetrateuch*). In addition, there remains a minority of scholars (Hölscher, Schulte, Freedman) who, in differing ways, have tried to expand the unit to include the historical books through Kings. Finally, an increasing number of scholars (Fohrer, Rendtorff) have expressed themselves in favour of returning to the terminology of a Pentateuch.

The criteria for source criticism

A striking characteristic of the modern debate over source criticism of the Pentateuch is the growing uncertainty in regard to the criteria for determining literary strands. In the classic introduction to the sources provided by H. Holzinger, the author was confident in having established a whole range of objective measurements which included historical, linguistic, and literary criteria. This scholarly tradition of literary criticism still finds a strong representation in the Introduction of Eissfeldt. However, a growing loss of confidence in this older approach was reflected in Noth's opinion that the presence of doublets remained the only certain criterion by which sources could be determined (*History of Pentateuchal Traditions*, 22). Noth has been supported in general by both Richter and Coats. Westermann (*Genesis*, BK, 764f.) is equally cautious, but, in a careful review of the traditional criteria, sustains their value when used with the needed discernment. The case for rejecting source criticism *in toto*, whether made by the students of Engnell or by Cassuto, does not appear to have gained a wide following.

An important new issue of source criticism has been raised from the side of structural studies of the biblical narrative. This method approaches the literary study of the Old Testament from a much broader base than is usually associated with traditional source criticism. M. Weiss and G. W. Coats (cf. bibliography on Genesis), and also N. Whybray (cf. bibliography on Samuel), have raised the question of how one relates the obvious literary creativity of a story to the source critical approach which has often been described in more or less mechanical terms. A significant attempt to exploit both approaches is offered by McEvenue's stylistic analysis of the Priestly source.

Individual sources: the Yahwist

In the works of both Noth and von Rad the role of the Yahwist source in the Pentateuch has been greatly expanded. Noth argued that the Yahwistic narrative constituted the literary basis for the oldest pentateuchal tradition, and that the E source was of minor importance. Von Rad attributed an even more significant role to the Yahwist by making him into the first major Hebrew theologian. The decisive moves in linking traditions such as the primeval history to the patriarchal tradition was described as the work of this creative genius. The importance of von Rad's move in individualizing the Yahwist can be seen in contrast to Gunkel, who envisioned the J source as the product of a school and not an individual.

The impact of von Rad's portrayal of the Yahwist has been very wide on several generations of scholars. In spite of Noth's reluctance to follow von Rad at this point, German scholarship continued to develop in von Rad's direction in attributing theological integrity to each of the sources. Ironically, as the literary profile of the various sources continued to blur, the theological profile took on new specificity. Wolff's essay, 'The Kerygma of the Yahwist', followed by popularizations by Ellis and Brueggemann among others, typified this extension of von Rad's theory. One can also recognize in this approach to the Yahwist the influence of New Testament redactional studies, which, beginning in the 50s, were attempting to recover the theological individuality of the evangelists. In my judgment, this extension of source criticism is highly questionable. The penetrating criticism of Rendtorff in *Das überlieferungsgeschichtliche Problem des Pentateuch* has also raised fundamental questions as to its methodological legitimacy.

Mention should also be made of the effort of Winnett and his students N. Wagner and J. Van Seters (cf. bibliography to Genesis) to redate the Yahwist source and to separate it into an earlier and post-exilic later strand. A somewhat similar move has been also attempted in Germany (H. H. Schmid). In my judgment, the major significance of these monographs has been to call into question many of the unexamined assumptions of the 'orthodox' literary critical method rather than to establish a convincing new hypothesis regarding the sources. However, it is too soon to assess the impact of the approach until further work has been done.

Of more significance in the current debate have been the several attempts to establish a motivation for the Yahwist's writing. Part of the problem has been in establishing a fixed date for the composition which has traditionally been set in the monarchial period, but which has oscillated between the ninth and tenth centuries. Some scholars, following von Rad's lead, have related the Yahwist's work to a theological crisis within tenth-century Israel (cf. Brueggemann). Others have stressed the political factors and seen his work as an attempt to legitimate the Davidic monarchy. F. M. Cross speaks of the Yahwist as propaganda in support of the interests of the national cult of the empire. Because the references to the monarch are so minor and such an oblique reading of the text is demanded in order to support the theory (cf. Hölscher, 31; Schulte, 203), it is doubtful whether any clarity will ever be achieved. Moreover, it is hard to suppress the feeling that the intense concern with this question derives from a larger hermeneutical assumption regarding the nature of all biblical literature rather than arising from problems within the text itself.

The Elohist source

The major debates over the nature and scope of the Elohist source occurred in the previous generation (cf. the survey by Craghan). Volz and Rudolph questioned the existence of E as a source and proposed seeing those passages which have usually been assigned to the Elohist as secondary glosses on the basic J narrative in a fashion somewhat akin to the old fragmentary hypothesis. Subsequently, Mowinckel argued for extending the scope of the Elohist into the first eleven chapters of Genesis (cf. Fuss's monograph listed in bibliography on Exodus). Again the major effect of these studies has been to point out difficulties in the classic source divisions rather than to establish a fresh consensus around a new proposal. The detailed defence of an E source by Noth, Fohrer and Eissfeldt, among others, has generally convinced a majority of the traditional position of E, but an important minority still remains sceptical of E's existence. Many scholars are inclined with Noth to reckon with a duplicate, parallel strand to J even when its fragmentary character is acknowledged. Finally, mention should be made of Wolff's similar attempt to sketch a 'kerygmatic' profile of E. In my opinion, the same problems which were outlined above, apply to Wolff's method, if anything in even more exacerbated form.

The Priestly source

The problem of the scope of P was posed by Noth – first in his Joshua commentary (1938) but especially in his *Überlieferungsgeschichtliche Studien* (1943) – when he challenged the traditional literary critical hypothesis of seeing the continuation of P into the book of Joshua. Noth contended that P ended with Deut. 34.1a, 7–9. A majority of scholars appear convinced by Noth's analysis; however, his conclusions have continued to call forth opposition from such scholars as Haran and Vink, who claimed to have isolated P material in passages such as Josh. 8.30–35 and 18. 1–10. The debate will continue, but it seems largely determined by the participants' overall understanding of the Pentateuch/Hexateuch rather than arguments on specific texts.

Probably the most controversial issue at present regarding the Priestly sources revolves about the issue of whether or not P should be considered an independent literary source or a redaction of earlier literary material. The issue is not a new one. Earlier attempts had been made by Löhr and others to describe P as a redactional layer without independent status. Such attempts were strongly resisted by such scholars as Budde, Eissfeldt, and Noth. Recently the redactional theory has received new stimulus from R. Rendtorff and F. M. Cross. Rendtorff (*Problem*) has sought to undermine a basic tenet of the source theory by showing that the P source was not a complete and continuous strand within the Pentateuch, but rather consisted of chronological notices and isolated theological passages which functioned to join together complexes of tradition. Similarly Cross has tried to demonstrate the redactional role of P material and the extent to which P assumed a prior knowledge of JE, especially regarding the Sinai covenant.

In my judgment, the debate as formulated especially by Cross may have posed a false alternative by its sharp contrast between source and redaction. It could well be that P, or a portion of it, was an independent source and also served a redactional role. The problem seems to be how to explain, on the one hand, P's obvious dependence on JE in places, and on the other hand, the apparently independent integrity of his narrative in other places. At least the great variety within the P material and the divergence of function within the strand – compare P in Gen. 1–11 with 12–25 – should caution against simple alternatives. Still the issue is an important one and calls for further research.

Another controversial issue focuses on the dating and redactional history of P within the Pentateuch. Since the period of the 30s the nature of the Priestly writing has been viewed in quite a different light. There is wide agreement that much of the material is pre-exilic and that it underwent an extended history of development within a circle of tradents before its final codification. Nevertheless, a post-exilic dating for the final shape of P has continued to represent a wide consensus. Divergent views would be Cross's sixth-century dating, or Vink's theory of a late dating in the Persian period.

When Kaufmann first argued for the priority of the P source to that of Deuteronomy, he did not gain much support for his formulation of the problem. However, more recently Noth's understanding of the redactional history of the Pentateuchal sources has offered some support for the approach first defended by Kaufmann. Noth has argued for a priestly redaction of the JE material, which had not first undergone a Deuteronomic redaction. The explanation accounts for the Deuteronomist's providing the last redactional frame in the editing of Deut. 34 and not the Priestly writer. Still it remains a highly contested problem to what extent Deuteronomic influence extends to the Tetrateuch.

A more important issue than settling an absolute date – a tentative enterprise at best – is that of determining the purpose and motivation behind the Priestly strand. According to the classic literary critical view the Priestly writings represented a tendentious projection back into the Mosaic age by the Jerusalem priesthood in order to legitimate the post-exilic cult and to provide a programme for it. Cross's interpretation also sees it as a propaganda programme but one written in preparation for and in hopes of the restoration. In a more cautious view, B. A. Levine (cf. bibliography on Leviticus) allows for a certain idealization rather than intentional fabrication, but also holds to a historical basis for many of the institutions described.

A very different view of the purpose of the Priestly writings is taken by Zimmerli and Elliger, who see reflected in P the situation of the exilic community, and who also argue that the dominant force in the shaping of P was theological rather than political. For Elliger the issue at stake was the presence of God in the midst of his exiled people. For Zimmerli the emphasis falls on understanding Israel's relation to God in terms of a covenant of grace. The difficulty of adjudicating between political and theological interpretations is obvious when such different exegetical assumptions lie at the heart of the issue.

Form criticism and traditio-criticism

Since the end of World War II form criticism and traditio-criticism of the Pentateuch have been dominated by the work of Alt, von Rad and Noth. This evaluation is not to suggest that the last thirty years have been a period of quiet consensus. Far from it! However, the major questions were set by these German scholars even when evoking strongest criticism, as for example in Mendenhall's well-known rebuttal.

In striking contrast to the situation of the last generation, the present debate, especially in regard to the study of the Pentateuch, is characterized by the dissolution of the older consensus and a search for new questions and answers. Otto Kaiser's apt characterization of contemporary German scholarship could be extended to include the English-speaking world as well: 'Old Testament scholarship . . . is again in a period of revolution in which the great conceptions, worked out between the two world wars, of amphictyony and covenant, of law and covenant, of covenant and prophecy . . . are being put in question' (*Introduction*, p.x.).

Von Rad's famous thesis respecting the Hexateuch had met initial opposition from scholars such as Weiser, whose own suggestion of a covenant festival at least shared a broad agreement with von Rad as to the centrality of Israel's cult. The attack on von Rad came from several sides. The debate which ensued with the discovery of the Hittite treaties was not decisive, but did erode the thesis in several ways. It pointed out a certain narrowness in his form-critical approach which had isolated itself from extra-biblical parallels. It also raised the question whether there could be a better explanation for the omission of the Sinai tradition from the Exodus tradition than the one proposed by von Rad. Even more crucial, the debate forced a thorough re-examination of Deuteronomy and the assumptions regarding Israel's cult on which much of von Rad's thesis rested. Increasingly, questions began to be raised as to whether the crucial force behind the formation of the Pentateuch was, in fact, the cult or whether the shape depended to much greater extent on a redactional process. Although Perlitt's book on *Bundestheologie* (1969) has continued to call forth much opposition, his thesis of the late development of a covenant theology had a strongly negative impact on von Rad's approach to the problem.

M. Noth had developed several of his brilliant theses around seminal ideas of Alt, including the amphictyony, and the relation of law and covenant. Surprisingly enough, the Albright school generally accepted, often quite uncritically, these reconstructions, particularly the so-called 'tribal league' thesis (cf. Bright, 140ff.; Cross, *Canaanite Myth*, 79ff.). But within Germany critical questions regarding the amphictyony began to be raised by S. Herrmann – there had been earlier attacks by Lewy and Orlinsky but without great impact – which later were continued by Fohrer, de Geus and others. This attack did not have a direct effect on the composition of the Pentateuch but its larger impact was important in blurring the sharp profile of the pre-monarchial period on which many literary constructions had been built. In addition, at least within Germany, the efforts of Kutsch, Jepsen, and Fohrer to challenge the traditional meaning of covenant also did much to undermine the elaborate construct which had been erected about covenant festivals.

Another sign of the dissolution of the older form-critical consensus can be seen in the continuing crisis over proper methodology. Form critics have attempted to move in several new directions, many of which have directly affected the study of the Pentateuch. Some have followed the lead of R. Knierim in trying to break out of the present impasse by a closer refining of form critical terminology. Others such as W. Richter have been strongly influenced by structuralism and have sought greatly to enlarge the range of questions beyond those raised by the previous generation.

Another impressive example of dissatisfaction within the older consensus is reflected in the recent attempt of Rendtorff to develop a new approach to the Pentateuch which would overcome some persistent weaknesses of his teachers. He focused on the problem of assuming uncritically that the methods of literary and traditio-criticism were complementary disciplines. In the course of his study he attacked the consensus on both literary critical and traditio-critical levels and sought another method for recovering the larger units within the Pentateuch. Rendtorff has undoubtedly broken new ground; however, it remains unclear how Rendtorff's proposals relate to the new redactional emphasis of scholars like Perlitt and Kaiser.

Among the calls for new methodology one should also include the appeal for broad-based sociological and *religionsgeschichtliche* studies according to the original programme of Gunkel rather than seeing traditio-criticism in more narrowly conceived literary terms. R. R. Wilson's monograph on biblical genealogies (cf. bibliography on Genesis) in the light of recent anthropological material and ancient Near Eastern parallels offers an interesting model for this school of thought. Similarly, N. Gottwald's forthcoming monograph is a creative attempt to employ modern sociological theory to the study of Israel's institutions.

During the years of the von Rad–Noth dominance of pentateuchal studies, the American school under Albright's influence often sought to defend the historicity of Israel's early traditions by appealing to ancient Near Eastern parallels. This approach received its classic formulation in John Bright's *History*. Over the years many of the alleged parallels, especially to Nuzi, have been abandoned under increasing attack (cf. J. Van Seters); interest in this somewhat apologetic line has flagged even within the school itself. Although it is certainly possible that the recent archaeological discoveries at Ebla will revive the approach, the students of Albright, particularly under Cross's leadership, have shifted the focus away from the older position. Cross's published essays outline a programme which envisions Israel's development in continual tension between forces arising from mythical roots in Canaanite culture and historical elements of her experience with Yahweh. Several of his well-known essays bear directly on pentateuchal studies and provide impressive models for his students. His appeal to the work of M. Parry and A. B. Lord as offering an important corrective to German form-critical work has been suggestive, but has not as yet been developed in any detail.

Another fruitful modern development within pentateuchal studies which has been represented by a whole team of international scholars is that of comparative law. Detailed comparative studies by J. J. Finkelstein, W. Moran, R. Frankena, A. Cazelles, M. Weinfeld, S. Paul, and B. A. Levine (cf. bibliographies on Exodus and Leviticus), to name but a few, have done much to correct many of the broad generalizations about law which were once current, and were still represented in Noth's influential treatise on Old Testament law. The continuing discovery of fresh cuneiform legal material can only aid in extending the importance of this discipline.

3. The Canonical Shape of the Pentateuch

Any attempt to offer a different approach to the study of the Pentateuch which does not take into account the achievements of historical critical scholarship over the last two hundred years is both naive and arrogant. One of the purposes of rehearsing the outlines of this history is to make certain that the canonical approach which follows is understood as a post-critical alternative. It seeks to take seriously both the successes and the failures evident from this history of scholarship, while at the same time mounting a case for a very different approach to the study of the Pentateuch and to the full range of problems which have been outlined.

As a result of the victory of the historical critical method, virtually every Introduction to the Pentateuch identifies its task as one of reconstructing the historical development through its various complex stages. Although I do not deny that such a historical enterprise is legitimate and at times illuminating, it is my contention that the study of the history of Hebrew literature in the context of the ancient Near East is a different enterprise from studying the form and function of the Pentateuch in the shape accorded it by the community of faith as its canonical scriptures. I am also aware that the study of the canonical shape of a biblical book cannot be simply divorced from knowledge of its historical development, but the relationship of these two dimensions of the text is an extremely subtle one which dare not be destroyed by crude identification. Because the present shape of the Pentateuch offers a particular interpretation of how the tradition is to be understood, the critical task at hand is both to describe the actual characteristics of the canonical shape and to determine the theological significance of that shape.

Terminology

Later Jewish tradition commonly spoke of the first five books as the Torah, the Torah of Moses, or the Book of the Law of Moses. However, at least by the beginning of the Christian era but probably long before, the term Torah designated the first five books within the Jewish canon. Moreover, already in the post-exilic period, in the later books of the Old Testament, there are references to 'the Book of Moses' (Ezra 6.18; Neh. 13.1; II Chron. 25.4), but it is not clear whether the entire Pentateuch is intended or only the legal sections. Subsequent Jewish tradition coined the technical term 'the five-fifths of the Law' (ḥ^amiššāh ḥûmšē hattôrāh) to describe the division of the Pentateuch into five parts. This tradition is old and already assumed by the Septuagint and all Hebrew manuscripts. The term *pentateuchus* is the Latin rendering of the Greek ἡ Πεντάτευχος, meaning the fivefold book.

Canonical form and function

The first issue at stake is to determine whether this fivefold division actually belongs to the canonical shape of the Old Testament or whether it is a post-Old Testament rabbinic development. From a study of the terminology the question remains ambiguous. Is there any literary evidence that these books were seen together as a canonical unit?

First of all, it is quite clear that the five books were seen as separate entities by the final biblical editor in spite of the obvious continuity of the one story which extended from the creation of the world (Gen. 1.1) to the death of Moses (Deut. 34). The book of Genesis is structured by means of a repeated genealogical formula (2.4; 5.1; 6.9, etc.) which ties the various parts of the book into a unity. Genesis closes with the death of the last patriarch; Exodus begins with the nation in Egypt. However, Ex. 1.1–5 recapitulates material from Genesis at the outset (Gen. 46.8ff.) in order to form an introduction to the new book. Similarly, the final chapter of Exodus concludes with the building of the tabernacle and summarizes its role in the future wanderings of the people.

The book of Leviticus continues the same historical setting of Moses' receiving the law at Sinai, but the different approach to the material serves to set the book off from Exodus. J. Milgrom (*IDB Suppl*, 541) aptly characterizes the difference: 'It (Leviticus) is thematically an independent entity. In Exodus, the P code describes the construction of the cultic implements . . ., whereas Leviticus converts this static picture into scenes from the living cult.' By structuring its material topically Leviticus often breaks the logical and chronological sequence of its continuity with Exodus (cf. chs. 8–10). Leviticus closes with a clear summary, marking it off from the fourth book.

The book of Numbers gives the least evidence of independent integrity of any book in the Pentateuch. Nevertheless, G. B. Gray (*Numbers*, p.xxiv) is far from the mark when he discerns absolutely no inner coherence and proposes a different division between the three middle books. In distinction from Leviticus, the book of Numbers focuses on the laws of the camp when on the march, thus the military order of the tribes, the census of the fighting force, and the laws related to the Levites, which are found only in Numbers. The book begins with a precise date formula which indicates a new section of material and concludes with a summary. The movement within the book is from Sinai, to Paran, to the Plains of Moab which are marked by chronological and geographical notices.

Few scholars doubt the sharp break which presently separates Numbers from Deuteronomy. Deuteronomy has both a clear introduction and conclusion which establishes it as an independent work although it shares the setting on the plains of Moab with the latter part of Numbers. In sum, there is clear editorial evidence to establish five divisions with the Pentateuchal material.

However, it is now necessary to push beyond the formal relationship of the five parts. Is there evidence to show a coherent inner relationship in terms of content as well? At the outset, it is evident that the three middle books share the same basic content, which has to do with the giving and receiving of the divine law by Moses at Sinai. The history at Sinai is connected within the three books in an explicit chronological sequence stating when Israel arrived, how long she encamped at Sinai, and when she departed. Moreover, the events of Sinai are preceded and succeeded by the account of the wilderness wanderings which led the people from Egypt to Sinai, and from Sinai to the edge of the promised land. Thus the close inner relationship of the three middle books is clear.

The more difficult issue is to determine the place of the first and fifth books in the Pentateuch. Even the casual reader must observe that the book of Genesis differs greatly in its style and content from the three middle books. In the main, it recounts the history of a family and does not yet speak of the nation Israel. Yet it is also evident that the patriarchal material has not just been accidentally attached to the story which follows, but is integrally connected. Indeed, the patriarchal stories have been consistently edited in such a way as to point to the future. In spite of a complex development within the tradition of the promise to the patriarchs (cf. Genesis), the continuing thread which ties together the material is the promise of a posterity and a land. Clearly Genesis was conceived of by the final redactor as the introduction to the story of Israel which begins in Exodus.

The role of Deuteronomy is even more difficult to determine and remains much contested (cf. ch. X, 'Deuteronomy'). It is set off sharply from the preceding book by its style which is that of a series of speeches by Moses to Israel. Although its content is often a repetition of earlier laws, the homiletical style is distinct. Deuteronomy 1 states the purpose of Moses' speech to Israel as 'explaining' the law. Whatever its original role in the development of Israel's law, the final editor of the Pentateuch understood Deuteronomy's role as providing a type of commentary to the preceding law. Moreover, the book was given a setting consciously different from the original declaration of the law at Sinai. Some forty years later, to a new generation, Moses interprets the meaning and purpose of the law of Sinai which he had once received in terms of a covenant. Deuteronomy emphasizes the unique role of Moses as mediator and interpreter of the divine will. It is, therefore, fully in order when Deuteronomy closes the Pentateuch with an account of the death of Moses. In sum, a study of the content of the five books gives additional evidence of an intentional structuring of these books into a purposeful whole.

The relation of the canonical shape of the Pentateuch to the complex development of its prehistory requires a more detailed study and will be pursued in the succeeding chapters on each separate book of the Pentateuch. However, the full force of the function of the Pentateuch as a unit gains further support when one realizes that the shape of the final editing of the five books into a unit ran counter to the natural order of the original tradition. The primary credit for seeing this issue goes to James Sanders in his book *Torah and Canon*. On the basis of early credal statements Sanders attempted to show that the epic traditions of Israel extended from the Egyptian exodus to the conquest of the land (Deut. 6.20ff.; 26.5ff.; Josh. 24.2ff.). Of course it was in recognition of this pattern that the nineteenth-century literary critics had spoken of a Hexateuch in order to include the traditions of the conquest. But then Sanders raised the basic canonical issue when he questioned why the original tradition was truncated by the position of Deuteronomy which excluded Joshua from the primary unit of the Torah. On the basis of a reconstruction of the literary history of the Pentateuch, Sanders offered his own solution, concentrating on the post-exilic period. He saw the exclusion of the book of Joshua as an important confessional statement regarding the nature of Torah. To the landless exilic community of Babylon possession of the land was not constitutive of Jewish faith, but a promise yet to be realized.

Although I question some of the details of Sanders' reconstruction of the literary history and would prefer to attribute the last redactional stage to the Deuteronomist rather than P, I agree fully with his theological assessment that the formation of a Pentateuch established the parameters of Israel's understanding of its faith as Torah. For the biblical editors the first five books constituted the grounds of Israel's life under God and provided a critical norm of how the Mosaic tradition was to be understood by the covenant people. The fundamental theological understanding of God's redemptive work through law and grace, promise and fulfilment, election and obedience was once and for all established. The story which continued in the book of Joshua was thus qualitatively distinguished from the Pentateuch by the shape given by the canon.

There is a further issue of great importance which is closely related to the canonical shaping of the Pentateuch. In his recent book *(Problem)* R. Rendtorff has been very successful in demonstrating that the present form of the Pentateuch can be attributed neither to traditional connections made on the oral stage nor to the literary strands of the Pentateuch, whether to J or P. A hiatus remains between the shape given the material by the last literary source and its final canonical shape. Rendtorff then describes traces of a comprehensive reworking of the Pentateuch which is reflected in such passages as Gen. 22.16; 23.6; 24.7; 50.24. Such an expression as 'the land which he swore to Abraham, to Isaac, and to Jacob', offers a holistic reading of the entire Pentateuch in terms of promise which goes beyond the individual sources in forming the parts of the Pentateuch into one continuous story. Similar linking passages are found also in Exodus (Rendtorff, 77).

In my judgment, Rendtorff's analysis allows one to draw some important canonical observations. The final form of the Pentateuch, which cannot be simply derived from the combination of literary sources, gives evidence of a canonical reading of the whole in its final stage of editing. The various parts were more closely united by means of cross-references, either to the promises of the past or to an anticipation of the future. In sum, a theological force which reflects a knowledge of the whole Pentateuch has given it a final order.

The Mosaic authorship and canon

There is one final issue which calls for discussion. In what sense is the claim of Mosaic authorship part of the canonical shape of the Pentateuch? The traditional view of the pre-critical era had assumed the Mosaic authorship on the basis of occasional references to Moses' literary activity. Support for this interpretation came from the Talmud, which made explicit the authorship of Moses, and from the New Testament. By the beginning of the twentieth century historical critical scholarship was virtually unanimous in denying the Mosaic authorship of the Pentateuch.

The evidence for a long period of historical growth appeared to rule out the possibility of his authorship when the term 'authorship' was construed in its usual modern sense. Occasional attempts to salvage the term by claiming that a kernel of the Pentateuch stemmed from the Mosaic age did little to win wide support. The most recent discussion of the Mosaic authorship, such as the section in J. A. Soggin's *Introduction* (80ff.), attempts to show that the whole idea of Mosaic authorship arose as a late development within Judaism and is of no importance for a modern understanding of the books. Bruce Vawter (*On Genesis*, New York 1977, p.15) seems to represent the modern Roman Catholic consensus when he writes: 'Mosaic authorship no longer forms a problem for practically anyone, and therefore that part of the issue has been resolved.'

In my judgment, the question of the Mosaic authorship of the Pentateuch has not been correctly formulated because the issue has been treated apart from its canonical function. On the one hand, critical historical scholarship defined the issue of authorship in a modern sense and investigated it as a strictly historical problem. It did not take much effort to demonstrate the obvious historical difficulties. On the other hand, conservative scholarship – whether in a Jewish, Protestant or Catholic form is almost immaterial – was equally willing to argue on strictly historical grounds (cf. Cornely, 320), coupled with an appeal to religious tradition, in order to build a first line of defence for the authority of Scripture. Mosaic authorship was thought crucial in supporting the historicity of the Bible on which authority was grounded by tying the composition of the books as closely as possible to the events themselves. Under increasing pressure conservatives sought to redefine authorship in order to broaden the term, but without much success. In the end, neither side in the debate did justice to the canonical understanding of Moses' relationship to the Pentateuch.

If one turns to the Pentateuch, it is clear that Moses' writing activity is closely tied to his mediatorial role in receiving the divine law at Sinai. Whereas God himself is portrayed as writing the decalogue (Ex. 34.1; Deut. 4.13; 10.4), Moses not only proclaims the 'words and ordinances' of God to the people (Ex. 24.3), but he is also commissioned to write them (v.4; cf. 34.27). The significance of Moses' writing of the law receives its clearest formulation in Deut. 31. The context of the chapter is the impending death of Moses, and his commissioning of the writing of the law. Several crucial points are made in the chapter. The law, which derived from God's speaking to Moses, applies to every successive generation of Israel (31. 11–13). It serves as a witness to God's will (v.28). The law of God has now been transmitted for the future generations in the written form of scripture. It is placed next to the ark in book form to be read to the people periodically (10ff.). Indeed, the original role of Moses as the unique prophet of God (34.10) who proclaims the word of God as a witness (31.27ff.) will be performed by the book of the law in the future (31.26ff.). Moses will shortly die, but his formulation of the will of God will continue. Throughout the rest of the Old Testament the identification of the divine law with Moses' writing of it in a book is continued (Ezra 6.18; Neh. 13.1; II Chron. 25.4). Although there is no explicit reference in the Old Testament which connects the book of Genesis to Moses, the move was made in Jewish tradition when the unity of the entire Pentateuch was assumed.

If then the Old Testament canon assigns an important role to Moses' writing the book of the law, how is one to explain the historical evidence that the canonical form of the Pentateuch contains much material which is obviously later than the age of Moses? In my judgment, the Old Testament does not provide direct evidence by which to answer this question. It is possible, for example, as some scholars have theorized, that the role of Moses was continued in an office and later persons accordingly added material in the name of Moses. But the evidence to support the theory is missing. However, in spite of the lack of historical evidence by which to trace the actual process, it would seem clear that the authorship of Moses did perform a normative role within a canonical context from a very early period. Thus laws attributed to Moses were deemed authoritative, and conversely authoritative laws were attributed to Moses.

The implication to be drawn from this understanding of the Mosaic authorship is that a theological judgment was at stake respecting the authority of Israel's law. The claim of Mosaic authorship functioned as a norm by which to test the tradition's authority. This was obviously not a historical judgment in the modern sense, but a measuring of the truth of a growing corpus of law by the tradition long experienced as authoritative. The appeal to Mosaic authorship derived its meaning only within the context of a community of faith for whom a body of written tradition had already been recognized as authoritative. The claim of Mosaic authorship therefore functioned theologically within the community to establish the continuity of the faith of successive generations with that which had once been delivered to Moses at Sinai. Unfortunately, in the nineteenth-century debate over authorship the canonical role of Moses in relation to the Pentateuch was misunderstood by both parties. When correctly interpreted, the Mosaic authorship of the Pentateuch is an important theological affirmation which is part of the canonical witness.

VI

GENESIS

Commentaries

M. M. Kalisch, 1858
J. P. Lange, ET, LCHS, 1868
F. Delitzsch, ⁵1899
A. Dillmann, KeH, ⁶1892
H. Holzinger, KHC, 1898
S. R. Driver, WC, 1904
J. Skinner, ICC, 1910
H. Gunkel, HKAT, ⁴1917
O. Procksch, KAT, ³1924
B. Jacob, *Das Erste Buch der Tora*, 1934
A. Richardson, TB (chs. 1–11), 1953

A. Clamer, SB, 1953
U. Cassuto, 1961–64
E. A. Speiser, AB, 1964
W. Zimmerli, ZBK (chs. 1–11), ³1967, ZBK (chs 12–25), 1976
D. Kidner, TOTC, 1967
G. von Rad, ET, OTL, rev. ed. 1972
R. Davidson, CNEB (chs. 1–11), 1973
C. Westermann, BK (chs. 1–11), 1974
B. Vawter, *On Genesis*, 1977

Bibliography

W. F. **Albright**, *From the Stone Age to Christianity*, Baltimore ²1957; L. **Alonso Schökel**, *The Inspired Word. Scripture in the Light of Language and Literature*, ET London and New York 1967; A. **Alt**, *Der Gott der Väter*, Stuttgart 1929=*KS* I, 1953, 1–78; ET *Essays* (see Pentateuch), 1–77; E. **Auerbach**, *Mimesis*, ET Princeton 1953, Oxford 1954; J. **Barr**, 'Reading the Bible as Literature', *BJRL* 56, 1973, 10–33; R. **Barthes**, 'The Struggle with the Angel. Textual Analysis of Genesis 32:23–33', *Structural Analysis and Biblical Exegesis*, ET Pittsburgh 1974, 21–33; P. **Beauchamp**, *Création et separation. Étude exégétique du chapitre premier de la Genèse*, Brussels 1969; J. **Blenkinsopp**, 'The Structure of P', *CBQ* 38, 1976, 275–92; D. **Bonhoeffer**, *Creation and Fall: A Theological Interpretation of Genesis 1–3*, ET London and New York 1959; J. **Bright**, see 'Pentateuch'; W. **Brueggemann**, 'David and his Theologian', *CBQ* 30, 1968, 156–81; 'Yahwist', *IDB Suppl*, 971–75; H. **Cazelles**, 'Patriarchs' *DBS* 7, 81–156; B. S. **Childs**, 'The Etiological Tale Re-examined', *VT* 24, 1974, 387–97; W. M. **Clark**, 'The

Flood Story and the Structure of the Pre-patriarchal History', *ZAW* 83, 1971, 184–211; R. E. **Clements**, *Abraham and David. Genesis XV and its Meaning for Israelite Tradition*, SBT II.5, 1967; D. J. A. **Clines**, 'The Theology of the Flood Narrative', *Faith and Thought* 100, London 1972–3, 128–42; 'Theme in Genesis 1–11', *CBQ* 38, 1976, 483–507; G. W. **Coats**, 'The Joseph Story and Ancient Wisdom: A Reappraisal', *CBQ* 35, 1973, 285–297; *From Canaan to Egypt. Structural and Theological Context for the Joseph Story*, Washington 1976; J. F. **Craghan**, 'The Elohist in Recent Literature', *BTB* 7, 1977, 23–35; F. M. **Cross**, 'The Religion of Canaan and the God of Israel', *Canaanite Myth and Hebrew Epic*, Cambridge, Mass. 1973, 3–75.

W. G. **Dever** and W. M. **Clark**, 'The Patriarchal Traditions' in *Israelite and Judaean History*, ed. J. H. Hayes and J. M. Miller, OTL, 1977, 70–148; D. S. **DeWitt**, 'The Generations of Genesis', *EvQu* 48, 1976, 196–211; H. **Donner**, *Die literarische Gestalt der alttestamentlichen Josephsgeschichte*, Heidelberg 1976; W. **Eichrodt**, *Die Quellen der Genesis von neuem untersucht*, BZAW 31, 1916; H. **Eising**, *Formgeschichtliche Untersuchung zur Jakobserzählung der Genesis*, Emsdetten 1940; O. **Eissfeldt**, 'Stammessage und Novelle in den Geschichten von Jakob und von seinen Söhnen', *Eucharisterion, Studien zur Religion und Literatur des A und NT* I, FS *H. Gunkel*, FRLANT 36, 1923, 56–77 = *KS* I, 1962, 84–104; 'Biblos Geneseōs', *FS E. Fascher*, Berlin 1958, 31–40 = *KS* III, 1966, 458–70; 'Jahwe, der Gott der Väter', *TLZ* 88, 1963, 481–90=*KS* IV, 1968, 79–91; A. **Eitz**, *Studien zum Verhältnis von Priesterschrift und Deuterojesaja*, Diss. Heidelberg, 1970; K. **Elliger**, 'Sinn und Ursprung der priesterlichen Geschichtserzählung', *ZTK* 49, 1952, 121–43=*KSAT*, Munich 1966, 174–98; J. A. **Emerton**, 'The Riddle of Genesis XIV', *VT* 21, 1971, 403–37; M. **Fishbane**, 'Composition and Structure in the Jacob Cycle (Gen. 25:19–35:22)', *JJS* 26, 1975, 15–38; J. P. **Fokkelman**, *Narrative Art in Genesis*, Assen 1975; T. E. **Fretheim**, *Creation, Fall and Flood. Studies in Genesis 1–11*, Minneapolis 1969; 'The Jacob Traditions. Theology and Hermeneutic', *Interp* 26, 1972, 419–36; 'Elohist', *IDB Suppl*, 259–63.

K. **Galling**, *Die Erwählungstraditionen Israels*, BZAW 48, 1928; J. **Goldin**, 'The Youngest Son or Where does Genesis 38 Belong', *JBL* 96, 1977, 27–44; C. H. **Gordon**, 'The Story of Jacob and Laban in the Light of the Nuzi Tablets', *BASOR* 66, 1937, 25–27; 'Biblical Customs and the Nuzi Tablets', *BA* 3, 1940, 1–12; 'Abraham and the Merchants of Ura', *JNES* 17, 1958, 28–31; W. H. **Green**, *The Unity of Genesis*, New York 1895; H. **Gressmann**, 'Ursprung und Entwicklung der Joseph-Sage', *Eucharisterion I, FS H. Gunkel*, 1923, 1–55; K. R. R. **Gros Louis**, ed., *Literary Interpretation of Biblical Narratives*, Nashville 1974; W. **Gross**, 'Jakob, der Mann des Segens. Zu Traditionsgeschichte und Theologie der priesterschriftlichen Jakobsüberlieferungen', *Bibl* 49, 1968, 321–44; H. **Gunkel**, 'Die Komposition der Joseph-Geschichte', *ZDMG* 76, 1922, 55–71; H. **Haag**, *Is Original Sin in Scripture?*, ET New York and London 1969; M. **Haran**, 'The Religion of the Patriarchs: An Attempt at a Synthesis', *ASTI* 4, 1965, 30–55; G. F. **Hasel**, 'The Polemical Nature of the Genesis Cosmology', *EvQu* 46, 1974, 81–102; M.-L. **Henry**, *Jahwist und Priesterschrift. Zwei Glaubenszeugnisse des Alten Testaments*, Stuttgart 1960; S. **Herrmann**, 'Joseph in Ägypten. Ein Wort zu J. Vergotes Buch "Joseph en Egypte"', *TLZ* 85, 1960, 827–30; J. **Hoftijzer**, *Die Verheissungen an die drei Erzväter*, Leiden 1956; P. **Humbert**, 'Die neuere Genesis-Forschung', *ThR* NF 6, 1934, 147–60, 207–28; 'Die literarische Zweiheit des Priester-Codex in der Genesis', *ZAW* 58, 1940–41, 30–57; W. L. **Humphreys**, 'Joseph Story, The', *IDB Suppl*, 491–3; A. **Hurwitz**, 'The Evidence of Language in Dating the Priestly Code', *RB* 81, 1974, 24–56.

J. J. **Jackson** and M. **Kessler**, ed., *Rhetorical Criticism, Essays in Honor of James Muilenburg*, Pittsburgh 1974; M. D. **Johnson**, *The Purpose of the Biblical Genealogies with Special Reference to the Setting of the Genealogies of Jesus*, Cambridge 1969; O. **Kaiser**, 'Stammesgeschichtliche Hintergründe der Josephgeschichte', *VT* 10, 1960, 1–15; C.-A. **Keller**, 'Die Gefährdung der Ahnfrau. Ein Beitrag zur gattungs-und motivgeschichtlichen Erforschung alttestamentlicher Erzählungen', *ZAW* 66, 1954, 181–91; 'Grundsätzliches zur Auslegung der Abraham-Überlieferung in der Genesis', *TZ* 12, 1956, 425–45; M. **Kessler**, 'Rhetorical Criticism of Genesis 7', *Rhetorical Criticism*, 1–17; I. M. **Kikawada**, 'The Shape of Genesis 11:1–9', ibid., 18–32; R. **Kilian**, *Die vorpriesterlichen Abrahams–Überlieferungen*, BBB 24, 1966; K. **Koch**, *The Growth of the Biblical Tradition*, ET London and New York 1969; S. R. **Kuelling**, *Zur Datierung der 'Genesis-P-Stücke'*, Kampen 1964; W. G. **Lambert** and A. R. **Millard**, *Atra-hasis: The Babylonian Story of the Flood*, Oxford 1969; E. R. **Leach**, *Genesis as Myth and Other Essays*, London 1969; M. R. **Lehmann**, 'Abraham's Purchase of Machpelah and Hittite Law', *BASOR* 129, 1953, 15–18; B. A. **Levine**, 'Priestly Writers', *IDB Suppl*, 683–87; J. **Lewy**, 'Les textes paléo-assyriens et l'Ancien Testament', *RHR* 110, 1934, 29–65; N. **Lohfink**, *Die Landverheissung als Eid*, SBS 28, 1967; B. O. **Long**, 'Recent Field Studies in Oral Literature and their Bearing on Old Testament Criticism', *VT* 26, 1976, 187–98.

A. **Malamat**, 'King Lists of the Old Babylonian Period and Biblical Genealogies', *JAOS* 83, 1968, 163–73; B. **Mazar**, 'The Historical Background of the Book of Genesis', *JNES* 28, 1969, 73–83; S. E. **McEvenue**, *The Narrative Style of the Priestly Writer*, Rome 1971; J. L. **McKenzie**, 'The Literary Characteristics of Genesis 2–3', *ThSt* 15, 1954, 541–72 = *Myths and Realities*, New York and London 1963, 146–81; A. **Meinhold**, 'Die Gattung der Josephsgeschichte und des Estherbuches. Diasporanovelle I', *ZAW* 87, 1975, 306–24; S. **Mowinckel**, *The Two Sources of the Predeuteronomic Primeval History (JE) in Gen I-XI*, Oslo 1937; '"Rachelstämme" und "Leastämme"', *Von Ugarit nach Qumran*, FS O. Eissfeldt, BZAW 77, 1958, 129–50; M. **Noth**, *History of Pentateuchal Traditions*, ET Englewood Cliffs, N.J. 1972; E. **Otto**, 'Jakob in Bethel–Ein Beitrag zur Geschichte der Jakobüberlieferung', *ZAW* 88, 1976, 165–90; R. H. **Pfeiffer**, 'A Non-

Israelitic Source of the Book of Genesis', *ZAW* 48, 1930, 66–73; R. **Polzin**, "'The Ancestress of Israel in Danger" in Danger', *Semeia III: Classical Hebrew Narrative*, ed. R. C. Culley, Missoula 1975, 81–98; A. **de Pury**, 'Genèse XXXIV et l'histoire', *RB* 76, 1969, 5–49; *Promesse divine et légende cultuelle dans le cycle de Jacob. Genèse 28 et les traditions patriarchales*, 2 vols., Paris 1975.

G. **von Rad**, 'The Promised Land and Yahweh's Land in the Hexateuch', (1943), ET *The Problem of the Hexateuch*, Edinburgh and New York 1966, 79–93; 'The Joseph Narrative and Ancient Wisdom' (1958), ET ibid., 292–300; D. **Redford**, *A Study of the Biblical Story of Joseph*, *SVT* 20, 1970; R. **Rendtorff**, 'Genesis 8,21 und die Urgeschichte des Jahwisten', *KuD* 7, 1961, 69–78; 'Hermeneutische Probleme des biblischen Urgeschichte', *FS Friedrich Smend*, Berlin 1963, 19–29; "'Der Jahwist" als Theologe? Zum Dilemma der Pentateuchkritik', *SVT* 28, 1974, 158–66; *Das überlieferungsgeschichtliche Problem des Pentateuch*, BZAW 147, 1977; H. **von Reventlow**, *Opfere deinen Sohn. Eine Auslegung von Genesis 22*, BSt 53, 1968; W. M. W. **Roth**, 'The Wooing of Rebekah: A Tradition Critical Study of Genesis 24', *CBQ* 34, 1972, 177–87; L. **Ruppert**, *Die Josephserzählung der Genesis. Ein Beitrag zur Theologie der Pentateuchquellen*, Munich 1965; N. M. **Sarna**, *Understanding Genesis*, New York 1966; J. M. **Sasson**, 'Generation, seventh', *IDB Suppl*, 354–56; J. **Scharbert**, 'Der Sinn der Toledot-Formel in der Priesterschrift', *Wort–Gebot–Glaube. FS W. Eichrodt*, Zürich 1970, 45–56; 'Patriarchentradition und Patriarchenreligion. Ein Forschungs—und Literaturbericht', *VF* 19, 1974, 2–24; W. H. **Schmidt**, *Die Schöpfungsgeschichte der Priesterschrift*, WMANT 17, ²1967; H. **Seebass**, *Der Erzvater Israel*, BZAW 98, 1966; E. A. **Speiser**, 'The Wife-Sister Motif in the Patriarchal Narratives', *Biblical and Other Studies*, ed. A. Altmann, Cambridge, Mass. and London 1963, 15–28; O. H. **Steck**, *Die Paradieserzählung*, BSt 60, 1970; 'Genesis 12, 1–3 und die Urgeschichte des Jahwisten', *Probleme biblischer Theologie*, *FS G. von Rad*, Munich 1971, 525–54; *Der Schöpfungsbericht der Priesterschrift*, FRLANT 115, 1975; P. E. S. **Thompson**, 'The Yahwist Creation Story', *VT* 21, 1971, 197–208; T. L. **Thompson**, *The Historicity of the Patriarchal Narratives: The Quest for the Historical Abraham*, BZAW 133, 1974; J. **Van Seters**, 'Jacob's Marriages and Ancient Eastern Customs', *HTR* 62, 1969, 377–95; *Abraham in History and Tradition*, New Haven and London 1975; 'Patriarchs', *IDB Suppl*, 645–8; R. **De Vaux**, 'Les Patriarches Hébreux et l'Histoire', *Studii Biblici Franciscani Liber Annuus* 13, Jerusalem 1962/3, 287–97; *The Early History of Israel*, ET, 2 vols., London and Philadelphia 1978; A. **Vergote**, *Joseph en Égypte*, Louvain 1959; W. **Vischer**, *The Witness of the Old Testament to Christ* I, ET London 1949; G. **Wallis**, 'Die Tradition von den drei Ahnvätern', *ZAW* 81, 1969, 18–40; H. **Weidmann**, *Die Patriarchen und ihre Religion im Licht der Forschung seit Julius Wellhausen*, FRLANT 94, 1968; P. **Weimar**, 'Aufbau und Struktur der priesterschriftlichen Jakobsgeschichte', *ZAW* 86, 1974, 174–203; M. **Weippert**, 'Abraham der Hebräer? Bemerkungen zu W. F.

Albrights Deutung der Väter Israels', *Bibl* 52, 1972, 407–32; M. **Weiss**, 'Einiges über die Bauformen des Erzählens in der Bibel', *VT* 13, 1963, 456–75; C. **Westermann**, 'Arten der Erzählung in der Genesis', *Forschung am Alten Testament*, Munich 1964, 9–91; *Genesis 1–11*, Darmstadt 1972; *Genesis 12–50*, Darmstadt 1975; 'Promises to the Patriarchs', *IDB Suppl*, 690–93; *Die Verheissungen an die Väter, Studien zur Vätergeschichte*, FRLANT 116, 1976; R. R. **Wilson**, *Genealogy and History in the Biblical World*, New Haven and London 1977; W. **Zimmerli**, 'Sinaibund und Abrahambund', *TZ* 16, 1960, 268–80=*Gottes Offenbarung*, Munich 1963, 205–16.

1. Historical Critical Problems

Because the broad historical critical problems of Genesis have already been discussed in the previous chapter on the Pentateuch, it will not be necessary to repeat the same material. This section will focus more narrowly on specific problems relating to the book of Genesis. No attempt will be made to provide a full survey of modern criticism, a task which has been met in part by Westermann's bibliographical surveys. Rather the following discussion will be limited to a selection of certain basic critical issues which will provide the proper context for subsequent canonical analysis.

The modern critical study of the book of Genesis has been strongly influenced by Hermann Gunkel's commentary (1901; [4]1917). His work established the foundation upon which much of the recent scholarship has been built, and thus it provides a good point of departure from which to assess recent critical research. A major contribution of Gunkel's commentary was his description of the material of the book as saga, a category which he had appropriated from such scholars as A. Olrik. Gunkel defined saga as an ancient form of poetic story dealing with persons and events of the distant past which was passed along orally in a circle of tradition (4th ed., viii). He saw the aetiological element as a major concern of the saga in providing an explanation for the source of the various aspects of nature and history experienced by the eponymic fathers. Gunkel concentrated his form-critical analysis largely on classifying types of saga and analysing their artistic features. Although it is now evident that Gunkel's new approach brought to an end the nineteenth-century form of debate over historicity and opened up a new perspective, it also initiated a heated debate on the critical problem of defining what is meant by saga.

The attack on Gunkel's understanding of the term has come from several different directions (cf. Van Seters, *Abraham*, 131ff. for a summary). André Jolles in *Einfache Formen* (Darmstadt[4] 1969) argued for describing saga after the pattern of Icelandic saga which dealt with domestic, family affairs rather than political or ethnic situations as envisioned by Gunkel. Jolles' lead has been vigorously pursued by Westermann, and with some modification by Koch. But as Van Seters has pointed out, Jolles' definition of saga has met with severe criticism from the field of modern folklore where the model of Icelandic saga is viewed as an idiosyncratic literary genre. Again, F. M. Cross (*Canaanite Myth*, 112) has suggested that the form of oral transmission described by A. B. Lord, *The Singer of Tales* (Cambridge, Mass. 1960), offered a major corrective to Gunkel's insistence on the priority of the smallest units within the development of saga, but so far the suggestion has remained untested. Perhaps the basic concern at stake has been best expressed by B. O. Long, who argues that a new definition of saga must be developed which rests on contemporary anthropological data, rather than on nineteenth-century observations on which Gunkel largely depended. However, it is ironical that the revisions have not as yet resulted in any great measure of illumination and have certainly produced no close rival to Gunkel's initial analysis of Genesis. It is also interesting to observe that von Rad – surely the most important commentator on Genesis since Gunkel – appears to have abandoned the task of redefining saga, but suggested that the problem of applying the term to Genesis lay elsewhere: 'One can now ask whether the designation "saga" is still appropriate for this material which is so permeated through and through by faith' (*Genesis*, rev. ed. 1972, 37).

Another important problem in Genesis, on which much energy has been expended since Gunkel's commentary, has been indicated by the shift from the discipline of form criticism to that of traditio-criticism (*Überlieferungsgeschichte*). As has often been pointed out, Gunkel's main interest lay in tracing the development of the individual sagas of Genesis. Although he observed different complexes of sagas and described significant features of interrelationship, the actual history of the development of the larger units of traditions remained largely undeveloped. Von Rad's monograph on the Hexateuch (1938), but especially Noth's *History of . . . Traditions* (1948) opened up a new direction which has dominated the modern study of Genesis for several decades. The great impact of von Rad's monograph lay in the simplicity of his solution for relating the tradition of the exodus to the primeval history, the promise to the Fathers, and Sinai. Von Rad and Noth were largely successful in convincing a consensus that behind the present form of Genesis lay a long and complex history of tradition. However, it remained a troubling factor that the attempts to unravel this history produced such speculative results. In Noth's analysis in particular the constant appeal to conjecture for lack of solid evidence only exacerbated the problem. The same high level of speculation characterized a large number of traditio-critical monographs on Genesis during the 60s and 70s as a new generation tried to build on Noth. Finally, in Westermann's huge commentary on Gen. 1–11 all the problems inherent in the traditio-critical method reached their zenith, but in a complexity which threatened to devour exegesis.

In reaction to the fragile nature of much of the traditio-critical work on Genesis, American scholars tended to fall back on archaeological and straight historical reconstructions (Speiser, Sarna, Vawter). Again it is ironical to observe that the reaction at times appears to have made a full circle and returned to a pre-Gunkel period. For example, Speiser's reflections on the historicity of the early patriarchal traditions and the early roots of monotheism (*Genesis*, lxix) would have been dismissed out of hand by Gunkel.

One of the more impressive aspects of Gunkel's commentary was his ability to hold together form criticism, *Religionsgeschichte*, and historical research within the one exegetical discipline. More recent scholarship has had much trouble keeping them all together. Those scholars who were interested in the historical problems of Genesis have tended to defend the tradition's historicity by opposing the form-critical method (Gordon, Albright, Bright). Conversely, those who have emphasized literary methods have usually lost contact with the sociological and historical dimensions of the text. Similarly, the recent counter-movement against Albright's position which has been mounted by Van Seters and T. L. Thompson has often succeeded in pointing out serious problems in the older historical reconstruction of the patriarchs, but it has not been any more successful in recovering a sense of the whole. Certainly the most impressive challenge to Alt's theory of the 'God of the Fathers' on which both Noth and von Rad were dependent, has come from the work of Frank Cross. Indeed Cross has projected a comprehensive historical reconstruction by which to understand all of Israel's earliest history. He envisions the key to this history to lie in the tension between its mythical and historical elements which form two sides of the one coin. However, it remains a serious question whether this overarching, ideological framework under which Cross and many of his students operate has not robbed the literary, form-critical and traditio-critical disciplines of much of their integrity.

One of the greatest contributions of Gunkel's commentary on Genesis which sets it completely apart from such representative commentaries as Keil, Dillmann, Skinner, and Procksch, was his remarkable literary sensitivity to the biblical narrative. Perhaps more by intuition than training, Gunkel was highly successful in entering into the world of the biblical writers and resonating to the full range of notes sounded. Much of the impact of von Rad's commentary derived from the same literary and aesthetic sensitivity. Within the last two decades and from very different sources there has emerged a growing concern to pursue the study of the Bible as literature on the synchronic level for its own sake (cf. the full bibliography on the subject by D. A. Robertson, *IDB Suppl*, 551). Not surprisingly much of the interest of this approach has focused on the book of Genesis. E. Auerbach's study of Hebrew narrative style on the basis of Gen. 22 has remained a classic without a close rival in its sheer brilliance and illumination. Again, in spite of much that is unconvincing, the essays of E. R. Leach and R. Barthes provide a good example of insights from the side of structuralist anthropology. The implications of James Muilenburg's 'rhetorical criticism' for the Genesis narrative have been explored by several of his students (cf. J. J. Jackson and M. Kessler). Finally, important contributions on the hermeneutics of biblical literature have been made by J. Barr, L. Alonso Schökel, W. Richter (see bibliography to previous chapter), and M. Weiss.

Although it is premature to attempt a full assessment of the new literary approach to Genesis because of the fluid state of the discipline, a number of basic critical questions have already arisen. What is the relationship between the diachronistic and synchronic dimensions of a biblical text? Does the literary method work successfully with only certain texts, such as Gen. 22 which is generally conceded to be a unified passage? Finally, is there a danger that the study of the structure of language can evolve into such an independent discipline as to lead away from the actual exegesis of the biblical text and focus on other concerns? Clearly both challenge and threat are involved.

The final issue to be raised turns on the problem of how one is to deal with the theological dimension of Genesis in the light of the modern historical critical debate. It is legitimate to raise this broader question in relation to Genesis because the handling of this book has functioned as an important barometer of the theological climate during the last few generations. In the period of the 30s several highly influential studies on Genesis (Bonhoeffer, Vischer) sought to recover a theology in conscious opposition to the reigning critical consensus. In a real sense, Karl Barth's exegesis of chs. 1–2 (*Church Dogmatics* III/1) stands in the same tradition. However, in spite of the powerful heuristic effect of these studies on Old Testament study in general, the major theological development within the field did not emerge from this direction. Rather, quite clearly the form-critical work, first by Zimmerli, and then above all by von Rad, provided an impressive union of theology and criticism. Significant popularization followed in English, such as the existential interpretation of A. Richardson (TB, 1950). It is unnecessary to review the evidence for the slow dissolution of the consensus (cf. above), but the effect can once again be charted in the theological handling of Genesis.

Wolff's attempt (see bibliography to 'The Pentateuch') to write a theology of the individual sources is certainly an extension of von Rad's method, but an unfortunate one, in my judgment. Not only does it rest on a fragile literary critical basis, but it virtually rules out the chance of doing theological justice to the narrative and canonical structure of Genesis. Moreover, the assumption that the major theological shaping of Genesis derives from the 'genius' of the Yahwist is highly vulnerable both from a historical critical and theological perspective.

Westermann's commentary on Genesis has moved in a different direction from that of Wolff and also represents a vigorous rejection of von Rad's understanding of *Heilsgeschichte*. Westermann is at great pains to do justice to the full range of disciplines, including particularly comparative Near Eastern studies, history of religions, and traditio-criticism. However, it seems already clear that his contribution will not lie primarily in the area of Old Testament theology. The concluding theological section, which rises as a vestige from a former generation, has been lost in the innumerable levels of literary and cultural development.

In sum, the problem of relating the theological dimensions of Genesis to the context of historical critical research is far from settled and emerges as a major critical issue for the coming generation. It is the thesis of this Introduction that neither the descriptive nor the constructive task of exegesis will be adequately performed without more serious attention to the canonical shape of the book of Genesis.

2. The Canonical Shape of Genesis

The structure of the book

It has long been recognized that the present form of the book of Genesis has been structured into a whole by means of a repeated genealogical formula, 'these are the generations (*toledot*) of. . . '. The formula with slight variation appears in 2.4; 5.1; 6.9; 10.1; 11.10; 11.27; 25.12; 25.19; 36.1(9) and 37.2. Commentators continue to disagree slightly on the semantic range of the term *toledot*, and whether exactly the same meaning is conveyed throughout the book (cf. the various translations in the RSV). But it is certain from the Hebrew syntax that the formula is always followed by the genitive of the progenitor and never of the progeny (Skinner, 41). The immediate significance of this observation is that the first occurrence of the formula in 2.4: 'these are the generations of the heavens and the earth .. ' serves as a superscription to the account which follows and can, under no circumstances, either be shifted to a position preceding 1.1, or treated as a subscription to 1.1–2.4a. (cf. B. Jacob, 71 for a list of the proponents of these theories).

The *toledot* formula is followed either by a genealogy or by a narrative account. Thus, a genealogy is introduced in 5.1; 10.1; 11.10; 25.12 and 36.1(9), and a narrative in 2.4; 6.9; 11.27; 25.19 and 37.2. Furthermore, it is significant to observe that the genealogies are of two different sorts. A vertical genealogy which pursues one line of descendants is found in two places. 5.1ff. traces the line from Adam to Noah; 11.10ff. from Shem to Terah. Three of the genealogies are segmented or horizontal in form indicating the relationship of various subgroups within a family. 10.1ff. traces the offspring of the sons of Noah, Japheth, Ham and Shem along with a description of their geographical distribution. 25.12ff. pursues the descendants of Ishmael, and 36.1 those of Esau, also with a brief account of geographical claims.

The crucial point to be made turns on the relationship between the two types of genealogy and the narrative material. The function of the vertical genealogies is to trace an unbroken line of descendants from Adam to Jacob, and at the same time to provide a framework in which to incorporate the narrative traditions of the patriarchs. The descendants of Adam are traced to Noah (5.1ff.) and the *toledot* formula in 6.9 introduces the traditions of the flood and Noah's sons in the chapters which follow. Next 11.10 continues the chosen line from Shem to Terah and the formula in 11.27 introduces the Abraham traditions. Again, in 25.19 the formula picks up the line with Isaac and introduces the Jacob narratives. Finally, the formula in 37.2 continues the story of Jacob's family by introducing the Joseph and Judah (ch. 38) stories. The three segmented genealogies (10.1; 25.12; 36.1) are placed in their proper sequential order, but remain tangential to the one chosen line which is pursued by means of narratives and vertical genealogies.

The function of the ten *toledot* formulae is to structure the book of Genesis into a unified composition and to make clear the nature of the unity which is intended. The role of the *toledot* formula in 2.4, which introduces the story of mankind, is to connect the creation of the world with the history which follows. This history includes both the generations of the special line and the general, as the two types of genealogy show. However, the major concern of the structure is to describe both creation and world history in the light of the divine will for a chosen people. The initial canonical implication to be drawn from the structure is that the continuity of the whole history cannot be threatened by overemphasizing other internal divisions, such as the primeval history (*contra* Westermann), which has now been subordinated to an overarching canonical framework.

Before one can adequately assess other significant effects of the present structure of Genesis, it is necessary to discuss the relation of the book's final form to its literary history. The general complexity of the source problem has already been discussed in a previous chapter. In terms of Genesis, the position is usually held, according to its classic formulation, that the Priestly source, extends from 1.1

to 50.12–13 and provides the framework of the book by means of its genealogies. At least two earlier sources, J and E, which had been united in the seventh century, were then joined to the P source by a post-exilic editor to give the present form of the book. In my judgment, there are several major problems with this theory which have resulted in a misunderstanding of the canonical shape of Genesis.

First of all, it has become increasingly doubtful whether one can speak of a Priestly source extending the whole length of Genesis (cf. Rendtorff, *Problem*; Cross). What one finds is a collection of very different types of material which share many of the characteristic priestly idioms and concepts. For example, in the book of Genesis there are only four blocks of narrative material represented by P, the creation (1.1–2.4a), the flood (6*–9*), the covenant with Abraham (17), and the burial of Sarah (23). The remaining material is either genealogical (5.1ff.; 10.1ff.; 11.1ff.; 25.12ff.) or extremely brief redactional notices which supplement a story with particular priestly tradition (16.1a, 3, 15–16; 21.1b, 2b–5; 26.34–35; 27.46–28.9, etc.). Moreover, only in the flood story has the Priestly strand been actually intertwined with the earlier sources. It is not at all obvious that all the priestly material formed an independent source before its being joined with JE.

However, the complexity of the prehistory of the tradition is such that the attempt to explain P material simply as a redactional level of JE is also unconvincing (*contra* Cross). The four major blocks of narrative material have their own integrity apart from the JE material, and when this P material is joined to the earlier material, the relationship is not redactional. The essential basis of this assertion is particularly clear in the fusion of strands within the flood story (cf. Gunkel's discussion). Moreover, there are different redactional levels within the Priestly material itself (cf. 2.4 and 5.1) which would speak against a unified priestly redactional activity.

In sum, the history of the Priestly writings is a highly complicated one. The source consisted of very different kinds of material some of which may well have been connected in strands, but other parts may have circulated separately (e.g. chs. 17 and 23; cf. Rendtorff, *Problem*, 128ff.). Then again some sections are clearly redactional and have no independent integrity apart from the earlier sources.

If one turns to examine the J and E sources in Genesis, the complexity of the history of composition is not diminished. The classic theory which recognized two independent strands still commends itself, in my judgment, but at times the E source appears in such fragmentary form that one might rather speak of a supplementary function without independent integrity. However, as Noth has readily admitted, there is frequently no objective evidence within the two strands by which to assign a source designation. The terminology simply serves as ciphers to mark doublets within a given passage. This complex situation offers another reason against attempting to isolate the Yahwist and the Elohist and assessing their work as 'creative theologians'. Moreover, efforts at determining the relative age of the sources must remain extremely provisional. Thus one concludes that the J and E sources often appear to reflect a common tradition, but the exact stages through which the development passed remains obscure. Occasionally on a given passage the priority of the J source over against E can be well asserted (cf. 12.10ff. and 20.1ff.), but even such judgments run the risk of assuming a unilinear theory of literary growth.

In the light of the complexity of the relationship among the sources of Genesis, several observations are in order regarding the book's final form and its literary history. Above all, it is essential to recognize that the present shape of the book of Genesis is not simply a juxtaposition of independent literary strands which previously had had nothing to do with one another. Rather, the development of the book underwent a complex process of growth and change in which different literary traditions mutually influenced each other in a dynamic interaction within the community of faith. Thus it seems increasingly evident from the close parallelism of sequence that the editors of the Priestly writings were aware of the earlier epic traditions and did not develop their composition in complete isolation as often suggested.

Two examples from Gen. 1–11 will illustrate the interdependence of the sources. The first two blocks assigned to P are 1.1–2.4a and 5.1–28, 30–32. But if one attempts to read these two sections in sequence, the discrepancy between the two passages is immediately apparent. 1.26ff. uses the noun 'Adam' in its generic sense of mankind, whereas 5.1 employs it as a proper name. The solution to this friction lies in the transition from a generic term to a proper name which the J source had made in chs. 2–4. The link between the P and J material lies on a far deeper level than is generally assumed. Both the form and content of P are shaped by the earlier sources.

The second example turns on the use of the priestly genealogical formula in 2.4a. The reasons have already been given why the formula must be interpreted as a superscription to the material which follows and not as a subscription to the priestly creation account (1.1–2.3). (The type-setting of 2.4 in Kittel's *Biblia Hebraica* is misleading and its interpretation has been unfortunately carried over in the RSV.) In 2.4 the formula 'these are the generations of the heavens and the earth' is the introduction to the J account in 2.4bff. The formula can neither refer to P's prior creation account, nor stand alone, nor refer to the next block of P material which follows in 5.1. One must therefore conclude that the priestly formula serves a redactional purpose of linking together the P and J creation accounts. Moreover, the formula in 2.4 must be on a different literary level from the Priestly creation account of which it is not an integral part. It appears to be a secondary redactional extension of the older P *toledot* series which had commenced in 5.1. In sum, the relation of the P and J material in Gen. 1–2 is far removed from being a mechanical linking of independent literary strands, but reflects a complex process of growth in which a mutual influence extended over the long period of composition. It is this interaction which we have identified as the canonical process occurring as the biblical literature is selected and ordered by its actual use in the community.

A second major effect of the structure of the canonical shaping of the book of Genesis emerges more clearly from this study of the earlier stages of composition lying behind the final form of the book. It has become increasingly obvious that a complex literary history preceded the present structure. Yet it is also clear that the present order has often assigned a different role to a passage from that which it originally performed. A classic example of this canonical shaping is found in Gen. 1 and 2. It is hardle necessary to rehearse all the reasons for the literary critical distinctions drawn between the two creation accounts of P(1.1–2.4a) and J(2.4b–3.24) (cf. Driver or Skinner for a review). However, it is equally true that the two originally different accounts have not been simply juxtaposed in Genesis as two parallel creation stories. To read them in this fashion as has usually been done (cf. Vawter's recent commentary) disregards the essential effect of the canonical shaping which has assigned the chapters different roles within the new context of the book of Genesis.

The introductory formula in 2.4 makes it clear that J's account has now been subordinated to P's account of the creation. What now follows proceeds from the creation in the analogy of a son to his father. Mankind is the vehicle of the *toledot*. Thus in spite of the partial overlapping in the description of creation, ch. 2 performs a basically different role from ch. 1 in unfolding the history of mankind as the intended offspring of the creation of the heavens and the earth. When the sequence of events in ch. 2 differs strikingly from ch. 1, the structure of the literature guides the reader to recognize in the shift of idiom a literary device by which further to illuminate the relationship between creation (ch. 1) and offspring (ch. 2). Conversely, on the basis of ch. 2 he now understands that the purpose of the creation in ch. 1 points to mankind and his history. In sum, the structure of the book has also altered the semantic level of the chapter in assigning ch. 2 a different function. Its new role in subordination to ch. 1 has been achieved by raising the chapter to a degree of figurative language once-removed from its original literal sense. By continuing to speak of the 'two creation accounts of Genesis' the interpreter disregards the canonical shaping and threatens its role both as literature and as scripture.

The canonical function of the promise

The great importance of the promises to the patriarchs in the book of Genesis has spurred a tremendous amount of secondary literature ever since a fresh impetus was first provided by Galling (1928) and Alt (1929). (Westermann's bibliography included 21 items and is selective, *IDB Suppl*, 693). The promises of God to the patriarchs appear in many different forms and are addressed to each father individually and as a group (50.24). The promises relate, above all, to posterity and land.

Recent critical scholarship has focused its study on a wide variety of problems. Form criticism has attempted to analyse the primary and secondary formulations and to bring some order to the great variation within the promises. Traditio-criticism has focused its attention on establishing a relationship among the various promises of land, children, and blessing, but without arriving at any broad consensus. Similarly, the original *Sitz im Leben* of the promises, which Alt had boldly hypothesized as being directed to the landless followers of the 'God of the Fathers', has continued to evoke heated debate with no clear agreement in sight.

It is not intended as a deprecation of this critical research to suggest that the canonical significance of the promises to the patriarchs should not be lost in the search to unravel the complex problems in the literature's early development. There is sufficient evidence to indicate that the promises, particularly of the land, were originally directed to the patriarchs with the prospect of imminent fulfilment. That is to say, there was nothing originally to suggest that an interval of hundreds of years including a period of slavery in Egypt was intended until the promise could be fulfilled in the conquest of Joshua. However, within the canonical context of the book of Genesis the promises to the patriarchs have been clearly assigned a different role. This new interpretation has been realized by means of several explicit passages (15.13) and by the larger framework into which the promises have been ordered. The divine words of assurance have been set within an eschatological pattern of prophecy and fulfilment which now stretches from Abraham to Joshua. The promises function only as a prelude to the coming exodus, and extend into the distant future.

The canonical effect of this new role for the ancient patriarchal promises is far reaching. All the individual stories of the Fathers have now been framed within a bracket of eschatology. The promise provides the constant element in the midst of all the changing situations of this very chequered history. In spite of the enormous variety within the individual traditions which the canonical process has retained, the portrayal of the patriarchs has been refocused about their one role as bearers of Israel's hope. What is historically an anachronism has become a theologically central confession. Moreover, the effect of the promise has a crucial impact on the actual exegesis of the book. The theological constant of the divine Word, which provides the stories with a referent, points to the future. To achieve this goal the canonical editor can employ originally parallel stories (chs. 12 and 20) to make two very different points respecting the promise of a son. Again, it is the threat to the promise which lies behind the story of Gen. 22 (cf. von Rad). The frequent attempt to recover a historical referent by means of alleged parallels from Canaanite culture (cf. Gunkel, Driver, Vawter) badly misses the point of the canonical text because it highlights those very elements which have long since been pushed into the background and overlooks the main thrust being made by the passage itself.

The canonical function of genealogy

One of the sharpest breaks with traditional Christian interpretation which the critical study of the Old Testament effected came in the handling of biblical chronology contained in the genealogies of Genesis. (Jewish interpretation followed a somewhat different approach.) As represented in classic form by Bishop James Ussher, but defended by countless others, the view has been that one could compute the history of the world since its creation in exact chronology by means of the Old Testament genealogies. Ussher arrived at the figures of 4004 BC for the date of creation and 2368 years for the historical period covered by the book of Genesis. The collapse of this understanding of chronology came largely from the impact of the natural sciences in the early nineteenth century.

From the side of biblical criticism, extra-biblical parallels to Genesis had long been known through Berossus, a Babylonian priest of the third century BC whose lists have survived in Greek. With the discovery of cuneiform literature the real source of ancient Near Eastern chronology in the Babylonian and especially the Sumerian king-lists became clear. As a result it first appeared that the biblical genealogies had lost all theological significance and were simply to be recognized as a somewhat garbled accommodation to ancient chronological tradition. However, in more recent years a more fruitful approach to the problem has emerged both from the side of cuneiform and from biblical studies.

The newer historical approach to ancient Near Eastern culture (cf. Malamat, Sasson, and R. R. Wilson) has sought to discover the sociological function of the genealogy, and has rejected the older starting point, still held by Gunkel, which saw genealogy as a vestige of an original narrative. Rather, genealogy in its various forms emerges as an independent and highly significant literary form of antiquity. It performed an important function of legitimating royal dynasties and registering the changing political claims of groups by adjusting their lineage to reflect the realities of the existing political order.

In the light of this original function of genealogy in the ancient Near East, it would seem that the book of Genesis stands in a relationship of both continuity and discontinuity with its inherited tradition. It frequently shares the same formal characteristics (segmented, vertical), and employs the huge numbers characteristic of the Babylonian and Sumerian lists. It also serves to legitimate existing social realities. Nevertheless, the major function of the genealogy in Genesis seems to differ from its analogue. The description of the structure of Genesis pointed out the role of the vertical genealogies in tracing the line of the chosen family. This is predominantly a theological function, indeed in relation to political entities outside the chosen line, but one which uses the old traditions not primarily for political legitimation but for religious affirmation.

Genesis 5 illustrates well the new function of the genealogy even though the form of the listing is unusual for the Old Testament. The age of the father is given before the birth of his child, then the age after the birth, and finally his total age. Everything focuses on the birth of the child who becomes the carrier of the promise. The genealogy marks the passing of time in an orderly sequence, but measured in terms of father and son rather than centuries. What is particularly striking in this understanding of time is that it is not reckoned in the form of absolute dates, but in the schematized pattern of descendants. When Bishop Ussher sought to translate biblical genealogy into scientific chronology and set a date for creation, he effected a major dislocation of the biblical approach to temporal reality.

It remains a debatable question to what extent the extravagant numbers in Genesis perform a specific canonical function. Occasionally the theory has been defended that the purpose of the numbers lay in their decreasing size which functions as a parallel tradition to the 'fall' of ch. 3. But the evidence for the theory is indecisive. Recently Westermann (BK, 480) has argued that the large numbers which are confined to the primeval history testify to the 'empowering of the blessing' with which mankind was blessed at the creation. Although this theory is suggestive, the issue has not been fully resolved. In my judgment, it seems likely that the numbers did acquire a specific interpretation within the canon because the Old Testament was always aware of the normal boundaries of human life (Ps. 90.10) which appeared to have been inoperative in the primeval days.

The shaping of the individual sections

A comprehensive study of the separate sections of Genesis in terms of canonical function lies beyond the scope of an Introduction and belongs to the task of a commentary. Nevertheless, a few observations are necessary to focus on some of the areas which will demand further investigations.

(a) Chapters 1–11

The problem of understanding the canonical role of the primeval history can be illustrated by contrasting the interpretations of von Rad and Westermann. Von Rad understands the purpose of these chapters to have been first determined by the Yahwist, who portrayed a history of increasing alienation from God. Starting with the expulsion from the Garden of Eden, sin expanded and grew, resulting in the murder of Abel, the illicit marriage of the angels, and the flood. This history of sin reached its climax in the Tower of Babel which threatened to return the creation into a chaos. The key to von Rad's *heilsgeschichtliche* interpretation lies in the call of Abraham (12. 1–3). The election of Israel provides the perspective from which this universal history of divine judgment and mercy toward human sinfulness is viewed in Genesis. It provides the major theological aetiology of Genesis by linking Israel's redemptive history to world history.

Westermann rejects several important features of von Rad's interpretation. He does not believe that Gen. 1–11 should be subordinated to the patriarchal traditions of chs. 12ff., but sharply distinguished in order to do justice to the integrity of the primeval history. Westermann stresses that these chapters do not move on the horizontal plane of history, but rather portray a vertical God-man dimension. They treat the universal reality of human existence which is not tied to a specific time or culture. Further, he makes the significant point that the biblical writers of chs. 1–11 have adopted texts which arose in the world outside of Israel and do not stem from the experience of Israel with Yahweh. He contests the theory that a growth of sin is intended, but argues for seeing only a portrayal of the variety and scope of the alienation. Finally, Westermann claims that the purpose of chs. 1–3 is not to portray a primeval age of innocence – there is no 'fall' for Westermann – but rather to deal with the issue of human existence in its frailty and limitation

To what extent do these two interpretations deal adequately with the canonical role assigned to these chapters within the book of Genesis? In my judgment, von Rad's attempt to interpret chs. 1–11 in close relation to the history of the patriarchs has a canonical warrant in the overall structure of the book. The line which is traced by means of the *toledot* formula explicitly unites the primeval history with that of the patriarchs. However, von Rad's attempt to subordinate the universal history to that of Israel runs into serious literary and theological problems. At this point one can recognize a persistent tension within von Rad's theological position. On the one hand, he designates the theological 'data' of the Old Testament to be Israel's witness to the divine acts of God, but on the other hand, he describes Old Testament theology as Israel's growth in self-understanding in the constant process of reworking older tradition. By reading the primeval history as an aetiology for Israel's election, von Rad has subordinated creation to redemption, which runs counter to the canonical shape of Genesis.

The canonical issues raised by Westermann's interpretation are the reverse of those of von Rad. He has made a genuine contribution by defending the integrity of the primeval history. Universal history is not a derivative of Israel's election. However, Westermann's attempt to substitute an existential interpretation of Gen. 1–2 in the place of *Heilsgeschichte* raises a host of new problems. There is no canonical warrant for interpreting these chapters as a description of the quality of life constitutive of being human. Rather, the point of the paradisal state is to contest the ontological character of human sinfulness. Mankind was not created in alienation either from God or his fellows.

To summarize: the canonical role of Gen. 1–11 testifies to the priority of creation. The divine relation to the world stems from God's initial creative purpose for the universe, not for Israel alone. Yet Israel's redemptive role in the reconciliation of the nations was purposed from the beginning and subsumed within the eschatological framework of the book.

(b) Chapters 37–50

One of the sections of Genesis which has been most actively pursued in recent years has been the Joseph cycle. Gunkel had noted its striking difference in form and use of tradition from the other patriarchal collections, and had designated it a 'novella'. However, it was the brilliant essay of von Rad in 1953, 'The Joseph Narrative and Ancient Wisdom', which sparked the new interest in the Joseph stories. Von Rad argued that the story's different form with its strong didactic flavour derived from its origin in wisdom circles. In the wake of his essay there have appeared numerous articles both supporting and contesting the thesis. However, throughout the whole debate there was little or no attention given to the canonical questions. What is the shape of the final chapters and what is their function within the book of Genesis as a whole?

The difficulty of the questions is raised immediately by the structure of the book of Genesis. The Joseph narratives are introduced by a *toledot* formula in 37.2 which places him in line with the other patriarchs. The stories of Joseph then occupy a position in the book roughly equal to those of Abraham and Jacob. Nevertheless, Joseph is clearly set apart from the earlier patriarchs. He does not form part of the triad to whom the promise of land and posterity is given, rather he becomes the first (Gen. 50.24) to whom the promise to Abraham, Isaac, and Jacob is reiterated. If Joseph is not the bearer of the promise in the same way as his forefathers, what then is his role in Genesis?

Certainly one of the keys to the canonical interpretation is given in the place assigned to the story of Judah (ch. 38). In the large majority of commentaries (cf. Gunkel, von Rad, etc.) the chapter is summarily dismissed as an unfortunate interpolation into the Joseph story. At best it serves a secondary literary role of marking the passage of time when Joseph journeyed into captivity. Only Benno Jacob, among modern commentators, reflects more seriously on the purpose of the chapter. Fortunately, several recent articles which approach the problem from the side of general literature, have again focused on the purpose of the chapter in its present position.

The first observation to make is that the *toledot* formula in 37.2 introduces the family of Jacob. Judah's story is as much a part of the history as is Joseph's, and the disproportionate length assigned to each is of little importance. The intention to deal with the whole family of Jacob is confirmed by the inclusion of all the twelve sons in Jacob's final testament in ch. 49. The 'blessings of Jacob' also reveal an important perspective of the tradition. It is from the line of Judah, not Joseph, that Israel's redemption is to come. The point of this last section seems to lie somewhere in the contrast between the stories of these two sons in relation to the promise. Joseph became the means of preserving the family in a foreign country (50.20), but also the means by which a new threat to the promise of the land was realized. Conversely, Judah demonstrated an unfaithfulness which threatened to destroy the promise of a posterity, which was only restored by the faithfulness of a Canaanite wife. In sum, the final section of the book of Genesis turns on the issue of the threat to the promise which leads inevitably to the book of Exodus.

3. Theological and Hermeneutical Implications

(a) Von Rad once wrote: 'For no stage in this work's long period of growth is really obsolete; something of each phase has been conserved and passed on as enduring until the Hexateuch attained its final form' (*Genesis*, rev. ed., 28). Certainly von Rad is right in suggesting that the final form of Genesis reflects the layering of tradition in which there has been no attempt to flatten out the diverse material into a monolithic whole. However, von Rad's traditio-critical approach, as a legacy of Gunkel, has failed to reckon seriously with the full implications of the canonical progress on the traditioning process. Above all, the final form of Genesis provides a hermeneutical guide by which to interpret this complex prehistory of the literature. It introduces a critical judgment in emphasizing certain features, subordinating others, and even suppressing some. To speak of Genesis as scripture is to acknowledge the authority of this particular viewing of Israel's tradition which in its particular form provided a critical theological standard for future generations of Israel.

(b) It was part of the great sensitivity of von Rad as an exegete to have discerned a unique feature of the Genesis saga: 'It reflects a historical experience on the relevant community which extends into the present time of the narrator' (*Genesis*, 34). However, rather than attributing this peculiarity to the nature of a literary genre, the canonical approach recognizes this feature of actualizing the biblical material as a major concern in its formation. This theological force is not an extrinsic category which was later imposed by religious interpreters, but is constitutive of the literature itself. The book of Genesis offers a powerful example of a process of editing in which an eschatological framework was finally allowed to become the dominant force in its shaping.

(c) One of the most difficult modern hermeneutical problems associated with the study of the book of Genesis turns on establishing the relationship between myth and history. More than one generation of scholars has sought to bring clarity to this issue. It would be presumptous to suggest that the canonical approach has suddenly resolved the problem, but it does aid in setting certain parameters for the discussion.

The same history-like story extends from Genesis 1 to 50 which is set in a genealogical framework of human history. No part of Genesis can be called 'history' in the narrow, modern usage of the term because of the tangential relationship to objective reality, even though different historical elements are evidenced throughout the book in varying degrees. Conversely, there is no Old Testament myth in exact analogy to ancient Near Eastern mythology. The Genesis material is unique because of an understanding of reality which has subordinated common mythopoetic tradition to a theology of absolute divine sovereignity. The book of Genesis reflects different degrees of intensity by which to portray representative and universal features of human life; however, the canonical structure of the composition guards against dissolving the narrative into ontological concerns to which the story only functions as illustration. The basic point to be made is that regardless of terminology – whether myth, history, or saga – the canonical shape of Genesis serves the community of faith and practice as a truthful witness to God's activity on its behalf in creation and blessing, judgment and forgiveness, redemption and promise.

History of Exegesis

Carpzov I, 67ff., *DBS* 7, 687–95; *DThC* 6, 1206ff., 2335ff.; *EB* 2, 323; *Augustine*, *La Genèse au sens littéral*, Oeuvres 48 (Bibliothèque Augustinienne, 7e série), Paris 1972, 67–79 (full bibliography of patristic exegesis); E. F. C. **Rosenmüller**, *Scholia in Vetus Testamentum* I, 1, Berlin ³1821, v–lii; *RGG*³ 2, 1377–79.

G. T. **Armstrong**, *Die Genesis in der alten Kirche*, Tübingen 1962; N. **Avigad**, and Y. **Yadin**, *A Genesis Apocryphon*, Jerusalem 1956; W. **Bacher**,

'Abraham ibn Ezras Einleitung zu seinem Pentateuch Kommentar', *Sitzungsberichte der Wiener Akademie*, Phil.-hist. Klasse 81, 1875, 362–444; R. H. **Bainton**, 'The Immoralities of the Patriarchs according to the Exegesis of the Late Middle Ages and of the Reformation', *HTR* 23, 1930, 39–49; G. **Bardy**, 'Melchisédech dans la tradition patristique', *RB* 35, 1926, 496–509; 36, 1927, 25–45; J. P. **Bouhot**, 'Pentateuque chez les Pères', *DBS* 7, 687–708; H. **Cazelles**, 'Pentateuque II. L'Époque Médiévale', *DBS* 7, 708–28; N. **Dahl**, 'The Story of Abraham in Luke-Acts', *Studies in Luke-Acts, FS P. Schubert*, ed. L. E. Keck and L. J. Martyn, Nashville 1966, London 1968, 139–58; J. **Daniélou**, 'La typologie d'Isaac dans le christianisme primitif', *Bibl* 28, 1947, 363–93; 'Abraham dans la Tradition Chrétienne', *Cahiers Sioniens* 5, Paris 1951, 160–79; R. **Devreesse**, 'Châines exégétiques grecques', *DBS* 1, 1084–1233; L. **Diestel**, *Geschichte des Alten Testament in der christlichen Kirche*, Jena 1869, 482–508; J. W. **Etheridge**, *The Targums of Onkelos and Jonathan Ben Uzziel on the Pentateuch*, 2 vols., London 1862–5; L. **Ginzberg**, *The Legends of the Jews*, 7 vols., Philadelphia 1911–38; E. **Gottlieb**, 'The Significance of the Story of Creation in the Interpretation of the Early Cabbalists' (Hebrew), *Tarbiz* 37, Jerusalem 1967–8, 294–317; P.-M. **Guillaume**, 'Joseph, chez Pères de l'église', *DS* 8.2, 1974, 1280–89.

H. **Hailperin**, *Rashi and the Christian Scholars*, Pittsburg 1963; J. **Hennig**, 'The First Chapter of Genesis in the Liturgy', *CBQ* 10, 1948, 360–75; H. D. **Hummel**, 'Critical Methodology and the Lutheran Symbols' Treatment of the Genesis Creation Account', *CTM* 43, 1972, 528–47; J. **Jervell**, *Imago Dei. Gen 1, 26f. im Spätjudentum, in der Gnosis und in den paulinischen Briefen*, FRLANT 76, 1960; C. W. **Jones**, 'Some Introductory Remarks on Bede's Commentary on Genesis', *Sacris Erudiri* 19, Steenbrugge 1969–70, 115–98; S. **Kierkegaard**, *Fear and Trembling*, ET London 1939, Princeton 1941; Y. **Laurent**, 'Le caractère historique de Gen 2–3 dans l'exégèse française au tourant de XIXe siecle', *ETL* 23, 1947, 36–69; H.-G. **Leder**, 'Arbor Scientiae. Die Tradition vom paradiesischen Apfelbaum', *ZNW* 52, 1961, 156–89; N. **Leibowitz**, *Studies in the Book of Genesis*, Jerusalem 1972 (including bibliography of medieval Jewish commentators); D. **Lerch**, *Isaaks Opferung christlich gedeutet*, Tübingen 1950; A. **Levene**, *The Early Syrian Fathers on Genesis*, London 1951; E. B. **Levine**, 'The Aggadah im Targum ben Uzziel and Neofiti I to Genesis', *Neophyti I*, ed. A. Díez Macho, II, Madrid 1970, 537–78; J. P. **Lewis**, *A Study of the Interpretation of Noah and the Flood in Jewish and Christian Literature*, Leiden 1968; H. **de Lubac** and L. **Doutreleaux**, 'Introduction', *Origène, Homilies sur la Genese*, SC 7, 1947; ²1976; E. **Mangenot**, 'Hexaméron', *DThC* 5, 2325–54; M. **Metzger**, *Die Paradieserzählung. Die Geschichte ihrer Auslegung von J. Clericus bis W. M. L. de Wette*, Bonn 1959; J. **Michl**, 'Der Weibessame (Gen 3,15) in spätjüdische und frühchristliche Auffassung', *Bibl* 33, 1952, 371–401, 476–505; A. A. **Miller**, 'The Theologies of Luther and Boehme in the Light of their Genesis Commentaries', *HTR* 63, 1970, 261–303; Y.

Moubarac, 'Abraham en Islam', *Cahiers Sioniens* 5, 1951, 196–212; M. **Müller**, *Die Lehre des hl. Augustinus von der Paradiesehe und ihre Auswirkung in der Sexualethik des 12. und 13. Jahrhunderts bis Thomas von Aquin*, Regensburg 1954. C. A. **Patrides**, 'Renaissance Interpretations of Jacob's Ladder', *TZ* 18, 1962, 411–18; M. **Philonenko**, *Joseph et Aséneth*, Studia Post-Biblica 13, Leiden 1968; A. **Posnanski**, *Shiloh. I. Die Auffassung von Genesis XLIX, 10 in Altertum bis zum Ende des Mittelalters*, Leipzig 1904; F. E. **Robbins**, *The Hexaemeral Literature. A Study of the Greek and Latin Commentaries on Genesis*, Chicago 1912; 'The Influence of Greek Philosophy on the Early Commentaries of Genesis', *AJT* 16, 1912, 218–40; F. **Ros**, 'The Creation of Eve in the Greek Fathers till Chrysostom', *Misc. Biblica B. Ubach*, Montserrat 1953, 31–48; S. **Rosowsky**, *The Cantillation of the Bible: The Five Books of Moses*, New York 1957 (cf. review by E. Werner, *JQR* 49, 1959, 287–92); S. **Sandmel**, *Philo's Place in Judaism: A Study of Conceptions of Abraham in Jewish Literature*, rev. ed. New York 1971; S. **Spiegel**, *The Last Trial*, New York 1967; N. H. **Steneck**, *Science and Creation in the Middle Ages: Henry of Langenstein on Genesis*, South Bend, Ind. 1976; W. **Trillhaas**, '"Felix Culpa". Zur Deutung der Geschichte vom Sündenfall bei Hegel', *Probleme Biblischer Theologie*, FS G. von Rad, Munich 1971, 589–602; G. **Vermes**, 'The Life of Abraham', *Scripture and Tradition in Judaism*, Leiden ²1973, 67–126; P. **Vignaux**, et al., *In Principio. Interprétations des premiers verses de la Genèse*, Études Augustiniennes, Paris 1973; A. **Williams**, *The Common Expositor: An Account of the Commentaries on Genesis, 1527–1633*, Chapel Hill, N.C. 1948; R. McL. **Wilson**, 'The Early History of Exegesis of Gen 1,26', *Studia Patristica* I, TU 63, 1957, 420–37; G. **Wuttke**, *Melchisedech der Priesterkönig von Salem. Eine Studie zur Geschichte der Exegese*, BZNW 5, 1927.

VII

EXODUS

Commentaries

M. M. Kalisch, 1855
C. F. Keil, BC 1864
A. Dillmann, V. Ryssel, KeH, ³1897
F. de Hummelauer, CSS, 1897
H. Holzinger, KHC, 1900
B. Baentsch, HKAT, 1903
S. R. Driver, CB, 1911
H. Gressmann, *SAT*, ²1922
P. Heinisch, HS, 1934
G. Beer, HAT, 1939

A. Clamer, SB, 1956
M. Noth, ET, OTL, 1962
G. Te Stroete, BOuT, 1966
U. Cassuto, 1967
G. H. Davies, TB, 1967
F. C. Fensham, POuT, 1970
J. P. Hyatt, NCeB, 1971
R. E. Clements, CNEB, 1972
B. S. Childs, OTL, 1974
F. Michaeli, CAT, 1974
W. H. Schmidt, BK, 1974ff.

Bibliography

M. **Aberbach** and L. **Smolar**, 'Aaron, Jeroboam and the Golden Calves', *JBL* 86, 1967, 129–40; A. **Alt**, 'The Origins of Israelite Law', *Essays* (see Pentateuch), 81–121; K. C. W. **Bähr**, *Symbolik des Mosaischen Cultus*, I-II, Heidelberg ²1874; K. **Baltzer**, *The Covenant Formulary*, ET Oxford 1971; James **Barr**, 'Some Semantic Notes on the Covenant', *Beiträge zur Alttestamentlichen Theologie, FS W. Zimmerli*, Göttingen 1977, 23–38; C. **Barth**, 'Zur Bedeutung der Wüstentradition', *SVT* 15, 1966, 14–23.; W. **Beyerlin**, *Origins and History of the Oldest Sinaitic Traditions*, ET Oxford 1965; 'Die Paränese im Bundesbuch und ihre Herkunft', *Gottes Wort und Gottes Land, FS H. W. Hertzberg*, Göttingen 1965, 9–29; F. S. **Bodenheimer**, 'The Manna of Sinai', *BA* 10, 1947, 1–6; C. **Brekelmans**, 'Exodus XVIII and the Origins of Yahwism in Israel', *OTS* 10, 1954, 215–24; 'Die sogenannten deuteronomistischen Elemente in Genesis bis Numeri', *SVT* 15, 1966, 90–96; M. **Caloz**, 'Exode, XIII, 3–16, et son rapport du Deutéronome', *RB* 65, 1968, 5–62; H. **Cazelles**, *Études sur le code d'alliance*, Paris 1946; 'Les Localisations de l'Exode et la critique littéraire', *RB* 62, 1955, 321–

64; B. S. **Childs**, 'A Traditio-Historical Study of the Reed Sea Tradition', *VT* 20, 1970, 406–18; W. M. **Clark**, 'Law', *Old Testament Form Criticism*, ed. J. H. Hayes, San Antonio, Texas 1974, 99–139; G. W. **Coats**, 'The Traditio-Historical Character of the Reed Sea Motif', *VT* 7, 1967, 253–65; *Rebellion in the Wilderness*, Nashville 1968; F. M. **Cross**, 'The Tabernacle', *BA* 10, 1947, 45–68; 'Yahweh and the God of the Patriarchs', *HTR* 55, 1962, 225–59; expanded as 'The Religion of Canaan and the God of Israel', *Canaanite Myth and Hebrew Epic*, 1973, 3–75; 'The Song of the Sea and Canaanite Myth', *God and Christ: Existence and Providence*, ed. R. W. Funk (*Journal of Theology and the Church* 5), New York 1968, 1–25; reprinted, *Canaanite Myth*, 112–44; F. M. **Cross** and D. N. **Freedman**, 'The Song of Miriam', *JNES* 14, 1955, 237–50.

D. **Daube**, *Studies in Biblical Law*, Cambridge and New York 1947, 74–101; G. I. **Davies**, 'The Wilderness Itineraries: A Comparative Study', *Tyndale Bulletin* 25, London 1974, 46–81; S. **De Vries**, 'The Origin of the Murmuring Tradition', *JBL* 87, 1968, 51–8; O. **Eissfeldt**, *Baal Zaphon, Zeus Kasios und der Durchzug der Israeliten durchs Meer*, Halle 1932; 'Die Komposition von Exodus 1–12', *KS* 2, Tübingen 1963, 160ff.; *Die Komposition der Sinai-Erzählung 19–34*, Berlin 1966; 'Palestine in the Time of the Nineteenth Dynasty. (a) The Exodus and Wanderings', *CAH* II/2, 1975, 307–30; K. **Elliger**, 'Sinn und Ursprung der priesterlichen Geschichtserzählung', *KSAT*, Munich 1966, 174–98; I. **Engnell**, 'Paesaḥ-Maṣṣot and the Problem of "Patternism"', *Orientalia Suecana* 1, Uppsala 1952, 39–50; reprinted as 'The Passover', in *A Rigid Scrutiny*, Nashville 1969 (=*Critical Essays on the Old Testament*, London 1970), 185–96; J. J. **Finkelstein**, 'Mishpat' (Hebrew), *EB* 5, 1968, 588ff.; G. **Fohrer**, *Überlieferung und Geschichte des Exodus*, BZAW 91, 1964; V. **Fritz**, *Israel in der Wüste*, Marburg 1970; N. **Fueglister**, *Die Heilsbedeutung des Pascha*, Munich 1963; W. **Fuss**, *Die deuteronomistische Pentateuchredaktion in Exodus 3–17*, BZAW 126, 1972; E. **Gerstenberger**, *Wesen und Herkunft des apodiktischen Rechts*, WMANT 20, 1965; H. **Gese**, 'Der Dekalog als Ganzheit betrachtet', *ZTK* 64, 1967, 121–38; M. **Greenberg**, 'Some Postulates of Biblical Criminal Law', *Y. Kaufmann Jubilee Volume*, Jerusalem 1960, 5ff.; 'The Thematic Unity of Exodus III-XI', *Fourth World Congress of Jewish Studies* I, Jerusalem 1967, 151–4; H. **Gressmann**, *Mose und seine Zeit*, FRLANT 18, 1913; J. H. **Gronbaek**, 'Juda und Amalek. Überlieferungsgeschichtliche Erwägungen zu Exodus 17, 8–16', *StTh* 18, 1964, 26–45; A. H. J. **Gunneweg**, 'Mose im Midian', *ZTK* 61, 1964, 1–9; H. **Haag**, 'Pâque', *DBS* 6, 1120–49; M. **Haelvoet**, 'La Théophanie du Sinaï', *ETL* 29, 1953, 374ff.; J. **Halbe**, *Das Privilegrecht Jahwes, Ex 34, 10–26*, FRLANT 114, 1975; M. **Haran**, 'Exodus, The', *IDB Suppl*, 304–10; S. **Herrmann**, *Israel in Egypt*, ET, SBT II.27, 1973; F. **Hesse**, *Das Verstockungsproblem im Alten Testament*, Berlin 1955; J. P. **Hyatt**, 'The Site and Manner of the Israelites' Crossing of the Sea', *Exodus*, NCeB, 1971, 156ff.

B. S. **Jackson**, 'The Problem of Exod. xxi 22–25 (ius talionis)', *VT* 23,

1973, 273–304; R. **Knierim**, 'Exodus 18 und die Neuordnung der mosaischen Gerichtsbarkeit', *ZAW* 73, 1961, 146–71; K. **Koch**, *Die Priesterschrift von Exodus 25 bis Leviticus 16*, Göttingen 1959; L. **Koehler**, 'Der Dekalog', *ThR* NF 1, 1929, 161–84; H.-J. **Kraus**, 'Zur Geschichte des Passah-Massot-Festes im Alten Testament', *EvTh* 18, 1958, 47ff.; A. **Kuenen**, 'Manna und Wachteln', *Gesammelte Abhandlungen zur biblischen Wissenschaft*, Freiburg 1894, 276ff.; A. **Kuschke**, 'Die Lagervorstellung der priesterschriftlichen Erzählung', *ZAW* 63, 1951, 74–105; E. **Kutsch**, 'Erwägungen zur Geschichte der Passafeier und des Massotfestes', *ZTK* 55, 1958, 1–35; *Verheissung und Gesetz*, BZAW 131, 1973; A. **Lauha**, 'Das Schilfmeermotiv im Alten Testament', *SVT* 9, 1963, 32–46; S. **Lehming**, 'Massa und Meriba', *ZAW* 73, 1961, 71–7; S. E. **Loewenstamm**, *The Tradition of the Exodus in its Development* (Hebrew), Jerusalem 1965; N. **Lohfink**, 'Zum "kleinen geschichtlichen Credo" Dtn 26,5–9', *Theologie und Philosophie* 46, Freiburg 1971, 19–39.

D. **McCarthy**, *Treaty and Covenant*, Rome 1963; G. **Mendenhall**, 'Ancient Oriental and Biblical Law' and 'Covenant Forms in Israelite Tradition', *BA* 17, 1954, 26–46, 50–76=*Law and Covenant in Israel and the Ancient Near East*, Pittsburgh 1955; E. **Meyer**, *Die Israeliten und ihre Nachbarstämme*, Halle 1906; S. **Mowinckel**, *Le Décalogue*, Paris 1927; J. **Muilenburg**, 'The Form and Structure of the Covenantal Formulations', *VT* 9, 1959, 347–65; 'A Liturgy of the Triumphs of Yahweh', *Studia Biblica et Semitica T. C. Vriezen dedicata*, Wageningen 1966, 238–50; E. **Nicholson**, *Exodus and Sinai in History and Tradition*, Oxford and Richmond, Va. 1973; 'The Interpretation of Exodus xxiv 9–11', *VT* 24, 1974, 77–97; 'The Decalogue as the Direct Address of God', *VT* 27, 1977, 422–33; E. **Nielsen**, *The Ten Commandments in New Perspective*, ET, SBT II.7, 1968; M. **Noth**, *Die Gesetze im Pentateuch*, Königsberg 1940; ET *The Laws in the Pentateuch and Other Studies*, Edinburgh 1966, Philadelphia 1967, 1–107; *A History of Pentateuchal Traditions*, ET Englewood Cliffs, N.J. 1972; E. **Osswald**, *Das Bild des Moses*, Berlin 1962; E. **Otto**, 'Erwägungen zum überlieferungsgeschichtlichen Ursprung und "Sitz im Leben" des jahwistischen Plagenzyklus', *VT* 26, 1976, 3–27; S. M. **Paul**, *Studies in the Book of the Covenant in the Light of Cuneiform and Biblical Law*, Leiden 1970; J. **Pedersen**, 'Passahfest und Passahlegende', *ZAW* 52, 1934, 161–75; L. **Perlitt**, *Die Bundestheologie im Alten Testament*, WMANT 36, 1969; 'Mose als Prophet', *EvTh* 31, 1971, 588–608; J. **Plastaras**, *The God of Exodus*, Milwaukee 1966; J. **Popper**, *Der biblische Bericht über die Stiftshütte*, Leipzig 1862; W. J. A. **Powers**, 'Glueck's Exploration in Eastern Palestine in the Light of Recent Evidence', *VT* 21, 1971, 118–23.

K. **von Rabenau**, 'Die beiden Erzählungen vom Schilfmeerwunder in Exod. 17–14,31', *Theologische Versuche*, ed. P. Wätzel, East Berlin 1966, 9–29; G. **von Rad**, *Die Priesterschrift im Hexateuch*, Stuttgart 1934; 'The Form-Critical Problem of the Hexateuch', *Problem* (see Pentateuch), 1–78; A. **Reichert**, *Der Jahwist und die sogenannten deuteronomistischen Erweiterungen* *im Buch Exodus*, Diss. Tübingen 1972; W. **Richter**, *Die sogenannten vor-prophetischen Berufungsberichte*, Göttingen 1970; L. **Rost**, 'Weidewechsel und altisraelitischen Festkalendar', *ZDPV* 66, 1943, 205–16; W. **Rudolph**, *Der 'Elohist' von Exodus bis Josua*, Berlin 1938; H. **Schmid**, *Mose: Überlieferung und Geschichte*, BZAW 110, 1968; H. H. **Schmid**, *Der sogenannte Jahwist*, Zürich 1976; H. **Schulz**, *Das Todesrecht im Alten Testament*, BZAW 114, 1969; H. **Seebass**, *Mose und Aaron, Sinai und Gottesberg*, Bonn 1962; J. B. **Segal**, *The Hebrew Passover*, London and New York 1963; R. **Smend**, *Die Entstehung des Alten Testaments*, Stuttgart 1978; J. J. **Stamm** and M. E. **Andrew**, *The Ten Commandments in Recent Research*, ET, SBT II.2, 1967; T. C. **Vriezen**, '"'ehje' ăser 'chje'"', *FS A. Bertholet*, Tübingen 1950, 498–512; 'Exodusstudien, Exodus 1', *VT* 17, 1967, 334–53; 'The Exegesis of Exodus XXIV, 9–11', *OTS* 17, 1972, 100–33.

K. **Walkenhorst**, *Der Sinai im liturgischen Verständnis der deuteronomistischen und priesterlichen Tradition*, Bonn 1969; P. **Weimar**, *Untersuchungen zur pries-terschriftlichen Exodusgeschichte*, Würzburg 1973; P. **Weimar** and E. **Zenger**, *Exodus. Geschichten und Geschichte der Befreiung Israels*, Stuttgart 1975;, J. **Well-hausen**, *Prolegomena to the History of Israel*, ET Edinburgh 1885, 83ff.; C. **Westermann**, 'Die Herrlichkeit Gottes in der Priesterschrift', *Wort–Gebot–Glaube, FS W. Eichrodt*, Zürich 1970, 227–49; M. **Weinfeld**, 'To the Origin of Apodictic Law in Ancient Israel' (Hebrew), *Tarbiz* 41, Jerusalem 1971–72, 349–60; H. **Wildberger**, *Jahwes Eigentumsvolk*, Zürich 1960; F. V. **Winnett**, *The Mosaic Tradition*, Toronto 1949; G. E. **Wright**, *God who Acts*, SBT I.8, 1952; E. **Zenger**, *Die Sinaitheophanie. Untersuchung zum jahwistischen und elohistischen Geschichtswerk*, Würzburg 1971; Z. **Zevit**, 'The Priestly Redaction and Interpretation of the Plague Narrative in Exodus', *JQR* 61, 1976, 193–211; W. **Zimmerli**, 'Ich bin Jahwe', *Geschichte und Altes Testament*, Tübingen 1953, 179–209=*Gottes Offenbarung*, Munich 1963, 11–40; 'Sinaibund und Abrahambund. Ein Beitrag zum Verständnis der Priesterschrift', *TZ* 16, 1960, 268–80=*Gottes Offenbarung*, 205–16; *The Law and the Prophets*, ET Oxford 1965; 'Erwägungen zum "Bund" ', *Wort–Gebot–Glaube*, 171–90.

1. Historical Critical Problems

The exegetical activity on problems relating to the book of Exodus since the end of World War II has been enormous. It is quite impossible to pursue the full scope of issues in any detail. The reader is referred to the full bibliographies in my Exodus commentary and that of W. H. Schmidt. Although there will inevitably be some overlapping with the previous section on the Pentateuch, this chapter will attempt to focus on problems specifically related to the book of Exodus, as much as it is possible.

Literary critical problems

In recent years attention to the source-critical problems of the book of Exodus has been less intense than in other areas. Many of the same problems encountered in the analysis of Genesis have continued into Exodus. The extreme difficulty of separating the J and E sources has long been recognized. In an effort to clarify the picture two major efforts have been made which closely parallel research on Genesis. Rudolph continued his study into Exodus proposing to eliminate the need for an E source. Fohrer sought to demonstrate the presence of a 'nomadic' (N) source in his study of chs. 1–15. Neither of these attempts succeeded in shaking the older consensus. A more representative analysis was offered by Noth, who still held to the classic divisions, but with considerably less confidence in his ability to separate precisely between the early strands. The extreme complexity of exact source division in Exodus is best illustrated in ch. 19, which has evoked the widest possible disagreement among scholars (cf. Childs).

There is another perplexing problem relating to source criticism in Exodus. It has to do with the criteria for determining the sources to which to assign the large blocks of legal material. Wellhausen first found three major strands of legal material in addition to the priestly source. He assigned the Book of the Covenant (21–23) to J, the Decalogue to E, and Ex. 34 to an independent source. However, after Kuenen's criticism Wellhausen agreed that the Book of the Covenant did not belong to J. This decision cleared the way for him to distinguish between E's 'ethical decalogue' (ch. 20) and J's 'cultic decalogue' (ch. 34). However, increasingly the opinion has grown that the legal material is largely independent of the traditional sources and, at best, can be assigned only a secondary role within a particular source.

A similar problem arises in connection with old poems such as Exodus 15 which only secondarily has been brought into relationship with literary sources. Often one has the impression of a very old core to which a later layer of material, akin either to P (Ex. 34.29ff.) or to D (19.3ff.) has been added. In many cases, the persistent effort to assign material to sources has resulted in such an atomizing of the strands that the classic documentary hypothesis has unintentionally given way to one which is closer to the old fragmentary hypothesis (cf. Beyerlin, *Origins*).

The problem of the priestly source in Exodus is a more complex one than in Genesis. First of all, the P source has been closely intertwined with earlier sources in many more chapters including the story of the plagues, the crossing, and the manna. As in the case of Genesis, it is not at all clear to what extent the priestly material should be considered an independent source or simply a redaction of the epic tradition (Cross). At least one should be cautious in posing the question in terms of a simple alternative. At times the P source clearly reveals the continuity of a unified source (cf. the crossing of the sea, ch.14). Then again, it seems to assume a knowledge of earlier sources and function as a priestly redaction (cf. Noth on 6.2ff.). Finally, there remains the much debated issue of the relationship of the narrative to the legal material within the priestly source. Elliger and Noth have expressed themselves strongly in favour of seeing an original level of the source in the narrative material to which the legal sections have been secondarily added. However, others such as B. A. Levine (*IDB Suppl*, 686) prefer to see a chronological overlapping of code and narrative with a mutual influencing process at work in the formation of both. The issue has not been fully resolved.

Another source-critical issue which is especially critical in Exodus has to do with the possibility of a Deuteronomic redaction. At the turn of the century Driver had pointed out the presence of Deuteronomic terminology in Exodus, but it was Baentsch who spoke of a Deuteronomic redaction in passages such as 12.24–27a, 13.3–16, and 19.3b–8. He has been followed by many recent commentators (Noth, Hyatt, Fuss, etc.). However, Lohfink, Brekelmans, Caloz and Reichert have pointed out problems with identifying these Exodus passages with a seventh-century Deuteronomic writer, and the term 'proto-deuteronomic' has been suggested to allow for an earlier dating. Other scholars see little evidence for such a redaction (Fohrer, Smend).

Finally, the issue of relating source criticism to form and traditio-criticism, has been forcefully posed by Rendtorff (*Problem des Pentateuch*), and to a lesser extent by H. H. Schmid. The issue is as complex as it was in Genesis and still unresolved. This nature of the problem can be well illustrated by pointing to the unreflecting manner in which Gressmann related the literary and oral dimensions of texts in his early form-critical study of Moses. He assumed that independent sagas extended from the oral stage directly into literary sources. Von Rad went considerably beyond Gressmann in seeing larger units on the oral level, but it was Noth who at least tried to face the issue by posing an intermediate stage in terms of a *Grundschrift* on which both J and E were dependent as later recensions of the common tradition. Rendtorff has initiated a new stage in the debate which has only begun.

Form-critical and traditio-critical issues

During the last three decades the centre of much of the most exciting work in the Old Testament has focused on the study of the oral traditions found in the book of Exodus. Until quite recently there would have been a broad consensus that some of the major discoveries had occurred in the field by applying Gunkel's insights to Exodus. Research on the traditions fell into two broad categories, which were always closely related. On the one hand, there appeared a series of detailed form-critical studies which concentrated on investigating a single tradition, such as the passover or Sinai tradition, and was designated *Traditionsgeschichte*. On the other hand, there were studies which sought to trace the growth and interrelationship between traditions, such as Sinai and Exodus, and were designated *Überlieferungsgeschichte*. Actually the method of research of the two forms of 'tradition history' was similar, differing only in emphasis, and they frequently flowed together.

Gunkel, followed shortly by Mowinckel, had stressed the dominant role of the cult in the formation of the Psalter. The same theory was soon applied to the traditions of Exodus. Mowinckel's early monograph on the Decalogue in 1929 did not make much impact at first even though the second part of the book extended his understanding of cult into the narrative material of Exodus. Rather, it was J. Pedersen's article on the passover in 1934 which first worked out a thorough-going cultic theory to explain the history of the tradition. He argued that the whole complex of Ex. 1–15 arose as a cultic legend which had historicized the various elements which constituted the original ceremony into a narrative form.

Although Pedersen provided the initial impetus, the monographs of von Rad and Noth shortly dominated the discussion. Von Rad brought much greater precision to bear in delineating the cultic traditions. He isolated several liturgical formulae in the Hexateuch which he argued were skeletal outlines of an early cultic ceremony (Deut. 6.20ff.; 26.5ff. etc.) Because these credal formulations lacked reference to the Sinai tradition, he posited two separate circles of traditions, suggesting a festival at Gilgal as the locus of the Exodus tradition and Shechem of the Sinai tradition. Noth greatly broadened the scope of the discussion in his 1948 monograph (ET *History of Pentateuchal Traditions*), but accepted basically von Rad's reconstruction along with the strong cultic emphasis.

In the period after World War II, von Rad's thesis evoked a huge amount of secondary literature in a long and heated debate. One group of scholars sought to extend and refine the method to include among others the traditions of the wilderness (Coats, Fritz), election (Wildberger), covenant (Baltzer), and Sinai (Beyerlin). The strongest opposition to von Rad's formulation came from the side of the Americans who rallied around Mendenhall's theory of Hittite treaties in order to construct a very different model for the development of Israel's early traditions. (cf. Nicholson for a history of this debate). In the course of the discussion von Rad's position was increasingly eroded, but conversely the difficulty of making any direct application of the Hittite parallels became apparent.

Another area of form-critical study of great importance for the book of Exodus centred on the study of Old Testament law. Although there has been a long, scholarly tradition of comparative legal studies, A. Alt's essay of 1934 set off a fresh wave of interest from the side of the form critics. Alt not only distinguished between two forms of law which he designated casuistic and apodictic, but he sought to establish a setting for each. He argued that casuistic law was common to ancient Near Eastern culture, but that apodictic law was unique to Israel. This distinction was accepted by many and exploited theologically by von Rad, Noth, Zimmerli, and others.

In Germany the form-critical study of law was continually refined in the studies of Gese, Gerstenberger, Richter, Schulz, among others. However, the law of diminishing returns began to set in and much of the original excitement surrounding Alt's original thesis was dissipated. Elsewhere on the international scene interest in law turned more to comparative ancient Near Eastern studies, exemplified in the work of S. Paul, Greenberg, F. C. Fensham, Finkelstein, and Cazelles.

It can be debated to what extent redactional criticism should be regarded as a separate discipline distinct from both literary and form criticism. However, as it emerged in Old Testament studies in the monograph of L. Perlitt, it represented a decided break with the form-critical and traditio-critical work which has just been described. Returning to a position somewhat akin to that of Wellhausen, Perlitt argued that the term covenant as a theological concept appeared relatively late in Israel and was first developed by Deuteronomy. His attempt to demonstrate that all earlier references to covenant stem from the hand of the school of Deuteronomy runs directly counter to the assumption on which von Rad and Noth had based their work. In this same context of changing models, Weinfeld's monograph on Deuteronomy (see bibliography there) was also significant in substituting the role of the scribe in the place of the cult.

Theology and history of religions

The form-critical method in Germany since the period of the 30s had been carried on closely allied with an intense interest in the theology of the Old Testament. The connection was particularly evident in the handling of the Exodus traditions. Whereas an earlier generation of scholars such as Gressmann, Jirku, and Alt, had pursued the traditions from an interest in history and comparative religions, a generation led by scholars such as Eichrodt and von Rad sought to place the new research within the framework of *Heilsgeschichte*. As popularized in America by G. E. Wright, all of Old Testament theology became a recital of the 'God who Acts'.

During the whole period of the hegemony of this theological approach, which had deep roots in post-war neo-orthodox theology, Scandinavian Old Testament research, particularly as represented by Engnell, Widengren and others, continued to pursue the history of religions with little interest in theological issues, at least not in the form proposed by von Rad. (This generalization does not apply to Mowinckel, who continued to act as a bridge to Germany.) An active interest in the history of religion continued in England and was represented by Oesterley and T. H. Robinson in the 30s and later by Hooke, A. Johnson, and J. B. Segal who mediated Scandinavian scholarship.

In America the rebirth of interest in comparative religion in relation to the Old Testament came from the side of Albright and took its most impressive form in the writings of Frank Cross. In his essays on 'The Divine Warrior' (*Canaanite Myth*, 79ff., 112ff.) Cross attempted a synthesis between the *Heilsgeschichte* school of von Rad and the history of religions approach of Engnell. Although he attempted to salvage a theological interest in establishing a symbiotic relationship between myth and history, his results reveal that Old Testament theology has been largely subsumed under an ideology of comparative religion. Once again Old Testament studies seem to have come full circle. The shift finds its clearest expression in the changing approaches to the book of Exodus.

2. The Canonical Shape of Exodus

The structure of the book

The structure of Exodus is very different from that of Genesis. There is no series of genealogical formulae to provide clearly marked divisions. Although there is an itinerary from the priestly source (12.37a; 13.20; 14.1f.; 15.22a; 17.1a; 19.2), it neither extends the whole length of the book nor provides an overarching framework. The itinerary is picked up again in Numbers.

We find the material of Exodus somewhat loosely arranged according to a historical sequence. After the introduction (1.1–17) establishes its connection with Genesis, the stories relate in order the birth of Moses, his return to Egypt, the deliverance, the journey to Sinai, the covenant at Sinai, and the establishment of the tabernacle. The chapters are very unevenly divided in terms of the detail by which the passage of chronological time is recorded. Exodus 12.41 fixes the period of the Egyptian captivity at 430 years, yet the bulk of chs. 1–12 relate to a very short period before the deliverance. Similarly, the last chapters from 19–40 cover a period of less than a year (19.1; 40.17). Even though a narrative sequence is retained within an established historical period, the interest of the writer falls on certain specific moments within the history. The frequent tensions within the narrative reveal a long history of development lying behind the final form in which diverse material has been formed into a loosely unified composition.

There is no obvious way to divide the book into its parts. Chapters 1–15 cover the exodus from Egypt, 15.22–18.27 the wilderness journey, and 19–40 the covenant at Sinai and its ordinances. Yet

such divisions are based on elements of general content and do not
rest on formal literary markers. It would seem that the general
structure of the book reveals little of conscious canonical shaping.
Rather, as we shall attempt to show, the canonical force left its
mark on the formation of the smaller units within the larger structure of the book, as, for example, in the form of the legal corpus
(19–24), the broken and restored covenant (32–34), and the
ordered and executed building of the tabernacle (25–31, 35–40).

The final shape in relation to prehistory

Several crucial issues have been posed by historical critical
research on the relationship of the complex history of composition
to the book's final form. Although the problems raised are to be
taken seriously, the crucial canonical issue at stake is whether or
not the process of the literature's development has been correctly
described.

The study of the oral traditions behind the present form of the
text has pointed out the various tensions which arose from the
complex history. For example, there is no organic unity between
the stories of Moses' birth (chs. 1–2) and his subsequent return to
Egypt (ch.5). The circumcision in 4.24ff. fits in poorly with the
commission (chs. 3–4). and the relation between the exodus from
Egypt after the plagues and the crossing of the sea appears artificial. One implication to be drawn is that the subsequent religious
use of the material by the community could tolerate a certain level
of literary friction within its scripture.

However, the problem of the prehistory became more complex
when von Rad, on the basis of a certain literary tension between the
exodus and Sinai traditions, posed the theory that the two complexes of material were treasured by separate groups and at different festivals within Israel until joined by the Yahwist in the tenth
century. If we put aside for the moment the criticisms which the
Yahwist's role in the theory has received from Noth, the basic
historical and theological issue at stake is whether the proposal
takes seriously the actual process by which tradition developed
within a community of faith. It seems a priori unlikely that traditions so basic to the faith of Israel as the exodus and Sinai could
have existed apart from one another in complete isolation for such a
long period. Von Rad's theory does not reckon seriously enough

with the fact that a traditioning process took place in the constant use by a community of faith. Far more likely is a theory which would explain the tensions between Exodus and Sinai in terms of peculiar liturgical usages which separated the material into schemata and thus left a mark on the subsequent confessional formulations. The canonical concern at this point should not be confused with an older conservative apologetic which measured the validity of tradition only in terms of its historicity. Rather, the issue at stake is the nature of the process by which Israel shaped and was shaped by those traditions whose divine authority was experienced, accepted, and confessed. In sum, the relationship in Exodus between the final form of the book and the oral tradition shows a continuity within a developing community of faith with which von Rad's theory fails to deal adequately.

An analogous issue of great importance in understanding the book of Exodus turns on how one envisions the relationship among the various literary strands. The problem can be best illustrated in terms of the priestly writings. The theory is usually held (Noth, Zimmerli, Koch) that P represents an independent source without any evidence of the Sinai covenant. According to this understanding, 19.1–2a connects directly to 24.15b–18 in P, thus showing no knowledge of the theophany and covenant of JE found in chs. 19–24. Zimmerli ('Sinaibund') pushes the literary analysis one step further by claiming an intentional omission of the Sinai material for theological reasons. Again, the issue at stake is not the presence of sources, but how one interprets their interrelationship and the process by which they were brought together to constitute the book of Exodus in its present form.

In my judgment, there is sufficient literary evidence to conclude that the priestly writer assumed the knowledge of the earlier traditions, and that the peculiar profile of the P material regarding the Sinai tradition arose from other reasons. First, the redactor's method in forming the unit 19–24 is significant. He apparently had a variety of different accounts of the Sinai tradition which he arranged within a continuous narrative framework. The parallel account in ch. 32 was put into a new context of covenant renewal. The Book of the Covenant (21–23) was related to ch. 20 by distinguishing between the people's fear and Moses' new role as covenant mediator. Finally, the covenant ceremony of ch. 24 was used to conclude the unit and to begin the tabernacle account in ch. 25. It seems likely that the restriction of the P material to 24.15–18 as an introduction to the tabernacle material stemmed in large part from the editor's technique and has little to say about P's knowledge of Sinai.

Secondly, the priestly portrayal of Moses' role in 24.15ff. and 34.29–35 indicates a knowledge of an ancient tradition of his office which had its original setting in the tent tradition (cf. Childs, *Exodus*, 347ff.) and presupposes a tradition of Sinai. Indeed, the whole point of the tabernacle tradition culminates in Moses' ancient office of mediator being replaced by the newly constituted priestly function of Aaron and his sons (40.12ff.; 40.34). Moreover, other portions of the priestly corpus, particularly the Holiness Code (Lev. 17–26; cf. especially ch. 19) presuppose the centrality of the Sinai covenant for P.

It is therefore, in my judgment, a misleading argument from silence to draw significant theological implications of priestly theology on the basis of an alleged profile from a reconstructed document. The basic error arises from failing to reckon with a continuing canonical process which was deeply involved in the shaping of the literature into a whole composition and which reflected the struggle of a religious community to come to terms with the diversity of its tradition. For this reason the whole of Exodus is far greater than the sum of its individual parts.

The relation of narrative to law

We have suggested that the principal effect of the canonical shaping of Exodus did not lie in an overarching structure of the book which served only loosely to connect the material in a chronological sequence. Rather, the arrangment of the independent parts better reflects the effect of canonical influence. The relation of the narrative to the legal portions of Exodus offers a good illustration. Critical study of Exodus has discovered that the history behind the narrative and legal traditions often developed along strikingly different lines. Moreover, the early historical development within the various collections of laws also show little uniformity, as a comparison of the Decalogue with the Book of the Covenant makes immediately clear. However, the canonical process which resulted in the present form of the book brought to bear on the material an obvious theological concern, which had not been fully developed in the prehistory, namely, the close interaction between narrative and law. It is theologically significant to observe that the events of Sinai are both preceded and followed by the stories of the people's resistance which is characteristic of the entire wilderness wanderings. The narrative material testifies to those moments in Israel's history in which God made himself known. For Israel to learn the will of God necessitated an act of self-revelation. Israel could not discover it for herself.

The placing of the decalogue in its present position supports the same theological point. The prologue (20.2) summarizes the previous narrative of the first eighteen chapters. The commandments are addressed to the people who have been rescued from slavery in Egypt. However, the decalogue also serves as an interpretative guide to all the succeeding legal material. From a traditio-critical perspective the position is secondary; from the theological perspective of the canonical shape it is pre-eminent. There is a comprehensiveness to the commandments which sets the decalogue apart from other series. Moreover, its simplicity derives from its not being addressed to a particular segment of the population during a specific period of history, but to every person within Israel.

Critical scholarship has done much to illuminate the original historical setting of the Book of the Covenant (21–23), yet its canonical position with Exodus has often been overlooked. The material is now placed within a narrative setting which legitimizes Moses' role as interpreter of the law (20.18ff.). The canon thus recognizes the different form of the divine law in the decalogue and the laws which follow, and it does not fuse the two. However, the canonical shaping has relativized the historical and literary differences by subsuming both under the rubric of revealed law from Sinai. Chapter 24 concludes the Sinai corpus by a return to narrative, thus providing the laws with an explicit commentary in the setting of a covenant-sealing ceremony. The commands are to be understood in closest relation to the God of the covenant who laid claim upon a people and pointed them to a new life as the people of God. When Wellhausen and Perlitt seek to relegate covenant to a late Deuteronomic stage in Israel's development, a literary judgment is made which runs in the face of the canonical estimate of its role. Moreover, it is highly suspect when the linguistic distinctions suggested by Kutsch for the term $b^e r\hat{\imath} t$ (covenant) can hardly be rendered into meaningful English (cf. Barr).

Worship and obedience

The complex prehistory of Ex. 32–34 has long been recognized and never fully resolved (cf. most recently Halbe). It is also clear that the individual chapters have been formed into an obvious theological framework of sin and forgiveness. To contrast a so-called 'ethical decalogue' (ch. 20) with a 'ritual decalogue' (ch. 34) completely misses the point. Rather, ch. 32 recounts the breaking of the covenant, ch. 34 relates to restoration. The chapters are held together by a series of motifs which are woven into a unifying pattern which includes judgment of disobedience, intercession for forgiveness, and prayer for the presence of God.

In its present position within the book of Exodus, this section performs an important canonical function in relation to the tabernacle traditions. The role of the tabernacle as portrayed in ch. 40 was to extend the Sinai experience by means of a permanent, cultic institution. Exodus 24.16f. describes the 'glory of Yahweh' settling on Mount Sinai with the appearance of a devouring fire on the top of the mountain. In 40.34 the same imagery is picked up and transferred from the mountain to the tabernacle. The presence of God which had once dwelt on Sinai now accompanies Israel in the tabernacle on her desert journey. Once the glory of God had filled the temple, 'Moses was not able to enter the tent of meeting' (40.35). His prophetic role had been absorbed into his new priestly function. Moses and Aaron together perform the priest's ritual ceremony before approaching the altar (40.31). Together they bless the people when they leave the tent (Lev. 9.23), but the ongoing institution by which God made known his will to Israel is through the perpetual priesthood of Aaron (40.15). The tent of meeting has become the centre of Israel's worship.

The canonical function of Ex. 32–34 is to place the institutions of Israel's worship within the theological framework of sin and forgiveness. Moses had not even descended from the mountain with the blueprint for worship (32.1ff.) before Israel turned to false worship. The covenant relationship stood under the shadow of human disobedience from the outset. The golden calf incident in ch. 32 is portrayed, not as an accidental misdeed, but as a representative reaction, constitutive to human resistance to divine imperatives. The worship inaugurated at Sinai did not reflect an ideal period of obedience on Israel's part, but the response of a people who were portrayed from the outset as the forgiven and restored community. If ever there were a danger of misunderstanding Sinai as a pact between partners, the positioning of Ex. 32–34 made clear that the foundation of covenant was, above all, divine mercy and forgiveness.

Original event and actualization

One of the most significant examples of canonical shaping in the book of Exodus involves the use of a literary technique which combined the account of an original event with the portrayal of the continuous celebration of that same event. The deliverance of Israel at the sea is first recounted in a prose narration in the third person (13.17ff.), but it is followed by a poetic account in the first person. The canonical effect of Ex. 15 in rehearsing the same event is to actualize the victory in the form of a liturgical celebration, concluding with the response, 'Yahweh will reign for ever and ever'. An event in past history has been extended into present time and freed for every successive generation to encouter.

Similarly, much of the tension in the story of the passover arises from the practice of juxtaposing the original event with its continuing celebration. 12.21ff., which is usually attributed to the J source, recounts the original events of the first passover in Egypt. But this description is preceded by an account in 12.1ff. which describes its cultic representation (12.11): 'throughout every generation, as an ordinance for ever' (v.17), and it is followed by the service for instructing the children in the meaning of the passover ceremony (v.16ff.). The canonical effect of this literary device is of profound theological significance. The original events are not robbed of their historical particularity; nevertheless, the means for their actualization for future Israel is offered in the shape of scripture itself.

3. Theological and Hermeneutical Implications

(a) The book of Exodus, no less than Genesis, has undergone a complex history of development. The final stage still reflects tensions and friction from this prehistory. Yet once again, the combined narrative is far more than the sum of its parts. Indeed, the decisive canonical witness is often found in the manner by which the parts have been combined. A literary analysis of sources is frequently of great help in hearing precisely the different witnesses within a passage. However, when the attempt is made to treat the sources as separate theological entities, an assumption of an isolation between sources is at work which runs counter to the canonical traditioning process and which disregards the way the material was used authoritatively within a community of faith and practice.

(b) For the theologian the book of Exodus provides a classic model by which to understand the proper relation between 'gospel and law'. The election of Israel was not conditional on obedience to the law (20.2), but derived solely from the mercy and kindness of God (19.4). Nevertheless, obedience to the will of God is constitutive of being the people of God and fulfils the purpose of election (19.5). Failure to respond in faith carries with it a special measure of divine judgment (34.6f.).

(c) The book of Exodus makes immediately evident that the canonical shaping of the material constituting Israel's scriptures has not sought to eliminate the miraculous elements by any form of reductionism. However, the canonical function of the miraculous within the story is also not an obvious one which can be deduced from a principle of supernaturalism. Rather, the subtle canonical shaping requires careful exegesis and strenuous reflection. At times the miraculous events play a role in convincing the Egyptians that God is opposing their action (14.24). Again, 'a great work' serves to engender Israel's faith in God (14.31) calling forth praise to God's incomparable power (15.11). The manna offers Israel a test by which to discern a gift of God. The plagues of Egypt serve, not to soften Pharaoh's heart, but rather to multiply signs in the world (Ex. 10.1f.),and thus reveal Yahweh's true nature (v.2). Finally, Moses' sister remains open to the mystery of God's plan for the child as it unfolds within a nexus of events (2.4ff.).

The book of Exodus makes much use of the miraculous as a varied and subtle medium for its witness as scripture. The force of the canon is to suggest that the witness is authoritative in a form not only once appropriate to Israel, but also shaped as a continuous vehicle of divine truth. However, it is within the context of the biblical canon that the material has its theological function which acts as a check against its misuse in the form of either rationalism on the left or of supernaturalism on the right.

(d) One of the effects of the historical critical study of Exodus is to demonstrate the difficulty of engaging in a 'quest for the historical Moses'. Yet it remains an unexplored challenge, whether or not one can speak meaningfully of a 'canonical Moses', by which one would mean a theological profile of Moses which would do justice to the canonical form of the literature which bore eloquent testimony to his place within the divine economy.

(e) Finally, there would be no better place in scripture on which to test the theological legitimacy of a 'theology of liberation' than the book of Exodus. Scripture reminds its hearers that the exodus from Egypt involved political activity in an historical arena for the sake of an oppressed people with the expectation of a new life. Yet Exodus also sets these events within the theological reality of human arrogance, divine judgment, and profound faith in the ultimate plan of God. The canonical shape of Exodus acts as a major deterrent against all forms of quietism, but offers no warrant for the politicizing of biblical redemption into a form of human self-fulfilment.

History of Exegesis

A. **Calmet**, *Dictionary of the Bible*, London 1732, III, 253ff.; **Carpzov** I, 97–99; *DThC* 5, 1761f.; *RGG*[3] 2, 831f.

H. **von Campenhausen**, 'Die Bilderfrage als theologisches Problem der alten Kirche', *Tradition und Leben* 1960, 216ff.; B. S. **Childs**, *Exodus*, OTL, 1974; J. **Daniélou**, *From Shadows to Reality*, ET London 1960; 'Exodus,' *Reallexikon für Antike und Christentum* 7, 22–43; R. **Le Déaut** and J. **Lécuyer**, 'Exode', *DS* 4.2, 1961, 1957–95; P. **Delhaye**, *Le Décalogue et sa place dans la morale chrétienne*, Bruxelles [2]1963; E. R. **Goodenough**, 'Philo's Exposition of the Law', *HTR* 27, 1923, 109ff.; R. M. **Grant**, 'The Decalogue in Early Christianity', *HTR* 40, 1947, 1–17; T. **Jansma**, 'Ephraim's Commentary on Exodus', *JSS* 17, 1972, 203–12; J. Z. **Lauterbach**, 'Introduction', *Mekilta de-Rabbi Ishmael*, Philadelphia and London 1933, xiii–lxiv; J. **Leclercq**, 'Moise', *DACL* XI, 2, 1648–89; N. **Leibowitz**, *Studies in the Book of Exodus*, 2 vols., New York 1975; E. B. **Levine**, 'Parallels to Exodus of Pseudo-Jonathan and Neophyti I', *Neophyti I*, ed. A. Díez Macho, II, Madrid 1970, 419–76; S. **Lowy**, *The Principle of Samaritan Bible Exegesis*, Studia Post-Biblica 28, Leiden 1977.

F. **Maschkowski**, 'Rashi's Einfluss auf Nikolaus von Lyra in der Auslegung des Exodus', *ZAW* 11, 1891, 268–316; G. F. **Moore**, 'Commentaries on the Laws', *Judaism* I, Cambridge, Mass. 1927, 135–49; E. **Norden**, 'Jahve und Moses in hellenistischer Theologie', *Festgabe für A. von*

Harnack, Tübingen 1921, 292–301; E. **Osswald**, *Das Bild des Mose*, Berlin 1962; E. **Preuschen**, 'Passah, altkirchliches und Passahstreitigkeiten', *RE*³ 14, 725ff.; B. **Reicke**, *Die Zehn Worte in Geschichte und Gegenwart*, BGBE 13, 1973; J. L. **Saalschütz**, *Das Mosaische Recht mit Berucksichtigung des spätern Jüdischen*, 2 vols. 1848, ²1853; R. **Smend**, *Das Mosebild von Heinrich Ewald bis Martin Noth*, BGBE 3, 1959; L. **Smolar** and M. **Aberbach**, 'The Golden Calf Episode in Postbiblical Literature', *HUCA* 39, 1968, 91–116; P. J. **Verdam**, *Mosaic Law in Practice and Study throughout the Ages*, Kampen 1959; G. **Vermes**, 'Circumcision and Exodus IV. 24–26. Prelude to the Theology of Baptism', *Scripture and Tradition*, Leiden ²1973, 178–92; N. **Walter**, *Der Thoraausleger Aristobulus*, TU 86, 1964.

VIII

LEVITICUS

Commentaries

C. F. Keil, BC, 1864
M. M. Kalisch, 1867–72
A. Dillmann, V. Ryssel, KeH ³1897
A. Bertholet, KHC, 1901
B. Baentsch, HKAT, 1903
D. Hoffmann, 1905–6
A. R. S. Kennedy, CeB, 1910
A. W. Streane, CB, 1914
H. Holzinger, HSAT, ⁴1922

P. Heinisch, HS, 1935
A. Clamer, SB, 1940
M. Noth, ET, OTL, 1965
K. Elliger, HAT, 1966
N. H. Snaith, NCeB, 1967
H. Cazelles, JB, ³1972
J. R. Porter, CNEB, 1976
G. J. Wenham, NICOT, 1979

Bibliography

A. **Alt**, 'The Origins of Israelite Law', *Essays* (see Pentateuch), 79–132; B. **Baentsch**, *Das Heiligkeitsgesetz. Lev. XVII-XXVI. Eine historisch-kritische Untersuchung*, Erfurt 1893; J. **Begrich**, 'Die priesterliche Tora', BZAW 66, 1936, 63–88; reprinted, *GSAT*, Munich 1964, 232–60; P. J. **Bidd**, 'Priestly Instruction in Pre-Exilic Israel', *VT* 23, 1973, 11–14; A. **van den Branden**, 'Lévitique 1–7 et le Tariff de Marseille, CIS i, 105', *Rivista degli Studi Orientali* 40, Rome 1965, 107–30; A. **Cholewiński**, *Heiligkeitsgesetz und Deuteronomium*, AnBib 60, 1976; R. E. **Clements**, *God and Temple*, Oxford and Philadelphia 1965; A. **Cody**, *A History of Old Testament Priesthood*, Rome 1969; F. M. **Cross**, 'The Priestly Houses of Early Israel', *Canaanite Myth and Hebrew Epic*, Cambridge, Mass. 1973, 195–215; K. **Elliger**, 'Das Gesetz Leviticus 18', *ZAW* 67, 1955, 1–25; 'Zur Analyse des Sündopfergesetzes', *Verbannung und Heimkehr. FS W. Rudolph*, Tübingen 1961, 39–50; L. E. **Elliott-Binns**, 'Some Problems of the Holiness Code', *ZAW* 76, 1955, 26–40; H. **Gese**, 'Die Sühne', *Zur biblischen Theologie*, Munich 1977, 85–106; R. **Gradwohl**, 'Das "fremde Feuer" von Nadab und Abihu', *ZAW* 75, 1963, 288–96; G. B. **Gray**, *Sacrifice in the Old Testament*, Oxford and New York 1925; P. **Grelot**, 'La dernière étape de la rédaction sacerdotale', *VT* 6, 1956, 174–89; J. M. **Grintz**, 'Do not Eat of the Blood', *ASTI* 8, 1972, 78–105; M. **Haran**, 'Studies in the Account of

LEVITICUS 181

the Levitical Cities', *JBL* 80, 1961, 45–54, 156–65; 'Holiness Code', *EJ* 8, 820–25; G. **Harford-Battersby**, 'Leviticus', *DB* 3, 102–9; E. W. **Hengstenberg**, 'The Sacrifice of Holy Scripture', *Ecclesiastes*, ET Edinburgh 1864, 367–409; J. **Hoftijzer**, 'Das sogenannte Feueropfer', *SVT* 16, 1967, 114–34.

H. **Jagersma**, *Leviticus 19. Identiteit-Bevrijding-Gemeenschap*, Studia Semitica Neerlandica 14, Assen 1972; R. **Kilian**, *Literarkritische und formgeschichtliche Untersuchung des Heiligkeitsgesetzes*, BBB 19, 1963; K. **Koch**, *Die Priesterschrift von Exodus 25 bis Leviticus 16*, FRLANT 71, 1959; L. **Koehler**, *Old Testament Theology*, ET London 1957, Philadelphia 1958; W. **Kornfeld**, *Studien zum Heiligkeitsgesetz*, Vienna 1952; B. A. **Levine**, 'Ugaritic Descriptive Rituals', *JCS* 17, 1963, 105–11; 'The Descriptive Tabernacle Texts of the Pentateuch', *JAOS* 85, 1965, 307–18; *In the Presence of the Lord*, Leiden 1974; B. J. **van der Merwe**, 'The Laying on of Hands in the Old Testament', *OuTWP* 5, 1962, 33–43; A. **Merx**, 'Kritische Untersuchung über die Opfergesetze Lev. I-VII', *ZWTh* 6, 1863, 41–84, 164–81; A. **Metzinger**, 'Die Substitutionstheorie und das alttestamentliche Opfer', *Bibl* 21, 1940, 159–87, 247–72, 353–77; J. **Milgrom**, 'The Biblical Diet Laws as an Ethical System', *Interp* 17, 1963, 288–301; *Studies in Levitical Terminology I*, Berkeley 1970; 'The Function of the Ḥaṭṭā't Sacrifice' (Hebrew), *Tarbiz* 40, Jerusalem 1970–71, 1–8; 'Sin Offering or Purification Offering', *VT* 21, 1971, 237–39; 'The Alleged Wave Offering in Israel and in the Ancient Near East', *IEJ* 22, 1972, 33–38; *Cult and Conscience*, Leiden 1976; 'Leviticus', *IDB Suppl*, 541–5; G. F. **Moore**, 'Leviticus', *Encyclopaedia Biblica*, ed. T. K. Cheyne and J. S. Black, vol. 3, London and New York 1902, 2776–93; J. **Morgenstern**, 'The Decalogue of the Holiness Code', *HUCA* 26, 1955, 1–27.

J. **Neusner**, *The Idea of Purity in Ancient Judaism*, Leiden 1973; M. **Noth**, *The Laws in the Pentateuch and Other Studies*, ET Edinburgh and New York 1966; W. **Paschen**, *Rein und Unrein. Untersuchung zur biblischen Wortgeschichte*, Munich 1970; G. **von Rad**, 'Form-Criticism of the Holiness Code', *Studies in Deuteronomy*, SBT I.9, 1953, 25–36; A. F. **Rainy**, 'The Order of Sacrifices in Old Testament Rituals', *Bibl* 51, 1970, 485–98; R. **Rendtorff**, *Die Gesetze in der Priesterschrift*, Göttingen [2]1963; *Studien zur Geschichte des Opfers im Alten Testament*, WMANT 24, 1967; H. **von Reventlow**, *Das Heiligkeitsgesetz formgeschichtlich untersucht*, WMANT 6, 1961; R. **Schmid**, *Das Bundesopfer in Israel. Wesen, Ursprung und Bedeutung der alttestamentlichen Schelamim*, Munich 1964; N. H. **Snaith**, 'Sacrifices in the Old Testament', *VT* 7, 1957, 308–17; 'The Sin-Offering and the Guilt-Offering', *VT* 15, 1965, 73–80; W. B. **Stevenson**, 'Hebrew 'Olah and Zebah Sacrifices', *FS A. Bertholet*, Tübingen 1950, 488–98; R. **de Vaux**, *Le Sacrifice dans l'Ancien Testament*, Paris 1964; 'Le Sacerdoce en Israël', *Populus Dei* I. *Israel. Studi in onore del Card. A. Ottaviani*, Rome 1969, 113–68; J. G. **Vink**, 'The Date and Origin of the Priestly Code in the Old Testament', *OTS* 15, 1969, 1–144; V. **Wagner**, 'Zur Existenz des sogenannten Heiligkeitsgesetzes', *ZAW* 86, 1974, 307–16; J. **Wilkinson**, 'Leprosy and Leviticus: The Problem of Description and Identification', *SJT* 30, 1977, 153–69; P. **Wurster**, 'Zur Charakteristik und Geschichte des Priesterkodex und der Heiligkeitsgesetzes', *ZAW* 4, 1884, 112–33.

1. Historical Critical Problems

There is a wide agreement regarding the structure of the book of Leviticus. Chapters 1–7 deal with the sacrificial system, 8–10 the inaugural service, 11–16 laws of impurities, and 17–26 laws of holiness. Chapter 27 is an appendix on various gifts to the sanctuary. Among a few scholars there remains some resistance to accepting Klostermann's theory of a 'Holiness Code' (17–26). For example, Hoffmann and Milgrom prefer to join ch. 17 to the preceeding section, but the disagreement is relatively minor.

Upon first glance the literary problems of the book seem fairly straightforward. The entire book has long been assigned to the priestly writings. Even though chs. 17–26 were thought to stem from an independent source, the same priestly hand which was responsible for the book as a whole has thoroughly accommodated the section within a unified perspective. However, literary critical research in the later part of the nineteenth century continued to discover tensions within the composition, and soon resorted to more complex subdivisions within the P code. The detailed analyses of Harford–Battersby and of Holzinger accurately reflect a common literary approach about the turn of the century. Other scholars such as Baentsch reached similar conclusions regarding the multi-layered quality of the Holiness Code, particularly in relation to Ezekiel, but the issue proved insoluble when viewed from the perspective of a unilinear growth of literary sources.

Once again, the form-critical approach appeared to offer a new avenue into the material which could break out of the impasse. Indeed, it became immediately apparent that the question of the original form and function of the priestly material was independent of its post-exilic codification within the P source. The early form-critical study of Begrich sought to recover the original function of instruction as 'preached law' within the priestly office. Likewise, von Rad tried to relate the form of the Holiness Code to the paraenetic role of the Levites. Rendtorff and Koch focused their atten-

tion on reconstructing the form of ancient rituals which lay behind
the laws of sacrifice. One of the most successful attempts to trace
the growth of tradition through several distinct stages was Elliger's
brilliant analysis of Lev. 18. However, that the form-critical
method also had its limitations was inadvertently demonstrated by
Reventlow. He argued that the Holiness Code had its original setting within an ancient Israelite covenant festival and that the different levels in the literature could be derived from a developing
paraenetic activity. In spite of some acute observations by the
author, a reaction against the extremes of tradition history began to
set in. Significantly, the last full-scale commentary on Leviticus by
Elliger returned to a predominantly literary critical analysis.

There is, however, another important dimension to the critical
study of the book of Leviticus which runs parallel to its literary and
form-critical study and was only indirectly affected. In the
English-speaking world in particular, the early research of W.
Robertson Smith and James Frazer drew much attention to questions of the background in comparative religion of Israel's priestly
institutions, and the origins of cult. Naturally investigation of the
Hebrew terminology always played an important role in the debate
over general theories of the meaning of sacrifice. G. B. Gray's book
was highly significant in subordinating the theoretical discussion of
origins to a comprehensive philological approach which attempted
to recover the meaning by appeal to usage rather than etymology.

Within recent years some of the most significant work has been
pursued by means of detailed analysis of sacrificial terminology.
Although much new insight has been achieved through the use of
comparative ancient Near Eastern studies, the newer attempts,
particularly of Milgrom, Levine, and Rainy, are characterized by a
sophisticated methodology which seeks to penetrate into the
priestly system without assuming an immediate identity between
ancient cultures. Neusner's book on the post-biblical use of ideas of
purity is also full of insight. Many of the larger questions once
posed so forcefully by W. R. Smith have not again been addressed,
but the more modest, limited concern with specific terminology will
certainly provide a solid foundation for dealing with the broader
issues.

Finally, a word is in order regarding the theological assessments
of the book of Leviticus which have continued to play an unusually
large role in the treatment of the material. On the one hand, from

the perspective of orthodox Judaism, David Hoffmann's learned commentary represents the last attempt to define the commentator's task explicitly as one of harmonizing the biblical text with later Jewish halachic tradition. As a result, Hoffmann's apologetics have virtually replaced exposition of the biblical text. On the other hand, the material of Leviticus has frequently been disparaged by modern Christian scholars. L. Koehler reflected a strong negative bias when he discussed Israel's cult under the rubric of 'self-salvation'. Then again, Noth's description of the late post-exilic understanding of law as an absolute entity devoid of its prior connection to covenant and community seemed largely to rest on a prior theological assumption. Finally, Eichrodt's tendency in his *Theology* to contrast negatively 'external action' within the cult with personal and spontaneous feelings of piety which constituted Israel's true religion, could hardly do justice to the book of Leviticus. It remains therefore to be seen whether or not Leviticus will receive a fresh theological handling which can avoid these old pitfalls.

2. The Canonical Shape of Leviticus

The first lead in assessing the canonical shape of Leviticus is offered by the structure of the book. Both the introduction (1.1) and conclusion (27.34) indicate that a continuity with the historical setting of the final section of Exodus is intended. The laws which comprise Leviticus were given to Moses by God at Sinai. This connection is made explicit in Lev. 8–9, which forms the literary continuation of Ex. 29, the inauguration of Aaron and his sons. Moreover, chs. 8–9 show the same redactional features as Ex. 35–40. The ceremony unfolds according to the exact execution of the will of God, 'as Yahweh commanded Moses' (8.9, 13, 17, 21, 29, etc.).

This same intention to bind the laws of Leviticus to Sinai is again made explicit in the concluding subscription to the laws of sacrifice (7.37f.). It has been generally recognized that chs. 1–7 form a secondary literary level within the book, and interrupt the original narrative sequence which joined ch. 8 directly to the erection of the tabernacle. Nevertheless, the editors of Leviticus have restructured the material in order to show that the sacrificial system which commenced with the inauguration of Aaron in chs. 8–9 stemmed from a divine revelation at Sinai through Moses (7.38). The sacrifices which Aaron initiated did not derive from custom, but from direct compliance with divine will. What Aaron instituted had already been established as a 'perpetual due' from the people of Israel throughout every succeeding generation (v. 36). Aaron's inauguration became an instance of obedient response of proper worship; Nadab and Abihu illustrated judgment on unholy disobedience (ch.10).

The laws of impurities which follow in chs.11–16 as well as the laws of holiness in 17–26 assume the establishment of a covenant between God and Israel at Sinai. God had separated Israel to himself as a holy people and sanctified them (21.23). Israel was to reflect the nature of God's holiness by separating from all that was unholy. The laws, therefore, spell out in detail the distinction between the holy and the common, the unclean and the clean (10.10). Israel does not achieve a state of holiness by performing duties. Holiness is not a process to be won. Rather, God has separated Israel to himself, and rendered his people holy in the deliverance from Egypt (22.31). However, holiness can be forfeited by contamination with the profane. By keeping the divine commandments Israel responds obediently to her status as an elect, holy nation. The imperative, 'Be holy as I am holy' (19.2) challenges Israel to realize the status and perform the role to which she has been called. The laws of Leviticus are grounded in the being of God who is the sole measure of holiness. The statutes for distinguishing holiness from unholiness are external, and so is the means of atonement which cleanses Israel's sin, thus restoring her before the presence of God (16.29ff.).

The status of a holy people, separated unto God, does not only control Israel's relation with the deity, but extends into the realm of human relations. Chs. 17–26 grounded Israel's ethical response in exactly the same manner as chs. 11–16 had done for the cult, namely in the nature of God's being as holiness (ch.19). The continual refrain: 'I am Yahweh, your God' (19.4ff.) links the revelation of the divine will to the covenant at Sinai, which was made fully known in the disclosure of the divine name (Ex. 6.2ff.).

The canonical effect of structuring the book in such a way as to connect all the material of Leviticus directly to the revelation at Sinai is of crucial importance in understanding how the book was shaped in its role as authoritative scripture for Israel. All the laws of Leviticus which stemmed originally from very different periods, and which reflected strikingly different sociological contexts, were subordinated to the one overarching theological construct, namely, the divine will made known to Moses at Sinai for every subsequent generation. This hermeneutical move is not to be characterized as simply a dehistoricizing of the material. It is strikingly different from the canonical process affecting 'Second Isaiah', for example. Rather, in the book of Leviticus one historical moment in Israel's life has become the norm by means of which all subsequent history of the nation is measured. If a law functions authoritatively for Israel, it must be from Sinai, and if it is from Sinai, it must be authoritative. Clearly a theological understanding of Sinai is at work in the canonical process which is of a different order from a modern reconstruction of the historical origins of Israel's cult.

There is a second important canonical effect from subordinating the material of Leviticus to a theological construct. The many and various historical rationales which once lay behind the original laws have also been drained of theological significance. Israel's laws of impurities are given for the purpose of distinguishing between clean and unclean and, like the laws of sacrifice, stem directly from the will of God. That is to say, no other reason lying behind a particular law is admitted. Laws were not given as a didactic technique, nor for reasons of Israel's health, nor to illustrate an ethical principle. Although, historically, such motivation may well have played a role, the canonical ordering of Leviticus has systematically ignored such influences and derived everything from the one divine will which called for the sole response of obedience.

Finally, the material of Leviticus has been structured in such a way that the laws are to serve as perpetual statutes. There is no hint that any are to be considered temporary, nor is their validity conditional upon subsequent historical circumstances. Again, there is no indication in the canonical shape that the legislation of Leviticus was understood as an idealization of a particular period or as a representative response of an obedient people. In sum, any periodization of Leviticus – whether in terms of *Heilsgeschichte* or legal dispensations – finds no warrant within the book itself.

3. Theological and Hermeneutical Implications

(a) A witness is given that the institutions and rites which determine how Israel is properly to worship God derived from divine revelation. Israel's cult is not her own invention. There is no tension between the spirit and the form of the covenant. Rather in the service of the tabernacle the sons of the covenant realize their new life of freedom to 'walk erect'. The canonical shape provides a critical theological judgment against any reading of the tradition which isolates the priestly elements of the tradition from the so-called prophetic, or plays the one against the other. When the priestly material of Leviticus is interpreted only in relation to an alleged post-exilic historical background, a major theological testimony of the book is threatened.

(b) The book of Leviticus offers a major example of the Old Testament's understanding of law. Israel's law presupposed the covenant of Sinai and the election of a holy people. The imperative of obedience to the law is grounded in the eternal will of God who promises to dwell in the midst of his people. Israel has been made holy by God's act of choosing a people and a response is demanded from Israel commensurate to the nature of God's holiness. Obedience to the law does not make Israel holy – only God can sanctify – but her disobedience can surely jeopardize the relation between God and people. To interpret the laws of Leviticus as a form of self-salvation which arose in contrast to the prophetic emphasis on divine grace is to misunderstand the canonical function of the book. In terms of Christian theology, the book of Leviticus contains both gospel and law.

(c) There is no sign within the shape of the book of Leviticus which would indicate any canonical intentionality to interpret the material in a way which would abstract, symbolize, or rationalize Israel's cult. Yet significantly neither Judaism nor Christianity have continued to observe the cult in its Old Testament form in spite of both religious communities' claim to accept the book of Leviticus as authoritative scripture. The grounds for a reinterpretation of the cultic prescriptions of Leviticus are unique to each of the two faiths. For Judaism the destruction of the temple which brought to an end the worship of the second temple was understood as a punishment of God. The cultic imperatives of sacrifice have been fulfilled in the study of Torah (cf. Lev. Rabbah vii), but the hope of the restoration of the original cult continues to constitute the future hope of Judaism (cf. Ber. 29b; Shab. 24a; Musaf to New Year's Service, Ex. Rabbah xxxi, etc.). For Christianity the cult has been reinterpreted christologically – particularly in the book of Hebrews – and placed within the category of the old foreshadowing the new.

What is of particular interest is that both Judaism and Christianity have used warrants from the larger canon, of course in conjunction with the new tradition either of the synagogue fathers or the gospel, by which to justify a non-literal interpretation of the laws. But in both cases the grounds for theological reinterpretation have not rested on the canonical shape of the book of Leviticus itself. Moreover, neither Judaism nor Christianity has appropriated the material according to the two most obvious options. Both rejected the move which would bind the authority of Leviticus to the literal observance of its laws, as demanded, for example, by various Jewish and Christian sects over the centuries. Both also rejected a consistently symbolic interpretation which would cut itself free from Israel's historic existence, according to the model of Philo. In sum, both communities appealed to a larger canonical interpretation by which to justify a unique appropriation of the sacred tradition.

The issue between the two faiths on their differing use of Leviticus remains a theological one which, however, relates closely to the question of canon. In spite of having only a portion of the biblical canon in common, it remains an important task for Jews and Christians to explore the divergent understanding of Leviticus in relation to the rest of the Hebrew Bible, as well as to the additional bodies of later tradition treasured by the two religious communities as authoritative.

History of Exegesis

Carpzov I, 116–19; *DThC* 9, 498; *EB* 2, 887f.; *RGG*[3] 4, 340.

J. **Daniélou**, 'La Fête des Tabernacles dans l'exégèse patristique', *Studia Patristica* I, TU 63, 1957, 262–79; C. F. **Keil**, *Manual of Biblical Archaeology* I, ET Edinburgh 1887, 16ff., 249f.; H. **Hirschfeld**, 'Sa'adyāh's Commentary on Leviticus', *JQR* 19, 1907, 136–61; D. **Hoffmann**, *Das Buch Leviticus*

I, Berlin 1905, 17f.; E. B. **Levine**, 'Parallels to Leviticus of Pseudo-Jonathan and Neophyti I', *Neophyti I*, ed. A. Díez Macho, III, Madrid 1971, 481–515; G. E. **Moore**, 'Commentaries on the Laws', *Judaism* I, Cambridge, Mass. 1927, 135–49; J. **Neusner**, 'The Jewish-Christian Argument in Fourth-Century Iran: Aphrahat on Circumcision, the Sabbath, and the Dietary Laws', *Journal of Ecumenical Studies* 7, Philadelphia 1970, 282–98; V. **Nikiprowetzky**, 'La Spiritualisation des sacrifices et le culte sacrificiel au temple de Jérusalem chez Philo d'Alexandrie', *Sémitica* 17, Paris 1967, 97–116; B. **Smalley**, 'Ralph of Flaix on Leviticus', *Recherches de théologie ancienne et médiévale* 35, Louvain 1968, 35–82; 'An Early Twelfth-century Commentator on the Literal Sense of Leviticus', ibid. 36, 1969, 78–99; H. **Wenschkewitz**, 'Die Spiritualisierung der Kultusbegriffe Tempel, Priester und Opfer im Neuen Testament', *Angelos* 4, Leipzig 1932, 70–230.

IX

NUMBERS

Commentaries

C. F. Keil, BC, 1865
A. Dillmann, KeH, ²1886
B. Baentsch, HKAT, 1903
H. Holzinger, KHC, 1903
G. B. Gray, ICC, 1905
H. Gressmann, *SAT*, ²1922
L. E. Elliott Binns, WC, 1927

P. Heinisch, HS, 1936
A. Clamer, SB, 1940
A. Drubbel, BOuT, 1963
N. H. Snaith, NCeB, 1967
M. Noth, ET, OTL, 1968
J. de Vaulx, SoBi, 1972
J. Sturdy, CNEB, 1976

Bibliography

W. F. **Albright**, 'The Oracles of Balaam', *JBL* 63, 1944, 207–33; 'The List of Levitic Cities', *Louis Ginzberg Jubilee Volume I*, New York 1945, 49–73; M. **Barnouin**, 'Remarques sur les tableaux numériques des Nombres', *RB* 76, 1969, 351–64; C. **Barth**, 'Zur Bedeutung der Wüstentradition', *SVT* 15, 1966, 14–23; A. **Bergman**, 'The Israelite Tribe of Half-Manasseh', *JPOS* 16, 1936, 224–54; J. A. **Bewer**, 'The Ordeal in Num., Chap. 5', *AJSL* 30, 1913, 36–47; U. **Cassuto**, 'The Sequence and Arrangement of the Biblical Sections' (1947), in *Biblical and Oriental Studies* 1, Jerusalem 1973, 1–6; G. W. **Coats**, *Rebellion in the Wilderness*, Nashville 1968; A. **Cody**, *A History of Old Testament Priesthood*, Rome 1969; F. M. **Cross**, 'The Priestly Houses of Early Israel', *Canaanite Myth and Hebrew Epic*, Cambridge, Mass. 1973, 195–215; S. **De Vries**, 'The Origin of the Murmuring Tradition', *JBL* 87, 1968, 51–8; B. D. **Eerdmans**, 'The Composition of Numbers', *OTS* 6, 1949, 101–216; O. **Eissfeldt**, 'Die Komposition der Bileam-Erzählung', *ZAW* 57, 1939, 212–41=*KS* II, Tübingen 1963, 199–226; 'Sinai-Erzählung und Bileamsprüche', *HUCA* 32, 1961, 179–190; 'Die Eroberung Palästinas durch Altisrael', *WO* 2, 1955, 158–71=*KS* III, 1966, 367–83; K. **Elliger**, 'Sinn und Ursprung der priesterlichen Geschichtserzählung', *ZTK* 49, 1952, 121–43=*KSAT*, Munich 1966, 174–98;

M. **Fishbane**, 'Numbers 5:11–31, A Study of Law and Scribal Practice in Israel and the Ancient Near East', *HUCA* 45, 1974, 25–45; V. **Fritz**, *Israel in der Wüste*, Marburg 1970. M. **Greenberg**, 'Levitical Cities', *EJ* 11, 136f.; H. **Gressmann**, *Mose und seine Zeit*, FRLANT 18, 1913; W. **Gross**, *Bileam. Literar- und formkritische Untersuchung der Prosa in Num 22–24*, StANT 38, 1974; A. H. J. **Gunneweg**, *Leviten und Priester*, FRLANT 89, 1965; M. **Haran**, 'The Uses of Incense in the Ancient Israelite Ritual', *VT* 10, 1960, 113–29; 'Studies in the Account of the Levitical Cities', *JBL* 80, 1961, 45–54; 'The Priestly Image of the Tabernacle', *HUCA* 36, 1965, 191–226; O. **Henke**, 'Zur Lage von Beth Peor', *ZDPV* 75, 1959, 155–63; J. **Hoftijzer**, 'The Prophet Balaam in a 6th Century Aramaic Inscription', *BA* 39, 1976, 11–17; G. **Hort**, 'The Death of Qorah', *Australian Biblical Review* 7, Melbourne 1959, 2–26; K. R. **Joines**, 'The Bronze Serpent in the Israelite Cult', *JBL* 87, 1968, 245–56; D. **Kellermann**, *Die Priesterschrift von Numeri 1,1 bis 10,10 literarkritisch und traditionsgeschichtlich untersucht*, BZAW 120, 1970; H.-J. **Kraus**, *Worship in Israel*, ET Oxford and Richmond, Va. 1966; A. **Kuenen**, 'Manna und Wachteln', *Gesammelte Abhandlungen zur biblischen Wissenschaft*, Freiburg 1894, 276ff.; J.-R. **Kupper**, 'Le recensement dans les textes de Mari', *Studia Mariana*, ed. A. Parrot, Leiden 1950, 99–110; A. **Kuschke**, 'Die Lagervorstellung der priesterschriftlichen Erzählung', *ZAW* 63, 1951, 74–105; S. **Lehming**, 'Massa und Meriba', *ZAW* 73, 1961, 71–77; 'Versuch zu Num. 16', *ZAW* 74, 1962, 291–321; B. A. **Levine**, 'Numbers, Book of', *IDB Suppl*, 631–5; J. **Liver**, 'Korah, Dathan and Abiram', *Scripta Hierosolymitana* 8, Jerusalem 1961, 189–217; 'The Ransom of the Half-Shekel', *HTR* 56, 1963, 182–98.

R. S. **Mackensen**, 'The Present Literary Form of the Balaam Story', *D. B. MacDonald Presentation Volume*, Princeton and London, 1933, 279–92; B. **Mazar**, 'The Cities of the Priests and Levites', *SVT* 7, 1960, 193–205; 'The Sanctuary of Arad and the Family of Hobab the Kenite', *JNES* 24, 1965, 297–303; G. **Mendenhall**, 'The Census Lists of Numbers 1 and 26,' *JBL* 77, 1958, 52–66; J. **Milgrom**, *Studies in Levitical Terminology* I, Berkeley 1970; S. **Mittmann**, 'Num 20, 14–21. Eine redaktionelle Kompilation', in *Wort und Geschichte. FS K. Elliger*, Neukirchen-Vluyn 1973, 143–9; K. **Möhlenbrink**, 'Die levitischen Überlieferungen des Alten Testaments', *ZAW* 52, 1934, 184–231; S. **Mowinckel**, 'Der Ursprung der Bil'āmsage', *ZAW* 48, 1930, 233–71; E. **Nielsen**, 'The Levites in Ancient Israel', *ASTI* 3, 1964, 17–20; M. **Noth**, *Das System der zwölf Stämme Israels*, BWANT IV 1 (=52), 1930; 'Der Wallfahrtsweg zum Sinai (4.Mose 33)', *PJB* 36, 1940, 5–28, reprinted in *Aufsätze zur biblischen Landes- und Altertumskunde*, ed. H. W. Wolff, I, Neukirchen-Vluyn 1971, 55–74; 'Num 21 als Glied der "Hexateuch"-Erzählung', *ZAW* 58, 1940–41, 161–89; reprinted in *Aufsätze* I, 75–101; 'Beiträge zur Geschichte des Ostjordanlandes', I-IV (1941–1959), reprinted in *Aufsätze* I, 345–543; *Überlieferungsgeschichtliche Studien* I, Halle 1943, 190–206; *History of Pentateuchal Traditions*, ET Englewood Cliffs

N.J. 1972; M. **Ottosson**, *Gilead, Tradition and History*, Coniectanea Biblica OT, 3, Lund 1969. L. **Pákozdy**, 'Theologische Redaktionsarbeit in der Bileam-Perikope', *Von Ugarit nach Qumran, FS O. Eissfeldt*, BZAW 77, 1958, 161–76; R. **Press**, 'Das Ordal im Alten Israel', *ZAW* 51, 1933, 121–40, 227–55; G. **von Rad**, *Die Priesterschrift im Hexateuch*, BWANT IV.13 (=65), 1934; G. **Richter**, 'Die Einheitlichkeit der Geschichte von der Rotte Korah (Num 16)', *ZAW* 39, 1921, 128–37; W. **Rudolph**, *Der 'Elohist' von Exodus bis Joshua*, BZAW 68, 1938; K. **Seybold**, 'Das Herrscherbild des Bileamsorakels Num 24, 15–19', *TZ* 29, 1973, 1–19; J. **Simon**, 'Two Connected Problems Relating to the Israelite Settlement in Transjordan', *PEQ* 79, 1949, 27–39, 87–101; *The Geographical and Topographical Texts of the Old Testament*, Leiden 1959, 233–66; E. A. **Speiser**, 'Census and Ritual Expiation in Mari and Israel', *BASOR* 149, 1958, 17–25; 'Background and Function of the Biblical *Nāśî'*, *CBQ* 25, 1963, 111–17; J. J. **Stamm**, *Erlösen und Vergeben im Alten Testament. Eine begriffsgeschichtliche Untersuchung*, Bern 1940; S. **Talmon**, 'Divergencies in Calendar-reckoning in Ephraim and Judah', *VT* 8, 1958, 48–74; J. **Van Seters**, 'The Conquest of Sihon's Kingdom: A Literary Examination', *JBL* 91, 182–97; R. **de Vaux**, *Ancient Israel: Its Life and Institutions*, ET London and New York 1961, 361–6; D. **Vetter**, *Seherspruch und Segensschilderung*, Stuttgart 1975; S. **Wagner**, 'Die Kundschaftergeschichten im Alten Testament', *ZAW* 76, 1964, 255–69; K. H. **Walkenhorst**, *Der Sinai im liturgischen Verständnis der deuteronomistischen und priesterlichen Tradition*, BBB 33, 1969; M. **Weippert**, *The Settlement of the Israelite Tribes in Palestine*, ET, SBT II.21, 1971; J. **Wellhausen**, *Prolegomena to the History of Israel*, ET Edinburgh 1885, 151–61; F. V. **Winnett**, *The Mosaic Tradition*, Toronto 1949; M. **Wüst**, *Untersuchungen zu den siedlungsgeographischen Texten des Alten Testaments*, I, *Ostjordanland*, Beihefte zum Tübinger Atlas der Vordern Orients, Wiesbaden 1975; A. H. **van Zyl**, *The Moabites*, Leiden 1960.

1. Historical Critical Problems

The book of Numbers has generally been regarded as the least unified composition within the Pentateuch. Noth found it difficult to discern any pattern in its construction (*Numbers*, 1). G. B. Gray described it as having been 'mechanically cut out of a whole' without any unity of subject matter (xxiv). Indeed, the book is characterized by very different kinds of material which stem from various historical periods.

Following the critical analyses of Kuenen and Wellhausen in the latter part of the nineteenth century, there was a widespread consensus that the book of Numbers had made use of material from an earlier (JE) and a later stratum (P), and that the same familiar literary strands which had been found in Genesis and Exodus were represented. There was a general agreement among such literary critics as Baentsch, Holzinger, and Gray in separating the priestly source from the earlier level. However, some disagreement continued in the details of dividing J and E, and in determining the different levels within P.

Within more recent years there has been considerable interest in reconstructing and dating the several poetic sections of Numbers (10.35; 21.14–15, 17–18, 27–30). Albright's essay on the Balaam oracles in particular opened up a brilliant new approach to the text, which his students have continued to pursue. Then again, Rudolph's attempt to dispense with the E source was also extended to Numbers, as was also von Rad's analysis of P. But clearly, the most influential new source-critical analysis of Numbers was carried on by Noth, both in a series of articles and in his two volumes on the history of Israelite traditions. The major thrust of Noth's argument was that the older source-critical model was misleading in its interpretation of the latter chapters of Numbers. He proposed a type of fragmentary hypothesis in order to demonstrate that the P source ended for Numbers with 27.12–23 which section connected directly to Deut. 34.1,7–9. He assigned the chapters which contained a conquest tradition (e.g. 21; 31; 32; 34.1–12) to a compositional level different from P. The issues raised by Noth are significant and are closely related to his understanding of a Deuteronomistic history.

H. Gressmann's highly influential book on Moses (1913) was the first attempt systematically to apply Gunkel's new insights to the stories of Numbers. In spite of the speculative nature of many of his reconstructions, Gressmann was successful in opening up the complex dimensions of the oral tradition which lay behind the sources. Consequently in the more recent period, form-critical research has tended to focus on individual traditions rather than to treat the book of Numbers as a whole. For example, significant work has been done on the twelve-tribe system (Noth), the ordering of the camp (Kuschke), the Levitical traditions (Möhlenbrink, Gunneweg), the murmuring traditions (Coats, Fritz), the Balaam cycle (Mowinckel, Gross), and the allotment of the land (Alt, Noth). The most ambitious attempt to offer a traditio-historical analysis of a large portion of Numbers is that of Kellermann. In spite of many good observations regarding the relative age of the material, the extreme complexity of the redactional analysis has blunted its impact.

Problems of history and comparative religion were also closely related in the study of Numbers. Of particular interest were the early conquest traditions which spoke of an attack on the Negeb, and the seizure of Transjordan (cf. Weippert). Debate on the history of the Levitical cities has also been intense (Albright, de Vaux, Mazar, Haran). Again, the book of Numbers has been studied critically for its references to the development of Israelite priesthood. Especially do the redactional levels of such stories as Korah, Dathan and Abiram (chs. 16–17) appear to reflect a complex history of the struggle within the priesthood which has been all but obliterated. Mazar has attempted to bring to bear archaeological evidence from Arad on the problem of the early priestly clans. Finally, Cross has offered a new synthesis which he sees as an alternative to Wellhausen's classic formulation.

One of the more significant attempts to interpret the high numbers reported in the two chapters of Numbers on the census has been offered by G. Mendenhall. He has argued that the term *'elef* did not originally designate the term 'thousand', but rather a contingent of troops under its own leader. The census lists contained old tradition from the period of the amphictyony, and its numbers were commensurate with other ancient Near Eastern records of the same period. Later the military system broke down with the rise of the monarchy and the original significance of the census was misunderstood.

With regard to the theology of the book of Numbers, credit is due to J. de Vaulx, who among all the recent commentators, stands virtually alone in attempting to develop a theology of the book in relation to the history of exegesis. Even though de Vaulx is not always successful in bridging the gap from traditional to critical interpretation, his reflections are always of theological interest.

2. The Canonical Shape of Numbers

The canonical problem of the book of Numbers is succinctly posed by Noth when he writes: 'We can scarcely speak of a special significance peculiar to the book of Numbers. It has its significance

within the framework and context of the greater Pentateuch whole'
(*Numbers*, 11). Equally challenging is Gray's suggestion (xxiv) that
a coherent reading of the material would be greatly improved by
assigning the first ten chapters of Numbers to the book of Exodus.
Is this really the case or is there also a canonical perspective on
Numbers which has not been fully grasped?

At the outset, we are immediately faced with the problem of
determining the structure of the book. There are certain chronological indicators given (1.1; 7.1; 10.11; 33.38) but it is highly unlikely
that these notices form a structure for the book. The year is missing
in 20.1 and 7.1 disrupts the temporal sequence of the narrative. The
remarkable disregard for recording the events during the period of
the forty years' wanderings would also belie the claim for a serious
chronological interest on the part of the biblical editors.

A more likely suggestion for structuring the book is provided by
the geographical features which are carefully registered when Israel
journeyed from Sinai to the plains of Moab. Gray thus divides the
book into three geographical sections: 1.1–10.10, the wilderness of
Sinai; 10.11–21.9, north of Sinai, west of the 'Arabah; 21.10–36.13,
east of the 'Arabah (Jordan valley). However, the problem of
determining the structure from the geographical indicators appears
most clearly in the division of 21.9. From a literary perspective a
major division at this point is far from obvious. Moreover, Noth
ends his second section at 20.13 before the beginning of the conquest traditions, and de Vaulx sets the break at 22.1 when Israel
encamped on the plains of Moab beyond the Jordan at Jericho.
This disagreement confirms the impression that there are no clear
indications within the text of how the editors wished to divide the
material at this juncture. For this reason, although geographical
features are significant, their importance in establishing a structure
should not be exaggerated. The biblical editors seem less concerned
with this literary problem than are modern commentators.

Chapters 1.1–10.10

Perhaps the best place to start a closer analysis of the book is at
the beginning. The first ten chapters up to the departure from Sinai
in 10.11 continue the same setting of the people at Sinai which
extended from Ex.19 through the entire book of Leviticus. The
heart of this section lies in chs. 1–4 which describe the census, the
organization of the camp, and the duties of the Levites in the ser-

vice of the tabernacle. Chapters 5–6 present various laws and regulations, and 7–10 offer additional cultic regulations, several of which are additions to previously discussed rites (8.1–4; 9.1ff.).

The literary form of these chapters is significant. Directives are given to Moses by God in the form of direct address (1.1; 2.1,etc.). Along with these prescriptions there are also descriptions of how the imperatives were executed in fulfilling the census (1.17ff.), and in numbering the Levites (4.34ff.). Chapter 7 describes the bringing of offerings by the leaders of the tribes at a period prior to 1.1. Although the presentation is related in a historical tense, the stereotyped repetition of the identical offerings for all twelve tribes once again reveals the intent to portray an ideal. Finally, 9.15ff. describe the cloud's appearance over the tabernacle as frequentative action which assumes a long history of experience on the march, even before the people have broken camp.

The point to be made from this peculiar literary form is that the writer is portraying a situation which combines both prescriptive and descriptive elements, and which also falls outside clearly defined temporal and geographical boundaries. The unifying force behind this apparent disorder lies in a theological construct which views the material from a unified sacerdotal perspective. The fundamental concern of this section lies in characterizing the nature of a holy estate, which is set apart absolutely from all profane and unholy elements, and thus provides the proper dwelling within Israel for the presence of God (5.3). To characterize the theological intent as an idealization of historical reality is misleading in so far as the contrast is not between the ideal and the actual, but between the holy and the profane. However, it is true that within this sacerdotal perspective the lines between the prescriptive (ideal) and the descriptive (historical) are not clearly drawn.

Chapters 1–4 set forth the sacred order of the camp. At the centre was the tabernacle, and arranged in concentric circles according to the degree of holiness were the Levitical families and the other tribes. (The pre-eminent position assigned to Judah in 2.3 is not explained historically, but set forth simply as part of the divine imperative.) The various laws which follow seem to be a miscellaneous collection. The 'law in case of jealousy' (5.11ff.) in particular appears to be a very ancient one. Other laws seem to be supplements to previously discussed subjects (5.5–10 // Lev. 5.20–26; 8.1–4// Ex. 25.31ff.; 8.5–22//3.5–13; 9.1–14// Ex.12.1ff.). Certain sections, such as 8.15–19, are borrowed almost entirely from other passages in Numbers (8.16a=3.9; 8.16b=3.12; 8.17=3.13; 8.18=3.12; 8.19a=3.7; 8.19b=1.53). But the decisive point to be made is that these apparently miscellaneous laws have been connected by way of association to chs. 1–4 about the central theme of holiness. All unclean persons are to be excluded from the camp (5.1–4). Even if an uncleanliness is only suspected, it is to be pursued and rooted out (5.11ff.). The law of the Nazirite (ch.7) focuses almost entirely on his 'separation' from the profane and even things generally regarded as clean. Again, the discussion of passover treats the problem of the proper procedure when anyone has been made unclean (8.6ff.). Similarly the cleansing of the Levites for their service offers the means of atonement for Israel and of preventing the plague which inevitably strikes against all uncleanliness (8.19). Finally, the Levitical blessing (6.22ff.) and the continuing cloud over the tabernacle (9.15ff.) describe the effect of the divine presence among an undefiled, sacral encampment.

In sum, chs. 1–10 portray the divine will for Israel in completely sacerdotal terms which not only relativize historical differences in the age and original setting of the material, but obscure the line between the prescribed and the actual forms. The effect is that the entire emphasis falls on characterizing the nature of being separated to God in preparation for becoming a pilgrim people on the move.

Chapters 10.11–22.1

The difficulty of establishing the exact conclusion of this section has already been discussed. Although it could possibly be set earlier in ch. 21, the arrival at the plains of Moab and the ensuing threats establish a decisive break in continuity with the period of the wilderness wanderings.

At first glance the literary situation of this section appears to be strikingly different from the first section. Whereas 1.1–10.10 derived exclusively from the priestly source, the succeeding section consists of a complex relationship between an earlier Pentateuchal stratum (JE) and various levels of a priestly strand. At times stories are made up entirely of the earlier sources (11 and 12), but more frequently the JE account has been closely intertwined with P material (chs. 13f.; 16f.; 20f.). The very different ways in which the priestly material relates to the older sources would support seeing P as a literary source in these chapters, rather than as simply a redactional layer. Finally, there is a series of laws which appear to fall outside of the narrative sequence, and thus are generally regarded as an even later priestly interpolation (chs. 15; 18; 19).

A closer examination reveals a similar intent to that of the first section. The editor of this section has used the earlier material in order to illustrate the disastrous effect of Israel's contamination with the unholy during the wilderness journey. The stories in chs. 11 and 12 serve to illustrate divine judgment on Israel's disobedience without any needed additions, but the effect of contamination is most clearly portrayed in the priestly additions to the remaining stories (14.37; 16.41ff.). Judgment by plague is particularly characteristic of divine wrath against the unclean.

Moreover, the same principle of association is at work in the inclusion of various cultic laws which appear to have no integral relation to the narrative. Chapter 15 deals with the laws concerning offerings, and the means of atonement for an error committed unwittingly by a whole population (v.26). The association with the preceding narrative is obvious since an entire generation has just been condemned to die in the desert because of its sin. Again, the connection of ch.18, the law of the priest's portion, with the preceding story of Korah, is made explicit in v.5: 'that there be wrath no more upon the people of Israel'. Similarly the function of the 'red heifer' in ch.19 is to provide an ongoing means of atonement for anyone who has been made unclean.

There is one additional feature to observe in the role assigned to these laws. The three chapters (15;18;19) share in common a function as a 'perpetual statute throughout the generations' (15.15, 21, 23, 37; 18.8, 11, 19, 23; 19.10, 21). There is no effort made to relate these laws to the narrative sequence because they are directed to future generations and provide them with a means of avoiding the contamination experienced by their fathers in the wilderness.

In sum, the second section is also ordered from a strictly sacerdotal perspective which has made use of historical material by which to contrast the clean and the unclean. The historical dimension is also disregarded and often obscured by a priestly concern which is largely atemporal and which extends its directives to encompass the future as well as the past.

Chapters 22.2–36.13

A new theme of the impending conquest of the promised land is introduced with the defeat of the Amorite kings in ch. 21. With the people's arrival at the plains of Moab, it becomes a recurring motif which is again interspersed with a variety of seemingly miscellaneous laws. Two initial threats endangered the people, that of Balaam (22–24) and of Baal Peor (25). However, in both instances the danger was overcome. The plague which struck because of the false sacrifices (25.8ff.) was stayed by the zeal of Phinehas, the priest. As a sign of a new nation which followed the death of the entire generation of the wilderness (26.63ff.) a new census was taken. Neither Aaron nor Moses could participate in the inheritance because they had failed to 'sanctify' God at Meribah (27.12ff.). Thus they also belonged to the unclean generation of the wilderness.

The laws which constitute the final section of the book again reflect different stages of literary development (cf. Noth), but also illustrate the editors' concern that the laws of holiness and the sacred allotment (34.1ff.) be maintained throughout every successive generation (35.29) lest the land be polluted in which God has chosen to dwell (35.33ff.). The establishment of the Levitical cities (ch.35) assures that no unjust blood be shed and the ruling respecting the daughters of Zelophehad (ch.36) prevents any family from losing its rightful inheritance.

In spite of its diversity of subject matter and complex literary development the book of Numbers maintains a unified sacerdotal interpretation of God's will for his people which is set forth in a sharp contrast between the holy and the profane. The holy is portrayed as the presence of God, the blessing of numbers, the laws of cleanliness, the service of the Levites, the atonement of Aaron, and the inheritance of a clean land. Conversely, the profane consists of all sorts of uncleanliness, and results in the wrath of God, his plagues of judgment, a lost inheritance by a dying people, and the pollution of the land.

3. Theological and Hermeneutical Implications

(*a*) The usual practice of critical commentators of evaluating the material of Numbers according to its degree of historicity runs the acute risk of misunderstanding the major theological categories into which the biblical writers have cast their material. By contrasting the allegedly historical elements with 'fictional' ones a polarity is established which is alien to the writers' purpose and obscures the basic cultic distinction between the sacred and the profane. Even the category of the 'ideal' versus the 'actual' must be used with extreme caution lest it obscure a close hearing of the biblical text by its philosophical assumptions. From a canonical perspective the hermeneutical problem is far from settled when one claims to have salvaged the historicity of an early tradition, but then assumes the tradition was subsequently misunderstood (e.g. Mendenhall on the census). In such instances, neither the attackers of the tradition nor its defenders have addressed the canonical issue which turns on its present function within scripture.

(b) The canonical process at work in the shape of Numbers incorporated much diverse material within the framework of an overarching theological construct. However, this move did not in this case drain these originally independent units of their original meaning. For example, the strong, eschatological note which was sounded in the final oracle of Balaam was left intact, even though it did not conform particularly well to the sacerdotal emphasis of the priestly editors. This canonical tolerance of diversity thus allowed the material to function freely on several levels. Such a hermeneutical effect is not to be confused with playing the reconstructed stages in a historical development against the final form of the text. The question as to how much independent life from an earlier stage was allowed to survive, e.g. the law of jealousy in ch. 5, can only be determined by a close exegesis within the canonical context.

(c) Even though the theological stance of the priestly editors of Leviticus and of Numbers appear to be the same, the canonical shape of the two book is quite different. Several different factors entered the process. Certainly the nature of the received traditions played a significant role, but also the particular role which was assigned to a composition resulted in a different shaping process. The book of Leviticus also focuses on the issue of the holy and the profane, but the theme of the march and conquest were first introduced in Numbers. A different perspective was thus opened up even in regard to the issue of the holy and the profane. The nature of a book's canonical function is not simply to be identified with motifs and themes.

History of Exegesis

Carpzov I, 133f.; *DThC* 9, 716; *EB* 2, 141; *RGG*³4, 1543.

B. S. **Childs**, *Exodus*, OTL, 1974, 293, 297; R. B. **Kenney**, *Ante-Nicene Greek and Latin Patristic Uses of the Biblical Manna Motif*, Diss. Yale University 1968; E. B. **Levine**, 'Parallels to Numbers of Pseudo-Jonathan and Neophyti I', *Neophyti I*, ed. A. Díez Macho, IV, Madrid 1974, 649–707; I. **Sonne**, 'The Paintings of the Dura Synagogue', *HUCA* 20, 1947, 301ff.; E. E. **Urbach**, 'Homilies of the Rabbis on the Prophets of the Nations and the Balaam Stories' (Hebrew), *Tarbiz* 25, Jerusalem 1956, 272–89; J. **de Vaulx**, 'Interprétations juive et chrétiennes', *Les Nombres*, SB, 1972, 41–50; G. **Vermes**, 'The Story of Balaam – The Scriptural Origin of Haggadah', *Scripture and Tradition in Judaism*, Studia Post-Biblica 4, Leiden ²1973, 127–77.

X

DEUTERONOMY

Commentaries

F. W. Schultz, 1859
C. F. Keil, BC, 1865
A. Dillmann, KeH, ²1886
S. R. Driver, ICC, ³1901
F. de Hummelauer, CSS, 1901
D. Hoffmann, 1913–1922
E. König, KAT, 1917
G. A. Smith, CB, 1918
K. Steuernagel, HKAT, ²1923

A. Clamer, SB, 1940
G. E. Wright, IB, 1953
P. Buis, J. Leclercq, SoBi, 1963
G. von Rad, OTL, 1966
A. Phillips, CNEB, 1973
J. A. Thompson, TOTC, 1974
P. C. Craigie, NICOT, 1976
H. Lamparter, BAT, 1977

Bibliography

A. **Alt**, 'Die Heimat des Deuteronomiums', *KS* II, Munich 1953, 250–75; O. **Bächli**, *Israel und die Völker*, Zürich 1962; K. **Baltzer**, *The Covenant Formulary*, ET Oxford 1971; W. **Baumgartner**, 'Der Kampf an das Deuteronomium', *ThR* NS 1, 1929, 7–25; A. **Bentzen**, *Die josianische Reform und ihre Voraussetzungen*, Copenhagen 1926; G. R. **Berry**, 'The Code found in the Temple', *JBL* 39, 1920, 44–51; J. A. **Bewer**, G. **Dahl** and L. B. **Paton**, 'The Problem of Deuteronomy: A Symposium', *JBL* 47, 1928, 305–79; H. **Breit**, *Die Predigt des Deuteronomisten*, Munich 1933; C. **Brekelmans**, 'Die sogenannten deuteronomischen Elemente in Gen.–Num. Ein Beitrag zur Vorgeschichte des Deuteronomiums', *STV* 15, 1966, 90–96; K. **Budde**, 'Das Deuteronomium und die Reform König Josias', *ZAW* 44, 1926, 177–225; C. M. **Carmichael**, *The Laws of Deuteronomy*, Ithaca, N.Y. and London 1974; B. S. **Childs**, 'Deuteronomic Formulae of the Exodus Traditions', *SVT* 16, 1967, 30–9; R. E. **Clements**, 'Deuteronomy and the Jerusalem Cult-Tradition' *VT* 15, 1965, 300–12; 'Covenant and Canon in the Old Testament', *Creation, Christ and Culture, FS T. F. Torrance*, Edinburgh 1976, 1–12; F. M. **Cross** and D. N. **Freedman**, 'The Blessing of Moses', *JBL* 67, 1948, 191–210; 'Josiah's Revolt against Assyria', *JNES* 12, 1953; 56–59.

P. **Diepold**, *Israels Land*, BWANT V.15 (=95), 1972; W. **Dietrich**, *Prophetie und Geschichte. Eine redaktionsgeschichtliche Untersuchung zum deuteronomistischen Geschichtswerk*, FRLANT 108, 1972; F. **Dumermuth**, 'Zur deuteronomischen Kulttheologie', *ZAW* 70, 1958, 59–98; W. **Eichrodt**, 'Bahnt sich eine Lösung der deuteronomischen Frage an?', *NKZ* 32, 1921, 41–51, 53–78; J. A. **Emerton**, 'Priests and Levites in Deuteronomy', *VT* 12, 1962, 129–38; R. **Frankena**, 'The Vassal-Treaties of Esarhaddon and the Dating of Deuteronomy', *OTS* 14, 1965, 122–54; K. **Galling**, 'Das Gemeindegesetz im Deuteronomium 23', *FS A. Bertholet*, Tübingen 1950, 176–91; 'Das Königsgesetz im Deuteronomium', *TLZ* 76, 1951, 133–8; H. **Gressmann**, 'Josia und das Deuteronomium', *ZAW* 42, 1924, 313–37; J. **Hempel**, *Die Schichten des Deuteronomiums*, Leipzig 1914; J. **Herrmann**, 'Ägyptische Analogien zum Funde des Deuteronomiums', *ZAW* 28, 1908, 291–302; G. **Hölscher**, 'Komposition und Ursprung des Deuteronomiums', *ZAW* 40, 1922, 161–55; F. **Horst**, *Das Privilegrecht Jahwes*, FRLANT 45, 1930; A. R. **Hulst**, *Het Karakter van den Cultus in Deuteronomium*, Diss. Groningen 1938; R. H. **Kennett**, *Deuteronomy and the Decalogue*, Cambridge and New York 1920; P. **Kleinert**, *Das Deuteronomium und der Deuteronomiker*, Bielefeld 1872; M. G. **Kline**, *Treaty of the Great King. The Covenant Structure of Deuteronomy*, Grand Rapids 1963.

J. **L'Hour**, 'L'Alliance de Sichem', *RB* 69, 1962, 5–36, 161–84, 350–68; J. **Lindblom**, *Erwägungen zur Herkunft der josianischen Tempelkunde*, Lund 1971; S. **Loersch**, *Das Deuteronomium und siene Deutung. Ein forschungsgeschichtlicher Überblick*, Stuttgart 1967; N. **Lohfink**, 'Der Bundesschluss im Lande Moab. Redaktionsgeschichtliches zu Dt 28,69 bis 32,47', *BZ* NF 6, 1962, 32–56; 'Die Bundesurkunde des Königs Josias', *Bibl* 44, 1963, 261–288; *Das Hauptgebot*, AnBib 20,1963; 'Zum "kleinen geschichtlichen Credo"', Deut. 26.5–9', *Theologie und Philosophie* 46, Freiburg 1971, 19–39; 'Deuteronomy', *IDB Suppl*, 229–32; V. **Maag**, 'Erwägungen zur deuteronomischen Kultzentralisation', *VT* 6, 1956, 10–18; S. Dean **McBride**, 'The Yoke of the Kingdom. An Exposition of Deuteronomy 6:4–5', *Interp* 27, 1973, 273–306; D. J. **McCarthy**, *Treaty and Covenant*, Rome 1963; R. P. **Merendino**, *Das deuteronomische Gesetz. Eine literarkritische, gattungs– und überlieferungsgeschichtliche Untersuchung zu Dt 12–26*, BBB 31, 1969; G. **Minette de Tillesse**, 'Sections "tu" et sections "vous" dans le Deutéronome', *VT* 12, 1962, 29–87; S. **Mittmann**, *Deuteronomium 1, 1–6, 3. Literarkritisch und traditionsgeschichtlich untersucht*, BZAW 139, 1975; W. L. **Moran**, 'The Ancient Near Eastern Background of the Love of God in Deuteronomy', *CBQ* 25, 1963, 77–87; E. W. **Nicholson**, *Deuteronomy and Tradition*, Oxford and Philadelphia 1967; M. **Noth**, *Überlieferungsgeschichtliche Studien* I, Halle 1943; T. **Oestreicher**, *Das deuteronomische Grundgesetz*, Gütersloh 1923; L. **Perlitt**, *Bundestheologie im Alten Testament*, WMANT 26, 1969; J. G. **Plöger**, *Literarkritische, formgeschichtliche und stilkritische Unter-*

suchungen zum Deuteronomium, BBB 26, 1967; G. **von Rad**, *Das Gottesvolk im Deuteronomiums*, BWANT III.11 (=36), 1929; *Studies in Deuteronomy*, ET, SBT I.9, 1953; 'Ancient Word and Living Word. The Preaching of Deuteronomy and our Preaching', *Interp* 15, 1961, 3–13; A. **Rofé**, 'The Strata of the Law about the Centralization of Worship in Deuteronomy and the History of the Deuteronomic Movement', *SVT* 22, 1972, 221–6; review of M. Weinfeld's *Deuteronomy and the Deuteronomic School* in *Christian News from Israel*, 24, 1974, 204–9; *Introduction to Deuteronomy, Part I* (Hebrew), Jerusalem 1975; M. **Rose**, *Der Ausschliesslichkeitsanspruch Jahwes*, BWANT VI.6 (=106), 1975; G. **Schmitt**, *Der Landtag von Sichem*, Stuttgart 1964; M. H. **Segal**, 'The Book of Deuteronomy', *JQR* 48, 1957–8, 315–51; G. **Seitz**, *Redaktionsgeschichtliche Studien zum Deuteronomium*, BWANT V. 13 (=93), 1971; P. W. **Skehan**, 'The Structure of the Song of Moses in Deuteronomy (Deut. 32:1–43)', *CBQ* 13, 1951, 153–63; C. **Steuernagel**, *Der Rahmen des Deuteronomiums*, Berlin 1894; M. **Weinfeld**, 'The Origin of Humanism in Deuteronomy', *JBL* 80, 1961, 241–7; 'Cult Centralization in Light of a Neo-Babylonian Analogy', *JNES* 23, 1964, 202–12; 'Deuteronomy – The Present Stage of Inquiry', *JBL* 86, 1967, 249–62; *Deuteronomy and the Deuteronomic School*, Oxford 1972; A. C. **Welch**, *The Code of Deuteronomy. A New Theory of its Origin*, London 1924, New York 1925; 'When was the Worship of Israel Centralized in the Temple?', *ZAW* 43, 1925, 250–5; 'The Problem of Deuteronomy', *JBL* 48, 1929, 291–306; *Deuteronomy: The Framework to the Code*, London and New York 1932; J. **Wellhausen**, *Prolegomena to the History of Israel*, ET Edinburgh 1885; H. M. **Wiener**, 'The Arrangement of Deut. 12–26', *JPOS* 6, 1926, 185–95; G. E. **Wright**, 'The Levites in Deuteronomy', *VT* 4, 1954, 325–30; 'The Lawsuit of God: A Form-Critical Study of Deuteronomy 32', *Israel's Prophetic Heritage, FS J. Muilenburg*, ed. B. W. Anderson and W. Harrelson, New York and London 1962, 26–67.

1. Historical Critical Problems

The importance of Deuteronomy for the history of critical research can hardly be overestimated. It provided the linchpin for the source-critical theory of the Pentateuch. Its decisive influence on the structure of the historical books was recognized at an early date. More recently, the role of a Deuteronomic circle in editing the prophetic books has been a major discovery of critical research. Moreover, the importance of Deuteronomy is further evidenced by the many modern scholars who hold that Deuteronomy constitutes the centre of Old Testament theology.

The history of critical research on the book of Deuteronomy has been reviewed many times and need not be rehearsed in detail (cf. Baumgartner, Lohfink, Loersch, Nicholson, Seitz). The frequently used method of tracing a chronological sequence in the history of research is helpful in pointing out the different focuses of interest and the changing methodologies. Starting with de Wette in 1806 the literary and historical critical approach continued to dominate throughout the nineteenth century and culminated in the twentieth century with the work of Steuernagel and Hempel. Beginning in the late 1920s the impact of form-critical and traditio-critical research began to be felt in the early studies of Welch, Horst, and Alt, but reached its height in the work of von Rad. More recently, a redactional critical approach – some prefer the name 'stylistic' approach – has again shifted the focus of research, and is exemplified in the monographs of Lohfink, Merendino, Seitz and others. M. Noth's work was an important influence in shifting the focus. Obviously there is a good bit of overlap in the different methods and the danger of oversimplification is acute in such a schematization. Therefore, it may be more helpful in summarizing the major critical issues to deal with the history of research in terms of pivotal problems.

Dating and authorship

Beginning with de Wette's epoch-making thesis, critical scholarship on the book of Deuteronomy has focused its continuous attention on the problem of the date and authorship of the composition. Several hypotheses have sustained themselves in spite of considerable modification since the original formulation by de Wette. First of all, most critics would still agree in seeing some relationship between Deuteronomy and the seventh-century reform programme of Josiah (II Kings 22f.), in spite of the great debate in the 1920s which was waged by Hölscher, Kennett, Welch and others. But beyond this broad consensus in recognizing a seventh-century stamp of a reform movement, many related details are still much contested. No consensus has emerged on the exact nature of the influence which arose from the reform, and few would hold any longer that Deuteronomy provided the major impetus for the 'programme' which is recorded in II Kings 23. Again, most scholars would contend that much of the material of Deuteronomy was far older than the seventh century, and many would insist on a level of redactional reworking of the book far later than the seventh century. Then again, the original attempt to see centralization of the cult as the key to dating and authorship has generally been abandoned and the issue placed within the much broader historical context of Assyrian decline (Bentzen). Nevertheless, that centralization played an important role for one layer of the book's composition (cf. ch.12) is still generally accepted in spite of the efforts of Oestreicher and Welch to eliminate it entirely as an issue.

Structure and unity of the book

There is an almost universal consensus in deriving the present form of the book of Deuteronomy from a long period of historical development. Again, there is a wide agreement in rejecting an easy equation between the 'Book of the Covenant' mentioned in II Kings 22 and the final shape of Deuteronomy. Beyond this, there is little agreement on the nature and scope of a 'Urdeuteronomium', or even of the criteria by which it could be isolated. The use of the variations between the singular and plural pronouns as a means of recovering the earliest level continues to resist a fully satisfactory solution, although the study of Minette de Tillesse has produced a far more positive response than Steuernagel's complex literary theories. Then again, the attempt to explain the various layers and duplications within the present structure of the book as different editions, according to the proposal of Wellhausen, has not been generally accepted. Lohfink is more representative of a majority view when he defends seeing a more complex development than simply having two versions of a homiletical framework (1–4 and 27; 5–11 and 28–30) enclosing an original law code (12–26).

Certainly the most influential theory of Deuteronomy's history of development among modern scholars has been proposed by Noth in his familiar hypothesis of a Deuteronomistic historian (*Überlieferungsgeschichtliche Studien* I). According to Noth, chs. 1–3(4) form the introduction to the Deuteronomistic historical work which encompasses Joshua, Judges, Samuel, and Kings, whereas chs. 5–11 provide the actual introduction to the Deuteronomic law. The strengths of Noth's theory are several. It places the problem of the structure of Deuteronomy within a broader literary context and resolves a complex literary problem with great simplicity. However, there are some disadvantages as well to the theory of a Deuteronomistic historical book. Critics such as Fohrer argue that the theory destroys the integrity of the book of Deuteronomy. We shall return to the issue in our own analysis of the book's canonical shape.

Form-critical and traditio-critical analysis

The issue of the structure of the book is closely involved with the problem of literary forms. Traditionally the book has been viewed as Moses' last will and testament (Philo), which he delivered in three final addresses to Israel. Although commentators seem to agree on the number of three addresses, upon closer examination one sees that there is considerable disagreement as to which chapters constitute each address. The scope of the third speech in particular has proven to be highly controversial (compare Keil, Hoffmann, Wright, and Thompson). Actually the close attention of P. Kleinert to the variety of superscriptions which appear throughout the book did much to destroy the traditional, unified concept of the book's composition and opened up the way to a history of traditions approach.

Within recent years several major theses have emerged which have addressed the form-critical problem. Building on the earlier insights of Klostermann, G. von Rad developed the theory that Deuteronomy was the reflection of a history of a paraenetic use of the law which had its provenance in the ancient Israelite cult of the amphictyony. Because of the emphasis on both the military and cultic traditions, von Rad argued for the Levites as the most likely tradents of the Deuteronomic tradition. Although his brilliant analysis of the paraenetic style has received wide acclaim, the Levite theory has continued to evoke criticism.

A very different approach to the traditions of Deuteronomy was first suggested by G. Mendenhall (see bibliography to Exodus) when he drew attention to the parallels between the Hittite suzerain treaties and the legal tradition of the Pentateuch. His insight was vigorously pursued by others who found in the structure of the book of Deuteronomy the best evidence for an influence from a common treaty pattern (Baltzer, McCarthy, Wright, Kline, etc.). Although very few scholars would contest the value of this ancient Near Eastern parallel – a few such as Nötscher rejected the parallel out of hand – no consensus has emerged in establishing a close historical or literary relationship, as was first suggested.

Finally, the most recent hypothesis regarding the form and tradition of Deuteronomy has been proposed by M. Weinfeld (*Deutero-nomy*). His central thesis is that Deuteronomy was composed by scribes and sages from the royal house of Judah during the eighth to seventh century BC and that the book reflects the wisdom of the ancient Near East as its major source. According to Weinfeld, the resemblance between the book of Deuteronomy and the suzerainty treaties of the surrounding nations derived from a literary imitation by a learned scribal office and was not a reflection of an actual cultic ceremony as proposed by Mendenhall and Baltzer. In spite of the many unresolved problems with Weinfeld's hypothesis – what is meant by wisdom and why should Jerusalem be considered the locus of the tradition? – his thesis has provoked a very interesting re-examination of the form-critical and traditio-historical dimensions of the book. Needless to say, the very fluid state of the research shows no signs of moving towards a consensus in respect to this set of issues.

Redaction-critical problems

Redactional criticism is closely akin to both the literary and traditio-historical problems on the composition, but it focuses its major attention on the intentionality of those who gave it a present shape rather than remaining with the earlier stages of the text's prehistory. Noth's study of the reworking of Deuteronomy by a Deuteronomistic editor who had before him 4.44–28.69 (EVV 29.1) provided a major stimulus for the newer approach. To this influence was joined the new interest in the stylistic features of the composition as a whole, exemplified by Lohfink's approach (*Hauptgebot*). Within the last decade a rash of highly technical studies have appeared, which, building on Noth, try to trace in great detail the nature of the Deuteronomistic redaction (Plöger, Merendino, Seitz, Mittmann).

Certainly the most incisive, and yet extreme conclusions, among the newer studies have been drawn by L. Perlitt in his *Bundestheologie*. He vigorously contests the widely held view that Israel's faith from the beginning centred in a covenant with Yahweh, but rather argued that the covenant theology was a late development in Israel derived from the Deuteronomistic authors of the seventh and sixth centuries in an effort to meet the crisis brought about by the destruction of the two Israelite kingdoms. The effect of this highly contested thesis is to bring the state of modern research into a full circle by drawing at least near to the position once defended by Wellhausen, but which had been widely assumed to be erroneous for the last forty years. The very success of Perlitt's attack on the antiquity of covenant theology has pointed out the danger among the current generation of scholars of building a superstructure on earlier theories such as those of von Rad and Noth, which were useful as working hypotheses, but disastrous when confused with incontrovertible fact.

The theological dimension

The history of critical research on the book of Deuteronomy illustrates well the varying degrees of creative interaction between the critical analysis of the book and the theological interest of the scholar. De Wette's original thesis reflected his own battle with the dominant orthodox Protestant theology of his period and bore a decidely anti-theological flavour which easily lent itself to the 'pious fraud' theory of the late nineteenth century.

By the time of Driver's famous commentary the effort to establish in a more positive way the theological significance of Deuteronomy on the basis of the new critical reconstruction had assumed a fixed form. For Driver Deuteronomy's theological significance lay in its attempt to inculcate 'religious and moral principle' in the late monarchial period. As a 'prophetical law-book', it expressed a 'great spiritual and moral ideal' which included monotheism, the ethical nature of God, and a holy people. However, Driver's concern with the theological did not really affect his analysis of the book's composition in any significant way, but simply reflected his more positive approach to the Bible in general.

The relation of A. C. Welch's theological interest to his critical analysis of Deuteronomy is more significant than in Driver's case. Welch's strong theological interest was clearly exhibited in his first major publication, which was in dogmatics rather than in biblical studies. Surprisingly enough, Welch's basic critical position respecting Deuteronomy was worked out in his first book on the subject, *The Code of Deuteronomy* (1924), without serious attention to the theological issues of Deuteronomy. Only in his second monograph, *Deuteronomy: The Framework to the Code* (1932) did he present the significance of his critical theories in a highly creative theological interpretation. He argued for a dynamic use of the law as a divine authority which needed to be adapted to the changing historical situation of Israel (27). He stressed the prophetic role of Deuteronomy whose setting he had earlier located in Northern Israel and which allowed him to draw theological connections between Deuteronomy and Elijah, Amos, and Hosea. But as with Driver, the theological interpretation of the biblical book appears to have followed from his prior historical critical analysis without seriously affecting the analysis itself.

One of the remarkable aspects of von Rad's work on Deuteronomy is to discern how his larger theological concerns greatly influenced his critical analysis, in fact, provided him with a tool by which to break out of the literary impasse of the 1920s. In his dissertation of 1929, *Das Gottesvolk in Deuteronomium*, von Rad rejected the usual literary critical starting point of II Kings 22f. and sought to find a new critical avenue into the material by pursuing the implications of Deuteronomy's theological understanding of the people of God. Only in his subsequent monographs did von Rad broaden the basis of his study with a close form-critical and traditio-critical investigation, but his initial breakthrough emerged from his new theological starting point. The creative effect of a strong theological interest on the critical study of Deuteronomy can also be seen in some of the monographs of the 1930s such as by Breit and Hulst.

It remains an intriguing question to what extent the newer redaction-critical studies of the late 60s and 70s reflect a changing theological model. Theological interest in Deuteronomy has certainly not diminished, but it has shifted away from the form which it had in the period after World War II. The effect has been that the complexity of the recent studies resembles much more the work of the 1920s before von Rad struck out in a new theological direction. It is too early to predict whether a study of the theological dimensions of the book will be a significant force in forming a new critical synthesis.

2. The Canonical Shape of Deuteronomy

The structure and style of the book as a whole

The present form of the book of Deuteronomy consists in a series of addresses by Moses to the people just before the entry into the promised land of Canaan. To these addresses are joined additional material which introduces a different narrative framework, namely the imminent death of Moses and the appointment of a successor (ch. 31). There then follows a concluding song (32), a blessing (33), and the report of the death of Moses (34).

Little significance has been attached to the editing process in establishing exact divisions between the various speeches. The variety among the superscriptions makes it difficult to lay much emphasis on the scope of each speech. The parts flow together, overlap, and repeat. In the end, the speeches appear as a single sermon of Moses (von Rad). Although the idea of Deuteronomy's being a farewell speech does not appear explicitly until the concluding chapters when the words of Moses are read in the light of the larger narrative – Moses has been excluded from entry into the land – the whole book functions canonically as his last will and testimony. Within this overarching framework of the final shape of the book the structure can tolerate various tensions and interpolations which reflect the stages in its long history of growth without being a serious distraction.

From a canonical perspective the critical issue at stake is whether or not one assumes that the function of the material at some early stage of its prehistory is determinative for a proper understanding of the book. Can one speak meaningfully of a canonical shape as the final form of the text in which the material has been cast? The canonical approach does not deny that forces from Deuteronomy's early history have left a stamp on the material, such as liturgical patterns from the cult (von Rad) or a common ancient Near Eastern treaty structure (Baltzer). However, the point of debate lies in determining how these earlier levels now function within the context of a canonical collection of sacred scripture.

Chapter 1 makes it immediately clear that the purpose of Moses' addressing the people is to 'explain the Torah' (v. 5). To the new generation who was about to cross into the land Moses interprets the Sinai covenant. He does not offer a new law, but by means of a rehearsal of the history of Israel since Sinai, he seeks to inculcate obedience to the divine law which had once and for all constituted the nation (5.22). Moses explains the law book by recapitulating what has happened as well as applying the divine law to the new situation in which the people would shortly enter. It is, therefore, built into the canonical function of Deuteronomy that a new application of old tradition is being offered, but a tradition which had already assumed a normative, written form. The homiletical style which belongs to the present shape of the book is an essential part of the explanation of the law. The new interpretation seeks to actualize the traditions of the past for the new generation in such a way as to evoke a response of the will in a fresh commitment to the covenant. The present form of the book of Deuteronomy reflects a dominant editorial concern to reshape the material for its use by future generations of Israel. The process can be termed canonical because it relates to the use of tradition as authoritative scripture rather than by initiating a liturgical actualization or legitimating a process of continuous reinterpretation.

It is obvious from the complex structure of the present book that the material has undergone a long history of development. Much effort has been expended by several generations of critics to reconstruct this history. Fohrer's sketch of the development (*Introduction*, 174ff.) offers a typical example of tracing the stages from the 'original lawbook to the present book'. Perhaps the suggested canonical approach can be more sharply focused by contrasting it with such a representative reconstruction of its growth.

(*a*) First, it seems to me very doubtful that one can distinguish the different levels of development as sharply as Fohrer suggests. The strikingly different theories of other scholars regarding the original stages of the material which Fohrer rejects in his treatment only emphasize the subjectivity of his proposal. Actually his schema assumes a larger concept of Israel's history of religion which the author simply illustrates from Deuteronomy.

(*b*) Secondly, Fohrer fails to reckon with the canonical process of transforming tradition into a collection of authoritative writings for a religious community. The different layers of the composition are either related to a given historical event, a political programme, or to a redactor's alleged intentionality, but never to the effect on the final form of the canonical text itself. Conversely, the continuous effect of the material on the very community which is shaping the tradition through its use is nowhere adequately reflected, but rather different reconstructed levels are set out in an externalized pattern of historical development.

(c) Thirdly, Fohrer's schema does not do justice to the process by which earlier features of the book's structure assume a different role and tensions are accommodated in a fresh way for a new purpose within the literary composition. To isolate elements from an early stage, such as the entrance of the so-called 'military laws', usually fails to describe how such material functions within the completed form of the book. One misses any attempt at a holistic reading of the literature.

The canonical role of the individual sections

Chapters 1–4

In spite of the different form and style of ch. 4, it now functions along with the first three chapters of the book as an introduction to the chapters which follow. The context for Moses' address is immediately given by the prologue. The words were delivered in the fortieth year, that is, at the end of the long wilderness wanderings period whose history had previously been related and was now assumed. The geographical setting is the plains of Moab on the edge of the promised land. Moreover, the content of the speech is described as having been given to Moses 'by Yahweh in commandment' (1.3) which again assumes a knowledge of the events of Sinai (Ex. 20.18ff.). This history is subsequently repeated in more detail in Deut. 4.9ff. and 5.22ff.

Deuteronomy 1.5 offers the first reference to 'this law' (*hattôrāh hazzō't*) and in the context of the chapter has its antecedent in the words which Moses had earlier received at Sinai. The full significance of Moses' 'explaining' (*bē'ēr*) the law has long been debated, but it would seem apparent that his task involved more than simply imparting information which had hitherto been only privy to Moses. Rather, the emphasis falls on his clarifying and interpreting the material in order to ensure its proper understanding by the people. This role does not in itself contradict the description of his address in 1.3, but does shift the focus.

It comes as an initial surprise to discover that the material which follows the prologue is not an explanation of law, but a rehearsal of the nation's history following the covenant at Sinai. Yet the selection of narrative material has been carefully chosen to describe the historical situation and to ground the theological argument which will occupy the rest of the book. Israel rebelled against God in refusing to accept the promise of the land. As a result, a divine judgment fell on the old generation which had been delivered from Egypt (1.35). Not one of them would enter the land, but only their children would inherit the promise. In addition, Moses himself, the mediator of the covenant, was also denied entrance and was to be replaced in his office by Joshua (Deut. 3.28). But the history which Moses reviewed did not just consist in rebellion and judgment. The new generation (2.16) had already experienced the truth of the promise. Israel had defeated their enemies, crossed into their possession east of the Jordan, and had begun to occupy their inheritance. Moreover, Moses' successor, Joshua, had already been chosen.

The purpose of this historical review is made clear in ch. 4. In the light of this experience of both judgment and mercy, Moses appeals to Israel to obey the commandments of God, to learn from the lessons of the past in order, and to take full possession of the land and its blessing. The rehearsal of the theophany at Sinai and the giving of the decalogue serves to ground Israel's life once and for all in the covenant, but at the same time to indicate that the new laws which Moses now delivers are extensions of the same divine will. Israel's new life in the land stands in direct relationship to the one divine will (4.14). In sum, the content of Moses' address stems from the one constitutive event of Israel's life, Sinai, but it is offered as a new formulation of the divine purpose in the light of that particular moment in the nation's life, standing between promise and fulfilment.

Von Rad was the first to have pointed out that the problem of actualizing of past tradition for a new generation was basic to Deuteronomy. This problem is closely related to the canonical shaping of chs. 1–4. Moses recapitulates Israel's past history in order to focus on the new and critical situation of the moment: a new generation, a new leadership, a new land. The concern of the book of Deuteronomy is how to actualize the covenant law in this new situation. It is highly significant to observe in chs. 1–4 the differing perspectives from which the issue of actualization is viewed. On the one hand, the change that history produces is strongly emphasized, and three different generations are delineated. There is the old 'evil generation' (1.34) who refused to enter the land. There is the 'second' generation of their children who would possess the land (1.39). Finally, there is the future generation who would become corrupt in the land (4.25ff.) and would call forth the divine judgment of exile. On the other hand, there is another perspective reflected in these same chapters which envisions only an unbroken continuity with the past. The same people, addressed as 'you' and 'we', participated in the Sinai covenant (4.11), the rebellion in the wilderness (1.26), the victory over Og and Bashan (3.1ff.), and the possession of the new land (4.40).

The shift in perspective which appears in chs. 1–4 is not to be resolved by means of a literary solution. Rather, the issue is a theological one. It turns on the problem of relating the elements of continuity and discontinuity within the tradition. There is only one covenant and one law, but there are different generations, facing new challenges. How does the old relate to the new? The problem has been introduced in chs. 1–4, and its resolution will occupy the rest of the book of Deuteronomy.

It should be clear from this analysis of the canonical function of chs. 1–4 that Noth's theory of chs. 1–3(4) as the introduction to the Deuteronomistic historical work is being called into question. In my judgment, his hypothesis seriously misunderstands the function of these chapters within the book of Deuteronomy, and destroys the basic link to the preceding Pentateuchal tradition.

Chapters 5–11

Chapter 5 begins with a new introduction, but actually it serves to continue the same context which was established in ch. 1. Moses addresses all Israel in order to explain the 'statutes and ordinances' just before the entrance into the land. However, once again, if the reader had expected an immediate description of the law to follow, he will be disappointed. Rather chs. 5–11 present an extended homiletical address which again reviews elements of Israel's past history and each time focuses on an appeal for new commitment to the covenant. For this reason, Wellhausen considered 5–11 to be simply a parallel to chs. 1–4 from a different edition of the book. Noth viewed chs. 5–11 as the real introduction to the Deuteronomic laws of 12–26, assigning 1–4 to the larger Deuteronomic historical work. In my judgment, neither of these alternatives have dealt adequately with the role of 5–11 within the canonical book of Deuteronomy.

In one sense, chs. 5–11 do not present anything different from that already offered by 1–4. The rather rambling homiletical style is akin to ch. 4. The chapters again repeat incidents from Israel's history which provide the grounds for the homily. The centrality of the Sinai experience is also evident throughout the chapters. In another sense, the effect of chs. 5–11 in their present role within the book is far from being a tedious repetition. Rather, these chapters serve to expand and develop the themes of the book in a highly effective and dramatic style, which is lost if the unity of the chapters is removed by some literary device, whether of Wellhausen or Noth.

Chapters 1–4 had raised the issue of actualization. Chapter 5 returns to the issue and develops it into a major theological proposition. The covenant at Horeb was not confined to that first generation of Israelites who participated historically in the event, but the homilist extends its actuality to the new generation as well: 'all of us who are alive this day' (5.3). The decalogue is then repeated as providing the unchanging and eternal will of God for all time. The theophany is reinterpreted in order to focus completely on the divine words, not on the form, as the bearer of the divine will. The words were written down on stone and made final: 'he added no more'. The writer of ch. 5 makes it absolutely clear that the decalogue formed the basis of the covenant and the new generation stood under its imperative in complete continuity with the first generation who had experienced the awesome event at the mountain.

Once the ground of the covenant has been reaffirmed as constitutive for every generation, the homily sets forth in great detail the role of Moses in his office as continuing mediator of the divine will (5.22ff.). Indeed 5.28ff. legitimates Moses' role as interpreter of the statutes and ordinances of the law which is to occupy the rest of the book. Whereas chs. 1–4 assumed this role of Moses on the basis of the tradition of Ex. 20, Deuteronomy eliminates all ambiguity in the tradition and sets forth fully the rationale for Moses' speech to the people.

In the chapters which follow, the writer preaches to the people by choosing as his text events in Israel's history – with the exception of Sinai – which had not been mentioned in the historical review of

1–4: exodus, manna, golden calf, the new tablets. Although the general purpose of the historical review is similar to chs. 1–4, to inculcate obedience to the covenant, the intensity of the appeal is far greater and forms a powerful introduction to the laws which finally appear in ch. 12. Although these chapters are multi-layered and reflect different historical stages in composition, the frequent warning to the future generation of an exile from the land does not fracture the movement of the chapters, but parallels the same transition between generations which occurred in 1–4. In sum, the final form of this section has easily accommodated the various stages of the book's prehistory to form an effective theological unity. The canonical shaping of these chapters is not to be identified with a strictly literary unity, but functions effectively in spite of tensions and repetitions. Although some of Lohfink's stylistic observations regarding the literary structures of the chapters are surely correct, the canonical function does not depend on a stylistic demonstration of artistic intentionality.

Chapters 12–26

The complex literary development of these central chapters has long been recognized and much of the effort of modern critical scholarship has been devoted to unravelling the history. It is fully clear that the laws are of different periods within Israel's history. A comparison with the laws of Exodus (cf. Driver) reveals a large duplication, but with significant changes and additions. Some laws reflect later institutions (ch. 17), or subsequent alterations of economic, political, and social conditions of the monarchial period (cf. 14.22ff.; 15.1ff.; 20.1ff.). At times critical research has been quite successful in tracing the different levels. It may even be possible to speak of a 'theological advance' in some of the later attempts at humanizing earlier laws (Weinfeld). However, these observations, important as they may be for certain questions, do not touch the heart of the theological issue of how these chapters have been shaped to function canonically within the final form of the book of Deuteronomy. Yet it is quite clear that the material has been subject to some characteristic ordering which gives it a particular shape.

First of all, the setting forth of the law is now set within the context of the new situation, hitherto unexperienced by Israel, of the entrance into the land (18.9; 19.1ff.). Israel is not to continue behaving as before (12.8), but is given a new charter by Moses. This means that the canon has recognized the very different character of the laws of Deuteronomy and sought to accommodate the change within the framework of the new historical condition of the conquest. Thus, the old tithe law is adjusted to the new situation 'when the way is too long for you' (14.24ff.), and the laws regarding slaughtering are desacralized on the grounds that the land has been enlarged, which demands that a new distinction be made between profane and holy slaughter (12.20ff.). The effect of this ordering of the laws within chs. 12–26 is to legitimate the principle of change within the law – God's will is not a lifeless statute – but at the same time to subordinate all the various forces at work in the historical development to one theological category. That is to say, the process of canonical ordering accommodates into the final form of the book a great variety of different laws, but virtually disregards the specific socio-political forces at work which actually produced the new forms of the law. In sum, the canon substituted one historical category which it interpreted theologically for a great variety of complex social and historical factors.

Secondly, the laws of Deuteronomy are described as regulating future occurrences in the land: 'if a prophet arises . . . ' (13.1), or when a king 'sits on the throne . . . ' (17.18). By projecting the new stipulations into the future the canonical shaping is able to accommodate a variety of later laws which could not possibly have functioned under Moses. Once again, this move recognizes the development of legal tradition which derived from new institutions, and seeks to accommodate the change in terms of the future orientation of the Mosaic law.

Thirdly, the laws of 12–26 have been provided with a redactional framework which has traditionally been characterized as centralization. It has long been noticed that the demand to worship Yahweh only 'in one place which he chose to let his name dwell' (12.5), is limited to a few chapters and additions (12.1ff.; 12.20ff.; 14.22ff., etc.), In my judgment, Welch made out a strong case that many of the laws of Deuteronomy originally functioned without a concept of cult centralization. He felt that originally the theological emphasis fell on the purity of Israel's worship rather than its unity. Be that as it may, the stress of ch. 12 on centralization as a means for both the unity and the purity of Israel's worship now functions as a prism through which the whole legal collection is viewed. In spite of the relatively late entry of centralization into the Deuteronomic corpus, the demand for purity of worship by means of centralization has been expanded into a major force within the canonical shape of the book.

Chapters 27–30

The long history of composition is again evident in the tensions within these chapters and a carefully structured literary unity certainly fails (cf. Fohrer, *Introduction*, 172). Chapter 27 is often thought to interrupt an original connection between 26 and 28 and disturb the logical blessing-and-cursing sequence. But these chapters do form a fitting conclusion to the laws of 12–26 by setting forth obedience to this divine law in terms of life and death (30.15). That these chapters reflect liturgical elements from an original covenant ceremony is certainly possible, but difficult to demonstrate. The present function of the chapters is to evoke an obedient response to the completed law from the generation who would enter the land. To that end Moses re-establishes the covenant with them in Moab on that day (29.11), and confirms the promise made to the fathers. But in the act of renewing the covenant with the 'second generation' Moses includes in the actualization, not only the new generation, but all future generations as well (29.14).

Chapters 31–34

Although these final chapters are often dismissed as a miscellaneous collection of unrelated passages, they constitute in fact an important example of canonical shaping of the final form of ancient tradition. Because critical attention has focused mainly on recovering the original setting of the poems (cf. Cross and Freedman; Wright), the basic theological function of this final section in relation to the book as a whole has been largely overlooked.

Chapter 31 provides a definite shift from the context of Moses' delivering an address to the people which has characterized the book so far. Now Moses enters into a series of actions. He ends his sermon, fixes it in written form (31.9), commissions Joshua as his successor, and deposits the law beside the ark. Moreover, he establishes a routine for the law to be read at set periods in order that the succeeding generations may hear and do the law (31.12). This written law is to function as a witness against future generations who rebel. Indeed, according to 31.20ff. Moses actually reckons with the certain disobedience of the succeeding generation. In line with this thought ch. 31 introduces the 'Song of Moses' which he teaches the people as a testimony against their future disobedience.

It has long been evident that ch. 32 has undergone a lengthy period of independent existence and only secondarily has been given its present context in relation to ch. 31. Still little attention has been paid to its new role in this final form. From a canonical perspective this question is crucial. The poem contrasts the unchangeable fidelity of God with the perversity of his faithless people. Moses is portrayed as offering a prophetic understanding of history in poetic dress which encompasses both past, present, and future. The song is addressed not to the contemporaries of Moses, but to later disobedient Israel, lying under the judgment of God. The great acts of redemption under Moses are described as belonging to the far distant past (32.7), and viewed from the perspective of the 'latter days' (31.29).

The significance of this new context in which the song now functions lies in the effect it generates on the interpretation of the previous legislation of the book. Chapter 32 confronts future, disobedient Israel with the same imperatives of the covenant God, but provides a hermeneutical key by which to understand the Mosaic law in the age of disobedience. Once again, the canonical setting addresses the issue of actualization directly. However, the move is not to 'update' the laws to meet the new situation. Rather, a theological judgment is offered regarding the nature of the covenant God – he remains faithful to his promise – and the implications are drawn for the people of God.

Chapter 33, the blessings of Moses, is similar to ch. 32 in also participating in a long period of independent life before assuming its present role within the book of Deuteronomy. However, the poem brings no exhortation or warnings, but simply offers an invocation of blessing for the future. The perspective is again prophetic in which Moses surveys the future of the nation, picking up the promises of Gen. 29, and seeing them fulfilled in a purely ideal manner. The poem begins with the glorious fact of the founding of the kingdom of God and concludes with reference to Yahweh as Israel's eternal refuge in whom his people find eternal salvation and hope. The poem ends by celebrating the good fortunes of a redeemed people.

The canonical function of ch. 33 serves to place the law fully within the perspective of divine sovereignty, shifting the focus from Israel's behaviour to God's ultimate purpose. The Mosaic legislation is thus subordinated to the overriding purpose of God for his people and the final eschatological realization of his will is attested to in spite of the nation's failure.

The final chapter of the book, ch. 34, brings the role of Moses to an end. Moses is allowed to view from afar the land promised to the fathers and about to be possessed. Joshua assumes the leadership and Moses' unique role as covenant mediator is evaluated. His significance is not to be perpetuated in a grave cult, but in the memory of his great deeds wrought for Israel through the power of God and now recorded in the law of Moses.

Peculiar features of the canonical stamp

A persistent problem in the history of Deuteronomic research is the widespread disagreement over the main purpose of the book. What was the reason for the book of Deuteronomy anyway? What was the purpose of its being written, how was it intended to be used, and by whom? To call it a law-book seems highly misleading, although it obviously contains law. Nor is it a programme with a clear historical focus, as has become evident from the failure to resolve the problem in terms of Josiah's reform. The various form-critical designations – last will, treaty form, homily – do not touch the heart of the problem, but describe isolated features of the text or address an early stage in the book's development. The inability to find a single focus has led some scholars, such as Hölscher, to suggest that the book is an ideal projection without any concrete historical roots. Although some of the examples of idealization are impressive, the theory as a whole is inadequate and distorts other historically conditioned features. Probably von Rad has wrestled hardest with this larger problem. Beginning in his 1929 dissertation he spoke of the 'atmosphere of the timeless' (p. 60), which hung over the book. Later he spoke of the book's 'Janus-like quality' which seemed to point in a priestly and cultic direction while at the same time exhibiting militaristic elements of nationalism.

It is my contention that most of the critical theories proposed for interpreting the purpose of the book have been based on some one correct observation, but have failed to do justice to the issue as a whole. Moreover, the major source of the problem lies in the failure to reckon with the canonical forces which emerged to shape the book in its role as authoritative literature of a community of faith. What were these forces and how did they affect the shape of Deuteronomy?

(a) First, there is an ideal, timeless quality about the book of Deuteronomy which moves against seeing in the book a specific historical programme. Certainly the problem of actualization has been an important factor in refashioning the material in this manner. It also provides the connection with the canon. The writer of Deuteronomy consciously relativizes the importance of chronological time when describing the new generation as being fully involved in the events of the past. By making every generation analogous to the generation at Sinai, the historical qualities of the people of God recede before an ideal of faith. Then again, the style of the writer to sermonize each concrete law and to address the will of the audience moves the point of the text out of the specific into the area of a moral principle. Nor does the existential note of the sermon – 'us, who are alive this day' (5.3) – work against this ideal quality, but simply ties down the imperative to the historicity of that moment.

However, it is crucial in properly evaluating this idealizing feature of the book to recognize that it did not arise out of whole cloth as a post-exilic projection which was devoid of all historical reality, but was part of a historical process of rendering ancient tradition accessible to future generations. Moreover, this idealizing tendency was restricted to a specific function in the portraying of faithful Israel and was therefore held in close check. As a result, many of the concrete historical elements of the tradition were left completely untouched in their original historical specificity. These concrete elements provide sufficient evidence to reject Hölscher's comprehensive theory of idealization.

(b) In spite of the timeless quality found in Deuteronomy, there is also a very definite eschatological movement within the book. It has remained a puzzlement to many how these seemingly mutually exclusive tendencies could coexist. Nevertheless, the category of promise and fulfilment is used as a major device by which to structure the diverse traditions into a unified address by Moses. Israel in the book of Deuteronomy stands on the banks of the Jordan about to enter the land of Canaan, a people caught in between the moment of election and realization. The promise of the land is still beyond reach. The rest from her enemies lies yet in the future. The required commitment demanded of the covenant people remains an unexecuted imperative. The theological force behind this eschatological perspective can be termed canonical in the sense that the traditions of the past have been wrenched from their mooring and made to provide a normative guide to successive generations of faithful Israel who anticipate the fulfilment of the covenant promise.

(c) Von Rad was the first to have clearly perceived that the book of Deuteronomy is dominated by a theological perspective which has forged divergent historical elements into one unifying principle. Deuteronomy speaks of one God, one people, and one revelation at Sinai. The laws of centralization of Israel's worship are actually only derived from this theology of purity which God demands from his people. Likewise the individuality of the twelve tribes has been subordinated to the overarching principle of the unity of the people of God. Yet it is a mistake to derive this dominant theological force from a private, individualistic notion of a given author. Such an explanation fails to reckon with the evidence of a long experience by the people with the material itself. In the history of the Deuteronomic tradition, which is reflected in the various layers of homiletical practice, the imperatives of the covenant appear to have left a mark even in the process of ordering and structuring the tradition itself. By its long use as an authoritative word of God the principle of theological unification gained a dominant role in shaping the book.

(d) Finally, a major canonical force in the shaping of Deuteronomy derived from the fixing of the Mosaic law in book form. A major contribution of Perlitt has been to describe a level of redaction which grounded Israel's existence in a collection of written scripture and not in a recurring covenant ceremony. In fact, von Rad also made explicit mention of the beginning of a canon consciousness in Deuteronomy's understanding of the law as contained in a fixed body of writing (*Theology* I, 189).

However, this correct literary analysis of a redactional influence on Deuteronomy is usually judged by scholars to be a breakdown of genuine Deuteronomic theology which was thought to be originally flexible and dynamic. Surely this evaluation seriously misses the mark. Rather, the fixing of the shape of Deuteronomy in a written form arose from a theological concern to guard the shape of the tradition which had assumed a normative role within the community's life and on whose authority faith was grounded. It did not destroy, but rather helped to maintain the richness of the tradition, but in such a way as to allow the Mosaic law to be mediated for successive generations who had no direct access to Sinai.

3. Theological and Hermeneutical Implications

The great importance of the canonical role of Deuteronomy lies in its providing the hermeneutical key for understanding the law of Moses, that is to say, the Pentateuch, in its role as the sacred scripture of Israel. Using the form of an address, Moses is portrayed as explaining the divine will to a new generation which had not itself experienced the formative events of its religious history. Deuteronomy, therefore, serves as a commentary on how future generations are to approach the law and it functions as a guide in establishing its canonical role. The book instructs future Israel on the manner in which past tradition is properly made alive in fresh commitment to the God of the covenant.

First, Deuteronomy emphasizes that God's covenant is not tied to past history, but is still offered to all the people. The continuity of the covenant relationship is in no way weakened by the passing of time, but in the act of commitment Israel of every age partakes of the selfsame event of Sinai.

Secondly, the promise of God to his people still lies in the future. Israel's existence is characterized by an election, but this only can anticipate in faith the possession of her heritage.

Thirdly, Deuteronomy teaches that the law demands a response of commitment. The writer of the book strives to inculcate the law into the will of his people. The purpose of God remains a dynamic imperative which evokes an active choice in order to share in the living tradition of God's people.

Finally, the ability to summarize the law in terms of loving God with heart, soul and mind is a major check against all forms of legalism. The Mosaic law testifies to the living will of God whose eternal purpose for the life of his people offers the only grounds for hope and salvation.

History of Exegesis

Carpzov I, 144f.; *DThC* 4, 664–672; *EB* 2, 618; *RGG*³ 2, 103.

J.-P. **Bouhot**, 'Pentateuque chez les Pères', *DBS* 7, 687–707; H. **Cazelles**, 'Pentateuque, II. L'Époque médiévale', *DBS* 7, 708–28; J. **Daniélou**, 'Das Leben, das am Holze hängt. Dt. 28,66 in der altchristlichen Katechese', *Kirche und Überlieferung. FS J. R. Geiselmann*, Freiburg 1960, 22–34; S. **Maybaum**, *Die ältesten Phasen in der Entwicklung der jüdischen Predigt*, Berlin 1901, 42ff.

PART THREE

THE FORMER PROPHETS

XI

INTRODUCTION TO THE FORMER PROPHETS

Bibliography

E. **Auerbach**, 'Die grosse Überarbeitung des biblischen Bücher', *SVT* 1, 1953, 1–10; R. **Bach**, 'Deuteronomistischen Geschichtswerk', *RGG*³ 2, 100f.; W. **Brueggemann**, 'The Kerygma of the Deuteronomistic Historian', *Interp* 22, 1968, 387–402; F. M. **Cross**, 'The Structure of Deuteronomic History', *Canaanite Myth and Hebrew Epic*, Cambridge, Mass. 1973, 274–89; W. **Dietrich**, *Prophetie und Geschichte. Eine redaktionsgeschichtliche Untersuchung zum deuteronomistischen Geschichtswerk*, FRLANT 108, 1972; O. **Eissfeldt**, *The Old Testament. An Introduction*, Oxford and New York 1965, 241–8; G. **Fohrer**, *Introduction to the Old Testament*, Nashville 1968, London 1970, 192–5; D. N. **Freedman**, 'Pentateuch', *IDB* 3, 711–27; 'Deuteronomic History', *IDB Suppl*, 226–8; E. **Jenni**, 'Zwei Jahrzehnte Forschung an den Büchern Josua bis Könige', *ThR* 27, 1961, 1–32, 98–146; A. **Jepsen**, *Die Quellen des Königsbuches*, Halle 1953, ²1956; O. **Kaiser**, *Introduction to the Old Testament*, ET Oxford and Minneapolis 1975, 168–75; N. **Lohfink**, 'Bilanz nach der Katastrophe: Das deuteronomistische Geschichtswerk', *Wort und Botschaft*, ed. J. Schreiner, Würzburg 1967, 196–208; E. W. **Nicholson**, *Deuteronomy and Tradition*, Oxford and Philadelphia 1967, 107ff.; *Preaching to the Exiles*, Oxford and New York 1970; M. **Noth**, *Uberlieferungsgeschichtliche Studien* I, Halle 1943; L. **Perlitt**, *Bundestheologie im Alten Testament*, WMANT 26, 1969, 54–128; O. **Plöger**, 'Reden und Gebete im deuteronomistischen und chronistischen Geschichtswerk', *Aus der Spätzeit des Alten Testaments*, Göttingen 1971, 50–66; G. **von Rad**, *Studies in Deuteronomy*, ET, SBT I.9, London 1953; A. N. **Radjawane**, 'Das deuteronomistische Geschichtswerk. Ein Forschungsbericht', *ThR* NS 38, 1973–4, 177–216; M. **Rose**, *Der Ausschliesslichkeitsanspruch Jahwes. Deuteronomische Schultheologie und die Volksfrömmigkeit in der späten Königszeit*, BWANT VI.6 (=106), 1975; G. **Sauer**, 'Die chronologischen Angaben in den Büchern Deut. bis 2 Könige', *TZ* 24, 1968, 1–14; R. **Smend**, 'Das Gesetz und die Völker', *Probleme biblischer Theologie, FS G. von Rad*, Munich 1971, 494ff.; J. A. **Soggin**, 'Deuteronomistische Geschichtsauslegung während des babylonischen Exils', *Oikonomia. FS O. Cullmann*, Hamburg 1966, 11–17; H. W. **Wolff**, 'Das Kerygma des deuteronomistischen Geschichtswerkes', *ZAW* 73, 1961, 171–86=*GSAT*, 308ff.; E. **Zenger**, 'Die deuteronomistische Interpretation der Rehabilitierung Jejachins', *BZ* 12, 1968, 16–30.

1. Introduction to the Historical Critical Problems

The traditional terminology of the Hebrew Bible included the books of Joshua, Judges, Samuel, and Kings within the second part of the Hebrew canon, which was designated 'Prophets' (*nᵉbî'îm*). That this division was at least as early as the Hellenistic period is testified to by the Prologue to the book of Sirach, and by Josephus, Philo, and the New Testament (cf. ch. II). The further traditional canonical division within the Prophets of the 'former' (*ri'šônîm*) and 'later' (*'aḥᵃrônîm*) distinguished the first four historical books from the prophetic books of Isaiah, Jeremiah, Ezekiel, and the Twelve. This terminology first emerged in the Middle Ages (cf. Sotah 48b). However, the two references in Zechariah to the 'former prophets' (1.4; 7.7) offer a certain biblical warrant for the later terminology.

Modern historical criticism has been almost unanimous in rejecting the traditional division of the Former Prophets as being of little value. Driver (*Introduction*⁹, 106) characterizes it as 'artificial'. Eissfeldt (242) regards the division as 'very imperfect'. In the place of the traditional division two major critical theories have been substituted to explain the composition of these historical books. The first theory, entitled the 'documentary' by Eissfeldt, assumes that sources similar to those found in the Pentateuch continue through at least part of the historical books. Basic to this analysis is seeing the book of Joshua in close connection with the first five books to form a Hexateuch. The second theory, entitled the 'fragment' hypothesis by Eissfeldt, arises from an analysis of M. Noth. It envisions an independent historical work consisting of the book of Deuteronomy and the four histories which a compiler, designated the Deuteronomistic historian (Dtr.), edited during the exilic period. Because Noth regarded Deuteronomy as the introduction to this historical work, the traditional Pentateuchal division is reduced to a Tetrateuch.

It is appropriate to examine these two rival critical theories in more detail in order to point out both the strengths and weaknesses. The first theory, which envisions sources forming a Hexateuch, supports its case by showing the strong lines of continuity between the promises of the land in the Pentateuch and its fulfilment in Joshua. The theory argues that the Pentateuch remains a torso without the concluding chapter which the book of Joshua supplies. The explicit correspondence between such commands as that in Deut. 27 to erect an altar in the land and their erection is closely observed in Josh. 8. Again, the parallel passages and duplicates found especially in Joshua and Judges appear to confirm the theory of literary strands which have been joined together much like those of the Pentateuch.

Nevertheless there remain several major problems in the successfull application of this theory. First of all, no consensus as to the specific nature and scope of the sources has emerged, not even concerning such a basic issue as the presence of the same Pentateuchal sources. Even more serious, the theory does not adequately explain the particular redactional influence of Deuteronomy on the material. If there were a unit such as a Hexateuch, it is difficult to imagine why there is so little trace of Deuteronomic influence on the first four books, and such a very strong one on the final book. Moreover, the obvious relation between Joshua and the later histories is thereby severed.

The second theory of a Deuteronomistic historical work was first proposed by Noth, and has subsequently received wide support from many other scholars. (A somewhat similar theory was developed by Jepsen independently of Noth, but his results were delayed in publication until 1953.) Several strengths of Noth's hypothesis are soon apparent. The theory of one Dtr. author does full justice to the strong Deuteronomic influence which extends through all four historical books, but is almost entirely missing in the earlier narrative material of the Pentateuch. Again, the theory offers an illuminating explanation of the multiple introductions in Deuteronomy and why Joshua is so dependent on what precedes it. Finally, the theory of a compilation of bundles of fragments rather than of continuous strands often appears to explain the historical development in a simpler fashion.

However, this second theory is also not without its difficulties as its major critics have continued to point out (Eissfeldt, Weiser, Fohrer). First of all, the removal of the book of Deuteronomy from the Pentateuch leaves a torso-like composition which has never been fully justified. Freedman (*IDB* 3, 717f.) speaks of two overlapping works. Then again, Noth's description of the Dtr. historical work as the unified composition of one author seems to have over-emphasized the Deuteronomic influence on these books as a whole. The tremendous variety within the historical books is not adequately explained by Noth's theory of a single sixth-century compilation, in spite of his appeal to different traditions underlying the composition. These problems have called forth several attempts to modify Noth's original theory by positing a number of different stages of Dtr. redaction (Cross). Finally, Noth's basically negative understanding of the purpose of the Dtr. author in composing his work has not evoked much agreement. As a result, many have sought to supplement or alter Noth's position by proposing a much more positive role for the composition in the life of Israel (Wolff, Cross).

One of the most noticeable effects of this impasse in the scholarly discussion of the Former Prophets has been the speculative nature of much of the exegesis on these books. In fact, Eissfeldt (247) concludes his discussion by admitting that much of the analysis which followed must remain 'largely of a hypothetical character', and would be greatly influenced by which of the theories of composition was accepted. In the light of this unfortunate effect a re-examination of the canonical shape of the Former Prophets is called for.

2. The Canonical Shape of the Former Prophets

The first major problem to be faced is the observation which has evoked much of the controversy in the critical study of the Former Prophets, namely, there is both a close connection with the early books, and yet a distinct separation from the Pentateuch. In my judgment, neither of the current theories of composition have succeeded because neither has taken seriously the task of describing the present canonical shape of the collection.

First of all, in the final form of the Hebrew Bible the first five books have been clearly separated from the subsequent history as a Pentateuch (cf. ch. V). Even though there are signs indicating that the division was of post-exilic origin and that it ran counter to an earlier ordering of the tradition which extended the sequence from

creation to the conquest (cf. Sanders, *Torah and Canon*) the final
shape of the Hebrew canon is unambiguous in maintaining the
literary integrity of the Pentateuch. The canon does not recognize
either a Hexateuch or a Tetrateuch. In the earlier chapter on the
book of Deuteronomy, we sought to draw out the full historical and
theological implications of this move. Deuteronomy performed a
critical canonical function, both in its authoritative reinterpretation
of the first four books as Torah and also in its effect on the subsequent historical books.

Although the strong lines of continuity between the Pentateuch
and Joshua are clear, the decisive factor to recognize is how the
canon established the relationship. Joshua is clearly dependent on
the laws of Deuteronomy, but Noth's understanding of this dependency fails to reckon with the new canonical role of Deuteronomy
within the Pentateuch. The book of Joshua does not function simply as an extension of the book of Deuteronomy. Rather, Joshua
cites Deuteronomy in its canonical form as the 'Book of the Torah'
(*sēper hattôrāh*). Moreover, within the canon Deuteronomy is never
assigned an integrity all its own apart from the laws of Exodus.
This means that Joshua's references to Deuteronomy includes the
entire law which is now encompassed within the Pentateuch.
Indeed, Freedman (*IDB* 3, 717) registers an important point
against Noth's view of the Dtr. history in stressing that this history
assumed a period from the creation of the world and did not just
begin with Moses. What Freedman failed to consider was the
canonical shaping which encompasses the larger historical perspective.

In the last chapters of Deuteronomy Moses is commanded to
write the 'words of the law in a book' (31.24) which book is to be
placed beside the ark. The significance of this act does not lie in
determining the exact limits of the writing, which is nowhere
clearly revealed, but in the new authoritative role which the written
form of the Torah now performs. Crucial for understanding the
place of Joshua in relation to the Pentateuch is to observe the
central position assigned to the Book of the Law (cf. 1.8; 4.10; 8.3,
32, 35, etc.). Joshua assumed the leadership of the nation in the
place of Moses, but his role was not a continuation of the Mosaic
office. Rather, he was dependent upon carrying out the divine law
which had not only been revealed to Moses, but which was
recorded in a book for future generations.

In sum, the canonical shape of Joshua in relation to the Pentateuch explains both the elements of continuity and discontinuity which critical scholarship has observed. The book of Joshua is sharply separated from the Pentateuch, and the Pentateuch's role as the written form of the law is stressed. Yet Joshua is closely connected to the Pentateuch by its dependence on the 'Book of the Law' and forms the introduction to a continuing story in the Former Prophets.

There is a second problem in understanding the shape of the Former Prophets from a canonical perspective which turns on the relation of Joshua to the other historical books. One of the most attractive features of Noth's theory of a Dtr. historical work is his recognition of the strong ties connecting the four historical books, which had been de-emphasized in the 'documentary' theory of a Hexateuch. Noth has mounted an impressive case for a post-exilic redaction of the four historical books from a Deuteronomic perspective. In my opinion, the effect of this complex historical process on the final canonical shape has not been adequately assessed by Noth.

The history of the nation from its conquest of the land to its destruction by the Babylonians is now arranged according to a clear literary pattern of prophecy and fulfilment. Even before the entrance into the land the consequences of disobedience to the divine law recorded by Moses were rehearsed in detail before the people (Deut. 28). The culmination of disobedience was explicitly described as being 'plucked off the land' and 'scattered among all peoples' (vv.63f.). The editorial shaping of the books which follow offers a theological interpretation of Israel's history in terms of the working out of the stipulations of the Book of the Law. Not only is the correspondence between the prophecy and fulfilment continually made clear, but at crucial points in the history long 'Deuteronomic' speeches are inserted, which interpret theologically the course of Israel's history in the light of the Book of the Law (Deut. 27f.; Josh. 1.2ff.; 22.1ff.; Judg. 2.6ff.; I Sam. 12; I Kings 8; II Kings 17 and 24).

A characteristic feature of the canonical shape is its insistence on viewing the actual historical occurrences of the sixth century from the perspective of the Book of the Law, which each successive generation of prophets reiterates to the nation. In order to assure that the exile is understood theologically as stemming from Israel's disobedience of the law, an exact correspondence of prophecy and fulfilment is established. What Noth interpreted as a sixth-century redaction by an exilic editor, from a canonical perspective is the final stage in a process of shaping the biblical text to bear witness to the inevitable working out of the prophetic word. The unique feature of the canonical interpretation is its using the actual events of the sixth century to provide a theological framework for the entire prophetic history, and thus obscuring the historical dimension in the development of the final shape of the text which the redactional criticism of Noth sought to recover. The effect of the canonical reading has been to encompass Israel's history within a theological interpretation without any concern for preserving the historical stages in the complex development of the literature.

There is an additional aspect of the canonical shape of the Former Prophets which is crucial in understanding the function of the material. The issue turns about the extent to which the diversity of the tradition was allowed to retain its original autonomy within the theological framework of the final redaction. In his effort to stress the unity of a Dtr. historical work Noth has emphasized the role of the compiler of the tradition as having the freedom of an 'author', who fashioned a new creation apart from any inherited structure. He has also stressed the non-official character of this redaction, assigning the Dtr. theology to the author's own private concept of history.

In my judgment, this assessment of the role of the Dtr. redactor does justice neither to the intention of the final editor, nor to the effect on the text which he left in stamping the tradition. The most characteristic feature of the Dtr. redaction is the tremendous diversity of material left within the Former Prophets. It is this observation which has caused scholars such as Weiser and Fohrer to contest Noth's theory of a unified Dtr. historical work. The major point to be made is that the overarching theological categories which unite the four historical books did not function in such a way as to flatten or seriously to alter the earlier stages of the material's development. Within its final shape the material was allowed to reflect an independent integrity which it had achieved from an earlier stage of its prehistory. For this reason there are enormous differences in tradition, institutional setting, and literary genres separating Joshua from Judges, and Samuel from Kings.

In its present canonical shape there is no evidence that the ma-

terial was transformed in such a way as to make only one major
'Deuteronomic' point. Rather, so much independence has been
allowed the material that no one clear-cut option emerges as to how
certain sections were to be understood within the broad framework.
For example, it is not obvious how the so-called 'pro-monarchial'
material in I Samuel relates to the general theology of the Davidic
kingdom in Israel.

The implications of this situation would further call into question
Noth's characterization of the Dtr. editor as exercising a private
disposition in his composition. A far more plausible explanation
would be to assume that the material which the final redactor
gathered and shaped had already exerted such an 'official' force on
the community by its use that he was unable or unwilling to
attempt a change. Far from being an idiosyncratic opinion of one
author, the shaping of the Former Prophets reflects a long process
within the community of Israel which incorporated the witness of
many earlier generations and thus acknowledged the authority
which previous stages of the literature had already exerted through
use.

3. Theological and Hermeneutical Implications

(a) Within the Hebrew canon the four historical books belong
within the division of the Prophets. The significance of this
classification lies in the canon's assessment of the nature of these
historical records. The object of this biblical witness is not to record
history per se – whatever that might be – but to bear testimony to
the working out of the prophetic word in the life of the nation. One
of the clearest indications that the canon regarded the prophetic
quality of these historical books to be of the same order as that of
the Latter Prophets appears in the frequent and wholesale incorpo-
ration of the historical material within the books of the prophets (cf.
Isa. 36–39// II Kings 18–20; Jer. 40.7–9// II Kings 25.23–26; Jer.
50.31–34// II Kings 25.27–30; Jer. 52.1ff.// II Kings 24.18ff.). A
similar theological purpose of both sets of writings within the division of the Prophets is confirmed. Thus the canonical shape lays
claim to a particular theological function for these books and is
critical of an exegetical stance which would use the historical books
only as 'sources' of other information. This assertion is not to deny
that the historical books can serve this function in a fully legitimate

fashion in certain contexts. But this non-canonical use cannot be allowed to overlook the particular canonical function to which the material has been assigned within the canonical collection.

(*b*) One of the striking features of the Former Prophets is the highly selective nature of the material which has been preserved. Certain periods of history have been dealt with in great detail (e.g. the rise of the kingdom in I Sam. 7ff.), whereas others have been hastily passed over or omitted entirely (e.g. Omri gets only a few lines, I Kings 16). Or again, strikingly different perspectives on the same period of Israel's history have been preserved. One implication to be drawn from this feature is that certain epochs were chosen because of their crucial theological significance. An even more important factor than the selection of particular periods was the manner in which the history was presented. Thus, the book of Joshua pictures obedient Israel taking full possession of the land in fulfilment of the divine promise (21.43), whereas Judges make quite a different point in viewing the failure to dislodge the Canaanites as the result of disobedience. By viewing this material as the canonical history of the prophetic word one is thereby cautioned against assuming the subject matter to be a simple – or even crude – form of history which is better reconstructed by means of modern scientific methods. By supposing that the function of the biblical witness is only meaningful in a referential sense, the selectivity and peculiar stance of the Bible is thereby judged deficient and needful of correction. Such a hermeneutical move fails to take seriously the canonical role of the Former Prophets and seriously jeopardizes the ability to hear the text on its own terms.

(*c*) Modern critical scholarship has continued to disagree on the overall purpose of the Deuteronomic shaping of the Former Prophets. Noth's well-known thesis that the purpose was largely a negative one to explain the destruction of the nation has met with little support. It is hard to imagine a negative cause as sufficient reason to compose and preserve the tradition. Von Rad sought to find a positive reason in the messianic hope which he found in the freeing of Jehoiachin from prison (II Kings 25.27ff.). Finally, Frank Cross argued that the original purpose of Dtr. was to outline a reform programme under Josiah's reign which later was rather clumsily modified in the light of Josiah's untimely death and the ensuing débâcle.

All these hypotheses have in common an attempt to explain the author's purpose in terms of a reconstructed political factor by means of which a concrete historical referent for focusing the book's concern is supplied. In my judgment, H. W. Wolff's interpretation has been closer to recovering the function of the canonical text. He tries to show that the book's rehearsing of the history of the destruction of the nation has the pattern of divine judgment and forgiveness built into it in such a way as to offer to the nation under judgment a renewed promise of forgiveness. In sum, the book has not been redacted primarily to offer an explanation of the past, but to function as scripture for the new generation of Israel who are instructed from the past for the sake of the future. Deut. 29.29 (Heb. v. 28) offers a classic formulation of this canonical principle: '. . . the things that are revealed belong to us and to our children for ever, that we may do all the words of this law.'

XII

JOSHUA

Commentaries

C. F. Keil, BC, 1857
A. Dillmann, KeH, ²1886
G. A. Cooke, CB, 1913
H. Gressmann, *SAT*, ²1922
C. Steuernagel, HKAT, ²1923
J. Garstang, 1931
A. Fernández, CSS, 1938
A. Gelin, SB, 1949
H. Freedman, SonB, 1950

H. W. Hertzberg, ATD, ²1952
M. Noth, HAT, ²1953
J. Bright, *IB*, 1953
Y. Kaufmann, 1959
J. Gray, NCeB, 1967
J. A. Soggin, ET, OTL, 1972
J. M. Miller, G. M. Tucker, CNEB, 1974

Bibliography

Y. **Aharoni**, 'Problems of the Israelite Conquest in the Light of Archaeological Discoveries', *Antiquity and Survival* 2, The Hague 1957, 131–50; 'The Province-List of Judah', *VT* 9, 1959, 225–46; W. F. **Albright**, 'Archaeology and the Date of the Hebrew Conquest of Palestine', *BASOR* 58, 1935, 10–18; 'The Israelite Conquest of Canaan in the Light of Archaeology', *BASOR* 74, 1939, 11–23; 'The List of Levitic Cities', *L. Ginzberg Jubilee Volume*, New York 1945, 49–73; B. J. **Alfrink**, 'Het "stil staan" van zon en maan in Jos x, 12–15', *Studia Catholica* 24, Nijmegen 1949, 238–69; A. **Alt**, *Die Landnahme der Israeliten in Palästina. Territorialgeschichtliche Studien*, Leipzig 1925; reprinted in *KS* I, 1953, 89–125; ET *Essays* (see Pentateuch), 133–69; 'Judas Gaue unter Josia', *PJB* 21, 1925, 100–16=*KS* II, 1953, 276–88; 'Das System der Stammesgrenzen im Buche Josua', *FS E. Sellin*, Leipzig 1927, 13–24=*KS* I, 1953, 193–202; 'Josua', in BZAW 66, 1936, 13–29=*KS* I, 1953, 176–92; O. **Bächli**, 'Von der Liste, zur Beschreibung, Beobachtungen und Erwägungen zu Jos. 13–19', *ZDPV* 89, 1973, 1–14; J. **Bright**, *Early Israel in Recent History Writing*, SBT I.19, 1959; K. **Budde**, 'Richter und Josua', *ZAW* 7, 1887, 93–166.

B. S. **Childs**, 'A Study of the Formula "Until this day"', *JBL* 82, 1963, 279–92; F. M. **Cross** and G. E. **Wright**, 'The Boundary and Province Lists of the Kingdom of Judah', *JBL* 75, 1956, 202–26; O. **Eissfeldt**, 'Die Eroberung Palästinas durch Altisrael', *KS* III, 1966, 367–83; V. **Fritz**, 'Die sogenannte Liste der besiegten Könige in Josua 12', *ZDPV* 85, 1969, 136–61; 'Das Ende der spätbronzezeitlichen Stadt Hazor Stratum XIII und die biblische Überlieferung in Josua 11 und Richter 4', *UF* 5, 1973, 123–39; K. **Galling**, 'Der Beichtspiegel', *ZAW* 47, 1929, 125–30; B. **Goff**, 'The Lost Jahwistic Account of the Conquest of Canaan', *JBL* 53, 1934, 24–9; N. K. **Gottwald**, 'Were the Early Israelites Pastoral Nomads?', in *Rhetorical Criticism: Essays in Honor of James Muilenburg*, Pittsburg 1974, 223–55; M. J. **Gruenthaner**, 'Two Sun Miracles of the Old Testament', *CBQ* 10, 1948, 271–90; J. **Halbe**, 'Gibeon und Israel', *VT* 25, 1975, 613–41; E. **Jenni**, 'Zwei Jahrzehnte Forschung an den Büchern Josua bis Könige', *ThR* NF 27, 1961, 118–29; Z. **Kallai-Kleinmann**, 'The Town Lists of Judah, Simeon, Benjamin and Dan', *VT* 13, 1958, 134–60; Y. **Kaufmann**, *The Biblical Account of the Conquest of Palestine*, Jerusalem 1953; H.-J. **Kraus**, 'Gilgal – ein Beitrag zur Kultusgeschichte Israels', *VT* 1, 1951, 181–99; F. **Langlamet**, *Gilgal et les récits de la traverseé du Jourdain*, Paris 1969; 'Josué, II et les traditions de l'Hexateuque', *RB* 78, 1971, 5–17, 161–83, 321–54; J. **L'Hour**, 'L'Alliance de Sichem', *RB* 69, 1962, 5–36, 161–84, 350–68; N. **Lohfink**, 'Die deuteronomistische Darstellung des Übergangs der Führung Israels von Moses auf Josue', *Scholastik* 37, Freiburg 1962, 32–44.

B. **Mazar**, 'The Cities of the Priests and Levites', *SVT* 7, 1960, 193–205; D. J. **McCarthy**, 'The Theology of Leadership in Joshua 1–9', *Bibl* 52, 1971, 165–75; G. E. **Mendenhall**, 'The Hebrew Conquest of Palestine', *BA* 35, 1962, 66–87; *The Tenth Generation*, Baltimore and London 1973; J. M. **Miller**, 'Joshua, Book of', *IDB Suppl*, 493–96; 'The Israelite Occupation of Canaan', *Israelite and Judaean History*, ed. J. H. Hayes and J. M. Miller, OTL, 1977, 213–84; K. **Möhlenbrink**, 'Die Landnahmesagen des Buches Josua', *ZAW* 56, 1938, 238–68; S. **Mowinckel**, *Zur Frage nach dokumentarischen Quellen in Josua 13–19*, Oslo 1946; *Tetrateuch-Pentateuch-Hexateuch*, Berlin 1964; M. **Noth**, *Das System der zwölf Stamme Israels*, BWANT IV. 1 (=52), 1930; 'Studien zu den historisch-geographischen Dokumenten des Josuabuches', *ZDPV* 58, 1935, 185–255 = *Aufsätze* I, 1971, 229–80; 'Bethel und Ai', *PJB* 31, 1935, 7–29; *Überlieferungsgeschichtliche Studien* I, Halle 1943, 40–47, 182–90; 'Überlieferungsgeschichtliches zur zweiten Hälfte des Josuabuches', *FS F. Nötscher*, BBB 1, 1950, 152–67; L. **Perlitt**, *Bundestheologie im Alten Testament*, WMANT 36, 239–84; H. H. **Rowley**, *From Joseph to Joshua*, London and New York 1950; J. F. A. **Sawyer**, 'Joshua 10:12–14 and the Solar Eclipse of 30 September 1131 BC', *PEQ* 104, 1972, 139–46; P. P. **Saydon**, 'The Crossing of the Jordan, Jos. chaps. 3 and 4', *CBQ* 12, 1950, 194–207; H. **Schmid**, 'Erwägungen zur Gestalt Josuas in Überlieferung und Geschichte', *Jud* 24, 1968, 44ff.;

K.-D. **Schunck**, *Benjamin. Untersuchungen zur Entstehung und Geschichte eines israelitischen Stammes*, BZAW 86, 1963.
G. M. **Tucker**, 'The Rahab Saga (Joshua 2): Some Form-Critical and Traditio-Historical Observations', *The Use of the Old Testament in the New and Other Essays. FS W. F. Stinespring*, Durham, N.C. 1972, 66–86; R. **de Vaux**, *The Early History of Israel* II, ET London and Philadelphia 1978; W. **Vischer**, 'Das Buch Josua', *Das Christuszeugnis des Alten Testaments* II, Zürich ²1946, 5–63; E. **Vogt**, 'Die Erzählung vom Jordanübergang, Josue 3–4', *Bibl* 46, 1965, 125–48; M. **Weippert**, *The Settlement of the Israelite Tribes in Palestine*, ET, SBT II.21, 1971; 'Das geographische System des Stamme Israel', *VT* 23, 1973, 76–89; G. J. **Wenham**, 'The Deuteronomic Theology of the Book of Joshua', *JBL* 90, 1971, 140–48; J. A. **Wilcoxen**, 'Narrative Structure and Cult Legend: A Study of Joshua 1–6', *Transitions in Biblical Scholarship*, ed. J. C. Rylaarsdam, Chicago and London 1968, 43–70; G. E. **Wright**, 'Epic of Conquest', *BA* 3, 1940, 25–40; 'The Literary and Historical Problems of Joshua 10 and Judges 1', *JNES* 5, 1946, 105–14.

1. Historical Critical Problems

In the preceding chapter some of the problems of relating Joshua to the Pentateuch have already been discussed. The aim of this chapter will be, therefore, to concentrate on specific issues within the book of Joshua itself, although some repetition cannot be fully avoided.

Many of the major critical problems of Joshua had already been adumbrated by A. Masius (1574), and emerged with sharp clarity in Eichhorn's *Einleitung*. Thus, he noticed apparent anachronisms (9.23), events occurring after the death of Joshua (Josh. 19.47// Judg. 18.1), later historical perspectives (15.15), and the lack of chronological order. Although conservative scholars sought to reconcile the difficulties (Carpzov, Jahn) and to defend the traditional view of the authorship of Joshua, by the middle of the nineteenth century even so staunch a conservative as Keil had abandoned this position, while still maintaining the book's unity and antiquity. By the last half of the nineteenth century critical scholars were assuming a long history of literary development behind the book and concentrating their efforts on tracing the steps of this prehistory in detail.

Chapters 1–12

Among modern scholars two somewhat different critical approaches to the first twelve chapters of Joshua have emerged. The first emphasizes a literary critical approach, and is represented by Eissfeldt and Fohrer. The second stresses a traditio-critical approach, and is advocated by Alt, Noth, and a large number of younger scholars (Kaiser, Soggin).

The literary critical approach is characterized by its attempt to see the first twelve chapters of Joshua as consisting of numerous literary strands, many of which are continuations from the preceding books, and hence constitute a Hexateuch. Although there remains considerable disagreement in the designating of the sources, some major features are held in common by supporters of the literary approach. It is maintained that the earliest literary account of the conquest is now found in Judg. 1.1–2.5 with only a few fragments of this account distributed throughout the book of Joshua (Josh. 15.13–19; 15.63; 17.11–13, etc.). This earliest account, which was organized geographically to survey the results of the occupation, provided the basis for a second stage of development in which the tradition of conquest was arranged sequentially and expanded with local aetiological material either in the J source or a *Grundschrift*. Subsequently, the figure of Joshua, who was a local Benjamite hero, was introduced into the account. Thus, there emerged a pre-Deuteronomic stage which was made up of composite strands. The decisive shape of the present book was formed by a major Deuteronomic reworking of the older material, often seen in two distinct stages. Finally, a few traces of a priestly source were discovered.

The major critical alternative to this schema was first proposed by Alt (1926) and later developed by Noth in detail. First of all, Noth rejected the idea of literary sources from the Pentateuch continuing into the book of Joshua. Rather, he envisioned the book's developing from an ancient collection of aetiological sagas which once existed independently of each other, but were collected about Gilgal. About the year 900 the local figure of Joshua was joined with the cycle and united with the military stories of chs. 10–11 to form a national epic of the conquest of West Jordan. The Deuteronomic material was attributed to the redactional work of the Dtr. historian who placed the older material within his history.

In spite of the real differences between these two currently held critical positions regarding the composition of chs. 1–12, there are large areas of agreement which are as significant as the disagreements. Both critical positions hold that the present account of the conquest is a historical construct with no clear-cut relationship to the actual historical events, which is thought to be more accurately portrayed by Judges 1. Actually the role which one attributes to aetiology – whether of primary or secondary importance within the tradition (Childs) – affects the degree of historical value ascribed to the material more than does the choice of critical approach. Finally, the major influence of a Deuteronomic editor is recognized by both approaches while a minor role is assigned to the priestly writers whose contributions are relegated to homiletical expansions.

Chapters 13–21

Modern critical scholarship is also sharply divided on the assessment of the chapters dealing with the division of the land. The older literary critical approach assigned these chapters mainly to a priestly writer, although the presence of an earlier composite source was often admitted. Generally the position was defended that the tribal boundaries were a theoretical or ideal projection. Mowinckel placed the material in the genre of 'learned literature', which like the last chapters of Ezekiel sketched an ideal programme for the future. Even Kaufmann, who defended the antiquity of the tribal divisions, held them to be largely a theological projection.

More recently, chiefly from the impetus of Alt and Noth, a different assessment of these chapters has increasingly gained the ascendancy. Noth in particular rejected assigning these chapters to the late priestly writer, but argued that two documentary sources formed the basis of the division. The one consisted of a system of tribal boundaries with a list of points which established the borders of the tribal territories in the period of the Judges. The other consisted of a list of twelve administrative districts of Judah from the time of Josiah. In spite of Mowinckel's argument that such an ancient list could not have survived, most modern scholars have tended to regard the Alt-Noth approach as a genuine critical advance. At the same time numerous suggestions for modification of the original theory have been offered, especially by Israeli scholars who have assumed the leadership in this area of research (cf. Cross and Wright, Kallai-Kleinmann, Aharoni, etc.).

To summarize: although no clear consensus regarding details has emerged, modern critical scholarship is agreed that the present book of Joshua represents only the last stage of a long and involved prehistory involving both oral and literary development. The traditional view which assessed the book as simply a unified composition of Joshua has surely been proven erroneous. The presence of an extended history with resulting literary and historical tensions cannot be successfully denied.

However, the historical critical approach with its concentration on recovering the history of the tradition has failed to assess the canonical role of the book of Joshua. The issue of how the tradition was formed and what role was assigned to the various parts has not been adequately studied. Our attention will, therefore, focus on this set of problems.

2. The Canonical Shape of Joshua

The interpretative framework

Few would contest the assertion that the main purpose of the book of Joshua was to show the fulfilling of the promises to the fathers regarding the gift of the land (Deut. 30.20). Not only did Israel defeat its enemies, but its actual possession of the promised inheritance was demonstrated by the division among the twelve tribes. Joshua 23.14 summarizes this theme: 'not one thing has failed of all the good things which Yahweh your God promised concerning you . . . ' (cf. 21.45).

However, the unique element of the book of Joshua is the way in which the theological significance of the possession of the land has been developed. The material, which critical scholarship has usually termed Deuteronomic, serves the role within the final form of the book of offering an elaborate and highly reflective theological interpretation of the conquest of the land. This level of redaction, which in this instance is not the last one, forms the dominant shape of the book by encompassing the earlier traditions within a new framework (chs. 1;12;23) and also by frequent expansion of the earlier literary levels (chs. 8;11;24).

Chapter 1 begins the history with a programmatic statement to Moses' successor. Joshua is to assume leadership and carry out the task of securing the land promised to Moses. The period of the

conquest is carefully restricted to the period extending from the
death of Moses (Josh. 1.1) to the death of Joshua (Judg. 1.1). The
continuity between the leadership is confirmed by a reiteration of
the promise to Moses of God's continual presence (Deut. 11.25), as
well as by the extent of the land's boundaries (Deut. 11.23f.). The
events of the conquest are linked in a *heilsgeschichtliche* pattern to the
redemptive events of the past, the crossing of the Jordan being
paralleled with the crossing of the Red Sea (4.23f.). However, the
figure of Joshua, especially in the first eleven chapters, is often
consciously set in a typological relation to Moses. He commands
the people to sanctify themselves before the great event (3.5//Ex.
19.10); he instructs the priests (4.10); he is exalted before the
people like Moses (4.14); he encounters the commander of God's
army (5.13//Ex. 3.1ff.); he intercedes for sinful Israel (7.6ff.//
Deut.9.25); he gives his last will just before his death (23.1//
31.2ff.).

An even more important factor in shaping the book of Joshua is
the normative role which the law of Moses is assigned. The relationship of Joshua to the divine law is clearly a different one from
that of Moses, the lawgiver. Joshua is fully dependent on the law of
Moses which has assumed an authoritative role in its written form.
The '*sepher* Torah' is 'not to depart out of your mouth' (1.8). Joshua
reads the blessings and the curses 'according to the book of the law'
(8.34), and he cites the book of the law in his last testament (23.6).
Still the main point lies not in contrasting a written with an oral
form of the law – a sharp distinction was not maintained – but
rather in the normative role of a closed corpus of divine law which
was attributed to Moses.

The major force for structuring the narrative derived from
Joshua's obedience to the law of Moses. Joshua 1.8 sets out this
relationship as absolutely crucial for Israel's success. Obedience or
disobedience to the law determines the immediate test of success or
failure. Thus, Joshua reads the blessings and curses to the people
before Mounts Gerizim and Ebal (ch. 8) according to the explicit
command of Moses (Deut. 27.1ff.), and sets up the cities of refuge
according to his instruction (20.1ff.//Deut. 19.1ff.). The Anakim
are wiped out as promised (Josh. 11.21//Deut. 9.2), and the 'hor-
net' is sent to expel the enemy (24.12//Deut. 7.20). The phraseo-
logy of Deuteronomy is constantly cited to ensure the divine
promise: 'no man can withstand you' (Josh. 1.5//Deut. 11.25),

'God fights for Israel' (Josh. 10.14; 23.10; Deut. 3.22). In addition, older tradition from the pre-Deuteronomic stage is given a new framework in order to make explicit the confirmation of the promise of divine aid (5.13ff.; 10.14).

Conversely, the negative illustrations of disobedience and failure are closely patterned after the Deuteronomic formulation of the Mosaic law. The defeat at Ai (ch. 7) examplified the threat already envisioned in Deut. 12. Or again, the explicit danger of intermarriage which is sounded in Joshua's last warning (23.12) is patterned after Deut. 7.3. Then again, the great apprehension of the tribes over the altar which was constructed by the Jordan (ch. 22) arose out of fear that the statutes of Deut. 12 were being disregarded in an overt act of cultic apostasy.

Finally, the effect of the Deuteronomic redaction on the canonical shaping of the book of Joshua is most noticeable in the future-oriented focus of the blessing and cursing ritual. In ch. 8 the words of the law have been read. In 23.15 Joshua reiterates 'the evil things' which God will bring upon the disobedient nation. However, this theme reaches its climax in ch. 24 with a ceremony in which Israel bears witness against herself lest she disobey the God of the covenant. The Deuteronomic formulation of the curse picked up by Joshua reflects the language of exile from the land. Israel will be destroyed 'off this good land' (23.13, 15). God will 'consume you' (24.20; cf. 22.24). However, the specific Deuteronomic reference to 'scattering' (Deut. 4.27; 28.64; 30.3) does not occur in Joshua.

It has long been noticed by scholars that when the law of Moses is cited in the book of Joshua, it is from the book of Deuteronomy (8.31; 20.2–9). This evidence does not seem strange in the light of the important Deuteronomic redaction which we have just sketched. However, it is crucial to point out in this regard that the canonical form of Joshua does not assign an independent integrity to the book of Deuteronomy. In spite of the scholarly custom of speaking of the 'Deuteronomic writer' or the 'Deuteronomic law', this description plays no role whatever for the canonical editors. Rather, the Mosaic law is everywhere intended. That it is cited according to its Deuteronomic formulation arises from the canonical role which Deuteronomy had assumed in providing the authoritative interpretation of the law for the later generations of Israel. Moreover, the constant reference to sacred events which are not mentioned in Deuteronomy confirms the view that the law as encompassed in the entire Pentateuch is assumed as normative (cf. 24.1ff.). In sum, from a canonical perspective no individual integrity has ever been assigned to the 'Deuteronomic law', but it serves as a normative formulation of the one divine will revealed to Moses at Sinai.

Canonical shaping and historical tradition

One of the most immediate results of taking seriously the shape of the book of Joshua within the canon is to force a re-evaluation of the historical problems raised by the critical method. It is evident that the process of transmitting the historical traditions within the community of faith often ran in the face of a strictly historical handling of the material.

First, critical scholars have long since pointed out the tension – it is usually called contradiction – in the portrayal of the conquest of the land. On the one hand, the conquest is pictured in the main source of Josh. 1–12 as a unified assault against the inhabitants of the land under the leadership of Joshua which succeeded in conquering the entire land (11.23; 18.1; 22.43). On the other hand, there is a conflicting view of the conquest represented by Judges 1 and its parallels in Joshua (15.13–19, 63; 16.10; 17.11–13; 19.47) which appears to picture the conquest as undertaken by individual tribes, extending over a long period beyond the age of Joshua, and unsuccessful in driving out the Canaanites from much of the land. Any number of variations on these two options are possible, such as the theory proposed by G. Mendenhall of an internal socio-political upheaval.

The issue at stake is not one which calls for the modern interpreter to seek a method of harmonizing the difficulty which removes the tension (cf. Wright). In my judgment, this approach has been tried all too frequently by conservative scholars and exegesis quickly turns into apologetics. Rather, the goal is to describe to what extent the canonical editors recognized a problem and how they sought to deal with it.

Usually the description of the conquest which portrays a complete conquest of the whole land under Joshua is assigned to the Deuteronomic redaction of the book. Joshua 1 sets out the promise of possession of the whole land in the classic Deuteronomic idiom:

'No man will be able to stand before you.' The divine word appears
to be unconditional. Chapter 12 then summarizes the history of the
conquest: 'So Joshua took the whole land, according to all that
Yahweh had spoken to Moses.' In this description there is no mention of a gradual conquest, nor of a partial success, nor of a remaining task. The land had been possessed and it now rested from war
(11.23).

It is significant to observe at the outset that Josh. 23, which is
also assigned to the Deuteronomic editor, has a somewhat different
portrayal of the conquest. Of course, the chapter has many features
in common with ch. 1. Yahweh has promised possession of the land
(v. 5); Yahweh fights for Israel (v. 3); no man can withstand Israel
(v. 9). The difference in the tense of the verbs arises from the logic
of the narrative because in ch. 23 Joshua, pictured as an old man,
reviews what has in fact already happened. However, along with
these clear elements of continuity appears a number of new features. A distinction is made between those nations 'already cut off'
and those that 'remain' to be conquered (v. 14). The conquest of
these remaining nations lies in the future (v. 5). The success of the
full conquest is now made conditional upon Israel's obedience to
the law of Moses. If Israel mixes with the Canaanite population,
then God 'will not continue to drive out the nations, but they shall
be a snare and a trap' (v. 13).

How is one to explain these new features which do not appear in
ch. 1? It is immediately clear that the editor of Josh. 23 is directly
dependent on earlier Deuteronomic material. Ex. 23.30 and Deut.
7.22 had spoken of God's driving out the enemy 'little by little' until
the land was possessed. Deut. 7 assigns an additional positive note
to the gradual conquest: 'lest the wild beasts grow numerous' (v.
22). Moreover, in both these chapters the successful conquest is
conditional on Israel's obedience to the command not to inter-
mingle with the Canaanite inhabitants. Thus the Deuteronomic
editor of Josh. 23 has expanded his description of the conquest by
making use of old Deuteronomic material. Any discrepancy posed
by Josh. 1 with the portrayal of Josh. 23 has been resolved by this
editor by appealing to earlier tradition of a gradual and conditional
conquest. In fact, the pattern of Josh. 23 has become the normative
interpretation for the Deuteronomic redaction of the book of
Judges. Chapter 2 records the disobedience of the people and, as a
result, God's refusal any longer to drive out any of the nations that

Joshua left. These nations, in turn, become the 'snare and trap' which call forth the need for a deliverer through the series of 'judges'.

Moreover, there is no evidence to suggest that the variation within the Deuteronomic tradition regarding the nature of the conquest reflects a traditio-historical development, as if Josh. 1 offered an earlier theology of Deuteronomy, whereas ch. 23 represents a subsequent adjustment of the tradition which sought to explain the actual historical process as gradual. Rather, the major elements in Josh. 23 are already found in Deut. 7. God fought for Israel, but the conquest was to be gradual and conditional on obedience.

There are several implications to be drawn from this line of argument. First, the apparent discrepancy in the portrayal of the conquest does not derive from a combination of different sources or fragments, but is contained within the same Deuteronomic tradition. Secondly, there is no strong evidence to suggest that the editors of Joshua even recognized this tension as being a problem. The Deuteronomic redactor of ch. 23 summarized the history of the conquest fully in line with the earlier Deuteronomic theology of the land.

How then is one to explain the peculiar features within Josh. 1–12 which present the conquest in the Deuteronomic idiom but as total, unconditional, and of short duration? In my opinion, this feature of the book of Joshua is not to be dismissed as a variant historical tradition, but understood as a unique theological perspective of the Deuteronomic editor which the final canonical shape has preserved as normative. The Deuteronomic editor of Joshua fashioned his material into a highly theological pattern which not only disregarded strictly historical method, but which also shifted the emphasis to a different focal point from that ordinarily represented by the Deuteronomic tradition. The editor of chs. 1–12 envisions the period of Joshua (Josh. 1.1–Judg.1.1) as a paradigm of obedient Israel. Joshua is presented in ch. 1 as the heir to the divine promises who calls a people to obedience to the Book of the Law and receives a unified response of faith. Because the conditions of obedience have been met, the purpose of this ideal is to demonstrate that the result is the complete and total victory of Israel as God fulfils his promise to the letter. But the theology of the conquest in chs. 1–12 is different from Deuteronomy only in emphasis, not in essence. That the conquest is in fact conditional upon obedience is made fully clear by the disastrous defeat at Ai 'when the people of Israel broke faith in regard to the devoted thing' (7.1), specifically prohibited by Deut. 7.25. The Gibeonite deception also reflects Israel's failure to observe closely enough the stipulations of Deut. 20 regarding the 'cities which are near'.

A further confirmation of this thesis that the portrayal of the conquest serves as a theological construct which bears witness to God's fulfilling his promise to his obedient people appears in the manner in which the writer handles his earlier tradition. Critical scholars have long recognized a different, and probably more ancient, tradition of the conquest in Judg. 1 and in parallel fragments in Joshua (15.13–19 63, etc.). The editor of Joshua has preserved this divergent material, but without destroying his theological witness. On the one hand, he has relegated the picture of a slow conquest by individual tribes to the period after the death of Joshua (Judg.1.1), which in effect marked the end of the ideal period of obedience. The portrayal in ch. 1 introduces the grounds for the divine judgment in 2.1ff. Even though this redactional move resulted in chronological difficulties (2.6), the theological pattern of obedient and disobedient Israel was firmly maintained. On the other hand, the Deuteronomic editor of Joshua has assigned all the fragments of the earlier conquest account within the book of Joshua to the section which treats of the distribution of the land. Thereby he has given this material another role within the tradition which did not destroy his theological pattern. Even faithful Caleb must secure his individual inheritance by means of distribution by lot (14.6ff.).

The distribution of the land

The chapters on the distribution of the land (Josh. 13–21) present an analogous problem to that of the conquest. Some passages suggest that the conquest was complete, and the land was distributed among the Israelites according to their divisions and tribes (12.7; 18.10; 21.43), whereas other passages speak as if the distribution had not yet been completed and lay in the future (18.2; 23.4). Moreover, critical commentators have rightly pointed out the complexity of the land division tradition. First, there are the difficult historical problems. How much land was actually taken in the initial invasion? How is one to assess the geographical descriptions of the land? Again, there are the literary problems. How is one to explain the need for two distributions with an interruption and change of location (chs. 13 and 18)? How does one evaluate the sources used in these chapters to describe the geography of the distribution? Finally, there are the theological problems. What is the theology of the land, inheritance, and rest?

The task of a canonical reading is to assess how the editing of the book affected these problems. First of all, the dominant theme of chs. 13–21 was to confirm that the promise of God regarding the land was fulfilled. The biblical record goes to great lengths to confirm an actual possession of the land. The emphasis falls on the concrete, real distribution. Alt's theory that historical documents of boundaries and administrative districts were used seems far more likely than Kaufmann's theory of an ideal projection. Regardless of what historical dating one assigns these lists, they served the biblical editors to document the promise of possession and they continued to function in this manner within the final canonical shape of the book. The same motif of the actual possession of the land is picked up in the final chapter. Both Joshua and Joseph are buried in their own inheritance (24.30,32).

However, there is another movement within these chapters which has retained a calculated tension between the land as an ideal inheritance and the land as actually possessed. At times the land is described as occupied and distributed by lot, whereas at other times it is clear that the possession lies still in the future (18.1,3; 11.23; 13.1; 23.5, etc.). Also this tension does not arise primarily from a combination of sources, but from the particular perspective from which the land is viewed. However, once this dialectical pattern was established, it proved to be a means of accommodating the older tradition which described that territory which had in fact not been conquered (15.63, etc.).

Finally, the tension between the ideal inheritance and the actual possession was used by the editor of the book of Joshua in a homiletical fashion to urge continuous obedience. Joshua 23.4 speaks of all the land being allotted in principle, but not yet possessed. The homilist then links the actual possession conditionally with the people's obedience. If Israel is disobedient, particularly to the Deuteronomic prohibition of intermarriage (v.12), then the nations who remain will become a 'snare and trap'. The formulation in the chapter of the punishment is clearly intended to adumbrate the exile from the land: 'you shall quickly perish from off the good land which he has given you' (23.16).

3. Theological and Hermeneutical Implications

(a) The book of Joshua was shaped in such a way as to preserve a good number of tensions within the text. The task of the interpreter who works seriously with the canonical shape is not to seek ways of resolving the tension, either by ploys of harmonization or reductionism, but by tracing the effect of the present form of the book on Israel's witness to the conquest. It is important to preserve the dissonance within the canonical whole which has sought neither a literary nor a conceptual unity in performing its scriptural task.

(b) The history of exegesis of Joshua has been dominated by a mode of ostensive referential interpretation, both from the side of the conservatives who sought to defend the book's historical accuracy, and from the side of the liberals who sought to correlate and correct the biblical portrait with scientific historical reconstructions. Because of the nature of the material in Joshua, it is not surprising that the problem of using the biblical text in reference to historical phenomena should be an acute one. However, the failure to distinguish between the task of biblical interpretation and historical reconstruction is of crucial significance. No one denies the legitimacy of the historical enterprise in stressing this point, but the issue at stake is to what extent understanding of the biblical message depends upon a critical reconstruction of a historical referent. The hermeneutic of the canon maintains the integrity of the biblical witness as the only means through which scripture instructs this community of faith in the meaning of the book of Joshua for faith and practice.

(c) The shaping of the book of Joshua is a good example of the canonical process of editing the tradition in such a way that the last redaction does not prove to be the decisive one, but rather an earlier stage performs that function. In the case of Joshua a penultimate editor of the Deuteronomic school provided the critical transformation of the tradition which the canon preserved. A hermeneutic which takes seriously the canonical shaping does not necessarily assign authority to the last development in the chronological sequence of redaction. Rather, it seeks to follow the lead within the book itself in a holistic reading as it forms the material to function authoritatively for future generations of Israel. The Deuteronomic editor of Joshua provided the decisive canonical interpretation of the tradition, but later redactors confirmed this move by working within this framework.

History of Exegesis

Carpzov I, 162–6; *DThC* 8, 1573; *EB* 3, 564; *RGG*³ 3, 1573.

J. **Daniélou**, 'Rahab, figure de l'Église', *Irénikon* 22, Chevetogne 1949, 26–45; F. J. **Dölger**, 'Der Durchzug durch den Jordan als Sinnbild der christlichen Taufe', *Antike und Christentum* II, Münster 1930, 70–79; A. **Jaubert**, 'Introduction', *Origène, Homélies sur Josué*, SC 71, 1960, 9–93; A. J. **Michalski**, 'Raschis Einfluss auf Nikolaus von Lyra in der Auslegung des Buches Joshua', *ZAW* 39, 1921, 300–7.

XIII

JUDGES

Commentaries

C. F. Keil, BC, 1868

E. Bertheau, KeH, ²1883

K. Budde, KHC, 1897

G. F. Moore, ICC, ²1898

W. Nowack, HKAT, 1902

M.-J. Lagrange, ÉB, 1903

G. A. Cooke, CB, rev. 1918

C. F. Burney, ²1920

R. Kittel, HSAT, ⁴1922

J. Garstang, 1931

R. Tamisier, SB, 1949

J. J. Slotki, SonB, 1950

A. Vincent, JB, ²1958

H. W. Hertzberg, ATD, ²1959

J. Gray, NCeB, 1967

R. G. Boling, AB, 1975

Bibliography

Zvi **Adar**, *The Biblical Narrative*, Jerusalem 1959; L. **Alonso Schökel**, 'Erzählkunst im Buche der Richter', *Bibl* 42, 1961, 143–72; A. **Alt**, 'The Formation of the Israelite State in Palestine', ET *Essays* (see Pentateuch), 171–237; A. C. **Auld**, 'Judges I and History: A Reconsideration', *VT* 25, 1975, 261–85; F. **Bächli**, *Amphyktonie im Alten Testament*, Basel 1977; A. **Besters**, 'Le sanctuaire central dans Jud. 19–21', *ETL* 41, 1965, 20–41; W. **Beyerlin**, 'Gattung und Herkunft des Rahmens im Richterbuch', *Tradition und Situation, FS A. Weiser*, Göttingen 1963, 1–29; 'Geschichte und heilsgeschichtliche Traditionsbildung im Alten Testament', *VT* 13, 1963, 1–24; J. **Blenkinsopp**, 'Ballad Style and Psalm Style in the Song of Deborah: a Discussion', *Bibl* 42, 1961, 61–76; 'Structure and Style in Judges 13–16', *JBL* 82, 1963, 65–76; R. G. **Boling**, 'In those Days there was no King in Israel', *A Light unto My Path: Old Testament Studies in Honor of J. M. Myers*, Philadelphia 1974, 33–48; H. **Cazelles**, 'Juges', *DBS* 4, 1394–1414; J. L. **Crenshaw**, 'The Samson Saga: Filial Devotion or Erotic Attachment?', *ZAW* 86, 1974, 470–504.

O. **Eissfeldt**, *Die Quellen des Richterbuches*, Leipzig 1925; 'Der geschichtliche Hintergrund der Erzählung von Gibeas Schandtat', *FS G. Beer*, Stuttgart 1935, 19–40; J. A. **Emerton**, 'Gideon and Jerubbaal', *JTS* NS

27, 1976, 289–312; G. **Gerleman**, 'The Song of Deborah in the Light of Stylistics', *VT* 36, 1966, 32–53; C. H. J. **de Geus**, *The Tribes of Israel. An Investigation into some of the Presuppositions of Martin Noth's Amphictyony Hypothesis*, Assen 1976; O. **Grether**, 'Die Bezeichnung "Richter" für die charismatischen Helden der vorstaatlichen Zeit', *ZAW* 57, 1939, 110–21; H. **Gunkel**, 'Simson', *Reden und Aufsätze*, Göttingen 1913, 38–64; D. M. **Gunn**, 'Narrative Patterns and Oral Tradition in Judges and Samuel', *VT* 24, 1974, 286–317; H. **Haag**, 'Gideon–Jerubbaal–Abimelek', *ZAW* 79, 1967, 305–14; H. W. **Hertzberg**, 'Die Kleinen Richter', *TLZ* 79, 1954, 285–90; A. **van Hoonacker**, 'Le voeu de Jephté', *Le Muséon* 11, Louvain 1892, 448–69; 12, 1893, 59–80; E. **Jenni**, 'Vom Zeugnis des Richterbuches', *TZ* 12, 1956, 257–74; 'Zwei Jahrzehnte Forschung an den Büchern Josua bis Könige', *ThR* NF 27, 1961, 129–36; J. **Kitto**, *Cyclopaedia of Biblical Literature*, new ed. revised, Edinburgh 1856, II, 173–9; E. **Kutsch**, 'Gideons Berufung und Altarbau, Jdc. 6,11–24', *TLZ* 81, 1956, 257–74.

A. **Malamat**, 'The Danite Migration and the Pan-Israelite Exodus-Conquest', *Bibl* 51, 1970, 1–16; A. D. H. **Mayes**, 'The Period of the Judges and the Rise of the Monarchy', in *Israelite and Judaean History*, ed. J. H. Hayes and J. M. Miller, OTL, 1977, 285–331; B. **Mazar**, 'The Sanctuary of Arad and the Family of Hobab the Kenite', *JNES* 24, 1965, 297–303; E. **Meyer**, 'Kritik der Berichte über die Eroberung Palaestinas (Num. 20,14 bis Jud. 2,5)', *ZAW* 1, 1881, 117–46; S. **Mowinckel**, 'The Background of Judges 17–18', *Israel's Prophetic Heritage*, ed. B. W. Anderson and W. Harrelson, New York and London 1962, 80–85; *Tetrateuch–Pentateuch–Hexateuch*, BZAW 90, 1964, 17ff.; E. **Nielsen**, *Shechem: A Traditio-Historical Investigation*, Copenhagen ²1959; M. **Noth**, *Überlieferungsgeschichtliche Studien* I, Halle 1943; 'Das Amt des Richters Israels', *FS A. Bertholet*, Tübingen 1950, 404–17; E. **O'Doherty**, 'The Literary Problem of Judges 1,1- 3,6', *CBQ* 28, 1956, 1–7; W. **Richter**, *Traditionsgeschichtliche Untersuchungen zum Richterbuch*, BBB 18, 1963, ²1966; *Die Bearbeitungen des 'Retterbuches' in der deuteronomischen Epoche*, BBB 21, 1964; 'Zu den "Richtern Israels"', *ZAW* 77, 1965, 40–71; 'Die Überlieferungen um Jeptah, Ri 10, 17–12,6', *Bibl* 47, 1966, 485–556; E. **Robertson**, 'The Period of the Judges', *BJRL* 30, 1946, 91–114; M. G. **Roger**, 'Judges, Book of', *IDB Suppl*, 509–14; H. **Schmid**, 'Die Herrschaft Abimelechs (Jdc 9)', *Jud* 26, 1970, 1–11; H. **Schulte**, *Die Entstehung der Geschichtsschreibung im Alten Israel*, BZAW 128, 1972; E. **Sellin**, *Wie wurde Sichem eine israelitische Stadt?*, Leipzig und Erlangen 1922; U. **Simon**, 'The Parable of Jotham (Judges 14, 8–15): The Parable, Its Application, and the Narrative Framework' (Hebrew), *Tarbiz* 34, Jerusalem 1964–5, 1–34; C. A. **Simpson**, *Composition of the Book of Judges*, Oxford 1957, New York 1958; S. **Talmon**, 'In those Days there was no King in Israel' (Hebrew), *Proceedings of the Fifth World Congress of Jewish Studies* 1969, I, Jerusalem 1971, 135–44=ET *Immanuel* 5, Jerusalem 1975, 27–36; E. **Täubler**, *Biblische Studien*, Tübingen 1958; R. **de Vaux**, *The Early History of Israel* II, 'The Period of the Judges', ET London and

Philadelphia 1978; W. **Vischer**, 'Das Buch der Richter', *Das Christuszeugnis des Alten Testaments* II, Zürich ²1946, 65–144; W. **Vollborn**, 'Die Chronologie des Richterbuches', *FS F. Baumgärtel*, Erlangen 1959, 192–6; M. **Weinfeld**, 'The Period of the Conquest and of the Judges as seen by the Earlier and the Later Sources', *VT* 17, 1967, 93–113; A. **Weiser**, 'Das Deboralied, eine gattungs- und traditionsgeschichtliche Studie', *ZAW* 71, 1959, 67–97; G. E. **Wright**, 'The Literary and Historical Problem of Joshua 10 and Judges 1', *JNES* 5, 1946, 105–14; H.-J. **Zobel**, *Stammesspruch und Geschichte. Die Angaben der Stammesspruch von Gen 49, Dtn 33 und Jdc 5 über die politischen und kultischen Zustände im damaligen 'Israel'*, BZAW 95, 1965; A. H. **van Zyl**, 'The Messenger Formula in the Book of Judges', *OuTWP* 1959, 61–64.

1. Historical Critical Problems

Critical discussion of the book of Judges has focused on a number of classic problems. First, it has long been observed that the work of different hands is reflected in the present composition of the book. The main body of the book consists of a collection of stories which are generally regarded as some of the oldest in the whole Old Testament (e.g. ch.5). In their original context the stories circulated independently of each other on the oral level and concerned local tribal heroes. At some later date in the history of tradition these stories were combined into a narrative cycle and expanded to refer to all Israel. The exact shape of this pre-Deuteronomic stage continues to be hotly debated among scholars. However, the older view which argued for continuous literary strands extending throughout the book has been generally abandoned.

Then again, there is a widespread consensus that the early cycle of stories, in varying degrees, has undergone an important Deuteronomic redaction. It consists of an editorial framework for the earlier material which interpreted the narratives according to a set theological pattern, and provided a chronological order to the 'judges'. Recent critical work has suggested that more than one Deuteronomic redaction can be discerned. For example, Richter (BBB 18) has traced an exceedingly complex line of development which works with three Deuteronomic redactions. The first had only chs. 3–9 as a *Vorlage* to which he added characteristic opening and closing sentences such as 6.1 and 8.28. The second redactor constructed the Othniel story, 3.7–11, as a paradigmatic example of the perspective of the frames. The final reworking combined this document with related material to produce the segment of a Deuteronomic history which extended from the conquest to the beginning of the monarchy. However one judges the success of this analysis, such refinement of the various redactional levels has resulted in a move away from Noth's identification of the author of the book of Judges with the one Deuteronomistic historian. A different stage of redaction is usually attributed to the addition of the present introduction in 1.1–25 and the two appendices (chs. 17–21).

A second classic problem turns about the issue of the office of the so-called judges. Alt first distinguished between the role of the major judges who were charismatic, military leaders and the list of judges who had chiefly a juridical function. Noth then further developed Alt's theory that this latter type represented a particular office ('die kleine Richter') which he assigned to Israel's pre-monarchial period in the amphictyony. He argued that these 'judges' were only secondarily combined with the charismatic heroes. More recently, scholars such as Fohrer (*Introduction*, 206f.) have contested Noth's reconstruction and derived the minor judges from a historical transition from tribal to city government. Nevertheless, there is considerable agreement regarding the presence of two different offices which originally performed different functions. The erosion of Noth's hypothesis of an amphictyony (e.g. by de Geus and Bächli) has also affected the problem of the minor judges.

The third problem focuses on chronological problems of the book of Judges, and was discussed long before the rise of modern historical criticism. In general, scholars of the pre-critical period offered different solutions by which to harmonize the period of 480 years mentioned in I Kings 6 with the chronology of Judges (cf. the summary in Kitto, II, 178). Either calculations which were based on an interregnum were proposed, or the Septuagint was used as a warrant for reducing the figures, or the minor judges were excluded from the calculations. In the critical period the attempt to reconcile the accounts has been generally abandoned. Eichhorn thought that the gaps in the chronology of Judges made exact calculation impossible. Others suggested that round numbers were being employed. The most recent full-scale discussion, that of Noth, assigned the chronology to an artificial construct of the post-exilic

Deuteronomistic historian. Needless to say, no positive consensus has yet emerged on this matter.

2. The Canonical Shape of Judges

Critical scholars are generally agreed on the main structural features of the book. They are an introduction (1.1–2.5), a main body of stories (2.6–16.31), and two appendices (chs. 17–21). But the significance of the structure is far from obvious and no consensus regarding its canonical effect has arisen.

Prologue and epilogue

The first observation turns on the effect of the beginning and ending on the book of Joshua as a whole. The introduction begins with the phrase 'after the death of Joshua' which marks both the end of the previous period of the conquest and the beginning of a new period. The era of the judges is thus clearly distinguished from the previous period by the death of Joshua, even though this sharp line results in later chronological inconsistency within the continuing narrative (cf. 2.6). However, in marked contrast to the role of the introduction, the two appendices do not serve to establish an end to the period of the judges. The two incidents reported are not presented in a chronological sequence with the previous stories of the judges, but are simply set in the broad period of the judges 'when there was no king in Israel'. Moreover, the period of the judges obviously extends beyond the book of Judges into the book of I Samuel. What are the implications of this observation?

Historical critics usually explain the present position of the introduction 1.1–2.5 as arising from a conflation of sources. Accordingly, the book of Judges really begins with the Deuteronomistic editor's introduction at 2.6ff., but at a later stage in the development of the book this older fragment from the original Hexateuch was assigned its present position. Weiser (*Introduction*, 149) is typical in disparaging its role as a 'foreign element' which distorts the historical purpose of the Deuteronomic writer. Likewise, Mowinckel (*Tetrateuch*) feels that Judg. 1.1ff. is a parallel to the book of Joshua which records a history long before the period of the judges, and which received its present place out of an embarrassing necessity to preserve this fragment somewhere. But these historical judgments on the development of the literature fail to reckon with the effect of this 'fragment' on the final shape of the book, whether originally intentional or not.

The function of the introduction is to mark the beginning of a period of disobedience which stands in sharp contrast to the period which preceded. A theological judgment is made by its characterization of the period. No leader after Joshua has arisen. The unity of the nation has been fractured. The successes from the divine blessing have given way to a failure to repel the enemy. That the introduction performs this negative role is made explicit in 2.1–5 which confirms the judgment of God on the nation's disobedience.

Regardless of the literary development behind its present shape, the introduction to the book of Judges performs a significant theological function, which would have been lost had the book simply begun with the Deuteronomic introduction of 2.6–23. The introduction of ch. 1 offers a theological judgment on the nature of disobedient Israel. The Deuteronomic introduction which follows assumes this breakdown. Indeed, it builds its first stage in its pattern of divine help on the fact of Israel's disobedience. But each time the nation lapses, it returns to the quality of life described in ch. 1. The point is thus made that in spite of the repeated intervention of divine aid, the period is correctly characterized by the state of the nation in the introduction. Far from being a foreign element or useless fragment, the introduction strikes the keynote to the whole witness of the book.

The two appendices perform an analogous role and together complete the framework about the Deuteronomic pattern of the judges. The final stories do not provide a chronological perspective, but describe a quality of life which picks up the elements of the introduction. Interestingly enough, the mention of the Danites in 1.34ff. recurs in chs. 17 and 18, and references to Judah, Jerusalem and Bethel (1.7, 8, 22) provide the setting for the scandal of Benjamin (chs. 20 and 21). The two stories portray Israel's growing idolatry and the scandal which threatens the unity of the nation. However, the major difference in perspective between the introduction and the appendix lies in the latter's looking forward to the future kingdom rather than back to the earlier period.

The main body of the book

There is the widest agreement that the main body of the book of Judges now bears the peculiar shaping of a Deuteronomic editor (cf. Kaiser, *Introduction*, 120). Yet the effect of this redaction on the understanding of the tradition of Judges has not been adequately explored. At the outset it is significant to note how different the Dtr. handling of Judges was from that of Joshua. The Dtr. level did not encompass the whole book of Judges nor provide the major bracket around earlier tradition. Rather, the earlier material of the pre-Deuteronomic introduction (1.1–2.5) and the pre-Deuteronomic appendices (17–21) functioned as a frame around the Dtr. section (2.6–16.31).

There is considerable evidence from the content of the Dtr. material which would speak against identifying this Dtr. editor with just one author's peculiar viewpoint to whom Noth ascribes the historical composition from Deuteronomy to Kings. The exilic perspective which portrayed Israel's early history as being already under the shadow of its subsequent destruction (cf. Josh. 23.13) is strikingly absent. Rather, Israel's disobedience results in its failure to drive out the nations but does not unleash the curse of the Deuteronomic law (Deut. 27). Again, the variety within the Dtr. frame of ch. 2, when compared with the Dtr. material within the stories, would seem to reflect a growth of tradition rather than one author's individual perspective.

What then is the canonical effect of the Deuteronomic redaction of the main body of the book? The main result is to provide a theological interpretation on how this period of Israel's history was to be understood. It is likely that the stories had been linked in some way in the pre-Deuteronomic stage, but this editor provided a uniform pattern into which he fitted a collection of very disparate events. The variety of different stories served the one common purpose of illustrating a recurring pattern within history. This schema relativized the historical differences in order to emphasize the repetition of Israel's disobedience, God's anger, Israel's repentance, and God's salvation.

Whereas the introduction to Judges (1.1ff.) described the period by portraying a contrast with the leadership, tribal unity and success under Joshua, the Dtr. redaction characterized the deliverance of Israel in such terms as to recover momentarily the divine promise which had been lost. The charismatic leader was successful in repulsing the enemy. Moreover, he ruled over all Israel, and Israel was faithful to God during his lifetime. Finally, the chronological interest of the Dtr. redactor is theologically significant. The length of the judge's rule is recorded as if to establish God's rule in a temporal sequence, whereas in neither the introduction nor the appendix is the chronology recorded. It is as though the historical sequence of disobedient Israel had no movement and thus no significance.

The appendices return to the same period of the introduction which had been temporarily interrupted by the history of the judges. Again this disobedient state is described in the two narratives as being religiously chaotic (18.31), without a leader (18.1; 19.1; 21.35), and in dire peril of permanently losing the unity of Israel as the people of God (21.3).

There is one final point to be made in characterizing the effect of the Deuteronomic redaction. Even though the framework served to order the narrative diversity within a stereotyped pattern, the pattern did not seriously alter the original shape of the stories. There was no massive rewriting of the earlier traditions with an eye to forcing them into one mould. Rather the framework allowed the stories much room to function freely within the larger theological construct. Thus, the Samson cycle (13–16) was also placed within the Dtr. frame even though its content of defeat and victory focused on the personal history of one man rather than the nation. Within the larger narrative, however, the story was illustrative of the nation's disobedience through an easy analogy which the reader could now draw between the one and the many. In a similar way, the story of Abimelech's history formed an analogous relationship to the nation's history within the larger pattern.

3. Theological and Hermeneutical Implications

(a) The study of the canonical shaping of the book of Judges makes clear that different functions can be assigned to different historical sources even within the same book. Thus, for example, ch. 1 uses the undigested details of an ancient historical account in its original form as a means of illustrating the breakdown of Joshua's legacy. Conversely, 2.6ff. has been placed within a heavily schematized theological framework which has sacrificed many original details for the sake of the pattern.

Regardless of the different handling of the historical material, each method performs a particular function within the canonical form of the book. Any attempt to exercise a value judgment on the sources in relation to an extrinsic norm of historicity makes neither literary nor theological sense in the context of the canon.

(b) Much effort has been spent on reconstructing the variety of offices subsumed under the title of judge, and a rich history of development has been uncovered. For the historical enterprise the endeavour of reconstruction is fully legitimate. Still it is far from obvious that this information must of necessity have theological significance, especially since the historical distinctions between offices have been lost in the canonical shaping. At best one could argue that a knowledge of the history of tradition in this instance could illuminate the question of why the final form of the book failed to transmit such historical information.

(c) The book of Judges affords an excellent example of how a secondary theological framework can function on a body of older tradition. Far from assuming that the framework established only one exclusive interpretation of the material, the canonical shaping of Judges allowed for great freedom within an overarching pattern. Nowhere was the relation of the parts to the framework so closely established as to dictate only one possible hearing of the text. Thus the charge that to take seriously the final shape is to impoverish the vitality of the literature is far from the truth.

History of Exegesis

Carpzov I, 192–4; *DThC* 8, 1861f., *RGG*[3] 5, 1097ff.

R. **Hermann**, *Die Gestalt Simsons bei Luther*, Theologische Bibliothek Töpelmann 2, Berlin 1952, 5–20; F. M. **Krouse**, *Milton's Samson and the Christian Tradition*, Princeton and London 1949; A. **Penna**, 'The Vow of Jephthah in the Interpretation of St Jerome', *Studia Patristica* 4, TU 79, 1961, 162–70.

XIV

SAMUEL

Commentaries

C. F. Keil, BC, 1875
F. de Hummelauer, CSS, 1886
O. Thenius, M. Loehr, KeH, 1842,
   ³1898
H. P. Smith, ICC, 1899
K. Budde, KHC, 1902
W. Nowack, HKAT, 1902
P. Dhorme, ÉB, 1910
S. R. Driver, ²1913
H. Gressmann, *SAT*, ²1921
R. Kittel, *HSAT*, ⁴1922

W. Caspari, KAT, 1926
A. Médebielle, SB, 1949
S. Goldman, SonB, 1951
A. van den Born, BOuT, 1956
K. Gutbrod, BAT, 1956–8
R. de Vaux, JB, ²1961
W. McKane, TBC, 1963
W. H. Hertzberg, OTL, 1964
H. J. Stoebe, KAT², I, 1973
P. Ackroyd, CNEB, 1971–77

Bibliography

A. **Alt**, 'Das Grossreich Davids', *TLZ* 75, 1950, 213–220=*KS* II, 66ff.; ET *Essays*, 239–59; K. **Baltzer**, *Die Biographie der Propheten*, Neukirchen-Vluyn 1975; B. C. **Birch**, *The Rise of the Israelite Monarchy: The Growth and Development of I Sam. 7–15*, Diss. Yale University, 1970 = SBL Dissertation Series 27, Missoula 1976; J. **Blenkinsopp**, 'Jonathan's Sacrilege. I Sm 14, 1–46: A Study in Literary History', *CBQ* 26, 1964, 423–49; 'Theme and Motif in the Succession History (2 Sam xi 2ff.) and the Yahwist Corpus', *SVT* 15, 1966, 44–51; 'The Quest of the Historical Saul', *No Famine in the Land. Studies in Honor of J. L. McKenzie*, Missoula 1975, 75–99; H. J. **Boecker**, *Die Beurteilung der Anfänge des Königtums in den deuteronomistischen Abschnittes des I. Samuelbuches*, WMANT 31, 1969; P. A. H. **de Boer**, 'Texte et traduction des paroles attribúees à David en II Samuel xxiii 1–7', *SVT* 4, 1957, 47–56; J. **Bourke**, 'Samuel and the Ark, A Study in Contrasts', *Dominican Studies* 7, Oxford 1954, 73–103; W. **Brueggemann**, 'David and his Theologian', *CBQ* 30, 1968, 156–81; H. **van der Bussche**, 'Le texte de la prophétie de Nathan sur la dynastie davidique (II Sam., VII– I Chron., XVII)', *ETL* 24, 1948, 354–94; M. **Buber**, 'Die Erzählung von Sauls Königswahl', *VT*

6, 1956, 113–73; A. F. **Campbell**, *The Ark Narrative (1 Sam 4–6, 2 Sam 6)*. *A Form-Critical and Traditio-Historical Study*, SBL Dissertation Series 16, Missoula 1975; R. A. **Carlson**, *David, the Chosen King. A Traditio-Historical Approach to the Second Book of Samuel*, Stockholm 1964; H. **Cazelles**, 'David's Monarchy and the Gibeonite Claim', *PEQ* 87, 1955, 165–75; R. E. **Clements**, 'The Deuteronomistic Interpretation of the Founding of the Monarchy in I Sam VIII', *VT* 24, 1974, 398–410.

L. **Delekat**, 'Tendenz und Theologie der David-Salomo Erzählung', *Das ferne und nahe Wort. FS L. Rost*, BZAW 105, 1967, 26–36; W. **Dietrich**, 'David in Überlieferung und Geschichte', *VF* 22, 1977, 44–64; O. **Eissfeldt**, 'Nocheinmal: Text-, Stil- und Literarkritik in den Samuelisbüchern', *OLZ* 31, 1928, 801–12; *Die Komposition der Samuelisbücher*, Leipzig 1931; 'The Hebrew Kingdom', *CAH* II/2, 570–80; K. **Elliger**, 'Die dreissig Helden Davids', 1935 = *KSAT*, Munich 1966, 72–118; J. W. **Flanagan**, 'Court History or Succession Document? A Study of 2 Samuel 9–20 and I Kings 1–2', *JBL* 91, 1972, 172–81; H. **Gese**, 'Der Davidsbund und die Zionserwählung', *ZTK* 61, 1964, 10–26; J. **Goettsberger**, 'Die Verwerfung des Saul, 1 Sm 13 und 15', *Festgabe für A. Knöpfler*, Freiburg 1917, 140–58; J. H. **Grønbaek**, *Die Geschichte vom Aufstieg Davids (1. Sam 15 – 2. Sam 5)*, Copenhagen 1971; D. M. **Gunn**, 'Narrative Patterns and Oral Tradition in Judges and Samuel', *VT* 24, 1974, 286–317; 'Traditional Composition in the "Succession Narrative"', *VT* 26, 1976, 214–29; C. E. **Hauer**, 'The Shape of Saulide Strategy', *CBQ* 31, 1969, 153–67; S. **Herrmann**, 'Die Königsnovelle in Ägypten und in Israel', *WZ Univ. Leipzig* 3, 1953–4, 51–62; I. **Hylander**, *Der literarische Samuel-Saul Komplex (I Sam. 1–15), traditionsgeschichtlich untersucht*, Leipzig 1932.

A. **Kapelrud**, 'König David und die Söhne des Saul', *ZAW* 67, 1955, 198–205; M. **Kessler**, 'Narrative Technique in 1 Sm 16, 1–13', *CBQ* 32, 1970, 543–54; L. **Krinetzki**, 'Ein Beitrag zur Stilanalyse der Goliathperikope (1 Sam. 17, 1–18,5)', *Bibl* 54, 1973, 187–236; F. **Langlamet**, 'Les récits de l'institution de la royauté (I Sam., VII-XII)', *RB* 77, 1970, 161–200; G. C. **Macholz**, *Untersuchungen zur Geschichte der Samuel-Überlieferungen*, Diss. Heidelberg 1966; A. D. H. **Mayes**, 'The Reign of Saul', *Israelite and Judaean History*, ed. J. H. Hayes and J. M. Miller, OTL, 1977, 322–31; D. J. **McCarthy**, 'II Samuel 7 and the Structure of the Deuteronomistic History', *JBL* 84, 1965, 131–8; J. L. **McKenzie**, 'The Dynastic Oracle: II Sam 7', *ThSt* 8, 1947, 187–218; 'The Four Samuels', *Biblical Research* 7, Amsterdam 1962, 3–18; I. **Mendelsohn**, 'Samuel's Denunciation of Kingship in the Light of the Akkadian Documents from Ugarit', *BASOR* 143, 1956, 17–22; T. N. D. **Mettinger**, '"The Last Words of David". A Study of Structure and Meaning in II Samuel 23:1–7', *SEA* 41–42, 1976–77, 147–56; F. **Mildenberger**, *Die vordeuteronomistische Saul-Davidsüberlieferung*, Diss. Tübingen 1962; J. M. **Miller**, 'Saul's Rise to Power: Some Observations concerning I Sam. 9.1–10.16; 10.26–11.15 and 13.2–14.46', *CBQ* 36, 1974, 157–74; P. D. **Miller** and J. J. M. **Roberts**,

The Hand of the Lord: A Reassessment of the 'Ark Narratives' of I Samuel, Baltimore and London 1977; K. **Möhlenbrink**, 'Saul's Ammoniterfeldzug und Samuels Beitrag zum Königtums des Saul', ZAW 58, 1940, 57–70; S. **Mowinckel**, ' "Die letzten Worte Davids", II Sam. 23,1–7', ZAW 45, 1927, 30–58.

M. L. **Newman**, 'The Prophetic Call of Samuel', Israel's Prophetic Heritage, ed. B. W. Anderson, New York and London 1962, 86–97; M. **Noth**, Überlieferungsgeschichtliche Studien I, Halle 1943; 'David and Israel in II Samuel VII' (1957), ET Laws in the Pentateuch, Edinburgh 1966, Philadelphia 1967, 250–9; 'Samuel und Shilo', VT 13, 1963, 390–400; H.-U. **Nübel**, Davids Austieg in der frühe israelitischer Geschichtsschreibung, Diss. Bonn 1959; R. H. **Pfeiffer**, 'Midrash in the Books of Samuel', Quantulacumque K. Lake, ed. R. P. Casey et al., London 1937, 303–16; R. **Press**, 'Der Prophet Samuel. Eine traditionsgeschichtliche Untersuchung', ZAW 56, 1938, 177–225; O. **Procksch**, 'Die letzten Worte Davids', FS R. Kittel, BWAT 13, 1913, 112–25; G. **von Rad**, 'Die Anfänge der Geschichtsschreibung in Israel', in GSAT, Munich 1958, 148–88=ET The Problem of the Hexateuch, Edinburgh and New York 1966, 166–204; 'Zwei Überlieferungen von König Saul', GSAT II, 1973, 199–211; R. **Rendtorff**, 'Beobachtungen zur altisraelitischen Geschichtsschreibung anhand der Geschichte vom Aufstieg Davids', Probleme biblischer Theologie, FS G. von Rad, Munich 1971, 428–39; H. N. **Richardson**, 'The Last Words of David: Some Notes on II Sam. 23, 1–7', JBL 90, 1971, 257–66; A. D. **Ritterspach**, The Samuel Traditions: An Analysis of the Anti-Monarchial Source in I Samuel 1–15, Diss. Graduate Theol. Union, California 1967; L. **Rost**, Die Überlieferung von der Thronnachfolge Davids, BWANT III.6 (=42), 1926.

F. **Schicklberger**, Die Ladeerzählungen des ersten Samuel-Buches, Würzburg 1973; J. **Schildenberger**, 'Zur Einleitung in die Samuelbücher', Studia Anselmiana 27–8, Rome 1951, 130–68; L. **Schmidt**, Menschlicher Erfolg und Jahwes Initiative, WMANT 38, 1970, 120–88; W. H. **Schmidt**, 'Kritik am Königtum', Probleme biblischer Theologie, FS G. von Rad, Munich 1971, 440–61; J. **Schreiner**, Sion-Jerusalem Jahves Königssitz, Munich 1963; H. **Schulte**, Die Entstehung der Geschichtsschreibung im Alten Israel, BZAW 128, 1972; K.-D. **Schunck**, Benjamin, BZAW 86, 1963, 30–138; H. **Seebass**, 'I Sam 15 als Schlüssel für das Verständnis der sogenannten königsfreundlichen Reihe I Sam 9:1–10:16, 11:1–15, 13.2–14:52', ZAW 78, 1966, 148–79; 'Traditionsgeschichte von I Sam 8,10f und 12', ZAW 77, 1965, 286–96; J. A. **Soggin**, Das Königtum in Israel, BZAW 104, 1967, 27–76; H.-J. **Stoebe**, 'Die Goliathperikope I Sam. xvii, l-xviii, 5 und die Textform der Septuaginta', VT 6, 1956, 397–413; 'David und Mikal', BZAW 77, 1958, 224–43; 'Gedanken zur Heldensage in den Samuelbüchern', Das ferne und nahe Wort. FS L. Rost, BZAW 105, 1967, 208–18; H. **Timm**, 'Die Ladeerzählung I Sam 4–6; II Sam 6 und das Kerygma des deuteronomistischen Geschichtswerkes', EvTh 26, 1966, 505–26; M. **Tsevat**, 'Studies in the Book of Samuel', Parts 1–5, HUCA 32–36, 1961–1965; 'Samuel, I and II',

IDB Suppl, 777–81; T. **Veijola**, *Die Ewige Dynastie. David und die Entstehung seiner Dynastie nach der deuteronomistischen Darstellung*, Helsinki 1975; W. **Vischer**, 'Die Bücher Samuelis und der Könige', *Das Christuszeugnis des Alten Testaments* II, Zürich ²1946, 145–280; G. **Wallis**, *Geschichte und Überlieferung*, Berlin 1968; A. **Weiser**, *Samuel. Seine geschichtliche Aufgabe und religiöse Bedeutung*, FRLANT 81, 1962; 'Die Legitimation des Königs David. Zur Eigenart und Entstehung der sogenannten Geschichte von Davids Austieg', *VT* 16, 1966, 325–54; A. C. **Welch**, *Kings and Prophets*, London 1952, New York 1953; J. **Wellhausen**, *Der Text der Bücher Samuel untersucht*, Göttingen 1871; R. N. **Whybray**, *The Succession Narrative*, SBT II.9, 1968; H. **Wildberger**, 'Samuel und die Entstehung des israelitischen Königtums', *TZ* 13, 1957, 442–69; E. **Würthwein**, *Die Erzählung von der Thronfolge Davids – theologische oder politische Geschichtsschreibung?*, Zürich 1974.

1. Historical Critical Problems

Because of the length and diversity of this corpus of biblical material, it should come as no surprise that a wide range of problems have emerged within the history of critical scholarship. The present concern of this review is not to pursue the whole history of this research, but rather to outline some of the main areas which have played a major role and will be most directly affected by the new proposals.

Scope and division of the books of Samuel

The problem of determining the integrity of the books of Samuel as a discrete entity appeared very early in the history of exegesis. Eusebius and Jerome reported that the material had been originally transmitted in the Hebrew Bible as only one book. However, the influence of the Septuagint's dividing of the books of Samuel and Kings into four parts under the title 'Book of Kingdoms' affected the Hebrew Bible and the division of Samuel into two books was adopted in the printed editions from the Bomberg Bible of 1517 onwards. As a result, many modern scholars (e.g. Weiser) have criticized the present division of the two books as arbitrary and clumsy, especially because the death of Saul is separated by the division.

An even more serious problem lies in the beginning and ending of the books of Samuel. Noth argued that the actual division of the material into epochs extended from Judg. 2.6ff. to I Sam. 12 and encompassed the 'period of the Judges'. The present break at I Sam.1 would at best mark a minor subdivision much like the introduction of a new leader as in Judg. 13. The manner in which II Samuel closed was thought by Noth to be even more disruptive of the original narrative in which the story of David's successor reached its climax in I Kings 1. Particularly if L. Rost's theory of II Samuel is followed, the canonical division at the conclusion of Samuel appears to be a major hindrance in understanding the tradition correctly.

In the light of the problems in determining the outer limits of the two books, it is not surprising to discover that the inner divisions are equally problematic. Keil represented the older traditional approach when he divided the two books into three parts, I Sam. 1–12, 13–31, and II Sam. 1–24, and assigned each division to a period of history under Samuel, Saul, and David. But this division does not reflect such important shifts in the story as the transition from Samuel and Saul (chs. 8ff.) to Saul and David (16ff.). For this reason most modern commentators have sought to divide the books into smaller units in terms of the subject matter. Kaiser's outline (*Introduction*, 153) is a typical modern attempt at a closer reading: I.1–7 (Eli and Samuel); I.8–15(Samuel and Saul); I.16–II.1 (Saul and David); II.2–12 (David and his kingdom); II.13–20 (David and his succession); II.21–24 (Additions). Still it remains a question whether this eminently reasonable division does reflect the editor's own intention. The problem is complex because the few obvious summaries of literary sections (I Sam. 7.15–17; 14.47–52; II Sam. 8.15–18; 20.23–26) do not coincide completely with the content divisions as suggested above (cf. particularly the discussion of Schildenberger). The problem is further complicated when a diachronistic dimension is introduced and the material is distributed among different redactions.

In sum, the difficulty of determining the structure of the book seems to arise from the long history of transmission. At various stages in the development the material functioned in different ways and vestiges of several organizational schemes are still evident. The lack of consensus among critical scholars stems largely from a hermeneutical disagreement as to what level constitutes a proper reading of the tradition.

Literary, traditio-historical, and redactional problems

Starting with Eichhorn, the tensions between the various stories in Samuel, especially when compared with Chronicles, were rigorously pursued. Eichhorn concluded that the present form of the material was not derived from contemporary accounts of Samuel, Gad, or Nathan, as had been traditionally supposed (I Chron. 29.29), but was a product of tradition which was distant from the events being described. The effort to determine more exactly the sources lying behind the final form of the story was further made by Thenius (1842) and culminated in the classic literary theory of Wellhausen (F. Bleek's *Einleitung*,[4] 1878).

According to Wellhausen one could separate two parallel strands, especially in chs. 8–14. To the one which he regarded as the earlier and pro-monarchial in sentiment, he assigned 9.1–10.16; 11.1–15; 13–14. To the second, described as later and anti-monarchial, he assigned chs. 7; 8; 10.17–27; and 12. The force of Wellhausen's analysis is testified to by the immediate support which his source divisions received. Of course there remained areas of disagreement among literary critics who basically accepted Wellhausen's position. The further issue of whether the two strands in Samuel could be related to Pentateuchal sources was pursued by Budde and Kittel. Also Wellhausen's dating of the two sources to the Deuteronomic and post-Deuteronomic era was contested, especially by Budde and Cornill who assigned both sources to a pre-Deuteronomic period.

Although the refinement of Wellhausen's solution was continued by Eissfeldt and Pfeiffer up to the period of the Second World War, another approach to the problem had opened up which offered a different solution for explaining the development of the books. Following the lead of Gunkel, Gressmann proposed seeing the narrative material in Samuel, not in terms of parallel strands, but as a collection of once independent stories which had subsequently been joined into a continuous narrative. The most successful example of this approach was the influential monograph of L. Rost on the 'succession narratives' (II Sam. 9–20 + I Kings 1–2). He argued for a continuous story being formed by a skilful joining of independent tradition to recount the history of the Davidic succession. In more recent years this method with its emphasis on the oral tradition has dominated research on Samuel. Monographs such as those of Nübel, Mildenberger, Grønbaek, and Carlson – in spite of significant differences in approach – fall into a broad classification as traditio-historical research and have sought to reconstruct the development of the cycle of David's rise to power (I Sam. 15–II. Sam. 5). Similar attempts have been made on the early Samuel stories and the ark narratives (Campbell).

A third approach in the history of Samuel research, which is closely associated with the first two, is redactional criticism. The emphasis focuses on determining the shape of the narrative in relation to an editor's intentionality and in exploring the forces contributing to this particular imprint. The basic work on Samuel was obviously M. Noth's *Überlieferungsgeschichtliche Studien* of 1943. Noth's great contribution lay in his theory that a Deuteronomistic editor had constructed a unified historical work which extended from Deuteronomy through Kings. The role of the Deuteronomist was not simply that of a compiler, but rather of an author who composed a new literary entity out of older traditions.

In terms of the book of Samuel, Noth argued that the redactional influence was generally less than in either Judges or Kings. In such cycles as the history of Saul (I Sam. 13–II Sam. 2) Noth felt that there was almost no certain signs of Dtr. redaction. Also in the history of David he assigned few places in which the editor had left his mark. However, Noth did attribute a decisive role to the Dtr. hand in the chapters treating the rise of the monarchy (I Sam. 7–13). He accepted in general Wellhausen's categories of a pro- and anti-monarchial source, although Noth preferred to speak of tradition rather than sources. However, he assigned the late, anti-monarchial perspective to the 'free combination' of the Dtr. writer and felt that it rested basically on the theological bias of this single writer.

Since the publication of Noth's seminal monograph, a flood of articles and books have emerged which have sought to support, correct, or modify Noth's redactional theories. In general, the various critical methods outlined above all continued to be used in differing combinations, and have usually been seen as complementary in nature.

The difficulty of arriving at a widely supported consensus because of the increasing complexity in methodology can best be illustrated by the two most frequently studied groups of passages, namely, the rise of the kingdom (I Sam. 7–15), and the 'succession narratives' (II Sam. 9–20 + I Kings 1–2). With regard to the first set of texts, the main lines of Wellhausen's theory of a pro- and an anti-monarchial source have continued to provide the standard starting point for most critical discussion. Noth's refinement of Wellhausen's position increased the tension within the material. In recent years the theory has evoked a heated response and has eroded considerably. First, it has been pointed out that the material does not break easily into two opposing views of the kingdom, but reflects far more complex attitudes (cf. Stoebe and Birch). Thus, the account in I Sam. 10.17–27 may well reflect an entirely different source (Eissfeldt, Wildberger). Weiser has entirely rejected the polarity set up by Wellhausen as misleading, and has argued for a variety of originally separate elements of local tradition each of which had a different concern and function. However, Weiser's ability to point out weaknesses in the older approach has been more acceptable than his own proposal.

Then again, Noth's attempt to identify the later level with the free compositional work of Dtr. has met with much opposition. Such recent studies as those of Birch and Ritterspach have argued for a pre-Deuteronomic redaction somewhat more akin to Budde's position. Again, Weiser has pointed out that the very complexity of attitudes toward the monarch even in the later strand of I Sam. 7–12 speaks against attributing it to the hand of the Dtr. In response Boecker has sought to defend Noth's position that a Dtr. redaction is not incompatible with a highly nuanced approach to its establishment. In sum, recent research has been successful in pointing out the weaknesses of the classic critical solution to the problems of chs. 7–15, but no one new approach has been able to win a consensus.

With regard to the 'succession narrative' (II Sam. 9ff.) the situation is quite similar. Rost's brilliant thesis provided a fresh perspective into the material, and was widely accepted as convincing. Again, there has been a growing dissatisfaction expressed during the last decade which has focused on several aspects of the hypothesis.

Immediately after its publication, Gressmann and Eissfeldt attacked Rost's attempt to link the ark in II Sam. 6 to the succession narrative by way of Michal's reaction as being a highly contrived interpretation, which did not do justice to the function of the chapter. Yet even at this point the level on which the narrative was being read by the various scholars remained unclear. Then again, scholars such as Delekat and Würthwein have accepted Rost's main literary analysis, but have attempted to interpret the purpose of the cycle in a strictly political, rather than theological manner. Finally, a more far-reaching criticism has been launched by Carlson, who rejects completely the theory of a succession narrative, but rather divides the material into two sections: David under the blessing (II Sam. 2–5) and David under the curse (II Sam. 9–24). One of the strongest features of Carlson's argument is to have delineated more closely the final redactional shape of II Samuel which – at least in its final form – has shifted the focus of the stories away from a succession narrative.

The purpose of this review of critical research is not to suggest that no insight into the books has been achieved. This is certainly not the case. Rather, it is to suggest that a deep-seated confusion in methodology still obtains, especially regarding the level on which one reads the material and the intention of the final shaping of the tradition. The result is that the options become almost endless, with little prospect of adjudicating between rival theories.

2. The Canonical Shape of Samuel

The structure of the books

The history of the critical study of Samuel has demonstrated the difficulty of establishing the structure of the books because of a long period of oral and literary development which has left vestiges from the earlier stages in the final form. The canonical shaping has not attempted a consistent and thoroughgoing removal of these earlier schemes of ordering the material. Nevertheless, the final canonical stamp on the material has offered rather clear structural indications for a particular perspective.

The introductory formula of I Sam. 13.1 now forms a major division within I Samuel. Saul's reign is introduced according to the pattern which later was assigned to each successive king, thus establishing him as the first king in the long history of Israel's monarchy. Saul's reign extends from ch. 13 to 31, with his death introducing a new division in II Sam.1.1. The first twelve chapters of I Samuel now form a section around the figure of Samuel. This section opens with Samuel's birth and closes with his farewell

speech in ch. 12. The book division of II Samuel separates the two
reports of Saul's death, but the effect of setting the division after I
Sam. 31 is to shift the focus, even of Saul's death, to the figure of
David whose reign covers the remaining chapters of II Samuel. The
present ending of II Samuel assigns the account of David's final
years to the reign of Solomon (I Kings 1–2), again allowing another
material principle to override a consistent historical sequence. In
sum, the divisions are now loosely grouped around the major figure
in each section, Samuel, Saul, and David.

It is significant to observe that the final structuring of the material has often left the earlier divisions intact, which now function
as subdivisions within the larger divisions, but do not always
closely mesh. Thus in I Sam. 1–12, ch. 7 still serves as a significant
division of the Samuel narrative. Saul's role as the last of the
'judges' is summarized in 7.15–17, and ch. 8 begins a new phase of
Israel's history with the rise of the monarchy. Similarly, after Saul's
initial disobedience in ch. 13 the remaining chapters in Saul's reign
are viewed in the light of David's rise to power (cf. 13.14; 15.28;
16.14). Finally, the reign of David as presented in II Samuel still
reflects earlier divisions and his successful rise to power is sharply
contrasted with his reverses following Nathan's curse.

The function of Hannah's song (I Sam. 2.1–10)

Literary critics have long observed that Hannah's song interrupts the narrative sequence of the chapters. Its strikingly different
poetic form, its peculiar vocabulary, and its reference to the king as
the anointed one, have caused many to regard it simply as a dis-
turbing interpolation. Only recently has the redactional function of
this chapter in relation to the book as a whole been pursued (cf.
Carlson, 246ff.). Significantly those very elements which the older
literary critics regarded as incompatible with the intention of the
Samuel cycle are picked up in the final chapters of Samuel, a section also regarded as secondary. Compare, for example, the clause
'there is no rock like our God' (I Sam. 2.2; II.23.3), the similar
epiphanic language (I.2.10; II.22.8ff.), the blessing to the king
(I.2.10; II.22.51), the motif of exalting and debasing (I.2.6;
II.22.28, and the participial phrase 'killing and making alive'
(I.2.6ff.; II.22.17ff.).

Carlson's interest in ch. 2 remains strictly on the redactional level and he tries to tie it to the editorial work of the 'D-group'. However, at this point the search for the canonical role of the chapter within the corpus of Samuel moves in a different direction from Carlson. The canonical question turns on the issue of how the chapter functions in relation to the final form of the biblical text. I Samuel 1 begins a new period of Israel's history with the divine intervention in the birth of Samuel who brought life out of barrenness. Chapter 2 then interrupts the narrative sequence to offer praise to this great God, and to describe his purpose and ways in history. However, the focus of this chapter is not on history in the abstract; rather it falls specifically on the history which unfolds in the books of Samuel. The God who 'brings low and also exalts', who 'judges the end of the earth', who 'will give strength to his king' reveals his nature in the stories which follow. Chapter 2 offers an interpretative key for this history which is, above all, to be understood from a theocentric perspective. The focus on God's chosen king, his anointed one, David, appears right at the outset, and reveals the stance from which the whole narrative is being viewed.

The role of the appendix (II Sam. 21–24)

Ever since Budde's detailed commentary of 1902, a wide consensus has developed that the last four chapters form an appendix to the book. The major evidence put forward in its support centres in the dislocation of the proper historical sequence by this addition. For example, II Sam. 21.1–4 relates closely to ch. 9 and is presupposed in Shimei's curse (II.16.7). However, it has also been recognized that the six sections comprising these chapters have been arranged in an artistic symmetry: two stories form the beginning and ending of the appendix; then two lists of heroes are included (21.15–22; 23.8–39), finally, two poems are joined at the centre (ch. 22; 23.1–7).

The significance of this appendix for the reading of the whole narrative has seldom been pursued. The older literary critics, such as Budde, developed an elaborate redactional theory that the chapters were first deleted by a Deuteronomic editor as unsuitable and then later clumsily restored at a post-Deuteronomic stage. The traditio-critical approach of Rost also had little positive to say about these chapters which were regarded as an unfortunate intrusion into the succession narrative. The most recent and thorough study, that of Carlson, has recovered much of the importance of these chapters, but has focused on the redactional issue without an adequate treatment of their significance for the final form. The one highly welcomed exception is offered by the commentary of Hertzberg who began to draw out the exegetical significance of the appendix. He has correctly seen that the psalm of ch. 22 offers a theological commentary on the entire history of David (cf. also Gutbrod).

If we review the function of these various sections, a very definite canonical perspective is offered as a hermeneutical guide for understanding the books of Samuel. Of course, the recovery of a canonical intentionality does not rule out the likelihood that other forces of traditional history were involved in the transmission and shaping of this particular block of material. Thus, for example, the case of Elliger's reconstruction of the background of David's thirty chief men (II.23.8ff.), or the role of possible aetiological motifs in ch. 24, are not affected by the concern for the function within the final form of the narrative.

At the outset the story of the Gibeonites and the house of Saul (21.1–14) picks up a dominant issue in David's relation to Saul which is reflected throughout both books of Samuel (I.24.20ff.; II.3.1; II.9.1ff.; II.16.7ff.; II.19.24ff.). The story is at pains to demonstrate that David was not the cause behind the destruction of the Saulites, but the guilt lay with Saul's transgression which called for his blood-guiltiness before the law (cf. Num. 35.33). David's own part consisted, rather, in an act of mercy and compassion to the house of Saul. David had acted in righteousness and not broken his oath to Saul.

The following section (21.15–22) relates four separate incidents in the continuous war with the Philistines, but focuses on David's last battle. The description of his weakness serves to shift the focus of this summary of David's achievements away from his glorification and forms a transition to his praise of God in ch. 22. The psalm title provides the historical context of the hymn from which it is to be understood. Only after David had been given victory from all his enemies does he review his career in order to praise God, his deliverer. The thanksgiving hymn picks up many of the same themes of the song of Hannah and thus reinforces the same theocentric emphasis now seen in retrospect. Again the theme of David's confession of righteousness (22.24ff.) continues to sound a note which was struck in the first section. The full credit for David's victories is attributed to God who delivered him from all his enemies. The hymn closes with a reference to the prophecy of Nathan (II Sam. 7) that David's house will forever sustain the divine blessing.

The 'last words of David' (II Sam. 23.1–7) are introduced with a lengthy description of David's various roles which serve to connect the themes in the previous chapter and also to establish the right tone of solemnity for his last important utterance. In the form of a wisdom saying, contrasting the way of the righteous and the godless, the *mashal* portrays the ideal ruler of Israel as a 'righteous one' (*ṣaddîq*), ruling in the fear of God on whose kingdom the blessing of God falls. David then affirms that his house conforms to this messianic ideal, and he prophesies a glorious future for his dynasty with God's help. Hertzberg characterizes the passages as 'the theological programme for the future of the dynasty' (399).

The final section (ch. 24) returns to a narrative of judgment and forgiveness which formally parallels the initial story within the appendix. Whatever the historical reason lying behind the census – some suggest a military reorganization of the state which intruded into the area of the sacred – the final editor of the book understood the action as a form of David's self-glorification. For his misdeed David is portrayed as repentant, and again the mercy of God toward him and Israel prevails. The choice of the temple site is David's last accomplishment, but it too is firmly set within the context of divine purpose.

In sum, the final four chapters, far from being a clumsy appendix, offer a highly reflective, theological interpretation of David's whole career adumbrating the messianic hope, which provides a clear hermeneutical guide for its use as sacred scripture.

David under the blessing and the curse

Rost's theory of a 'succession narrative' forms a red thread by which to unite the disparate traditions of II Samuel into a unified history and cannot be lightly dismissed. His theory remains an attractive hypothesis by which to explain certain important features within the narrative. However, it seems more and more evident that the intention reconstructed by Rost is no longer shared by the final editor of the book. Rost's theory that chs. 9–20 were written *in majorem gloriam Salomonis* can hardly be maintained as the dominant theme of these chapters. If one takes the canonical shaping seriously, one recognizes that the climax of this alleged succession narrative has been sharply separated from the books of Samuel and assigned a different function in the subsequent history of Solomon. Again, the messianic reading of the book which is suggested both by the song of Hannah and the last words of David moves the narrative in a direction quite different from Rost's.

However, the strongest evidence for seeing a different principle of arrangement operative has been presented by Carlson. He argues for a D-group redaction which sees II Sam. 2–5 as 'David under the Blessing', and II Sam. 9–24 as 'David under the Curse'. Without debating the merits of trying to assign this ordering of the material to a particular redactional group – an interpretation which often seems very fragile – the analysis of the material of II Samuel into two different parts around the Bathsheba incident seems highly convincing. The statement in II Sam. 5.12 that Yahweh had 'exalted his kingdom for the sake of his people' summarizes the period of David's success as the 'shepherd of Israel' (5.2). In contrast, the execution of Nathan's curse (12.11ff.): 'I will raise up evil against you out of your own house', forms a dominant force in the succeeding chapters, and is repeatedly taken up in explicit reference to the curse (16.22, etc.).

In the final shape of the book Nathan's promise to David in II Sam. 7 plays a crucial role for the composition as a whole. The chapter is integrally joined to the ark story of ch. 6, but even though it climaxes the theme of blessing on David and his house, it is set apart with a different role from the blessings of chs. 2–5. The chapter takes up the theme of blessing, but projects it into an eschatological, messianic promise. The blessings are 'for ever' on the house of David (v.29). Thus II Sam. 7 both confirms the initial messianic note sounded in the song of Hannah and is reiterated as valid even after the period of the curse had passed (II Sam. 23.5). David's sin has been judged by the loss of the blessing, but in the end the messianic promise to his house remains unchanged in force.

The crucial significance of II Sam. 7 can also be discerned in the structure of I Samuel. In the same chapter in which Saul's reign over Israel was begun, Samuel announced that Saul's kingdom would not endure forever. God was seeking for a man 'after his own heart' to replace him. Again, in ch. 15 Saul was rejected from being king and the kingdom given to a 'neighbour of yours, who is better than you' (v.28). From the perspective of the final editor Saul's kingship was a false start from the beginning which never partook of the messianic promise to David and therefore could not endure.

The canonical perspective on the rise of the monarchy

Our earlier review of historical critical research pointed out the difficulty of the various attempts made to interpret the complex history of the rise of the monarchy which is reported in I Sam. 7–15. Since Wellhausen's incisive formulation of the problem few would deny that the relationship among the different accounts within these chapters is far from obvious. Whether or not one accepts the classic literary critical formulation of a pro- and an anti-monarchial source, the problem of reconciling at least two strikingly different approaches to this history remains. Significantly the shape which the final form of the book took did not seek to suppress either of the accounts, or to harmonize the approaches in such a way as to remove the tensions within the text. However, a strong case can be made that the present ordering of the chapters offers a particular canonical interpretation of the diversity within the traditions.

As we have seen, Wellhausen's classic solution of the problem has already been modified considerably in recent debate. However, if one starts with Wellhausen's formulation of a pro-monarchial source (A), and an anti-monarchial source (B), the intention of the final editor emerges with equal clarity:

8.1–22	9.1–10.16	10.17–27	11.1–15	12.1–25
B	A	B	A	B

The editor suppresses neither of the traditions. Each is allowed its full integrity and only minor alterations are made to preserve the continuity of the narrative (11.14). However, the two traditions are not just juxtaposed, but carefully intertwined. The scope of the section is also marked with 8.1 serving as an introduction and ch. 12 bringing it to a close. Although ch. 13 may once have belonged to the A strand, it has now been separated from the section and begins a new unit within the Samuel corpus.

What is the effect of this editorial process? How does one read the story in the light of its canonical shaping? Clearly the B source (tradition?) with its anti-monarchial tone has been given the pre-eminence. It now encloses the A source, coming both at the beginning and end. The people think that they are solving an immediate problem with the demand for a king, but the dominant note is the prophetic warning of Samuel against the dangers of their being 'like other nations'. Nevertheless, the message of the A source remains of great importance and its emphasis is enhanced by its new editorial function. The establishment of the kingdom – even though arising out of disobedience – is not to be viewed as a purely secular act. Although the establishment of a monarchy was not according to the original divine plan, God is still deeply involved. When Samuel anoints Saul, the divine blessing is given and the Spirit of God brings him the victory. Chapter 12 functions to summarize the perspective of the combined accounts. The basic issue of Israel's faith has not been determined by the change of the political structure. Israel, along with its new king, must still decide for or against God. 'If you still do wickedly, you shall be swept away, both you and your king!' (12.25). The canonical shaping provides a theological solution to the difficulty of the two traditions by relativizing the importance of the historical change. However, this is a literary and theological solution, and the historical problem of the rise of the kingdom is left largely unresolved in its canonical form.

3. Theological and Hermeneutical Implications

(a) The history of Israel as recorded in the two books of Samuel has been refashioned in the light of an overarching theological perspective which views the history in the light of a divine purpose. Both the hymnic introduction of ch. 2 and the thanksgiving psalm at the book's conclusion (ch. 22) establish a dominant eschatological, messianic perspective for the whole. Israel's history reflects the ways of God in the world which typologizes events into patterns of divine response. God exalts the poor and debases the proud. Although David's human weaknesses are not suppressed and at times even highlighted, his final role as the ideal righteous king emerges with clarity. The effect of this theologizing of history by the canon is to provide a bridge between the reading of Samuel and that of Chronicles. The canonical effect is to draw these two blocks of material closer together rather than to stress their differences.

(b) The frequent attempt of modern Old Testament theologians to see the significance of Samuel to lie in the perfecting of a new sense of God's working in history through an immanental cause and effect chain of human events (von Rad) is in acute danger of overstatement. A warrant for such a claim does lie in the new approach to historical writing reflected in Samuel. However, it is crucial for the theological question to recognize that this approach to history has been subordinated within the canonical context and that the theological importance of this history has been located elsewhere. No one within the canonical process appears to have drawn the theological implications of a new historiography suggested by von Rad. The theological weight of interpretation in the canonical perspective rests on a history which has been harmonized, typologized, and even proverbialized! To disregard this canonical shaping and to extrapolate the theological significance from a reconstructed philosophy is to rest the theological discipline on a very fragile basis indeed.

(c) In spite of the dominant, overwhelming canonical rendering of the material which rules out a move to historicize the tradition, the material is still allowed enormous freedom of movement with the larger canonical outlines. For example, even though David's career has been carefully structured within the rubrics of divine blessing and curse, some of David's most profoundly religious reactions occur within the period of the curse (II Sam. 16.9ff.). Similarly, Saul's reign is portrayed under the shadow of David's coming reign after ch. 13, and yet Saul is never stereotyped into a lifeless symbol of the rejected. To speak of a canonical reading is not to suggest that the flexibility of the text as religious literature was strangled or its inherent possibilities with a vibrant tradition have been quashed.

(d) Finally, the canonical perspective for reading this material serves as the major channel by which later generations within Israel sought to appropriate the sacred tradition. It is clear from Pss. 78 and 132 that the messianic hope of divine blessing, which was promised to the house of David forever, continued to inform the faith of the community and provided the assurance of a future for Israel in times of greatest crisis. Similarly the book of Chronicles affords additional evidence that the hope of the nation even in the exilic period found its grounds in the canonically interpreted history of the house of David.

History of Exegesis

Carpzov I, 228–33; *DThC* 13, 2804f.; *RGG*³ 5, 1360f.

J. **Daniélou**, 'David', *RAC* 3,594–602; R. **Devreesse**, *Les anciens commentateurs grecs de l'Octateuque et des Rois*, Studi e Testi 201, Rome 1959; P. **Dhorme**, 'La tradition exégètique', *Les Livres de Samuel*, ÉB, 1910, 13–15; D. C. **Duling**, 'The Promises to David and their Entrance into Christianity', *NTS* 20, 1973/4, 55–77; A. M. **La Bonnardière**, 'Les livres de Samuel et des Rois . . . dans l'oeuvre de Saint Augustin', *Revue des Études Augustiennes* 2, Paris 1956, 335–63; A. **Saltman**, 'Pseudo-Jerome on the Commentary of Andrew of St Victor 'on Samuel', *HTR* 67, 1974, 195–253; 'Introduction', *Pseudo-Jerome Quaestiones on the Book of Samuel*, Studia Post-Biblica 26, Leiden 1975; I. **Sonne**, 'The Paintings of the Dura Synagogue', *HUCA* 20, 1947, 316–20; H.-J. **Stoebe**, 'Die Geschichte der Forschung', *Das erste Buch Samuelis*, Gütersloh 1973, 32–52.

XV

KINGS

Commentaries

K. C. W. F. Baehr, ET, LCHS, 1872
C. F. Keil, BC, 1876
O. Thenius, M. Loehr, KeH, ³1898
I. Benzinger, KHC, 1899
R. Kittel, HKAT, 1902
C. F. Burney, 1903
J. Skinner, CeB, 1904
A. Šanda, EH, 1911–12
H. Gressmann, *SAT*, ²1921
O. Eissfeldt, *HSAT*, ⁴1922
A. Médebielle, SB, 1949

I. W. Slotki, SonB, 1950
J. Montgomery, H. S. Gehman, ICC, 1951
A. van den Born, BOuT, 1958
R. de Vaux, JB, ²1958
J. Gray, OTL, ²1970 (³1977)
H. A. Brongers, POuT, 1967–70
M. Noth, BK, 1968
J. Fichtner, K. D. Fricke, BAT, 1964–72
J. Robinson, CNEB, 1972, 1976
E. Würthwein (I), ATD, 1977

Bibliography

P. R. **Ackroyd**, 'Historians and Prophets,' *SEA* 33, 1968, 18–54; 'An Interpretation of the Babylonian Exile: A Study of 2 Kings 20, Isa. 38–39', *SJT* 27, 1974, 329–52; 'Kings, I and II', *IDB Suppl*, 516–19; W. F. **Albright**, 'King Joiachin in Exile', *BA* 5, 1942, 49–55; 'The Judicial Reform of Jehoshaphat', *A. Marx Jubilee Volume*, New York 1950, 61–82; B. **Alfrink**, 'Die Schlacht bei Megiddo und der Tod des Josias (609)' *Bibl* 15, 1934, 173–84; A. **Alt**, 'Israels Gaue unter Salomo', 1913, *KS* II, 1953, 76–89; 'Das Gottesurteil auf dem Karmel', 1935, *KS* II, 1953, 135–49; 'Der Stadtstaat Samaria', 1945, *KS* III, 1959, 258–302; 'The Monarchy in the Kingdoms of Israel and Judah', ET *Essays* (see Pentateuch), 1966, 239–59; J. **Barr**, 'Story and History in Biblical Theology', *JR* 56, 1976, 1–17; I. **Benzinger**, *Jahwist und Elohist in den Königsbüchern*, BWA[N]T II 2 (=27), 1921; K.-H. **Bernhardt**, 'Der Feldzug der drei Könige', *Schalom. Studien zu Glaube und Geschichte Israels. A. Jepsen dargebracht*, Berlin 1971, 11–22; J. **Bright**, *A History of Israel*, Philadelphia and London ²1972; R. P.

Carroll, 'The Elijah-Elisha Sagas', *VT* 19, 1969, 400–15; B. S. **Childs**, *Isaiah and the Assyrian Crisis*, SBT II.3, 1967; F. M. **Cross**, 'The Themes of the Book of Kings and the Structure of the Deuteronomic History', *Canaanite Myth and Hebrew Epic*, Cambridge, Mass. 1973, 274–89; F. M. **Cross** and D. N. **Freedman**, 'Josiah's Revolt against Assyria', *JNES* 12, 1953, 56–8.

J. **Debus**, *Die Sünde Jerobeams. Studien zur Darstellung Jeroboams und der Geschichte des Nordreichs in der deuteronomistischen Geschichtsschreibung*, FRLANT 93, 1967; W. **Dietrich**, *Prophetie und Geschichte. Eine redaktionsgeschichtliche Untersuchung zum deuteronomistischen Geschichtswerk*, FRLANT 108, 1972; H. **Donner**, 'The Separate States of Israel and Judah', *Israelite and Judaean History*, ed. J. H. Hayes and J. M. Miller, OTL, 1977, 381–434; O. **Eissfeldt**, *Der Gott Karmel*, Berlin 1954; 'Die Komposition von I Reg 16,29–II Reg 13,25', *Das ferne und nahe Wort. FS L. Rost*, BZAW 105, 1967, 49–58; I. **Engnell**, *Studies in Divine Kingship in the Ancient Near East*, Uppsala 1943, Oxford ²1967; G. **Fohrer**, *Elia*, Zürich ²1968; K. **Galling**, 'Der Gott Karmel und die Ächtung der fremden Götter', *Geschichte und Altes Testament. FS A. Alt*, Tübingen 1953, 105–25; 'Der Ehrenname Elisas und die Entrückung Elias', *ZTK* 53, 1956, 129–48; P. L. **Garber**, 'Reconstructing Solomon's Temple', *BA* 14, 1951, 2–24; D. W. **Gooding**, 'The Septuagint's Rival Versions of Jeroboam's Rise to Power', *VT* 16, 1967, 173–89; H. **Gunkel**, *Elias, Jahwe und Baal*, Tübingen 1906; E. **Haag**, 'Die Himmelfahrt des Elias nach 2 Kg. 2,1–15', *Trierer TZ* 78, Trier 1969, 18–32; E. **Haller**, *Charisma und Ekstasis. Die Erzählung von dem Propheten Micha ben Jimla, I Kön. 22, 1–28a*, TheolEx NF 87, 1960; W. W. **Hallo**, 'From Qarqar to Carchemish: Assyria and Israel in the Light of New Discoveries', *BA* 23, 1960, 33–61; B. **Halpern**, 'Sectionalism and Schism', *JBL* 93, 1974, 519–32; 'Levitical Participation in the Reform Cult of Jeroboam I', *JBL* 95, 1976, 31–42; M. **Haran**, 'The Rise and Decline of the Empire of Jeroboam ben Joash', *VT* 17, 1967, 266–97; G. **Hentschel**, *Die Elijaerzählungen*, Erfurter theologische Studien 33, Leipzig 1977; G. **Hölscher**, 'Das Buch der Könige, seine Quellen und seine Redaktion', *Eucharisterion. FS H. Gunkel* I, FRLANT 36, 1923, 158–213; *Geschichtsschreibung in Israel*, Lund 1953; E. **Janssen**, *Judah in der Exilszeit*, FRLANT 69, 1956; A. K. **Jenkins**, 'Hezekiah's Fourteenth Year. A New Interpretation of 2 Kings xviii 13–xix 37', *VT* 26, 1976, 284–98; A. **Jepsen**, *Die Quellen des Königsbuches*, Halle ²1956; 'Gottesmann und Prophet. Anmerkungen zum Kapitel 1 Könige 13', *Probleme biblischer Theologie, FS G. von Rad*, Munich 1971, 171–82; A. R. **Johnson**, *Sacral Kingship in Ancient Israel*, Cardiff 1955; J. **Liver**, 'The Book of the Acts of Solomon', *Bibl* 48, 1967, 75–101; N. **Lohfink**, 'Die Bundesurkunde des Königs Josias. Eine Frage an die Deuteronomiumsforschung', *Bibl* 44, 1963, 261–88, 461–98.

A. **Malamat**, 'The Last Kings of Judah and the Fall of Jerusalem', *IEJ* 18, 1968, 137–56; J. **McKay**, *Religion in Judah under the Assyrians 732–609 BC*, SBT II.26, 1973; T. N. D. **Mettinger**, *Solomonic State Officials: A Study of the*

Civil Government Officials of the Israelite Monarchy, Coniectanea Biblica OT, 5, Lund 1971; J. M. **Miller**, 'The Elisha Cycle and the Accounts of the Omride Wars', *JBL* 85, 1966, 441–54; 'The Fall of the House of Ahab', *VT* 17, 1967, 307–24; K. **Möhlenbrink**, *Der Tempel Salomos. Eine Untersuchung seiner Stellung in der Sakralarchitektur des Alten Orients*, BWANT IV.7 (=59), 1932; J. A. **Montgomery**, 'Archival Data in the Books of Kings', *JBL* 53, 1934, 46–52; N. **Na'aman**, 'Sennacherib's "Letter to God" on his Campaign to Judah', *BASOR* 214, 1974, 25–39; B. D. **Napier**, 'The Omrides of Jezreel', *VT* 9, 1959, 366–78; M. **Noth**, *Überlieferungsgeschichtliche Studien* I, Halle 1943, 103–29; B. **Oded**, 'Judah and the Exile', *Israelite and Judaean History*, ed. J. H. Hayes, 435–88; A. **Parrot**, *The Temple of Jerusalem*, ET London and New York 1957; L. **Perlitt**, *Bundestheologie im Alten Testament*, WMANT 36, 1969; I. **Plein** (= **Willi-Plein**), 'Erwägungen zur Überlieferung von 1 Reg 11, 26–14, 20', *ZAW* 78, 1966, 8–24; O. **Plöger**, *Die Prophetengeschichten der Samuel- und Königsbücher*, Diss. Greifswald 1937; B. **Porten**, 'The Structure and Theme of the Solomon Narrative (1 Kings 3–11)', *HUCA* 38, 1967, 93–128; O. **Procksch**, 'König Josia', *Festgabe für T. Zahn*, Erlangen 1928, 19–53.

G. **von Rad**, 'The Deuteronomistic Theology of History in the Book of Kings', *Studies in Deuteronomy*, ET, SBT I.9, 1953, 74ff.; M. **Rehm**, *Textkritische Untersuchungen zu den Parallelstellen der Samuel-Königsbücher und der Chronik*, Münster 1937; A. **Rofé**, 'The Classification of Prophetical Stories', *JBL* 89, 1970, 427–40; 'Classes in the Prophetical Stories', *SVT* 26, 1974, 143–64; H. H. **Rowley**, 'Elijah on Mount Carmel', *BJRL* 43, 1960–1, 190–219; W. **Rudolph**, 'Die Einheitlichkeit der Erzählung vom Sturz der Atalja (2 Kön 11)', *FS A. Bertholet*, Tübingen 1950, 473–8; H.-C. **Schmitt**, *Elisa. Traditionsgeschichtliche Untersuchungen zur vorklassischen nordisraelitischen Prophetie*, Gütersloh 1972; H. **Schulte**, *Die Entstehung der Geschichtsschreibung im Alten Israel*, BZAW 128, 1972; H. **Seebass**, 'Zur Königserhebung Jerobeams I', *VT* 17, 1967, 325–33; 'Der Fall Naboth in I Reg xxi', *VT* 24, 1974, 474–88; R. **Smend**, 'Das Gesetz und die Völker', *Probleme biblischer Theologie*, FS G. von Rad, Munich 1971, 494ff.; 'Der biblische und der historische Elia', *SVT* 28, 1975, 167–84; 'Das Wort Jahwes an Elia', *VT* 25, 1975, 525–43; J. A. **Soggin**, *Das Königtum in Israel*, BZAW 104, 1967, 77ff.; 'The Davidic-Solomonic Kingdom', *Israelite and Judaean History*, ed. J. H. Hayes, 332–80; J. J. **Stamm**, 'Elia am Horeb', *Studia Biblica et Semitica T. C. Vriezen dedicata*, Wageningen 1966, 327–34; O. H. **Steck**, *Überlieferung und Zeitgeschichte in der Elia-Erzählungen*, WMANT 26, 1968.

R. **de Vaux**, 'Les prophètes de Baal sur le mont Carmel', *Bulletin du Musée de Beyrouth* 5, Beirut 1941, 7–20; ET in de Vaux, *The Bible and the Ancient Near East*, New York 1971, London 1972, 238–51; *Ancient Israel*, ET London and New York 1961, 312–30; H. **Weippert**, 'Die "deuteronomistischen" Beurteilungen der Könige von Israel und Juda und das Problem der Redaktion der Königsbücher', *Bibl* 53, 1972, 301–39; J. **Wellhausen**,

Die Composition des Hexateuch und der historischen Bücher des Alten Testaments, Berlin ³1899; P. **Welten**, 'Naboths Weinberg (I Kön 21)', *EvTh* 33, 1973, 18–32; C. F. **Whitley**, 'The Deuteronomic Presentation of the House of Omri', *VT* 2, 1952, 137–52; H. W. **Wolff**, 'Das Kerygma des deuteronomistischen Geschichtswerkes', *ZAW* 73, 1961, 171–86; E. **Würthwein**, 'Die Erzählung vom Gottesurteil auf dem Karmel', *ZTK* 59, 1962, 131–46; 'Zur Komposition von I Reg 22,1–38', *Das ferne und nahe Wort. FS L. Rost*, BZAW 105, 1967, 245ff.; 'Elijah at Horeb, Reflections on I Kings 19.9–18', *Proclamation and Presence. OT Essays in Honour of G. H. Davies*, ed. J. I. Durham and J. R. Porter, London and Richmond, Va. 1970, 152–66; E. **Zenger**, 'Die deuteronomistische Interpretation der Rehabilitierung Jejachins', *BZ* NF 12, 1968, 16–30.

Selected Bibliography on the Chronology of Kings

Cf. the full bibliographical information in A. Jepsen and R. Hanhart (below), 48; A. Jepsen, *VT* 18, 1968, 31; E. R. Thiele (below), 2nd ed., 219–26; D. Shenkel (below), 138ff.; D. N. Freedman and E. F. Campbell (below), 215–19; J. H. Hayes and J. M. Miller, eds., *Israelite and Judaean History*, 678–81.

W. F. **Albright**, 'The Chronology of the Divided Monarchy of Israel', *BASOR* 100, 1945, 16–22; 'New Light from Egypt on the Chronology and History of Israel and Judah', *BASOR* 130, 1953, 4–11; K. T. **Andersen**, 'Die Chronologie der Könige von Israel und Judah', *StTh* 23, 1969, 69–114; J. **Begrich**, *Die Chronologie der Könige von Israel und Juda*, Tübingen 1929; D. J. A. **Clines**, 'Regnal Year Reckoning in the Last Year of the Kingdom of Judah', *Australian Journal of Biblical Archaeology* 2, Sydney 1972, 9–34; S. J. **De Vries**, 'Chronology, OT', *IDB Suppl*, 161–6; D. N. **Freedman** and E. F. **Campbell**, 'The Chronology of Israel and the Ancient Near East', *The Bible and the Ancient Near East, FS W. F. Albright*, ed. G. E. Wright, New York 1961, 203–28; D. N. **Freedman**, 'The Babylonian Chronicle', *BA* 19, 1956, 50–60; W. W. **Hallo**, 'From Qarqar to Carchemish', *BA* 23, 1960, 34–61; A. **Jepsen** and R. **Hanhart**, *Untersuchungen zur israelitisch-jüdischen Chronologie*, BZAW 88, 1964; A. **Jepsen**, 'Noch einmal zur israelitisch-jüdischen Chronologie', *VT* 18, 1968, 31–46; S. **Mowinckel**, 'Die Chronologie der israelitischen und jüdischen Könige', *AcOr* 10, 1932, 162–277; V. **Pavlovsky** and E. **Vogt**, 'Die Jahre der Könige von Juda und Israel', *Bibl* 45, 1964, 321–47; G. **Sauer**, 'Die chronologische Angaben in den Büchern Deut. bis 2 Kön.', *TZ* 24, 1968, 1–14; J. D. **Shenkel**, *Chronology and Recensional Development in the Greek Text of Kings*, HSM 1, 1968; H. **Tadmor**, 'Chronology of the last Kings of Judah', *JNES* 15, 1956, 226–30; 'Chronologie' (Hebrew), *EB* 4, 1962, 254–310; E. R. **Thiele**, *The Mysterious Numbers of the Hebrew Kings*, Exeter and Grand Rapids, Mich. ²1965; W. R. **Wifall**, 'The Chronology of the

Divided Monarchy of Israel', *ZAW* 80, 1968, 319–37; D. **Wiseman**, *Chronicles of Chaldaean Kings (626–556 BC) in the British Museum*, London 1956.

1. Historical Critical Problems

Critical research on the book of Kings has focused on the standard problems of text, sources, dating, and authorship (cf. the detailed review in the *Introductions* of Eissfeldt, Fohrer, and Kaiser). In addition, the special problem of chronology within Kings has continued to evoke much attention (cf. special bibliography). On the issues of traditio-historical criticism and redactional criticism the basic monograph of Noth has been at the centre of the debate. The appearance of Jepsen's book on the sources, which was written independently of Noth, offered an additional confirmation of this new scholarly direction.

Much of the impact of Noth's hypothesis regarding the Deuteronomistic historian rested on the simplicity of his theory which seemed to be able to resolve a whole series of critical problems in a fresh way. Noth argued for a Dtr. author who had created a historical composition, extending from Deuteronomy to Kings, which reflected a unified theological perspective. Although this biblical writer had used various earlier collections of stories and other traditions, he had not functioned simply as a collector or even as a redactor, but rather he had exercised the creative literary freedom of an author. (Noth's distinction between an author and a redactor in the light of his whole theory is not always illuminating.)

Noth pointed out that the handling of the history of the Kings presented the Dtr. author with a set of problems different from those which he had encountered in the earlier material. Whereas the material comprising the earlier part of his history, especially in Samuel, had already been formed into connected narrative traditions, no such unifying literary forces had yet been at work in the period of Kings. The Dtr. writer was thus able to create his historical composition directly from a variety of sources which were available to him, and to reflect his overall theological purpose in clearest fashion. Particularly impressive was Noth's defence of one unified chronological framework extending throughout the entire history (60ff.). Finally, Noth offered a simple solution to the question of the author's purpose and the date of composition. He attributed the composition to a single author who wrote during the exile from Palestine (c.550) in order to demonstrate how Israel's continual disobedience to the laws of God finally caused the nation to be destroyed through divine judgment.

The immediate effect of Noth's theory of a Dtr. author was to call into serious question the earlier critical attempts of scholars to see the literary development of the Former Prophets in an analogy to that of the Pentateuch as consisting of literary strands (cf. ch. XI). Almost overnight the older paradigm was abandoned by the majority of scholars in favour of the new model. However, this move does not suggest an uncritical acceptance of Noth's entire theory. Rather, the last three decades have been dominated by various attempts to modify, correct, and alter the hypothesis. In the first place, questions were raised about the adequacy of Noth's concept of a single author composing a unified historical work. Jepsen's detailed study seemed to indicate a much more complicated prehistory to the material than that envisioned by Noth (cf. also Dietrich and Schmitt). The sharp contrast between seeing the Deuteronomist as an author and as a redactor seemed to erode considerably in the debate. Moreover, the insistence on identifying the author with a single personage who was unattached to a larger group seemed to many unconvincing.

A second area in which modifications have been proposed lies in the question of dating the work of the author. Fohrer (*Introduction*, 167ff.) is representative of a good number of scholars in holding that the basic Dtr. redaction is pre-exilic. Dtr.'s unfamiliarity with the Babylonian exile and his description of Josiah's death point to a period before 609. Subsequently in the post-exilic period, the history was extended at least to 561 and the release of Jehoiachin. Similarly, Cross (287 ff.) argues that the recognition of two stages of redaction explains certain historical puzzles and apparent contradictions in the historical perspective. He attributes the primary edition to an author in the time of Josiah (Dtr.[1]) and sets the later supplementary reworking during the exile (Dtr.[2]). He links both editions to specific historical referents.

Finally, there has been much discussion concerning the general purpose of the entire work. Noth's view that the writer's concern was solely a negative one, namely to register the divine judgment which destroyed the nation, has called forth many rejoinders. Von

Rad has argued for the continuation of the promise to David, especially demonstrated at the end of the Dtr.'s work by the release of Jehoiachin from prison. H. W. Wolff has emphasized the continuing theme of repentance as being essential to the purpose of the author, and forming a paradigm of faith for later Israel to emulate. F. M. Cross also addresses this issue, but argues that an original theme of hope was overwritten and contradicted by the last editor, thus causing the present confusion for the modern reader.

Modern historical scholarship has, of course, also engaged itself with a large variety of other problems in the book of Kings which are not directly related to Noth's thesis. Particularly fruitful has been the vast literature surrounding the study of the Elijah stories. Impressive numbers of prominent scholars of the past have tried their hand at resolving the literary, historical, and theological problems of the cycle (cf. Gunkel, Alt, Eissfeldt, Galling, de Vaux, Fohrer, Rowley). Interest has not diminished, to judge by the more recent contributions of Smend, Steck and Würthwein. Steck's monograph in particular demonstrates the breakdown in methodological consensus and has called forth heated responses (cf. Smend). Research on the Elisha cycle has been far less, but is not different in kind (cf. Schmitt).

Finally, it is important to observe that attention to the difficult historical questions raised in the book of Kings has continued to be evoked (cf. especially the volume on *Israelite and Judaean History*, ed. J. H. Hayes and J. M. Miller, for full bibliographies on these issues). In spite of much critical analysis, such events as Sennacherib's invasion and Josiah's reform have not come to any certain resolution, and continue to evoke fresh discussion. In addition, interest in the peculiar textual problems of the book of Kings has been strong (J. W. Wevers [see bibliography to ch. IV above], J. D. Shenkel), but much work still lies ahead.

2. The Canonical Shape of Kings

The structure of the book

In the Hebrew Bible the book of Kings was transmitted as a unity and was only divided into two separate books in the fifteenth century under the influence of the Greek and Latin versions. The present division into two books is not particularly fortunate. It separates the history of Ahaziah and carries the Elijah cycle into II Kings in an arbitrary fashion. Some scholars have attributed the division to the mechanical need of fitting the book equally on two scrolls. The precedent for beginning books with the formula 'after the death of N' (cf. Josh. 1.1; Judg. 1.1; II Sam. 1.1) may also have exerted an influence.

The material within the books of Kings falls into three sections according to its content and follows the pattern established in Samuel:

1. I Kings 1–11, Solomon.
2. I Kings 12–II Kings 17, History of the Kings of Israel and Judah until the Destruction of the Northern Kingdom.
3. II Kings 18–25, History of the Kings of Judah.

The first two sections conclude with an appropriate summary. The final section describes the destruction and exile of Judah along with the additional note on the fate of Jehoiachin.

The use of sources

It is evident that the books of Kings represent only a skeletal account of a history which extends from the accession of Solomon to the destruction of Jerusalem in 587. A most striking feature is the conscious principle of selection which is operative throughout the book. Not only is the reader continually told where he can find additional information about each king ('now the rest of the acts of N ... are they not written in the book of the ... '), but also there is no attempt whatever to give a detailed account of each king's reign. The obvious lack of concern for a detailed survey would confirm the conclusion that the writer's purpose in the history lay elsewhere. Several indices reveal the author's true intention. First of all, the writer makes it clear that he conceives of his task as describing a unified history of events of one people within a cir- cumscribed period. In spite of the political division into two king- doms the writer refuses to treat them separately, but shuttles back and forth between them. The history ends with the loss of the land and the exile of the people. However, the threat of this disaster appears from the beginning of the history and connects the various reigns like a red thread. The writer continually recapitulates prior events and adumbrates future ones in order to enforce his theologi- cal interpretation of the whole history as a unified entity.

Secondly, the writer's consistent attempt to offer reasons for the impending judgment further confirms his intention to explain as well as to describe why Israel was destroyed. Sometimes he uses a stereotyped expression to characterize a reign ('he did not turn from the sins of Jeroboam', II Kings 3.1; 10.28; 13.2, etc.), but at other times he reveals an essential feature of his composition by assigning a lengthy theological explanation to justify the divine judgment (I Kings 11.9ff.; II Kings 17.7ff.). The author's concern to see an inner connection between the various epochs of Israel's history sets his work apart from the various sources which he had at his disposal.

The manner in which the reader is constantly referred back to the writer's sources indicates that he did not envision his composition to be in contradiction with his sources. He was not attempting to rewrite history nor to supply hitherto unknown information. Neither was he writing a 'theological history' which operated on its own principles apart from the history found in the official records. Event and interpretation belonged together and he needed only a selection from a larger historical sequence to demonstrate his thesis.

Prophetic history

Within the Hebrew canon the book of Kings has been assigned to the Former Prophets. That the biblical author conceived of his history in the closest relation to the prophets is manifested throughout. The blame for the nation's destruction did not lie with Israel's God, above all because Yahweh had 'warned Israel and Judah by every prophet and seer' (II Kings 17.13). Indeed, the intense involvement of the prophets extends the entire length of the books of Kings beginning with Nathan (I Kings 1.45), including Ahijah (I.11.29–40; 14.5f.), Shemaiah (I.12.21–24), Elijah (I.17.1ff.), Micaiah (I.22.8ff.), Elisha (II.2.1ff.), Jonah (II.14.25), Isaiah (II.19.1ff.), Huldah (II.22.14ff.) and others.

Moreover, von Rad pointed out the full significance of the prophecy-fulfilment pattern in the book of Kings. In some twelve cases beginning with the house of Eli (I Sam. 2.27–36) a prophecy is given which is explicitly picked up at a later date as having been fulfilled 'according to the word of Yahweh' (e.g. II Sam. 7.13//I Kings 8.20; I Kings 11.29ff.// I Kings 12.15; I Kings 13// II Kings 23.16–18, etc.). The prophetic word is thus conceived of as a 'history-creating force' (von Rad) which is unleashed in the world and accomplishes its purpose. The prophetic element does not lie simply in the predictive nature of the oracle, but in its integral connection with the whole historical process in which divine judgment and salvation unfolds.

Although it is customary in the modern scholarly discussion to distinguish sharply between a prophetic view of history and the Dtr. historian's, this difference is not registered in the canonical interpretation of the book of Kings. Rather, the writer of Kings clearly identifies his interpretation of Israel's history with that of the prophets. From the canonical perspective the editor of Kings cannot be regarded as representing a private or idiosyncratic point of view. Rather, he sees himself standing alongside the generation of prophets who had foretold the coming destruction. In fact, the canonical shaping did not result in a flattening out of the variety of messages which was actually within the different prophetic traditions, as one can discern by comparing the Elijah and Elisha cycles.

Law and covenant

Martin Noth designated the author of the book of Kings with the name 'Deuteronomistic' because he felt that the dominant influence upon him derived from the book of Deuteronomy. However, long before Noth's new formulation of the issues, it had been generally assumed by biblical scholars that the author of Kings used as his primary criterion for evaluating the rulers of Israel and Judah a norm of cultic purity which was found only in Deuteronomy. As von Rad expressed it, opposition to all continuing Canaanite high places had become for Deuteronomy the *articulus stantis et cadentis ecclesiae*. On the grounds of this criterion all the kings of Israel are condemned because they all 'walked in the way of Jeroboam, the son of Nebat'. The kings of Judah fare only slightly better. Five receive qualified approval and only two unqualified.

Usually modern critical scholars have characterized the Deuteronomic criterion as 'cultic orthodoxy' and viewed it as extremely narrow. The writer of Kings was also felt to lack all genuine sense of historical writing and his stance was contrasted negatively with the historical acumen of the author of the 'succession narrative' of II Samuel. Von Rad has attempted to undercut the force of this evaluation in several ways (*Problem of the Hexateuch*,

206ff.). First, he argued that the Dtr. writer's historical criterion of an 'either-or' stemmed from a peculiar theological attitude and should not be rejected all too quickly in the light of modern historical method. Secondly, he resisted the charge that the cultic norm was totally anachronistic by trying to show that such a norm was at least adumbrated in the age of the ancient Israelite amphictyony.

Although von Rad's interpretation has undoubtedly helped to recover a more sympathetic reading of the book of Kings, he has not reached to the heart of the problem, in my judgment. I would argue that the author of the book of Kings, far from being idiosyncratic, actually reflects a canonical perspective in his use of Deuteronomy as a theological norm for his history. At the outset, it is important to recognize how the author of Kings derives his criterion. He does not speak simply of traditions, but of a fixed written form which he designates as a 'book' (II Kings 22.1), as the 'book of law' (II.22.8, 11), as 'the law book of Moses' (II Kings 14.6), and 'book of the covenant' (II.23.2). The Torah of the Dtr. editor has not only received a written form, but it has already assumed its role as providing the authoritative framework for interpreting the earlier narrative and legal material. The author of Kings identifies himself, not just with a book, but with that religious community which was constituted by the Torah of Moses, as interpreted by Deuteronomy. In other words, the criterion of so-called 'cultic orthodoxy' was not a peculiar perspective of a Dtr. author or of a Deuteronomic school, but one representing the authoritative reading of the Mosaic law by a larger canonical tradition. Although the historical evidence is lacking by which to bring into sharper focus the exact historical contours of this socio-historical group, the theological significance lies in seeing the author of Kings, not as an innovator, but as a faithful representative of a canonical perspective which ultimately became coextensive with all of Judaism. The elevation of the opposition to Canaanite cults to a central position of Hebrew faith derives, therefore, not from an idiosyncratic position of one person, but arises from the particular shape of Israel's normative religious tradition which the book of Deuteronomy provided.

The function of Deuteronomy further explains the sharp 'either-or' stance of the Dtr. writer in evaluating each king's performance. The Deuteronomist set up his history in the light of the Mosaic law. Deut. 27–28 in particular had portrayed the blessings of obedience and the curses of disobedience to the Sinai covenant. It thus followed that history written from the perspective of obedience or disobedience, blessing or curse, would fall into an either-or pattern. In the actual development of his historical composition, the writer modified this theological perspective, not by introducing a third possibility, but by reference to the long-suffering mercy of God who continued to postpone executing the judgment which the disobedience to the covenant rightly entailed (I.11.34ff.; I.21.29; II.17.7ff.; II.22.18ff., etc.).

The promise to David

Von Rad has been the leading advocate of those wanting to see in the book of Kings not just a word of judgment, but a word of promise directed to the house of David and fulfilling itself in spite of the national catastrophe (*OT Theology* I,344ff.). Von Rad argued that there is a definite 'messianic motif' in the Dtr. history. He makes reference to the continual measuring of the Judaean kings as to whether or not they walked before God as David who was 'wholly true to Yahweh' (cf. I Kings 9.4; I.11.4, 6; I.14.8; I.15.3, etc.). Von Rad concludes that 'the anointed who stands as a standard and type behind the Deuteronomist's melancholy picture of the monarchical period is the completely righteous man who keeps all the commandments with his whole heart'(345). At the same time, von Rad is forced to concede that this understanding of the king in Dtr. represents a theology of history which is furthest removed from the position of the book of Deuteronomy.

Von Rad's interpretation of a messianic motif in Kings has been sharply attacked by both Wolff and Cross ('Themes', 276f.). The most recent criticism comes from Perlitt (47ff.) and focuses on the issue of a covenant with David. Perlitt contests von Rad's messianic interpretation and argues that neither the pre-Dtr. tradition nor the Dtr. writer himself speaks of a 'covenant' with David. Dtr. speaks only of promises to David which collapsed when the kings of Judah displayed their disobedience to the law. Passages such as II Sam. 7 and 23, Pss. 89 and 132, which speak of an 'eternal covenant' and a 'dynasty for ever', Perlitt assigns to a late, post-exilic period.

Once again, in my judgment, the issue has not been seen in clear enough focus. In spite of his keen observations, von Rad has sought to ground his messianic interpretation on a traditio-historical development without serious attention to the canonical shape which the biblical editors assigned to the David material. As a result, he is not only unable to make a successful bridge from the Deuteronomic concept of kingship to that of Dtr., but he is extremely vulnerable to Perlitt's literary critical attack on the dating of the Davidic traditions.

As we observed in our chapter on Samuel, the earlier traditions were given a redactional shape in II Sam. 7 and especially in the appendix II Sam. 21–24 which envisioned David as the ideal, righteous king. Without eliminating the historical features of David's chequered past, the Davidic traditions were cast in a messianic light by means of redactional shaping. The crucial point to make is that the Dtr. figure of David which appears in the book of Kings closely reflects this same canonical picture. A comparison of the vocabulary of II Sam. 22 with the Deuteronomic references to David reveals some remarkable similarities. David is the 'righteous one' (II Sam. 22.21; cf. I Kings 9.4), who is 'whole' (*tammîm*) before God (II Sam. 22.24/I Kings 9.4), obeying the 'ordinances and statutes' (II Sam. 22.23/I Kings 11.38), 'keeping his ways' (I Sam. 22.22/I Kings 11.33). Again, God shows his 'steadfast love to his anointed' (II Sam. 22.51/I Kings 8.23; Ps. 89. 1,28), and promises him an 'eternal covenant' (II Sam. 23.5/Ps. 89.3). In sum, von Rad's characterization of the Deuteronomist's ideal king is precisely that of the canonical David.

In the light of these observations, the issue of the Dtr. interpretation of the figure of David cannot be settled by an attempt to assign all the passages which speak of a Davidic covenant to a late post-exilic period (*contra* Perlitt). Rather, the Dtr. portrayal of David clearly stands within an exegetical tradition – we have called it canonical – which extends in time both before and after the age of the author of Kings. The close parallels between the redactional shaping of Samuel (II Sam. 22) and the vocabulary of Kings are best explained by reference to a common traditional understanding of the Davidic material which the two books shared.

To summarize: the stereotyped portrayal of David by the author of Kings as the model of the righteous king is not to be regarded as an idiosyncratic idealization of one author, but rather reflects a common canonical stance which was grounded in a particular understanding of Israel's sacred literature and which was testified to in its shaping.

The hope for a future

How was the book of Kings to be used by future generations of Israelites when its main purpose lay in portraying the destruction of the nation which had broken the covenant? The case for seeing a messianic hope has already been made. But does this one theme exhaust the positive role of the book for later generations of Israelites? In my judgment, H. W. Wolff has made out a good case for recognizing in this history a pattern of repentance and forgiveness which served as a model to be followed. Particularly in the final form of Solomon's prayer of dedication (I Kings 8), reference is made to a people 'who are carried away to the land of the enemy' (v.46) and the assurance is sought that repentance would issue in divine forgiveness. Moreover, because the writer of Kings does not restrict the presence of God to either the temple or the land, the possibility of renewed blessing is left open to the hope of future generations.

3. The Problem of the Chronology in the Book of Kings

The chronological data in the book of Kings present a cluster of special problems which call for separate attention. The elements of the chronological system of Kings are easily described. First, the dating of the accession year of the king of one of the kingdoms has been sychronized with the regnal year of the contemporary king of the other kingdom, and *vice versa*. Secondly, the length of the reign of each king is given. Finally, the death of the king and his successor are listed. Additional elements are provided for Judah such as the king's age on his accession and the name of the king's mother. Beside this stereotyped pattern, additional chronological notices have sought to synchronize major historical events which involve foreign nations with the regnal year of the Hebrew kings (e.g. I Kings 14.25; II Kings 15.17ff; II.16.1ff.; II.17.6; II.18.9ff.; II.23.29ff., etc.). Of course, such data have provided the information on which attempts to construct an absolute ancient Near Eastern chronology have been based (cf. Freedman).

The enormous difficulty of reconciling all the chronological information into a coherent schema has continued to baffle biblical scholars. Many of the factors which complicate the problems of Israelite chronology have long been recognized. The diversity in the method of calculating regnal years, the use of different calendars, and the practice of co-regencies have often been rehearsed (cf. Begrich, 55ff.; Thiele, 16ff.). In addition, the strikingly divergent chronological figures which appear in the Greek versions and in Josephus have added to the difficulty. Finally, the attempt to relate the biblical figures to the ever-growing body of extra-biblical data – Egyptian, Babylonian, Greek – has further taxed the learning and ingenuity of biblical scholars.

The chief purpose of this brief review of the chronological problems is not to offer a new solution which obviously lies outside the purview of an Introduction. Rather, it is to raise the literary and theological question of the canonical function of the chronology within the book of Kings. In order to sharpen the issue, we shall briefly rehearse some of the major representative approaches which have emerged in the history of research.

(a) There have been repeated attempts since the last part of the nineteenth century to demonstrate that the chronology of Kings is entirely a theoretical construction and does not rest on genuine, ancient tradition (cf. E. Krey, 1877, cited by Begrich, 10ff.). The theory is plausible to the degree in which it has correctly recognized that some of the chronological data, such as the number 480 in I Kings 6.1, appear to represent a round figure with a typological function (12 x 40). Yet a wide consensus has emerged in rejecting this interpretation for the major portion of Old Testament chronology. Even Wellhausen's important modification of the hypothesis (1875) in limiting the free construction to the synchronistic data (cited by Begrich, 1ff.) has been generally abandoned. The recovery of ancient Near Eastern parallels to both chronological elements of Kings, the regnal years and the synchronistic reckoning, has greatly weakened the probability of assigning any element totally to free construction.

(b) A second representative approach to Old Testament chronology has its most vigorous and learned representative in W. F. Albright. He, along with his students, envisioned the primary task to lie in the reconstruction of an absolute chronology on the basis of extra-biblical sources. Thus, Freedman can simply assert as obvious: ' ... the Biblical dates must be modified in accordance with the pattern of Near Eastern chronology now firmly established for the second and first millennia BC' ('Chronology', 203). Although few modern critical scholars would contest that the relating of the biblical chronologies to the extra-biblical is a part of the larger problem, some would question whether the integrity of the biblical text in its diverse roles within the Old Testament is threatened by elevating this one issue to a position of primacy. Albright's approach in studying the Bible as a source for historical information is one-sided, to say the least.

(c) A third approach to the problem of chronology is best represented by the classic continental studies of Begrich, Mowinckel, and Jepsen. These scholars, in spite of their individual diversity, hold in common a concern to distinguish the problems of Old Testament chronological *traditions* from that of establishing an absolute chronology for the ancient Near East. Begrich concludes that five chronological systems can be recovered in the book of Kings, and Jepsen argues for a pre-Dtr. synchronistic chronicle forming the earliest literary level of the book. But particularly with Begrich's results, many scholars remain unconvinced that he has correctly described the prehistory of the chronology of Kings. The complex reconstruction of five different systems arises in large measure from Begrich's own assumption of a highly rational process in Israel which appears to be without foundation. A more likely reconstruction of the development of the chronological traditions in Kings would reckon with historical overlappings and mutual influencing among fewer traditions. Jepsen's proposals for modifying Begrich's system seem more fruitful.

(d) The work of E. R. Thiele must also be considered representative of one school of 'conservative' American scholarship. Thiele shares a common concern with Albright to harmonize biblical chronology with an absolute chronology of the ancient Near East, but he diverges from Albright in holding that the biblical chronology can be brought completely into harmony with extra-biblical data as a fully coherent, rational system. In order to achieve this harmonious system, Thiele is forced to project innumerable coregencies, to reconstruct a complex interchange of calendars, and to fall back on unique patterns of calculation. In spite of his great learning and remarkable ingenuity, he has found few followers of his system apart from those who are committed apologetically to a doctrine of scripture's absolute harmony.

(e) Finally, the fresh perspective on the problem which has been opened up by the brilliant dissertation of J. D. Shenkel must be seriously considered by all future research. Shenkel, who has built on the textual work of F. M. Cross, was able to demonstrate that the variant chronological data of the Old Greek textual recension of Reigns represents an ancient and integral chronological tradition, and is not simply to be dismissed as a late, secondary reinterpretation of the Masoretic text. Moreover, Shenkel has dealt a severe blow to such reconstructions as those of Begrich and Thiele which have depended solely on the MT for recovering the original tradition. In addition, he has shown the textual basis for some of the tension in the present MT and has seriously damaged Thiele's explanation of co-regencies. However, Shenkel's own attempt to describe the historical process by which the various chronologies were related makes use of several projections of how biblical books were redacted which are far from obvious. Thus, at what period in Israel's history can one reckon with a close, midrash-like attention to adjust conflicting chronologies such as Shenkel assumes? Or again, how does one understand the relation between the narrative traditions of Kings and the various chronological schemata? Shenkel's final chapter lacks an important form-critical dimension which would test the traditio-historical development of the book against his logical reconstructions.

To summarize up to this point. The history of research has demonstrated the enormous difficulties involved in Old Testament chronology, and revealed some important advances which different representative methodologies have produced. However, it is equally revealing that the question of the canonical function of the chronology of Kings has not been seriously addressed. What then can be said to this issue?

First of all, it is apparent that the various chronological patterns in the book of Kings serve to establish a sequence in the historical experience of Israel. The use of a detailed chronology is the most obvious way of registering this cumulative nature of the nation's past history. I Kings 6.1 thus records that the building of the temple began in the second month of the fourth year of Solomon's reign, but it also establishes this crucial point in her history in reference to the nation's deliverance from Egypt, namely, in the 480th year after the deliverance from slavery. Conversely, the cumulative effect of Israel's misdeeds, personified by the reign of Jeroboam I and culminating in the destruction of the nation, is also registered by the chronology (e.g. I Kings 15.33f.; II Kings 17.1ff.).

Secondly, the use of chronology in Kings, especially its synchronism, provides the story of Israel with a comprehensive character
which embraces the whole people of God. The synchronism
accommodates the political realities of Israel's divided history, and
yet establishes the interrelatedness of the two kingdoms. It is
significant to note that the synchronistic schema does not impose a
temporal category which is conceptually foreign to a timeless,
anecdotal tradition, but rather fixes in a specific chronological
sequence an interrelatedness which is fully indigenous to the narrative traditions themselves. For example, the chronology establishes
a temporal framework for the Northern Kingdom's attack on
Jerusalem (II Kings 14.1ff.), and synchronizes the abortive assault
on Ramoth-gilead by King Ahab of Israel and King Jehoshaphat of
Judah. Indeed, even after the destruction of the Northern Kingdom, its history still has an important effect on Judah's experience
(II Kings 18.13ff.).

Thirdly, the chronology in Kings serves to establish the inter-
relatedness of Israel's history beyond that of the divided nation, by
including her experience within the framework of world history.
Thus, II Kings 15.19 records when Menahem offered tribute to the
Assyrian king, Tiglath-Pileser. II Kings 18.13ff. recounts when
Sennacherib invaded Judah and II Kings 25.1ff. specifies when
Nebuchadnezzar destroyed Jerusalem.

The hermeneutical implications of these various functions of
chronology within Kings are far-reaching, and require further
explication. The issue is particularly relevant to the current discussion in the field of Biblical Theology, which has attempted to
describe Israel's tradition in terms of 'story' rather than history (cf.
Barr). Indeed there is a wide consensus that the older use of the
term 'history' as a comprehensive category to encompass the whole
of the Old Testament is seriously deficient. Clearly much of the
biblical material does not reflect history in the modern sense of the
term. Yet is the term 'story' an adequate substitute? In his
illuminating essay James Barr seeks to describe the nature of the
biblical story in terms of its cumulative and unitary features. In my
judgment, reflection on the hermeneutical implications of Old Testament chronology, especially in the light of the canonical shape of
the book of Kings, would include several additional elements as
constitutive to this particular form of the biblical story.

It seems clear that at some point the biblical writer has borrowed chronological schemata from ancient Near Eastern tradition by which to shape the biblical traditions. He employed categories which constituted an essential part of ancient Near Eastern historical writing in order to render Israel's own story. The basic hermeneutical issue does not turn on the semantic problem of determining to what extent this category can be considered really historical in the modern sense, but rather on the biblical intention in adopting this common form by which to recount her experience.

The move certainly implies that Israel's story was understood as both unitary and cumulative in nature, but also that this story – at least in Kings – was considered analogous to the history recorded by Babylon and Egypt. The two accounts could be synchronized because they were of one piece and did not relate as different orders of profane or secular history. Moreover, the biblical writer cites his sources and challenges the reader to study the evidence from the public record. This use of chronology implies a hermeneutical move which is the exact opposite of other options which we have frequently discovered within the canonical process. In Kings the presentation of Israel's history is particular rather than representative, common rather than confessional, archival rather than midrashic. The use of chronology to render Israel's experience implies an element of historical particularity which strains the term 'story' almost as much as as it does that of modern history. Even the more flexible term of Hans Frei (*The Eclipse of Biblical Narrative*, 258) which designates the biblical material as 'history-like narrative' needs to have its content informed by the elements of chronology as much as it does from other analogues. It may be that the term 'story' is the best choice, but this choice also runs the risk, unless carefully qualified, of losing important features which are essential to Israel's witness.

There is one final aspect of the problem to be considered. Biblical chronology functions in closest contact to the biblical narrative. The point should be emphasized against the approach of Thiele that its proper canonical role does not depend on eliminating all the inner tension of the chronology, nor in reconstructing a harmonious system. In fact, Thiele's approach runs in the face of the canonical intention by its recourse to hypothetical reconstruction and systems of calculations long forgotten or unknown to the final form of the biblical account. Rather, biblical chronology functions in order to render accessible the historical feature of the narrative. The choice between rival chronological traditions often turned on the decision as to which chronology best functioned to ensure this result (cf. e.g. the effect on the narrative in II Kings 3 of the differing chronologies in the Old Greek and the MT).

To summarize: in spite of the many unresolved problems related to biblical chronology, the chronological shape of the material in the book of Kings performs an important canonical function by the manner in which it renders accessible Israel's narrative tradition in terms of particular, cumulative, and critical historical experience.

4. Hermeneutical Implications of Canonical Shaping

The study of the book of Kings provides a good example by which to contrast the method of redactional criticism with a canonical reading of the text. Noth's great contribution lay in his brilliant analysis of the work of the Dtr. writer, but in the end Noth characterized the Dtr. author as expressing a private, even idiosyncratic theology, apart from any group or institution. Or again, Frank Cross sought to relate the peculiar shape of the Dtr. edition of Kings to two different historical periods in which the peculiar needs of each period determined the shape of the redaction. Both of these interpretations are agreed that a correct modern interpretation of the book of Kings depends upon an accurate reconstruction of the book's historical development.

The decisive difference in the canonical approach which is being defended lies in the concern to understand the effect of a redactional layer on the text itself in its final form. It resists the corollary of most redactional criticism that the key to a text's shape lies in some force outside the text requiring a reconstruction of the hidden indices. Rather, the canonical approach seeks to employ the tool of redaction criticism to the extent that it aids in a more precise hearing of the edited text, but at the same time seeking to understand the expressed intentionality of that interpreted text.

A redactional critical approach like Noth's attributed the peculiar shape of Kings to the theology of an editor who had experienced the exile. A canonical approach would see the intention of the biblical writer to describe the execution of the curses of Deuteronomy, which had been rehearsed by successive generations of prophets, against a disobedient covenant people. The historical and literary insights from Noth's precise analysis of the redactional layers can be used with profit within the canonical approach in bringing the different elements which constitute the canonical text into sharper focus. For example, Solomon's prayer in I Kings 8 clearly reflects an elaborate concern with exile and captivity which affords a different intensity to this part of the text from its nucleus. However, a canonical approach differs markedly from redactional criticism in its commitment not to reverse the priorities of the canonical text, either by bringing to the foreground features left in the background, or by providing a referential position from which to evaluate the rightness or wrongness of the canonical intent.

Finally, the contrast in method can be illustrated on the figure of David. Whereas the redactional critical approach would tend to speak of a post-exilic idealization of David as stemming from a traditio-historical or psychological development within certain groups or specific institutions of Judaism, a canonical approach would interpret the portrait of David in Kings and Chronicles as perspectives derived from common reading of the tradition within the religious community in accordance with the prior canonical shape of the Samuel traditions.

History of Exegesis

Carpzov I, 192–4; *DThC* 13, 2084; *EB* 4, 1157; *RGG*³ 3, 1706.

M. **Aberbach** and L. **Smolar**, 'Jeroboam and Solomon: Rabbinic Interpretations', *JQR* 59, 1968, 118–32; K. C. W. **Bähr**, *Der Salomonische Tempel*, Karlsruhe 1848; 11ff.; J. D. **Eisenstein**, 'Temple in Rabbinical Literature', *JE* 12, 92–7; M. **Hayek**, 'Élie dans le tradition syriaque', *Études Carmelitaines* 35, I, Paris 1956, 159–78; J. **Leclercq**, 'Salomon', *DACL* 15, 588–602; R. E. **Murphy** and C. **Peters**, 'Élie (le prophète)', *DS* 4.1, 1959, 564–72; M.-J. **Stiassny**, 'Le prophète Élie dans le judaisme', *Études Carmelitaines* 35, II, 1956, 199–255; A. **Wiener**, *The Prophet Elijah in the Development of Judaism*, London 1978.

PART FOUR

THE LATTER PROPHETS

XVI

INTRODUCTION TO THE LATTER PROPHETS

Bibliography

P. R. **Ackroyd**, 'Isaiah i-xii: Presentation of a Prophet', *SVT* 29, 1978; K. **Baltzer**, *Die Biographie der Propheten*, Neukirchen-Vluyn 1975; R. V. **Bergren**, *The Prophets and the Law*, Cincinnati, 1974; H. **Birkeland**, *Zum hebräischen Traditionswesen*, Oslo 1938; K. **Budde**, 'Eine folgenschwere Redaktion des Zwölfprophetenbuches', *ZAW* 39, 1921, 218–29; A. **Büchler**, 'The Reading of the Law and Prophets in a Triennial Cycle', *JQR* 5, 1893, 420–68; 6, 1894, 1–73; R. E. **Clements**, *Prophecy and Tradition*, Oxford and Philadelphia 1975; 'Patterns in the Prophetic Canon', *Canon and Authority*, ed. G. W. Coats, 42–55; B. S. **Childs**, 'The Canonical Shape of the Prophetic Literature,' *Interp* 32, 1978, 46–68; G. W. **Coats** and B. O. **Long**, eds., *Canon and Authority: Essays in Old Testament Religion and Theology*, Philadelphia 1977; C. H. **Cornill**, *Der israelitische Prophetismus*, Berlin [13]1920; A. B. **Davidson**, *Old Testament Prophecy*, Edinburgh and New York 1904; B. **Duhm**, *Israels Propheten*, Tübingen [2]1922; O. **Eissfeldt**, 'The Prophetic Literature', *The Old Testament and Modern Study*, ed. H. H. Rowley, Oxford and New York 1951, 115–61; F. **Ellermeier**, *Prophetie in Mari und Israel*, Herzberg am Harz 1968; I. **Engnell**, 'Prophets and Prophetism in the Old Testament', ET in *A Rigid Scrutiny*, Nashville 1969 (=*Critical Essays on the Old Testament*, London 1970), 123–79; H. G. A. **von Ewald**, *Commentary on the Prophets of the Old Testament*, ET, 5 vols, Edinburgh 1875–1881.

G. **Fohrer**, 'Tradition und Interpretation im Alten Testament', *Studien zur alttestamentlichen Theologie und Geschichte (1949–1966)*, BZAW 115, 1969, 54–83; J. **Fürst**, *Der Kanon des Alten Testaments*, Leipzig 1868, 15–54; H. M. I. **Gevaryahu**, 'Biblical Colophons: A Source for the "Biography" of Authors, Texts and Books', *SVT* 28, 1975, 42–59; H. **Gunkel**, *Die Propheten*, Göttingen 1917; A. H. J. **Gunneweg**, *Mündliche und schriftliche Tradition der vorexilischen Propheten*, Göttingen 1959; W. W. **Hallo**, 'New Viewpoints on Cuneiform Literature', *IEJ* 12, 1962, 13–26; G. **Hölscher**, *Die Profeten*, Leipzig 1914; J. C. K. **Hofmann**, *Weissagung und Erfüllung*, 2 vols., Erlangen 1841–44; A. **Jepsen**, *Nabi*, Munich 1934; P. **Katz**, 'The Old

Testament Canon in Palestine and Alexandria', *ZNW* 47, 1956, 191–217; A. **Kuenen**, *The Prophets and Prophecy in Israel*, ET London 1877; W. G. **Lambert**, 'Ancestors, Authors and Canonicity', *JCS* 11, 1957, 1–14; J. C. H. **Lebram**, 'Aspekte der alttestamentlichen Kanonbildung', *VT* 18, 1968, 173–89; J. **Lindblom**, *Prophecy in Ancient Israel*, ET Oxford 1962, Philadelphia 1963; S. Z. **Leiman**, *The Canonization of Hebrew Scripture*, Hamden, Conn. 1976; W. E. **March**, 'Prophecy', *Old Testament Form Criticism*, ed. J. H. Hayes, San Antonio, Texas 1974, 141–77; M. **Margolis**, *The Hebrew Scriptures in the Making*, Philadelphia 1922; R. **Melugin**, *The Formation of Isaiah 40–55*, BZAW 141, 1976; W. L. **Moran**, 'New Evidence from Mari on the History of Prophecy', *Bibl* 50, 1969, 15–56; S. **Mowinckel**, *Prophecy and Tradition*, Oslo 1946; G. **von Rad**, *Old Testament Theology* II, ET London and New York 1965; T. H. **Robinson**, 'Die prophetischen Bücher im Lichte neuer Entdeckungen', *ZAW* 45, 1927, 3–9; H. E. **Ryle**, *The Canon of the Old Testament*, London 1892, 94–118.

J. A. **Sanders**, 'Hermeneutics in True and False Prophecy', *Canon and Authority*, ed. G. W. Coats, 21–41; N. H. **Sarna**, 'The Order of the Books', *Studies in Jewish Bibliography, History and Literature in Honor of J. Edward Kiev*, ed. C. Berlin, New York 1971, 407–13; W. Robertson **Smith**, *The Prophets of Israel*, London ²1895; H. L. **Strack**, 'Kanon des Alten Testaments', *RE³* 9, 741–68; H. B. **Swete**, 'Title, Grouping, Number, and Order of the Books', *Introduction to the Old Testament in Greek*, Cambridge ²1914, reprinted New York 1968, 197–230; S. **Talmon** and M. **Fishbane**, 'The Structuring of Biblical Books, Studies in the Book of Ezekiel', *ASTI* 10, 1976, 129–53; G. M. **Tucker**, 'Prophetic Superscriptions and the Growth of a Canon', *Canon and Authority*, ed. G. W. Coats, 56–70; R. R. **Wilson**, 'Form-critical Investigation of the Prophetic Literature: The Present Situation', *SBL Seminar Papers* 1973, 100–27; 'Prophecy and Society in Ancient Israel: The Present State of the Inquiry', ibid., 1977, 341–58; R. E. **Wolfe**, 'The Editing of the Book of the Twelve', *ZAW* 53, 1935, 90–129; T. **Zahn**, 'Zählungen der biblischen Bücher', *Geschichte des neutestamentlichen Kanons* II,1, Erlangen und Leipzig 1890, 318–43; W. **Zimmerli**, *The Law and the Prophets*, ET Oxford 1965, New York 1967.

The traditional Jewish and Christian interpretation of the Hebrew prophets assumed that the prophetic books were literary compositions which were written by the prophets themselves. The rise of the historical critical approach to the Bible fundamentally altered this picture. The prophetic books were seen to be the product of a long history of development, passing through many different hands, and reflecting many different historical layers. During the period of the dominance of the literary critical method, scholars such as A. Kuenen, B. Duhm, and C. H. Cornill sought to distinguish carefully between 'genuine' and 'non-genuine' elements within each composition in an effort to recover the original words of the prophet. This effort supported a major concern of some late nineteenth-century scholars (B. Duhm, G. Adam Smith) to uncover the inner personal experience of the prophet which was thought to hold the key to the message. G. Hölscher's influential book of 1914 did succeed in broadening the basis of research on the prophets by introducing a new sociological and comparative religion dimension, but it did not seriously undercut the dominant literary approach to the text (cf. Jepsen).

The most important break with literary critical interpretation came in the early decades of the twentieth century with the discovery of the significance of oral tradition for the Hebrew prophets. The terminology of books, authors, and glosses was replaced with that of tradition, circles, and collections. Beginning with Hermann Gunkel and his school, and shortly expanding into the rest of the scholarly world (Mowinckel, Birkeland) a vigorous effort was undertaken to trace the history of the prophetic oracles from the earliest units of speech to their final written form. The development of the form-critical method opened up a fresh avenue in demonstrating the nature of the stereotyped patterns of oral speech which the prophets employed, and in establishing a sociological context (*Sitz im Leben*) from which to understand the original function of these speech patterns. The traditio-historical method pursued the growth of the traditions from smaller to larger complexes, and traced the role of the various circles who shared in its transmission.

In an article in 1927, which was cited approvingly by both Eissfeldt and Mowinckel, T. H. Robinson sought to sketch three stages in the growth of the prophetic material. The first concerned the original independent prophetic oracle and its reception and transmission by a circle of disciples. The second stage involved the growth of the smaller collection into larger complexes, the addition of fresh material including anonymous sayings, and the arrangement of the collections into patterns. The third stage involved fixing the various units into a final literary form. Robinson's article was significant in setting out the various areas in which critical scholarship would focus its attention for the next fifty years. But it is equally clear in retrospect that the major concentration of research has fallen in the first two stages of Robinson's outline. Decidedly less interest has been evoked in studying the development and effect of the final form of the prophetic books. Rather, the field has been dominated by questions of the relation of prophet to cult, of law and covenant, and of history and tradition. The positive fruits of the last two generations of form-critical and traditio-critical work can best be appreciated in the second volume of von Rad's *Old Testament Theology*, and in the commentaries of H. W. Wolff and W. Zimmerli.

Only in relatively recent years has a new interest in the canonical shape of the prophetic books begun to appear which has developed a variety of different critical techniques for interpretation. First of all, fresh attention to the Hebrew scribal practices, when seen against their broad ancient Near Eastern background, has begun to throw new light on the final stage of collecting and ordering of the biblical books. Scholars such as Hallo, Talmon, Sarna, and Gevaryahu – to name but a few – have entered a relatively unexplored area and produced some fresh insights. Secondly, new research into the form and structure of the various prophetic collections within a book has shifted attention to a new set of questions which go beyond those posed by form and traditio-criticism. The research of Ackroyd, Clements, Melugin, among others, has been especially creative in this area. Finally, the larger theological problems of the effect of the canonical process on the growth of its various parts, particularly the relation of law and prophets, has been pursued with much insight by W. Zimmerli, R. E. Clements, and J. A. Sanders. Of particular importance is Clements' attempt ('Patterns') to trace the canonical development by which Old Testament prophecy could be summarized as a unified message of future salvation (cf. Sirach 48.17ff.; Acts 3.24; I Peter 1.10–12).

Before an attempt is made to pursue the issue of the canonical shaping of the various prophetic books, it is first necessary to raise the question about the canonical function of the particular ordering of the books with the present Hebrew canon. As is well known, the second division of the Hebrew canon distinguishes between the 'former' (*ri'šônîm*) and the 'latter' (*'aḥªrônîm*) prophets, including among the former Joshua, Judges, Samuel, and Kings, and among the latter Isaiah, Jeremiah, Ezekiel, and the Twelve. It is often conjectured that the canonization of the latter prophets extended secondarily to the former prophets.

Unfortunately, the historical factors at work in the collecting and ordering of the prophetic books remain very obscure (cf. ch. II), and one is largely dependent upon the implications which have been drawn from internal evidence of growth. Even such an obvious problem as explaining how twelve independent prophetic collections were united into a single book has remained unresolved although various forces at work in the process have been correctly observed by R. E. Wolfe, K. Budde, W. Rudolph and others. At times it would seem that concern for chronological order exerted an important influence on the arrangement, or that catchword connections between books were operative (e.g. Amos 1.2 and Joel 3.16). At other times mechanical factors such as length of the scroll played a role. T. Zahn has rightly emphasized the important part which mechanical features had in the numbering of the books of the Hebrew canon, and which continued to be reflected in the later rabbinical discussion on how books were to be copied. Similarly the later adaptation of the codex by the Christian church to replace the rolls also affected the attitude toward canonical sequence.

The order of the books within the section of the Latter Prophets varies considerably within the Jewish lists. The Talmudic order has the sequence: Jeremiah, Ezekiel, Isaiah, the Twelve; the French and German manuscripts the tradition: Jeremiah, Isaiah, Ezekiel, the Twelve; the Masoretic and Spanish manuscripts the order: Isaiah, Jeremiah, Ezekiel, the Twelve (cf. Ryle, Excursus C; Swete, 200). The discussions on the variation in order within the Talmud (Baba Bathra 14b–15a) indicate the later puzzlement over the divergent traditions. The rabbinic explanations are clearly homiletical rather than historical in nature.

The Greek orders vary extensively from the Hebrew. A different sequence is followed for the Minor Prophets. Although the order of the oldest Hebrew tradition (Isaiah, Jeremiah, Ezekiel) is the dominant one in the Greek orders, it is by no means universal. The later Latin order even inverted the sequence between the Former and Latter Prophets. More importantly, Daniel is included in the Septuagint either before or after Ezekiel and Lamentations is appended to Jeremiah. The assumption of both Strack and Swete that the order of the Hebrew canon was original and it was only later dislocated by the Septuagint can no longer be maintained (cf. Lebram, Katz). The major implication to be drawn from this evidence is that the Hebrew canon assigned an important role to its tripartite division, which set it apart from the Greek. However, the order of the prophetic books within the collection of the Latter Prophets assumed no great canonical significance and thus differed from the attitude shown to the order within the Pentateuch. The major effect of the canonical process lay in the shaping of the individual prophetic books, and in producing a new entity of a prophetic collection which functioned within the canon as a unified block over against the Torah.

History of Exegesis

W. **Baumgartner**, 'Die Auffassung des 19. Jahrhunderts von israelitischen Prophetismus' (1922), reprinted in *Zum Alten Testament und seiner Umwelt*, Leiden 1959, 27–41; R. E. **Clements**, *A Century of Old Testament Study*, Guildford and Philadelphia 1976, 51–75; E. **Cothenet**, 'Prophétisme dans le Nouveau Testament', *DBS* 8, 1222–1337; B. **Decker**, *Die Entwicklung der Lehre von der prophetischen Offenbarung von Wilhelm von Auxerre bis zu Thomas von Aquin*, Breslau 1940; L. **Diestel**, *Geschichte des Alten Testamentes in der christlichen Kirche*, Jena 1869, 650–60, 760–73; W. **Hübner**, *Die Prophetenforschung des Alten Testaments seit der Mitte des 18. Jahrhunderts*, Diss. Heidelberg 1957; H.-J. **Kraus**, *Geschichte der historisch-kritischen Erforschung des Alten Testaments*, Neukirchen-Vluyn ²1969, 144ff., 205ff., 275ff.; E. **von Matter**, *Die Auffassung der alttestamentlichen Prophetie von Eichhorn bis Volz*, Diss. Halle-Wittenberg 1923; A. J. **Reines**, *Maimonides und Abrabanel on Prophecy*, Cincinnati 1970; H. H. **Rowley**, 'The Nature of Old Testament Prophecy in the Light of Recent Study', *The Servant of the Lord*, London ²1965, 95–134; E. **Sehmsdorf**, *Die Prophetenauslegung bei J. G. Eichhorn*, Göttingen 1971; T. **Sherlock**, 'The Limitation of Prophecy', in *Religious Thought in the Eighteenth Century*, ed. J. M. Creed and J. M. Boys Smith, Cambridge and New York 1934, 61–64; H. **Witsius**, *Miscellaneorum sacrorum libri quatuor* I, Leyden 1736, 1–317.

XVII

ISAIAH

Commentaries on Chs. 1–66

W. Gesenius, 1821
J. A. Alexander, 1846–7
F. Delitzsch, BC, ⁴1889
J. Knabenbauer, CSS, 1881
T. K. Cheyne, ⁵1889
G. A. Smith, ExB, 1888–90, (²1927)
J. Skinner, CB, 1896–98
K. Marti, KHC, 1900
G. W. Wade, WC, 1911

B. Duhm, HKAT, ⁴1922
F. Feldmann, EH, 1925–26
J. Fischer, HS, 1937–39
E. J. Kissane, 1941–43
L. Dennefeld, SB, 1946
I. W. Slotki, SonB, 1949
G. Fohrer, ZBK, 1960–65
E. J. Young, NICOT, 1965–72
A. Schoors, BOuT, 1972

Commentaries on Chs. 1–39

G. B. Gray, ICC (1–27), 1913
O. Procksch, KAT, 1930
R. B. Y. Scott, *IB*, 1956
W. Eichrodt, BAT, 1960–67

P. Auvray, SoBi, 1972
O. Kaiser, ET, OTL, 1972–74
H. Wildberger, BK (1–12), 1972;
    BK (13–27), 1978

Commentaries on Chs. 40–66

K. Budde, *HSAT*, ⁴1922
P. Volz, KAT, 1932
J. Muilenburg, *IB*, 1956
C. R. North, 1964
J. D. Smart, 1965
G. A. F. Knight, 1965

J. L. McKenzie, AB, 1968
C. Westermann, ET, OTL, 1969
P.-E. Bonnard, ÉB, 1972
R. N. Whybray, NCeB, 1975
K. Elliger, BK (40–45), 1978

Bibliography on Isaiah 1–39

P. R. **Ackroyd**, 'A Note on Isaiah 2,1', *ZAW* 75, 1963, 320f.; 'An Interpretation of the Babylonian Exile: A Study of 2 Kings 20, Isaiah 38–39', *SJT*

27, 1974, 329–52; O. T. **Allis**, *The Unity of Isaiah*, Philadelphia 1950, London 1952; A. **Alt**, 'Jesaja 8, 23–9,6. Befreiungsnacht und Krönungstag', *FS A. Bertholet*, Tübingen 1950, 29–49 = *KS* II, 1953, 206–25; H. **Barth**, *Israel und das Assyrerreich in den nichtjesajanischen Texten des Protojesajabuches*, Diss. Hamburg 1974=*Die Jesaja-Worte in der Josiazeit*, WMANT 48, 1977; J. **Becker**, *Isaias – der Prophet und sein Buch*, Stuttgart 1968; S. H. **Blank**, *Prophetic Faith in Isaiah*, New York and London 1958; W. H. **Brownlee**, 'The Text of Isaiah vi 13 in the Light of DSI[a]', *VT* 1, 1951, 296–8; G. **Brunet**, *Essai sur l'Isaïe de l'Histoire*, Paris 1975; K. **Budde**, 'Über die Schranken, die Jesajas prophetischer Botschaft zu setzen sind', *ZAW* 41 1923, 154–203; *Jesaja's Erleben. Eine gemeinverständliche Auslegung der Denkschrift des Propheten (Kap. 6,1–9,6)*, Gotha 1928; 'Zu Jesaja 1–4', *ZAW* 49, 1931, 16–40, 182–211; 50, 1932, 38–72; 'Das Immanuelzeichen und die Ahaz-Begegnung, Jes. 7', *JBL* 52, 1933, 22–54; T. K. **Cheyne**, *Introduction to the Book of Isaiah*, London and New York 1895; B. S. **Childs**, *Isaiah and the Assyrian Crisis*, SBT II.3, 1967; J. **Coppens**, 'La prophétie de la 'Almah. Is. 7,14–17', *ETL* 28, 1952, 648ff.; C. H. **Cornill**, 'Die Composition des Buches Jesajas', *ZAW* 4, 1884, 83–105.

W. **Dietrich**, *Jesaja und die Politik*, Munich 1976; H. **Donner**, *Israel unter den Völkern*, Leiden 1964; J. H. **Eaton**, 'The Origin of the Book of Isaiah', *VT* 9, 1959, 138–57; I. **Engnell**, *The Call of Isaiah: an Exegetical and Comparative Study*, Uppsala 1949; S. **Erlandsson**, *The Burden of Babylon*, Lund 1970; A. **Feuillet**, 'Le signe proposé à Achaz et l'Emmanuel (Isaïe 7.10–25)', *RSR* 30, 1940, 129–51; R. **Fey**, *Amos und Jesaja*, WMANT 12, 1963; J. **Fichtner**, 'Jesaja unter den Weisen', *TLZ* 74, 1949, 75–80=*Gottes Weisheit*, Stuttgart 1965, 18–26; 'Jahwes Plan in der Botschaft des Jesaja', *ZAW* 63, 1951, 16–33=*Gottes Weisheit*, 27–43; G. **Fohrer**, 'Entstehung, Komposition und Überlieferung von Jesaja 1–39', *Annual of the Leeds Oriental Society* 3, 1961–2, 3ff.=*Studien zur alttestamentlichen Prophetie (1949–65)*, BZAW 99, 1967, 113–47; 'Jesaja 1 als Zusammenfassung der Verkündigung Jesajas', *ZAW* 74, 1962, 251–68=*Studien zur . . . Prophetie*, 148–66; 'Der Aufbau der Apokalypse des Jesajabuchs (Jesaja 24–27)', *CBQ* 25, 1963, 34–45=*Studien zur . . . Prophetie*, 170–81; K. **Fullerton**, 'Viewpoints in the Discussion of Isaiah's Hopes for the Future', *JBL* 41, 1922, 1–101; H. L. **Ginsberg**, 'Gleanings in First Isaiah', *M. Kaplan Jubilee Volume*, New York 1953, 245–59; 'Reflexes of Sargon in Isaiah after 715 BCE', *JAOS* 88, 1968, 47–53; H. **Gressmann**, *Der Messias*, Göttingen 1929; H. **Gunkel**, 'Jesaja 32, eine prophetische Liturgie', *ZAW* 42, 1924, 177–208.

E. **Hammershaimb**, 'The Immanuel Sign', *StTh* 3, 1949, 321–39; G. F. **Hasel**, *The Remnant*, Berrien Springs, Mich. 1972; J. H. **Hayes**, 'The Tradition of Zion's Inviolability', *JBL* 82, 1963, 419–26; M.-L. **Henry**, *Glaubenkrise und Glaubenbewährung in den Dichtungen der Jesajaapokalypse*, Stuttgart 1967; H.-J. **Hermisson**, 'Zukunftserwartung und Gegenwartskritik in der Verkündigung Jesajas', *EvTh* 33, 1973, 54–77; S. **Herrmann**, *Die prophetischen Heilserwartungen im Alten Testament*, Stuttgart 1965;

H. W. **Hertzberg**, 'Die Nachgeschichte alttestamentlicher Texte innerhalb des Alten Testaments', *Werden und Wesen des Alten Testaments*, ed. P. Volz, BZAW 66, 1936, 110–21=*Beiträge zur Traditionsgeschichte und Theologie des Alten Testaments*, Göttingen 1962, 69–80; H. W. **Hoffmann**, *Die Intention der Verkündigung Jesajas*, BZAW 136, 1974; F. **Huber**, *Jahwe, Juda und die anderen Völkern beim Propheten Jesaja*, BZAW 137, 1976; A. K. **Jenkins**, 'Hezekiah's Fourteenth Year. A New Interpretation of 2 Kings xviii 13– xix 37', *VT* 26, 1976, 284–98; E. **Jenni**, 'Jesajas Berufung in der neueren Forschung', *TZ* 15, 1959, 321–39; D. R. **Jones**, 'The Traditio of the Oracles of Isaiah of Jerusalem', *ZAW* 67, 1955, 226–46; 'Exposition of Isaiah chapter one verses one to nine', *SJT* 17, 1964, 464–77; 'Exposition of Isaiah chapter one verses twenty-one to the end', *SJT* 21, 1968, 320–29; O. **Kaiser**, 'Die Verkündigung des Propheten Jesaja im Jahre 701', *ZAW* 81, 1969, 304–15; M. M. **Kaplan**, 'Isaiah 6.1–11', *JBL* 45, 1926, 251–9; C. A. **Keller**, 'Das quietistische Element in der Botschaft des Jesaja', *TZ* 11, 1955, 81–97; R. **Kilian**, *Die Verheissung Immanuels. Jes. 7,14*, Stuttgart 1968; R. **Knierim**, 'The Vocation of Isaiah', *VT* 18, 1968, 47–68; L. **Köhler**, 'Zum Verständnis von Jes. 7.14', *ZAW* 67, 1955, 48–50.

R. **Lack**, *La Symbolique du Livre d'Isaïe. Essai sur l'image littéraire comme élément de structuralisme*, AnBib 59, Rome 1973; T. **Lescow**, 'Jesajas Denkschrift aus der Zeit des syrisch-ephraimitischen Krieges', *ZAW* 85, 1973, 315–31; L. J. **Liebreich**, 'The Position of Chapter Six in the Book of Isaiah', *HUCA* 25, 1954, 37–40; 'The Compilation of the Book of Isaiah', *JQR* 46, 1955–6, 259–77; 47, 1956–7, 114–38; J. **Lindblom**, *Die Jesaja-Apokalypse Jes. 24–27*, Lund 1938; *A Study of the Immanuel Section in Isaiah, Isa. 7,1–9,6*, Lund 1958; R. J. **Marshall**, 'The Structure of Isaiah 1–12', *BiblRes* 7, 1962, 19–32; J. **Milgrom**, 'Did Isaiah Prophesy during the Reign of Uzziah?' *VT* 14, 1964, 164–82; S. **Mowinckel**, 'Die Komposition des Jesajabuches Kap 1–39', *AcOr* 11, 1933, 267–92; *Prophecy and Tradition*, Oslo 1946; H.-P. **Müller**, *Ursprünge und Strukturen alttestamentlichen Eschatologie*, Berlin 1969; W. E. **Müller**, *Die Vorstellungen vom Rest im Alten Testament*, Leipzig 1939; J. **Muilenburg**, 'The Literary Character of Isaiah 34', *JBL* 59, 1940, 339–65; P. A. **Munch**, 'The Expression bajjôm hāhū. Is it an Eschatological Terminus Technicus?', *ANVAO* II, (Hist.-Filos. Klasse) 1936, No. 2; B. **Otzen**, 'Traditions and Structures of Isaiah xxiv-xxxii', *VT* 24, 1974, 196–206; G. **von Rad**, 'Die Stadt auf dem Berge', *EvTh* 8, 1948–9, 439–47 = *GSAT* I, Munich 1958, 214–24; 'Das Werk Jahwes', *Studia Biblica et Semitica T. C. Vriezen dedicata*, Wageningen 1966, 290–324; Y. T. **Raday**, *The Unity of Isaiah in the Light of Statistical Linguistics*, Hildesheim 1973; M. **Rehm**, *Der königliche Messias im Licht der Immanuel-Weissagungen des Buches Jesaja*, Kevelaer 1968; L. G. **Rignell**, 'Isaiah Chapter 1', *StTh* 11, 1957, 140–58; E. **Robertson**, 'Isaiah Chapter 1', *ZAW* 52, 1934, 231–36; W. **Rudolph**, *Jesaja 24–27*, BWANT IV.10 (=62), 1933; J. M. **Schmidt**, 'Gedanken zum Verstockungsauftrag Jesajas (Is. vi)', *VT* 21, 1971, 68–90; A. **Schoors**, 'Isaiah, the Minister of Royal Anointment?',

OTS 20, 1977, 85–107; R. B. Y. **Scott**, 'The Literary Structure of Isaiah's Oracles', *Studies in Old Testament Prophecy*, *FS T. H. Robinson*, ed. H. H. Rowley, Edinburgh and New York 1950, 175–86; W. **Staerk**, *Das assyrische Weltreich im Urteil der Propheten*, Göttingen 1908; J. J. **Stamm**, 'La prophétie d'Emmanuel', *RThPh* 32, 1944, 97–123; 'Die Immanuel-Weissagung, ein Gespräch mit E. Hammershaimb', *VT* 4, 1954, 20–33; 'Die Immanuel-Perikope im Lichte neuerer Veröffentlichungen', *ZDMG*, Suppl I, 1969, 281–98; 'Die Immanuel-Perikope. Eine Nachlese', *TZ* 30, 1974, 11–22; O. H. **Steck**, 'Bemerkungen zu Jesaja 6', *BZ* NF 16, 1972, 188–206; 'Beiträge zum Verständnis von Jesaja 7,10–17 und 8,1–4', *TZ* 29, 1973, 161–78; 'Rettung und Verstockung. Exegetische Bemerkungen zu Jesaja 7,3–9', *EvTh* 33, 1973, 77–90.

J. **Vermeylen**, *La composition littéraire du livre d'Isaïe I-XXXIX*, 2 vols., Paris 1977; W. **Vischer**, *Die Immanuel-Botschaft im Rahmen des königlichen Zionfestes*, Zürich 1955; J. **Vollmer**, *Geschichtliche Rückblicke und Motive in der Prophetie des Amos, Hosea und Jesaja*, BZAW 119, 1971; G. **Wanke**, *Die Zionstheologie der Korachiten in ihrem traditionsgeschichtlichen Zusammenhang*, BZAW 97, 1966; W. **Whedbee**, *Isaiah and Wisdom*, Nashville 1971; H. **Wildberger**, 'Die Völkerwallfahrt zum Zion', *VT* 7, 1957, 62–81; F. **Wilke**, *Jesaja und Assur*, Leipzig 1905; H. W. **Wolff**, *Frieden ohne Ende. Jesaja 7,1–17 und 9,1–6 ausgelegt*, BSt 35, 1962; W. A. **Wordsworth**, *En-Roeh. The Prophecies of Isaiah*, Edinburgh 1939; E. **Würthwein**, 'Jesaja 7,1–9, Ein Beitrag zu dem Thema: Prophetie und Politik', 1954; reprinted in *Wort und Existenz*, Göttingen 1970, 127–43; E. J. **Young**, *Studies in Isaiah*, London 1954; W. **Zimmerli**, 'Jesaja und Hiskia', *Wort und Geschichte*, ed. H. Gese und H. R. Rüger, Neukirchen-Vluyn 1973, 199–208.

Bibliography on Isaiah 40–55

D. **Baltzer**, *Ezechiel und Deuterojesaja*, BZAW 121, 1971; K. **Baltzer**, 'Zur formgeschichtliche Bestimmung der Texte vom Gottesknecht im Deuterojesaja-buch', *Probleme biblischer Theologie*, *FS G. von Rad*, Munich 1971, 27–43; J. **Begrich**, 'Das priesterliche Heilsorakel', *ZAW* 52, 1934, 81–92; *Studien zu Deuterojesaja*, Stuttgart 1938, reprinted Munich 1963; A. **Bentzen**, 'On the Ideas of "the Old" and "the New" in Deutero-Isaiah', *StTh* 1, 1948–9, 183–7; W. A. M. **Beuken**, '*Mišpaṭ*. The First Servant Song and Its Context', *VT* 22, 1972, 1–30; S. H. **Blank**, 'Studies in Deutero-Isaiah', *HUCA* 15, 1940, 1–46; P. A. H. **de Boer**, *Second Isaiah's Message*, Leiden 1956; P.-E. **Bonnard**, *Le Second Isaïe, son disciple et leur éditeurs, Isaïe 40–66*, Paris 1972; D. J. A. **Clines**, *I, He, We and They: A Literary Approach to Isaiah 53*, Sheffield 1976; F. M. **Cross**, 'The Council of Yahweh in Second Isaiah', *JNES* 12, 1953, 274–7; A. B. **Davidson**, 'The Book of Isaiah ch. XLff.', *The Expositor*, II.6, London 1883, 81ff.; K. **Elliger**, *Deuterojesaja in seinem Verhältnis zu Tritojesaja*, BWANT IV.11 (=63), 1933; I. **Engnell**, 'The 'Ebed Yahweh Songs and the Suffering Messiah in "Deutero-

Isaiah'", ET, *BJRL* 31, 1948, 54–93; G. **Fohrer**, 'Die Struktur der alttestamentliche Eschatologie', *TLZ* 85, 1960, 401–20=*Studien zur alttestamentlichen Prophetie*, BZAW 99, 1967, 32–58; H. **Gressmann**, 'Die literarische Analyse Deuterojesajas', *ZAW* 34, 1914, 254–97; *Der Messias*, Göttingen 1929, 285–323. H. **Haag**, ' 'Ebed–Jahwe–Forschung 1948–58', *BZ* NF 3, 1959, 174–204; M. **Haran**, 'The Literary Structure and Chronological Framework of the Prophecies in Is. XL-XLVIII', *SVT* 9, 1963, 127–55; G. H. **Jones**, 'Abraham and Cyrus: Type and Anti-type?', *VT* 22, 1972, 304–19; O. **Kaiser**, *Der königliche Knecht*, Göttingen 1959; Y. **Kaufmann**, *The Babylonian Captivity and Deutero-Isaiah*, New York 1970; K. **Koch**, 'Die Stellung des Kyros im Geschichtsbild Deuterojesajas und ihre überlieferungsgeschichtliche Verankerung', *ZAW* 84, 1972, 352–6; L. **Köhler**, *Deuterojesaja stilkritisch untersucht*, BZAW 37, 1923; J. **Lindblom**, *The Servant Songs in Deutero-Isaiah*, Lund 1951; N. **Lohfink**, ' "Israel" in Jes 49,3', *Forschungen zur Bibel. FS J.* Ziegler, Würzburg 1972, 217–29; R. F. **Melugin**, 'Deutero-Isaiah and Form Criticism', *VT* 21, 1971, 326–37; *The Formation of Isaiah 40–55*, BZAW 141, 1976; S. **Mowinckel**, *Der Knecht Jahwäs*, Giessen 1921; 'Die Komposition des deuterojesanischen Buches', *ZAW* 49, 1931, 87–112; C. R. **North**, 'The Former Things and the New Things in Deutero-Isaiah', *Studies in Old Testament Prophecy*, ed. H. H. Rowley, Edinburgh and New York 1950, 111ff.; D. **Odendall**, *The Eschatological Expectation of Isaiah 40–66 with Special Reference to Israel and the Nations*, Philadelphia 1970; L. **Rignell**, *A Study of Isaiah, Ch. 40–55*, Lund 1956; H. W. **Robinson**, 'The Hebrew Conception of Corporate Personality', *Werden und Wesen des Alten Testaments*, ed. P. Volz, BZAW 66, 1936, 49–62; H. H. **Rowley**, *The Servant of the Lord and Other Essays on the Old Testament*, London ²1965.

A. **Schreiber**, 'Der Zeitpunkt des Auftretens von Deuterojesaja', *ZAW* 84, 1972, 242f.; A. **Schoors**, 'Les choses antérieures et les choses nouvelles dans les oracles deutéro-isaïens', *ETL* 40, 1964, 19–47; *I am God Your Saviour: A Form-critical Study of the Main Genres in Is. 40–55*, SVT 24, 1973; S. **Smith**, *Isaiah, Chapters XL–LV*, Schweich Lectures 1940, London 1944, New York 1946; H. C. **Spykerboer**, *The Structure and Composition of Deutero-Isaiah*, Diss. Groningen 1976; C. **Stuhlmueller**, '"First and last" and "Yahweh-Creator" in Deutero-Isaiah', *CBQ* 29, 1967, 495–511; D. Winton **Thomas**, 'A Consideration of Isaiah LIII in the Light of Recent Textual and Philological Study', *ETL* 44, 1968, 79–86; C. C. **Torrey**, *The Second Isaiah*, Edinburgh and New York 1928; E. **von Waldow**, *Anlass und Hintergrund der Verkündigung des Deuterojesaja*, Diss. Bonn 1953; 'The Message of Deutero-Isaiah', *Interp* 22, 1968, 259–87; C. **Westermann**, 'Das Heilswort bei Deuterojesaja', *EvTh* 24, 1964, 355–73; 'Sprache und Struktur der Prophetie Deuterojesajas', *Forschung am Alten Testament*, Munich 1964, 92–170; R. N. **Whybray**, *The Heavenly Counsellor in Isaiah xl*, Cambridge and New York 1971; L. E. **Wilshire**, 'The Servant-City: A New Interpretation of the "Servant of the Lord" in the Servant Songs of

Deutero-Isaiah', *JBL* 94, 1975, 356–67; W. **Zimmerli**, *'Παῖς Θεου*, AT',
TWNT 5, 653–76=*TDNT* 5, 654–77; 'Der "neue Exodus" in der Verkündigung der beiden grossen Exilspropheten', 1960, reprinted *Gottes Offenbarung*, Munich 1963, 192ff.

Bibliography on Isaiah 56–66

R. **Abramowski**, 'Zum literarischen Problem von Jes. 56–66', *ThStKr*
96–97, 1925, 90–143; K. **Elliger**, *Die Einheit Tritojesajas*, BWANT III.9
(=45), 1928; 'Der Prophet Tritojesaja', *ZAW* 49, 1931, 112–40; W. **Kessler**, 'Zur Auslegung von Jes. 56–66', *TLZ* 81, 1956, 335–8; H.-J. **Kraus**,
'Die ausgebliebene Endtheophanie. Eine Studie zu Jes. 56–66', *ZAW* 78,
1966, 317–32; F. **Maass**, 'Tritojesaja?', in *Das ferne und nahe Wort. FS L.
Rost*, ed. F. Maass, BZAW 105, 1967, 156–63; H. **Odeberg**, *Trito-Isaiah
(55–66)*, Uppsala 1931; K. **Pauritisch**, *Die neue Gemeinde: Gott sammelt
Ausgestossene und Arme (Jesaja 55–66)*, Rome 1971; E. **Sehmsdorf**, 'Studien
zur Redaktionsgeschichte von Jesaja 56–66', *ZAW* 84, 1972, 517–76; W.
Zimmerli, 'Zur Sprache Tritojesajas', 1950, reprinted in *Gottes Offenbarung*, Munich 1963, 217–33.

1. The Historical Approach to the Book of Isaiah

The initial impact of the critical method

In the light of the great importance attached to the book of Isaiah,
especially by the Christian church, it is not surprising that the
historical critical study of the prophets began with Isaiah. Indeed
the battle over the right of critical research during the nineteenth
century was fought over the book of Isaiah with an intensity second
only to the Pentateuch.

The first major critical issue turned on the unity of the book. In
spite of certain hints dropped by Ibn Ezra and others, the credit for
developing a full-blown theory of dual authorship is usually
assigned to J. C. Döderlein (1775) and J. G. Eichhorn (1780–83) in
the latter part of the eighteenth century. In the debate which
ensued three arguments emerged for attributing chs. 40–66 to a
sixth-century author:

(*a*) The historical setting of chs. 40ff. reflects the exilic period
because Jerusalem is pictured as having fallen and the captives
deported.

(*b*) The striking differences in language, style, and concepts be-

tween the first and second parts of the book point to different
authors.

(c) The role of the Hebrew prophet involved addressing the
people of his day with contemporary issues in the light of God's
commands. If chs. 40ff. were spoken by an eighth-century prophet
to the needs of an exilic people some 150 years in the future, it
would be a situation without parallel in the rest of the Old Testament (cf. the case made by G. A. Smith, *Isaiah* II).

Conservative scholars, both Protestant and Catholic, reacted
vigorously with the following rebuttal.

(a) The present literary context attributes the whole book to
Isaiah which tradition is supported by rabbinic and New Testament authority.

(b) There are enough similarities in language and concepts to
maintain a unified authorship. The differences are to be explained
by the new subject matter and altered intention of the prophet.

(c) The supernatural quality of the prophecy is jeopardized if chs.
40ff. were written in the sixth century rather than in the eighth.

However, by the end of the nineteenth century the force of the
historical critical arguments against a unified authorship appeared
to have convinced the great majority of Old Testament scholars.
The appointment of A. Dillmann to Hengstenberg's chair in Berlin,
and the reversal of positions by Franz Delitzsch in the fourth edition of his commentary, marked the end of the last serious opposition to the critical view within Germany. In Britain A. B. Davidson's defence of the new position in 1883 – even when made with
great caution – broke the back of the conservative resistance and
cleared the way for G. A. Smith's immensely popular commentary
of 1890 and S. R. Driver's definitive *Introduction* of 1891. In America
the conservative position continued to find support for several more
decades from the Old Princeton school, but it represented increasingly an isolated, minority opinion.

Whereas at the close of the nineteenth century both G. A. Smith
and S. R. Driver felt the need to mount an extended case for the
critical perspective, by the beginning of the twentieth century this
position was more and more taken for granted. Likewise the hermeneutical principle became virtually axiomatic that a biblical
book could only be properly understood when interpreted in the
light of its original historical setting. This historical review is not to
suggest that conservative opposition ceased, but that its defence by

scholars such as O. T. Allis and E. J. Young did not advance substantially beyond the defensive lines set by Hengstenberg a century earlier. When some conservative scholars, such as W. A. Wordsworth, tried to defend the traditional stance with new historical evidence, the results were highly unconvincing and just as speculative as the arguments which they contested. As late as 1905 the Pontifical Biblical Commission supported the book's unity, but the position was generally abandoned by Catholic scholars after the new encyclical of 1943. Conservative Jewish scholarship never had the same stake in the traditional authorship of Isaiah as they had in the Pentateuch, and by the early twentieth century Jewish scholars generally went along with the new critical position (cf. e.g. Y. Kaufmann).

One of the immediate effects of the new critical consensus was that the study of the book of Isaiah became sharply separated into two distinct sections. Increasingly commentaries on the two parts of the book were assigned to different authors, and the history of critical research for each book went its separate way.

Critical problems of First Isaiah

B. Duhm's epoch-making commentary of 1892 made abundantly clear that chs. 1–39 were by no means a unity, but rather reflected a complex literary entity. Duhm divided First Isaiah into several small collections (1–12, 13–23, 24–27, etc.), and he traced the growth of various sections well into the Maccabean era. He attributed an original nucleus of two small collections (6.1ff.; 7.2–16; 8.1–18 and 28.1–30) to Isaiah himself, who wrote them for his disciples after the débâcle of the Syrian-Ephraimic crisis. Although Duhm did project a general theory for the composition of the whole book, his major interest lay in isolating the 'genuine' oracles of Isaiah from the subsequent 'non-genuine' layers of accretion. The goal of his critical endeavour was to recover the religious personality of the prophet himself.

In the period following Duhm there have been several detailed attempts, mainly from a literary critical perspective, to trace the history of the book's development (Budde, Mowinckel, Liebreich, Scott, Fohrer). In general, two major critical positions developed, one which followed Duhm's theory of originally independent sections finally being collected into a book, and the other which fol-

lowed the model of Budde who saw an original book as the nucleus
for later expansions and rearrangements. In spite of the great differences in the details of the reconstructions, certain observations
were held in common and formed the starting point for the analyses. First, such literary features as the broken sequence of oracles
with the same refrain (5.25; 9.12ff.) seemed clearly to indicate that
the present form of the book revealed literary dislocations which
had occurred in the course of the book's growth. Other such features pointing to a development were repetitions within the superscriptions (1.1; 2.1; 13.1), duplication of oracles (2.1ff.//Micah
4.1ff.), and the abrupt shift from poetry to prose (e.g. 3.16ff. and
3.18ff.; 10.5ff. and 10.12; 11.1–9 and 11.10ff.). Secondly, passages
within First Isaiah appeared to reflect very different historical
periods even though often juxtaposed. The grounds for this judgment did not arise explicitly from the texts themselves, but were
discovered obliquely through attention to historical allusions
(13.17), shifts in language (1.1.), and conceptual variations (26.19).

On the basis of such indications Mowinckel projected three different collections of prophecies. The first (6.1–8.22) was written by
the prophet himself at the time of the Syrian-Ephraimic war, and
twice supplemented by his disciples, once after 701 (1.1–31) and
again about 640 (portions of chs. 2, 5, 9, 10, 28, 29, 30 etc.). These
three collections were first arranged and later enlarged with
numerous eschatological additions, the oracles against the nations,
and the historical chapters (36–39).

Scott's proposal was even more detailed. He divided the book's
growth into seven different periods and worked extensively with
insertions and additions of an original Isaianic corpus. Finally,
Fohrer proposed a recurring literary pattern by which to trace the
growth of the composition. Accordingly, the sections fell into
schemata by which a basic corpus of judgment oracles had been
expanded by fragments of oracles and promises (e.g. 6.1–8.18;
8.19,21–22; 9.1–6).

If one were to try to summarize this history of research, it is fair
to say that only certain broad lines of consensus have emerged.
There appears to be an Isaianic core joined with several different
layers of material, some of which stem from redaction on the core
and others from additions of new collections. The material therefore reflects both pre- and post-exilic periods. Nevertheless, the
frustrating part of this history of research is that the material has

not lent itself readily to this kind of detailed literary reconstruction. Many of the crucial critical questions remain unresolved. Did Isaiah's original message contain promise as well as judgment? Did the prophet's message respecting Jerusalem and Assyria remain constant in the course of his ministry? What was the nature of the continuity between master and disciple?

In the light of the literary critical impasse various attempts have been made, beginning in the first quarter of the twentieth century, to overcome the narrowness of the predominantly literary critical approach of Duhm and his followers. The Scandinavians, particularly Engnell and Birkeland, stressed the work of an 'Isaiah school' which established a sense of continuity between the different ages and levels. Mowinckel himself (*Prophecy*) sought to revise his earlier analysis to include the traditional dimension. Finally, the essay of D. R. Jones ('Traditio') was one of the more insightful attempts to establish a different context for investigating the problem of composition. Jones was concerned to study both the tradition and tradition bearers of the material, and thus he placed the growth of the material within a process which dealt more adequately with its actual religious use by those who treasured it.

Of course, these reactions against the exclusively literary critical approach to Isaiah were part of the larger change within the discipline produced by the rise of the form-critical method. In terms of First Isaiah the major contribution lay in exploring the nature of the traditions on which Isaiah was dependent. In the work of von Rad and his students in particular the key roles played by the Zion and Davidic traditions were pursued. As a result, a profile of Isaiah's message emerged which was far different from that projected by Duhm (cf. von Rad, *OT Theology* II). Moreover, the recognition of Isaiah's independence from the Exodus traditions also set him apart more sharply from Hosea, Jeremiah, and Deutero-Isaiah.

Another highly significant contribution to the exegesis of Isaiah was performed by the study of the various genres within the corpus. Alt's well-known essay on Isa. 8.23–9.6 brought new insight by his suggestion of a coronation festival's providing the form of a fixed genre for the oracle which was then applied in a specific historical setting. Again, the form-critical analyses of Isa. 6 by Knierim and Steck correctly interpreted the relation of ch. 6 to chs. 7 and 8, and did much to destroy the widespread psychological analysis of the prophet's call. Finally, the implications of wisdom elements within the collection which literary critics had dismissed as secondary were fruitfully explored by Fichtner and Whedbee among others, thus recovering a rich diversity within the book which had been largely lost.

In the last decade several new directions can be observed in the study of First Isaiah. A new interest in the literary questions has returned in the form of redaction criticism which is consciously post-form-critical in orientation and not simply a return to the literary approach of Duhm. However, within this broad framework there is much diversity. Kaiser's most recent commentary on chs. 13–39, which is strikingly different from his earlier form-critical handling of chs. 1–12, is typical of one of the new directions and seeks to analyse the various layers of the books as intentional editorial reworking of the text. Similarly H. Barth's insightful dissertation seeks to recover a redactional activity in the seventh century relating to Assyria which occurred in between Isaiah's original ministry and the later post-exilic editing of the book. That such an approach involves dangers akin to those of the older literary critical method cannot be fully denied.

Another fruitful side of the new redactional interest in First Isaiah has been to explore the 'afterlife' (*Nachgeschichte*) of an early prophetic text as it was picked up and re-used in a different context. J. Becker's book was stimulating in pointing out some of the possibilities of such research. P. R. Ackroyd in particular has been a leader in England in pursuing the redactional function which lay behind the structuring of a collection of oracles. He has broken new ground in viewing the larger problems of prophetic composition from the inner perspective of the historic community's own understanding of the received tradition.

Critical problems of Second and Third Isaiah

The first major issue of Deutero-Isaiah which was to occupy much attention from the start turned on how one assessed the form of the oracles. Two very different opinions emerged in the ensuing debate. On the one hand, scholars such as Gressmann, Mowinckel, and Begrich saw in Second Isaiah a collection of oracles which had once functioned independently in an oral stage, and were only subsequently linked. Mowinckel went so far as to argue that the linkage was completely artificial and established by a mechanical catchword connection. Within this school of thought the definitive form-critical work was done by Begrich, whose success in recovering Second Isaiah's unusual speech forms convinced many of the correctness of his interpretation of the broad problems of composition. On the other hand, scholars such as Torrey and Muilenburg argued that the oracles were different in kind from those of the earlier prophets, notably Amos and First Isaiah. Rather the oracles of Second Isaiah formed a unified whole with a discernible progression of thought and reflected the structure of a literary composition instead of being a collection which was composed of smaller discrete units. Muilenburg went to the furthest extreme in regarding the whole composition of chs. 40–66 as a unified literary entity with a discernible strophic structure.

Within recent years a growing consensus has developed, led by C. Westermann and carefully documented by R. Melugin, that an intermediate position is closer to the truth than either of the two extreme formulations. The oracles reflect far more the features of a piece of literature composed by an author than the early form critics had recognized. Nevertheless, the influence of the older traditional forms on the present structure is far greater than either Torrey or Muilenburg had admitted. The exact nature of the forces within Israel which led to this type of composition has not as yet been adequately understood.

A second major issue of Deutero-Isaiah focused on the complex problem of the so-called 'servant songs', first isolated by Duhm as consisting of the following oracles: 42.1–4; 49.1–6; 50.4–9; and 52.13–53.12. The history of research on this issue has been reviewed so thoroughly that a detailed account is unnecessary (cf. North, Rowley). However, it is obvious that the problem has not been resolved in spite of the enormous effort which has been expended. In the period after World War II a reaction set in against isolating the servant songs from the rest of Deutero-Isaiah (cf. Kissane, Bonnard, etc.), but the exegesis which resulted neither broke new ground nor appeared to resolve the perennial problems. For a short while Engnell's attempt to interpret the songs within a mythical pattern of the death and rebirth of a divine king evoked much debate, but soon the alleged ancient Near Eastern parallels dissolved under close scrutiny. Nor has the once highly influential hypothesis of a 'corporate personality' proposed by H. Wheeler

Robinson fared much better. The most recent form-critical work of Westermann, Zimmerli, and Baltzer has shown the very great diversity of forms within Duhm's classification, but no new overarching solution has yet emerged. Nevertheless, this detailed form analysis does provide a good check against over simplifications of the problem as, for example, recent attempts to interpret the servant symbolically as the city of Jerusalem (Wilshire).

Finally, the issue of the unity of chs. 40–66 has continued to call forth heated debate. As is well known, Duhm first separated chs. 56–66 off from Deutero-Isaiah and attributed these final chapters to a Trito-Isaiah. His major reason for this move, apart from an alleged change in literary style, arose from his conviction that the historical setting of the latter chapters was different from Second Isaiah, and that Trito-Isaiah reflected the post-exilic Jewish community which had returned to Jerusalem. He argued that the reference to the temple, to sacrifice and sabbaths set apart the chapters from Second Isaiah but also antedated the work of Ezra and Nehemiah. In general, the majority of scholars have followed Duhm in his analysis; however, there remains an important minority which is still unconvinced (Maass). There is also disagreement whether or not to see Trito-Isaiah as a unified composition of one author (Elliger), or as a subsequent collection from many different hands.

Some of the most insightful work has been the attempt to analyse the parallel language of Deutero- and Trito-Isaiah. Zimmerli has interpreted the relationship as one of 'Nachgeschichte' (afterlife) in which earlier texts continued to be used in a different setting for a new function. His interpretation of the elements of continuity and discontinuity does, however, rest on a particular reconstruction of the historical setting of the chapters and would suffer if a different critical theory were substituted. A similar observation can be made respecting Sehmsdorf's redactional study.

An assessment of the historical critical study of the book

How is one to assess this history of scholarship which has just been reviewed? Surely it would be a grave misunderstanding to disparage the contribution of this enormous effort by generations of critical scholars. Because problems have been raised without clear-cut resolutions this result cannot be used as indictment against the critical approach. Moreover, it belongs to the nature of the enterprise that one critical theory is continually being replaced by another. The statement can hardly be denied that modern research has brought a new philological, historical, and literary precision to bear which was unknown in the pre-critical period. A measure of this critical accomplishment can be seen when one contrasts modern exegesis with a pre-critical commentary such as John Calvin or an anti-critical one such as E. J. Young. Moreover, recognition of the remarkable diversity within the book of Isaiah, the presence of literary seams, and the signs of redactional reworking are not to be gainsaid, but welcomed by anyone seriously concerned with understanding the biblical text.

Nevertheless, from the perspective of the community of faith and practice which confesses a special relationship to the Bible, the critical study of Isaiah has brought with it a whole set of new problems which have grown in size rather than diminished over the years. First of all, critical scholarship has atomized the book of Isaiah into a myriad of fragments, sources, and redactions which were written by different authors at a variety of historical moments. To speak of the message of the book as a whole has been seriously called into question, and even such relatively conservative scholars as W. Eichrodt have been forced to isolate a small number of 'genuine' or 'central' passages from which to interpret the rest of the book. Again, critical exegesis now rests upon a very hypothetical and tentative basis of historical reconstructions. Since it is no longer possible to determine precisely the historical background of large sections of Isaiah, hypotheses increase along with the disagreement among the experts. Finally, the more the book of Isaiah has come into historical focus and has been anchored to its original setting, the more difficult it has become to move from the ancient world into a contemporary religious appropriation of the message.

Of course, many of these problems have been recognized by scholars from within the critical discipline of biblical study, and the efforts of form criticism and traditio-criticism have sought to establish a sense of continuity between the different ages and levels of tradition. The attempt to find meaningful patterns in the compositional stamp of the book has at times recovered a sense of the book's wholeness and checked the endless process of atomization.

However, it is the thesis of this Introduction that the problems posed by historical critical exegesis require a far more radical hermeneutical solution than is achieved by simply adjusting individual features within the critical methodology. Rather, the community of faith for whom the book of Isaiah functions as scripture still seeks a much more basic understanding of the relation of canon to criticism than has been provided up to now. How then does a reckoning with canon affect the understanding of the book of Isaiah?

2. The Canonical Shape of the Book of Isaiah

The new theological context of Second Isaiah

Historical critical scholarship has made out a strong case for holding that the oracles of chs. 40ff. were originally addressed to Hebrew exiles in Babylon by an unnamed exilic prophet during the sixth century. However, the present canonical shape of the book of Isaiah has furnished these chapters with a very different setting. Chapters 40ff. are now understood as a prophetic word of promise offered to Israel by the eighth-century prophet, Isaiah of Jerusalem.

It is a basic misunderstanding simply to disregard the present context as a historical fiction. Rather, the present non-historical setting into which the canon has placed these traditions is a highly reflective, theological context. Moreover, it was considered so important that the original historical context of Second Isaiah – whatever it was exactly – has been almost totally disregarded by those who transmitted the material. What is left of the original context is, at best, scattered vestiges which explains why the attempt to reconstruct it as a basis for exegesis has proven so unsatisfactory and hypothetical. Even though the message was once addressed to real people in a particular historical situation – whether according to the model of Begrich or Muilenburg is indecisive – the canonical editors of this tradition employed the material in such a way as to eliminate almost entirely those concrete features and to subordinate the original message to a new role within the canon.

The characteristic feature of Second Isaiah, in striking contrast to Amos or Jeremiah, is that these chapters have no real historical context once they are removed from their present canonical setting within the book of Isaiah. These chapters begin with no superscription which is unlike all the other books of Old Testament prophets. There are no date formulae used, no concrete historical situations addressed. Rarely does the prophet speak to a specific historical need with which, for example, Amos abounds. The prophet does not confront persons or officials within the community as did Isaiah of Jerusalem. The one notable exception to this generalization is the reference to Cyrus (44.28–45.1), but even here the references to the historical events associated with Cyrus are minimal. Cyrus has become such a theological projection, an instrument in the hand of God, that his role blurs into the description of Abraham, who was also 'chosen . . . called from the ends of the earth . . . called from its farthest concerns . . . and upheld with a victorious right hand' (41.8ff.). The oracles within these chapters are either the words of God or of his servant. With a possible exception in ch. 40, no one else speaks. In Third Isaiah there are a few more historical references – one hears of eunuchs and foreigners – but basically the situation is the same. The theological context completely overshadows the historical. To what extent this literary situation reflects an intentional removal of historical data or was simply the result of a peculiar transmission process can be debated, but this judgment is not crucial for understanding the effect on the present text.

What then was the effect on these chapters of the loss of their original historical particularity? First, by placing the message of Second Isaiah within the context of the eighth-century prophet his message of promise became a prophetic word not tied to a specific historical referent, but directed to the future. A message which originally functioned in a specific exilic context in the middle of the sixth century has been detached from this historical situation to become fully eschatological. In its new context its message no longer can be understood as a specific commentary on the needs of exiled Israel, but its message relates to the redemptive plan of God for all of history. The announcement of forgiveness to downtrodden Israel – 'her warfare is ended, her iniquity is pardoned' – is not confined to a particular historical situation. Rather, in its canonical context it is offered to sinful Israel as a promise of God's purpose with his people in every age. Indeed, the loss of an original historical context has given the material an almost purely theological shape. In the context of sin and judgment, these chapters testify to Israel's real future.

One of the major critical arguments for separating Second Isaiah from First Isaiah turned on Israel's being offered forgiveness which seemed inappropriate for the unrepentant nation before the exile. Indeed, there is some historical force to the argument. First Isaiah was commissioned to preach a message of relentless judgment to a hardened people. Nevertheless, this line of argument fails to reckon seriously enough with the new function which the collectors of the material assigned to the original prophetic words. In their collected form as sacred writings the oracles did not serve primarily as historical records of a prophet's lifework, but as a continuing message of God's plan for his people in all ages. By placing the oracles into a topical and often non-historical context which subordinated their original function, a theological description of Israel as the recipient of both divine judgment and forgiveness was delineated. Historically First Isaiah spoke mainly of judgment to pre-exilic Israel. Conversely Second Isaiah's message was predominantly one of forgiveness. But in their canonical context these historical distinctions have been frequently blurred in order to testify to a theology which was directed to subsequent generations of Israelites. Sinful Israel would always be the object of divine terror; repentant Israel would receive his promises of forgiveness. To assure this theological understanding, the redaction of the book as a whole also assigned promise to First Isaiah and judgment to Second (and Third) Isaiah.

The opinion has been frequently aired by commentators that Second Isaiah's promise to the exiles was a noble concept, but was actually frustrated because the return of the exiles did not usher in the expected paradise. Begrich in particular rested much of his interpretation upon this psychological hypothesis. But by placing the message of Second Isaiah within its present theological context, the canonical shaping ruled out this psychological interpretation. Second Isaiah's message was not a hyperbolic commentary on the events of the exile, nor did it arise simply from the imagination of a poetic spirit. Rather, these prophetic words faithfully testified to God's will for Israel: 'God will come with might, and his reward is with him. He will feed his flock like a shepherd and will gather the lambs in his arms' (40.10f.). Surely this is poetry, but it is also a word which bears testimony to God's reality and his coming rule. The discrepancy between what happened after the exile and the prophet's eschatological description of God's will is not a criticism of the truth of the promise, but rather an indication of how little the exilic community partook of the promised reality.

The relation of First and Second Isaiah

The theological context which the canon gave Second Isaiah bears testimony to the history of the prophetic word. The message of Second Isaiah is not an interpretation of history as such. Its meaning does not derive from a referential reading based on events recorded in the sixth century; rather, its message turned on the fulfilment of the divine word in history. The distinction is a crucial one and supplies an important reason why the message of Second Isaiah cannot be properly understood apart from First Isaiah.

The testimony of Second Isaiah is that the great events of history which usher in the new age of redemption have been previously announced. At the outset of ch. 40 this central theme is sounded: 'The grass withers, the flower fades, but the word of our God will stand for ever' (v. 8). The deliverance through Cyrus and the rebuilding of Jerusalem are cited as evidence that God confirms the word of his prophet (44.26). Indeed, 'as the rain and snow come down from heaven and return not hither, but water the earth ... so shall my word be that goes forth from my mouth; it shall not return to me empty' (55.10). The canonical context of Second Isaiah affirms this history of the word. What the exilic prophet announced as fulfilling itself is the plan which First Isaiah had previously proclaimed and had been adumbrated in the events of 36–39. When Second Isaiah is separated from its canonical context, then the essential connection between prophecy and fulfilment within the book is lost.

An essential feature of the message of Second Isaiah is the recurrent theme of the 'former and latter things'. The phrase in slightly varying form occurs some ten times in chs. 40–55. In the contest with the false gods, the prophet challenges them: 'Set forth your case ... bring your proofs ... tell us the former things, what they are or declare to us the things to come' (41.21ff.). Later on, the divine assertion is made: 'The former things I declared of old, ... then suddenly I did them and they came to pass' (48.3). Finally, 'the former things have come to pass, and new things I now declare; before they spring forth I tell you of them' (42.9; cf. also 43.9; 43.16–19; 44.6–8; 45.9–13; 45.20f.; 46.9–11).

The problem of understanding the significance of this phrase has long been debated (cf. A. Bentzen, C. R. North, M. Haran, A.

Schoors). On the one hand, critical scholars argued that the phrase
'former things' must refer to events which were prior to the standpoint of the speaker. The events which were then experienced by
both the speaker and the addressee confirmed the truth of the
earlier prediction regarding these 'former things'. Then on the basis
of this confirmation, the prophet made a fresh prediction for the
future in terms of 'the latter things'. Therefore, the coming of Cyrus
was described as a predicted 'former thing' (41.25; 44.24ff.), which
had been confirmed. The coming deliverance of Israel from Babylon through Cyrus was then announced for the future as a 'new
thing' (48.3ff.). Because the logic of the idiom demanded that the
speaker be standing in between the former and latter things, the
prophecy could not have been written by the eighth-century prophet Isaiah, but only by the sixth-century Second Isaiah (cf. G. A.
Smith, 'Introduction', *Isaiah* II, for the development of the argument).

On the other hand, this usual historical interpretation could find
no convincing reference to a prophecy regarding Cyrus which Second Isaiah had pronounced (*contra* North), even though the force of
the whole argument rested on the fulfilment of a former word. It
was usually assumed that the oracles at issue either could not be
determined (Skinner) or had been lost. As a result, although the
exilic setting of Second Isaiah came into sharp focus, the message
itself was deemed to be only a torso.

In my judgment, recognition of the new theological context provided by the canon affords a way out of this impasse. Critical
exegesis has correctly described the original setting of the speaker,
but has missed the basic theological witness by disregarding its new
canonical shape. The 'former things' can now only refer to the
prophecies of First Isaiah. The point of Second Isaiah's message is
that this prophetic word has been confirmed. Once the connection
between First and Second Isaiah is severed, then the latter is indeed
only a confused fragment. The canonical shape testifies to the continuity of God's plan with Israel which was first announced in chs.
1–39 and confirmed in chs. 40ff. In the light of the present shape of
the book of Isaiah the question must be seriously raised if the
material of Second Isaiah in fact ever circulated in Israel apart
from its being connected to an earlier form of First Isaiah.

Certainly the force of much of the imagery of both Second and
Third Isaiah is missed unless the connection with First Isaiah is

recognized. The schema of before and after, of prophecy and fulfilment, provides a major bracket which unites the witnesses. The proclamation of the forgiveness of God (40.1) is set against the background of his former anger (1.5ff.; 3.1ff.; 42.25; 57.16). The theme of Jerusalem as the forsaken city (1.7ff.) is picked up in 62.4 and contrasted with the new city of joy. First Isaiah had spoken of the false worship of Israel; Second Isaiah speaks of true worship (58.6ff.). The pattern of seeing the new heavens and earth as a fulfilment of an earlier promise is made explicit in 65.25 by the citation of 11.6,9. Similarly, the description of God's 'stirring up' Cyrus from the north (41.25) picks up the same verb used in 13.17, 'I am stirring up the Medes. . . .' From the canonical perspective Second Isaiah's message of God's final and decisive redemption of Israel is not qualitatively different from the prophecies of First Isaiah.

Of course, there are important differences between the two collections both in form and content which were preserved in the final canonical ordering. Much that is revealed in ch. 40 as actually breaking forth is only adumbrated in the earlier chapters. First Isaiah speaks in mysterious tones of God's hidden and strange plan (28.24ff.); in Second Isaiah the divine purpose has become manifest to the world. First Isaiah alone sees the glory of the Holy One of Israel in a temple vision; Second Isaiah witnesses to all people's experiencing the glory together. The first prophet testifies to God as king (ch. 6), but his coming to Zion is only announced by the second messenger (56.7). To hear the different notes within the one book is an essential part of taking seriously the canonical shape.

The theological shaping of First Isaiah

Recognition of the context of the canon further explains why First Isaiah has been edited according to a topical pattern. It is certainly erroneous to treat First Isaiah as mainly pre-exilic oracles of the eighth-century prophet to which a block of exilic and post-exilic material was later attached in chs. 40ff. This false assessment led to the view of some early literary critics that the attachment of Second Isaiah to First Isaiah arose from an accidental linkage of two separate manuscripts and was simply the result of a mechanical error. However, the coupling of collections arose from a far more complex process of editing and gives clear evidence of a more profound understanding in the skilful intertwining of traditions. First Isaiah now contains a large amount of later material which is scattered throughout the entire collection. Moreover, both its older and newer elements have been structured into a clear theological pattern which is integrally connected with Second Isaiah.

Second Isaiah begins in ch. 1 with a theological summary of the message of the entire Isaianic corpus by using material from several periods of Isaiah's ministry (cf. Fohrer). The disaster of the year 701 provides the perspective from which the whole is viewed, and which indicates the lack of an exact chronological interest from the outset. Israel has rebelled against God and become totally estranged. The divine judgment has fallen and the country lies in desolation. Israel tries to appease Yahweh by false worship, but God seeks to woo his people back to himself. He promises that salvation will come and Zion will one day be called a faithful city.

The theme of judgment and eschatological redemption extends throughout the main portion of chs. 2–11. The sharp alterations between the two contrasting themes are juxtaposed in 2.1–5 and 2.6ff., in 3.1ff. and 4.2ff., and in 9.8ff. and 11.1ff. This same thematic sequence now encloses an early core of material in 6.1–8.22. The date formula in 6.1 sets the call at the beginning of the prophet's ministry (*contra* Kaplan, Milgrom), during the last year of the reign of Uzziah, which is chronologically prior to the material both preceding and following. The significance of this editorial structure is that the words of judgment and of redemption are grounded in a divine decision regarding Israel which is made known to the prophet in his call. Yahweh, as the Holy One of Israel, is revealed to Isaiah in his kingly majesty and the prophet only then perceives the full dimension of the nation's sin. After he is cleansed from his own guilt he is commissioned as a messenger to deliver the verdict of divine judgment which has already been rendered in the heavenly council (cf. Knierim). The call of Isaiah is not to be interpreted psychologically (*contra* G. A. Smith, Kaplan, and others), nor does his message derive from the prophet's own sense of discouragement. Rather the role of hardening (vv. 9f.) rests on the divine decision for the destruction of the nation. The close connection of ch. 6 to chs. 7 and 8 indicates the working out of the judgment in the crisis of the Syrian-Ephraimic war of 734.

The redactional process reflected in the formation of these chapters is strikingly different from that found in the handling of Second

Isaiah. The historical particularity of Isaiah's call has been largely retained. In fact, the historical moment of the prophet's own experience becomes the theological magnet around which the collection of material in 1–12 is finally ordered (cf. P. R. Ackroyd). The historical moment of Isaiah's call is indissolubly linked to the moment of divine decision which pronounced the destruction of Israel. Even though this time-conditioned role of Isaiah within the divine economy is tied to the events of the Syrian-Ephraimic war, the message with all its historical particularity transcends the historicity of the prophet himself. His words of judgment which had not been received by that sinful generation were to be collected by his disciples for a later age. Even in the period 'when God was hiding his face', there was the beginning of a new generation of faith (6.13b; 7.14; 8.17; 11.1ff.). The communal litany of ch. 12 concludes the first major section of the book and testifies to the continuing role of the community of faith which liturgically in its praise anticipates the promise of the coming salvation.

The section which follows in First Isaiah comprises oracles against the nations (chs. 13–23). The evidence is very strong that the individual oracles derive from different periods, some early and some late. From the perspective of the canonical editors these chapters receive their interpretation in the oracles of chs. 24–27 in which one again hears the liturgy of the redeemed community. The concrete judgment spoken against the individual nations in chs. 13ff. is understood to be illustrative of the final and universal judgment against all the world which will usher in Israel's redemption. The redactional connection between chs. 13 and 24 point to Babylon's representative role among the nations, which function is not to be lost by an over-historicizing of the material (*contra* Erlandsson). God will protect his pleasant vineyard (27.1; cf. 5.1ff.) and all the nations will worship at the mountain of Jerusalem (27.13; cf. 2.1ff.). Chapters 28–35 follow the pattern of initial judgment against the haughty drunkards of Ephraim and Jerusalem (28.1ff.) and the rebellious leaders of Judah (30.1ff.) to conclude with a picture of Zion's future redemption from judgment in chs. 34–35 which closely resembles the idiom of Second Isaiah.

The concluding section of First Isaiah, chs. 36–39, which forms a duplicate to II Kings 18–20, has been assigned a very important new function within the book of Isaiah. P. R. Ackroyd has mounted a convincing case for holding that these chapters were intentionally inserted between First and Second Isaiah. They were edited in such a way as to anticipate the Babylonian exile of chs. 40ff. (cf. particularly 39.6, 'nothing shall be left') and thus they provided a historical context for Second Isaiah's message of hope. These chapters in their canonical context have assumed a new metaphorical role as a commentary on the death and rebirth of the nation.

In sum, a major aim of the theological redaction of First Isaiah was to assure that its message was interpreted in the light of Second Isaiah. An interesting dialectic movement was thus established when one recalls that the reverse effect was discernible in the editing of Second Isaiah.

The canonical function of Third Isaiah (chs. 56–66)

In a previous section the critical debate over the analysis of the concluding chapters of the book of Isaiah was briefly discussed. That there are some distinctive features in these chapters few would wish to contest. What is their canonical function within the book?

W. Zimmerli has raised a crucial issue when he mounted a case for understanding the language of Third Isaiah as a later, post-exilic re-use of the earlier language of Second Isaiah. He argued that one could clearly discern the differences between the two authors by comparing the parallel passages. In several places Zimmerli found that Third Isaiah was employing verbal citations from his predecessor (e.g. 58.8b = 52.15b; 62.11 = 40.10; 60.4a = 49.18a, etc.). In other places the relationship was one of loose imitation of language and literary form. Zimmerli concluded from his study that one could discern in Third Isaiah a tendency to soften and spiritualize the message of Second Isaiah. In the place of realistic eschatological language, closely tied to events in history, one perceived a growing abstraction from historical reality which was characteristic of pious convention.

In spite of many insightful observations, in my judgment, Zimmerli's analysis has not done justice to a canonical reading of these chapters and as a result his theological conclusions are not fully in focus. The basic exegetical problem lies in Zimmerli's setting the message of Second Isaiah within a reconstructed, 'original' historical setting which he then contrasts with a more spiritualized interpretation of Third Isaiah. However, in its present canonical context the message of Second Isaiah has already been raised to a new semantic level, which is at least one step removed from Zimmerli's reconstruction in its quality of literal speech. In fact, the spiritualizing tendency of Third Isaiah is similar to that of Second Isaiah when the latter is read in its canonical context. From a historical perspective Third Isaiah may well be dependent upon Second Isaiah and have undergone a different history of transmission. However, from the canonical perspective of the final form and function, there is no real tension between these two sections and they both perform a similar function in relation to First Isaiah. It is undoubtedly the force of this canonical shaping which has continually evoked a strong minority opinion among some critical scholars who contest designating chs. 56–66 as an independent entity.

The problem of the 'servant songs' within the canon

The shape of the canonical editing of Isaiah is important in the way in which it interprets elements of discontinuity and strangeness within the Isaianic tradition. Far from being an attempt to level the variety within the prophetic message into a monolithic whole, the canonical editors have preserved – particularly in one case – a remarkable tension within the tradition.

Certainly the most difficult and controversial problem within chs. 40ff. turns on the problem of understanding the 'servant of Yahweh' passages. Briefly the issue is as follows: throughout Second Isaiah Israel's role in the economy of God is described in terms of the servant of Yahweh. In 41.8 Israel is introduced as his servant, who has been specifically chosen and promised divine aid on a mission. Yet the picture of the servant of Yahweh is so divergent that the majority of scholars feel constrained to speak of two different figures under the same image. On the one hand, the servant is viewed as collective Israel; on the other, he is an individual. Collective Israel is pictured as blind and deaf, unable to understand, a people robbed and plundered (42.18ff.), whereas the other servant is described as alert and sensitive to the word of God (50.4ff.). Collective Israel is guilty of her punishment; the other servant is innocent. Collective Israel suffers from the abuse of the nations, whereas the other servant is rejected by his own people. Finally, collective Israel is portrayed in typical, representative language, while the other servant appears as a historical figure who suffered and died at a particular time.

Of course, these contrasts within the picture first caused B. Duhm to separate the servant songs from the rest of Second Isaiah. Since Duhm's first attempt to identify the individual servant with some historical figure within Israel, almost every known and unknown figure of importance within the Old Testament has been suggested (Moses, Jeremiah, Zerubbabel, even Second Isaiah). Indeed, the whole discussion since Duhm has been characterized by its highly speculative nature. In my judgment, the breakdown in exegetical method has been caused by the failure to take seriously the canonical shape of the book. As a result, those features which the tradition has sought to emphasize have been disregarded and information has been repeatedly sought which the canonical process has, either consciously or unconsciously, blurred beyond recovery. What then can one say about the effect of the canonical process on the servant of Yahweh problem?

First, there has been no attempt made within the chapters of Second Isaiah to identify the servant with any figure in First Isaiah. In the light of the consistent pattern of prophecy and fulfilment, it is a remarkable fact that nowhere do the editors seek to identify the servant with the royal eschatological figure of First Isaiah (9.1ff.; 11.1ff.;). The imagery of the two portrayals is completely different and there is no redactional effort whatever to unite them. The canonical shape has simply retained the message of the servant as a new and hitherto unknown word of prophecy.

Secondly, the servant is consistently identified with Israel throughout the book. Nowhere is there a hint of another name or another person which ever functioned with the title within the tradition. This means that even though some of the description of the servant appears historical and not representative, efforts to recover the identity of a historical personage are doomed to failure. Only the biblical tradition knows of the servant, and it is silent on the issue beyond making a straightforward identification with Israel.

Thirdly, the canonical process has preserved the tradition of the servant in a form which reflects a great variety of tensions. The polarity remains between the servant as a corporate reality and as an individual, between the typical features and the historical, between a promised new Israel of the future and a suffering and atoning figure of the past. Nowhere is there any effort made to resolve the tension by means of a historical sequence, or by a theological pattern, or by an explanatory commentary (contrast the Targum). This observation implies that in regard to this portion of the message of Second Isaiah the canonical process preserved the material in a form, the significance of which was not fully understood. The diversity within the witness could not be resolved in terms of Israel's past experience, rather the past would have to receive its meaning from the future.

3. Theological and Hermeneutical Implications

(a) There is no book in the Old Testament in which the signs of growth in the history of its composition are more patent than Isaiah. However, we have argued in the preceding analysis that the contribution of historical criticism to exegesis does not lie in separating so-called genuine from non-genuine oracles, nor in seeking to recover the faith of the community at different stages in the book's composition. Wherein then does the value of critical research lie in the exegesis of scripture?

Specifically in terms of the book of Isaiah, critical study has made both positive and negative contributions. On the negative side, it has aided in resisting a historicizing of the biblical prophecies by making clear that the book is not ordered chronologically. It has offered good form-critical evidence for rejecting the widespread psychologizing of Isaiah's call in ch. 6. It has also done much to undercut the rationalistic interpretation of supernaturalism by establishing a sixth-century dating of these chapters. On the positive side, it has demonstrated the extent to which the prophetic word has been refracted through a community of tradents. Although the bearers of the tradition have sought to hide their own identity, their great significance within the process of composition has emerged in the selection of oracles, in the many signs of literary arrangement, and in the transmission of an interpreted text. This knowledge of the history of the book's composition thus forces the serious biblical interpreter to come to grips with the theological issues of canon, community of faith, and spirit. Theological reflection is no longer a luxury which is secondary to basic exegesis, but is constitutive of the task of interpretation itself.

(b) The nature of the biblical understanding of prophecy and fulfilment is made clear by the canonical form of the book of Isaiah. The Old Testament is not a message about divine acts in history as such, but about the power of the word of God. The divine word which proclaims the will of God confirms itself in bringing to completion its promise. History is an important medium of God's activity, but history receives its meaning from the divine word, and not *vice versa*. Fulfilment is not measured by a correspondence theory of historical truth, but in terms of the entrance of the reality testified to by the prophetic word. Thus, the redactional framework in which the Isaianic material now functions, far from being a historical fiction, is a faithful testimony to the promise and execution of God's salvation to his people.

(c) It has become axiomatic for much of modern exegesis to describe the biblical message as so historically oriented to its original setting that it required alteration whenever the historical situation changed. Westermann's formulation is typical: 'Deutero-Isaiah in his day had to speak the word appropriate to a different situation. It is quite impossible to disassociate the prophetic word from the time at which it was uttered ... Thus, God's word can never be of the nature of general teachings – perennially valid without reference to its original context' (*Isaiah 40–66*, 9f.).

In my judgment, this exegetical principle reflects a misunderstanding of what the Old Testament means by the living word of God. This modern hermeneutical theory can probably be explained as an existential rejection of the concept of eternally valid ideas which was popular in the idealistic philosophy of the nineteenth century. However, Westermann's exegetical rule renders virtually impossible the task of taking seriously the canonical shape of the biblical text. Specifically in terms of Second Isaiah, the final form of the literature provided a completely new and non-historical framework for the prophetic message which severed the message from its original historical moorings and rendered it accessible to all future generations. Although the canonical shaping of the Isaianic traditions allowed a great variety of different forms to continue, the various witnesses hold in common a concern to testify to the ways of God with Israel and the world, both in judgment and in redemption. This characterization is not to suggest that the Bible in its canonical form became a book of doctrine approximating to the Book of Concord or the Westminster Confession. Nevertheless, the dogma of modern hermeneutics which rejects as alien to the

Old Testament everything which even approaches a theological doctrine or biblical principle cannot be sustained from the Bible itself.

(d) The problem of the later appropriation of the Old Testament by Jewish and Christian writers after the Old Testament period is an extremely important but highly complex one, and it lies beyond the scope of this Introduction. At least the point should be made that the New Testament shared a broad understanding with contemporary rabbinic interpretation in studying the text within the context which the canonical process had provided. For both communities the message of Second Isaiah was not tied to a sixth-century referent, but was understood to address an eschatological hope to future Israel. The disagreement between Jews and Christians in the use of Isaiah remains a theological one – what is the nature of the promise and who is Israel? – and cannot be resolved by appeals to 'objective, scientific exegesis'.

History of Exegesis

Carpzov III, 122–6; *DBS* 4, 728f.; *DThC* 8, 77f.; *EB* 3, 935f.; *RGG*³ 3, 611.

F. M. **Abel**, 'Le Commentaire de Saint Jérôme sur Isaïe', *RB* 25, 1916, 200–25; J. M. **Allegro**, 'More Isaiah Commentaries from Qumran's Fourth Cave', *JBL* 77, 1958, 215–21; L. **Alonso Schökel**, 'Isaïe', *DS* 7.2, 1971, 2077–9; E. **Fascher**, *Jesaja 53 in christlicher und jüdischer Sicht*, Berlin 1958; L. **Finkelstein**, 'Introduction', *The Commentary of David Kimhi on Isaiah*, Columbia University Oriental Series 19, New York 1926, xvi-xcvi; H. A. **Fischel**, 'Die deuterojesanischen Gottesknechtlieder in der jüdischen Auslegung', *HUCA* 18, 1943–4, 53–76; S. **Gozza**, 'De S. Hieronymi commentario in Isaiae librum', *Antonianum* 35, Rome 1960, 49–80, 169–214; J. **Jeremias**, 'Zum Problem der Deutung von Jes. 53 im palästinischen Spatjüdentum', *Mélanges M. Goguel*, Neuchâtel-Paris 1950, 113–19; E. **Künzli**, 'Zwinglis Jesaja-Erklärungen', *Zwingliana* 10, Zürich 1957, 488–91; A. **Neubauer** and S. R. **Driver**, *The Fifty-third Chapter of Isaiah According to the Jewish Interpreters*, 2 vols., London 1876, reprinted New York 1970; J. A. **Sanders**, 'From Isaiah 61 to Luke 4', *Christianity, Judaism and Other Greco-Roman Cults*, ed. J. Neusner, Part I, Leiden 1975, 75–106; J. F. **Stenning**, *The Targum of Isaiah*, Oxford and New York 1948; G. **Théry**, 'Commentaire sur Isaïe de Thomas de Saint Victor', *La Vie Spirituelle* 47, Paris 1936, 146–62; H. W. **Wolff**, *Jesaja 53 im Urchristentum*, Halle 1942, ³1950.

XVIII

JEREMIAH

Commentaries

F. Hitzig, KeH, ²1866
C. F. Keil, BC, 1880
J. Knabenbauer, CSS, 1889
B. Duhm, KHC, 1901
C. H. Cornill, 1905
F. Giesebrecht, HK, ²1907
L. Elliott Binns, WC, 1919
J. W. Rothstein, *HSAT*, ⁴1922
P. Volz, KAT, ²1928
G. A. Smith, ⁴1929

A. Condamin, ÉB, ³1936
L. Dennefeld, SB, 1946
H. Freedman, SonB, 1949
J. P. Hyatt, *IB*, 1956
H. Lamparter, BAT, 1964
J. Bright, AB, 1965
A. Weiser, ATD, ⁵1966
W. Rudolph, HAT, ³1968
A. van Selms, POuT, 1972–4
E. W. Nicholson, CNEB, 1973–75

Bibliography

P. R. **Ackroyd**, 'Aspects of the Jeremiah Tradition', *Indian Journal of Theology* 20, Serampore 1971, 1–12; F. **Augustin**, 'Baruch und das Buch Jeremia', *ZAW* 67, 1955, 50–56; H. **Bardtke**, 'Jeremia der Fremdvölkerprophet', *ZAW* 53, 1935, 209–39; 54, 1936, 240–62; A. **Baumann**, 'Urrolle und Fasttag. Zur Rekonstruktion der Urrolle des Jeremiabuches nach den Angaben in Jer. 36', *ZAW* 80, 1968, 350–73; W. **Baumgartner**, *Die Klagedichte des Jeremia*, BZAW 32, 1917; J. M. **Berridge**, *Prophet, People and the Word of Yahweh*, Zürich 1970; H. **Birkeland**, *Zum hebräischen Traditionswesen*, Oslo 1938, 41ff.; S. H. **Blank**, 'The Confessions of Jeremiah, and the Meaning of Prayer', *HUCA* 21, 1948, 331–54; *Jeremiah, Man and Prophet*, Cincinnati 1961; J. **Bright**, 'The Date of the Prose Sermons in Jeremiah', *JBL* 70, 1951, 15–35; 'The Prophetic Reminiscence: Its Place and Function in the Book of Jeremiah', *Biblical Essays, Proceedings: Die Ou-Testamentiese Werkgemeenskap*, Stellenbosch 1966, 11–30; 'Jeremiah's Complaints', *Proclamation and Presence, Essays in honour of G. H. Davies*, ed. J. I. Durham and J. R. Porter, London and Richmond, Va. 1970, 189–214; W. **Brueggemann**, 'Jeremiah's use of Rhetorical Questions', *JBL* 92,

1973, 358–74; K. **Budde**, 'Über die Capitel 50 und 51 des Buches Jeremia', *Jahrbücher für deutsche Theologie* 23, Leipzig 1878, 428–70, 529–62.

U. **Cassuto**, 'The Prophecies of Jeremiah concerning the Gentiles', *Biblical and Oriental Studies, I: The Bible*, Jerusalem 1973, 178–226; H. **Cazelles**, 'Jérémie et le Deutéronome', *RechSR* 38, 1951, 5–36; 'Sophonie, Jérémie et les Scythes en Palestine', *RB* 74, 1967, 24–44; B. S. **Childs**, 'The Enemy from the North and the Chaos Tradition', *JBL* 78, 1959, 187–98; J. L. **Crenshaw**, *Prophetic Conflict*, BZAW 124, 1971; O. **Eissfeldt**, 'Jeremias Drohorakel gegen Ägypten und gegen Babel', *Verbannung und Heimkehr. FS W. Rudolph*, Tübingen 1961, 31–37; W. **Erbt**, *Jeremia und seine Zeit*, Göttingen 1902; G. **Fohrer**, 'Jeremias Tempelwort 7,1–15', *TZ* 5, 1949, 401–17; E. **Gerstenberger**, 'Jeremiah's Complaints', *JBL* 82, 1963, 393–408; A. H. J. **Gunneweg**, 'Konfession oder Interpretation im Jeremiabuch', *ZTK* 67, 1970, 395–416; S. **Herrmann**, *Die prophetischen Heilserwartungen im Alten Testament*, BWANT V.5 (=85), 1965, 159ff.; 'Die Bewältigung der Krise Israels. Bemerkungen zur Interpretation des Buches Jeremia', *Beiträge zur alttestamentlichen Theologie, FS W. Zimmerli*, Göttingen 1977, 164–78; 'Forschung am Jeremiabuch. Problem und Tendenzen ihrer neueren Entwicklung', *TLZ* 102, 1977, 481–90.

T. R. **Hobbs**, 'Some Remarks on the Composition and Structure of the Book of Jeremiah', *CBQ* 34, 1974, 257–75; W. L. **Holladay**, 'Style, Irony and Authenticity in the Book of Jeremiah', *JBL* 81, 1962, 44–54; 'Prototypes and Copies: A New Approach to the Poetry-Prose Problem in the Book of Jeremiah', *JBL* 79, 1966, 351–67; 'A Fresh Look at "source B" and "source C" in Jeremiah', *VT* 25, 1975, 394–412; *The Architecture of Jeremiah 1–20*, Lewisburg and London 1976; F. **Horst**, 'Die Anfänge des Propheten Jeremia,' *ZAW* 41, 1923, 94–153; W. J. **Horwitz**, 'Audience Reaction to Jeremiah', *CBQ* 32, 1970, 555–64; F.-L. **Hossfeld** and I. **Meyer**, 'Der Prophet vor dem Tribunal', *ZAW* 86, 1974, 30–50; J. P. **Hyatt**, 'Torah in the Book of Jeremiah', *JBL* 60, 1941, 381–96; 'Jeremiah and Deuteronomy', *JNES* 1, 1942, 156–73; 'The Deuteronomic Edition of Jeremiah', *Vanderbilt Studies in the Humanities*, 1, Nashville 1951, 71–95; 'The Beginnings of Jeremiah's Prophecy', *ZAW* 78, 1966, 204–14; J. G. **Janzen**, *Studies in the Text of Jeremiah*, HSM 6, 1973; M. **Kessler**, 'Form-Critical Suggestions on Jer. 36', *CBQ* 28, 1966, 389–401; 'Jeremiah Chapters 26–45 Reconsidered', *JNES* 27, 1968, 81–8; 'Rhetoric in Jeremiah 50 and 51', *Semitics* 3, Pretoria 1973, 18–35; H.-J. **Kraus**, *Prophetie in der Krisis*, Neukirchen 1964; H. **Kremers**, 'Leidensgemeinschaft mit Gott im Alten Testament: Eine Untersuchung der "biographischen" Berichte im Jeremiabuch', *EvTh* 13, 1953, 122–40; O. **Loretz**, 'Die Sprüche Jeremias in Jer. 1.17–9.25', *Ugaritforschungen* 2, Neukirchen 1970, 109–30.

G. C. **Macholz**, 'Jeremia in der Kontinuität der Prophetie', *Probleme biblischer Theologie, FS G. von Rad*, Munich 1971, 306–34; H. G. **May**, 'Towards an Objective Approach to the Book of Jeremiah: The Biographer', *JBL* 61, 1942, 139–55; 'The Chronology of Jeremiah's Oracles',

JNES 4, 1945, 217–27; J. W. **Miller**, *Das Verhältnis Jeremias und Hesekiels sprachlich und theologisch untersucht*, Assen 1955; S. **Mowinckel**, *Zur Komposition des Buches Jeremia*, Kristiania 1914; *Prophecy and Tradition*, Oslo 1946, 61ff.; P. K. D. **Neumann**, 'Das Wort, das geschehen ist . . . Zum Problem der Wortempfangsterminologie in Jer. I–XXV', *VT* 23, 1973, 171–217; E. W. **Nicholson**, *Preaching to the Exiles*, Oxford and New York 1970; E. **Nielsen**, *Oral Tradition*, ET, SBT I.11, 1954; T. W. **Overholt**, *The Threat of Falsehood*, SBT II.16, 1970; 'Some Reflections on the Date of Jeremiah's Call', *CBQ* 23, 1971, 165–84; K.-F. **Pohlmann**, *Studien zum Jeremiabuch*, FRLANT 118, 1978; G. **von Rad**, 'Die Konfessionen Jeremias', *EvTh* 3, 1936, 265–70; R. **Rendtorff**, 'Zum Gebrauch der Formel *nᵉ'* um jahwe im Jeremiabuch', *ZAW* 66, 1954, 27–37; H. Graf **von Reventlow**, *Liturgie und prophetisches Ich bei Jeremia*, Gütersloh 1963; C. **Rietzschel**, *Das Problem der Urrolle*, Gütersloh 1966; T. H. **Robinson**, 'Baruch's Roll', *ZAW* 42, 1924, 209–21; L. **Rost**, *Israel bei den Propheten*, BWANT IV. 19 (=71), 1937, 54–71; H. H. **Rowley**, 'The Prophet Jeremiah and the Book of Deuteronomy', *Studies in Old Testament Prophecy*, FS *T. H. Robinson*, ed. H. H. Rowley, Edinburgh and New York 1950, 157–74; 'The Early Prophecies of Jeremiah in Their Setting', *BJRL* 45, 1962–3, 198–234.

W. **Schottroff**, 'Jeremia 2,1–3. Erwägungen zur Methode der Prophetenexegese', *ZTK* 67, 1970, 263–94; F. **Schwally**, 'Die Reden des Buches Jeremia gegen die Heiden XXV. XLVI-LI', *ZAW* 8, 1888, 177–217; J. **Skinner**, *Prophecy and Religion*, Cambridge and New York 1922; B. **Stade**, 'Bemerkungen zum Buche Jeremia', *ZAW* 12, 1892, 276–308; 'Der "Völkerprophet" Jeremia und der jetziger Text von Jer. Kap, 1', *ZAW* 26, 1906, 97–123; H.-J. **Stoebe**, 'Seelsorge und Mitleiden bei Jeremia', *WuD* NF 4, 1955, 116–34; 'Jeremia, Prophet und Seelsorger', *TZ* 30, 1964, 385–409; 'Geprägte Form und geschichtliche, individuelle Erfahrung im Alten Testament', *SVT* 18, 1969, 212–19; W. **Thiel**, *Die deuteronomistische Redaktion von Jeremia 1–25*, WMANT 41, 1972; D. Winton **Thomas**, 'Again "the Prophet" in the Lachish Ostraca', *Von Ugarit nach Qumran*, FS *O. Eissfeldt*, BZAW 77, 1958, 244–9; E. **Tov**, 'L'incidence de la critique textuelle sur la critique littéraire dans le livre de Jérémie', *RB* 79, 1972, 189–99; G. **Wanke**, *Untersuchungen zur sogenannten Baruchschrift*, BZAW 122, 1971; H. **Weippert**, *Die Prosareden des Jeremiabuches*, BZAW 132, 1973; A. **Weiser**, 'Das Gotteswort für Baruch Jer. 45 und die sogenannte Baruchbiographie', reprinted in *Glaube und Geschichte im Alten Testament*, Göttingen 1961, 321–9; A. C. **Welch**, *Jeremiah. His Time and His Work*, Oxford and New York 1951; C. F. **Whitley**, 'The Term Seventy Years Captivity', *VT* 4, 1954, 60–70; H. **Wildberger**, *Jahwewort und prophetische Rede bei Jeremia*, Diss. Zürich 1942; F. **Wilke**, 'Das Skythenproblem im Jeremiabuch', *FS R. Kittel*, BWA[N]T 13, 1913, 222–54.

1. Historical Critical Problems

It seems hardly necessary to review in detail the history of research on the book of Jeremiah because this task has been performed many times and is readily available in English (cf. Bright, Nicholson, and Kaiser, *Introduction*). The critical problems within the book are many and are well-known. The composition reflects no clear chronological patterns. There are remarkable duplications in which oracles are separated from the report of the event itself without an obvious reason (chs. 7 and 26; 25 and 36, etc.). Again, the length and order of the Greek text varies considerably from the Hebrew. However, the major critical problem on which modern critical research has focused turns on the relation between the poetic and prose sections of the book.

The first sharply delineated formulation of this basic critical problem is usually attributed to B. Duhm, who in 1901 distinguished three sources within the book. He spoke of the authentic poetic oracles of Jeremiah, of biographical stories about Jeremiah, and a 'supplementer' (*Ergänzer*) who, at a much later post-exilic period, transformed the prophet into a preacher of judgment and morals. This approach was picked up and further refined in Mowinckel's monograph of 1914; he designated these three sources as A, the authentic poetic, B, the biographic prose, and C, the Deuteronomic redaction. In 1946 Mowinckel modified his earlier position somewhat by speaking of three levels of 'tradition' rather than literary sources. The basic outlines of this analysis have been accepted by leading scholars including Birkeland, Pfeiffer (*Introduction*), Rudolph, and Hyatt, among others. Of course, there have been strong dissenting voices (Holladay, Rietzschel, Weippert). As one might expect, Mowinckel's classification of the material has also been applied to the problem of trying to recover the original form of the scroll mentioned in ch. 36 as the first step in the composition of the book. Although the majority of scholars have tended to identify the original scroll with a selection of poetic material within chs. 1–25 from the A source, an impressive minority opinion continues to defend the prose material of C with the scroll (Eissfeldt, T. H. Robinson, Miller).

In recent years the critical discussion has focused mainly on establishing the historical relationship between the poetic tradition of A and the prose tradition of C. On the one hand, a large group of scholars in the tradition of Duhm and Mowinckel would consider the prose material of C to be an exilic (or even post-exilic) level of tradition, formulated by a Deuteronomistic school which may contain some authentic Jeremianic material but which is basically unhistorical in its present form. The emphasis falls on the historical discontinuity between the poetry and the prose (cf. particularly Hyatt). A theological modification of this basic critical position regarding the historical value of the prose material is represented by scholars such as Nicholson and Thiel, who would not defend the historicity of the prose material any more than Mowinckel, but who would assign a new positive theological value to the Deuteronomistic redaction of the tradition. These scholars would argue that the function of C material was not to provide an accurate historical record but to actualize through preaching the old traditions for a new historical situation of the exile. Yet the emphasis remains on historical discontinuity.

On the other hand, there is another group of critical scholars who, in various ways, seek to establish a strong sense of historical continuity between the poetic and prose layers. A variety of different suggestions have merged which have sought to overcome the sharp division first proposed by Duhm. Cornill sought to blur the distinction between Jeremiah's use of poetry and prose, and he defended an authentic historical level of prose which he attributed to Jeremiah. Weiser, Miller, and others have tried to link both Jerusalem and Deuteronomy to a common liturgical language and thus retain Jeremianic authorship for Deuteronomically flavoured prose. Then again, Holladay ('Prototypes'), and most recently Weippert have sought to establish a close literary relationship between poetic prototypes which recur in a prose copy, thus recovering a historical continuity.

Above all, John Bright has mounted an impressive case for historical continuity. In his 1951 article Bright was able effectively to destroy the theory that Jeremiah's prose exhibited many post-exilic features common with Ezekiel and Second Isaiah, which H. G. May had proposed. Moreover, Bright argued against identifying Jeremiah's prose with a Deuteronomic redaction and he sought to demonstrate statistically that the prose of Jeremiah was distinctive from the stereotyped prose of the Deuteronomist. He concluded that Jeremiah had a prose style of his own, which was commensurate with other seventh-century Hebrew literature. This prose represented a historically accurate 'gist' of what the prophet had been remembered saying by his disciples. In a subsequent article in 1966 Bright sought to show that the language of the biographer's prose B and that of C was indistinguishable. Since the B writer, who was usually identified at that time with Baruch, was historically linked to Jeremiah, the closeness in style and content with C would further substantiate the historicity of C's picture of the prophet.

The purpose of this review is not to offer a full evaluation of the strengths and weaknesses of these different positions – there are recent critiques by Holladay (*VT*, 1975,) and Herrmann (*TLZ*) – but rather to illustrate the nature of the present impasse regarding the relation of the poetic and prose traditions. What has emerged from half a century of debate is the recognition that literary and historical elements both of strong discontinuity and of continuity are present within the Jeremianic tradition. On the one hand, those scholars who stress the sharp differences between the poetic and prose levels have correctly seen that a significant redactional process has been at work. The prose tradition now bears a shape which is so strikingly different from the poetry of the prophet and so remarkably similar to the prose of the Deuteronomist that the arguments for seeing the influence of a different hand at work in the prose far outweigh in probability all other explanations – whether literary, historical, or psychological – which would seek to derive all the various levels from the historical Jeremiah. Even Bright's A[1] source reflects a clearly discernible redactional level of Dtr. material.

On the other hand, elements of genuine literary and historical continuity cannot be denied. Efforts to establish a significant temporal distance between the life of Jeremiah and the prose redaction in order to account for the transformation within the tradition have broken down. For several very strong reasons the prose level must have developed shortly after the death of Jeremiah. First, the language of C is seventh-century and exilic, not post-exilic. Secondly, the biographical prose narratives, often attributed to Baruch and clearly resting on historical tradition, already reflect the Deuteronomist's concept of Jeremiah's ministry and are even at times a literary abbreviation of the C material (cf. Wanke for current debate over the B material). Finally, the prose material of

Jeremiah exerted an influence on Ezekiel which would further mili-
tate against a late dating.

In sum, the critical problem remains a highly complex issue
which is unlikely to reach a clear-cut historical resolution in the
foreseeable future. The theological issue lies in determining to what
extent responsible exegesis is dependent upon first solving these
critical problems. Once again it is the thesis of this Introduction
that attention to the canonical shaping of this book shifts the priority of questions being addressed to the text.

2. The Canonical Shape of Jeremiah

The two forms of proclamation

The first feature to observe is that the book of Jeremiah in its
present form takes explicit notice of two different ways in which
Jeremiah delivered his oracles, indeed of two distinct literary forms
of his preaching. Chapters 25 and 36 relate a crucial event which is
dated in the fourth year of Jehoiakim, in the year 605, which was
the first year of Nebuchadnezzar's reign. The prophet has met such
resistance to his preaching that he is physically prevented from
public proclamation in the temple (36.5ff.). He dictates his message
on a scroll to Baruch who is commissioned to read it in the temple.
Chapter 25 describes the contents of the scroll (cf. also 36.2) as a
summation or précis of Jeremiah's preaching for the last twenty-
three years which was evoked as a final effort to call the people to
repentance before the impending judgment.

The historical critical discussion has tended to focus its attention
on the account of the destruction of the scroll by Jehoiakim, and
Jeremiah's subsequent preparation of a new scroll to which 'many
similar words were added' (36.32). However, the most significant
feature of the biblical account from the perspective of the tradition
itself is that two different forms of the prophetic proclamation are
described and are attributed to two different settings. For some
twenty-three years the prophet preached to the people orally. (The
probability that his oral delivery was in metrical form is not registered explicitly by the tradition itself, and was not given a particular canonical significance.) Then in the year 605, in the light of a
specific historical situation, Jeremiah fixed his message in writing.
He selected, condensed, and emphasized certain features toward

achieving a definite purpose, namely, a call to repentance. The reaction of the nobles on hearing the words read confirms the threatening content of the message.

If we now translate the tradition's account of the prophet's two modes of preaching into critical terminology, the tradition attributes to Jeremiah a level of oral communication from Josiah's reign through Jehoiakim (source A) and a written condensation of prophetic threat (source C). Moreover, according to the tradition the content of Jeremiah's scroll interpreted the prophet's ministry in the light of Israel's sacred scripture, namely, Deuteronomy. Jeremiah saw himself as standing in the line of a series of prophets (25.4) who preached the law and called for repentance. From the tradition's perspective the events of Israel's history – the hardness of the people, the wickedness of the king, the rise of Nebuchadnezzar – led to the prophet's reshaping of his message in the light of scripture.

The book of Jeremiah recognizes these two forms of proclamation which it attaches to different stages of Jeremiah's ministry. However, it was the later role as a preacher of judgment after the mode of Deuteronomy that became the dominant pattern by which the prophetic message was shaped. In the light of the ensuing events of history, culminating particularly in the destruction of Jerusalem in 587, Jeremiah was understood as the prime example of the messenger of God – a picture shared and decisively formed by the scriptural tradition of Deuteronomy – who forecast the divine judgment.

From a historical critical perspective the authentic poetic tradition of Jeremiah was transformed by cloaking the prophet's message in the later, prose language of the Deuteronomic tradition. From the perspective of the tradition a new understanding of Jeremiah emerged from the events of history, which, far from being a distortion, confirmed the prior word of scripture. The canonical shaping of the Jeremianic tradition accepted the Deuteronomic framework as an authentic interpretation of Jeremiah's ministry which it used to frame the earlier poetic material.

The canonical perspective thus confirms both the continuity and discontinuity within the tradition, but it does this in a particular manner. On the one hand, the canonical shaping of the tradition is explicit in attempting to derive the two forms of the prophetic proclamation from the actual experience of the prophet. A definite continuity is grounded in the self-understanding of the prophet himself. In this respect, the levels of tradition are integrally linked to the prophet in a way which is not the case, for example, between First and Second Isaiah. On the other hand, the force which has shaped the prose tradition combines theological and non-historical elements in such a way that historical continuity in the scientific sense of the discipline has been seriously eroded. The element of discontinuity entered because the prose level of material has been reinterpreted in the light of the Deuteronomic understanding of a divine prophet to such an extent as to absorb its original historical profile. A new form has emerged which cannot be adequately described – either historically or theologically – as only a 'gist' (Bright).

The canonical shaping of the book confirmed as authentic the later picture of Jeremiah's ministry which was portrayed in the light of the larger canon and which it used along with the uninterpreted poetic oracles. The present form of Jeremiah's oracles goes beyond a historical recounting of the prophet's activity. Rather, the memory of his proclamation was treasured by a community of faith and consciously shaped by theological forces to serve as a witness for future Israel. One of the major forces arose from hearing the prophet's words in conjunction with the law of Moses, and in placing Jeremiah in a chain of divine messengers who warned of Jerusalem's destruction. Indeed, for that generation which experienced the truth of Jeremiah's prophecy, his role acquired an even greater relevance.

The Deuteronomic framework

A second feature of the canonical shaping of the present form of the book of Jeremiah is the perspective provided by the Deuteronomic flavoured prose sections which now frame the entire Jeremianic corpus. The decision to attach a verbatim excerpt from II Kings 24 to the book of Jeremiah, following the explicit conclusion to the prophet's own words (51.64), is a further confirmation that his words are viewed as a prophecy leading up to the events reported in II Kings. Equally important is the role of the Dtr. prose account at the introduction. The call of Jeremiah is part of the early poetic level, but the true significance of the call is explained in language reminiscent of Deuteronomy (Jer. 1.15ff.). The same interpretative pattern can be discerned throughout chs. 1–25. The early poetic tradition has been preserved, usually quite untouched, but it has been placed within larger blocks of prose which interpreted Jeremiah's role in the light of the fuller canon, especially Deuteronomy (cf. 7.1ff.; 11.1ff.; 21.1ff.; 25.1ff.).

Many of the stages within this process of canonical shaping can no longer be fully recovered. John Bright has made the interesting suggestion that another symbol, A[1], should be used to designate a type of material in Jeremiah which is a series of autobiographical prose accounts written in the first person which are *ex post facto* reminiscences of actions already performed. He lists such passages as 1.4–19; 13.1–11; 18.1–2; and 19.1–12 on which most scholars have been divided as to source. From a redactional point of view the interesting feature is the contrasting way in which this material (A[1]) has been handled in comparison to the poetic. Invariably A[1] material has been reinterpreted in the light of Deuteronomy and brought into closest contact with the preaching style of C material (18.10ff.; 19.5ff.; 24.9ff.). However the point to be made is that, in spite of a different history of editing in which many elements are not clear, in the end both A and A[1] material function similarly within the interpretative framework of the larger canon. This observation is not to suggest that the 'original poetic Jeremiah' has been destroyed. Even in the final form of the book his oracles have been transmitted largely unredacted in all their rich diversity. Rather, the Deuteronomic framework serves to interpret the significance of Jeremiah's ministry for the life of the nations within the larger economy of God's plan.

The function of the biographical material

There is another important and unusual feature in the canonical shaping of the book of Jeremiah. The reader is given a deeper insight into the life of the prophet than is found with any other Old Testament prophet. This biographical interest is registered in two different sorts of material. Within the poetic material there is a collection of poems, often entitled 'the Confessions of Jeremiah' (11.18–12.6; 15.10ff.; 20.7ff., etc.). In addition, and far more extensive, there is a second major block of material extending from chs. 26–45 (excepting chs. 30–33) which contains stories about Jeremiah's prophetic activity from the beginning of Jehoiakim's reign, through the fall of Jerusalem, and during the final period of his life in Egypt.

One of the striking features of this biographical material is that many of the events recorded in this section contain abbreviated summaries of oracles which are found elsewhere in the earlier collections in addition to descriptions of incidents in the prophet's life. The classic example is the paralleled account of the temple speech in Jer. 7.1–15 and 36.1ff. It seems quite evident that the biographical material, called B by Mowinckel, has undergone its own particular history. With a few exceptions (cf. Wanke), the general historical accuracy of the accounts has not been seriously challenged. Often the composition of the material has been attributed to Baruch, not only because of his close association with the prophet during this period and his explicit role as amanuensis, but especially because of the private oracle in ch. 45 which appears to conclude the collection. However, these critical issues have not been fully resolved.

Scholars have argued at great length as to the purpose of the biographical accounts within the book as a whole. H. Kremers' suggestion of seeing the aim of the stories to portray the 'passion of Jeremiah' (*Leidensgeschichte*) has been accepted by some scholars, but appears to many as unconvincing. More recent studies, especially that of Nicholson, have emphasized that the chief interest of the stories does not really fall on the personal suffering of the prophet. His suffering serves as only a secondary element within a larger framework. Rather, the stories reflect a theological interest in demonstrating from his history 'the rejection of the Word of God' spoken by his prophets (Nicholson, 55). Thus the reaction to Jeremiah's temple speech (ch. 26) is followed by a similar story regarding another prophet, Uriah, who was murdered because of his message of judgment. Again, Nicholson has made an illuminating point in showing the conscious typological effort to contrast the rejection of Jeremiah's message by the wicked king, Jehoiakim, with the earlier acceptance by the repentant king, Josiah (II Kings 22).

The inclusion of biographical stories is of great importance in the final shaping of the Jeremianic material by the canonical tradition. First, it is an indication that Jeremiah's proclamation consisted not just of his words, but was represented by his whole life. The prophet not only consistently warned of the coming divine judgment upon the nation, but he participated himself in the judgment of his people. The collectors of Jeremiah's words moved in a direction quite different from that taken by the editors of the eighth-century prophets. They acknowledged by their inclusion of his life story that a complete understanding of his ministry demanded elements of both speech and action. Similarly, von Rad has made an illuminating interpretation of the so-called 'confessions' in showing that the central issue in recording the inner struggles of the prophet turned on the nature of the prophetic office and the full dimensions of divine judgment as a theological issue.

There is an additional element of significance to be observed regarding the canonical role of the biographical material. Previously we discussed the problem of relating the poetic material (A) with the Dtr. flavoured prose (C). The biographical material (B) forms an important link in the redactional process. The false impression of this process has often been engendered that the Dtr. framework imposed a layer of foreign accretion upon the genuine poetic portrait of Jeremiah. That this approach is a basic misunderstanding of the tradition's growth emerges clearly from the inclusion of the biographical material. It is of crucial significance to recognize that both Jeremiah's message and his office were immediately understood by his audience in terms congruent with the Dtr. interpretation of the C prose. The biographical tradition of Jeremiah is not built upon the early poetic material, but rather is fully in accord with the Dtr. portrayal. The picture of Jeremiah as a preacher of judgment did not, therefore, arise from a tendentious literary programme, but was formed by the events of history, such as the temple speech, when seen in the light of scripture, and was so perceived by both circles of disciples.

The oracles of promise

Another feature of basic importance in the canonical shaping of the book of Jeremiah is to be found in the role which has been assigned to the so-called 'salvation oracles' of the prophet. These oracles which focus on the future hope of Israel are found particularly in the collection of chs. 30–33, but there are many other examples of an eschatological hope found elsewhere in the book. What is the nature of this hope and how have these oracles been employed in the total message of the book?

Within the final form of the book the element of salvation appeared right at the outset of Jeremiah's ministry and was assigned a programmatic function within his call. His prophetic commission was both 'to destroy and overthrow, to build and plant'. This theme of a dual role continues to be echoed throughout the book in separate prose sayings (18.5ff.; 24.6; 31.28; 42.10; 45.4). The prophetic book bears witness to the belief that, regardless of the severity of the divine judgment on Israel, the ultimate goal in the divine economy was redemption. The editors of Jeremiah's oracles indicate the outcome of the drama before beginning the story in order to remove any doubt respecting the ultimate plan of God. However, this theological affirmation of God's purpose does not undercut the intensity with which Jeremiah struggled for Israel's future (8.22ff.; 32.1ff.), nor does it protect against his moments of genuine despair (6.27ff.; 20.14).

There is another indication that the oracles of salvation have undergone a significant redactional reshaping. Scholars such as P. Volz (KAT, 274ff.) have made a strong case for seeing that the message of a promised return to the land was originally directed to the survivors of the long since destroyed Northern Kingdom. The promise was directed to 'the remnant of Israel' (31.7), who will 'again plant vineyards upon the mountains of Samaria' (v. 5) when God restores 'the fortunes of the tents of Jacob' (30.18), and Rachel's children are 'brought back from the north country' (cf. also 3.12f.). However, in the present form of the book of Jeremiah these original promises have been combined with oracles of promise which include Judah as well (31.23ff., 27ff.; cf. 3.14ff.). The promises have thus been loosened from their original historical moorings and given a fully eschatological function. Both Israel and Judah – and every successive generation of God's people – live from this same promise of divine faithfulness.

The major section of promises have been collected in chs. 30–33 and precede the account of Jerusalem's fall (39.1ff.). The effect of this ordering of the material re-emphasizes the belief that promise was a part of the divine plan from the outset. It did not arise from a last-minute feeling of compassion to salvage something from the debacle. Moreover, pursuant to the redactor's pattern Jeremiah's poetic oracles of salvation (chs. 30f. and 33) have been combined with a prose account in which Jeremiah himself experienced the promise (ch. 32). There seems to have been a deliberate redactional concern to anchor the promise, not only in the tradition, but in the self-understanding of the prophet himself. The point is significant because such a redactional interest is relatively rare within the Old Testament.

One final feature respecting the oracles of promise calls for discussion. Older commentators such as J. Skinner (74ff.) and more recently S. Herrmann (*Heilserwartungen*, 159ff.) have observed the unusual way in which threats and promises are formulated in both an absolute and a conditional form (cf. chs. 7; 18). This observation is not to suggest that the fulfilment of the divine promises in the theology of Jeremiah must await Israel's fulfilling of certain conditions. The unconditional formulation (31.1ff.) runs directly in the face of this interpretation. Nevertheless, the language of a covenant, indeed of a new covenant (31.31ff.) implies a loyalty from the side of Israel. God's commitment to Israel is as fixed as the orders of the stars (31.35ff.). In sum, the oracles of promise in their final edited form did not serve to engender passive waiting in the generations who looked for the promise, but functioned to order the life of the community who lived in expectation toward righteousness.

The oracles to the nations

The final section of the book of Jeremiah contains a message to the nations (chs. 46–51). As is well known, the Masoretic order of these chapters differs from the Greek which has inserted these chapters in ch. 25. It is very possible that the Greek order represents an earlier stage of the formation of the book. Janzen (115ff.) derives the Masoretic order from a mechanical textual problem which caused new material to be sewn to an older manuscript as an appendix. A more likely explanation, in my judgment, is that the larger pattern found in other prophetic books of reserving the oracles against the nations to the last influenced the Masoretic tradition. The major effect of the Masoretic order is to maintain the close connection between the oracles in chs. 1–25 and the biographical events in chs. 26–45. Moreover, the final chapter which describes the destruction of Jerusalem 'by the nations' is closely linked both with the preceding oracles and the initial call of Jeremiah in ch. 1. The result emphasizes the claim of Yahweh, the God of Israel, over the course of history, including the nations. However, the issue of the order of the oracles does not emerge as a major redactional problem which would seriously affect the book's witness. The same theology is implied in the Greek tradition as the Hebrew. The Masoretic text appears simply to have preferred a more logical position within the total book. The historical perspective of this section often covers events of the later period which now function in the canonical shaping to confirm the oracles of the prophet.

3. Theological and Hermeneutical Implications

(a) First of all, by taking seriously the canonical shape of the book of Jeremiah a different stance emerges as to how one evaluates the different levels of tradition within the book. It has been typical of the critical method, shared by such varying approaches as Duhm, von Rad, and Bright, to seek to recover the 'authentic Jeremiah' by making use chiefly of the poetic oracles. As a result, the explicit structure by which the prophetic material was shaped is consistently removed as late and tendentious. Over against this hermeneutical reflex a canonical approach to the book strives to understand the full dimension of the interpreted testimony. Although it does not burden the canonical profile with claims of historicity, it acknowledges the normative theological shaping of the material by the canon. It does not seek to play off the various levels of tradition against each other, but rather follows the leads within the composite as to how the parts relate theologically.

(b) Secondly, a most significant feature of the canonical shaping lies in the close relation established between the law and the prophets. Whereas critical scholarship has concentrated much of its effort in seeking to discover how the historical Jeremiah reacted to the Josianic reform in order to forge a bridge to the book of Deuteronomy, the biblical tradition itself passed over the incident in complete silence. Rather, it placed Jeremiah within the tradition of preachers of the law and provided the later community with a prophetic interpretation of how the law properly functioned within the divine economy. To take this interpretation seriously rules out both an alleged conflict between the law and the prophets, and also a legalistic subordination of the latter into a minor role.

(c) Finally, the canonical approach speaks to the issue of prophetic collections as scripture. In my judgment, attention to the canon calls forth a very different model from that currently employed by the majority of critical scholars. The theological function of the book of Jeremiah is not adequately treated by using it as a referential source for historical reconstruction, whether or not one's approach is liberal (Hyatt) or conservative (Bright). Likewise, a redactional approach which views the book as an historical actualization of exilic preaching rests upon a non-canonical reconstruction in its effort to make the book serve theologically. It renders interpretation dependent upon recovering a depth dimension within the text when it has not been assigned a canonical function. Moreover, this approach to actualization as a response to the community's needs fails to reckon with the critical force unleashed by Israel's scriptures in establishing a new context from which to interpret the growing tradition. Finally, the canonical approach affirms that the witness of the book for the community of faith, Jewish and Christian, which confesses its authority, lies in the form which it received by the tradition in order to mediate the prophetic word for every future generation.

History of Exegesis

Carpzov III, 174–7; *DThC* 8, 884–8; *EB* 3, 885; *RGG*³ 3, 590.

C. **Kannengiesser**, 'Jerémé. II. chez les pères de l'Élise', *DS* 8.1, 1974, 889–901; C. A. **Moore**, *Daniel, Esther, and Jeremiah: The Additions*, AB, 1977; G. **Montico**, *Geremia profeta nella tradizione ebraica e cristiana*, Padua 1936; W. **Naumann**, *Untersuchungen über den apokryphen Jeremiasbrief*, BZAW 25, 1913; P. **Nautin**, 'Introduction', *Origène, Homélies sur Jérémie* I, SC 232, Paris 1976, 15–191; C. **Wolff**, *Jeremia im Frühjudentum und Urchristentum*, TU 118, 1976.

XIX

EZEKIEL

Commentaries

E. W. Hengstenberg, 1869
R. Smend, KeH, ²1880
C. F. Keil, BC, 1882
C. H. Cornill, 1886
J. Knabenbauer, CSS, 1890
A. B. Davidson, CB, 1892
A. Bertholet, KHC, 1897
J. Herrmann, KAT, 1924
G. A. Cooke, ICC, 1936
A. Bertholet, K. Galling, HAT, 1936

L. Dennefeld, SB, 1946
F. Fisch, SonB, 1950
G. Fohrer, K. Galling, HAT², 1955
H. G. May, IB, 1955
J. B. Aalders, COuT, 1955–57
H. Lamparter, BAT, 1968
W. Zimmerli, BK, 1969
J. W. Wevers, NCeB, 1969
W. Eichrodt, ET, OTL, 1970

Bibliography

J. G. **Aalders**, *Gog en Magog in Ezechiël*, Kampen 1951; P. R. **Ackroyd**, *Exile and Restoration*, OTL, 1968, 103–17; P. **Auvray**, 'Le problème historique du livre d'Ézéchiel', *RB* 55, 1948, 503–19; 'Ézéchiel', *DBS* 8, 1970, 759–91; D. **Baltzer**, *Ezechiel und Deuterojesaja*, BZAW 121, 1971; E. **Baumann**, 'Die Hauptvisionen Ezechiels in ihrem zeitlichen und sachlichen Zusammenhang untersucht', *ZAW* 67, 1955, 56–67; G. R. **Berry**, 'The Composition of the Book of Ezekiel', *JBL* 58, 1939, 163–75; E. **Broome**, 'Ezekiel's Abnormal Personality', *JBL* 65, 1946, 277–92; K. **Budde**, 'Zum Eingang des Buches Ezechiel', *JBL* 50, 1931, 20–41; M. **Burrows**, *The Literary Relations of Ezekiel*, New Haven 1925; K. W. **Carley**, *Ezekiel among the Prophets*, SBT II.31, 1975; U. **Cassuto**, 'The Arrangement of the Book of Ezekiel', *Biblical and Oriental Studies* I, Jerusalem 1973, 227–40; H. J. **van Dijk**, *Ezekiel's Prophecy on Tyre*, Rome 1968; L. **Dürr**, *Die Stellung der Propheten Ezechiel in der israelitisch-jüdischen Apokalyptik*, Münster 1923; W. **Eichrodt**, 'Der Sabbat bei Hesekiel. Ein Beitrag zur Nachgeschichte des Prophetentextes', *Lex tua veritas*, *FS H. Junker*, Trier 1961,

65–74; 'Der neue Tempel in der Heilshoffnung Hesekiel', *Das ferne und nahe Wort*, *FS L. Rost*, BZAW 105, 1967, 37ff.; K. **Elliger**, 'Die grossen Tempelsakristeien im Verfassungsentwurf des Ezechiel (42, 1ff.)', *Geschichte und Altes Testament*, *FS A. Alt*, Tübingen 1953, 79–103.

G. **Fohrer**, 'Die Glossen im Buche Ezechiel', *ZAW* 63, 1951, 33–53; *Die Hauptprobleme des Buches Ezechiel*, BZAW 72, 1952; *Die symbolischen Handlungen der Propheten*, Zürich 1953; D. N. **Freedman** 'The Book of Ezekiel', *Interp* 8, 1954, 446–71; F. S. **Freedy**, 'The Glosses in Ezekiel i-xxiv', *VT* 20, 1970, 129–52; J. **Garscha**, *Studien zum Ezechielbuch*, Berne and Frankfurt 1974; H. **Gese**, *Der Verfassungsentwurf des Ezechiel (Kap. 40–48) traditionsgeschichtlich untersucht*, BHT 25, 1957; 'Ez 20,25f und die Erstgeburtsopfer', *Beiträge zur alttestamentlichen Theologie*, *FS W. Zimmerli*, Göttingen 1977, 140–51; M. **Greenberg**, 'On Ezekiel's Dumbness', *JBL* 77, 1958, 101–5; 'The Citations in the Book of Ezekiel as a Background for the Prophecies' (Hebrew), *Beth Mikra* 50, Jerusalem 1973, 273–8; M. **Haran**, 'Ezekiel's Code (Ezek. xl-xlviii) and its Relation to the Priestly School' (Hebrew), *Tarbiz* 44, Jerusalem 1974–5, 30–53; J. **Harvey**, 'Collectivisme et individualisme, Ez. 18, 1–32 et Jér. 31,29', *Sciences Ecclésiastiques* 10, Montreal 1958, 167–202; V. **Herntrich**, *Ezechielprobleme*, BZAW 61, 1932; S. **Herrmann**, *Die prophetischen Heilserwartungen im Alten Testament*, BWANT V.5 (=85), 1965, 241ff.; G. **Hölscher**, *Hesekiel. Der Dichter und das Buch*, BZAW 39, 1924; F. **Horst**, 'Exilsgemeinde und Jerusalem in Ez viii-xi. Eine literarische Untersuchung', *VT* 3, 1953, 337–60; C. G. **Howie**, *The Date and Composition of Ezekiel*, New Haven 1950; W. A. **Irwin**, *The Problem of Ezekiel*, Chicago 1943; 'Ezekiel Research since 1943', *VT* 3, 1953, 54–66; G. **Jahn**, *Das Buch Ezechiel auf Grund des Septuaginta hergestellt*, Leipzig 1905; K. **Jaspers**, 'Der Prophet Ezechiel. Eine pathographische Studie', *Arbeiten zur Psychiatrie, Neurologie und ihren Grenzgebieten*, *FS K. Schneider*, Heidelberg 1947, 77–85.

P. **Katz**, 'Zur Textgestaltung der Ezechiel-Septuaginta', *Bibl* 35, 1954, 29–39; C. **Kuhl**, 'Zur Geschichte der Hesekiel-Forschung', *ThR* NF 5, 1933, 92–118; 'Neuere Hesekielliteratur', *ThR* NF 20, 1952, 1–26; 'Der Schauplatz der Wirksamkeit Hesekiels', *TZ* 8, 1952, 401–18; 'Zum Stand der Hesekiel-Forschung', *ThR* NF 24, 1956–7, 1–53; J. D. **Levenson**, *Theology of the Program of Restoration of Ezekiel 40–48*, HSM 10, 1976; H. G. **May**, 'The Departure of the Glory of Yahweh', *JBL* 56, 1937, 309–21; J. W. **Miller**, *Das Verhältnis Jeremias und Hesekiels sprachlich und theologisch untersucht*, Assen 1955; W. L. **Moran**, 'Gen. 49,10 and its Use in Ez. 21,32', *Bibl* 39, 1958, 405–35; M. **Noth**, 'La catastrophe de Jérusalem en l'an 587 avant Jésus-Christ et sa signification pour Israël', *RHPhR* 33, 1953, 81–102=*GSAT*, ²1960, 346–71; R. A. **Parker** and W. **Dubberstein**, *Babylonian Chronology 625 BC–AD 45*, Brown University Studies 19, Providence 1956; K. **von Rabenau**, 'Die Entstehung des Buches Ezechiel in formgeschichtlichen Sicht', *WZ Halle* 5, 1955–6, 659–94; 'Das prophetische Zukunftswort im Buche Hesekiel', *Studien zur Theologie der alttestamentlichen*

Überlieferungen, Neukirchen 1961, 61–80; H. Graf **von Reventlow**, 'Die Völkern als Jahwes Zeugen bei Ezechiel', *ZAW* 71, 1959; 33–43; *Wächter über Israel. Ezechiel und seine Tradition*, BZAW 82, 1962; H. H. **Rowley**, 'The Book of Ezekiel in Modern Study', *BJRL* 36, 1953, 146–90; reprinted in *Men of God*, London and New York 1963, 163ff.; A. **van Selms**, 'Literary Criticism of Ezekiel as a Theological Problem', *OuTWP* 4, 1961, 24–37; James **Smith**, *The Book of the Prophet Ezekiel: A New Introduction*, London and New York 1931; S. **Spiegel**, 'Ezekiel or Pseudo-Ezekiel?', *HTR* 24, 1931, 245–321; 'Toward Certainty in Ezekiel', *JBL* 44, 1935, 145–71.

S. **Talmon** and M. **Fishbane**, 'The Structuring of Biblical Books: Studies in the Book of Ezekiel', *ASTI* 10, 1976, 129–53; C. C. **Torrey**, *Pseudo-Ezekiel and the Original Prophecy*, New Haven and London 1930; M. **Tsevat**, 'The Neo-Assyrian and Neo-Babylonian Vassal Oaths and the Prophet Ezekiel', *JBL* 78, 1959, 199–204; N. **Turner**, 'The Greek Translators of Ezekiel', *JTS* 7, 1956, 12–24; R. R. **Wilson**, 'An Interpretation of Ezekiel's Dumbness', *VT* 22, 1972, 91–104; J. **Ziegler**, 'Zur Textgestaltung der Ezechiel-Septuaginta', *Bibl* 34, 1953, 435–55; W. **Zimmerli**, 'Das Gotteswort des Ezechiel', *ZTK* 48, 1951, 249–62=*Gottes Offenbarung*, Munich 1963, 133ff.; *Erkenntnis Gottes nach dem Buche Ezechiel*, Zürich 1954=*Gottes Offenbarung*, 41ff.; 'Die Eigenart der prophetischen Rede des Ezechiel', *ZAW* 61, 1955, 1–26=*Gottes Offenbarung* 148ff.; 'Das Wort des göttlichen Selbstweises (Erweiswort), eine prophetische Gattung', in *Mélanges A. Robert*, Paris 1957, 154–64; 'Der Wahrheitserweis Jahwes nach der Botschaft der beiden Exilspropheten', *Tradition und Situation, FS A. Weiser*, Göttingen 1963, 133ff.; *Ezechiel. Gestalt und Botschaft*, BSt 62, 1972; 'Deutero-Ezechiel?', *ZAW* 84, 1972, 501–16.

1. Historical Critical Problems

The impact of the historical critical method upon the book of Ezekiel was surprisingly slow in being felt. Well into the twentieth century the critical consensus remained confident of the book's literary unity and integrity of authorship (cf. S. R. Driver, *Introduction*). However, once the critical problems were opened up – usually G. Hölscher is given credit for the initial impetus – the widest possible disagreement regarding the book developed. Modern critical opinion still remains in a far greater state of flux than with any of the other major prophets.

In broad terms, the problem of the book lies in the inability to construct a picture of Ezekiel conforming even in general to the main features of Hebrew prophecy which critical scholarship has come to expect. The book appears to lack the sharp contours of a given historical period, of a definite geographical locality, and of genuine prophetic preaching to a concrete group of listeners. For example, in the introduction the inaugural vision is assigned to the fifth year of King Jehoiachin's captivity (593) and the latest date mentioned in 29.17 is the twenty-seventh year of the captivity (571). Yet many scholars are convinced that materials of a much earlier and later date are evidenced throughout the book. Then again, the prophet seems to oscillate back and forth between Babylon and Jerusalem without ever reflecting a concrete historical addressee in either community. Finally, the style of prophetic address lacks most of the traditional forms of oral speech (invective, threat, disputation), but rather abounds in allegory, symbolic acts, and visions.

Much of the history of modern critical scholarship during the twentieth century can be seen as an effort to address these issues.

(a) G. Hölscher argued in 1924 that the prophet Ezekiel was actually a spirit-filled poetic writer whose work had been reworked by an unimaginative prose redactor of the fifth century who had transformed radically the nature of the original composition. By means of literary surgery Hölscher was able to recover about one-seventh of the book for the original author. With somewhat similar conclusions, W. Irwin argued that the original oracles of the prophet had been misunderstood by a later commentary which he sought to remove in order to recover the pristine form of Ezekiel himself. More recently, S. Herrmann, followed by O. Kaiser (*Introduction*, 257), has maintained that the original message of the prophet contained no expectation of salvation and he assigned those oracles in the present text which spoke of promise to a later hand.

(b) The difficulty of fixing a specific historical period for Ezekiel's ministry along with a concrete audience has resulted in two very different critical reactions. On the one hand, several scholars (e.g. James Smith) have assigned Ezekiel to an early period in Northern Israel by claiming that the book reflects the abuses of Manasseh's age. On the other hand, other scholars, notably C. C. Torrey, have described the book as a pseudepigraph from the third century BC which was completely a literary creation without any real historical roots.

(c) In an effort to explain the dual geographical foci of the book on Jerusalem and Babylon various theories have been put forth which also rely heavily on redactional activity. Herntrich proposed the theory that the genuine Ezekiel was active only in Jerusalem before the exile, and that a post-exilic editor reworked chs. 1–39, adding his own material in order to portray the prophet as also working during the exile. Various less radical modifications of Herntrich's thesis have also been proposed, such as that suggested by Bertholet and Pfeiffer (*Introduction*), which would allow a genuine historical ministry to the prophet at different periods within his life, but which would eliminate the need for ecstatic transport between the two localities.

(*d*) Then again, various theories have been suggested to explain the peculiarities of Ezekiel's ecstatic behaviour in terms of psychological disturbances or physical illness (cf. especially K. Jaspers), but in general these attempts have met with little positive reception by critical commentators and have left only an indirect influence on the history of research.

(*e*) Finally, the history of modern critical research on the book of Ezekiel has not been adequately surveyed until the work of W. Zimmerli has been assessed. It is certainly fair to say that he has succeeded in inaugurating a new phase in the study of the book by his numerous articles and massive commentary. Not only has Zimmerli attempted a continual critical dialogue with all his predecessors, but in addition, he has presented his own thorough solutions to the book's many problems. Zimmerli's contributions are numerous but they can be roughly divided into two main areas.

First, Zimmerli has sought to understand the peculiar forms of prophetic speech found in Ezekiel by means of an exhaustive form-critical and traditio-critical investigation. In an exciting new way he was able to demonstrate Ezekiel's dependence upon ancient Hebrew tradition in the call narrative, in the historical recitals, and in the exodus and election themes. Above all, he demonstrated the social-legal setting of the book, which has close parallels in the Holiness Code of Leviticus (chs. 17–26), from which Ezekiel constructed his oracles.

Secondly, Zimmerli developed his theory of a text's 'afterlife' (*Nachinterpretation*) to explain the different levels of growth reflected in the final form of the book. He argued that the words of Ezekiel continued to evoke a process of reinterpretation on the part of his followers, and that most of the complex literary issues raised, for example by Hölscher, could best be explained by this subsequent accretion on an original Ezekiel kernel (*Grundtext*) by a post-exilic 'school'.

In my judgment, Zimmerli's research has been a major advance in the right direction toward an understanding of the critical problems of the book. He has succeeded in undercutting most of the radical literary and traditio-critical theories of his predecessors – and successors (Garscha) – by means of his own incisive and frequently convincing analysis. It is difficult to believe that critical scholarship will ever return to a pre-Zimmerli stage in evaluating the book. Nevertheless, in my judgment, there are some inadequacies in Zimmerli's commentary. Above all, I do not think that he has correctly assessed the canonical shape of the book, but has rested his interpretation on a critically reconstructed pre-canonical form of the book. In this regard he has retained too close a continuity with the assumptions of the historical critical methodology. It is significant to observe that, although much of Zimmerli's research has been accepted by younger scholars, it has often been used in a form without Zimmerli's theological concerns and made to function fully within the older critical framework. I shall return to a more thorough evaluation of Zimmerli's method once I have presented my own thesis regarding the canonical shape of the book.

2. The Canonical Shape of Ezekiel

The present shape of the book derives from a long and complex canonical process which collected and shaped the material to function as authoritative writing within the Jewish community. In the history of research on the book of Ezekiel, similar to the handling of other prophetic books, the advocates of the usual historical critical methods strove to relate each passage to a particular historical event or situation. Particularly in Ezekiel's case, the changing geographical locale, the fluid historical perspective, and the symbolic forms of speech proved a major stumbling-block to this approach. Unfortunately, evidence of other forces at work which mitigated the direct historical stimuli was dismissed as unimportant accretion or redactional misunderstanding.

In addition, there is another peculiarity to the book of Ezekiel which complicated the issue and made an understanding of the canonical shape of the book even more elusive. The uniqueness of

Ezekiel among the major prophets derives from the unusual relationship between the original function of the oracles and its subsequent canonical shaping. I would argue the thesis that Ezekiel's original historical role was shaped by forces closely related to those which have been characterized as canonical. The effect of this joining of influences has been that there has emerged the strongest continuity between the original oracles and the final canonical shape. The prophetic material in this case did not undergo a major literary or historical transformation in order to serve its new canonical role. Indeed, there was a canonical process extending over a lengthy period of time in which different editorial activity can be discerned, but the development was one of closest continuity between the various stages of the literature. Because of this close relation between the form and function of Ezekiel's original oracles and the later canonical use of the material, it is important to study these features of the original oracles which lent themselves so easily to later canonical adoption.

Ezekiel's radical theocentric orientation

The dominant feature of the book of Ezekiel is its stark theological understanding which views everything from a radical theocentric perspective. A different understanding of reality, including time and space, resulted from this theological orientation which affects every aspect of Ezekiel's oracles. It accounts, in large measure, for the inability of modern scholars to fit Ezekiel into the usual prophetic patterns. Thus, even when his oracles are fixed within a chronological framework, these temporal moorings are immediately transcended when the prophet describes the plan of God for Israel in terms completely freed from temporal limitation. For example, in chs. 12, 16, and 20, in the period before the fall of Jerusalem when Ezekiel is being instructed by the word of God concerning the impending destruction of the nation, the message of judgment inevitably includes a word of God's ultimate will for Israel in the future which is salvation.

Or again, when the prophet proclaims his message to the people, the historical addressee takes on such a highly theological profile that the concrete features of time and place fade into abstraction. Thus, in ch. 14 Ezekiel begins by addressing 'certain of the elders of Israel' who sat before his house. But as the oracle proceeds, the address suddenly incorporates all of Israel (v. 5; cf. Zimmerli, *Gottes Offenbarung*, 152). The specific groups of exiles lose their features of historical particularity and are caught up into larger theological categories of disobedient or redeemed Israel. Often it is impossible to know whether the oracles are directed to the remnant at Jerusalem or to the exiles of Babylon. In the same way the important spatial distinctions between these two localities Babylon and Jerusalem have become entirely relativized because the people of God are viewed as one entity from the divine perspective.

The office of Ezekiel is also completely shaped from the same theocentric perspective. The oracles of the prophet consist almost entirely of the word of God to Ezekiel. The prophet's task as a watchman is to proclaim the radical divine 'either/or'. He is not to negotiate, intercede or persuade (3.16ff.; 33.1ff.). Only rarely is there any sign of direct confrontation. Ezekiel speaks of the divine will for sinful Israel with the initiative for judgment and restoration lying solely in the hands of God (37.1ff.).

The effect of this theocentric concentration is that Ezekiel's message never takes on the particularity of the usual prophetic activity in which specific issues and groups are addressed in invective and threat. By viewing history from the divine perspective – to speak of idealization is not fully accurate – the prophet moves in an atemporal dimension of divine decision. However, because of these features, the need for actualizing the message for a later generation is not present to the same degree. The original theological formulation serves each generation equally well. The ultimate challenge to Israel 'to know that I am Yahweh' requires no canonical reformulation.

Traditions and forms used by Ezekiel

One of the major contributions of Zimmerli's form-critical research on Ezekiel has been his ability to explain the reasons lying behind some of the strangeness of the prophet's language. Particularly in such difficult chapters as 14, 18, and 33 he has made a strong case for Ezekiel's use of priestly language derived from Israel's ancient sacral-legal tradition. The propensity to cloak his prophetic message in forensic terminology has a far-reaching effect on its content. First, Israel's history of disobedience is not addressed in the typical prophetic invective, but rather in the impersonal form of the case study (18.1ff.). Secondly, the addressee is not directly confronted, but his case is viewed in terms of priestly judgments of righteous or unrighteous action (14.1ff.). As a result, Ezekiel's message appears to reflect an abstract, impersonal tone and seems more ideal than actual.

Frequently in the history of Ezekiel research, scholars have attempted to draw important theological implications directly from these peculiar stylistic features which were usually of a derogatory nature, e.g., Ezekiel was an unfeeling priest, a rigid legalist, or an individualist who repudiated corporate responsibility. Zimmerli has gone a long way in destroying the foundation of this basic misunderstanding of the prophet's language. He has been able to show, particularly in the use of casuistic legal terminology, Ezekiel's effort to formulate a fresh and vigorous imperative which made use of the traditional language of the cult. When correctly interpreted, the prophet's message was highly existential! (cf. Zimmerli, BK 1, 406ff.). Nevertheless, the effect of this peculiar idiom is such that the message does not share in the same level of historical particularity as does Amos or Jeremiah. Because of its formulation, the legal principles of right and wrong on which the covenant was based applied equally well to each successive generation who faced life or death decisions under covenant law.

Then again, the widespread use of symbolic action, visions, and allegories by the prophet clearly lent itself to subsequent use within the canon. Ezekiel couched his message in a language which proclaimed a message by way of analogy. The disastrous politics of Zedekiah were vigorously condemned by means of the eagle allegory (ch. 17). Jerusalem's unfaithfulness to Yahweh was pictured in terms of an ungrateful foundling (ch. 16). Even the historical traditions of the exodus, wilderness, and conquest became schematized into typological patterns of the past (20.1ff.) and of the future (20.33ff.). The effect was to render Ezekiel's message in a form one stage removed from direct historical stimuli. This characterization is not to suggest that Ezekiel's message is an unreal idealization of history – the issue of reality is certainly not at stake – but rather that he portrayed a divine message in such a way as to address the future as well as the present generation with the unchanging will of God.

The role of scripture

Surely one of the most important aspects of Ezekiel's message was its dependence upon the activity of interpretation within the Bible itself. Not only was Ezekiel deeply immersed in the ancient traditions of Israel, but the prophet's message shows many signs of being influenced by a study of Israel's sacred writings. The impact of a collection of authoritative writings is strong throughout the book. Obviously the mediating of Israel's tradition through an authoritative written source represents a major canonical interest. The evidence that such an activity was a major factor in the formulation of Ezekiel's original oracles would also account for the ease with which the canonical process adopted his oracles without great change.

Thus, for example, in ch. 20 Ezekiel is not only making use of the great traditions of the Egyptian slavery, exodus, and conquest, but he offers a detailed and radical reinterpretation of the law of the first-born found in Ex. 22.28. Again, the vision of the seventy elders of Israel 'each with a censer in his hand' is not understood unless this cultic abuse is seen in the light of the covenant ceremony in Ex. 24.9ff. and the judgment of Korah in Num. 16.16ff. Or again, in the portrayal of Gog and Magog (chs. 38–39) one can recognize the influence of Isa. 5.26ff.; Jer. 4.29ff.; and Ps. 46. The image of the furnace in 22.18 is dependent on Isa. 1.22, the pot in 24.3ff. on Jer. 1.13. Again, the portrayal of the glory of Yahweh in ch. 1 reflects an exegetical influence from Isa. 6. This preoccupation with scripture on the part of Ezekiel should come as no surprise since the importance of the 'scroll' which is eaten is stressed right from the start (3.1ff.).

It is also very likely a sign of exegesis within the Bible that the same images continue to be used throughout the book often with a different meaning, but nevertheless calling up echoes of the other passages. The caldron image as an utterly irresponsible boast (11.3) is transformed in ch. 24 into a dreadful word of judgment. The imagery of the vine is played upon in chs. 15, 17, and 19, each time with a different set of nuances. Similarly the figure of the sword is repeated (chs. 11 and 21), and the great cedar (chs. 17 and 31).

To summarize: particular features within Ezekiel's prophetic role which shaped both the form and content of his message contained important elements which the later canonical process found highly compatible to adapt without serious reworking for its own purpose of rendering the tradition into a corpus of sacred writing.

The structure of the book

In spite of the close continuity between the original message of Ezekiel and its final canonical form, there are many signs which point to the influence on the book's composition which derived from the subsequent process of collecting and ordering the material. The most obvious sign of this canonical process lies in the closely integrated structure of the book as a whole. In fact, it was the early recognition of the perspicuous arrangement of the various sections within the book which first deceived critical scholars into thinking the book was a simple composition of a single author. The present structure is divided into four clearly defined sections, 1–24, 25–32, 33–39, 40–48.

The backbone of the structure is provided by a chronological framework which extends throughout the book and joins the sections together. Generally the pattern follows the historical sequence from the fifth year of the exile (1.2) to the twenty-fifth (40.1) with some slight variation in the middle sections. Although it has often been remarked that the dates apply only to those passages explicitly recorded, the literary effect of the framework is clearly intended to include the other passages as well within the larger temporal pattern. The canonical ordering has thus tied the material more closely to a fixed historical sequence than was evidenced at the book's first stage of development. The reason behind the preoccupation with the chronology of the oracles is clearly revealed and is theological in nature. Ezekiel's message is confined to one of divine judgment on Jerusalem until the city's destruction (3.16ff.; 24.25ff.; 33.21ff.). Whatever Ezekiel's dumbness may once have entailed, the motif within the present canonical context serves to limit the prophet's preaching rather than to silence him completely.

Nevertheless, within the chronological framework into which the canonical process has fixed the material, several other moves can be discerned. First, there are several signs to indicate that the original oracles of the prophet have been subsequently expanded to make use of later historical events. The most obvious example is in ch. 12, in which a sign-act of the prophet has been expanded to include references to the abortive attempt at escape by Zedekiah (vv. 12ff.). The frequently disparaging characterization of such an addition as a *vaticinium ex eventu* (Fohrer, Wevers) has misunderstood the theological intention behind this redactional activity. The editor saw in this event an historical instance confirming the prophecy of imminent judgment which the sign-act had already unleashed. The editorial addition enriched the original oracle but did not undercut the theological function of the chronology in limiting the content of Ezekiel's message according to its relation to Jerusalem's fate. Other examples of such expansions can be found in 20.27ff.; 29.6ff.; and 30.20ff.

Then again, one can see that the chronological framework which defines the content of Ezekiel's message to Israel in its canonical setting does not restrict the ultimate purpose of God toward his people. The eschatological promise of salvation beyond the judgment is pictured throughout the book, and transcends completely the temporal framework (cf. 11.16ff.; 16.59ff.; 17.22ff.; 20.33ff.; 34.11ff.; 36.22ff.; 37.1ff.; 39.25ff.; 40.1ff.). Although there is no convincing evidence to suggest that the original oracles of Ezekiel lacked the element of promise, the later canonical shaping has ordered the oracles of salvation in such a way as to emphasize the ultimate will of God for Israel's restoration even at every stage of the nation's impending destruction. The theocentric perspective of Ezekiel's original oracles has been further radicalized by the canonical structuring of the whole.

In addition to the chronological framework, there are several other significant examples of the interpretative role of the present structure. The description of the prophet's office as that of a watchman appears to have had its original setting in the oracle of ch. 33. However, in the present structure of the book the oracle has been combined with a section from ch. 18 and placed in ch. 3 to serve as an introduction to the prophet's ministry. This reordering of the original material into a new form has raised one description of the prophet's role into an overarching category by which to interpret Ezekiel's whole ministry.

The placing of the oracles against the nations (chs. 25–32) within the present structure clearly reflects a later canonical ordering. This material now interrupts the literary sequence which joined 24.27 with 33.21ff. Although the reasons behind this move are not always certain, this intentional positioning does effect a theological reinterpretation of the material. The nations – Ammon, Moab, Edom, Philistia, Tyre and Egypt – are judged for different reasons from those applying to Israel. Usually the grounds for condemnation have to do with their vengeance against Israel and their arrogance. The nations are judged before the restoration of Israel usually by means of similar images: the destroying sword, the desolation of the land, the felling of the cedars. However, the goal of this judgment is the same as that of Israel's: 'that you may know that I am Yahweh' (25.11, 17, etc.). Significantly, the prophecies against Gog and Magog (chs. 38–39) have not been included within the framework of chs. 25–32, but these nations are explicitly envisioned as attacking the restored and forgiven Jerusalem. The eschatological hope thus expressed is closely akin to that of Joel 3 and Zech. 14 in which the divine destruction of the enemy is a constitutive part of the restoration of Israel.

It is also theologically significant that the concluding section of the book, chs. 40–48, portrays the restored people of God as a community demonstrating the proper worship of God. These chapters form a conscious contrast with the earlier portrayal of Israel's disobedience in terms of an abuse of worship, particularly chs. 8–11. On the one hand, the canonical shape has not sought to spiritualize the description of the new temple and the new land in order to soften the concrete features of Israel's hope. On the other hand, the description of the transformation of the land in terminology reminiscent of paradise (47.1ff.) emphasizes the divine source of the new creation, commensurate with Israel's resurrection from the dead (37.1ff.).

Exegesis of the Bible by the Bible

Perhaps the most significant sign of canonical shaping within the book of Ezekiel has to do with a process of expansion of the original oracles by means of exegetical activity within the Bible. To what extent this expansion represents a reworking of the original material by the prophet himself or by a later 'school' cannot always be determined, but both possibilities are likely. Certainly one of the great contributions of Zimmerli's commentary has been in showing the extent of this process of continuing interpretation.

The process of reinterpretation of the original text takes a variety of different forms. At times there is an explicit attempt within the canonical process to link Ezekiel's message to previous prophecies. 38.17 refers to the earlier prophets who foretold the coming of the enemy from the north. Ezekiel's prophecy against Gog and Magog (chs. 38f.) is then seen as fulfilling these earlier prophecies and the language of Isa. 5, Jer. 4–6, and Ps. 46 is brought into Ezekiel's passage to assure the connection between prophecy and fulfilment.

At other times an original passage of Ezekiel shows signs of being expanded in the light of the larger canon, which material functions in the form of an interpretative commentary. The initial theophany of God in ch. 1 has been greatly embellished by bringing in the imagery of other theophanies from Ex. 24.9ff., Isa. 6.1ff., and Ps. 18.11. The description of the Day of Yahweh in 7.19 seems to have been enriched by borrowing from Zeph. 1.15. Or again, the effect of Isaiah 2 on Ezekiel 40 can be discerned in the elaborate picture of the holy mountain.

Even more characteristic of Ezekiel's method of internal exegesis is the interpreting and expanding of one of the chapters in the light of another. One of the clearest examples of this activity can be seen by the introduction of the theophanic descriptions of God of ch. 1 into the theophany of chs. 8–11. The theological implication is obvious. The same God who appeared in all his glory is the self-same one who departed in judgment from sinful Jerusalem. Again, the literary relationship between chs. 16 and 23 is complex, but a mutual influence upon each other appears most likely. Moreover, the form of expression reveals that this conflation is not simply a textual problem, but an intentional exegetical expansion.

The re-use of images

Finally, there are signs within the final canonical shaping of a text of an original passage being reapplied to a new situation within the community in a way which is quite different from its original role. Some of this process of reapplication simply derives from the autonomy of the symbolic language which has stimulated a wide variety of differing reactions. In ch. 23 the unusual feature is that the language of the original allegory has been detached from the figure of speech and applied literally as a warning to the women in exile (23.48). Although Zimmerli judges this expansion of the original text to be a 'surprising rationalization' of the allegory which has distorted the text (vol. 1, 555), this evaluation does not do justice to the versatility of the image to serve a new function. A similar phenomenon seems to be present in ch. 16 with elements of the allegory being applied homiletically to the exiles apart from the original figure of speech.

Canonical interpretation contrasted with others

Perhaps it will aid in sharpening the focus of the discussion to contrast the exegetical method which is being suggested with W. Zimmerli's understanding of a text's 'afterlife' (*Nachinterpretation*). Because of the great erudition and penetrating insight of his research, all subsequent Ezekiel research will have to measure itself against Zimmerli's work. My own dependence upon his research is readily acknowledged.

I fully agree with Zimmerli's analysis that the present Hebrew text of the book of Ezekiel shows clear evidence of subsequent expansion. This amplification has resulted from a process in which later hands – Zimmerli prefers to speak of a 'school' rather than redactors – have worked on the original text in the light of other passages of scripture and of new historical events. In various ways this later expansion has reshaped the text, either by interpolation, further commentary, or by reorganizing the structure.

However, I differ with Zimmerli in the evaluation of this process within his practice of the exegetical discipline. Zimmerli understands his task first to be a recovery of the original '*Grundtext*' which he reconstructs by means of textual, literary and form-critical techniques. It is this *Grundtext* which provides Zimmerli with the basis for interpreting each passage. However, greatly to his credit, he does not simply dismiss the additional material as worthless accretion, which is the standard approach of Hölscher, Fohrer, and Wevers, but seriously attempts to understand the subsequent growth as commentary on the original text. Often Zimmerli judges the expansion to be an enrichment of the original text, but occasionally (cf. ch. 23) he argues that the subsequent commentary has seriously misunderstood the original meaning of the text.

My criticism of Zimmerli's method of treating the text's growth can only be briefly outlined under the following points. First, Zimmerli has, in effect, substituted his own reconstructed basic text for the canonical Hebrew text (cf. ch. IV above). As a result, his basic interpretation rests on the same precarious subjective basis as does all such critical reconstructions. But there is an even more serious objection: Zimmerli's method, like the usual historical critical approach, has missed the significance of the canonical process in which the experience of Israel with the use of its authoritative writings has been incorporated into the text itself as part of the biblical witness. The canonical shaping not only registered that history by its shaping of the tradition, but it also brought that process to an end when it fixed its canon. Everything thereafter was commentary, not text. Zimmerli disregards this fundamental canonical decision by substituting a pre-canonical stage in the text's development for the normative canonical text, and by judging a significant part of the canonical text as merely commentary. It also follows that Zimmerli's exegesis makes little theological use of the history of exegesis since it no longer shares a common text with the past.

Secondly, Zimmerli's method of working from a reconstructed *Grundtext* to which has been appended commentary runs the danger of losing the inner dynamic of the full canonical passage. To divide a passage historically into stages often destroys the synchronic dimension of the text. A literary entity has an integrity of its own which is not to be identified with the sum of its parts. Zimmerli's method is vulnerable to the criticism of mishandling the text as literature.

Thirdly, Zimmerli's method shares the widespread assumption of historical criticism that the introduction of a historical dimension necessarily aids in illuminating the biblical text. Continually the reader is instructed which verses are historically later within the text than others. At times some of these observations are helpful; at other times the judgments are hypothetical and fragile. Frequently he has overestimated the significance which this historical dimension brings to the text of Ezekiel. This bias towards the historical often blocks an understanding of the final canonical form which has consciously introduced theological elements into the text in order to blur the common historical perspective.

3. Theological and Hermeneutical Implications

(a) The book of Ezekiel provides a good example of how an understanding of the original oracles of the prophet has contributed to the understanding of the final, canonical shape. Because these two stages in the development of the book are in such close continuity, failure to comprehend the unique form and content of the historical ministry of Ezekiel, such as we find in Hölscher, Herntrich, and Irwin, seriously impairs the ability to understand the canonical shape as well. However, the genuine contributions of the form-critical method, if pursued apart from an understanding of the canonical process, can also fail to do justice to the final form of the book.

(b) The theological importance of the book of Ezekiel for the total biblical witness has often been jeopardized by the preoccupation of critical scholarship with the literary, historical, and psychological problems. When the book is properly understood in its canonical form, it addresses most of the major theological issues which have exercised Israel from the beginning: God, people, covenant, law, land, sin, judgment, forgiveness, restoration, and kingdom of God. The canonical approach to Ezekiel does not attempt to supply any one interpretation of this subject matter. This enterprise can only be accomplished by exegesis itself. However, the canonical approach does contribute theologically by resisting those critical categories which denigrate the book's individual integrity. Such a typical move is one which sees the book of Ezekiel as only a transitional link between 'early prophecy' and 'late apocalypticism'. The canonical approach serves a theological function in liberating both the text and its interpreter from such stultifying preconceptions.

(c) The canonical form of Ezekiel reflects a delicate theological balance portraying Israel's faith in terms which are both concrete and spiritual, historical and ideal, present and future. The 'glory of God' speaks of both the revealed and the hidden side of God. The new temple describes in precise architectonic detail an outline of the proper spiritual worship of restored Israel. The promised land of the new creation is divided by boundaries much like the old, but its trees resemble those of Eden. To undercut these elements of acute tension is to lose the unique theological testimony of this prophet's witness.

History of Exegesis

Carpzov III, 225–7; *DThC* 5, 2041f.; *EB* 3, 653; *RGG*³ 2, 851.

J. **Daniélou**, 'La vision des ossements desséchés (Ezéchiel 37,1–14) dans les Testimonia', *RSR* 53, 1965, 220–33; J. **Grassi**, 'Ezekiel XXXVII.1–14 and the New Testament', *NTS* 11, 1964–5, 162–4; G. **Haendler**, 'Altkirchliche Auslegungen zu Ez 3, 17–19', *TLZ* 90, 1965, 167–74; J. **Harvey**, 'Ézéchiel', *DS* 4.2, 1961, 2204–20; W. **Neuss**, *Die Entwicklung der theologischen Auffassung des Buches Ezekiel zur Zeit der Frühscholastik*, Bonn 1911; *Das Buch Ezekiel in Theologie und Kunst bis zum Ende des 12. Jahrhunderts*, Münster 1912; S. **Poznanski**, 'Introduction' (Hebrew), *Kommentar zu Ezechiel und den XII. Kleinen Propheten von Eliezer aus Beaugency*, Warsaw 1910–13; A. **Vanhoye**, 'L'utilisation du livre d'Ézéchiel dans l'Apocalypse', *Bibl* 43, 1962, 436–76.

THE BOOK OF THE TWELVE

XX

HOSEA

Commentaries

C. F. Keil, BC, 1868
F. Hitzig, H. Steiner, KeH, ⁴1881
J. Knabenbauer, CSS, 1886
G. A. Smith, ExB, 1896, (²1928)
W. R. Harper, ICC, 1905
A. van Hoonacker, ÉB, 1908
E. Sellin, KAT, ²⁻³1929
S. L. Brown, WC, 1932
S. M. Lehrman, SonB, ²1952
D. Deden, BOuT, 1953

E. Osty, JB, ²1958
A. Deissler, SB, 1961
T. H. Robinson, HAT, ²1964
É. Jacob, CAT, 1965
J. Ward, 1966
W. Rudolph, KAT², 1966
A. Weiser, ATD, ⁵1967
C. van Leeuwen, POuT, 1968
J. L. Mays, OTL, 1969
H. W. Wolff, Herm, 1974

Bibliography

P. R. **Ackroyd**, 'Hosea and Jacob', *VT* 13, 1963, 245–59; A. **Allwohn,** *Die Ehe des propheten Hosea in psychoanalytischer Beleuchtung*, BZAW 44, 1926; A. **Alt**, 'Hosea 5,8–6,6. Ein Krieg und seine Folgen in prophetischer Beleuchtung', *NKZ* 30, 1919=*KS* II, Munich 1953, 163–87; R. **Bach**, *Die Erwählung Israels in der Wüste*, Diss. Bonn 1952; E. **Baumann**, '"Wissen um Gott" bei Hosea als Urform von Theologie?', *EvTh* 15, 1955, 416–25; S. **Bitter**, *Die Ehe des Propheten Hosea. Eine auslegungsgeschichtliche Untersuchung*, Göttingen 1975; W. **Brueggemann**, *Tradition for Crisis. A Study in Hosea*, Richmond 1968; K. **Budde**, 'Der Schluss des Buches Hosea', *Studies presented to C. H. Toy*, New York 1912, 205–11; 'Der Abschnitt Hosea 1–3' *ThStKr* 96/97, 1925, 1–89; M. J. **Buss**, *The Prophetic Word of Hosea*, BZAW 111, 1969; R. E. **Clements**, 'Understanding the Book of Hosea', *Review and Expositor* 72, Louisville, Ky. 1975, 405–23; J. F. **Craghan**, 'The Book of Hosea: A Survey of Recent Literature', *BTB* 1, 1971, 81–100; I. **Engnell**, 'Hoseaboken', *Svenskt Bibliskt Uppslagsverk* 1, Gävle 1948, 847–83; G. **Fohrer**, 'Umkehr und Erlösung beim Propheten Hosea', *TZ* 11, 1955, 161–85=*Studien zur . . . Prophetie*, BZAW 99, 1967, 222–41; H. **Frey**, 'Der

Aufbau der Gedichte Hoseas', *WuD* 5, 1957, 9–103; H. L. **Ginsberg**, 'Studies in Hosea 1–3', Y. *Kaufmann Jubilee Volume*, Jerusalem 1960, 50–69; 'Hosea's Ephraim, more Fool than Knave', *JBL* 80, 1961, 339–47; E. M. **Good**, 'The Compositions of Hosea', *SEA* 31, 1966, 21–63; 'Hosea 5,8–6,6: An Alternative to Alt', *JBL* 85, 1966, 276–86; R. **Gordis**, 'Hosea's Marriage and Message: A New Approach', *HUCA* 25, 1954, 9–35.

H. **Hellbardt**, *Der verheissene König Israels. Das Christuszeugnis des Hoseas*, Munich 1935; P. **Humbert**, 'Osée le prophète bédouin', *RHPhR* 1, 1921, 97–118; É. **Jacob**, 'L'Héritage cananéen dans le livre du prophète Osée', *RHPhR* 43, 1963, 250–9; 'Der Prophet Hosea und die Geschichte', *EvTh* 24, 1964, 281–90; Y. **Kaufmann**, *The Religion of Israel*, ET Chicago 1960, London 1961, 371ff.; J. **Lindblom**, *Hosea, literarisch untersucht*, Åbo 1928; N. **Lohfink**, 'Zu Text und Forum von Os 4,4–6', *Bibl* 1961, 303–32; H. G. **May**, 'The Fertility Cult in Hosea', *AJSL* 48, 1932, 73–98; H. S. **Nyberg**, *Studien zum Hoseabuch*, Uppsala 1935; G. **Ostborn**, *Yahweh and Baal. Studies in the Book of Hosea and Related Documents*, Lund 1956; H. W. **Robinson**, *Two Hebrew Prophets: Studies in Hosea and Ezekiel*, London 1948; H. H. **Rowley**, 'The Marriage of Hosea', *BJRL* 39, 1956–7, 200–33=*Men of God*, London 1963, 66–97; W. **Rudolph**, 'Präparierte Jungfrauen?', *ZAW* 75, 1963, 65–73; N. H. **Snaith**, *Mercy and Sacrifice. A Study on the Book of Hosea*, London 1953; W. F. **Stinespring**, 'A Problem of Theological Ethics in Hosea', *Essays in Old Testament Ethics, J. P. Hyatt in Memoriam*, ed. James Crenshaw and J. T. Willis, New York 1974, 131–44; J. **Vollmer**, *Geschichtliche Rückblicke und Motive in der Prophetie des Amos, Hosea und Jesaja*, BZAW 119, 1971; T. C. **Vriezen**, 'La tradition de Jacob dans Osée 12', *OTS* 1, 1942, 64–78; J. M. **Ward**, 'The Message of the Prophet Hosea', *Interp* 23, 1969, 387–407; I. **Willi-Plein**, *Vorformen der Schriftexegese innerhalb des Alten Testaments*, BZAW 123, 1971; H. W. **Wolff**, '"Wissen um Gott" bei Hosea als Urform von Theologie', *EvTh* 12, 1952–3, 533–54=*GSAT*, Munich 1964, 182–205; 'Der grosse Jezreeltag', *EvTh* 12, 1952–3, 78–104=*GSAT*, 151–81; 'Hoseas geistige Heimat', *TLZ* 81, 1956, 83–94=*GSAT*, 232–50.

1. Historical Critical Problems

The difficulty of interpreting the book of Hosea has long been felt. Jerome's often quoted characterization of the book has not been greatly improved upon: 'Commaticus est [= in short sections] et quasi per sententias loquens' (*Praef. ad xii proph.*). The problems are intense and varied. At the outset, the nest of problems surrounding Hosea's marriage in chs. 1–3 continues to resist the emergence of a consensus. Again, the lack of a clear order within the book remains baffling. Especially for chs. 4–14 even the effort to establish the broad lines of divisions evokes much debate. Finally, the Hebrew text of Hosea is generally regarded as one of the poorest in the Old Testament.

Within these different areas several generations of modern critical scholars have expended great energy with only varying degrees of success. The attempt to reconstruct the historical circumstances surrounding Hosea's marriage has been consistently frustrated (cf. the surveys of Rowley and Bitter). Form-critical analysis has provided a useful, if mainly negative, service in emphasizing the impossibility of penetrating behind the text by means of psychoanalysing the prophet, or by speculating on a theory of prolepsis in order to remove the offence. Wolff has made out a good case for seeing the form of both chs. 1 and 3 to be a prophetic sign-act. Yet the difficulty of maintaining a consistent interpretation from this perspective has not been overcome (cf. Rudolph's criticism of Wolff). The perennial attempt even by such modern scholars as Gressmann to resort to a symbolic interpretation of the marriage is a further confirmation of the impasse in recovering the original event.

Similarly, the attempt to resolve the form-critical problems of the book has met with persistent obstacles. Indeed, form-critical work has at times succeeded in bringing certain sections into sharper historical focus. For example, Alt has made out a good case for relating 5.8ff. to the crisis of the Syrian-Ephraimic War of 734. Then again Wolff has uncovered portions of prophetic disputation oracles, of *memorabilia*, judgment oracles, and prophetic promises. What emerge frequently are bits and pieces of fragmented oracles. Often Wolff is forced to posit several different voices in a passage or to suggest a shift in audience in an effort to find coherence. In the end, he speaks of a larger 'kerygmatic' structure which has blurred this original level of proclamation into a loose topical arrangement of association. Although the modern form critic suspects that Hosea's oracles once functioned in a way analogous to those of Amos, this judgment remains unproven and the present form of the book has apparently obliterated this earlier level almost beyond recovery. In part, Buss's attempt to provide a more comprehensive stylistic approach to the book arose from the inability of form criticism alone successfully to analyse the form of the book.

The history of the book's redactional development is equally perplexing. Certainly the credit for pursuing this issue with the greatest thoroughness belongs again to Wolff. He argues for three different transmission complexes. Chapters 1–3 contain a portion of the prophet's own *memorabilia* which are written in the first person form of address. This material has been added to and expanded by a disciple in 1.2–6, 8f. A second complex (chs. 4–11) reflecting many different periods, was written down in kerygmatic units within Hosea's circle of disciples shortly after being delivered. A third complex (12–14) does not go back to the prophet himself, but stems from his circle of disciples and is dated in the last period of the Northern Kingdom. These three complexes were later transmitted by a Deuteronomic redaction which added the superscription and 'updated' a few passages. Finally, a few places such as 1.7 and 3.5 show signs of an early Judaic editing. However, it remains a moot question whether the evidence available can really support such a detailed reconstruction of the book's literary history. A good number of commentators remain unconvinced (Rudolph, Fohrer, Buss, etc.).

A far simpler, but impressive attempt to trace the redactional history of the book has recently been offered by R. E. Clements. He seeks to demonstrate that knowledge of the history of the book's development offers the most reliable key for its interpretation, and, among other things, serves an important negative function. On the one hand, it refutes the psychological interpretation of Hosea's message which derives it from his marital experience (H. Wheeler Robinson, Rowley, etc.). On the other hand, it offers a check to the 'confused and wooden' reflection of Engnell who infers from the final form of the text that Hosea had a partisan preference for Davidic kings. Clements argues positively that the essential character of Hosea's preaching was a warning of the coming destruction of the Northern Kingdom and that the elements of promise are almost entirely secondary and emerged only after the threats had been fulfilled. (11.8–9 is seen as an exception to this rule.) We shall return later to the hermeneutical implications of Clements' interpretation.

An even more controversial aspect of Wolff's interpretation is his attempt to reconstruct the historical and sociological background of Hosea's preaching. Two of his theses have been especially bold. First, with the aid of Herodotus' account he has sought to interpret the divine command in 1.2 to 'take a wife of harlotry', as reflecting a form of cultic prostitution which had infiltrated the Northern

Kingdom and which had polluted the entire nation in the eyes of the prophet. Secondly, he has argued for Hosea's kinship with the Levites as the circle from which he gained his interest in the cult, opposition to the priesthood, and knowledge of Northern Israelite tradition. In both instances Wolff has succeeded in stimulating a fresh and interesting debate, but support has remained divided, with some of the sharpest rebuttal coming from Rudolph.

Finally, regarding the textual problems, clearly the pendulum has swung away from the extreme distrust of the Masoretic text which the classic literary critics shared (e.g. Harper, ICC). Nevertheless, in spite of the persistent attempts of Nyberg to rehabilitate confidence in the accuracy of the MT, many of his suggested contributions appear highly artificial and not very illuminating (cf. e.g. 4.4–6). The textual issue is, of course, a part of a larger methodological controversy, but it remains particularly acute for the book of Hosea.

2. The Canonical Shape of Hosea

It is our contention that there is another way of approaching the material which can do justice both to the book's literary development and to its final form. The canonical method does not assume either that the prophet's message was conveyed correctly only on the original level or that a reconstruction of the historical stage is essential to a correct interpretation. Rather, it focuses its attention on determining how the tradition was heard, shaped, and preserved by the community of faith to serve as scripture. It seeks to do justice to the logic of the material in its canonical context without subjugating the prophetic testimony to any theories of correlation with an allegedly objective historical reality.

Multiple layers in Hosea and the canonical process

If one attempts to trace the various stages through which the Hoseanic material has progressed prior to its final form, there is good evidence to postulate that the original stage stemmed from the proclamation of the prophet Hosea himself. To state the case negatively, there is no reason to suggest that the book is a pseudepigraphical composition from the post-exilic era. The language and background of the book reflect a historical ministry of Hosea during the latter half of the eighth century. The message of Hosea is directed, by and large, to the inhabitants of the Northern Kingdom, although it is likely that at least in one place (5.8ff.) the prophet addressed the Southern Kingdom as well. Although chs. 4–14 do not pretend to report particular oracles directed to specific historical situations – the summary, compilatory nature of the present collection is only too obvious – it is nevertheless clear that Hosea was addressing real people in a given period of history. The main thrust of his words focused on a continual attack upon Israel's syncretistic religious worship which had transformed the worship of Yahweh into a fertility cult. Israel took over from Canaanite mythology the concept of a symbiotic relationship between deity and land which was actualized in the rites of sacred marriage (4.11f.). The centre of Hosea's message lay in his passionate rejection of this understanding of Israel's faith, which he described as 'harlotry' to the God of Israel's history.

However, Hosea did not attack Israel's religion simply by rehearsing the older traditional formulae. He boldly adapted the older language to the new situation. Yahweh, not Baal, was the Lord of the land, who was Israel's faithful lover and forgotten provider of bounty. Hosea confronted the mythological concepts of Canaanite religion with a 'realistic' language which laid claim to all areas of life in the name of Yahweh. The sign-acts of Hosea's marraige to Gomer in ch. 1 and again his purchase of a woman in ch. 3 belong in the context of this realistic confrontation with the mythological distortion of Israel's religion. The sign-act functioned as a history-creating expression of divine judgment which actualized the threat in the giving of the ominous names. On this primary level of Hosea's historical ministry, it seems clear that his words and deeds provided the basis for the tradition.

However, it is important to recognize that there was a second level in the development of the tradition, as is the case in all the prophets. Hosea's words were recorded in some form and gathered into a collection. This process of collection in itself involved a critical activity of selecting, shaping, and ordering of the material. We have no direct evidence of how this collecting process took place, by whom it was executed, or at what precise period. However, there is some indirect evidence which throws some light on the issue in the numerous references to Judah within the book (cf. 1.7; 2.2[EVV

1.11]; 4.15; 5.5, 10, 14; 6.4, 11; 8.14; 10.11; 12.2). These references are of different kinds. 5.10, 14 appear to belong to the primary level of Hoseanic preaching. Most of the remaining passages seem to be redactional. The significance of this observation lies in the information which it provides of the use which was made of Hosea's preaching. The Judaean references indicate that chs. 4–14 were used and applied to the Southern Kingdom, probably as a collection of oracles. It is highly unlikely that Hosea himself preached in Judah. Rather, at a later date, most probably during the last two decades of the eighth century, his words were used and their original scope was extended to include Judah also within the impending judgment. Prophetic authority was not tied to an office, nor to a particular mode of delivery, but lay in the prophetic word itself.

The nature of this subsequent use of Hosea's original words indicates an important hermeneutical shift in the function of the material. In its original role Hosea's preaching and symbolic action arose in confrontation with Israel's distorted syncretistic religion. Hosea's use of language was 'realistic', that is, it opposed the Canaanite mythological concept of deity and land with a theological alternative: Yahweh was Israel's 'lord' (Baal) and lover. Hosea chose to stand within the mythological world-view and shatter it by introducing a new referent for the old language. But a generation later, to a different people and situation, Hosea's realistic language was understood metaphorically. 'Harlotry' was only an image apart from any mythological concept of sacred marriage which could be applied to Judah because of her disobedience, i.e., unfaithfulness to God's covenant (4.15.). A further indication that the prophet was seen as one who speaks metaphorically or symbolically is reflected in 12.11: 'I spoke to the prophets; it was I who multiplied visions, and through the prophets *gave parables* (analogies, *ᵃdammeh*).' This shift from a realistic to a metaphorical use of language did not involve a drastic metamorphosis, but was simply an extension of the figurative dimension already within the language. Nevertheless, this semantic possibility allowed for an extension of Hosea's ministry which functioned apart from the original office and afforded an independent integrity to the prophetic collection.

There is a third stage in the development of the book which one can trace to some degree. The hypothesis of another level is supported, first of all, by the strikingly different references to Judah in

the first three chapters. In these chapters Judah's positive relation
to Yahweh is contrasted with Israel's negative one. Judah is the
recipient of promise, Israel of judgment (1.7; 2.2 [EVV 1.11]; cf. 3.5
'David their king'). How is this shift to be explained in the light of
the earlier extension of Hosea's words of judgment to include Judah
as well in chs. 4–14? The solution appears to lie in the particular
shaping which the material of chs. 1–3 has been given. Several
observations regarding these chapters are in order. Regardless of
the prehistory behind the two sign-acts in chs. 1 and 3, the present
editing of these chapters has given a decidedly symbolic interpretation to this material. Chapters 1 and 3 are not connected integrally,
but stand as independent blocks which are separated by ch. 2,
rather than being two parts of one story. This redactional shape, or
in this case lack of shape, flies in the face of all attempts at interpretation which would reconstruct out of the two chapters a history of
Hosea's marriage. Again, the redactor's intention that the sign-acts
be understood metaphorically is made explicit in both chapters (cf.
1.2, 4f., 6f., 9; 3.1, 4, 5). In addition, the present position of ch. 2
serves to render it into an extended metaphor of the unfaithful wife
and provides the editor's key for interpreting the two more difficult
chapters which now frame it.

To summarize the argument up to this point. We have tried to
mount a case that the material of chs. 4–14 which once functioned
realistically on the primary level when directed to the Northern
Kingdom was later heard metaphorically and applied to Judah
secondarily. A similar process seemed to be at work in chs. 1–3. On
the primary level Hosea's sign-act of marrying an adulterous
woman functioned to actualize the threat of divine judgment in the
historical moment of the prophet's call. The marriage was not an
allegory, nor a vision, nor a proleptic recapitulation, but a prophetic event in Israel's history. Yet when this symbolic action was
added to the earlier collection of prophetic sayings of chs. 4–14, it
had already been understood in a symbolic way.

Hosea's message of hope

There is another feature in the editing of chs. 1–3 which is of
great importance in addition to the metaphorical role to which the
imagery has been assigned. The issue turns on how to understand
the message of hope in the book which contrasts sharply with the

words of rejection and judgment. Critical scholars continue to debate whether this hope of a future restoration reflects the primary level of Hosea's preaching or the secondary. Wolff and Rudolph argue for the primary, Clements for the secondary. Regardless of what one decides – my preference is for the former – the relating of judgment and salvation within chs. 1–3 has now been placed within a *heilsgeschichtliche* schema. Israel must remain punished in exile for a time (3.4) before its restoration to the new people of God. It is possible that the redaction of chs. 1–3 fell in the period after the destruction of the Northern Kingdom when the Southern Kingdom of Judah understood its role within the divine economy to be a different one from that of the Northern Kingdom. Perhaps the promise in 1.7 reflects the preaching of Isaiah, and would indicate the period of Sennacherib's abortive attack on Jerusalem. However, that may be, the new redactional shaping of chs. 1–3 within a redemptive pattern offers a different interpretation of Judah's future from that found in chs. 4–14. Judah has now inherited the promise which disobedient Israel had once spurned.

An interesting sign of this change of application within the Judaean redaction may well be reflected in the textual problems of 12.1 (EVV 11.12). On an earlier level, Judah's relation to God paralleled that of disobedient Israel (12.3a, EVV 2a), but at a later date in the context of the whole book including chs. 1–3, Judah was contrasted positively with Israel (cf. the versions on this passage).

However, the larger exegetical issue still remains. What is the canonical significance of this multi-layered text and of this redactional process? How does the historical dimension aid in interpreting the final form of the book? Although the present shape of chs. 1–3 appears to derive from a later editorial stage than chs. 4–14, the first section now provides the exegetical key in the framework from which the entire book is to be read. The effect is twofold. First, Hosea's marriage and the birth of the children have been raised to a metaphorical level of language. Although the original oracles of the prophet arose in the historical milieu of eighth-century Northern Israel, the language functions symbolically to address every generation of Israelite, beginning with Judah. Secondly, judgment and salvation are inextricably joined in the purpose of God for his people. They are placed in an eschatological relationship which holds them together in the one divine plan. The message which follows in chs. 4–13 sets out in detail God's controversy with his people which forms the grounds for his judgment. But interspersed with his threat comes the note of redemption (11.8–9) which reaches its climax in ch. 14. The inner dynamic of God's intention toward Israel varies considerably in chs. 4–11 from that given in the first section. Yet the intensity of the divine struggle and the paradoxical relationship of love and anger has grown even stronger.

A major point to be made in regard to Hosea's message of hope is that it did not arise out of the personal experience of the prophet in his marriage, nor can it be located in the prophet's self-understanding. Rather, it is a theological judgment which bears witness to God's continual and passionate loyalty to his people in the face of Israel's flagrant and persistent disloyalty. Clements is surely right in seeing an important negative function of historical criticism to lie in undercutting this erroneous interpretation.

The conclusion of the book

There is one final element to be observed which affects the understanding of the message as a whole. The book of Hosea concludes with a wisdom saying (14.9): 'Whoever is wise, let him understand these things ... for the way of Yahweh is right.' Although many of the Old Testament prophetic books show signs of wisdom influence – particularly Amos and Isaiah – the influence is not on the final redactional level, but often belongs to the primary prophetic proclamation itself. Only in the book of Hosea does a wisdom saying function in a redactional role which has its parallel in Prov. 30.5 or Eccl. 12.13. What is the redactional function of this final verse?

The verse functions as an explicit directive to the reader to instruct him in the proper understanding of the collection. The reader is admonished 'to be wise' and to 'discern' the ways of God which are surely right, but not obvious. Reflection and meditation are required to penetrate their meaning. The prophet's words are seen to lead the reader into right and wise action. By characterizing the collection of Hosea's oracles as wisdom, the canonical editor offers another indication that the metaphorical function of this prophetic language has been recognized by its being tied to the mysteries of God's purpose. The message of the prophet was true and faithful above all for later generations within Israel, but the reality of the symbolic language required the insight and penetration of the wise in order to comprehend.

3. Theological and Hermeneutical Implications

(a) We have attempted to trace the history of the development of the book of Hosea as it functioned authoritatively within a community of faith. We have used the tools of redactional criticism but toward a different end from that normally envisioned, namely, toward the better understanding of the canonical text. The historical dimension has proven valuable in bringing this context into sharper focus. However, the redactional stages remained subordinated to its present canonical function, which in the case of Hosea, was not correlated to the different levels of the book's historical growth.

The methodological contrast between redactional criticism and the canonical approach can best be illustrated by reference to the insightful article of R. E. Clements. The redactional analysis which I have offered is similar in its broad outlines to that of Clements. However, Clements uses his recovery of the various levels in a very different way from the one being suggested. He still derives the major authority of Hosea's message from the original level of the prophet's preaching. However, because the message of hope is largely secondary in his analysis, he is forced into a theologically reductionist position. Hosea's message of hope, which emerged shortly after 732 BC, was mistaken in failing to see that an even greater disaster lay ahead. Nevertheless 'at its deepest level' what Hosea attested to was truth, for it insisted that God's love does triumph (423). In my judgment, an approach which follows the canon's intent in subordinating the editorial process avoids this pitfall and allows for the true historical dimensions of the book.

(b) The book of Hosea provides an excellent example of canonical shaping which effected a change in the semantic level on which the message functioned. The original prophetic words of Hosea which were addressed to the people of the Northern Kingdom in the eighth century were extended to confront a different people and situation. Finally they were transformed into symbolic language which continued to offer judgment and hope to future generations far beyond the temporal confines of Hosea himself.

384 THE LATTER PROPHETS

(c) By taking seriously the canon's role of determining the level of the book's *sensus literalis*, many of the pitfalls of allegorizing, psychologizing, and historicizing the message of Hosea can be avoided. In regard to the book of Hosea, the symbolic interpretation of his message arises from a descriptive analysis of the book itself in its new context as scripture, and provides the best critical check against misunderstanding the text through anachronistic categories.

History of Exegesis

Carpzov III, 296–301; *EB* 2, 806; *RGG*³3, 457.

J. M. **Allegro**, 'A Recently Discovered Fragment of a Commentary on Hosea from Qumran's Fourth Cave', *JBL* 78, 1959, 144–7; S. **Bitter**, *Die Ehe des Propheten Hosea. Eine auslegungsgeschichtliche Untersuchung*, Göttingen 1975; H. **Cohen**, 'Introduction', *The Commentary of Rabbi David Kimhi on Hosea*, Columbia Univ. Oriental Series 20, New York 1929, ix-xli.

S. **Coleman**, *Hosea-Concepts in Midrasch und Talmud*, Diss. Bloemfontein 1960; H. **Hailperin**, 'Nicholas de Lyra and Rashi: The Minor Prophets', *Rashi Anniversary Volume*, New York 1941, 115–47; D. **Hill**, 'On the Use and Meaning of Hosea vi.6 in Matthew's Gospel', *NTS* 24, 1977, 107–19; G. **Krause**, *Studien zu Luthers Auslegung der kleinen Propheten*, BHT 33, 1962; A. **Neher**, *Les petits prophètes dans le Talmud*, Diss. Strasbourg 1947; A. **Wünsche**, *Der Prophet Hosea (c.1–7) . . . mit Benutzung der Targumim, der jüdischen Ausleger Raschi, Aben Ezra und David Kimchi*, Leipzig 1868; 'Der Prophet Hosea in der haggadischen Auslegung des Jalkut Schimeoni', in *Vierteljahrsschrift für Bibelkunde. Talmudische und patristische Studien*, hrsg. von M. Altschüler, I, Berlin 1903, 66–127.

XXI

JOEL

Commentaries

K. A. Credner, 1831
C. F. Keil, BC, 1868
G. A. Smith, ExB, 1896, (²1928)
S. R. Driver, CB, 1898
J. Wellhausen, 1898
A. van Hoonacker, ÉB, 1908
J. Bewer, ICC, 1911
G. W. Wade, WC, 1925
E. Sellin, KAT, ³1929
D. Deden, BOuT, 1953

M. Bič, 1960
M. Delcor, SB, 1961
D. R. Jones, TB, 1964
T. H. Robinson, HAT, ³1964
C. A. Keller, CAT, 1965
A. Weiser, ATD, ⁵1967
W. Rudolph, KAT², 1971
L. C. Allen, NICOT, 1976
H. W. Wolff, Herm, 1977

Bibliography

G. W. **Ahlström**, *Joel and the Temple Cult of Jerusalem*, SVT 21, 1971; W. **Baumgartner**, 'Joel 1 und 2', *FS K. Budde*, BZAW 34, 1920, 10–19; J. **Bourke**, 'Le Jour de Yahwé dans Joël', *RB* 56, 1959, 5–31, 191–212; K. **Budde**, '"Der von Norden" in Joel 2,20', *OLZ* 22, 1919, 1–5; 'Der Umschwung in Joel 2', *OLZ* 22, 1919, 104–10; W. W. **Cannon**, '"The Day of the Lord" in Joel', *Church Quarterly Review* 103, London 1927, 32–63; L. **Dennefeld**, *Les Problèmes du livre de Joël*, Paris 1926; B. **Duhm**, 'Anmerkungen zu den zwölf Propheten', *ZAW* 31, 1911, 184–8; *Israels Propheten*, Tübingen ²1922; H. T. **Fowler**, 'The Chronological Position of Joel among the Prophets', *JBL* 16, 1897, 146–54; G. B. **Gray**, 'The Parallel Passages in Joel and their Bearing on the Question of Date', *The Expositor* IV, 8, London 1893, 208–25; E. W. **Hengstenberg**, *Christology of the Old Testament* I, ET Edinburgh and New York 1854, 285ff.; H. **Holzinger**, 'Sprachcharakter und Abfassungszeit des Buches Joel', *ZAW* 9, 1889, 89–131; A. **Jepsen**, 'Kleine Beiträge zum Zwölfprophetenbuch', *ZAW* 56, 1938, 85–96; A. S. **Kapelrud**, *Joel Studies*, Uppsala 1948; A. F. **Kirkpatrick**, *The Doctrine of the Prophets*, London ³1917, 46–79; E. **Kutsch**, 'Heu-

schreckenplage und Tag Jahwes in Joel 1 und 2', *TZ* 18, 1962, 81–94.
H. P. **Müller**, 'Prophetie und Apokalyptik bei Joel', *Theologia Viatorum* 10, Berlin 1965, 231–52; J. M. **Myers**, 'Some Considerations Bearing on the Date of Joel', *ZAW* 74, 1962, 177–95; E. **Nestle**, 'Miscellen I. Zur Kapiteleinteilung in Joel', *ZAW* 24, 1904, 122–7; M. **Plath**, 'Joel 1, 15–20', *ZAW* 47, 1929, 159f.; O. **Plöger**, *Theocracy and Eschatology*, ET Oxford and Philadelphia 1968; G. **von Rad**, *Old Testament Theology* II, ET Edinburgh and New York 1965, 133–7; B. **Reicke**, 'Joel und seine Zeit', *Wort–Gebot–Glaube, FS W. Eichrodt*, Zürich 1970, 133–41; W. **Rudolph**, 'Wann wirkte Joel?' *Das ferne und nahe Wort, FS L. Rost*, BZAW 105, 1967, 193–8; O. R. **Sellers**, 'Stages of Locust in Joel', *AJSL* 52, 1935–6, 81–5; M. **Smith**, *Palestinian Parties and Politics that Shaped the Old Testament*, New York and London 1971; F. R. **Stephenson**, 'The Date of the Book of Joel', *VT* 19, 1969, 224–9; J. A. **Thompson**, 'Joel's Locusts in the Light of Near Eastern Parallels', *JNES* 14, 1955, 52–5; 'The Date of Joel', *A Light unto my Path: Old Testament Studies in Honor of J. M. Myers*, Philadelphia 1974, 453–64; A. C. **Welch**, 'Joel and the Post-exilic Community', *The Expositor* VIII, 20, London 1920, 161–80; H. W. **Wolff**, *Die Botschaft des Joel*, TheolEx NF 109, Munich 1963.

1. Historical Critical Problems

The problems of the book's literary integrity and its dating have been closely intertwined in the history of critical research. Nevertheless, these are separate problems and can be treated in turn for the sake of clarity.

Literary integrity

During the last half of the nineteenth century the unity of chs. 1–2 and 3–4 (EVV 1.1–2.27 and 2.28–3.21) was firmly defended by many scholars by interpreting the portrayal of the locust plague in chs. 1–2 as a prophetic word without a historical basis which pointed to a future event (Hengstenberg, Merx – see below, p. 394). But the artificiality of the approach, which was particularly evident in the handling of ch. 1, gave way to the more natural view that the locust plague had already been experienced and lay in the past. However, once this move was made, the unity of the book became a major issue because the last two chapters were clearly eschatological in nature.

Duhm developed the classic literary critical approach in dividing the book into two parts. Chapters 1 and 2 dealt simply with a locust plague. Later, when the Maccabean author of chs. 3–4 added his eschatological material, he also entered a series of interpolations into chs. 1 and 2 (1.15; 2.1b, 2a, 10a, 11b). Duhm's approach has been widely followed with slight modifications by G. A. Smith, Bewer, T. H. Robinson, and others. However, the difficulties involved in such a theory have also been pointed out. Jepsen (86) made the incisive observation that to eliminate all the eschatological elements in ch. 1 would logically entail the further elimination of 1.2–4 as well. Weiser's attempt to hold to a single author and to a two-stage theory of composition cannot be considered successful.

Within more recent years there have been several notable attempts made to develop a new theory of the book's unity. In 1948 Kapelrud defended the unity of Joel by postulating a single liturgical function for the book which he connected to an enthronement festival of Yahweh. However, cultic interpretation in the form presented by Kapelrud has not been widely accepted. A more impressive defence of the book's unity has been made by H. W. Wolff. He has argued for the striking literary and form-critical symmetry of the entire book which he considers to be strong evidence for single authorship. In the following section Wolff's theory will be discussed in more detail.

Date of composition

The traditional Masoretic placing of Joel between Hosea and Amos within the collection of the Book of the Twelve at first lent a predisposition toward an early pre-exilic dating, even though the book's superscription was silent on the subject. However, very shortly the great majority of critical scholars had decided upon a post-exilic date, indeed assigning the book to the Persian period. The reasons for this evaluation turned on such evidence as Joel's heavy dependence on earlier written prophets (Isa. 13; Obad. 17, etc.), and the alleged historical allusions to the late period (1.9; 4.6). (cf. Bewer, Wolff and Eissfeldt, *Introduction*, 394, for a summary of the evidence). Although it is correct to say that a post-exilic dating still represents the majority opinion, there remains a strong minority who continue to defend a pre-exilic dating. Kapelrud and Rudolph in particular have argued for a seventh-century dating by describing a cultic activity in the pre-exilic period which is akin to that of Joel, and by denying that the reference to Greeks in 4.6 (EVV 3.6) is a decisive factor for post-exilic dating.

The major purpose of the book

It is instructive to trace the effect of the various critical theories regarding date and composition on the general interpretation of the book. The older generation of literary critics, strongly under the influence of Wellhausen and Duhm, were basically negative in their theological evaluation of Joel. He represented a nationalistic cult prophet devoid of any ethical criticism of Israel (cf. G. A. Smith, Bewer, T. H. Robinson, and also W. Rudolph).

However, within recent years there has been any number of attempts at a fresh appraisal of Joel, usually built on a new literary analysis. Eissfeldt (*Introduction*, 394) has argued that Joel's major concern was with the problems of everyday life, such as the economic problems resulting from the locust plague, and that the eschatological elements were only a type of literary device to high-light the present distress of the community. But the theory is really a *tour de force* and reverses the present emphasis of the book which finds its climax in chs. 3 and 4.

A very different interpretation of Joel has been put forward by O. Plöger (96ff.) as part of his programme to delineate different religi-ous parties within the post-exilic community. Plöger argues that traditional eschatological statements about the Day of the Yahweh were de-eschatologized by a circle which was connected with the institution of the cult in order to limit the eschatological expecta-tions (2.19ff.). However, a reaction set in from another circle which held fast to the eschatological tradition and even added a new historico-eschatological interpretation of the prophetic message in ch. 4. Subsequently ch. 3 was added as a further conventicle-type limitation of salvation to those within Israel who shared in the outpouring of the spirit. It is obvious that Plöger's theory assumes a very complex literary development behind the present form of the book. Even if such a growth could be shown, it remains a very speculative enterprise to reconstruct an unknown period of Israel's post-exilic history on the basis of literary tensions within a text which seem to have been both set up and resolved in order to confirm the historical thesis.

Finally, Rudolph's interpretation is far less complex. He also argues that the function of the cultic sections of the book (2.18ff.) was to assure Israel of her future safety from all threats of judgment such as those found in ch.1. Therefore, a fear of the Day of Yahweh which affected God's people adversely was judged to be erroneous. Joel preached a message of full salvation to Israel and complete judgment on the nations. After describing his message in this manner, Rudolph characterizes Joel as a *Heilsprophet* akin to Hananiah (Jer. 28), and of no enduring theological importance. It remains a puzzlement in Rudolph's interpretation how such an erroneous message was ever retained after the catastrophe of the exile and was heard by successive generations of Jews in such a different way from that outlined by this learned commentator (cf. Qumran, NT, midrashim).

2. The Canonical Shape of Joel

In my judgment, H. W. Wolff has been highly successful in showing the literary unity of the book which is characterized by its striking symmetry. The lament (1.4–20) parallels the promise (2.21–27), the announcement of a catastrophe (2.1–11) matches the promise of better days (4.1–3, 9–17), and the summons to repentance (2.12–17) is set over against the promise of the spirit (3.1ff.). Such obvious paralleled expressions in 2.27 and 4.17 (EVV 3.17) speaks against sharply separating the first two chapters from the last.

However, the issue of canonical function is not identical with literary unity. Wolff's study has demonstrated that the four chapters have been consciously structured into a unity, and that the message is impaired if the book is fragmented. However, the issue has not been settled whether or not this literary unity derives from a single author or is a redactional creation. It is a difficult issue to decide as is evidenced by the lack of a scholarly consensus. I tend to think that the unity is redactional. However, the effect on reading the book as a unity is not dependent on one's ability to resolve this literary critical problem.

The crucial issue from a canonical perspective turns on how one reads the book in its present form. What are the canonical guidelines for its interpretation? Wolff interprets Joel as a fresh prophetic word of the prophet in the Persian period which had been evoked by a devastating locust plague. Joel makes use of ancient traditions – the Day of Yahweh, the enemy from the north, the restoration of the land – some of which had already assumed written form, to contest the prevalent view that God's promise to his people had run its course and was now powerless. The prophet transformed an 'almost forgotten theme' into a new and existential threat of impending judgment which issued in a call for repentance. Then on the basis of Israel's obedient response of repentance, Joel prophesied a change in the Day of Yahweh from one of judgment to salvation by means of a liturgy. The major effect of Joel's new prophetic interpretation was to reorder the eschatological sequence. Repentant Israel would be delivered (3.5), the nations who threatened Jerusalem would be destroyed (4.1ff.), and the earth would return to its paradisal state (4.18).

I do not deny that much of Wolff's exegesis is insightful and true to the intent of the canonical text. However, I do not feel that his interpretation is fully on target. In my judgment, it has been overly influenced by his reconstruction of an alleged fourth-century historical context from which he understands the book. The result is that he reads into the text a variety of themes, such as the 'almost forgotten theme' of the Day of Yahweh, or the opposition to the *status quo* established by Ezra and Nehemiah. In effect, Wolff has replaced the canonical setting with his reconstructed historical one and emphasized features which are, at most, in the background of the prophet's message.

The crucial issue in the interpretation of Joel centres in the relationship between chs. 1–2 and 3–4 (EVV 1.1–2.27 and 2.28–3.21). Joel's original prophecy in ch. 1 grew out of the devastation from the locust plague which the prophet saw as a sign of the coming divine judgment. The Day of Yahweh was not one of salvation, but of doom, dread, and darkness. In ch. 2 the prophet developed the theme of impending judgment on the basis of traditional biblical imagery, which he used to pose (v. 11) the basic existential question: Who can endure it?

One of the important sections in Wolff's interpretation involves his handling of 2.1–17. He holds that a sharp distinction should be made between the oracles in ch. 1 and ch. 2. In ch. 1 the locust plague lies in the past, whereas in ch. 2 the threat is of an invading army and is future oriented. Then again, the form of speech in ch. 1 is the communal complaint, whereas in ch. 2 the 'call to alarm' and the appeal for repentance dominate. Wolff's insistence on a sharp demarcation between the chapters has been strongly criticized by Rudolph. In my judgment, Wolff is correct in seeing important differences between the two chapters, especially in insisting that the future tenses in ch. 2 be taken seriously. Yet he has de-emphasized the important features which bind the chapters together. The promise of restoration of 2.25 identifies the locusts of ch. 1 and the army of 2.11. The basic point to be made is that the prophet can move freely from the threat of a past historical event to the coming eschatological judgment because he sees both as sharing the self-same reality. To posit two totally separate and distinct historical events recorded in these two chapters not only misses the subtle literary manner of shifting from past to future, but seriously threatens the theological understanding of prophetic eschatology which spans temporal differences.

That there is a tension in chs. 1 and 2 between past and future, between a this-worldly plague and cosmological threat, and between local and universal judgment cannot be denied. However, it should not be dissolved, as Duhm suggested, by describing one layer as a strictly historical event which he then contrasts with a subsequent eschatological interpolation. The pattern of chs. 1 and 2 belongs to the integral shape of the canonical book and forms the basis for its subsequent expansion in chs. 3 and 4.

On the basis of Joel's message of imminent judgment and his call for repentance (2.12), a fast is called. The text uses the idiom and form of traditional liturgy (2.15ff.). Moreover, by means of a remarkable shift into narrative style in which the hand of an editor is visible, the response of God to the people's repentance is recorded in 2.18: 'Yahweh ... had pity on his people.' It issues in a new prophetic word of divine forgiveness and promise (2.19–27). The language of the promise returns to the agricultural imagery of ch. 1, and testifies that God's favour toward Zion has already begun (2.21), and will continue in the restoration of the land to a condition before its recent devastation by the plague (2.25).

Joel's original prophecy arose out of the crisis wrought by the locust and was addressed to the generation who immediately experienced the harsh event. However, the crucial canonical shaping occurred when an editor took up this prophecy and fashioned it into a message for future generations according to the canonical intent explicitly stated in 1.3. The second layer was addressed to the latter days (3.1 and 4.1; EVV 2.28; 3.1). The editor applied Joel's prophecy to this new situation and proclaimed Israel's new role in God's plan for the world. Although the Day of Yahweh had been prefigured in the sign of the locust, judgment lay still in the future. Again there would be signs in the heavens and on earth of 'blood and fire'. Yet just as in the past God's mercy was extended to Israel because of repentance, once again the same word of salvation was held out for the future. 'All who call upon the name of Yahweh shall be delivered' (3.5; EVV 2.32). The community of the future would stand before the same imperatives as did the people of the past. Neither the final judgment nor the ultimate salvation had yet occurred. (This formulation is indebted to an unpublished paper of Melanie Morrison.)

Joel's original prophecy had been aimed solely at Israel, but in its new canonical form the judgment was now expanded to include all the nations. The cosmological dimension of the final judgment had been briefly touched upon in ch. 2, but these features were now fully extended. Likewise, the earlier restoration of the land now became only a prefiguration of the eschatological return of the paradisal promise.

An important aspect of the canonical shape of Joel is the editor's frequent use of Israel's growing body of sacred writings. The constant reference to older prophetic words has long been observed as characteristic of the book (cf. Obad. 17 in 3.15; Isa. 13.16 in 1.15; Amos 1.2 in 4.16; Wolff, *Joel*, 10 for a full listing of the parallels). Interestingly enough, it is the last two chapters which are particularly heavy with citations from earlier prophets. Thus the new prophetic formulation was grounded in the authority of the past and made use of the old tradition for the new generation. Joel's prophecy was deemed a true and faithful testimony and it was confirmed by similar authoritative words of other prophets. The authority of Joel's message lay in confronting God's people with a living call to renewed faith, a characteristic which also describes the force behind the canonical process.

3. Theological and Hermeneutical Implications

(a) The theological dimensions of the book of Joel are misunderstood when they are grounded upon a historical critical attempt to date the book according to absolute chronology in order to reconstruct its true historical setting. Rather, the theological significance of Joel derives from its role within the canonical process of reaffirming and reinterpreting Israel's tradition of divine revelation. The true historical dimension of the book lies in the history of God's people who wrestled with the hard realities of their life in the light of the renewed prophetic promise of a coming new divine order.

(b) Undoubtedly there were different historical groups within Israel's post-exilic history which can be analysed in part by modern sociological and historical methodologies, such as those suggested by O. Plöger and M. Smith. However, this historico-sociological approach to the Old Testament is deficient when it fails to reckon with the inner canonical process which, in the case of Joel, has largely obscured these historical differences among groups and replaced them with a normative literature. The significance of the canon is that these sacred writings became the norm by which religious identity was measured within the community of faith, and for establishing what degree of tension could be sustained. It is characteristic of the canonical process that original sociological groupings have been subordinated to a theological definition of what constitutes the people of God. This observation does not imply that the historical enterprise is illegitimate, but it does call into question an exegetical method which feels itself so dependent on historical research as to overlook the explicit testimony of the literature itself in its canonical form.

(c) The canonical shape of Joel also attests to the important role played by the typological relationship between the past and the future in God's purpose with his people. Far from being a denigration of history, it actually confirms its significance by drawing out its representative feature of the life of faith in its struggle for obedience in the world.

(d) The prophetic word is actualized by retelling Joel's story. By repeating the account of the locust plague, of Israel's repentance, and of God's pity the message unfolds before its hearers. No technique is required to extract Joel's message from its form. All that is needed is that true witness is borne: 'Tell your children of it, and let your children tell their children, and their children another generation' (1.3).

History of Exegesis

Carpzov III, 312f.; *DBS* 4, 1102f.; *DThC* 8, 1495; *RGG*³ 3, 802.

A. **Kerrigan**, 'The "Sensus Plenior" of Joel III, 1–5 in Act. II, 14–36', *Sacra Pagina* II, Paris 1959, 295–313; B. **Lindars**, *New Testament Apologetic*, London 1961, 36ff.; A. **Merx**, *Die Prophetie des Joel und ihre Ausleger. Von den ältesten Zeiten bis zu den Reformation. Eine exegetisch-kritisch und hermeneutisch-dogmengeschichtliche Studie*, Halle 1879; C. **Roth**, 'The Teacher of Righteousness and the Prophecy of Joel', *VT* 13, 1963, 91–95; G. **Widmer**, *Die Kommentare von Raschi, Ibn Ezra, Radaq zu Joel. Text, Übersetzung und Erläuterung mit einer Einführung in die rabbinische Bibelexegese*, Basle 1945.

XXII

AMOS

Commentaries

C. F. Keil, BC, 1868
F. Hitzig, H. Steiner, KeH, ⁴1881
G. A. Smith, ExB, 1896, (²1928)
S. R. Driver, CB, 1897
W. R. Harper, ICC, 1905
A. van Hoonacker, ÉB, 1908
H. Gressmann, *SAT*, ²1921
E. Sellin, KAT, ²⁻³1923
R. S. Cripps, ²1955

M. Delcor, SB, 1961
T. H. Robinson, HAT, ³1964
S. Amsler, CAT, 1965
A. Weiser, ATD, ⁵1967
J. L. Mays, OTL, 1969
E. Hammershaimb, 1970
W. Rudolph, KAT², 1971
H. W. Wolff, Herm, 1977

Bibliography

P. R. **Ackroyd**, 'A Judgment Narrative between Kings and Chronicles? An Approach to Amos 7.9–17', *Canon and Authority*, ed. G. W. Coats and B. O. Long, Philadelphia 1977, 71–87; R. **Bach**, 'Gottesrecht und weltliches Recht in der Verkündigung des Propheten Amos', *FS G. Dehn*, Neukirchen 1957, 23–34; E. **Balla**, *Die Droh- und Scheltworte des Amos*, Leipzig 1926; K. **Barth**, *Church Dogmatics* IV/2, ET Edinburgh and Grand Rapids, Mich. 1958, 445–52; W. **Baumgartner**, *Kennen Amos und Hosea eine Heilseschatologie?*, Diss. Zürich 1913; A. **Bentzen**, 'The Ritual Background of Amos 1,2–2, 3', *OTS* 8, 1950, 85–99; W. **Berg**, *Die sogenannten Hymnenfragmente im Amosbuch*, Bern 1974; W. **Brueggemann**, 'Amos 4,4–13 and Israel's Covenant Worship', *VT* 15, 1965, 1–15; K. **Budde**, 'Zu Text und Auslegung des Buches Amos', *JBL* 43, 1924, 46–131; J. F. **Craghan**, 'The Prophet Amos in Recent Literature', *BTB* 2, 1972, 242–61; K. **Cramer**, *Amos. Versuch einer theologischen Interpretation*, BWANT III. 15 (=51), 1930; J. L. **Crenshaw**, 'The Influence of the Wise upon Amos. The "Doxologies of Amos" and Job 5:5–16, 9:5–10', *ZAW* 79, 1967, 45–52; *Hymnic Affirmation of Divine Justice: the Doxologies of Amos and Related Texts in the Old Testa-*

ment, SBL Diss. Series 24, Missoula 1975; F. **Crüsemann**, 'Kritik an Amos im deuteronomistischen Geschichtswerk. Erwägungen zu 2 Könige 14,27', *Probleme biblischer Theologie, FS G. von Rad*, Munich 1971, 57–63. E. L. **Dietrich**, *Die endzeitliche Wiederherstellung bei den Propheten*, BZAW 40, 1925; R. **Fey**, *Amos und Jesaja*, WMANT 12, 1963; H. **Gese**, 'Kleine Beiträge zum Verständnis des Amosbuches', *VT* 12, 1962, 417–38; R. **Gordis**, 'The Composition and Structure of Amos', *HTR* 33, 1940, 239–51; H. **Gottlieb**, 'Amos und Jerusalem', *VT* 17, 1967, 430–63; N. K. **Gottwald**, *All the Kingdoms of the Earth*, New York 1964, 94–114; A. H. J. **Gunneweg**, 'Erwägungen zu Amos 7,14', *ZTK* 57, 1960, 1–16; S. **Herrmann**, *Die prophetischen Heilserwartungen im Alten Testament*, BWANT V.5 (=85), 1965, 118–26; G. **Hölscher**, *Die Profeten*, Leipzig 1914, 94–114; H. W. **Hoffmann**, 'Zur Echtheitsfrage von Amos 9,9f.', *ZAW* 82, 1970, 121f.; F. **Horst**, 'Die Doxologien im Amosbuch', *ZAW* 47, 1929, 45–54=*Gottes Recht*, Munich 1961, 155–66; A. S. **Kapelrud**, *Central Ideas in Amos*, Oslo ²1961; U. **Kellermann**, 'Der Amosschluss als Stimme deuteronomistischer Heilshoffnung', *EvTh* 29, 1969, 169–83; K. **Koch**, 'Die Rolle der hymnischen Abschnitte in der Komposition des Amos Buches', *ZAW* 86, 1974, 504–37; K. **Koch** et al., *Amos untersucht mit den Methode einer strukturalen Formgeschichte*, 3 Teile, Neukirchen-Vluyn 1976; L. **Koehler**, 'Amos-Forschungen von 1917–1932', *ThR*, NF 4, 1932, 195–213; S. **Lehming**, 'Erwägungen zu Amos', *ZTK* 55, 1958, 145–69.

V. **Maag**, *Text, Wortschatz und Begriffswelt des Buches Amos*, Leiden 1951; L. **Markert**, *Struktur und Bezeichnung des Scheltworts. Eine gattungskritische Studie anhand des Amosbuches*, BZAW 140, 1977; L. **Monloubon**, 'Amos', *DBS* 8, 1972, 706–24; J. **Morgenstern**, 'Amos Studies', *HUCA* 11, 1936, 19–140; 12–13, 1937–8, 1–53; 15, 1940, 59–305; E. **Nielsen**, *Oral Tradition*, SBT I.11, 1954, 64–79; S. M. **Paul**, 'Amos 1:3–2:3: A Concatenous Literary Pattern', *JBL* 90, 1971, 397–403; H. Graf **Reventlow**, *Das Amt des Propheten bei Amos*, FRLANT 80, 1962; L. **Rost**, *Israel bei den Propheten*, BWANT IV.19 (=71), 1937, 6–20; H. H. **Rowley**, 'Was Amos a Nabi?', *FS O. Eissfeldt*, Halle 1947, 191–98; W. **Rudolph**, 'Die angefochtenen Völkersprüche in Amos 1 and 2', *Schalom. FS A. Jepsen*, Berlin 1971, 45–9; H. H. **Schmid**, 'Amos. Zur Frage nach der "geistige Heimat" des Propheten', *WuD* NF 10, 1978, 85–103; W. H. **Schmidt**, 'Die deuteronomistische Redaktion des Amosbuches', *ZAW* 77, 1965, 168–93; H. **Schulte**, 'Amos 7,15a und die Legitimation des Aussenseiters', *Probleme biblischer Theologie, FS G. von Rad*, Munich 1971, 462–78; R. **Smend**, 'Das Nein des Amos', *EvTh* 23, 1963, 404–23; S. **Spiegel**, 'Amos versus Amaziah', 1957, in *The Jewish Expression*, ed. J. Goldin, New York 1970, 38–65; H.-J. **Stoebe**, 'Der Prophet Amos und sein bürgerlicher Beruf', *WuD* 5, 1957, 160–81; 'Überlegungen zu den geistlichen Voraussetzungen der Prophetie des Amos,' *Wort–Gebot–Glaube, FS W. Eichrodt*, Zurich 1970, 209–25.

S. L. **Terrien**, 'Amos and Wisdom', *Israel's Prophetic Heritage, Essays in Honor of J. Muilenburg*, New York and London 1962, 106–14; J. **Tolk**,

Predigtarbeit zwischen Text und Situation, Beiträge zur evangelischen Theologie 62, Munich 1972; G. M. **Tucker**, 'Prophetic Authority (A Form-Critical Essay on Amos 7: 10–17)', *Interp* 27, 1973, 423–34; P. **Volz**, 'Zu Amos 9,9', *ZAW* 38, 1919–20, 105–11; S. **Wagner**, 'Überlegungen zur Frage nach den Beziehungen des Propheten Amos zum Südreich', *TLZ* 96, 1971, 653–70; J. M. **Ward**, 'Amos', *IDB Suppl*, 21–23; J. D. W. **Watts**, 'An Old Hymn Preserved in the Book of Amos', *JNES* 15, 1956, 33–9; A. **Weiser**, *Die Prophetie des Amos*, BZAW 53, 1929; J. **Wellhausen**, *Die kleinen Propheten*, Berlin ³1898; I. **Willi-Plein**, *Vorformen der Schriftexegese innerhalb des Alten Testaments*, BZAW 123, 1971; H. W. **Wolff**, *Amos' geistige Heimat*, WMANT 18, 1964; ET *Amos the Prophet*, Philadelphia 1973; *Die Stunde des Amos*, Munich 1969; 'Das Ende des Heiligtums in Bethel', *Archäologie und Altes Testament, FS K. Galling*, Tübingen 1970, 287–98; E. **Würthwein**, 'Amos Studien', *ZAW* 62, 1950, 10–52.

1. Historical Critical Problems

During the pre-critical period, and well into the early nineteenth century, it was generally assumed that the book of Amos had been written by the prophet himself in its present form except for parts of ch. 7. The article in Smith's *Dictionary of the Bible* by G. E. L. Cotton (1860) used as evidence for Amos' authorship that the book was 'logically and artistically connected in its several parts'.

The rise of modern literary and historical criticism altered this assessment sharply. The book was judged to contain not only the 'genuine' oracles of the prophet, but non-genuine additions which later editors had supplied. The promises in ch. 9 in particular were thought to be spurious along with the oracle against Judah (2.4f.). Increasingly the final form of the book was judged to reflect elements of disorder, especially in the sequence of the visions. Great effort was expended throughout the literary critical period of the late nineteenth century and early twentieth centuries by such commentators as J. Wellhausen and W. R. Harper to recover the *ipsissima verba* of Amos who was held in great esteem as the earliest written prophet and exponent of ethical monotheism. Indeed, the credit for recovering Amos' literary skill which overturned Jerome's disparaging characterization (*imperitus sermone*) goes largely to these literary critics. For the English-speaking world G. A. Smith's eloquent Victorian commentary played no small role in the new assessment of the prophet's true significance.

The first serious form-critical work on Amos arose from within Gunkel's circle of students (H. Gressmann, W. Baumgartner, E. Balla). Balla in particular sought to delineate more precisely the nature of the oral forms used by Amos while continuing to employ Gunkel's terminology of 'threat and invective' (*Droh- und Schelt-worte*). This form-critical interest has continued vigorously up to the present, and has its most impressive representative in H. W. Wolff.

Along with the study of prophetic forms went an effort to recover the oral traditions used by Amos. Whereas the older literary critics usually conceived of Amos as an isolated individual of great creativity, the work of traditio-criticism altered this picture dramatically. Amos was seen to stand in much closer continuity with Israel's sacred traditions. Würthwein and Rowley, following Mowinckel's original suggestion, pursued the theory of Amos as a cultic prophet. Again, Reventlow's controversial monograph pushed hard the thesis that Amos was dependent throughout on inherited liturgical patterns. More recently, often in reaction to the cultic emphasis, other institutional settings have been proposed, especially that of wisdom (Wolff, Terrien). Unfortunately, one sees how little consensus has been reached in the matter of the book's setting by comparing the modern commentaries of Wolff and Rudolph.

Most recently, in an effort to get beyond the apparent impasse respecting oral tradition, more attention has been paid to the redactional history of the book. The method usually assumes the critical results of both literary and form criticism, but it seeks to understand the process of the book's formation in relation to the particular *Tendenz* of its editors. W. H. Schmidt's provocative article in 1965 attempted to attribute a decisive editorial activity to the work of a Deuteronomistic redactor. His conclusions have been picked up and debated by a number of younger scholars (Crüsemann, Kellermann). Again, the monograph of Willi-Plein is representative of the newer approach in seeking to interpret the redactional role of the alleged glosses in Amos rather than simply deleting them as 'non-genuine' after the manner of the older literary critics.

Finally, the major credit in bringing together and developing the newer lines of critical research on Amos certainly goes to the incisive commentary of H. W. Wolff. His work has been at the forefront of the critical debate for the last decade and, particularly in the form of a new English translation, will continue to be at the centre of critical research on the book of Amos for the foreseeable future.

Wolff's commentary is characterized by a consistent and detailed use of the form-critical and redaction-critical methods which he employs in developing his 'kerygmatic' exegesis. I shall focus on Wolff's commentary because the hermeneutical and exegetical issues at stake emerge here in their sharpest focus.

According to Wolff, the composition of the book of Amos has passed through a lengthy process of oral and literary transmission. He suggests that one can distinguish some six different levels within the book. The first three he attributed to Amos himself and his contemporaries in the eighth century. These include the oldest kernel of the book found in chs. 3–6, the five vision reports (7.1–8; 8.1f.; 9.1–4) and the earliest level of redaction by the 'Amos school' found in such additions as 1.1b, 7.10–17, etc. Wolff designates the last three levels as arising from the text's 'afterlife' (*Nachinterpretation*). New material has been added by way of commentary in an attempt to actualize the older message for a new situation. These levels include the three strophes of a hymn (4.13; 5.8f.; 9.5f.), the important Deuteronomic redaction (1.1, 9–11; 2.4f.; 3.1f.; 3.7; 5.25f.) and a post-exilic addition of promise in 9.11–15.

The basic issue at stake in the interpretation of Amos does not turn on whether Wolff is correct in every detail of his literary analysis – a conclusion hardly likely – but rather it turns on the historical critical model of exegesis which is best illustrated by Wolff's approach and is widely shared by his contemporaries. It is certainly not my intention to disparage the efforts of modern critical scholarship – a glance at E. B. Pusey's commentary on the Minor Prophets (1860) serves as a reminder of how far the discipline has come – but seriously to question the manner in which the critical method is employed in the exegesis of Amos.

2. The Canonical Shape of Amos

Historical critical research has demonstrated convincingly, in my judgment, that the present form of the book of Amos has been reached only after a lengthy history of development which has shaped the material both in its oral and literary stages. That the present text of Amos is multi-layered is clear. How does one understand this text which has been so formed? Instead of trying to recover the original message of the prophet Amos by separating it from later expansions, the goal of canonical interpretation is to discern in the final composition how the message of Amos was appropriated and formed to serve as authoritative scripture within the community of faith. I believe there is much evidence to show that the book of Amos reflects a theological context which has transformed the original message of Amos in a variety of ways toward the goal that the prophetic word functions as a critical norm for future generations within Israel. Following my analysis of the canonical shape, I shall try to contrast my suggested canonical reading with that of Wolff's.

The superscription of the book

The book begins with a lengthy superscription which has often been judged as overloaded with phrases reminiscent of Deuteronomy. It is very possible that a shorter version once introduced an earlier collection of Amos' words such as, 'The words of Amos ... of Tekoa which he saw concerning Israel ... two years before the earthquake' (cf. Wolff; W. H. Schmidt). Be that as it may, the present superscription now serves an important canonical function for the entire book. First, the expanded superscription has been strongly influenced both by the vocabulary and the content of ch. 7. The superscription thus presupposes the message of the book as a whole. The clause, 'The words ... which he saw' (*ḥāzāh*) picks up the verb from ch. 7 and indicates that both the words and the visions which are found in the rest of the book are included.

Secondly, Amos' message is directed 'against Israel'. Within the book of Amos the term Israel stands for two closely related, but distinct entities. On the one hand, it designates the political state of Northern Israel under the rule of Jeroboam II (3.12). On the other hand, it refers to the group who was rescued from Egypt, and who was constituted as the people of God in the promised land (2.10; 9.7). The immediate reference to the two political divisions of the nation, each ruled by a separate king, would confirm the judgment that in the superscription the term Israel refers to the Northern Kingdom. The point to be stressed is that the historical particularity of Amos' original addressees has not been weakened or generalized in the title. Even though for Amos the inhabitants of the Northern Kingdom continue in their identity as the people of Yahweh, *pars pro toto*, the historical reference of the original eighth-century historical entity has been explicitly retained in its canonical form. The full significance of this hermeneutically restrictive move will appear later.

The phrase 'two years before the earthquake' originally appears to have served a chronological function for an early generation who remembered this event. Indeed, some have argued that Amos' initial authority derived from his prediction of a coming earthquake which was confirmed within two years. However, its original function, regardless of what it may have been, has certainly been replaced by the preceding date formula which includes Amos within the larger framework of the nation's history. The date formula serves to identify the prophet within a historical sequence for those generations who no longer remembered the earthquake. Amos' place within a specific period of Israel's history has, thereby, been securely anchored and not loosened. The reference to an earthquake has now been closely tied to Yahweh's roaring from Jerusalem and thus it assumes a metaphorical connotation which continues to reverberate throughout the book (2.13ff.; 9.1ff.).

The superscription is closely joined to the first oracle of Amos (1.2). This once independent oracle now functions in this prominent position to provide a thematic introduction to the entire composition. The traditional language of God's dwelling in Zion and Jerusalem has been employed, not as a sign that the addressee has shifted from Israel to Judah, but to indicate that the God who once offered divine protection to his people by inhabiting Zion now roars in anger against them. The oracle emphasizes the overriding theological concern of the entire book. Amos speaks prophetically of the nature and will of the God of Israel. His passion for social justice arises from this basic theological perspective.

Israel and the nations, 1.3–2.16

The unit 1.3–2.16 forms the longest section within the book. Much scholarly discussion has focused on recovering the original setting of this oracle (cf. especially Bentzen's theory of Egyptian execration texts as an analogue). However, it seems unlikely that the prehistory of the text is of crucial importance in determining the present editorial role within the book. At most the knowledge of its exact historical setting would aid in understanding how Amos used a stereotyped form in his original proclamation. Usually oracles against the nations follow those directed against Israel (First Isaiah, Jeremiah, Ezekiel). The reversal of this normal prophetic pattern indicates the stance which controls the editing of the book of Amos. The oracles against the nations reflect a theological perspective which transcends the personal and historical vision of Amos, both in terms of geographical scope and extent of time. The judgment of Yahweh begins against the nations of the world for crimes perpetuated over a period of several hundred years. Only after this universal divine claim has been announced does the judgment fall on the Northern Kingdom and the focus narrow to the historical period involving Amos.

There is a rather wide consensus (Wellhausen, G. A. Smith, Harper, Wolff, Mays) that the original oracle of Amos against the nations has been expanded to include an oracle against Judah (2.4f.; cf. also 2.9f., 11f.). Indeed, the oracle does reveal significant differences in form and content from the dominant pattern. In recent times the expansion has been often attributed to the work of a Deuteronomic redaction (W. H. Schmidt). I tend to agree that 2.4f. does represent a secondary level within the text of Amos. However, the evidence for seeing a different hand at work is neither as clear nor as decisive as Schmidt and Wolff would suggest (cf. Kellermann). Be that as it may, the crucial exegetical issue turns on determining the effect of the Judah oracle on the interpretation of the passage in its larger context.

In 2.6ff. Amos climaxes his judgment against the nations by turning his attack upon Israel. It seems most likely that the Northern Kingdom is the addressee which is consistently the object of Amos' polemic (cf. Rost). Nevertheless, the Northern Kingdom is seen as the bearer of the sacred tradition (2.10) and it is consistent with Amos' idiom to employ the broader connotation of the term Israel when referring to the nation's sacred tradition (9.7). The reference in 2.4f. to Judah does not alter the semantic range of the term Israel in 2.6, as if Judah were originally included in the term. Rather, the reference extends the judgment to Judah as one of the nations without weakening or abstracting from the original historical reference to the Northern Kingdom. This move to extend the judgment in 2.4f. is similar to that found in 3.1b (cf. Wolff). The canonical significance of the inclusion of Judah is to rule out any attempt to see a contrast in the divine plan for the Northern and Southern Kingdom (contra Wellhausen). Specifically, it is no longer possible to explain the promises in ch. 9 as a reference to Judah's continuation in the post-exilic period. Thus, although the message of judgment was originally directed by Amos solely to the Northern Kingdom, there was never a positive future held out for Judah.

Words and visions, chs. 3–9

There follows in chs. 3–6 a collection of oracles, reflecting different oral patterns, which were once delivered at different times and to various audiences. Form-critical research has been especially helpful in bringing into sharper focus the form and function of these stereotyped patterns of address. By understanding the manner in which forms were traditionally used, the reader often discerns with greater clarity the radical twisting of emphasis which Amos gave his material. Thus, the funeral dirge (5.1) was pronounced over fallen Israel, the 'call to worship' (5.4) imitated a summons to transgress at Bethel, and the 'torah liturgy' of the priests (5.21–24) was used to condemn Israel's sacrifices as effecting only God's disgust.

However, it is significant to observe that the collecting and structuring of these oracles into their present form has assigned them a different role from their original one. The oracles have been formed into a book with little effort to preserve an original historical setting and often lack a specific addressee. They have been joined into larger topical units, usually, however, without destroying the contours of the original oracles. (The editorial process for the book of Amos was very different from that of Hosea.) The oracles have been loosely linked under such rubrics as 'hear this word' (3.1; 4.1; 5.1), or 'woe to those who . . . ' (5.18; 6.1, 4). A continuity of content has been established which oscillates between prophetic invectives of accusation (4.1ff.; 6.1ff., etc.) and divine words of judgment (3.14f.; 4.12; 6.8). An original distinction has often been maintained between the prophet's own words of accusation and the words of God which von Rad (*Theology* II, 130–8) has rightly described as characteristic of Amos. However, this distinction plays an insignificant role in the final editing process and it carries no special theological weight for the interpretation of the canonical text. A different type of oracle (3.3–8) which reflects a sapiential disputation form in its rhetorical questions has been placed at the head of this section to provide an initial justification of the prophet's office. He speaks such oracles of judgment out of a sense of divine compulsion. God has made known his will and when he speaks, who can be silent!

There is another similar redactional feature to observe which has influenced the canonical shaping of the book. A series of five visions begins in ch. 7 and extends through to ch. 9. What appears to have been an earlier collection of visions has now been incorporated within the same broad topical framework of chs. 3–6. The original vision sequence has first been disrupted by the interpolation of the historical confrontation between Amos and Amaziah (7.10–17). The position of the oracle appears to have been dictated, at least in part, by a catchword association (7.9 and 10f.). The effect of this passage is to pick up and reinforce the earlier theme of divine compulsion (3.3ff.) while illustrating at the same time the resistance of Israel's religious institutions and officials to the divine word. Again, the same type of invective and divine judgment oracle which was found in chs. 3–6 has been placed between the fourth and fifth visions (8.4ff.). This move would indicate that the editorial shaping established no theological significance between Amos' words and his visions, but assigned the same function to these originally different prophetic media.

The hymns of Amos

There is an additional feature of redactional activity within these same chapters which is of canonical significance. In three different places within chs. 4–9 there appear passages which have been correctly designated as 'hymns' (4.13; 5.8–9; 9.5–6). Not only does each passage reflect the hymnic style of the Psalter – the subject of praise is characteristically described by means of the active participle – but each passage shares a similar metre and common refrain: 'Yahweh is his name'. These last features in particular have been used as evidence by some to argue that the hymnic fragments comprise three stanzas of the one psalm. The position of each of these hymns is usually regarded as a redactional feature, but no consensus has emerged to explain its particular use within the book in spite of the enormous concentration of effort in recent years (cf. Horst, Wolff, Crenshaw, Berg, Koch). Horst's theory of a later liturgical use of the prophet's words in the form of a confession of sin, followed by a doxology of the community, has inadequate warrant from the text itself. Again, Wolff's modification of Sellin's hypothesis of the doxologies being connected to the destruction of Bethel has been severely weakened by the criticism of Rudolph.

An exegesis which works from the canonical text shifts the major focus away from the use of the hymns in Israel's prehistory and seeks to determine the effect of the doxologies on the present reading of the book. In their present literary position the hymns serve as a type of commentary – indeed in a liturgical form – which elaborates on the nature of the God of Israel whose threatening appearance in judgment has been announced. There seems to be no one literary device used in fixing the position of these hymns within the whole. In 5.8f. a simple catchword principle appears to have been at work. In 9.5ff. there is an explicit recapitulation of 8.8 in 9.5 which has the effect of the hymn's becoming a type of commentary on the entire preceding chapter. In sum, the redactional use of a series of hymnic fragments to interpret the nature of God is primarily a theological move determined by the content of the whole book, which was probably already in its written form. The over-all result is to reinforce the primary theological focus of the editor's work. Amos' attack on Israel during the reign of Jeroboam warns of the anger of God whose power in creation and judgment continues to be celebrated by the community of faith.

The function of chapter 9

The final and perhaps most significant sign of canonical shaping of the book of Amos for use as scripture appears in ch. 9. The major exegetical problem centres on how to interpret the sudden shift from a message of total judgment for Israel to one of promise. Wellhausen's caustic remark: 'Roses and lavender instead of blood and iron' (96), is typical for a generation of scholars who felt the shift to be absolutely irreconcilable with the message of Amos.

There has been a variety of different approaches to the problem since Wellhausen's day in an effort to solve the problem of the sudden transition, which is usually set at v. 8b.

(a) A large number of scholars have continued to accept the classic position of Wellhausen that the latter portions of ch. 9 stem from a later – usually post-exilic – addition (e.g. Fohrer, *Introduction*). However, within this group several modifications have been made. Some scholars limit the later additions to vv. 8b, 11–15, and maintain the authenticity of vv. 9–10. Others have accepted the broad lines of Wellhausen's literary analysis, but have opposed his theological characterization. So, for example, Wolff and Mays have sought to interpret the addition in a more positive light as a process of later actualization which felt constrained to soften Amos' harsh judgment. Kellermann has tried to place the verses within the orbit of Deuteronomic theology.

(b) A strong minority of scholars has sought to salvage all or a portion of 9.11ff. as an authentic oracle of Amos by different means. Sellin's literary solution suggested that 9.11–15 originally belonged to Amos' word to Amaziah in 7.16f. Again, the early form critics, such as Gressmann, as well as contemporary ones like Reventlow, contested the criterion of logical consistency. They assigned the oracle to a different oral setting within the genuine proclamation of Amos (also Hammershaimb). More recently, Rudolph has defended the authenticity of 9.11–15 by means of literary and historical arguments, but in the end characterized Amos' hope for a restoration of the Davidic kingdom as ill-conceived and erroneous.

In my judgment, the literary and historical evidence for regarding 9.11–15 as secondary to the primary level is strong. However, I do not believe that the solutions to the problem, either from the left or the right of the theological spectrum, have dealt seriously enough with the central issue of the canonical function of these verses within the final form of the book.

Let us return to the problem of ch. 9. The decisive shift from judgment to promise comes in the second half of 8: 'The eyes of Yahweh God are upon the sinful kingdom, and I will destroy it from the surface of the earth, except that I will not utterly destroy the house of Jacob.' In my judgment, one of the strongest arguments for holding v. 8b to be redactional lies in the structure of the complete oracle (vv. 7–10). The last two verses (9–10) do not reckon with the restriction of 8b, but join directly to 8a (contra Rudolph). In v. 9 the metaphor is of shaking Israel with a large mesh sieve (cf. Volz) 'among' or 'by means of' the nations. The good grain falls through, but the worthless refuse of sticks and stones remains in the sieve (cf. Sir. 27.4). In this case, nothing falls through. All of the sinful kingdom is doomed for destruction. This message is fully consistent with the rest of the book of Amos which has announced the absolute end of Israel (7.7ff.; 8.2; 9.1).

However, in the present form of ch. 9 two additions have been made, namely, vv. 8b and 11–15. The effect of including 8b within Amos' final oracle of judgment (7–10) is to offer an important restriction. The restriction does not lie in a contrast between the Northern and Southern Kingdoms, as if the addition were simply a post-exilic legitimation of Judah's existence. The term 'house of Jacob' (8b) never refers to the Southern Kingdom in the book of Amos (cf. 3.13; 7.2; 8.7). Nor does the redactional restriction lie in contrasting Jeroboam's dynasty with the larger political state of Israel. Nor does the contrast lie between a political entity (sinful kingdom) and a religious one (God's people).

Rather, the restriction which is introduced in 8b assumes the complete destruction of the kingdom of Israel (9–10). It does not weaken or undercut the severity or extent of the judgment. No segment of Israel escapes the judgment, as Amos had truly prophesied. The restriction has to do with the ultimate purpose of God in the future of Israel. The discourse moves into the realm of eschatology (11, 13). It turns on the possibility of a new existence after the end has come. The promise concerns the raising up of the shattered 'booth of David' – that is, David's larger kingdom, which can again lay claim on the land. No human ruler can achieve this feat; the initiative lies solely with God. The hope is miraculous and logically incomprehensible. It is placed within the eschatological framework of the latter days. That the continuity which the new shares with the old has been established from God's side is indicated by the mythopoetic language of the return of paradise.

The redaction of ch. 9 does not soften Amos' message of total judgment against sinful Israel by allowing a pious remnant to escape. The destruction is fully confirmed (vv. 9b, 11). Rather, the editor effects a decisive canonical shaping of the book by placing Amos' words within a broader, eschatological framework which transcends the perspective of the prophet himself. Only from the divine perspective is there a hope beyond the destruction seen by Amos. This theological stance is made explicit in the little noticed hymnic expansion which concludes the first oracle of promise in v. 12b. The reference to God's name over all the nations, and the hymnic style, 'Yahweh the one who does this', stands in close continuity with the earlier hymnic expansions. The effect of the canonical shaping of ch. 9 is to place Amos' words of judgment within a larger theological framework, which, on the one hand, confirms the truth of Amos' prophecy of doom, and, on the other hand, encom-

passes it within the promise of God's will for hope and final redemption. In its canonically interpreted form the historically conditioned ministry of the eighth-century prophet of judgment serves
as a truthful witness of scripture for the successive generations of
Israel.

The canonical approach contrasted with others

At least three important differences distinguish the canonical
approach to the book of Amos from historical critical exegesis,
which is best represented by H. W. Wolff.

(a) Wolff's method assumes that each redactional level of the
biblical text has arisen in reaction to a specific historical impetus
which effected a continual 'updating' of the text. A correct theological understanding of this multi-layered text, therefore, depends on
correlating the form of the text to a precisely defined historical
referent. 2.4f. is judged to be a sixth-century Deuteronomic addition; 9.11ff. a post-exilic expansion. Speculation is constitutive to
the method since the very information needed for such literary and
historical judgment is largely missing from the biblical text and
must be supplied. By the linking of exegesis directly to historical
reconstruction the integrity of the biblical text and the theological
enterprise is seriously jeopardized.

In contrast, an exegesis in the context of the canon sees the
purpose of the text's growth to be a shaping of the message to serve
as Israel's authoritative scripture. The decisive force at work in the
book's formation is theological in nature. It arises through Israel's
continuous engagement with the word of God and does not depend
directly upon external forces of historical change. Actualization has
already been built into the canonical text. Thus, the book of Amos
is not a dead relic of the past which needs to be made relevant.

(b) Wolff's historical interpretation of the redactional layers of
Amos has the effect of reading the biblical text from a perspective
which often runs counter to that demanded by the literature itself.
For example, 9.11ff. is interpreted as a commentary on the exile, an
event which the biblical editor had already experienced. In contrast, the canonical approach attempts to identify with the perspective of the literature itself in an effort to comprehend the interpreted
text. Significantly, for ch. 9 both the threat of the destruction of the
nation and the promise of its rebirth are events still lying in the
future.

(c) In spite of his continuous insistence that biblical revelation is time-conditioned and situation-oriented, Wolff is forced to move to a higher level of abstraction, both historically and theologically, when he seeks to apply the text to a 'goal' (*Ziel*). The bridge between yesterday and today is sought in some analogical structure, usually typology or recurring situations (cf. the incisive criticisms of J. Tolk). Moreover, Wolff's use of the New Testament as a guide for theological application of Amos fails to reckon with the canonical reading of the Old by the New which is of a different order from Wolff's critical reconstruction. In my judgment, there is no greater indictment of the critical method than the theological bankruptcy of its homiletical model.

3. Theological and Hermeneutical implications

(a) It is of great theological importance that a high degree of historical particularity has been preserved in Amos' preaching. Above all, his prophetic ministry has been assigned a particular place within a larger *heilsgeschichtliche* framework. Amos' role was not to evoke repentance, but to pronounce the total judgment of God on that Israelite kingdom at that particular moment in history. The book's superscription ties Amos inextricably to the reigns of Jeroboam and Uzziah. The truth of Amos' oracles was demonstrated to Israel in the destruction of the Northern Kingdom by the Assyrians within a generation after Amos' prophecy.

The particularity of Amos' prophecy against Israel was left largely untouched by the canonical editors in order that his attack on the Israel of his age could provide a normative criticism of distorted religion for the subsequent community of faith. The burden of his preaching was to make clear that Israel's manner of life reflected a basic misunderstanding of divine election, worship, justice, covenant, and promise. He resorted to drastic rhetorical devices to press home his attack. In Amos' proclamation Israel was given a prophetic word to serve continually against persistent and recurring abuses of religion which threaten true faith. Far from blunting the edge of the message, the canon preserved it razor-sharp.

(b) In addition to preserving the historical particularity of Amos' message, the canonical shaping provided the material with a powerful theological framework which transcended the perspective of the historical Amos. The God who was revealed to Israel in the time-conditioned witness of the Hebrew prophet was not confined within the limitations of human perspective. The editors arranged the material by the use of editorial commentary, hymnic doxologies, and eschatological expansions to confront the hearer with the eternal God, the Creator and Redeemer of Israel, who was a living and active force both in the past, present, and future. The book is consistently theocentric in perspective.

(c) Finally, the book of Amos in its canonical shape functions for the contemporary church and synagogue, not to provide a model on how the modern clergyman is to become a prophet like Amos for his day – the prophetic 'office' is time-bound in God's economy – but rather the book serves as a faithful witness to the God of Israel whose will we now understand more clearly through the medium of scripture. This living God calls his people into obedient worship which is tested by the standard of God's justice and righteousness (5.24).

History of Exegesis

Carpzov III, 329f.; **Darling**, I, 708–11; *DThC* 1, 1120; *EB* 6, 286; *RGG*³ 1, 331.

M. **Blechmann**, *Das Buch Amos im Talmud und Midrasch*, Leipzig n.d.; G. **Bouwman**, *Des Julian von Aeclanum Kommentar zu den Propheten Osee, Joel und Amos*, AnBib 9, 1958; J. **Knabenbauer**, *Commentarius in Prophetas Minores*, Paris 1886, 4ff.; J. **Touzard**, *Le livre d'Amos*, Paris 1909.

XXIII

OBADIAH

Commentaries

C. P. Caspari, 1842
C. F. Keil, BC, 1868
P. Kleinert, ET, LCHS, 1874
J. Wellhausen, [3]1898
G. A. Smith, ExB, 1898, ([2]1928)
T. T. Perowne, CB, 1898
A. van Hoonacker, ÉB, 1908
J. A. Bewer, ICC, 1911
K. Marti, HSAT, [4]1923
G. W. Wade, WC, 1925

E. Sellin, KAT, [2-3]1929
G. C. Aalders, COuT, 1958
A. Deissler, SB, 1961
T. H. Robinson, HAT, [3]1964
C. A. Keller, CAT, 1965
A. Weiser, ATD, [5]1967
J. D. W. Watts, 1969
W. Rudolph, KAT[2], 1971
L. C. Allen, NICOT, 1976
H. W. Wolff, BK, 1977

Bibliography

H. **Bekel**, 'Ein vorexilisches Orakel über Edom in der Klagestrophe–die gemeinsame Quelle von Obadja 1–9 and Jeremia 49,7–22', *ThStKr* 80, 1907, 315–42; M. **Bič**, 'Eine verkanntes Thronbesteigungsfestorakel im Alten Testament', *ArOr* 19, 1951, 568–78; 'Zur Problematik des Buches Obadjah', *SVT* 1, 1953, 11–25; É. **Bonnard**, 'Abdias', *DBS* 8, 693–701; W. W. **Cannon**, 'Israel and Edom: The Oracle of Obadiah 1', *Theology* 14, London 1927, 129–40, 191–200; A. **Condamin**, 'L'unité d'Abdias', *RB* 9, 1900, 261–8; F. **Delitzsch**, 'Wann weissagte Obadja?', *Zeitschrift für die lutherische Theologie und Kirche* 12, Leipzig 1851, 91–102; A. H. **Edelkoort**, 'De profetie van Obadja', *NedThT* 1, 1946–7, 276–93; G. **Fohrer**, 'Die Sprüche Obadjas', *Studia Biblica et Semitica T.C. Vriezen dedicata*, Wageningen 1966, 81–91; N. **Glueck**, 'The Boundaries of Edom', *HUCA* 11, 1936, 141–57; J. **Gray**, 'The Diaspora of Israel and Judah in Obadiah v.20', *ZAW* 65, 1965, 53–9; M. **Haller**, 'Edom im Urteil der Propheten', *FS K. Marti*, BZAW 41, 1925, 109–17; U. **Kellermann**, *Israel und Edom. Studien zum Edomhass Israels in 6.-4. Jahrhundert vor Chr.*, Münster

1975; P. K. **McCarter**, 'Obadiah 7 and the Fall of Edom', *BASOR* 221, 1976, 87–91; J. **Muilenburg**, 'Obadiah, the Book of', *IDB* 3, 578f.; J. M. **Myers**, 'Edom and Judah in the Sixth-Fifth Centuries BC', *Near Eastern Studies in Honor of W. F. Albright*, Baltimore 1971, 377–92; J. M. **Rinaldi**, 'In librum Abdiae', *Verbum Domini* 19, Rome 1939, 148–54, 174–9, 201–6; T. H. **Robinson**, 'The Structure of the Book of Obadiah', *JTS* 17, 1916, 402–8; W. **Rudolph**, 'Obadja', *ZAW* 49, 1931, 222–31; J. M. P. **Smith**, 'The Structure of Obadiah', *AJSL* 22, 1905–6, 131–8; H. W. **Wolff**, 'Obadja – ein Kultprophet als Interpret', *EvTh* 37, 1977, 273–84.

1. Historical Critical Problems

Two main issues have dominated the critical discussion of the book of Obadiah: historical setting and literary integrity. In spite of its being the shortest book in the Old Testament, Obadiah's two problematic issues have generated much debate and little concord.

Because the superscription affords no evidence as to the background of the prophet or of his age – the order of Obadiah within the collection was disregarded early in the history of research – the interpreter is dependent upon internal evidence for establishing a setting. Although there are many gaps in the history of Edom in relation to Israel, the description of Edom's ruthless role in exploiting the devastation of Jerusalem points most clearly to the Babylonian attack of 587. The parallel passages (Ps. 137.7; Lam. 4.21f.; Ezek. 25.12; 35.5, 12; Isa. 34.8) focus on the treachery of the Edomites in harassing their kinsmen, the Jews, precisely at Judah's moment of greatest humiliation. The vividness of the description would appear to indicate a period of composition not too far removed from the beginning of the exile.

However, this line of argument for fixing a historical setting has been complicated by another important literary consideration. Certain verses of Obadiah have a close parallel with Jer. 49 (Obad. 1b–4 // Jer. 49.14–16; v. 5 // 49.9; v. 6 // 49.10a). Ever since the thorough study of Caspari (1842) the opinion has generally dominated which held that Obadiah had the priority and that Jeremiah was dependent upon his composition (cf. Keil, van Hoonacker, Rudolph). However, a minority opinion has continued to defend the priority of Jeremiah (Bonnard, 697 ff.). Wolff has sought to avoid the impasse by opting for a common oral tradition underlying both passages.

For those who defended the priority of Obadiah a further question emerged which affected the problem of dating the book. It was usually assumed that Jer. 49 was written in the fourth year of Jehoiakim before the destruction of Jerusalem. How then could Obadiah be dated in the exile? Caspari sought to avoid the difficulty by interpreting the destruction of Jerusalem and Edom's treachery as prophecies, written in the historical tense, but this move received little acceptance because of its extreme artificiality. Another attempt to avoid the difficulty was put forward by Kleinert and Keil who sought to relate the encounter with Edom to an earlier event, such as the battle reported in II Chron. 21.8–11 during the reign of Joram. But again the evidence is very strained and the identification has not commended itself. In more recent times the issue has usually been resolved by holding to a later post-exilic date for that section in Jer. 49 which parallels Obadiah. It is instructive to observe that even such early commentators as Calvin held firmly to the exilic dating of Obadiah, relating the book to the destruction of Jerusalem. It should also be mentioned that some scholars (e.g. Bewer) follow the lead of Wellhausen in relating certain of the references to the attack on Edom by the Nabataeans in the first half of the fifth century.

The second major critical issue turns on the literary integrity of the book. The two extreme positions in the spectrum of opinion are, on the one hand, represented mainly by older commentators who held to one unified work, and, on the other hand, scholars such as Robinson and Fohrer who find half-a-dozen fragments within the book. Occasionally the book's unity has been defended by an appeal to a cultic role (Bič, Watts), but the suggestion is without adequate evidence to convince. Likewise, Wolff's most recent attempt to understand the book as an actualization of older prophetic words against Edom by the cult prophet, Obadiah, is forced to supply many of the elements on which the hypothesis rests.

Probably the most convincing analysis of the book's structure has been put forth by Rudolph who refined Wellhausen's divisions. Rudolph describes two main oracles, 2–14, 15b and 15a, 16–18, to which an appendix has been added in 19–21. In the first oracle, which is a judgment on Edom, the nations functioned as agents in Edom's punishment, and the judgment was confined to the historical plane. In the second oracle, which is an eschatological judgment on the nations, the perspective borders on the apocalyptic.

2. The Canonical Shape of Obadiah

The canonical issue has frequently entered the discussion in an indirect fashion with the question: why would Israel have ever preserved this short, bitter polemic against Edom? Often the answer offered a theological condemnation of Israel's nationalism to which its hatred of Edom was attributed. The element which is missing in such an appraisal is the failure to recognize that the words of Obadiah have been placed within a larger context to serve a canonical function. Only after this shaping has been understood can one begin to address the theological questions involved in preserving these traditions.

In the first place, the threat against Edom which was grounded in the treacherous action at the moment of Jerusalem's destruction (vv. 5–9) has been closely linked to the larger, all-inclusive eschatological judgment on the nations. Even if Rudolph were correct in his opinion that the oracle in vv. 2–14 was originally delivered as a fully this-worldly, temporal judgment on Edom, the significance of the punishment has been enlarged and transformed in the final form of the book. Moreover, the point should not be overlooked that in vv. 1–4 it is the pride of Edom which is the affront to God, not the conduct toward Judah. Clearly, the threat to the sovereignty of God is the initial focus of the divine anger.

The next hint of its new eschatological interpretation is given in the formula in v. 8, 'in that day'. The connection is made even more explicit in the manner in which the two oracles have been joined in v. 15. From a strictly literary perspective Wellhausen, Rudolph, and Wolff are right in reversing the order of 15a and 15b. Verse 15b summarizes the theme of retribution in the preceding oracle whereas 15a strikes the new eschatological chord of the succeeding verses. Nevertheless, the present order does not seem to reflect simply an accidental textual mishap, but fits in smoothly with a larger redactional reshaping.

The effect of v. 15 in its present sequence is to interpret the oracle against Edom as part of the coming 'Day of Yahweh' which is directed to all the nations. The inversion also firmly joins the oracle in 16–18 into a unity with 2–15. Whereas 2–15 begins with Edom and ends with an eschatological judgment on all the nations, 16–18 begins with the nations and ends with the utter destruction of

Edom. Thus, Edom and the nations are not to be separated into different prophetic oracles, but represent different aspects of the same event within the divine judgment. The effect of the new framework is to ensure that Edom is now understood as a representative entity, namely, the ungodly power of this world which threatens the people of God. The canonical shape of the book addresses Edom as an example of what lies ahead for the pagan world.

Secondly, the prophet speaks of the coming redemption of Israel after her deepest humiliation. The climactic note of the coming of God's kingdom sounds the central theme of the final oracle, and once again interprets Edom's defeat not as a boastful achievement of Israel against its arch-rival but as a sure demonstration of God's rule over all the nations. Verse 17 had made the point, not only that there would be a holy remnant, but the house of Jacob would again possess its land. It is highly significant that this promise of the land was neither rendered into an abstraction nor spiritualized in any way. Rather, the commentary on v. 17 which is offered by vv. 19–21 serves the opposite function. The possession of land is made even more concrete. Its borders are described and the exiles who recover their lost inheritance are specifically portrayed as an essential part of the future hope.

In sum, the canonical shape of the oracles of Obadiah has interpreted the prophetic message as the promise of God's coming rule which will overcome the evil intent of the nations, even Edom, and restore a holy remnant to its inheritance within God's kingship.

3. Theological and Hermeneutical Implications

(a) It is significant to note in the history of the exegesis of the book of Obadiah that even such a staunchly conservative scholar as C. F. Keil, who was usually alert to theological issues, shared fully in the hermeneutical axiom of the historical critical method. He argued against seeing any representative features in Obadiah on the basis that 'all the prophecies are occasioned by distinct, concrete relations and circumstances belonging to the age from which they sprung' (339). Although this axiom contains a measure of truth, it fails to reckon with the decisive canonical reworking of the original material for a new role of sacred scripture within the continuing community of faith. This canonical force often moved the tradition in a direction which undercuts completely the legitimacy of applying the axiom to the final form of the biblical text.

(b) The history of research on Obadiah also illustrates an important indirect effect of critical scholarship on the canonical understanding of an Old Testament book. The literary relationship between Obadiah and Jer. 49 has no major canonical significance. The interpretation of Obadiah is not seriously affected by the reader's recognizing a literary relationship. At most it offers an interesting illustration of how a similar text can function canonically in another setting. However, a correct critical analysis has an important indirect role in undercutting an interpretative move by Keil and Kleinert which would substitute a logical deduction regarding authorship for hearing the biblical text itself. The difference between a flat biblicistic reading, which is often rationalistic, and a genuine canonical interpretation can be well illustrated from this small book.

History of Exegesis

Carpzov III, 343f.; *DB* 1, 22f.; *DBS* 8, 701; *RGG*[3] 8, 701.

K. **Baltzer** and H. **Koester**, 'Die Bedeutung des Jakobus als Oblias=Obdias', *ZNW* 46, 1955, 141f.; G. **Krause**, *Studien zu Luthers Auslegung der Kleinen Propheten*, BHT 33, 1962; D. **Neiman**, 'Sefarad: The Name of Spain', *JNES* 22, 1963, 128–32.

XXIV

JONAH

Commentaries

C. F. Keil, BC, 1868
F. Hitzig, H. Steiner, KeH, ⁴1881
G. A. Smith, ExB, 1898, (²1928)
A. van Hoonacker, ÉB, 1908
J. A. Bewer, ICC, 1912
W. Nowack, HKAT, ³1922
G. W. Wade, WC, 1925
E. Sellin, KAT, ²⁻³1929
G. A. F. Knight, TB, 1950

J. D. Smart, IB, 1956
A. Feuillet, JB, ²1960
M. Delcor, SB, 1961
T. H. Robinson, HAT, ³1964
C. A. Keller, CAT, 1965
A. Weiser, ATD, ⁵1967
W. Rudolph, KAT², 1971
H. W. Wolff, BK, 1977

Bibliography

G. C. **Aalders**, *The Problem of the Book of Jonah*, London 1948; E. J. **Bickermann**, *Four Strange Books of the Bible*, New York 1967; S. H. **Blank**, '"Doest Thou Well to be Angry?" A Study in Self Pity', *HUCA* 26, 1953, 29–41; W. **Böhme**, 'Die Composition des Buches Jona', *ZAW* 7, 1887, 224–84; K. **Budde**, Vermutungen zum 'Midrasch des Buches der Könige', *ZAW* 12, 1892, 40–51; M. **Burrows**, 'The Literary Category of the Book of Jonah', *Translating and Understanding the Old Testament, Essays in Honor of H. G. May*, ed. H. T. Frank and W. L. Reed, Nashville 1970, 80–107; R. E. **Clements**, 'The Purpose of the Book of Jonah', *SVT* 28, 1975, 16–28; G. H. **Cohn**, *Das Buch Jona im Lichte der biblischen Erzählkunst*, Assen 1965; J. **Ellul**, *The Judgment of Jonah*, ET Grand Rapids 1971; G. I. **Emmerson**, 'Another Look at the Book of Jonah', *ExpT* 88, 1976, 86f.; I. H. **Eybers**, 'The Purpose of the Book of Jonah', *Theologia Evangelica* 4, Pretoria 1971, 211–22; P. **Fairbairn**, *Jonah. His Life, Character and Mission*, Edinburgh 1849, reprinted Grand Rapids 1964; A. **Fáj**, 'The Stoic Features of the Book of Jonah', *Annali dell' Istituto Orientale di Napoli* 34, Naples 1974, 309–45; A. **Feuillet**, 'Les sources du livre de Jonas', *RB* 54, 1947,

161–86; 'Le sens du livre de Jonas', *RB* 54, 1947, 340–61; T. E. **Fretheim**, *The Message of Jonah*, Minneapolis 1977.

S. D. **Goitein**, 'Some Observations on Jonah', *JPOS* 17, 1937, 63–77; H. **Gunkel**, *Ausgewählte Psalmen*, Göttingen 1904, 239–246; 'Jonabuch', *RGG²*, 3, 366–369; E. **Haller**, *Die Erzählung von dem Propheten Jona*, TheolEx 65, 1958; A. **Jepsen**, 'Anmerkungen zum Buche Jona', *Wort–Gebot–Glaube, FS W. Eichrodt*, Zurich 1971, 297ff.; Jörg **Jeremias**, *Die Reue Gottes*, BSt 65, 1975, 98ff.; A. R. **Johnson**, 'Jonah 2, 3–10. A Study in Cultic Phantasy', *Studies in Old Testament Prophecy presented to T. H. Robinson*, ed. H. H. Rowley, Edinburgh and New York 1950, 82–102; O. **Kaiser**, 'Wirklichkeit, Möglichkeit und Vorurteil. Ein Beitrag zum Verständnis des Buches Jona', *EvTh* 33, 1973, 91–103; Y. **Kaufmann**, *The Religion of Israel*, ET Chicago 1960, London 1961, 282–86; C. A. **Keller**, 'Jonas, le portrait d'un prophète', *TZ* 21, 1965, 329–40; E. G. **Kraeling**, 'The Evolution of the Story of Jonah', *Hommages à André Dupont-Sommer*, ed. A. Caquot and M. Philonenko, Paris 1971, 305–18; C. **Kuhl**, 'Die Wiederaufnahme—ein literarkritisches Prinzip?', *ZAW* 64, 1952, 1–11.

G. M. **Landes**, 'The Kerygma of the Book of Jonah', *Interp* 21, 1967, 3–31; N. **Lohfink**, 'Jona ging zur Stadt hinaus (Jona 4,5)', *BZ* NF 5, 1961, 185–203; O. **Loretz**, 'Herkunft und Sinn der Jona-Erzählung', *BZ* NF 5, 1961, 18–29; J. **Magonet**, *Form and Meaning. Studies in Literary Techniques in the Book of Jonah*, Berne and Frankfurt 1976; G. **von Rad**, *Der Prophet Jona*, Nurnberg 1950=*Gottes Wirken in Israel*, Neukirchen-Vluyn 1974, 65–78; A. **Rofé**, 'Classes in the Prophetical Stories: Didactic Legenda and Parable', *SVT* 26, 1974, 153–64; W. **Rudolph**, 'Jona', *Archäologie und Altes Testament, FS K. Galling*, Tübingen 1970, 233–9; H. **Schmidt**, *Jona, eine Untersuchung zur vergleichenden Religionsgeschichte*, FRLANT 9, 1907; L. **Schmidt**, *De Deo. Studien zur Literarkritik und Theologie des Buches Jona, des Gesprächs zwischen Abraham und Jahwe in Gen. 18,22ff. und Hiob 1*, BZAW 143, 1976; U. **Steffen**, *Das Mysterium von Tode und Auferstehung, Formen und Wandlungen des Jona-Motivs*, Göttingen 1963; R. D. **Wilson**, 'The Authenticity of Jonah', *PTR* 16, 1918, 280–98, 430–56; H. W. **Wolff**, *Studien zum Jonabuch*, BSt 47, 1964, ²1975; A. G. **Wright**, 'The Literary Genre Midrash', *CBQ* 28, 1966, 105–38, 417–57.

1. Historical Critical Problems

The history of the interpretation of the book of Jonah has been reviewed many times and need not be rehearsed in detail (cf. Bickermann). The attempt to interpret the book as a straightforward historical report met with resistance at a very early date. The search for alternative theories of interpretation led, on the one hand, to various allegorical and typological moves, and, on the other hand, to innumerable rationalistic ploys, e.g. that Jonah had dreamed the story, or that the ship which rescued him was named 'the great fish'! During the last century research has focused on the study of the extra-biblical parallels from folklore (H. Schmidt), and on determining the literary genre of the story (cf. Wolff, Rofé, L. Schmidt). A rather wide consensus has developed in assigning a post-exilic dating to the composition of the book, chiefly because of the language and vagueness in the historical references to Nineveh. Bickermann and Fáj have sought to demonstrate features within the book which are distinctly Hellenistic in character. The apparent knowledge of the book by Sirach (49.10) and Tobit (14.4, 8) sets a definite *terminus ad quem* for its composition.

During the latter part of the nineteenth century various attempts were offered which questioned the literary integrity of the book (G. A. Smith, II, 509ff. [²1928, 497ff.]), and a variety of sources were posited to account for the literary tensions. From this endeavour only two observations have received much support. The secondary nature of the psalm in ch. 2 has been widely accepted and a possible dislocation of 4.5 has been defended. But even here a minority opinion has continued to resist these moves (cf. Landes and Lohfink). In sum, the basic unity of the book has been strongly maintained by modern critical scholarship.

The effort to specify the literary genre of the book of Jonah has met with less agreement. It has been characterized as a fable, didactic novel, prophetic legend, and parable. Others have described the book as a midrash or even as an allegory. Recently, Keller has tried to demonstrate the book's affinity to the so-called 'Confessions of Jeremiah', and L. Schmidt has coined the phrase *'erzählte Dogmatik'* (narrated dogmatics) in an effort to pinpoint its peculiar features. In the end, many commentators opt for a mixed genre with the presence of many eclectic elements.

The most crucial and perplexing problem of the book turns on the interpretation of its major purpose. Broadly speaking, two major interpretations have emerged in the history of exegesis, of course, with innumerable variations within each group. The first alternative interprets the book of Jonah as focusing on some aspect of unfulfilled prophecy. The main issue is described either as Jonah's effort not to be a false prophet, or as analysing the relation of conditional to unconditional prophecy, or as dealing with the lack of fulfilment of the prophecy against the nations. This position has generally been advocated by Jewish interpreters (Goitein, Bickermann, Weinreb [see below, p. 427]), but also by an impressive number of non-Jewish exegetes (Calvin, Hitzig). The recent interpretations of Keller and Clements would fit broadly into this first category.

The second major pattern of interpretation sees the point of the book to lie in the attempt to extend the message of salvation to the Gentiles against the resistance of the Jews. This interpretation has mainly been defended by Christian scholars (Haller, Rudolph, Wolff), although a variation of this approach is reflected in the early Jewish defence of Jonah who is pictured as fleeing lest he bring indirect judgment on Israel by converting the heathen (cf. Bickermann).

The impasse has arisen because both exegetical positions find warrants in the text to use as support, but then again both positions reflect serious weaknesses as well. The first theory of interpretation points out the connection of the Jonah story with the prophetic figure in II Kings 14. In this sole reference to Jonah, the prophet is remembered because his word had been fulfilled. Again, the reason for Jonah's flight, explicitly stated in 4.2, focuses on his knowledge that the judgment against Nineveh would not be carried out. Finally, Jonah's call in ch. 1 also relates to the larger problem of the role of prophecy in Israel.

However, there are persistent difficulties with this approach which have not been adequately resolved. The office of prophet does not ever seem to be at stake in such a way as might have been expected in this interpretation. Again, the message that all prophecy is ultimately conditional was already a truism within Israel (cf. Jer. 18), and hardly needing an elaborate defence. The lesson that God was both just and merciful was also fully obvious to every Hebrew. Even the theme of God's right to change his mind does not seem to be the point of the book, but an implicit assumption.

The second interpretation which focuses the book on the conversion of the Gentiles seeks to support its theory by pointing out Jonah's use in 4.2 of the ancient Hebrew formula which provided the grounds for Israel's election (Ex. 34.6f.). Again, the contrast between Jonah the Hebrew, and the heathen of ch. 1 seems to have a parallel in ch. 3. Finally, the lesson from the plant in ch. 4 turns on God's concern for his whole creation rather than with the issue of prophecy *per se*. Nevertheless, serious obstacles also emerge for this interpretation. The book does not reflect any antagonism between Jew and Gentile, nor does the role of Nineveh as the enemy of Israel play any role. The descriptive formulae are all bland and stereotypical. It is also not obvious that Jonah was understood as a representative figure, especially as a caricature of Hellenistic Judaism.

In sum, neither of the major interpretations has been able to achieve a clear consensus nor to do justice to the full range of exegetical problems in the biblical text.

2. The Canonical Shape of Jonah

In an effort to describe how the book of Jonah functions in its canonical context, it seems wise to begin with the form-critical problem. What is the form and function of the Jonah story? It has long been noticed that the book reaches a climax in ch. 4 with a didactic point. Indeed once this point has been made, the book comes to an abrupt end. Moreover, the retrospective explanation in 4.2 succeeds in closely tying the preceding scenes to the didactic point of the final chapter. It is crucial to observe how the point is made. It emerges from the dialogue between God and Jonah and is self-contained. It does not need to be explained by the author of the story. The form-critical implication to be drawn from this observation is that the story now functions in a way analogous to that of a parable. In spite of the probability that the elements of the story may have once circulated independently of its present form, the story now functions as a unit in which the audience receives the word in unmediated form from the narrative itself.

However, there are several reasons why we prefer the term 'parable-like' rather than making an immediate identification of the Old Testament book with the form of the parable. First, the nature of the genre of parable is itself a highly controversial issue, particularly from the side of New Testament scholarship, and the term introduces into the discussion many extraneous issues. The logic of the book is not affected by making more precise the exact relationship of the Old Testament story to the complexities within the genre. Secondly, there are certain unique features within the book

of Jonah which are not part of the parabolic form. The book begins
with the stereotypical literary formula of the prophetic books: 'the
word of Yahweh came to Jonah'. Although the book of Jonah is not
a collection of prophetic words, but rather a story about the prophet, the author has adapted the prophetic formula to his own
didactic purposes. By beginning with this formula, the author has
cast his story into the style of the other prophecies. Finally, there is
considerable flexibility within the form which must not be
sacrificed to an overly rigid formal classification.

The significance of this parable-like form of the book can be
elucidated by contrasting its form and function with other suggested genres. The story is different from a prophetic legend whose
meaning is supplied by means of a redactor's framework imposed
upon the story (e.g. I Kings 16.29ff.). Again, the story of Jonah is
not symbolic action which points to another dimension of reality by
means of carefully contrived adumbration. Moreover, the story
does not belong to the genre of midrash even though there are
elements of midrashic technique involved because the major concern of the narrative does not turn on explaining a difficulty in a
biblical text. Finally, the story does not function as an allegory
which requires the proper key in order for its hearers to perceive its
meaning. However, although this form-critical analysis of how the
story functions does rule out certain interpretations, it does not
offer in itself a criterion for adjudicating between the two conflicting
interpretations which were discussed above. To resolve this problem, we shall have to seek evidence of canonical shaping in the final
form of the book.

The majority of critical scholars are convinced that the prayer in
ch. 2 is a later interpolation into the original story. Among the
various reasons brought forward against the originality of the
prayer, two stand out. It is argued that the prayer has not only
disturbed the structure of the story, but also has introduced a confusing note into the one clear message of the book. In terms of the
original structure, the first and second commissions to Nineveh are
clearly parallel (1.1 and 3.1). In each of these two chapters the
focus of the story falls on the heathen reaction, the threat of judgment, the prayer for deliverance, and the ensuing rescue. Chapter 4
shifts the perspective to Jonah. His reaction to Nineveh's repentance is described, which in turn evokes the lesson in a divine
response.

In this reconstruction of the original story Jonah never changes in voicing his opposition to his mission. He first flees, but is compelled to return by God's direct intervention. He then carries out his commission, but is angry at its success. His explanation (4.2) indicates his consistent resistance from the beginning. He knows in advance that God will not carry through with his threat. The issue turns on the fulfilment of the prophet's word. Jonah resisted because he did not want to be a false prophet. In his response God defends his right as Creator to let his mercy to his creation override the prophetic word. By the removal of ch. 2 the sharp lines of the original story emerge, thus confirming the interpretation which related the purpose of the book to the issue of unfulfilled prophecy.

But what is the effect on the story when in its final form the lengthy prayer of Jonah is introduced in ch. 2? This move appears to have been a crucial one in the canonical shaping. First of all, the structure of the book is substantially altered by the introduction of the prayer of ch. 2. As has been convincingly demonstrated by Landes, ch. 2 now functions as a parallel to ch. 4. The similar introductory formulae as well as the consistent structure serve as literary evidence for an intentional structural paralleling of the chapters. The effect of the parallel is that the meaning of ch. 4 is now strongly influenced by ch. 2.

In ch. 2 Jonah prays to God from the belly of the fish. The prayer is not a cry for help, but is a prayer of thanksgiving for deliverance already experienced. The Hebrew text is unequivocal in its use of verbs of completed action in striking contrast to the Septuagint's attempt to remove this problem. In its present narrative context the threat to Jonah's life lay in his being drowned in the sea. The large fish was the divine means of deliverance! The prayer of Jonah is a veritable catena of traditional phrases from the Psalter. Jonah prays in the stereotypical language of the psalms which every faithful Jew had always used. He first describes the threat to his life in the language of the complaint psalm, which, however, because of the context of the ongoing narrative, works to provide a new and remarkable dimension of historical specificity. Jonah is thankful for his rescue and ascribes praise to his God: 'Deliverance belongs to Yahweh'! (v. 10; EVV v. 9).

In ch. 4 Jonah again prays to his God and once again he makes use of traditional language. The formula of v. 2 appears first in Ex. 34.6 in the giving of the covenant to Israel at Sinai, but has become an integral part of the liturgical language of the Psalter as well (Pss. 86.15; 103.8; 111.4; 112.4; 116.5; 145.8). This time, however, the appeal to the same divine attribute of mercy evokes a negative response from the prophet. He is angry because God has 'repented of the evil' intended for Nineveh (cf. Jörg Jeremias). If his anger had once stemmed from concern over the fulfilment of the prophetic word, there has been a noticeable shift in the expanded narrative. The structural parallelism of chs. 2 and 4, which contrasts the two prayers of Jonah, refocuses the narrative. The issue now turns on the scope of divine mercy. Jonah is thankful for his own deliverance, but resentful of Nineveh's inclusion within the mercy which had always been restricted to Israel. This interpretation is further supported by the prayer of the king. His response: 'who knows, God may yet repent and turn from his fierce anger', is a citation from Joel 2.14, and a continuation of the same covenant formula which Jonah uses in 4.2. Clearly the issue is now on the recipient of the divine mercy.

The inclusion of the prayer of Jonah in ch. 2 has had another effect on the interpretation of the story. The prayer affords the reader an avenue into the faith of the prophet. Obviously, Jonah's personality is not the issue, but rather Jonah is portrayed as a typical Jew who shares Israel's traditional faith. In his trouble he renders thanksgiving to God and is confident of divine rescue. In sum, the effect of the prayer from a canonical perspective is to typify Jonah! The lesson which was directed to Jonah now also serves a larger audience. The book addresses those other faithful Jews who have been set apart from the nations by the Mosaic covenant, and who were sustained by the sacred traditions of their Psalter.

There are several other observations which can be made in regard to the effect of the prayer in ch.2 on the interpretation of the book as a whole. The initial characterization of the book as a parable-like story which directly communicates its message to its hearers still holds. Nevertheless, the inclusion of the prayer has had the effect of complicating the simple parabolic form which is an additional reason for characterizing the final form of the story with the less precise terminology. The story has been given a different literary structure and another internal dynamic has been set in motion. Jonah no longer serves simply as the reluctant messenger of God to whom the message in ch. 4 is directed. Rather his role has been expanded by fashioning him into a representative figure and thus establishing a link between Israel and the heathen. Of course, it is the complexity of the form within the final shape of the book which has caused the difficulty of interpretation and has afforded genuine warrants for the various critical analyses.

The crucial question now arises as how one is to relate these two different interpretations found in the book. If the above analysis is at all correct, the final form of the story does seek to address the issue of God's salvation being extended to the nations as well as to Israel. Moreover, this redactional stamp has not obliterated the earlier form of the story, but refocused it. In my judgment, the final reworking of the story simply extended the original point. In the 'first edition' the theological point turned on God's right as Creator to override his prophetic word for the sake of his entire creation. The 'second edition' merely amplified the point respecting the whole creation in terms of the nations, but it did not alter the basic creation theology by substituting one of election.

Is it possible to make any further observations as to the historical process lying behind the development of the canonical shape of the story? There is no evidence to suggest that the two levels of the story were separated by a long historical development. Not only is the language of one piece, but the midrashic method of handling the tradition is represented just as much by the reconstructed first stage as by the final form. It seems more likely to suggest that the force which effected a shift in the function of the book derived from the canonical process itself. When the book was collected within a corpus of other sacred literature, the need arose to specify the addressee as the covenant community. Thus the original prophetic problem of unfulfilled prophecy against the nations was expanded. Again, the effect of ordering the book within a larger collection can be seen on the new reading of the significance of Nineveh. To be sure the idiom within the biblical text is neutral and lacks any specific reference to Israel's historical relationship to the Assyrians. But this larger historical dimension is now supplied by the role of the larger canon. Thus, the reader brings to the story a common memory respecting the Ninevites to whom Jonah was sent with a message of repentance, and he has in his canon the book of Nahum!

Finally, the canonical setting of the story in the period of Jeroboam II (II Kings 14), rather than placing it in the post-exilic period, ensures seeing the issue raised by the book as constitutive to the theological relation between Israel and the nations. The issue is not to be historicized and derived from an allegedly post-exilic narrowness of Hellenistic Judaism (*contra* Wolff), but serves as a critical prophetic judgment on Israel in line with the rest of the prophetic witnesses of the Old Testament.

3. Theological and Hermeneutical Implications

(a) By determining that the book of Jonah functions in its canonical context as a parable-like story the older impasse regarding the historicity of the story is by-passed as a theological issue. Because the book serves canonically in the role of an analogy, it is as theologically irrelevant to know its historicity as it is with the Parable of the Good Samaritan. In both instances historical features have been incorporated within the narrative, but this determination does not affect the canonical role which the book plays (*contra* Aalders). This is a judgment respecting the canonical function of Jonah and is not to be generalized into a principle that history is unimportant for the Bible.

(b) The canonical shape of the book of Jonah offers an example of an editorial process which retained intact elements of an earlier interpretation. A subsequent editing of the book shifted the focus, but did not eliminate the earlier level. To the extent to which the earlier interpretation has been retained in the final shape of the book, it continues to offer a genuine canonical witness. In the case of the book of Jonah, the final form did subordinate one interpretation to another and offered a clear guideline as to the primary message. Thus, the two interpretations reflect an inner relationship within the canon and are not to be played off against each other.

(c) The form of the book of Jonah is unique in the Book of the Twelve. The book does not contain the oracles of Jonah, nor is the material biographical in the strict sense. Rather, the authority of the book rests on the prophetic function of the book as bearer of a message. All attempts, therefore, to defend the prophet's reputation – he fled out of love of Israel (Rashi), or he resisted the divine decision from concern over God's glory – miss the purpose of the book within the canon. Such apologetics serve to weaken rather than enhance the truth of the book.

(d) The canonical shape of the book of Jonah resists the attempts of both Jew and Christian to politicize the biblical message. On the one hand, the divine attack on Jonah's resistance is not to be derived from post-exilic narrowness, but is theologically grounded in the nature of God as Creator. On the other hand, the case for seeing Jonah's resistance arising because of the inclusion of the nations is not to be dismissed as a later Christian bias, but is a genuine Old Testament witness directed against a misunderstanding of the election of Israel.

History of Exegesis

Carpzov III, 367–70; *DBS* 4, 1130f.; *DThC* 8, 1498ff.; *EB* 3, 612; *RGG*[3] 3, 855f.; H. W. **Wolff**, *Jona*, BK, 1977, 70–72.

E. **Bickermann**, 'Jonah', *Four Strange Books in the Bible*, New York 1967, 1–49; R. H. **Bowers**, *The Legend of Jonah. Fifty Odd Interpretations of Jonah from the New Testament through the English Renaissance*, The Hague 1971; Y.-M. **Duval**, *Le livre de Jonas dans la littérature chrétienne grecque et latine, sources et influences du commentaire sur Jonas de Saint Jérôme*, 2 vols., Paris 1973; 'Jonas (le livre de)', *DS* 8.2, 1974, 1264–67; R. A. **Edwards**, *The Sign of Jonah in the Theology of the Evangelist and Q*, SBT II.18, 1971; P. **Friedrichsen**, *Kritische Übersicht der verschiedenen Ansichten von dem Buche Jonas*, Leipzig [2]1841; L. **Ginzberg**, *The Legends of the Jews* 4, Philadelphia [6]1954, 239–53; J. **Jeremias**, 'Iōnas', *TWNT* 3, 410–13 = *TDNT* 3, 406–10; J. **Leclercq**, 'Jonas', *DACL* 1.2, 2572–631; A. **Penna**, 'Andrea di S. Vittori: il suo commento a Giona', *Bibl* 36, 1955, 305–31; S. **Poznanski**, 'Targoum Yerouschalmi et son commentaire sur le livre de Jonas', *REJ* 40, 1900, 130–53; K. H. **Rengstorf**, 'Das Jona-"Zeichen"', *TWNT* 7, 231f.=*TDNT* 7, 233f.; E. **Stommel**, 'Zum Problem der frühchristlichen Jonasdarstellungen', *Jahrbuch für Antike und Christentum* 1, Münster 1958, 112–15; F. **Weinreb**, *Das Buch Jonah. Der Sinn des Buches Jonah nach ältesten jüdischen Überlieferung*, Zürich 1970.

XXV

MICAH

Commentaries

C. P. Caspari, 1852
C. F. Keil, BC, 1868
F. Hitzig, H. Steiner, KeH, ⁴1881
J. Wellhausen, ³1898
G. A. Smith, ExB, 1898 (²1928)
A. van Hoonacker, ÉB, 1908
J. M. P. Smith, ICC, 1911
W. Nowack, HKAT, ³1922
G. W. Wade, WC, 1925

E. Sellin, KAT, ²⁻³1929
A. Deissler, SB, 1964
T. H. Robinson, HAT, ³1964
A. Weiser, ATD, ⁵1967
R. Vuilleumier, CAT, 1971
W. Rudolph, KAT², 1975
A. S. van der Woude, POuT, 1976
J. M. Mays, OTL, 1976
L. C. Allen, NICOT, 1976

Bibliography

W. **Beyerlin**, *Die Kulttraditionen Israels in der Verkündigung der Propheten Micah*, FRLANT 72, 1959; A. **Bruno**, *Micah und der Herrscher aus der Vorzeit*, Leipzig 1923; K. **Budde**, 'Das Rätsel von Micha 1', *ZAW* 37, 1917–8, 77–108; 'Micha 2 und 3', *ZAW* 38, 1919–20, 2–22; 'Verfasser und Stelle von Mi. 4,1–4 (Jes. 2,2–4)', *ZDMG* 81, 1927, 152–58; M. **Collin**, 'Recherches sur l'histoire textuelle du prophète Michée', *VT* 21, 1971, 281–97; A. **Condamin**, 'Interpolations ou transpositions accidentelles?', *RB* 11, 1902, 379–87; J. **Coppens**, 'Le cadre littéraire de Michée V, 1–5', *Near Eastern Studies in Honor of W. F. Albright*, Baltimore 1971, 57–62; M. **Crook**, 'The Promise in Micah 5', *JBL* 70, 1951, 313–20; K. **Elliger**, 'Die Heimat des Propheten Micha' (1934)=*KSAT*, Munich 1966, 9ff.; I. H. **Eybers** 'Micah, the Morashthite: The Man and His Message', *OuTWP* 11, 1968, 9–24; G. **Fohrer**, 'Micha 1', *Das ferne und nahe Wort. FS L. Rost*, BZAW 105, 1967, 65–80; V. **Fritz**, 'Das Wort gegen Samaria Mi 1,2–7', *ZAW* 86, 1974, 316–31; A. **George**, 'Le livre de Michée', *DBS* 5, 1952, 1252–63; H. **Gunkel**, 'The Close of Micah: A Prophetical Liturgy', 1924, ET in *What Remains of the Old Testament*, London and New York 1928, 115–49.

E. **Hammershaimb**, 'Einige Hauptgedanken in der Schrift des Propheten Micha', *StTh* 15, 1961, 11–34; J. **Harvey**, 'Le "Rib-Pattern"', réquisitoire prophétique sur la rupture d'Alliance', *Bibl* 43, 1962, 179–96; P. **Haupt**, 'The Book of Micah', *AJSL* 27, 1911, 1–63; J. P. **Hyatt**, 'On the Meaning and Origin of Micah 6:8', *AThR* 34, 1952, 232–39; K. **Jeppesen**, 'New Aspects of Micah Research', *JSOT* 8, 1978, 3–32; Jörg **Jeremias**, 'Die Bedeutung der Gerichtsworte Michas in der Exilszeit', *ZAW* 83, 1971, 330–53; A. S. **Kapelrud**, 'Eschatology in the Book of Micah', *VT* 11, 1961, 392–405; T. **Lescow**, 'Das Geburtsmotiv in den messianischen Weissagungen bei Jesaja und Micha', *ZAW* 79, 1967, 172–207; 'Redaktionsgeschichtliche Analyse von Micha 1–5', *ZAW* 84, 1972, 46–85; 'Redaktionsgeschichtliche Analyse von Micha 6–7', *ZAW* 84, 1972, 182–212; J. **Lindblom**, *Micha literarisch untersucht*, Åbo 1929; J. L. **Mays**, 'The Theological Purpose of the Book of Micah', *Beiträge zur alttestamentliche Theologie*, FS W. *Zimmerli*, Göttingen 1977; E. **Nielsen**, *Oral Tradition*, SBT I.11, 1954, 79–93; W. **Nowack**, 'Bemerkungen über das Buch Micha', *ZAW* 4, 1884, 277–94; B. **Reicke**, 'Liturgical Traditions in Micah 7', *HTR* 60, 1967, 349–68; B. **Renaud**, *Structure et attaches littéraires de Michée IV–V*, Paris 1964; *La Formation du Livre de Michée*, Paris 1977; L. P. **Smith** 'The Book of Micah', *Interp* 6, 1952, 210–27; B. **Stade**, 'Bemerkungen über das Buch Micha', *ZAW* 1, 1881, 161–72; 'Weitere Bemerkungen zu Micha 4.5', *ZAW* 3, 1883, 1–16; 'Micha 1,2–4 und 7,7–20, ein Psalm', *ZAW* 23, 1903, 163–77; H.-J. **Stoebe**, 'Und demütig sein vor deinem Gott', *WuD* 6, 1959, 180–94; H.-M. **Weil**, 'Le chapitre 2 de Michée expliqué par Le Premier Livre des Rois, chapitres 20–22', *RHR* 121, 1940, 146–61; I. **Willi-Plein**, *Vorformen der Schriftexegese innerhalb des Alten Testaments*, BZAW 123, 1971, 70–126, 306–8; J. T. **Willis**, 'A Note on wǎ'ōmar in Micah 3,1', *ZAW* 80, 1968, 50–54; 'The Structure of Micah 3–5 and the Function of Micah 5.9–14 in the Book', *ZAW* 81, 1969, 191–214; 'The Authenticity and Meaning of Micah 5.9–14', *ZAW* 81, 1969, 353–68; 'The Structure of the Book of Micah', *SEA* 34, 1969, 5–42; 'A Reapplied Prophetic Hope Oracle', *SVT* 26, 1974, 64–76; H. W. **Wolff**, 'Wie verstand Micha von Moreschet sein prophetisches Amt?', *SVT* 29, 1978, 403–17; A. S. **van der Woude**, 'Micah in Dispute with the Pseudo-prophets', *VT* 19, 1969, 244–60; 'Deutero-Micha: ein Prophet aus Nord-Israel?', *NedThT* 25, 1971, 365–78; 'Micah IV 1–5: An Instance of the Pseudo-Prophets quoting Isaiah', *Symbolae Biblicae et Mesopotamicae F.M.T. de Liagre Böhl dedicatae*, Leiden 1973, 396–402.

1. Historical Critical Problems

Historical critical research on the book of Micah began with the question of the literary integrity of the book. In the mid-nineteenth century diverse authorship and dating were first suggested by Ewald and others. In 1878 Wellhausen argued that 7.7–20 was post-exilic and akin to Isaiah 40ff. (Bleek's *Einleitung*, [4]1878, 425). However, the crucial essay for the literary critical approach was Stade's famous article of 1881 in which he assigned chs. 4–5 in their entirety to the post-exilic period, thus shattering any lingering tradition of unity. By the beginning of the twentieth century literary critics were generally agreed that only chs. 1–3 could with confidence be regarded as genuine (excepting of course 2.12f.), that chs. 4–5 and 7.7ff. were definitely post-exilic, and that uncertainty over dating remained only in respect to 6.4–7.7 (cf. the succinct review of G. A. Smith, I, 358f. [[2]1928, I, 384], and most recently Renaud, *Formation*).

Once again, the credit for shifting the focus of research in a new direction goes to H. Gunkel. In a brilliant article in 1924 he pointed out that 7.7ff was not oracular material, but was liturgical in form and content. The chapter consisted of psalm-like material and reflected the same fixed forms which he had described for the Psalter. Gunkel's essay served to check the increased fragmentation of the book along the older literary critical lines, but it also focused attention on the fundamental question of how the prophetic material was used by the later Jewish community. Gunkel's form-critical approach was later applied to the whole book of Micah by Lindblom, but with considerably less success.

In recent years other approaches have been adopted for the study of the book which are actually extensions of the earlier literary and form-critical methods. Detailed redactional analyses have been offered by Lescow, Jeremias, Mays, Willi-Plein, van der Woude and Renaud in order to interpret the growth of the book's composition. Although these scholars all agree on a complex history of redaction which passed through many stages, the analyses are so strikingly different that no common conclusions have emerged. Clearly the issue turns on the larger model which one uses. We shall return to a more detailed criticism of several of these attempts.

In addition to these redactional studies there have been several efforts at a structural analysis of the book, particularly with a concern in showing an intentional coherence in the present form of the book (Nielsen, Willis, Mays). Of these various attempts Renaud's study of 1964 ranks as the most extensive study of the structural features of chs. 4–5. Of particular significance is Renaud's attempt to show the effect upon Micah of a post-exilic school which was strongly under the influence of the Isaianic corpus. However, in spite of his close attention to the biblical idiom, his analysis of the structure has been criticized as too subjective. Indeed, in *Formation* Renaud has largely abandoned his earlier methodology in favour of a more standard redactional historical approach.

In sum, few books illustrate as well as does Micah the present crisis in exegetical method. In spite of many good insights and interesting observations of detail, the growing confusion over conflicting theories of composition has increasingly buried the book in academic debris. Needless to say, no general consensus of the book's form or function appears in sight.

2. The Canonical Shape of Micah

Literary structure and historical development

The book of Micah gives every evidence of being arranged in a clear pattern of alternating sections of judgment and salvation. Thus, oracles of judgment occur in 1.2–2.11 followed by salvation in 2.12–13. The same pattern repeats itself twice more: 3.1–12 followed by 4.1–5.4 (EVV 5.5); 6.1–7.7 followed by 7.8–20. The occurrence of the lead word 'hear' (*šim'û*) in 1.2, 3.1, and 6.1 tends to support this analysis (but cf. 3.9). The more usual division of the books into sections 1–3, 4–5 and 6–7 arises clearly from a historical critical evaluation of the history of the book's composition – 2.11f. is eliminated as a misplaced later interpolation – and does not do justice to the present shape of the book.

Recently James Mays (OTL) has offered a different interpretation of the structure which must be closely considered. His method shares the concern that the book's present context should not be dissolved in an effort to relate each passage to a reconstructed historical situation. Mays also argues for a particular theological shaping of the material: 'a persistent intention has been at work to bring the individual units under the control of broader kerygmatic purposes' (3). He divides the book into two major parts, 1.2–5.15 and 6.1–7.20, and finds evidence for this division in the parallel structure. The first part is addressed to a universal audience of all peoples. Yahweh's judgment of Samaria and Jerusalem (1.3–3.12) and his redemption of Zion and Israel (4.1–5.9) serve as a witness to the nations, forcing them to submission (4.1–4) or punishment (5.10–15). The second part of the book is addressed to Israel and portrays her under judgment (6.1–7.6), but also before the salvation of God (7.8–17) through divine forgiveness (7.18–20).

Clearly Mays has brought a fresh perspective to the problem of the book's structure. Still I have difficulty seeing sufficient evidence that the oracles addressed so prominently to Israel in chs. 1–3 are to be read as subordinate to a message to the nations in chs. 4–5. Again, Mays is forced to reinterpret 2.12f. into an oracle of judgment which seems artificial. In sum, I remain unconvinced that the motif of Yahweh's reign over the nations does serve as a 'kerygmatic' focus for ordering chs. 1–5.

Before one attempts to assess the effect of the book's pattern on its canonical interpretation, it is significant to raise the question of historical development. Is it likely that the literary pattern of alternating oracles of judgment and salvation stems from the prophet Micah himself, or does it arise from the editorial process? One's answer may affect how one hears the full canonical text. In my judgment, the pattern shows evidence of being part of a redactional activity, although this observation does not rule out the possibility that the original material may itself have contained oracles of alternating judgment and salvation.

The major reasons for suggesting that the literary pattern is part of an editorial process are as follows:

(a) The links by which the two types of oracle have been joined appear to be literary rather than historical, and the connection which has been established is often quite harsh (cf. especially 2.12f.; 4.1ff.).

(b) The oracles which make up different parts of the pattern seem to stem from very different periods (cf. 4.10ff.; 7.11, etc.) and reflect varying perspectives.

(c) Elements from the pattern reflect the influence from other books which is best explained as arising from a circle of tradents who transmitted the corpus of prophetic tradition.

To what extent can one recover the historical development which lay behind the present redactional pattern? Certainly the extreme difficulty of the task is evident from the history of critical research. Nevertheless, if one could succeed, even to a limited extent, in sketching some of the main lines of the book's redaction, this historical information might aid in interpreting the present shape of the canonical text. Of course, the threat that such information can confuse and mislead the interpreter is also present, but the risk can hardly be avoided within the present context of the discipline.

Redactional critics generally agree that the editing process extended over a considerable period and was not completed until the post-exilic era. If one works with this hypothesis – it seems reasonable enough – the major issue at stake is to determine the most likely redactional model. As we have already seen, the suggestions have differed dramatically. The theory of Lescow that the major redactional force was the liturgical use of the material for a service of lament and a festival of dedication of the temple has not found much support. Similary, Willis' structural theories have been criticized for being too arbitrary and hypothetical. Much more influential has been the analysis proposed by J. Jeremias. He has argued that the re-use of the Micah oracles in the period of the exile – he uses Zimmerli's hypothesis of *'Nachinterpretation'* – resulted in a shift of the addressee (1.5; 2.3f.; 3.4), in a broadening of the indictment beyond the specific historical group (1.5b–7; 5.10–14), and in a readjustment of the temporal form of the original prophecy to refocus the fulfilment (2.3f.; 3.4). Although I do not contest the rationale behind this theory of a text's 'afterlife', I have difficulty being convinced by the evidence presented for the book of Micah. Although I freely admit that there are tensions within the text at numerous places, I do not find that they fall into the schema proposed by Jeremias. The analysis appears to me as over-refined.

Jeremias' work has strongly influenced both Mays (OTL, 24) and Renaud (*Formation*). Indeed, in his second book on Micah Renaud has sought to buttress and further to refine some of Jeremias' conclusions. He has analysed the book's development into three major redactional stages, the most controversial of these being an alleged Deuteronomic level which he patterns after W. H. Schmidt's analysis of Amos. In my judgment, even when there are occasional signs of secondary glossing, the case for a unified redactional layer is very weak. Therefore, in spite of the many detailed contributions in Renaud's second volume, I find his broad analysis less illuminating than his earlier work. Particularly his arguments for posing an anti-Samaritan redaction for transforming 2.12f. to a position following 4.7 appear very tenuous.

Finally, A. van der Woude, in his learned Dutch commentary as well as in several earlier essays, has defended an even more radical redactional theory. He suggests a 'Deutero-Micah' in chs. 6–7 whose writings were later incorporated into Micah's prophecy by a Deuteronomic editor. He also argues that oracles of the pseudo-prophets against whom Micah fought have been erroneously attributed to Micah himself (e.g. 2.12f.; 4.9, 11–13), thus causing the present confusion in chs. 2 and 4. Again, enormous assumptions respecting the transmission and editing of the tradition are involved which strongly affect the analysis.

It is significant to notice, regardless of which editorial hypothesis is used, that the redactional model assumes the written tradition was 'actualized' for a later historical period in Israel's history by a process of updating the material. The major incentive lying behind the editorial process was to adjust the biblical tradition, which was already in some sort of written form, to a different historical need. In my judgment, this assumption which underlies the various redactional models is theoretically far from obvious, and, specifically in terms of Micah, highly misleading.

Rather, I would argue the case that the major force lying behind the redaction of Micah appears to have been the influence exerted upon its editors by the larger corpus of other prophetic material, particularly the oracles of Isaiah. The point is not to deny that later historical events influenced the redactors, but to contest a direct and intentional move on their part to adjust the tradition to each new historical situation. Rather, the editors of Micah sought to understand God's purpose with his people Israel by means of interpreting the growing body of sacred literature. Thus the effect of the changing historical situation was mediated through an interpretation of scripture and was only an indirect influence. The direct force in the shaping process came from one set of traditions upon another. The effect of this process of 'exegesis' within the Bible did not follow any one channel. It occurred in various liturgical settings, through preaching and teaching, and in the study of scripture itself.

Micah tradition and the Isaianic corpus

There is abundant evidence to show that the traditions of Micah were transmitted and reshaped by a circle of editors similar to those who treasured the Isaianic corpus. When one considers that the period of prophetic activity overlapped, that they were geographically close to one another, and, above all, that their messages had so many elements in common – Messiah, remnant, plan of God, etc. – the idea of a common circle of tradents is not unreasonable. The book of Micah shares with 'First Isaiah' a similar theological pattern of judgment and salvation, and to such an extent that it forms the warp and woof of the book. Here the contrast with other prophetic books is striking since elsewhere this alternation in pattern plays only a superficial role (Amos 9; Ezek. 40ff.). Again, a key passage in establishing the pattern of weal and woe appears in both books (Micah 4.1–4 // Isa. 2.1–4). Increasingly a consensus has emerged among critical scholars that this duplication cannot be explained by supposing that one of the prophets borrowed from the other (cf. Renaud, *Formation*, for the arguments). Rather, a common tradition was given a peculiar redactional function within each separate book.

Then again, both books show a similar liturgical influence in their redaction (cf. Isa. 12; 25; 33; Micah 7.8ff.). Of course, a liturgical influence is not totally missing from other of the prophetic books (Amos 4.13; 5.8; 9.5f.; Hab. 3, etc.), but the liturgical material has a particular structure in these two books which has much more in common. Not only is there the common form of a 'prophetic liturgy' (Gunkel), but the redactional role of the liturgy within the structural pattern of the book is similar.

Finally, a detailed study of the formulae and style of the redactional material of both books reveals a common source. Renaud has made a close study of the parallels (*Structure*). His research did not have its proper impact on the field because he failed to distinguish adequately in his first book between the original composition of a prophetic oracle and its subsequent redaction. His earlier claim that Micah 4–5 was composed in its entirety by a redactor is an overstatement and has been subsequently modified. Both the composition of First Isaiah and that of Micah reflect an integrity and independence of one another even when sharing common themes. However, when one focuses on the redactional level, the evidence for a mutual influence from a common circle of editors becomes strong indeed.

The following elements of redactional similarity are particularly to be noted:

(*a*) Both First Isaiah and Micah use the formula 'in that day' (*bayyôm hahû'*) as a major redactional device to link later material (Isa. 7.18ff.; 22.8ff.; Micah 4.6; 5.9; 7.12). Although the formula occurs frequently in the prophetic literature in a general adverbial usage, as Munch has shown (see bibliography to Isaiah), Duhm's original observation (*Jesaja*) of its particular redactional function in First Isaiah is to be sustained. Only in the late post-exilic period did the use of the formula outside this one circle become widespread (Joel 4.18; Zech. 9.16, etc.).

(*b*) The very rare expression 'from now and ever more' (*mē'attāh w'ʿad-'ôlām*) is clearly a liturgical formula which occurs in the Psalter (113.2; 115.18; 121.8, etc.) and again only in the redaction of Isaiah (9.6; 59.21) and Micah (4.7).

(*c*) The expression 'for the mouth of Yahweh has spoken' (*kî-pî yhwh-ṣ'ba'ôt dibbēr*) is another rare expression which is found in a redactional role only in Isa. 1.20; 40.5; 58.14 and in Micah 4.4.

(*d*) The expression 'he (or Yahweh) will reign in Mount Zion' (*malak Yhwh b'har ṣiyyôn*) occurs only twice in the Old Testament and both times in a redactional role (Micah 4.7; Isa. 23.23).

In sum, the evidence is strong that the tradition of Micah was transmitted by the same or a similar circle of tradents as those who were responsible for the editing of parts of the Isaianic corpus. Moreover, the redactional group would appear to have been located in Jerusalem and to have been at work from the beginning of the seventh century throughout the early post-exilic period. Undoubtedly further study of this editorial process could bring even more specificity to the group at work.

The effect of the canonical process on Micah

If we assume that these broadly drawn lines of historical development are generally correct, we can turn to the central problem of assessing the effect of the redaction on the interpretation of Micah's prophecy. Our major criticism of the usual practice of redactional criticism is its failure to take this aspect of the discipline seriously. First of all, Micah's prophecy has been arranged within a sharply defined theological pattern of recurring divine judgment and divine redemption. Moreover, the events which are instrumental in executing both the judgment and the redemption extend far beyond the historical period of the prophet himself. The book of Micah speaks of the Babylonian exile and the return from captivity. This assessment of the nature of the book would imply that the present prophetic collection is not simply recording Micah's original oracles, but has used them along with other material for another purpose. The oracles seek to describe in the prophetic idiom the full plan of God with Israel. The purpose of the book is not to provide sources for the recovery of the 'historical Micah' but rather to incorporate Micah's witness within a larger theological framework. The original proclamation by Micah of judgment and salvation has been extended to bear testimony to the larger intent of God with Israel.

During the time in which the oracles of Micah were being collected and used in some sort of authoritative way (cf. Jer. 26.17ff.) the predicted destruction both of Samaria and of Jerusalem had occurred. Events which originally served as prophecy became past history and now served a new role as an awe-inspiring confirmation of the truth of the prophetic message. However, the canonical shaping of the book did not simply retain these oracles as a past record, but placed them within a framework which supplied a theological interpretation to the meaning of the original oracles. The events assumed a typological dimension within a recurring pattern. The judgment of which Micah spoke was only illustrative of a continuing plan of God. Judgment and salvation for the people of God lay in the future as much as in the past. By placing the original oracles within a conscious pattern, the canonical editors rendered a theological judgment on how Micah's oracles were to be understood by every succeeding generation of Israel.

Secondly, the oracles of Micah have also been given a liturgical stamp within the final canonical shape. This mark has its clearest example in ch. 7. What is its effect on the reading of the book? The liturgical ending again offers a profoundly theological interpretation of how the community of faith understands itself in relation to the prophetic proclamation. The pattern of judgment and salvation does not serve as a timetable of future history, nor does it sketch a *Heilsgeschichte* whose progress can be objectively measured. Rather, the community of faith is assigning its role as the worshipping body, standing in between God's judgment and salvation, and possessed by both memory and anticipation. The liturgical ending of Micah offers a directive to the later community in regard both to its place of standing and its appropriation of the ancient witness.

Thirdly, the present shaping of Micah's prophecy has interpreted the book by placing it within a larger context shared by the prophet Isaiah. This common moulding has the effect that Isaiah serves as a commentary on Micah and *vice versa*. The use of a verbatim passage in such a central position consciously directs the reader to the other collection of prophecy. The two messages are not to be fused since each has been preserved with a distinct shape as a discrete entity. Yet the two are to be heard together for mutual enrichment within the larger corpus of prophecy. The canonical shaping thus emphasizes an affinity which is far closer than that established by belonging to the prophetic division of the Hebrew canon.

3. Theological and Hermeneutical Implications

(*a*) A basic assumption of the historical critical method is that a proper exegesis depends on a correct assessment of the age of various oracles within a book. That this type of historical judgment is necessary for reconstructing the development of a composition cannot be denied. However, this historical enterprise should not be confused with the exegetical task of understanding how a community of faith heard its traditions, and bore witness to their authority in the very process of treasuring them. The study of the book of Micah again illustrates how the concentration on the questions of historical dating proved to be a major deterrent in understanding the book's canonical function. Not only was the larger structure misinterpreted through the application of literary historical criteria, but also the basic theological patterns were distorted by introducing theories of historical development.

(*b*) The redactional process of editing the book of Micah within a theological framework shared by Isaiah points to the effect of a growing sense of a unified prophetic corpus within the canon of scripture. Although there were obviously many historical forces at work which can only be dimly perceived, it seems clear enough that the process of linking blocks of material was not an arbitrary act of harmonization. Rather, the canonical process developed, extended, and broadened a basic affinity which the two prophets shared. Moreover, the liturgical framework indicates that the process of canonization took place in the actual use of the prophetic material. The final canonical shaping reflected a function of the material which was not simply imposed, but which had exerted itself upon the tradents.

(c) Although our study has emphasized the liturgical force at work in the shaping process, the hermeneutical significance of this observation does not necessarily support a continuing liturgical use. An important theological distinction is here at issue. To describe the forces which affected the canonical shape is not to suggest that these forces themselves achieved canonical status. It is not the process which is normative for the later community, but the scriptures which reflect the process. The writings possess a canonical integrity apart from the historical process. Indeed, the canonical shape has frequently either eliminated or subordinated interest in the historical forces at work. To transfer the canonical authority to the historical process is to run counter to the whole intention behind the canonization of scripture. Nevertheless in the case of Micah, the liturgical setting of the book which originally functioned to provide a point-of-standing between judgment and salvation for the worshipping community suggests a stance which is still very compatible for its ongoing liturgical use. Yet the effect of the liturgical shaping does not restrict its future use to any one form of accommodation.

History of Exegesis

DBS 8, 736f.; *DThC* 10, 1667f.; *EB* 4, 891; *RGG*[3] 4, 931.

D. **Barthélemy** and J. T. **Milik**, *Discoveries in the Judaean Desert* I, Oxford and New York 1955, 77f.; C. P. **Caspari**, *Über Micha den Morasthiten und seine prophetische Schrift*, Christiana 1852, 449–58; H. **Englander**, 'Joseph Kara's Commentary on Micah in Relation to Rashi's Commentary', *HUCA* 16, 1941, 157–62; J. T. **Milik**, 'Fragments d'un midrash de Michée dans les manuscrits de Qumrân', *RB* 59, 1952, 412–18.

XXVI

NAHUM

Commentaries

C. F. Keil, BC, 1868
P. Kleinert, ET, LCHS, 1874
F. Hitzig, H. Steiner, KeH, [4]1882
A. B. Davidson, CB, 1896
G. A. Smith, ExB, 1898, (1928[2])
A. van Hoonacker, ÉB, 1908
J. M. P. Smith, ICC, 1911

E. Sellin, KAT, [2-3]1930
W. A. Maier, 1959
H. Lamparter, BAT, 1960
F. Horst, HAT, [3]1964
K. Elliger, ATD, [6]1967
C. A. Keller, CAT, 1971
W. Rudolph, KAT[2], 1975

Bibliography

W. R. **Arnold**, 'The Composition of Nahum 1–2,3', *ZAW* 21, 1901, 225–65; K. J. **Cathcart**, 'Treaty-Curses and the Book of Nahum', *CBQ* 35, 1973, 179–87; D. L. **Christensen**, 'The Acrostic of Nahum Reconsidered', *ZAW* 87, 1975, 17–30; S. J. **De Vries**, 'The Acrostic of Nahum in the Jerusalem Liturgy', *VT* 16, 1966, 476–81; A. **George**, 'Nahum (Le livre de)', *DBS* 6, 291–301; H. **Gunkel**, 'Nahum 1', *ZAW* 13, 1893, 223–44; A. **Haldar**, *Studies in the Book of Nahum*, Uppsala 1946; P. **Haupt**, 'The Book of Nahum', *JBL* 26, 1907, 1–53; P. **Humbert**, 'Essai d'analyse de Nahoum 1,2–2,3', *ZAW* 44, 1926, 266–80; 'Nahoum 2,9', *REJ* 83, 1927, 74–6; 'La vision de Nahoum 2,4–11', *AfO* 5, 1928–9, 14–19; 'Le problème du livre de Nahoum', *RHPhR* 12, 1932, 1–15; Jörg **Jeremias**, *Kultprophetie und Gerichtsverkündigung in der späten Königszeit Israels*, WMANT 35, 1970; C. A. **Keller**, 'Die theologische Bewältigung der geschichtlichen Wirklichkeit in der Prophetie Nahums', *VT* 22, 1972, 399–419; P. **Kleinert**, 'Nahum und der Fall Ninives', *ThStKr* 83, 1910, 501–34; J. L. **Mihelic**, 'The Concept of God in the Book of Nahum', *Interp* 2, 1948, 199–208; H. **Schulz**, *Das Buch Nahum. Eine redaktionskritische Untersuchung*, BZAW 129, 1973; R. **Weiss**, 'A Comparison between the Massoretic and the Qumran texts of Nahum III, 1–11', *RQ* 4, 1963–4, 433–9.

1. Historical Critical Problems

Although the superscription of the book makes no mention of the date of the composition, on the basis of internal and external evidence there is a widespread agreement in setting the date between the destruction of No-Amon (Thebes, 3.8) in 662 and the fall of Nineveh in 612. The major critical issues have turned rather on the problems of the structure of the book and the history of its composition.

The discovery of acrostic elements in the introductory hymn of ch. 1 at the end of the nineteenth century focused much scholarly attention on an attempted reconstruction of the original psalm. Over the years a growing consensus has developed that the present hymn is only a fragment and that it is pointless to seek to reconstruct a full acrostic psalm. However, there remains much debate on dating the psalm and interpreting its role within the book. Gunkel was the first to emphasize the sharp differences between the style and content of the psalm and the prophetic oracles which follow. He felt that the psalm was a later interpolation. More recently the tendency has been to view the psalm as an integral part of the book which has been intentionally structured by the succeeding verses of the chapter. Still it remains hotly contested how to understand the shift from the third person of the hymn to a style which oscillates between threats to the enemy (1.10f., 14; 2.2) and promises to Judah (1.12f.; 2.1–11).

The second major portion of the book (2.4ff.) contains far fewer problems. Although the exact divisions between units vary among the commentators, traditional elements of prophetic oracles have been usually recognized such as the dirge (3.18f.), the taunt (3.8ff.), the judgment oracle (2.14), and the vision (2.3ff.).

Of course, the discussion of the book's structure has been closely connected to the discussion of the larger problems of the history of composition. Scholars such as Humbert and Sellin have argued in different ways for seeing the book of Nahum as a prophetic liturgy which was composed after the fall of Nineveh and which celebrated a New Year's festival. Alleged evidence for the theory is the hymnic material of ch. 1, the different voices of the addressee of ch. 1, and the retrospective perspective of the concluding dirge. Fohrer (*Introduction*) has modified the position but still purports to find two prophetic liturgies which were artfully assembled and played a role in a less closely defined cultic ceremony. In general, this approach has played down the elements of future prophecy in terms of cultic re-enactment after the event, although Fohrer attempts to retain both elements. The cultic interpretation has been sharply rejected by many scholars (Elliger, Rudolph, Jeremias) and shows little signs of winning a majority. Finally, Haldar's somewhat idiosyncratic theory of the book as a political propaganda document which arose among cult prophets about 614, and identified Assyria with mythological figures, has received little support.

Most recently, two new studies by Jörg Jeremias and H. Schulz have attempted fresh redaction-critical analyses of the book. Jeremias' conclusion that the threat against Nineveh was originally directed to Judah has met some sharp rejoinders (cf. Rudolph, Schulz). To what extent exegetical techniques akin to later midrash were being practised at this time, such as are envisioned by Jeremias, remains a moot question. In my judgment, it is also unlikely that Schulz's redactional analysis will make a great impact. He derives the book's composition from the post-exilic period and envisions a redactional intent to reinterpret the exile in final eschatological terminology. Undoubtedly Schulz has seen some important redactional features (e.g. the role of the superscription, the intertwining of promise and threat, etc.), but his overarching schema is highly speculative and assumes a history of composition which strains the imagination.

Finally, the role of Nahum as a form of *Heilsprophet* (ET optimistic prophet?) has played an important role in the literary and theological evaluation of the book. Although expressed somewhat harshly, J. M. P. Smith's characterization of Nahum as 'a representative of the old, narrow and shallow prophetism' (281), is typical of a widespread negative judgment which is frequently contrasted with the 'ethical' notes of Amos and Hosea.

In my opinion, neither the literary nor the theological character of the book in its canonical function has been adequately assessed up to this point.

2. The Canonical Shape of Nahum

The content of the book of Nahum is clearly characterized from the outset in the two titles. The book contains a prophetic vision and it concerns the destruction of Nineveh. One of the immediate implications to be drawn is that any interpretation which overlooks the prophetic oracular nature of the book as addressing the future history of Israel and the world has failed to deal seriously with its canonical role within the Old Testament. For this reason, even if one could show that a cultic ceremony of the post-exilic community played a decisive role in the book's formation – I personally do not believe this possible for Nahum on either form-critical or redactional grounds – such a reconstruction of the book's prehistory could not, in any case, be identified with its final canonical function.

In my judgment, the first key to the canonical understanding of Nahum's prophecy is provided by the role of the introductory psalm of 1.2–8. The psalm offers a theological interpretation of how to understand the oracles of judgment which constitute the main portion of the book. Gunkel's contribution lay in his first drawing attention to the exact idiom of the psalm and thus enabling the interpreter to hear the text with a new precision. A close examination of the psalm itself and the verses which follow in 1.9–2.3 makes it clear that the original psalm has been intentionally reworked, expanded, and reinterpreted. Thus vv. 2b–3a have disregarded the poetic form of the original acrostic psalm to develop the theological role of the psalm in its new context. Likewise the implications of the divine claims voiced in the psalm are spelled out in the second half of the chapter in the direct addressing of the two historical entities, Assyria and Judah.

In the first place, the destruction of Nineveh is now explicitly derived from the nature of God – 'a jealous God' ... 'keeping wrath for the enemies', 'a stronghold in the evil day' – who claims dominion over the world. From a canonical perspective the threat against Nineveh does not, therefore, stem from the personal hatred of its Jewish author against Assyria, nor is it evoked by some particular historical event of the seventh century such as the death of Ashurbanipal in 630. Rather, the biblical author uses the psalm to establish the theological context for the prophecy of Nahum. What nation can withstand the God who overcame the primordial chaos? Moreover, the effect of the psalm is to subordinate the particularity of Nineveh's claim of power to the universal claims of God. Although the prophetic oracles of chs. 2 and 3 retain all the sharp historical individuality of the seventh century, the redactional framework provided by the psalm reduces Nineveh's role to that of an illustration of divine power against human evil and nationalistic arrogance. The canonical use of the psalm has relativized the historical particularity of Nineveh's destruction by viewing it as a type of a larger and recurring phenomenon in history against which God exercises his eternal power and judgment.

Secondly, the nature of the divine judgment against such evil is illuminated by the intertwining of oracles of woe and weal within the succeeding verses. It can be debated to what extent the particular contours of the passage reflect a cultic pattern from an early stage of composition, or whether the contrast of addressee is a literary feature of a final editor. Moreover, even the issue of whether the present shape derives from an intentional patterning or reflects elements of accidental dislocations within the final form of the text cannot be absolutely settled.

However, in my judgment, a strong case can be made for a conscious redactional shaping of 1.9–2.3. These latter verses pick up the contrast within the psalm between the enemy and those seeking God's protection, and develop the polarity. However, even if the present form of the Hebrew text – the issue is no different in the Greek – derived from unknown causes of dislocation and even textual corruption, the effect of the contrasting themes of ch. 1 appear to have been assigned a canonical function within the whole book. In sum, there is no good evidence, either textual or literary, for removing the tension between the addressees by reconstructing the passage into a consistent oracle of salvation (*contra* Rudolph).

In sum, the present intertwining of oracles of judgment and salvation interprets these two effects of divine intervention as being part of the one event. The word of consolation for Judah is not a corollary of Nahum's nationalism, nor does it issue from a particular prophetic office. Rather, it stems from a divine claim which encompasses both elements within the one theological purpose.

Thirdly, the psalm in ch. 1 functions to transform the visions of Nahum which foretold the historical destruction of Nineveh into an eschatological prophecy of the end time. This observation is not to suggest that the original oracles in chs. 2 and 3 were totally devoid of eschatological elements (cf. 2.11), but certainly the eschatological dimension has been greatly intensified by its editing (cf. Schulz). This interpretative move has been achieved, above all, by the linking of Nineveh's destruction to the nature of Yahweh whose creative power spans the beginning (1.4) and the end (1.8f.) of creation. However, the repeated reference to 'no more' (1.12b, 14a; 2.1b, 14; cf. 1.9b) contrasts the prior examples of divine intervention with the ultimate encounter. In its present canonical shape, the book of Nahum confirms the promise of divine justice to suffering Israel, whether suffering from the domination of Assyria, Babylon, or Rome.

Finally, the concluding dirge serves the canonical editor as a means of confirming the absolute certainty of the prophecy. To use it as evidence for fixing a post-exilic date completely overlooks its canonical function. The change of tone to timeless resignation also serves as a literary device, halting the feverish activity of the fall of the city and pointing back to the inexorable character of the divine purpose with Nineveh to which the initial psalm had testified.

3. Theological and Hermeneutical Implications

(a) The canonical process of actualizing the prophecy of Nahum to function as scripture was not achieved by updating the material to match the new problems of the post-exilic age, nor was it accomplished by means of a cultic dramatization by successive generations of Jews. Rather, the original prophecies were placed within an interpretative framework which provided a theological appropriation of Nahum's original message. This shaping did not require a dehistoricizing of the time-conditioned oracles. Indeed, they remained virtually untouched in their particularity, but a new role was assigned the oracles. They now functioned as a dramatic illustration of the final, eschatological triumph of God over all his adversaries. From this testimony within scripture each generation of suffering Israel derived its hope.

(b) The usual theological criticism directed toward Nahum's message is misplaced when it grounds its disparagement of features within Nahum's personality, office, or religious perspective. However, the significance of analysing the canonical process lies in showing that the inner theological reworking of material did not turn on these issues, but the book was assigned its role to address a different set of issues. To criticize Nahum from the perspective of Amos' theology fails to reckon seriously with the function of a collection of writings which together exercised its authority upon a community of faith.

History of Exegesis

Carpzov III, 395f.; H. Höpfl, *Introductio specialis in libros Veteris Testamenti*, [5]1946, 520f.; *RGG*[3] 4, 1298.

J. M. **Allegro**, 'Further Light', *JBL* 75, 1956, 90–93; 'More Unpublished Pieces of a Qumran Commentary on Nahum (4Qp Nah)', *JSS* 7, 1962, 304–8; A. **George**, 'Nahum: L'influence ultérieure sur le judaïsme', *DBS* 6, 299f.; W. **Windfuhr**, *Der Kommentar des David Kimchi zum Propheten Nahum*, Giessen 1927.

XXVII

HABAKKUK

Commentaries

F. Delitzsch, 1843
C. F. Keil, BC, 1868
P. Kleinert, ET, LCHS, 1874
A. B. Davidson, CB, 1896
G. A. Smith, ExB, 1898, (²1928)
K. Marti, KHC, 1904
A. van Hoonacker, ÉB, 1908
W. H. Ward, ICC, 1911

E. Sellin, KAT, ²⁻³1930
J. H. Eaton, TB, 1961
F. Horst, HAT, ³1964
M. Delcor, SB, 1964
K. Elliger, ATD, ⁶1967
C. A. Keller, CAT, 1971
W. Rudolph, HAT², 1975

Bibliography

W. F. **Albright**, 'The Psalm of Habakkuk', *Studies in Old Testament Prophecy, FS T. H. Robinson*, ed. H. H. Rowley, Edinburgh and New York 1950, 1–18; W. H. **Brownlee**, 'The Placarded Revelation of Habakkuk', *JBL* 82, 1963, 319–25; 'The Composition of Habakkuk', *Hommages à André Dupont-Sommer*, Paris 1971, 255–75; K. **Budde**, 'Die Bücher Habakuk und Zephanja', *ThStKr* 66, 1893, 383–93; 'Habakuk', *ZDMG* 84, 1930, 139–47; W. W. **Cannon**, 'The Integrity of Habakkuk 1–2', *ZAW* 43, 1925, 62–90; E. **Cothenet**, 'Habacuc', *DBS* 8, 791–811; B. **Duhm**, *Das Buch Habakuk*, Tübingen 1906; J. H. **Eaton**, 'The Origin and Meaning of Habakkuk 3', *ZAW* 76, 1964, 144–71; J. A. **Emerton**, 'The Textual and Linguistic Problems of Habakkuk II.4–5', *JTS* NS 28, 1977, 1–18; Donald E. **Gowan**, *The Triumph of Faith in Habakkuk*, Atlanta 1976; M. J. **Gruenthaner**, 'Chaldeans or Macedonians?', *Bibl* 8, 1927, 129–60, 257–89; P. **Humbert**, *Problèmes du livre d'Habacuc*, Neuchâtel 1944; W. A. **Irwin**, 'The Mythological Background of Habakkuk Chapter 3', *JNES* 15, 1956, 47–50; Jörg **Jeremias**, *Theophanie*, WMANT 10, 1965; *Kultprophetie und Gerichtsverkündigung in der späten Königszeit Israels*, WMANT 35, 1969, 11ff.; P. **Jöcken**, *Das Buch Habakuk*, BBB 48, 1977.

C. A. **Keller**, 'Die Eigenart des Propheten Habakuks', *ZAW* 85, 1973

156–67; B. **Margulis**, 'The Psalm of Habakkuk: A Reconstruction and Interpretation', *ZAW* 82, 1970, 409–22; S. **Mowinckel**, 'Zum Psalm des Habukuk', *TZ* 9, 1953, 1–23; E. **Nielsen**, 'The Righteous and the Wicked in Habaqquq', *StTh* 6, 1953, 54–78; J. W. **Rothstein**, 'Über Habakkuk, Kap. 1 und 2', *ThStKr* 67, 1894, 51–85; H. **Schmidt**, 'Ein Psalm im Buche Habukuk', *ZAW* 62, 1950, 52–63; S. **Schreiner**, 'Erwägungen zum Text von Hab. 2.,4–5', *ZAW* 86, 1974, 538–42; B. **Stade**, 'Habakuk', *ZAW* 4, 1884, 154–9; W. **Staerk**, 'Zu Habakuk 1,5–11: Geschichte oder Mythos?', *ZAW* 51, 1933, 1–29; M. **Stenzel**, 'Habakuk 2,1–4.5a', *Bibl* 33, 1952, 506–10; 'Habakkuk II, 15–16, *VT* 3, 1953, 97–9; C. C. **Torrey**, 'The Prophecy of Habakkuk', *Jewish Studies in Memory of G. A. Kohut*, New York 1935, 565–82; W. **Vischer**, *Der Prophet Habakuk*, BSt 19, 1958; H. H. **Walker**, N. W. **Lund**, 'The Literary Structure of the Book of Habakkuk', *JBL* 53, 1934, 355–70; A. S. **van der Woude**, ' "Der Gerechte wird durch seine Treue leben". Erwägungen zu Habakuk 2:4f', *Studia Biblica et Semitica T.C. Vriezen dedicata*, Wageningen 1966, 367–75; J. **Ziegler**, 'Konjektur oder überlieferte Lesart? Zu Hab. 2,5', *Bibl* 33, 1952, 366–70.

1. Historical Critical Problems

In spite of the brevity of this book the extreme difficulty of its interpretation is reflected in the wide divergence of scholarly opinion which has persisted (cf. Jöcken for an exhaustive survey). Surprisingly enough, it is not the structure of the book which has posed the major problem. In this regard there is a rather wide modern consensus in describing the various parts of the book. The first section (1.2–2. 4[5]) constitutes a unity made up of a complaint (1.2–4), a divine response (5–11), a second complaint (12–17), and a divine answer (2.1–4). There then follows a series of woe oracles (2.6–20), and a concluding psalm in ch. 3. The two chief areas of continuing debate regarding the structure focus on whether verses 2.4f. actually form the 'vision' which the prophet was commanded to write, and whether the series of woe oracles begins in 2.6 or earlier. Unfortunately, the decision is hampered by the difficult textual problems in these verses (cf. Emerton).

The basic critical problem of the book focuses on determining the historical reference of the oracles and their dating. The problem arises immediately in the first complaint (1.2–4). Who are the wicked of v. 4 who threaten justice and evoke the prophetic complaint? The most natural explanation would be to see the source of the evil as arising from within Israel which Habakkuk attacks in the classic prophetic rhetoric. Then the divine response in 1.5–11 announces the punishment of the evil within the nation by means of the Babylonians. Subsequently, in the second complaint the Babylonians themselves become the major source of the oppression, evoking the prophet's query regarding the justice of God's activity in human history. However, there are several difficulties with this common interpretation which refers the wickedness to the internal affairs of the nations. First of all, the coming of the Babylonians in vv. 5–6 is predicted as something new, but in vv. 7–11 their activity is already fully known. Indeed 2.17 implies a long history of pillage under which Judah suffered. Secondly, if the prophecy in vv. 5ff. is to be interpreted as a prophetic foretelling of future events, it would have to precede the events of 605 BC, in which the Babylon's ascendancy over Egypt becomes obvious to all. However, it is difficult to maintain this same pre-exilic dating for the rest of the book which disregards the internal evil of Israel and focuses completely on the destruction of the nations.

In the light of these problems, an alternative interpretation argues for seeing an external threat of outside oppression as the object of the prophet's complaint in 1.1–4. Since the Babylonians are then announced as the agent by whom the punishment is executed, the outside threat can only be identified with the Assyrians. The advantage of this approach is that it seems to allow a consistent historical dating of the oracles within Israel's history as Assyria's hegemony was replaced by Babylon's. Once again, there are some difficulties. First, it seems strange to refer the wickedness of 1.1–4 to an external force when the idiom is the traditional prophetic rhetoric for attacking Israel, e.g. 'the law is slacked and justice never goes forth'. Again, the traditional prophetic linkage of Israel's captivity under the Babylonians with a period of disobedience to the covenant is fully lost if an outside nation is made the subject of the wickedness. Finally, there is no explicit mention of Assyria anywhere else in the book, rather the whole weight falls on Babylon. To identify Assyria in 1.1–4 is to find the key to the book's interpretation by means of a logical, but fragile historical deduction.

In an effort to escape the horns of this dilemma several alternate proposals have been suggested which depend upon a critical ploy. Budde's classic literary critical approach transferred 1.5–11 after

2.4 and read 1–4, 12–17 as a consistent description of Assyrian oppression. However, the suggestion has obviously cut the Gordian knot rather than untying it. Another typical move sought to introduce a factor of historical development and set the oracles of chs. 1 and 2 at different periods within the span from 612–587 (cf. Driver, *Introduction*). However, solid literary evidence for seeing a process at work is lacking. Again, Duhm's well-known theory sought to resolve the tension by placing the entire book in the period of Alexander the Great, emending the text of 1.4 to read 'Kittim'. Finally, Staerk sought to dehistoricize the passage by interpreting the language of 1.5ff. as stereotyped, mythopoetic language associated with the enemy from the north which lacked any specific historical referent. However, I think it fair to say that none of these various interpretative moves has been judged by a consensus as convincing.

More recent scholarship has moved in a different direction in an attempt to resolve the problem. Generally a literary unity of the book has been defended, particularly among scholars such as Sellin and Humbert, who derived this unity from a cultic function of the book. Their approach went beyond simply recognizing liturgical material within the book such as in ch. 3, but portrayed Habakkuk as a cultic prophet whose role within a ritual accounted for the particular fusion of elements of complaint, response, vision, and theophany.

Another approach for defending the present unity of the book arose from a redaction-critical analysis which posited a consistent reworking of old material from the perspective of an exilic or postexilic editor. Thus both Elliger and Jeremias argue that the original function of many oracles, especially 2.6ff., had a different referent and the oracles were only secondarily edited to address the crisis of the exile. Evidence of a redaction of older material is also seen by Kaiser and Galling in allegedly secondary expansions such as 2.14, 18–20; 3.17–19, etc.

In my judgment, the genuine contribution of this history of scholarship has been to point out a variety of difficult problems which, when once seen, prevent all efforts at glossing over homiletically. However, I do not feel that the canonical shaping of this book has been adequately understood nor the theological dynamic correctly interpreted.

2. The Canonical Shape of Habakkuk

The structure of the book

One of the first keys in discerning the canonical shape is to be found in the manner by which traditional forms of speech, both psalmodic and prophetic, have been reworked to form a unified larger composition. Within 1.2–2.4 the traditional complaint psalm, followed by a divine response, is clearly reflected. But within the sequence of Habakkuk there have been several important alterations. First, the usual *Heilsorakel*, which is offered as a word of divine comfort in response to a complaint, has been turned on its head. 1.5–11 does not offer the usual assurance but rather announces an attack by a cruel nation which will set Israel's wickedness right by a devastating judgment. This move then allows a second complaint (12ff.) to expand and intensify the complaint which once again results in a new divine answer forming the climax of the unit. In sum, the traditional individual parts of oral speech have been fashioned into a larger literary composition. Although one cannot be fully sure of the original motivation behind the formation of this larger unit, the effect on reading the book is significant.

Secondly, the material has been placed within an autobiographical framework. The initial superscription designated Habakkuk as the prophet who received the revelation. Chapter 2.1 introduces the first person pronoun in a narrative style which describes the prophet's reception of the oracle. The traditional complaint and answer sequence is thus integrally tied to the personal experience of the prophet. The full significance of this move will be seen in its effect on ch. 3.

Chapter 3 is introduced by a title and concluded with a type of colophon which would seem to indicate an independent existence of this poem at some stage in its prehistory. However, it has been reworked into the book so skilfully as to form again a unified section which picks up and completes earlier themes by use of a complementary vocabulary. The main portion of the psalm (3.3–15) has the traditional form of the hymn with God being addressed in the familiar style which fluctuates between the third and second personal pronouns. The present form of the psalm has been expanded at both the beginning and the end with a first person autobiographical style which ties closely to 2.1ff. Chapter 3 now functions as a response of the prophet to the oracle of ch. 2. To suggest with Fohrer that ch. 3 actually serves the role of replacing the missing vision of ch. 2 is, in my judgment, badly to misunderstand its present role and to introduce unnecessary confusion.

Then again, one can see a reshaping of earlier traditional forms in the series of woe oracles of 2.6ff. Although it is possible at some earlier period in the material's prehistory that the oracles functioned in a different capacity (so Jeremias), the role of the oracles in the present composition has been clearly defined by means of a superscription in v. 6 and they have no independent life apart from the setting of the title. The woe oracles are attributed to the nations (2.6) and directed against the Babylonians on whom the full weight of divine judgment now falls. Moreover, the expansions within the oracles seem to reflect the influence of ch. 3 by introducing a strongly eschatological dimension (2.14) and by contrasting the impotence of idols (2.18f.) with the power of Yahweh, the description of which immediately follows.

Although the book of Habakkuk is filled with liturgical material, in my judgment, the present shape of the composition is not to be attributed to the influence of the cult. The autobiographical shaping moves in quite the opposite direction. The cultic influence is to be assigned a role in an earlier stage of development in providing traditional forms, but not in constructing the final literary composition.

A theological interpretation of history

The previous discussion of the difficulty which the critical method had encountered in establishing a consistent historical setting and date for chs. 1 and 2 touches on a crucial issue of canonical shaping. The present form of the book appears to reflect a historical situation before the rise of the Babylonians which focuses on Israel's disobedience, but at the same time it reflects a period subsequent at least to the first exile (597), and probably also to the second (587), which concentrates on the coming destruction of this enemy.

The careful literary construction of the book as a whole speaks against the suggestion that this tension has arisen accidentally. There would have been many ways in which to have resolved the problem if the biblical editor had so wished. Rather, it seems more likely that the final editor has purposefully arranged his material for a specific effect. First of all, the author has arranged the materials of chs. 1–2 in such a way as to disregard the complexities of the original historical setting of these oracles. The changing historical situation of the ancient Near East between 605 and 587 is not carefully registered. Rather, the precise historical background of the original oracles has been sacrificed to a new theological perspective which views human history from the divine perspective. The prophet learns that both the punishment of disobedient Israel by means of the Babylonians, and the subsequent destruction of that arrogant nation, belong to the one consistent purpose of God. The canonical shaping has thus condensed temporal differences of human history into a larger theological pattern.

However, it is crucial in understanding the special contours of Habakkuk to trace more precisely the new theological shaping. The historical differences in Israel's history have been condensed, but not in such a way as to substitute a timeless theological abstraction. Instead, the prophet is made to view human history from the perspective of a divine history, a *Heilsgeschichte*, in which temporal differences are still maintained. The prophet stands in the period before the end (2.3), and suffers with Israel under the divine judgment (3.17ff.). He is taught to await the end even though it seems slow in coming (2.3). The crucial role of ch. 3 is to ground this *Heilsgeschichte* in the nature of God himself. The historical perspective from which the prophet now views world events is thoroughly eschatological. From the perspective of the God whose work both begins and ends history, human events are measured in terms of judgment and redemption.

Nevertheless, there is a crucial point which links the course of human history with the divine will. It is revealed to the prophet in the gnomic form of an oracle in 2.4f. Righteousness is not judged by human capacity to understand the mind of God in world history, but rather in a faithful response of obedience which lives in God's promise. The prophet's testimony (3.18f.) witnesses to this faith which rejoices in God's salvation and awaits the end in spite of a human situation which oppresses the people of God (3.17). When viewed through the categories of redactional history, the book of Habakkuk may well reflect a literary layer of post-exilic material. But from a canonical perspective both earlier and later levels of literary development have been reshaped into a consistent and new theological pattern.

Habakkuk and Nahum compared

Perhaps it will help in sharpening the profile of Habakkuk's canonical shaping to contrast it with the book of Nahum which shares some similar historical and literary features. In both books the canonical process extended over a period of time, and signs of an original function of the oracles different from the later canonical one can still be discerned. In both cases the older material was assigned a new role by a final redactional stamp which fashioned earlier parts into a literary unity. Again, there is a similarity in the important interpretative role which a psalm had in providing a framework by which to refocus the older material. However, in Nahum the psalm introduced the book, in Habakkuk it concluded it. Moreover, the canonical process was more complex in Habakkuk and the redactional reworking of such a diversity of earlier forms required a much more thorough shaping of each section.

Although the theological understanding of God and his eschatological purpose for the world is similar in both psalms, the final effect of the canonical shaping of the two books does vary considerably. In Nahum the reader begins with the theocentric perspective of the hymn and secondarily derives the meaning of human events from the divine purpose. In Habakkuk the order is reversed. The reader begins with the problems of human history and only subsequently are they resolved in the light of a divine oracle. In Nahum the historical particularity of Nineveh's destruction is maintained and used to illustrate the divine plan. In Habakkuk the historical sequence is replaced by a new theological pattern of redemptive history which blurs the original historical settings to make its theological point.

3. Theological and Hermeneutical Implications

(a) The frequent assumption of the historical critical method that the correct interpretation of a biblical text depends upon the critic's ability to establish a time-frame for its historical background breaks down in the case of Habakkuk. The danger is acute that a doctrinaire application of historical criticism not only fails to find an access into the heart of the book, but by raising a series of wrong questions it effectively blocks true insight. The task of biblical interpretation is a far more subtle enterprise. Of course, in this endeavour the critical study of Habakkuk can play a useful role by pointing out the historical and literary tensions within the text and by resisting easy psychological harmonization. Yet the key to Habakkuk's canonical role lies in understanding rather than resolving these very tensions.

(b) The theological message of Habakkuk has been actualized in scripture for later generations in several different ways. In the autobiographical style of the confession the prophet himself serves as an example of a faithful response of one person living between the promise of the end and its arrival. The timeless quality of the gnomic form of the oracle in 2.4 also allows a flexibility in addressing both the individual and the entire community with the call of faith (note the plural in 1.5 and 3.16).

(c) The book of Habakkuk has been reworked in a way similar to Nahum to serve a particular canonical rule. The shaping process often involves a new theological focus which eliminates an original historical role. Extreme caution must be exercised in criticizing the scope of a prophet's message, e.g. he did not preach repentance to his own people, which disregards the particular role assigned the book within the canon.

History of Exegesis

Carpzov III, 411f.; *DThC* 6, 2010; *RGG*³ 3, 4.

A. J. **Baumgartner**, *Le prophète Habakuk. Introduction critique et exégése avec examan spécial des commentaires rabbiniques, du Talmud et de la Tradition*, Leipzig 1885; W. H. **Brownlee**, *The Text of Habakkuk in the Ancient Commentary from Qumran*, JBL Monograph Series 11, 1959; 'The Habakkuk Midrash and the Targum of Jonathan', *JJS* 7, 1956, 169–86; M. **Burrows**, *The Dead Sea Scrolls of St Mark's Monastery* I, New Haven 1950; S. **Coleman**, 'The Dialogue of Habakkuk in Rabbinic Doctrine', *Abr Nahrain* 5, Leiden 1964–5, 57–85; E. **Cothenet**, 'Habacuc VIII. Influence d'Habacuc', *DBS* 8, 806–11; K. **Elliger**, *Studien zum Habakuk-Kommentar vom Toten Meer*, Tübingen 1953; A. **Feuillet**, 'La citation d'Habacuc II, 4 et les premiers chapitres de l'épître aux Romans', *NTS* 4, 1959–60, 52–80; P. **Jöcken**, *Das Buch Habakuk*, BBB 48, 1977; J. A. **Sanders**, 'Habakkuk in Qumran, Paul and the Old Testament', *JR* 38, 1959, 232–44; A. **Strobel**, *Untersuchungen zum eschatologischen Verzögerungsproblem auf Grund der spätjüdisch- urchristlichen Geschichte von Habakuk 2, 2ff.*, Supplements to *Novum Testamentum* 2, Leiden 1964; J. **Ziegler**, 'Ochs und Esel in der Krippe. Biblisch-patristische Erwägungen zu Jes 1, 3 und Hab 3,2 (LXX)', *Münchener Theologische Zeitschrift* 3, Munich 1952, 385–402.

XXVIII

ZEPHANIAH

Commentaries

C. F. Keil, BC, 1868
P. Kleinert, ET, LCHS, 1874
F. Hitzig, H. Steiner, KeH, ⁴1881
A. B. Davidson, CB, 1896
G. A. Smith, ExB, 1898 (²1928)
K. Marti, KHC, 1904
S. R. Driver, CeB, 1906
A. van Hoonacker, ÉB, 1908
J. M. P. Smith, ICC, 1911

G. G. V. Stonehouse, WC, 1929
E. Sellin, KAT, ²⁻³1930
A. George, JB, ²1959
J. Eaton, TB, 1961
F. Horst, HAT, ³1964
K. Elliger, ATD, ⁶1967
C. A. Keller, CAT, 1971
W. Rudolph, KAT², 1975

Bibliography

M. **Bič**, *Trois prophètes dans un temps de ténèbres: Sophonie-Nahoum-Habaquq*, Paris 1968, 39–42, 51–73; H. **Cazelles**, 'Sophonie, Jérémie et les Scythes en Palestine', *RB* 74, 1964, 24–44; C. H. **Cornill**, 'Die Prophetie Zephanjas', *ThStKr* 89, 1916, 297–332; F. C. **Fensham**, 'Zephaniah, Book of', *IDB Suppl*, 983f.; G. **Gerleman**, *Zephania textkritisch und literarisch untersucht*, Lund 1942; H. **Gese**, 'Zephanjabuch', *RGG³* 6, 1901f.; J. P. **Hyatt**, 'The Date and Background of Zephaniah', *JNES* 7, 1948, 25–29; A. S. **Kapelrud**, *The Message of the Prophet Zephaniah: Morphology and Ideas*, Oslo 1975; G. **Langohr**, *Le Livre de Sophonie et la critique d'Authenticité*, Analecta Lovaniensia Biblica et Orientalia II.17, Louvain 1976; L. **Sabottka**, *Zephanja. Versuch einer Neuübersetzung mit philologischem Kommentar*, Rome 1972; F. **Schwally**, 'Das Buch Ssefanjâ, eine historisch-kritische Untersuchung', *ZAW* 10, 1890, 165–240; L. P. **Smith** and E. R. **Lacheman**, 'The Authorship of Zephaniah', *JNES* 9, 1950, 137–42; W. **Staerk**, *Das Assyrische Weltreich im Urteil der Propheten*, Göttingen 1908, 165–79; D. L. **Williams**, 'The Date of Zephaniah', *JBL* 82, 1963, 77–88.

1. Historical Critical Problems

In spite of some earlier attempts to contest the historical setting of the book which is offered in the book's superscription (Hyatt, L. P. Smith and Lacheman), there is a wide agreement among modern scholars in accepting the period of Josiah's reign (639–609). There remains some disagreement as to the exact period within his reign. Generally the argument for the period before the reform in 621 has gained acceptance in the light of the description of the religious abuses in ch. 1. However, a few scholars have suggested a somewhat later period on the basis of the phrase 'remnant of Baal', holding that the reform had already begun. The issue is not of great importance.

There is also general agreement on the structure of the book. The material falls into a familiar tripartite pattern: threats against Judah (1.2–2.3), threats against the nations (2.4–3.8), and promises (3.9–20). In 3.1ff. an original threat against Jerusalem has been expanded to bring the oracle within the orbit of the nations. Of course, there remains some disagreement on the detailed divisions, especially regarding ch. 3, as a comparison between Elliger and Rudolph will demonstrate. The unusually lengthy genealogy of the superscription has evoked some interest, but the message of the book seems unaffected regardless of the identification of Hezekiah.

The major critical problem of the book turns on the issue of the integrity of the oracles. A broad consensus among critical scholars holds that the present form of the book reflects a layer of genuine, late pre-exilic oracles to which has been attached a layer of post-exilic material. The earlier literary critical terminology of 'non-genuine' passages has been usually replaced by reference to 'primary' and 'secondary' material. The reasons for this judgment focuses on an allegedly post-exilic perspective in 3.4ff., the language and concepts akin to Ezekiel and Second Isaiah, and an eschatological description of a universal disaster which borders on the apocalyptic. Usually signs of this post-exilic redaction are found in 3.9–14 and 2.7, 8, 9a, 10–11, although some commentators such as Driver and Rudolph – rightly in my judgment – resist the move to characterize all oracles of promise as secondary and post-exilic.

2. The Canonical Shape of Zephaniah

There are several clear indications that the material comprising the book has undergone a period of development before reaching its present form. Recent redactional study has been helpful in identifying different layers within the book, but, in my judgment, has failed to relate the book's prehistory to the canonical process.

The present form of the book has selected and collected a variety of oracles which reflect the traditional forms of prophetic speech. The original form of the invective-threat (3.1–8), oracles against foreign nations (2.4–15), and the promise (3.9–13) has been preserved from an early oral stage, even if in somewhat altered state. However, there are signs pointing to an editorial activity which goes beyond the mere collecting of individual oracles. As most recent commentators agree, ch. 1 is comprised of many parts of original oracles which have now been formed into a larger literary unit around the subject of the 'day of Yahweh'. Rudolph designates it a 'kerygmatic unit'. Moreover, by connecting the woe oracles of 2.4ff. integrally with the preceding oracles (note the *kî* of v. 4) the level of eschatological intensity in the oracles against the nations has been raised appreciably and they have been drawn within the orbit of the one great divine event. Finally, the promise of salvation in 3.8ff. has been placed within a traditional pattern which has the oracles of promise following upon threat and concluding the book. In my judgment, it seems very likely that the oracle of promise belongs to an early level in the development, and should not be dismissed as a late and foreign accretion. The signs of two different layers within the passage would argue against seeing the whole passage (3.9–20) as post-exilic.

In addition to these early stages through which the book has developed, the final shape of Zephaniah appears to bear the stamp of a post-exilic redaction. In the first place, the oracle of salvation in ch. 3 has been expanded in the rhetoric of the return of the exiles (3.20). The effect of the post-exilic theology of the remnant has also left its impress on the oracles against the nations (2.7, 8, 9), and the destruction of the enemy is contrasted with the possession of the land by those righteous who survived the judgment. Finally, and a most important alteration in the structure of the book, the nations have been assigned a new role in the promise of God which breaks out of their traditional role as mere recipients of divine judgment. 2.11 first introduces a new note by describing the conversion of the nations, but in 3.9f. the new period of promised salvation actually begins with the conversion of the nations which precedes the promise to Israel. (Elliger's emendation of 3.9 must be rejected.) The universalism of the threatened judgment is closely paralleled by a universal redemption.

In reviewing the history of the book's composition, it is important to observe that crucial canonical shaping occurred both in the early and later periods of the book's growth. In ch. 1 early prophetic oracles have been selected, ordered, and condensed to form a compendium of teaching on the topic of the 'day of Yahweh'. Not only has the chapter retained a dominant theocentric perspective by its use of the first person of the divine speech, but it offers the basic theological starting point from which to understand the movement of the entire book. Once the message focuses on the eschatological intervention of God on his day of reckoning, it belongs to the logic of prophetic theology to include within this event both the judgment against Israel and the nations. Moreover, if one begins with a theology of God in terms of his eschatological work, the move to include the oracles of promise as an essential part of the selfsame event follows easily. The effect of the canonical process has been to restructure the prophetic material within a theological understanding of the nature of God and his work. For this reason Martin Bucer (*In Sophoniam enarrationes*, 1554) has rightly designated the book as a 'compendium' of prophetic teaching.

The crucial point to be made is that in the canonical process material has been organized about a theological centre. The 'day of Yahweh' theme includes a word of judgment and promise which is directed to Israel and the nations. Because of this overriding eschatological perspective, temporal differences have been transcended. The misunderstanding in the usual application of the historical critical method arises from assuming that each prophetic passage must be interpreted from a specific historical setting. When the canonical process has disregarded historical differences and organized the material theologically, the effect of the critical approach is to fragment the book into various editions and thus misunderstand the total witness. Indeed, the historical distinction between the pre- and post-exilic passages of Zephaniah can be highly misleading when disconnected from its canonical function. However, the inner logic of the book is clear once the theocentric starting point of the book is recognized.

The major effect on the understanding of the book arising from the post-exilic additions lies in delineating more precisely the result of the divine intervention among the nations (2.9ff.), and in painting the promise of future salvation in the specific colours of the exilic period. However, these final redactional expansions only continued a use of the material which had already received its decisive canonical role at a prior stage. The post-exilic redaction, when viewed from its effect on the canonical text, was not an attempt to make older material relevant by tying it to the exile, but rather the reverse. It gave the exile its true meaning in the light of the divine promise.

3. Theological and Hermeneutical Implications

(a) The theological centre from which the material was structured allowed the editors to change the historical perspective from pre-exilic to post-exilic and beyond without destroying the integrity of the biblical witness. Because of the nature of God who encompasses in his will both the past and the future, every successive generation of Israel found an immediate access to the prophetic message of judgment and salvation.

(b) In spite of the radically theocentric perspective which focuses fully on the eschatological nature of God in alone fulfilling his purpose, the response of faith from Israel's side is not overlooked. The will of God calls forth 'a people humble and lowly' who 'do no wrong and utter no lies' (3.12f.). From the biblical perspective eschatology and ethics are not in tension but stem from the same divine source.

(c) The richness and versatility of the canonical process is further illustrated by recalling the similarities and differences between the shaping of Amos and Zephaniah. There are several central themes shared by both such as the 'day of Yahweh', the fierce anger of God, the judgment against the nations, and the priests who profane the law. However, the differences are equally striking and reveal clearly the different canonical processes through which the two books were formed. In Amos the later stages of growth have left the original layer largely intact and the expansions come as interpolations and additions. In Zephaniah the original layer of prophetic preaching has been largely obscured. His message has been condensed and epitomized into topical units. Moreover, Zephaniah's words have been blended with other prophetic voices (First and Second Isaiah, Amos) which have been used in fashioning a prophetic compendium. In sum, the process of shaping the two collections was very different, but the final effect is similar and testifies to the strong lines of continuity in the hearing of the different prophets and in the fixing of consistent theological parameters for the prophetic message.

History of Exegesis

Carpzov III, 421f.; T. K. **Cheyne** and J. S. **Black**, eds., *Encycl. Bibl.* 4, Edinburgh and New York 1903, 5408f.; *RGG*[3] 6, 1902.

XXIX

HAGGAI

Commentaries

A. Köhler, 1860
C. F. Keil, BC, 1868
F. Hitzig, H. Steiner, KeH, ⁴1881
T. T. Perowne, CB, 1886
J. Wellhausen, ³1898
G. A. Smith, ExB, 1898 (²1928)
K. Marti, KHC 1904
A. van Hoonacker, EB, 1908
H. G. Mitchell, ICC, 1912
E. W. Barnes, CB², 1917
E. Sellin, KAT, ²⁻³1930

A. Deden, BOuT, 1956
A. Gelin, JB, ³1960
P. R. Ackroyd, Peake rev., 1962
F. Horst, HAT, ³1964
K. Elliger, ATD, ⁶1967
J. L. Koole, COuT, 1967
T. Chary, SoBi, 1969
J. G. Baldwin, TOTC, 1972
W. Rudolph, KAT², 1977
R. Mason, CNEB, 1977

Bibliography

P. R. **Ackroyd**, 'Studies in the Book of Haggai', *JJS* 2, 1951, 163–76; 3, 1952, 1–13; 'The Book of Haggai and Zechariah 1–8', *JJS* 3, 1952, 151–56; 'Some Interpretative Glosses in the Book of Haggai', *JJS* 7, 1956, 163–7; 'Two Old Testament Historical Problems of the Early Persian Period', *JNES* 17, 1958, 13–27; *Exile and Restoration*, OTL, 1968, 153–70; R. **Bach**, 'Haggai', 'Haggaibuch', *RGG³*, 24–26; J. **Begrich**, 'Die priesterliche Tora', *Werden und Wesen des Alten Testaments*, BZAW 66, 1936, 63–8, reprinted *GSAT*, Munich 1964, 232–60; W. A. M. **Beuken**, *Haggai-Secharja 1–8*, Assen 1967; P. F. **Bloomhardt**, 'The Poems of Haggai', *HUCA* 5, 1928, 153–95; T. **Chary**, 'Le culte chez les prophètes Aggée et Zacharie', *Les Prophètes et le culte à partir de l'exil*, Paris 1955, 119–59; A. **Deissler**, 'Aggée', *DBS* 8, 701–6; D. N. **Freedman**, 'The Chronicler's Purpose', *CBQ* 23, 1961, 436–42; K. **Galling**, 'Serubbabel und der Wiederaufnahme des Tempels in Jerusalem', *Verbannung und Heimkehr, FS W. Rudolph*, Tübingen 1961, 67–96; A. **Gelston**, 'The Foundation of the

Second Temple', *VT* 16, 1966, 232–5; P. D. **Hanson**, *The Dawn of Apocalyptic*, Philadelphia 1975, 140ff.; F. **Hesse**, 'Haggai', *Verbannung und Heimkehr*, 109–34.

F. **James**, 'Thoughts on Haggai and Zechariah', *JBL* 53, 1934, 229–35; K. **Koch**, 'Haggais unreines Volk', *ZAW* 79, 1967, 52–66; R. A. **Mason**, 'The Purpose of the "Editorial Framework" of the Book of Haggai', *VT* 27, 1977, 415–21; H. G. **May**, '"This People" and "This Nation" in Haggai', *VT* 18, 1968, 190–97; F. S. **North**, 'Critical Analysis of the Book of Haggai', *ZAW* 68, 1956, 25–46; O. **Procksch**, *Die kleinen prophetischen Schriften nach dem Exil*, Stuttgart 1916; J. W. **Rothstein**, *Juden und Samaritaner. Die grundlegende Scheidung von Judentum und Heidentum*, BWA(N)T 3, 1908; G. **Sauer**, 'Serubbabel in der Sicht Haggais und Secharjas', *Das ferne und nahe Wort, FS L. Rost*, BZAW 105, 1967, 199–207; E. **Sellin**, *Studien zur Entstehungsgeschichte der jüdischen Gemeinde nach dem Babylonischen Exil*, 2 vols., Leipzig 1900–1901; K. **Seybold**, 'Die Königserwartung bei den Propheten Haggai und Sacharja', *Jud* 28, 1972, 69–78; R. T. **Siebeck**, 'The Messianism of Aggaeus and Proto-Zacharias', *CBQ* 19, 1957, 312–28; O. H. **Steck**, 'Zu Haggai 1, 2–11', *ZAW* 83, 1971, 355–79; T. N. **Townsend**, 'Additional Comments on Haggai II, 10–19', *VT* 18, 1968, 559f.; H. W. **Wolff**, *Haggai*, BSt 1, 1951.

1. Historical Critical Problems

Literary critical problems

For the last hundred years the literary critical questions in respect to the book of Haggai have turned on the unity and integrity of the composition, especially focusing on the passage 2.10–19. Certain critical decisions regarding the composition of this passage have been widely accepted which seriously influence one's understanding of the entire book. A review of this evidence is first called for.

The difficulty of following the logic of the latter half of ch. 2 (vv. 15–19) has long been felt (cf. A. Köhler). Both the shift in tone and the peculiarities of the chronology seemed puzzling. At first the suggested corrections involved only the removal of a few phrases (Wellhausen, Marti), or a reinterpretation of the Hebrew syntax in order to by-pass the problems (Keil, van Hoonacker). Later a more ambitious attempt toward resolving the difficulties was made by E. Sellin (*Studien* II, 50ff.). He argued that the date formula in 1.15a represented a fragment from a passage which had been lost. Since 1.12ff. spoke of the beginning of the work on rebuilding the temple, and 2.1ff. already described the building as well under way some seven weeks later, Sellin reasoned that the report of the laying of the foundation stone must have occurred in between these two passages. He concluded that the passage in Haggai had been suppressed because the dating of the laying of the foundation stone conflicted with the Chronicler's report (Ezra 3.8ff.).

Sellin's suggestion was next picked up by Rothstein (53ff.) who argued that Sellin's lost passage was actually preserved in 2.15–19 and that, when joined to 1.15a, it formed the missing oracle. Rothstein adduced a variety of literary and historical proofs for supporting his case that the present unit, 2.10–19, was an artificial construct of two totally different passages. With slight variation (e.g. Mitchell, Horst, Elliger) Rothstein's reconstruction of the original setting of two separate passages has been widely accepted (cf. Wolff, Hesse, von Rad, *OT Theology* II, 282–5).

Rothstein's reconstruction of 2.10–14 has been of crucial importance for an evaluation of the entire book. He argued that Haggai made use of the form of the priestly decision to justify his rejection of the request of the Samaritans to participate in the rebuilding of the temple (cf. Ezra 4.1ff.). The original force of this harsh judgment on 'this people ... this nation' (v. 14) was lost when the referent was shifted from the Samaritans to the Jewish community by adding vv. 15–19. The important effect of this historical interpretation can be immediately sensed in the commentaries. Sellin characterized the decision of Samaritan exclusion as 'the actual moment of birth for post-exilic Judaism' (*Zwölfprophetenbuch*, 463). Elliger (92) wondered if the rejection of the Samaritans was more formative for the Jewish community than the rebuilding of the temple.

The effect of Rothstein's reconstruction had also a profound effect on the interpretation of 2.15–19. The promise of a new period of blessing was now made to synchronize exactly with the laying of the foundation stone in the sixth month. Unquestionably this reconstruction of the original sequence of events has succeeded in bringing the passage into sharper focus, but at the cost of losing several phrases as secondary misunderstandings. Thus, the reference in 2.18 to the twenty-fourth day of the ninth month has been generally eliminated as a confused gloss. Only recently has Rothstein's hypothesis been seriously questioned by Koch.

Redaction-critical problems

Ever since the early 50s the problem of the book's transmission has increasingly attracted the attention of scholars (cf. especially Ackroyd's articles). The most formidable attempt to deal with the entire history of the book's development, particularly the circles in which it was transmitted, has been offered by Beuken. Although the parallelism in the content between the Chronicler and Haggai had long been recognized (Hag. 2.3 // Ezra 3.12, etc.), Beuken tried to establish the decisive role of the Chronicler in the formation of the material by means of form-critical and traditio-critical arguments. Indeed, the parallels in the use of formulae, the chronological role of the superscriptions, and the structure of the oracles exhibit some striking similarities with the Chronicler. Nevertheless, in my judgment, the evidence is insufficient to establish the circles of tradents in as much detail as Beuken proposes. Even such a factor as Haggai's very different use of scripture from that of the Chronicler would make one hesitate to suggest too close an identification.

Again, the attempt to explain the redaction of the present shape of the book has not been successful. Beuken himself rejects the usual explanation for the 'dislocation' in ch. 2 as having arisen in an effort to harmonize the date of the laying of the foundation stone with that of Ezra 5.16. However, in the end he still characterizes the final shape of the book as an unfortunate disturbance of an original order (215f.).

The theology of Haggai in critical perspective

In general Haggai's theological contribution to Israel has not been highly regarded in modern times. It is fair to say that it has been eroded even further by the critical reconstruction of his oracles. He is usually judged to be a minor prophet indeed. Often he is thought to epitomize the exclusivism of post-exilic Judaism. Sellin spoke of 'crude materialism' in picturing the period beginning with Haggai (Zwölfprophetenbuch, 448). Hanson is typical in trying to employ modern sociological categories by which to interpret the period. Haggai is characterized as a leader in the 'hierocratic party' (e.g. temple programme, Zadok control, etc.) which he then contrasts with the 'visionary group'. Needless to say, his description does not enhance Haggai's contribution. Occasionally, Haggai is commended for his zeal in maintaining the purity of Israel's faith (Eichrodt, *Theology*), but again it is his motivation rather than his message which is appreciated.

2. The Canonical Shape of Haggai

The final form of the book of Haggai reflects the clear structure of four prophetic oracles, each of which is introduced by a date formula (1.1; 1.15b–2.1; 2.10; 2.20). Within this structure a variety of different oral forms of speech have been preserved (disputation, warning, promise, priestly decision, etc.). The reference to Haggai in the third person, as well as the structuring of his oracles, makes it obvious that the book has been edited by someone other than the prophet himself.

In the present form of the book the unity of 2.10–19 is recognized by the explicit reference in 2.20 to the 'second' oracle on the same day. However, a closer look at this text, which has, of course, been the contribution of the historical critical study, makes it evident that the unity of this passage is of a secondary nature and belongs to the redactional activity of the editors. This judgment stems from a number of observations. First of all, the oracle of priestly pronouncement (2.10–14) still retains a well-preserved form from its original historical function (Begrich) even though this function has been redirected into a prophetic allegory by the addition of vv. 15–19. Again, the lack of a close connection between the two parts of the passage – either in form or content – would suggest a secondary linkage of two once independent oracles. Finally, the extreme difficulty of following the logic of the last section would corroborate the sense of some dislocation in the text through the restructuring of the original oracles. Although Koch has made some important observations on the structure of this passage in relation to 1.2–8, and I fully agree with his rebuttal of Rothstein, nevertheless, in my judgment, the symmetry is of a redactional nature and does not represent an original prophetic genre.

In spite of the presence of some friction between the first and second parts of this unit, there are several signs which point to an intentional linking of the parts. 2.14 speaks of 'this people . . . and

this nation ... every work of their hands' (ma῾ᵃśeh yᵉdêhem) being
unclean. The same vocabulary recurs in v. 17 in a divine judgment
against Israel: 'I smote you and all the works of your hands ... '
(ma῾ᵃśeh yᵉdêkem). The repetition of the same phrase serves to form a
bridge between the third person addressee of 2.1–14 and the second
person of vv. 15–19. Again, the recurrence in v. 18 of the date of the
superscription in v. 10 further binds the sections together. That the
redactional effort of moulding the two passages into one has not
been fully successful is testified to by the unusual difficulty of
interpreting the combined unit.

What is the effect of this redactional activity on the interpretation of the prophetic traditions of Haggai? First of all, the connection alleged by Rothstein of vv. 10–14 to a historic decision by
Haggai to exclude the Samaritans from rebuilding the temple, even
if originally made, which is very uncertain, has been fully obliterated. There is no hint in the present text to relate the antecedent of
v. 14 to the Samaritans. Indeed, only one people is ever referred to
within the book and that is clearly the Jewish remnant. The redactional shaping of this oracle has removed the possibility of regarding the passage as an archaizing historical footnote concerning the
Samaritans, but rather fashioned it into a homily addressed to the
Jews. The priestly decision (10–14) now functions in a figurative
manner ('so it is ... ') to highlight Israel's sinfulness. When
Beuken (215f.) argues that the original sense of the passage as a
judgment against the Samaritans could not have been lost because
this issue remained of such great theological significance, he is
disregarding the effect of the canonical shaping which apparently
did not share this evaluation.

The function of the second part of the oracle (2.15–19) has also
been sharply altered by the new role which the redactor has
assigned it. By attaching this oracle to the priestly decision on the
twenty-fourth day of the ninth month the promise of blessing has
been given a new focus. Rather than the promise being attached
directly to the day on which the foundation-stone was laid (so
Rothstein), it has now been redirected to the day on which the
oracle of Israel's sinfulness was proclaimed. As a result, the laying
of the foundation-stone has lost its independent significance and
has been made into a sign of something else, namely, of Israel's
repentance. The failure to rebuild the temple, which God then
judged with crop failure, was a sign of Israel's failure to repent (v.

17). Conversely, the laying of the stone, for which blessing was promised, was a sign of a new spirit (1.14). In sum, the canonical shaping has reinterpreted the historical event in terms of its true religious significance and thereby provided it with a different context.

Much of the difficulty of interpreting the role of the foundation-stone turns on the dating of 2.18. If this verse is interpreted to mean that the laying of the foundation took place on the twenty-fourth day of the ninth month, then there is a flat contradiction with 1.14f. where the date for the laying of the foundation-stone is set at the twenty-fourth day of the sixth month. In my judgment, both the Hebrew syntax of 2.18 (cf. *l^emin hayyôm*) and the structure of 2.10–19 as a whole speak against the link to the ninth month. The passage in 2.15–17 is an exhortation to consider *today* what will come to pass by remembering what has transpired in the past *before* the laying of the foundation. The passage in 2.18–19 is an exhortation to consider *today* what will come to pass by remembering what has transpired in the past *since* the laying of the foundation until the present. By this call to consider, Haggai sets before the people the choice of blessing or curses. However, the choice revolves about repentance and not about the rebuilding of the temple. It is not tied to a political event such as the rejection of the Samaritans, but is an ever-present word 'from this day onward' setting before the people life and death, sin and repentance. (I am indebted to an unpublished paper by Melanie Morrison for certain of these formulations.)

There is another element to the canonical shaping of the prophetic tradition which emerges in the larger structure of the book. In the four separate oracles of the book, two major themes have been carefully intertwined. In the first and third oracles (1.1–15; 2.10–19) the prophet relates the present poverty of the people directly to the disregard of God's temple. In the second and fourth oracles (2.1–9; 2.20–23) the promise is reiterated that Israel's traditional eschatological hope is still valid. Significantly, the two themes have been carefully related to each other in the present shaping of the oracles. The promise to Zerubbabel which renews the messianic hope is now placed chronologically on the same day as the proclamation of Israel's sinfulness and the blessing of obedience. The promise is joined to Israel's obedience, not to her rejection of Samaria (*contra* Elliger). Once again the earthly temple is only a sign which adumbrates the heavenly temple (1.8; 2.8f.). The present poverty of this age is contrasted with the splendour of the *eschaton* which God will usher in. In sum, a theological dynamic is established by the intertwining of oracles which is only correctly understood by a holistic reading of the book. The attempt to reconstruct an original chronological sequence has failed to deal seriously with this dimension of the canonical text.

3. Theological and Hermeneutical Implications

(*a*) The message of Haggai in its canonical form retains a delicate balance between this-worldly political action and eschatological, divine intervention. Haggai, perhaps more than any other prophet, was committed to a political programme, namely, the restoration of the temple. The canonical shaping of the tradition has not withdrawn this major element of Haggai's proclamation. He remains a political activist! But the canonical shaping has carefully placed this message within a larger theological context. The people are urged to build 'that (God) may appear in (his) glory' (1.8). Certainly it is a pitiful structure which emerges, but God promises to transform it into a magnificent house on that day when all the world is judged in the great eschatological shaking (1.3ff.; 2.6ff.). Haggai is not 'building' the kingdom of God, but the divine blessing does not come without the building. The canonical shaping makes clear that there is no simple causal connection between human work and divine promise. The human political programme of rebuilding the temple was given divine sanction, but the eschatological promise is not collapsed into a material effect of the rebuilding.

(*b*) The attempt of critical scholarship to bring a biblical passage into sharper historical focus by means of historical reconstruction runs the acute danger of destroying the particular theological witness which the passage carries in its final canonical shape. Particularly in the case of Haggai, the prophet's alleged rejection of the Samaritans has been assigned a fundamental theological significance in spite of the book's own silence on the matter. Even more serious, the hermeneutical axiom that meaning is acquired only through ostensive reference, which controls this type of critical interpretation, renders the exegete incapable of hearing the canonical witness because it is often quite different from the original historical level.

(c) The problem of a prophetic promise failing to materialize has loomed large in the history of modern scholarship (cf. the classic analysis of A. Kuenen, *Prophecy and the Prophets in Israel*, ET London 1877). How is one to explain the authority attached to Haggai's prophecy in the light of his apparent joining of the coming new age with the building of an earthly temple? Moreover, the completion of the temple in 516 obviously preceded the prophecy of Haggai being assigned an authoritative role among the sacred writings. The canonical shaping of the tradition offers clear evidence of how the prophetic word was heard. Quite obviously the modern category of a word being 'time-conditioned' was not employed. Rather, the truth of the prophecy was firmly maintained, but its realization was conditioned, either by an appeal to a divine schedule ('in a little while ... ' 2.6; 'on that day', 2.23) or to Israel's response (2.17). Thus the prophetic word became the criterion by which to judge history instead of the reverse move which has dominated historical critical scholarship (cf. Zech. 8.9ff.; Hebrews 12.26ff.).

History of Exegesis

Carpzov III, 434f.; *DBS* 8, 704f.; *DThC* 1, 564–573; *RGG*[3] 3, 26.

A **Köhler**, 'Einleitung', *Die Weissagungen Haggai's*, Erlangen 1860, 1–33.

XXX

ZECHARIAH

Commentaries

C. F. Keil, BC, 1868
F. Hitzig, H. Steiner, KeH, ⁴1881
Ewald, ET, 1881
T. T. Perowne, CB, 1886
J. Wellhausen, ³1898
G. A. Smith, ExB, 1898 (²1928)
K. Marti, KHC, 1904
A. van Hoonacker, ÉB, 1908
H. G. T. Mitchell, ICC, 1912
E. W. Barnes, CB², 1917

E. Sellin, KAT, ²⁻³1930
P. R. Ackroyd, Peake rev., 1962
D. R. Jones, TB, 1962
M. F. Unger, 1963
F. Horst, HAT, ³1964
K. Elliger, ATD, ⁶1967
T. Chary, SoBi, 1969
J. G. Baldwin, TOTC, 1972
W. Rudolph, KAT², 1977
R. A. Mason, CNEB, 1977

Bibliography

P. R. **Ackroyd**, 'The Book of Haggai and Zechariah I–VIII', *JSS* 3, 1952, 151–6; *Exile and Restoration*, OTL, 1968, 171–217; S. **Amsler**, 'Zacharie et l'origine d'apocalyptique', *SVT* 22, 1972, 227–31; W. A. M. **Beuken**, *Haggai-Sacharja 1–8*, Assen 1967; D. **Buzy**, 'Les symboles de Zecharie', *RB* 15, 1918, 136–91, 323–405; M. **Delcor**, 'Deux passages difficiles: Zech xii 11 et xi 13', *VT* 3, 1953, 67–77; B. **Duhm**, 'Anmerkungen zu den zwölf Propheten, XII–XIII', *ZAW* 31, 1911, 189–200; R. **Eckardt**, 'Der religiöse Gehalt von Sacharja 9–14', *ZTK* 3, 1893, 311–31; W. **Eichrodt**, 'Vom Symbol zum Typos. Ein Beitrag zur Sacharja-Exegese', *TZ* 13, 1957, 509–22; K. **Elliger**, 'Ein Zeugnis aus der jüdischen Gemeinde in Alexanderjahr 332 v Chr. Eine territorialgeschichtliche Studie zu Sach 9, 1–8', *ZAW* 62, 1950, 63–115; H. **Frey**, 'Der siebenflammige Leuchter und die Oelsöhne. Beitrag zu einer theologischen Deutung von Sach. 4', *In Piam memoriam A. von Bulmerincq*, Riga 1938, 20–63; K. **Galling**, 'Die Exilwende in der Sicht des Propheten Sacharja', *VT* 2, 1952, 18–36=*Studien zur Geschichte Israel im persischen Zeitalter*, Tübingen 1964, 109–26 'Serubbabel und der Wiederaufbau des Tempels in Jerusalem', *Verbannung und*

Heimkehr, FS W. Rudolph, Tübingen 1961, 67–96; 'Serubbabel und der Hohepriester beim Wiederaufbau des Tempels in Jerusalem', *Studien*, 1964, 127–48; H. **Gese**, 'Anfang und Ende der Apokalyptik, dargestellt am Sacharjabuch', *ZTK* 70, 1973, 20–49=*Vom Sinai zum Zion*, Munich 1974, 202–30; —, 'Die Deutung der Hirtenallegorie Sach 11, 4ff.', *Vom Sinai zum Zion*, 231–8.

P. D. **Hanson**, 'Zechariah 9 and the Recapitulation of an Ancient Ritual Pattern', *JBL* 92, 1973, 37–59; *The Dawn of Apocalyptic*, Philadelphia 1975, 240ff., 280ff.; P. **Haupt**, 'The Visions of Zechariah', *JBL* 32, 1913, 107–22; E. W. **Hengstenberg**, *Dissertations on the Genuineness of Daniel and the Integrity of Zechariah*, ET Edinburgh and New York 1846, 293–315; A. **Jepsen**, 'Kleine Beiträge zum Zwölfprophetenbuch', *ZAW* 61, 1945–8, 95–114; C. **Jeremias**, *Die Nachtgesichte des Sacharja. Untersuchungen zu ihrer Stellung im Zusammenhang der Visionsberichte im Alten Testament und zu ihrem Bildmaterial*, FRLANT 117, 1976; D. R. **Jones**, 'A Fresh Interpretation of Zech IX–XI', *VT* 12, 1962, 241–59; A. **Köhler**, *Die Weissagungen Sacharjas*, 2 vols., Erlangen 1861–63; J. **Kremer**, *Die Hirtenallegorie im Buche Zacharias auf ihre Messianität hin untersucht*, Münster 1930; M.-J. **Lagrange**, 'Notes sur les prophéties messianiques des derniers prophètes', *RB* NS 3, 1906, 67–83; P. **Lamarche**, *Zacharie IX–XIV. Structure littéraire et messianisme*, Paris 1961; É. **Lipiński**, 'Recherches sur le livre de Zacharie', *VT* 20, 1970, 25–55; H.-M. **Lutz**, *Jahwe, Jerusalem und die Völker. Zur Vorgeschichte von Sach 12, 1–8 und 14, 1–5*, WMANT 27, 1968; K. **Marti**, 'Zwei Studien zu Sacharja', *ThStKr* 65, 1892, 207–45, 716–34; 'Die Zweifel an der prophetischen Sendung Sacharjas', *Studien zur semitischen Philologie und Religionsgeschichte J. Wellhausen gewidmet*, BZAW 27, 1914, 279–97; R. A. **Mason**, 'The Relation of Zech. 9–14 to Proto-Zechariah', *ZAW* 88, 1976, 227–39; H. G. **May**, 'A Key to the Interpretation of Zechariah's Vision', *JBL* 57, 1938, 173–84; K. **Möhlenbrink**, 'Der Leuchter im fünften Nachtgesicht des Sacharja', *ZDPV* 52, 1929, 257–86.

R. **North**, 'Zechariah's Seven-Spout Lampstand', *Bibl* 51, 1970, 183–206; 'Prophecy to Apocalyptic via Zechariah', *SVT* 22, 1972, 47–71; B. **Otzen**, *Studien über Deuterosacharja*, Copenhagen 1964; A. **Petitjean**, *Les Oracles du Proto-Zacharie*, Paris 1969; O. **Plöger**, *Theocracy and Eschatology*, ET Oxford and Philadelphia 1968; R. **Press**, 'Das erste Nachtgesicht des Propheten Sacharja', *ZAW* 54, 1936, 43–8; M. **Rehm**, 'Die Hirtenallegorie Zach 11, 4–14', *BZ*, NF 4, 1960, 186–208; Y. T. **Ridday** and D. **Wickmann**, 'The Unity of Zechariah Examined in the light of Statistical Linguistics', *ZAW* 87, 1975, 30–55; L. G. **Rignell**, *Die Nachtgesichte des Sacharja*, Lund 1950; L. **Rost**, 'Erwägungen zu Sacharjas 7. Nachtgesicht', *ZAW* 58, 1940, 223–8; 'Bemerkungen zu Sacharja 4', *ZAW* 63, 1951, 216–21; J. W. **Rothstein**, *Die Nachtgesichte des Sacharja*, BWA[N]T 8, 1910; M. **Saebø**, *Sacharja 9–14*, WMANT 34, 1969; 'Die deuterosacharjanische Frage. Eine forschungsgeschichtliche Studie', *StTh* 23, 1969, 115–40; G. **Sauer**, 'Serubbabel in der Sicht Haggai und Sacharjas', *Das ferne und nahe*

Wort, *FS L. Rost*, BZAW 105, 1967, 199–207; H. **Schmidt**, 'Das vierte Nachtgesicht des Propheten Sacharja', *ZAW* 54, 1936, 48–60; E. **Sellin**, 'Der Stein des Sacharja', *JBL* 50, 1931, 242–9; 'Noch einmal der Stein des Sacharja', *ZAW* 59, 1942/3, 59–77; K. **Seybold**, 'Spätprophetische Hoffnungen auf die Wiederkunft des davidischen Zeitalters in Sach 9–14', *Jud* 29, 1973, 99–111; B. **Stade**, 'Deuterozacharja', *ZAW* 1, 1881, 1–96; 2, 1882, 151–72, 275–309; W. **Staerk**, *Untersuchungen über die Komposition und Abfassungszeit von Zech 9–14*, Halle 1891; N. L. A. **Tidwell**, *'wā'ōmar* (Zech. 3:5) and the Genre of Zechariah's Fourth Vision', *JBL* 94, 1975, 343–55; G. **Wallis**, 'Erwägungen zu Sacharja VI 9–15', *SVT* 22, 1972, 232–7; J. **Wellhausen**, 'Zechariah', *Encyclopaedia Biblica*, ed. T. K. Cheyne and J. S. Black, vol. 4, London and New York 1903, 5390–95; I. **Willi-Plein**, *Prophetie am Ende. Untersuchungen zu Sacharja 9–14*, BBB 42, 1974; C. H. H. **Wright**, *Zechariah and his Prophecies in relation to Modern Criticism*, London 1879.

1. Historical Critical Problems

The extreme difficulty of interpreting the book of Zechariah has been felt from the earliest times (cf. Jerome's well-known characterization: *obscurissimus liber*). The additional factor that the book played such a significant role in the New Testament only added to the frustration of Christian scholars (cf. the statistics in P. Lamarche, 9). Nor did Jewish efforts fare much better, to judge from the striking differences of interpretations among the classic commentators (cf. the convenient edition of Kimchi by A. M. M'Caul [see p. 487 below], with references to Rashi, Ibn Ezra, and Abarbanel). The difficulty of the book is further attested by a review of the present state of critical research.

Chapters 1–8

The major critical problems in these chapters have to do with the present editorial shape of the section. To the series of 'night visions' (1.7–6.8) there has been added – usually by means of interpolation – a variety of other interpretative material. Fohrer's analysis (*Introduction*, 463) shares a consensus among literary critics when he designates the following as secondary additions to the visions: 1.16f.; 2.12f., 14, 15f. (EVV 2.8f, 10, 11f.); 3.8f.; 4.7αβ–10α. Moreover, chs. 7–8 are considered to be a loose collection of sayings which have been drawn into the orbit of an original legal discussion regarding fasting.

Ever since Wellhausen's incisive commentary, it has been generally accepted that the major reason behind the alteration in the form of the original visions resulted from an attempt to bring the text in line with the changing political situation. Thus Wellhausen considered Zerubbabel to have been the person who was originally crowned in 6.11, but was replaced by Joshua and a future messianic figure (cf. also 3.8) when Zerubbabel's political career was suddenly cut short. A similar attempt to reflect the political realities is also thought to lie behind the complex imagery of the lampstand in 6.11f.

Recent critical scholarship on these first eight chapters (e.g. Elliger, Ackroyd, Petitjean, Galling, Rignell, Beuken, etc.) has generally built on the literary analysis of Wellhausen and Rothstein, but has then sought to determine more exactly the nature of the traditions and the circles responsible for their transmission. Often the larger question of the rise of apocalypticism has played a role in the posing of the questions (Gese, Plöger, Hanson). It is difficult to speak of any consensus having emerged on these larger historical issues.

Chapters 9–14

The history of research of these chapters has been exhaustively handled by Otzen (11–34) and briefly summarized in English by Hanson (287–90). A further recapitulation seems therefore unnecessary. It is sufficient to state that a very wide consensus has developed among critical scholars since the middle of the nineteenth century in assigning these chapters to an author or authors different from the first eight chapters.

The most interesting and yet frustrating aspect of this research has been in the strikingly divergent assessment by the critics of so-called 'Deutero-Zechariah'. Throughout most of the nineteenth century the critical position which was dominant regarded much within these chapters to be pre-exilic. Indeed chs. 9–11 were usually assigned to the eighth century. The evidence for this decision rested mainly on the mention of the Northern and Southern Kingdoms (9.10, 13; 10.6), the reference to Assyria and Egypt, and the historical portrayal of Syria-Palestine in ch. 9. However, following Stade's article of 1881, a majority began to accept his arguments for assigning Deutero-Zechariah to the early Greek period. Stade's evidence turned on the historical reference to the Greeks in 9.13, on seeing in the reference to the Assyrians and Egyptians a cryptic cipher for the Seleucid and Ptolemaic kingdoms, and on emphasizing the close parallels in ch. 9 with Alexander's invasion. In addition, he sought to place these chapters within a historical development of Israel's religion which would further demonstrate a late post-exilic stage. Moreover, the complexity of the problem has once again been demonstrated by Otzen's extremely learned defence of the pre-exilic dating of the chapters. It would seem that critical opinion has come full circle and the same issues are being as hotly debated today as in 1881.

The inability to reach a consensus on the dating of the book has left unresolved the historical context for interpretation. As a result, few Old Testament books reflect such a chaos of conflicting interpretations. If further evidence for the breakdown of method within the discipline is needed, the reader is challenged to compare the recent proposals made by Lamarche, Otzen, Hanson and Seybold. Although I am aware of the danger of offering still another approach, perhaps attention to the canonical shape of the book can aid rather than exacerbate the problem.

2. The Canonical Shape of Zechariah

Chapters 1–8

The initial observation to make is that the present book of Zechariah reflects a definite redactional shaping of the visions. The visions which begin in 1.7 have been set within a specific chronological sequence. An absolute date has been provided in 1.7: the twenty-fourth day, the eleventh month, in the second year of Darius' reign, that is, 519 BC. In addition, the introduction to the visions (1.1–6) places the visions within a *heilsgeschichtliche* sequence as well. The history of disobedience testified to by the 'former prophets' is summarized along with the repentance of the fathers. The grounds for a shift in God's purpose for Israel has been prepared. Something new is in store for them.

What then follows is a series of visions. It was particularly the essay of Kurt Galling ('Die Exilwende') which for the first time demonstrated clearly the tension between the present literary framework and the original function of the various individual visions. Each vision appears to have originally functioned independently and addressed a particular historical situation. Thus, for example, the first vision (1.7ff.) pictures the nations 'at ease' and Jerusalem still suffering the 'indignation of seventy years'. The tradition of the seventy years of humiliation is familiar from Jer. 25 and Dan. 9. The vision offers a promise that the period is about to end and God will again have compassion on Jerusalem. Clearly this message refers to the deliverance of the exiles under Cyrus which still lies in the future. Again, the vision of the four horns (2.1ff., EVV 1.18ff.) portrays the imminent judgment on the Babylonians who had once inflicted destruction on Judah. The vision originally predated Cyrus's victory. Similarly, the final vision of the four chariots (6.1ff.) testifies to the gracious outpouring of the divine spirit on the exiles in Babylon, as Ewald correctly saw, and would again be set in a period close to the deliverance. However, the sixth vision (5.1ff.) clearly reflects a subsequent period when the returning exiles are promised divine vindication on those who sought to steal their land.

In my judgment, Galling has failed to draw the proper implications from his exegetical observations. Because of the tension between the message to the Babylonian exiles and the date given to the visions by Zechariah (519 BC), Galling sought to find historical evidence for shifting the date of the return from the exile away from 539 to one much closer to 519. Actually the issue at stake in Zechariah is of a different order. The basic problem here is not historical, but theological. The canonical shaping reflects a new theological interpretation. The original function of the various visions has been altered to allow the visions to perform a different role within the book of Zechariah. The prophetic visions are set in the second year of Darius, that is to say, some twenty years after the return from Babylon. The deliverance from the Babylonian exile now lies in the past. Although the traditional language of the 'second exodus' has been retained, it has been given a new reference. The language of hope now points to a still future event in which Israel's deliverance lies. Thus, the original focus on the end of the Babylonian rule has been interpreted eschatologically within its new literary framework and projected out into the future. The traditional identification of the new redemptive age, particularly as found in Second Isaiah, has been dissolved by a fresh eschatological vision which reckons with the return as a past historical event (cf. Galling, 'Exilwende', 117).

There is a second major sign of canonical shaping within chs. 1–8 which emerges clearly in the present expansion of the original visions by means of additional interpretative material. As has already been described, the visions have been supplemented by the addition of oracles. The two most obvious examples are the interpolations in chs. 2 and 4. These secondary additions to the original visions provide a very definite interpretation of the visions to which they have been joined. The oracle which begins in 2.10 (EVV 2.6) assumes the traditional form of the herald's cry. In a striking parallel to Isa. 48.20; Jer. 50.8ff.; 51.6, the oracle urges the exiles to flee from Babylon to Jerusalem. The eschatological intent appears most clearly in v. 11 with the conversion of the nations proclaimed 'in that day'. Verse 9 is of particular importance for its eschatological emphasis. The verse reflects the tradition of the 'final shaking' (Hag. 2.6) with the familiar theme of the 'plundering of the plunderer' (Isa. 14.2; 33.1).

What is the effect of the oracle on the interpretation of the vision? The oracle has made use of the traditional language of the second exodus and the final convulsion of the end time. Since the deliverance from Babylon now lies in the past, the language of the second exodus can only refer to a future redemption. The language is old, but the referent is new. A similar redactional role can be seen in the oracle in ch. 4. Through the outpouring of the divine spirit (Isa. 11.2) the mountains are transformed into a plain (Isa. 40.3f.) and the foundation of the earthly temple built by Zerubbabel adumbrates the heavenly temple of the new age (Ezek. 40ff.). In sum, both oracles now serve further to support the new eschatological role which the framework has assigned to the visions.

The expansion of the original sequence of the visions also includes sign-acts. In ch. 6 the sign-act consists in the crowning of Joshua. Wellhausen's argument that originally Zerubbabel was the recipient of the crowning has been followed by many modern commentators (Mitchell, Horst, Elliger, etc.), but even if this were the case, this level of the tradition has been completely eliminated (cf. the LXX). Joshua's crowning now functions symbolically to foreshadow the coming of the future messianic figure of the 'Branch'.

The sign-act in ch. 3 has also been fashioned by the redactor to function as one of the visions within the series of night visions (cf. v. 1), but along with this move, a divine oracle has also been added

(vv. 6ff.). The oracle betrays immediately the eschatological intention of the editor. Again the divine word speaks of the coming
Branch, of the final cleansing of the land, and the realization of the
traditional prophetic hope of peace (cf. Micah 4.4).

The similarity in the editing of the visions by means of oracles
and sign-acts points to the same level of redaction. The same formula 'you will know that Yahweh of Hosts has sent me' occurs
both in the oracles (2.13, 16 [EVV 2.9, 12]; 4.9) as well as in the
sign-act (6.15). Both oracles and sign-acts have a similar
eschatological orientation, and employ a similar literary technique
of attaching secondary material to the original vision by means of
block interpolation.

Finally, consideration of the function of chs. 7 and 8 is in order.
One is impressed immediately by the similar signs of redactional
activity. The passage is introduced by a date formula consistent
with 1.1, 7. The cultic question is raised in 7.3 but receives its
answer only in 8.18ff. by means of a divine oracle. Between the
question and answer is a series of divine oracles which sound
eschatological notes similar to those found in the earlier chapters.
Whereas in the preceding chapters the hortatory emphasis was
confined mainly to the introduction in 1.3ff. (cf. 3.7; 6.5), this
traditional element of prophetic proclamation has been greatly
expanded. The predominantly eschatological concern of the editor
has not undercut the ethical imperatives of the covenant. The similar reference to the preaching of the 'former prophets' in 1.4 and
7.12 (cf. 8.9) gives strong evidence of being shaped by the same
editorial hand.

To summarize: chs. 1–8 reflect a variety of different materials
(visions, sign-acts, priestly Torah oracles) which, however, have
been fashioned into a consistent pattern, probably by the same
redactor. The effect of the shaping is to afford the present chapters
with a role often quite different from the original function of both
the visions, sign-acts and Torah oracles. The message of chs. 1–8
has been firmly attached to the immediate period following the
return from Babylon and has transformed the traditional hope in
the second exodus to an eschatological portrayal of a still further
redemption.

Chapters 9–14

At the outset, it appears clear that chs. 9–14 do not exhibit any features which would cause one to assign them to the same redactional level which we have just described in chs. 1–8. Chs. 9–14 are divided into two separate sections, each introduced by a superscription (9.1 and 12.1), which seemed to have functioned independently, not only of chs. 1–8 but also of each other. There is no direct literary dependence of 9–14 on 1–8 such as a conscious patterning, a midrashic expansion, or a prophecy-fulfilment relationship. The immediate implication to be drawn is that the canonical process which resulted in shaping the book of Zechariah was of a very different order than that which fashioned the Isaianic corpus (cf. ch. XVII).

Chapters 9–11

These chapters consist of a variety of traditional prophetic forms which have been subsequently collected together. There are genres of threat, promise, herald's cry, invective, and allegory. The final collection does not exhibit a closely honed structural unity, but there is some parallelism of content between 9.1ff. and 11.1ff.

Because the forms appear to have arisen in a definite historical situation, it is natural that much scholarly attention has focused on specifying the original setting. The high density of specific historical and geographical references in ch. 11 further supports this scholarly effort. But the apparent ability of the divine words of judgment against Syria/Palestine to refer equally well to Sargon, Tiglath-Pileser, or Alexander would suggest that the role of the oracle lies in something else besides historical reference. Indeed the historical specificity has not been replaced by a move toward abstraction, but the oracles seem to describe a pattern of divine judgment which refers just as well to the past as to the future. Likewise, it does not appear significant for the chapters that the ciphers Egypt and Assyria could equally well designate the political forces opposed to God in the pre-monarchial or Maccabaean periods. The incongruity arises in that the historical detail does not refer to any one given period in history. Therefore, in spite of the highly plausible historical reconstruction of a Stade for the Greek period, and an Otzen for the pre-exilic setting, the canonical intention as it is reflected in the present role assigned to the material appears to lie elsewhere.

A similar observation can be made regarding the famous 'shepherd allegory' (11.4–17). Evidently at some stage in the transmission of the material a definite historical reference was intended. Moreover, the allegory, which may well have been originally a prophetic sign-act, has arisen in close dependence on the prior tradition of Jer. 23 and Ezek. 34. A remarkable density of historical particularity is present in the specific mention of the three shepherds destroyed in one month, the two phases of judgment in the annulling of the covenants, and the wages paid of thirty shekels of silver. However, the inability of critical research to establish a convincing case for one period is further evidence that the present canonical text has been dislocated from its original moorings. Elements of historical detail have been retained which in spite of their ambiguity and even incongruity the biblical author has used faithfully to testify to an eschatological pattern of divine judgment. In the contrast between the good and the bad shepherd a theological reality emerges in a typological handling of history. The allegory's capacity to illuminate both past and future events of the divine dealing with Israel is additional warrant for seeing a peculiar canonical use of historical material for a theological goal.

Chapters 12–14

The task of assessing the role of chs. 12–14 is far easier than with the previous section. The chapter is introduced with the familiar messenger formula proclaiming divine judgment against all the nations which lay siege on Jerusalem. What then follows – excepting 13.7–9 – is a series of loosely joined oracles of promise which have been linked with the recurring formula 'in that day'. There is some sense of progression of thought in the sequence of oracles which moves from judgment, through salvation, to the new Jerusalem, but it is not a closely-knit logical one. Rather, there is much repetition and overlapping of associated traditional motifs to form a rich mosaic which depicts the end time. The historical particularity of the previous chapters is lacking in 12–14 and a consistently eschatological message prevails throughout. The close dependence on motifs which appeared chiefly in the post-exilic period provide the warrant for most critical scholars' assigning a late date to this material. Among traditions in this category are usually included the attack on Jerusalem by the nations (Ezek. 38–39; Joel 4), the end of true prophecy (Neh. 6.10ff.), the eschatological transformation of Jerusalem (Isa. 65.17ff.), and the conversion of the nations (Isa. 56.6ff.).

The relation of chs. 9–14 to chs. 1–8

In spite of the need to handle the two sections of the book of Zechariah separately, the basic question of the canonical shape of 9–14 cannot be adequately posed until one considers the relationship of the entire last six chapters to the first part of the book. It has been the argument up to now that chs. 9–14 were edited by different hands from those of chs. 1–8 at a considerably later date. Moreover, chs. 9–11 could well have circulated independently, even of 'Deutero-Zechariah'. The implication of this assessment is that chs. 9–14 were not intentionally structured on the basis of 1–8. Rather, canonical intentionality was achieved by the effect of chs. 9–14 being attached to chs. 1–8 and thus assigned a role different from its original. However, before examining more closely the effect of joining the two sections within one canonical collection, it should be carefully noted that there is a surprising compatibility between the two books of material. This situation arises from similar religious traditions being reflected upon by the Jewish community during both periods. Indeed, the same blocks of authoritative scripture – notably Isaiah, Jeremiah, Ezekiel – probably already in some written form were exercising an effect on the composition of both sections of Zechariah. Therefore, although the juxtaposition did not derive from the intention of an original author, it did not result in a completely arbitrary linkage of two totally disparate collections of prophetic material.

Some of these elements of congruity should be noted. Zech. 2.5 speaks of a new Jerusalem without walls which experiences the special protection of Yahweh. Both 9.8 and 14.11 repeat the theme of Jerusalem's special security through divine care. The return of a paradisal fertility occurs in 8.12, while 14.8 speaks of living waters flowing from Jerusalem and 14.6 of perpetual light. The ancient covenant formula reiterated as a promise appears in 8.8 and 13.9. Again, 5.3 pictures the curse which went out over the land whereas 14.11 describes a time when the ban has been removed. Both sections deal with the divine judgment on the nations (2.1ff. [EVV 1.18] and 14.6) and both envision their ultimate conversion (2.15[EVV 2.11]; 8.22; 14.6) and worship of Yahweh (8.20; 14.16). The collection of the exiles is a theme in 8.7 and 10.9ff. That the new age results in a change in the cultic rites finds expression both in 8.18ff.

and 14.20. Both speak of the outpouring of the spirit which evoked the transformation (4.6; 12.10) and the cleansing away of those who swear falsely in the name of God (5.4; 13.3). Finally, the messianic figure of one who triumphs, not by might, but in humility is shared by 3.8; 4.6 and 9.6ff.

The case for compatibility of content between the first and second parts of the book should not be overstated. Often the vocabulary differs between the chapters, even when there is a close parallel in content. However, there is not a direct literary dependency of one section on the other. Nor does Lamarche's evidence for a highly structured unity in 9–14 appear fully convincing to us. Nevertheless, to suggest (cf. Eissfeldt, *Introduction*) that the book of Malachi could just as easily have also been attached to the book of Zechariah is equally misleading and underestimates the similarity between the sections.

What then is the effect of linking chs. 9–14 with 1–8? In my judgment, the effect is to expand, develop, and sharpen the theological pattern of the end time which had begun to emerge in Proto-Zechariah. The redaction of chs. 1–8 had reworked the older language of the second exodus in the light of the historical deliverance from Babylon in order to make it bear witness to an eschatological hope which still lay in the future. This move offered a major shift from an earlier eschatology which had envisioned the coming of the new age falling together with the return from Babylon. Now a new prophetic pattern emerges which distinguishes between the return from the exile and the coming of the end time. Israel had returned to the land, but the promise of redemption still lay in the future.

How then is one to understand the present period of history in relation to the end time? According to both Haggai and Zechariah the coming of the new age was linked to the faithful rebuilding of the temple at Jerusalem. Even in chs. 1–8 of Zechariah the prophet's focus concentrates on describing the new age. No clear word is given in chs. 1–8 for understanding the present age beyond the appeal to covenant faithfulness in ch. 8 which is commensurate with the 'seasons of joy' of the coming age. With the addition of chs. 9–14 to the book a prophetic word is offered by which to understand the period before the end. These chapters develop in detail the contours of a new eschatological pattern which addresses, not only the eschatological hope, but the community's present history as well.

Chapters 9–14 describe the period preceding the end in a manner which is barely adumbrated in chs. 1–8. They include God's severe judgment against the nations (9.1–8; 11.1–3). But they also picture renewed divine anger against God's own people who languish through their disobedience under false leaders, a flock scattered without a shepherd (10.1ff.; 11.15ff.; 13.7ff.). The 'shepherd allegory' (11.4ff.) speaks further of a period of indignation in which the covenant of grace and union are broken and Israel lies rejected under the abusive hand of the false shepherd. Moreover, the land is filled with pollution and false prophecy.

Then a change is marked in the divine economy. Once again God has compassion on his people (10.6) and signals the change with an outpouring of a 'spirit of mercy and supplication' (12.10). The land is purged in a fearful cleansing. Two-thirds perish and only a third is left alive. A repentant Jerusalem (12.10ff.) hears the renewed covenant promise (13.8f.) and responds in faith (v. 9). Chapter 14 focuses completely on the end time when God has again miraculously redeemed the remnant of suffering Jerusalem. The chapter forms a kaleidoscope of pictures of the new age and the kingship of God (14.9). Significantly, the traditional language of the second exodus, even in the altered form of Proto-Zechariah, is completely missing. Rather, the end is portrayed in the language of the apocalyptic vision. It is characterized by the sharpest polarity possible between the destruction of the cosmic forces of evil (14.2; cf. Ezek. 38–39; Joel 4), and the completely transformed new Jerusalem which is filled with 'living water' (v. 8), completely holy to God (vv. 20ff.), and without either night or winter (vv. 6f.).

It is important to recognize that the editorial joining of the two parts of Zechariah not only serves to alter the reading of the first chapters in terms of the last, but the reverse dynamic is also set in motion. The presence of Proto-Zechariah significantly affected how the community heard the message of the last chapters. To suggest that the late apocalyptic writers had lost interest in the everyday ethical responsibilities of the covenant because of a fixation on the coming age fails to reckon with the canonical shape of the book as a whole. The strong imperatives of ch. 8 which the editors link inextricably with the coming age serve as a constant warning against misunderstanding the nature of the coming kingdom. Judah's repentance is described in 13.9 by a repetition of the same ancient covenant formula found explicitly in 8.8. Thus ch. 8 provides the content to the imperatives which ch. 13 signals and links the two parts of the book closely together.

Finally, a word about the final shape of the book in relation to the larger Old Testament canon. Zechariah stands in an obvious historical and theological relationship to Haggai and continues many of the themes first raised by this contemporary prophet. Yet perhaps an even more important relationship exists between Zechariah and Daniel. Whereas Daniel portrays the period of Israel's 'indignation' before the coming of the new age from the perspective of the nations, and only deals with Israel's sufferings in conjunction with the agony of the end time, the reverse emphasis is found in Zechariah. The book in its present form develops a portrayal of the period before the end from the inner perspective of Israel and only brings in the judgment of the nations as sharing in the preparation for the new age. The history of exegesis has often illustrated the dangers of attempting to force Daniel's pattern upon the book of Zechariah, particularly in ch. 11. Nevertheless, there is a theological relationship between these two differing witnesses which adds great richness to a complete understanding of Israel's hope for the future.

3. Theological and Hermeneutical Implications

(a) The major witnesses expressed in the canonical shaping of the book of Zechariah are in danger of being lost when the two parts of the book are separated. The function of developing a prophetic picture of the end time for the community of faith which had already experienced in its history the return from exile is realized only in the combined process of theological reflection preserved in the whole book. From the canonical perspective the tension between the two sections of the book does not call into question the necessity for a holistic reading.

(b) The referential reading of Zechariah which assumes that its text can only be illuminated when it is properly correlated with the historical moment from which it emerged has been an utter disaster for exegesis. Because the text has not lent itself to this requirement of historical scholarship, the result has been that the interpretation of Zechariah has been dominated by historical speculation and theological fragmentation. Repeatedly commentators conclude that a passage is meaningless because its original reference is no longer available. By taking seriously the canonical shape the community of faith sought to discern in its scripture the intentionality of the biblical text which found its true reference in the divine will for God's people. Obviously, the text referred at times to discernible historical events, but the measure of its truth could not be determined by a theory of correspondence which was blind to that very divine reality to which the canonical text was pointing.

(c) The peculiar features in the formation of the book of Zechariah lie in the manner in which the historical changes affecting the community – return from exile, rebuilt temple, inner conflict and party strife – were interpreted to form a more mature and developed testimony to the ultimate hope of the nation. The historical experience of the exilic community became an integral part of the canonical process. Nevertheless, this experience registered itself theologically not by focusing on the historical processes themselves, but in providing a prophetic picture of God's plan for his people by which to instruct every future generation of Israel who awaits the coming of the kingdom. Indeed the book of Zechariah is anchored to the reign of Darius. It retains the specificity associated with Zerubbabel's building of the temple and the office of Joshua as high priest. At the same time the text points beyond these events to God's final purpose with his people which far transcends the boundaries of the sixth century. To attempt to interpret the book as the result of a conflict between 'visionaries' and 'realists' can only result in the worst kind of reductionism.

(d) The canonical shape of Zechariah points to a dimension of reality which is intense, bizarre, and overwhelming. Its prophetic testimony resists every effort to categorize it in sociological terms. 'I heard him – like a crazy man – talking of horses – lamps – chariots – famine – horns that sprout . . . ' The inability to unify the variety of images into a conceptual pattern does not vitiate its canonical shape, but challenges its hearers to wrestle with the book's content in other forms of actualization such as in art, poetry, and drama. (I am indebted to an unpublished paper by Mary Deeley for this formulation.)

History of Exegesis

Carpzov III, 451f.; *EB* 2, 928; *RGG*³ 5, 1265.

S. H. **Blank**, 'The Death of Zechariah in Rabbinic Literature', *HUCA* 12, 1937, 327–46; F. F. **Bruce**, 'The Book of Zechariah and the Passion Narrative', *BJRL* 43, 1961, 336–53; L. **Doutreleau**, 'Introduction', *Didyme l'aveugle sur Zacharie* I, SC 83, 1963, 13–186; G. **Diettrich**, Iŝo'dadhs Stellung *in der Auslegungsgeschichte des Alten Testaments an seinen Kommentaren zu . . . Sach 9–14 veranschaulicht*, BZAW 6, 1902; L. **Hartman**, *Prophecy Interpreted*, Lund 1966, 118f., 166f.; A. **Köhler**, 'Einleitung', *Die Weissagungen Sacharjas*, I, Erlangen 1861, 1–27; J. **Kremer**, *Der Hirtenallegorie im Buche Zacharias auf ihre Messianität hin untersucht, zugleich ein Beitrag zur Geschichte der Exegese*, Münster 1930; K. G. **Kuhn**, 'Die beiden Messias in den Qumrantexten und die Messiasvorstellung in der rabbinischen Literatur', *ZAW* 70, 1958, 200–8; A. **M'Caul**, *Rabbi David Kimchi's Commentary on the Prophecies of Zechariah*, London 1837.

XXXI

MALACHI

Commentaries

C. F. Keil, CB, 1868
F. Hitzig, H, Steiner, KeH, ⁴1881
T. T. Perowne, CB, 1890
G. A. Smith, ExB, 1898 (²1928)
J. Wellhausen, ³1898
K. Marti, KHC, 1904
A. van Hoonacker, ÉB, 1908
J. M. P. Smith, ICC, 1912
E. W. Barnes, CB², 1917
E. Sellin, KAT, ²⁻³1930
A. von Bulmerincq, 1926–32

R. C. Dentan, *IB*, 1956
A. Gelin, JB, ³1960
D. R. Jones, TB, 1962
F. Horst, HAT, ³1964
K. Elliger, ATD, ⁶1967
T. Chary, SoBi, 1969
P. A. Verhoef, COuT, 1972
J. G. Baldwin, TOTC, 1972
W. Rudolph, KAT², 1977
R. A. Mason, CNEB, 1977

Bibliography

W. A. M. **Beuken**, *Haggai-Sacharja 1–8*, Assen 1967; H.-J. **Boecker**, 'Bemerkungen zur formgeschichtlichen Terminologie des Buches Maleachi', *ZAW* 78, 1966, 78–80; K. **Budde**, 'Zum Text der drei letzten kleinen Propheten', *ZAW* 26, 1906, 1–28; K. **Elliger**, 'Maleachi und die kirchliche Tradition', *Tradition und Situation*, *FS A. Weiser*, Göttingen 1963, 43–48; I. H. **Eybers**, 'Malachi – The Messenger of the Lord', *Theologia Evangelica* 3, Pretoria 1970, 12–20; J. A. **Fischer**, 'Notes on the Literary Form and Message of Maleachi', *CBQ* 34, 1972, 315–20; O. **Holtzmann**, 'Der Prophet Maleachi und der Ursprung des Pharisäertums', *ARW* 29, 1931, 1–21; R. **Pautriel**, 'Malachie(le livre de),' *DBS* 5, 739–46; E. **Pfeiffer**, 'Die Disputationsworte im Buche Maleachi', *EvTh* 19, 1959, 546–68; J. **Swetnam**, 'Malachi 1.11: An Interpretation', *CBQ* 31, 1969, 200–9; C. C. **Torrey**, 'The Prophecy of "Malachi"', *JBL* 17, 1898, 1–15; T. C. **Vriezen**, 'How to understand Malachi 1:11', *Grace upon Grace*, *Essays in Biblical Theology presented to L. Kuyper*, ed. J. I. Cook, Grand Rapids 1975,

128–36; G. **Wallis**, 'Wesen und Struktur der Botschaft Maleachis', *Das ferne und nahe Wort*, *FS L. Rost*, BZAW 105, 1967, 229–37; A. C. **Welch**, *Post-exilic Judaism*, Edinburgh 1935, 113–25.

1. Historical Critical Problems

The book of Malachi has not received the same amount of critical scrutiny as have many of the other Minor Prophets. This situation probably arises from a feeling that the problems of the book seem neither as complex nor as important as some of the other prophets. Critical scholarship reflects a rather broad consensus in dating the book in the first half of the fifth century before the reforms of Ezra and Nehemiah. There is also wide agreement regarding the essential unity of the book. As to its form , the book consists largely of a collection of disputations (cf. especially the analysis of Pfeiffer). The book is usually divided into six sections: 1.2–5; 1.6–2.9; 2.10–16; 2.17–3.5; 3.6–12; 3.13–21 (EVV 3.13–4.3). Occasional glosses have been suggested (1.11–14; 2.11–12), but most of the proposals have not been widely accepted, e.g. Sellin's theory regarding 2.10–16. The only widespread suspicion falls on 3.22–24. Nevertheless, there are a number of critical issues which seriously affect the interpretation of the book and which are addressed by all modern commentaries.

(*a*) The first part of the superscription has evoked considerable notice. The phrase 'oracle of the word of Yahweh' (*maśśā' d'bar yhwh*) occurs only three times in the Old Testament, namely Zech. 9.1, 12.1, and Mal. 1.1. From this evidence the conclusion has usually been drawn that the phrase introduces three anonymous oracles which were appended at the conclusion of the collection of the Book of the Twelve. In the course of transmission the first two oracles became attached somehow to Zechariah, whereas the last oracle attained an independent status (cf. Eissfeldt, *Introduction*, 440, Fohrer, *Introduction*, 469, and Dentan, for variations of this argument). We shall return to the issue later for an examination of its merits.

(*b*) The second part of the superscription relates to the problem of the book's authorship. The Hebrew *mal'ākî* (Malachi) is rendered by the LXX as ἀγγέλου αὐτοῦ ('his messenger'). The Targum adds the clause 'whose name was Ezra the Scribe'. The

Babylonian Talmud (Megilla 15a) and Jerome share this same tradition. Accordingly, the evidence from the versions, the philological problem of taking the noun as a proper name, and the lack of any historical information concerning such a person, has convinced the majority of scholars that the word does not refer to a person, but is an appellative. There is, however, an additional aspect to the problem. Sellin is typical of most modern commentators in suggesting that the word was secondarily introduced into the superscription by a redactor from 3.1. In other words, the editor of the superscription identified the messenger who was announced in ch. 3 with the prophetic author of the book. Again, a closer scrutiny of this consensus will be in order.

(c) There is general agreement on the critical assessment of the last three verses (3.22–23, EVV 4.4–6) as consisting of two separate appendices. The evidence turns chiefly on the form and content of these concluding verses. Verse 4 is thought to be a summarizing admonition stemming from a 'legalistic' rather than prophetic editor (so. J. M. P. Smith, ICC). The last two verses offer a secondary attempt to identify the figure promised in 3.1. Dentan (*IB*) characterizes the verses as 'a bit of speculative exegesis'. Rudolph has argued for seeing these verses as a final redactional conclusion to all the prophetic books.

(d) The final problem turns on the issue of the book's original addressee. The form of the book still reflects clearly the original disputation between the prophet and an antagonist. Who were these persons? The frequent harshness of the response has caused some commentators (e.g. Elliger) to suggest that at least part of the message must have originally been directed to non-Jews, such as the Samaritans. Indeed, many commentators have rested much of their interpretation on distinguishing between the 'godless', i.e. the Samaritans and the 'discouraged pious', the faithful Jewish remnant (cf. Wellhausen on 3.16). For these commentators Malachi's distinction between the godless and the pious is considered as the first step toward the later development of the Hasidim within later Judaism (cf. ICC, *IB*). Again, this important issue needs to be closely re-examined.

How do these various issues appear in the light of the canonical shape into which the present book of Malachi has been fashioned?

2. The Canonical Shape of Malachi

The superscription

We turn to the first portion of the superscription. Is it so evident that because of the occurrence of the same formula in Zech. 9.1, 12.1 and Mal. 1.1 we can conclude that three anonymous oracles were quite arbitrarily assigned their present place within the canon? In my judgment, the issue is far more complex than has usually been assumed in the standard explanation of the phrase 'oracle of the word of Yahweh'.

In the first place, the similarity between the three occurrences of this word cluster is immediately reduced when one reckons with the strong possibility that the first word *maśśā'* (oracle) is used in its absolute form as a separate superscription in Malachi. The confusion regarding the syntax of the word is clearly reflected in the RSV's inconsistent translation of the three identical phrases. In the two passages in Zechariah, the term is translated absolutely, that is, 'oracle'; however, in Mal 1.1. it is translated in a construct chain, 'the oracle of the word of Yahweh'. The NEB is fortunately more consistent.

The evidence in the Hebrew Bible is insufficient to trace the function of the term *maśśā'* as a superscription, but it clearly had its own history and development. It has been used in an absolute state in two difficult texts in Proverbs, 30.1 and 31.1. Again, it functions as a superscription which is attached to the object of the oracle chiefly in Isaiah (13.1; 15.1; 17.1; 19.1, etc.; cf. the parallels in Jer. 46.2; 48.1, etc.). Apparently the term played a role in the original ordering of oracles according to their content, but also in the joining and arrangement of oracles within a collection. The history of this development remains too obscure to call for speculation.

The three verses in which the word cluster appears actually reflect striking differences in both form and function when seen in their entirety. Indeed, the elements of similarity are very superficial ones. Thus, for example, Zech. 9.1 – with the exception of the first word *maśśā'* – is not a superscription at all, but part of a larger poetic oracle. In contrast, the entire first half of Zech. 12.1 clearly functions as a superscription and parallels a form shared by many other prophetic superscriptions in which the content of the oracle is expressed by the preposition *'al* ('concerning', cf. Jer. 14.1; 46.1).

Then again, Mal. 1.1 differs from both and shares its characteristic features as a superscription with other passages in the Old Testament besides Zech. 9.1 and 12.1.

If we examine Mal. 1.1 more closely, certain basic features can be observed which do not appear in the two verses of Zechariah. First, the phrase 'word of Yahweh' (*d'bar yhwh*) appears without a verb. This usage is a feature of late Hebrew prose (e.g. II Chron. 35.6, etc.) and may reflect the influence of the Chronicler. It may possibly indicate a theological development in which the mediatory role of the prophet had receded. Secondly, the addressee is denoted by the preposition *'al* ('to', 'for') which is again a feature known especially in late Hebrew (Zech. 4.6). Finally, the role of the author is described by means of the preposition *b'yad* ('by') which has its closest parallels in Jer. 50.1; Hag. 1.1 and in Chronicles (cf. Beuken, 27ff.).

The point of this study is to demonstrate both the integrity and consistency of the title of Malachi with other features in post-exilic literature, and to show its completely different function from the two passages in Zechariah. The conclusion is far more obvious that the three passages had a history independent of one another than the suggestion of a dependency on the basis of a superficial resemblance. Moreover, the problem of authorship of the book of Malachi is an independent question which cannot be decided from an alleged similarity to anonymous passages in Zechariah. One could even argue that the closer parallels in Isa. 13.1 and Nah. 1.1 rather support a specific authorship within the prophetic tradition. In sum, the present independent status of Malachi did not arise from an arbitrary decision which separated it from the book of Zechariah. Rather, its separate status is deeply rooted in the book's own tradition.

Authorship of the book

We next turn directly to the problem of the book's authorship. Of course it is significant that the LXX translates the noun *mal'akî* as an appellative and not as a proper noun. Nevertheless, the Greek translation also raises a problem by its use of the third person ('his messenger') rather than the first person of the Masoretic text. If the Greek text were original, then the alleged connection of the superscription with 3.1 is no longer so obvious.

Again, the philological evidence for rejecting this formation as inconsistent with a contracted Hebrew name pattern (mal'ᵃkiyyāh = messenger of Yahweh) is inconclusive. The parallels between 'ᵃbî (II Kings 18.2) as compared with 'ᵃbiyyāh (II Chron. 29.1), or 'ûrî (I Kings 4.19) with 'ûriyyāh (I Chron. 6.29) cannot be easily denied. It is also possible to construe the name in a genitive relationship rather than subject and predicate. More recently, W. Rudolph has defended the interpretation as a proper name and finds no serious philological evidence against it.

There is, however, still an important point to make. The concern to question the critical theory of the book's anonymity does not arise from a traditional conservative stance which seeks to defend the book's historicity by establishing its authorship. The issue at stake is of a very different order, and is hermeneutical in nature. What are the implications for interpreting the book when one assumes that the appellative 'my messenger' was a late editor's attempt to identify the prophetic author of the book with the promised messenger of 3.1? Such an identification wreaks havoc with the entire message of the book. If an editor believed that the prophet himself had already functioned as the announced eschatological figure in 'preparing the way of Yahweh', then he misunderstood completely the prophetic hope expressed elsewhere with the same formula (cf. Isa. 40.3; 57.14; 62.10). The preparation envisioned by Isaiah has transformed sinful Israel in such a way that the people are ready to greet their coming king. One could perhaps argue that the redactor has not identified the person of 1.1 with the eschatological messenger of 3.1 but that the analogies lie only in having a similar task. It does appear from 2.7 that the term 'messenger' covers a number of different roles. However, this move to defend an appellative interpretation is not convincing because of the explicit use of the first person in 1.1. which links the term to 3.1 and not to 2.7.

Then again, the appellative interpretation stands in direct contradiction to the final two verses which still envisage a future messenger who will effect the restoration. In my judgment, this approach to the tradition which is embodied in the appellative rendering is highly unlikely. It does not reflect a development consistent with the process we have described as canonical shaping, but rather renders the prophetic text with a confused and unintelligible meaning. In spite of the difficulty associated with the authorship of the book, most commentators would agree that the book's style, historical specificity, and theological content point to a genuine prophetic figure as the source of the tradition. Conversely, there is no sign in the text of an intentional typological move which would emphasize the office to the detriment of the original prophet. Although it is certainly possible that the name of the prophet was lost in the history of transmission, it seems to be equally the case that the word *mal'ākî* was understood by the Masoretic tradition as a proper name. In its canonical shape, 3.1 serves as a word-play on the prophet's name in the superscription.

The addressee of the book

The superscription designates the addressee of the book as 'Israel'. The editors of the final form are consistent in maintaining this perspective throughout the whole composition. Jacob, the father of the nation, is contrasted with Esau, the father of Edom (1.2–5). The covenant with the fathers (2.10) is mentioned. It is 'the whole nation' which has robbed God (3.9). The law of Moses is 'for all Israel' (3.22; EVV 4.4). Regardless of groups within Israel being singled out, e.g. the priests (1.6; 2.1), 'those who feared Yahweh' (3.16), 'the arrogant and all evildoers' (3.19; EVV 4.1), these groups are pictured as part of the nation. Indeed Israel can be contrasted with the nations (3.12), but there is never a move to politicize groups within the nation, such as 'god-fearers' and 'evildoers', which would dissolve the solidarity of the nation.

In the present form of the book there is no evidence to support the theory that the harsh words of rejection (3.19ff.) were directed to those outside of Israel, i.e. the Samaritans, whereas the 'discouraged pious' were handled more gently. Therefore, the frequently suggested emendation of 3.16 (cf. Wellhausen, Sellin, etc.) which identifies the words of 3.13–15 which those 'who feared Yahweh' (v. 16) arises from a psychological attempt to establish a distinction within Israel which runs counter to the present canonical intention. The explicit reiteration in 3.19 (EVV 4.1) of the vocabulary of the arrogant and the evildoers from 3.15 rules out assigning any independent status to the category of the 'discouraged pious'. In sum, the prophetic message of Malachi is addressed solely to Israel; however, within the nation a distinction is made between the righteous and the wicked on the grounds of obedience to God (3.18).

The appendices

The evidence for regarding 3.22 (EVV 4.4) as an appendix from a different hand turns mainly on the particular style and theological perspective of the verse. In my opinion, the suggestion that we see a secondary level of interpretation in this appendix is probably right. However, Rudolph's theory that the appendix was intended as a conclusion to the entire prophetic collection, and matches the 'introduction' in Josh. 1.2, is not convincing. Rather the significance of 3.22 (EVV 4.4) lies in the effect it has as a concluding appendix on the interpretation of the book as a whole. To dismiss it as a 'legalistic corrective' stemming from some disgruntled priestly editor, is to misunderstand the process by which the Hebrew scriptures were collected. The imperative in 3.22 serves to establish an important critical perspective from within the tradition in the light of which Malachi's prophetic disputation assumes its proper theological place. The imperative calls to memory that the whole nation of Israel still stands under the law of Moses which still functions as the unchanging authority for the whole community. The imperative does not weaken Malachi's attack on the nation's sins, but it sets a check against any misuse of the prophet's words which would call into question national solidarity in the name of additional requirements for the pious.

The second appendix (3.2f.; EVV 4.5f.) is of even greater significance in its effect on the reading of the prophet's message. It first identifies the eschatological messenger of 3.1 with Elijah the prophet, who will precede the final day of judgment. The use of the eschatological vocabulary of Joel 3.4 (EVV 2.31) removes any ambiguity as to what day is meant. Elijah's task is to restore the spiritual unity of God's people in preparation for the coming of God to establish justice.

By identifying the eschatological messenger with a figure from Israel's tradition, namely Elijah, the editors again provided a theological context in which Malachi's message was to be understood. Clearly the identification went beyond the original message of the prophet, but arose from the compatible relationship between the Elijah tradition and the prophetic proclamation. Like Malachi, Elijah addressed 'all Israel' (I Kings 18.20). The people of Israel were severely fragmented by indecision of faith (18.21). A curse had fallen on the land (18.1 // Mal. 3.24, EVV 4.6). Elijah challenged all Israel to respond to God by forcing a decision between the right and the wrong (// Mal. 3.18). He did it by means of the right offering (// Mal. 3.3) and a fire which fell from heaven (// Mal. 3.3, 19). Of course, Elijah could return because he had not died, but had been taken alive into heaven.

The effect of identifying Malachi's eschatological prophet with Elijah was not only to establish in great detail the role of the prophet in respect to Israel's restoration, but also to describe theologically the condition of the addressee through this typological analogy. The appendix served to equate the hearers of Malachi's prophecy – along with future generations who heard his words in scripture – with the disobedient, vacillating people whose national allegiance to the God of their fathers was in danger of being dissolved. This redactional identification went beyond the prophet's original message, but it did not do injustice to it. Rather, it served to bring together elements from his preaching into a sharper focus, and to set them in a picture, which was enriched by Israel's fuller traditions.

The narrative report

There is one final indication of canonical shaping which comes in 3.16. At the outset the style is noteworthy (cf. Joel 2.18). A narrative reports the reaction of a group to a disputation between the prophet and the slanderers of God (3.13–15). Verse 16 does not recount the activity of the prophet, but shares a narrative perspective apart from the original disputation. The verse reports a historical response – the contrast is deliberately made with the repetition of the vocabulary (3.13//16) – and then adds a historical judgment which is obviously of a theological order: God heard them and reckoned their response to their credit. Then the original prophetic words of promise (vv. 17ff.) are attached to this historical group of faithful Israelites. The verse is clearly redactional. It reflects a layer different from the original setting of disputation and provides a new theological perspective.

The effect of the verse is to establish in the traditional prose of Hebrew narrative style that God 'heard' the response of the faithful as he had heard the prayers of Abraham, Moses and the psalmist. The historical report thus established a historical – not typological – continuity between faithful Israel in the past and in Malachi's age. It testifies to the fact that the promise of a righteous Israel was not simply a promise, but was even then a historical reality. Thus the theological integrity of Israel as the people of God was maintained.

To summarize: the original message of the prophet Malachi was placed within a larger theological context drawn from Israel's tradition which rendered the original prophetic words appropriate as scripture for successive generations of the people of God. The larger context acted both to enrich the prophet's message by the use of typological analogy, as well as to guard against a sectarian misuse of the prophet which would fragment the national solidarity in the name of reform.

3. Theological and Hermeneutical Implications

(a) Although the book of Malachi has been described in *religionsgeschichtliche* terms as enhancing the growth of sectarianism within Judaism, the canonical shaping of the book moves strongly in the opposite direction. In fact, the final form of the book reflects a profoundly theological understanding of the people of God. It can be debated to what extent the original role of the prophet contained the same theological emphasis. However, in its present shape a delicate balance obtains which affirms the solidarity of the entire nation as God's people against all attempts of pietism to establish 'spiritual norms'. At the same time the election of Israel does not alter the judgment of God who establishes a division between the righteous and wicked of Israel in terms of obedience to the divine law.

(b) The theological relation between the law and the prophets is strikingly illustrated by Malachi. The prophet utters a condemnation of the priestly cultic worship which is as penetrating and critical as any of the eighth-century prophets. Yet the final appeal to the normative role of the Mosaic law serves not to restrict, nor soften the prophet's proclamation, but rather to reaffirm the ground of Israel's existence testified to in the entire Old Testament. The canonical form of Malachi bears witness to Israel's conviction that the law and the prophets were not in opposition to each other, but constituted an essential unity within the divine purpose.

(c) The problem of criteria for determining canonical shaping is clearly illustrated in the issue of God's eschatological messenger.

Critical commentators often suggest that two secondary attempts at identification are represented by 1.1 and 3.23f. (EVV 4.5f.). The usual procedure is then to disparage both of the interpretations as secondary and individualistic distortions. The appeal to a process of canonical shaping has sought to show how the alleged identification in 1.1 cannot be designated a canonical interpretation. The effect of this identification would be to render the rest of the book unintelligible. Conversely, the secondary interpretation of the concluding appendix served a canonical function and did, in fact, establish the normative stance by which later readers interpreted the book. In sum, the tradition itself has established critical criteria in terms of continuity of tradition, integrity of the composition, and subsequent testimony of later Israel by which to determine the canonical shape.

History of Exegesis

Carpzov III, 464–6; *DBS*, 4, 610; *DThC* 9, 1759f.; *RGG*³ 4, 629.

A. **von Bulmerincq**, *Einleitung in das Buch des Propheten Maleachi. Der Prophet Maleachi* I, Dorpat 1926; J. **Carmignac**, 'Vestiges d'un Pesher de Malachie', *RQ* 4, 1964, 97–100; J. **Jeremias**, 'Die Elias Wiederkunft', *TWNT* 2, 933–36 = *TDNT* 2, 931ff.; J. **Knabenbauer**, *Prophetae Minores* II, Paris 1886, 430–45; A. **Köhler**, 'Einleitung', *Die Weissagungen Maleachi's*, Erlangen 1865, 1–27.

PART FIVE

THE WRITINGS

XXXII

INTRODUCTION TO THE WRITINGS

Bibliography

J. **Bloch**, *On the Apocalyptic in Judaism*, JQR Monograph Series 2, 1952; H. **Gese**, 'Die Entstehung der Büchereinteilung des Psalters', *Vom Sinai zum Zion*, Munich 1974, 159–67; G. **Hoelscher**, *Kanonisch und Apokryph*, Leipzig 1905; J. **Fürst**, *Der Kanon des Alten Testaments*, Leipzig 1868; P. **Katz**, 'The Old Testament Canon in Palestine and Alexandria', *ZNW* 47, 1956, 191–217; J. C. H. **Lebram**, 'Aspekte der alttestamentlichen Kanonbildung', *VT* 18, 1968, 173–89; S. **Leiman**, *The Canonization of Hebrew Scripture*, Hamden, Conn., 1976; M. **Margolis**, *The Hebrew Scriptures in the Making*, Philadelphia 1922; C. A. **Moore**, *Esther*, AB, 1971, XXIff.; D. **Rössler**, *Gesetz und Geschichte. Untersuchung zur Theologie der jüdischen Apokalyptik und der pharisäischen Orthodoxie*, WMANT 3, 1962; H. E. **Ryle**, *The Canon of the Old Testament*, London 1892, 119ff., 210ff.; S. **Segert**, 'Zur literarischen Form und Funktion der Fünf Megilloth', *ArOr* 35, 1965, 451–62; A. C. **Sundberg**, *The Old Testament of the Early Church*, Cambridge, Mass. and London 1964; R. D. **Wilson**, 'The Book of Daniel and the Canon', *PTR* 13, 1915, 352–408; 'The Silence of Ecclesiasticus concerning Daniel', *PTR* 14, 1916, 448–74; L. B. **Wolfenson**, 'Implications of the Place of the Book of Ruth in Editions, Manuscripts, and Canon of the Old Testament', *HUCA* 1, 1924, 151–78; W. **Würthwein**, 'Der Fünf Megilloth als Sammlung', *Die Fünf Megilloth*, Tübingen 1969, iii.

Modern critical scholarship has attributed little significance to the Hebrew canon's division of a final section called the Writings or Hagiographa (*kᵉtûbîm*). The reasons for this evaluation are not difficult to discover. First, the third division of the Hebrew canon appears to be a catch-all which lacks coherence. Even those subsections which do exhibit some degree of inner relationship, such as the five Megilloth, derive this unity from a post-Talmudic liturgical practice, and contribute little to the interpretation of the Hebrew text.

More importantly, critical research has discovered that a study of the biblical material according to the divisions of content provides a more useful avenue into the history and interpretation of the individual books. Thus, the major books within the Writings have usually been treated under such rubrics as psalmody, wisdom literature, the Chronicler, and apocalyptic. The smaller, more difficult books to classify such as Song of Songs, Ruth, and Esther have been often squeezed into other categories such as Hebrew lyric or folk tale. Moreover, critical research of the last hundred years has shown that the development of the various blocks of material such as the psalms and the apocalyptic literature have proceeded along independent lines which crossed only in a peripheral way, often at a very advanced stage of growth.

The one aspect in the final division of the Hebrew Bible which has continued to evoke the interest of critical scholarship lies in its contribution to the history of canonization. In chapter II we raised some of these important, but difficult questions. Unfortunately, almost every aspect connected with the formation of the Writings remains highly contested. It is not clear how the collection developed, nor when and where it was closed. The relation of the Writings to the other two Hebrew canonical divisions is also much debated. Some of the disagreement turns on the definition of canonicity which one employs (cf. the conflict of T. Zahn and A. Harnack on the concept of the canon for the New Testament). It does seem evident that the Writings contain much old material, such as the Psalms and the Proverbs, and yet also some of the youngest material of the Hebrew Bible (Dan. 8ff.). It is probable that books within the Writings achieved some recognition of their authority before canonicity was accorded the larger collection.

A brief glance at the great variation in the order of the books of the Writings indicates the degree of fluidity within the canonical division. The printed editions of the Hebrew Bible follow the sequence of the German and French manuscripts: Psalms, Proverbs, Job, Five Megilloth, Daniel, Ezra-Nehemiah, and Chronicles. However, the Talmudic order of Baba Bathra (13b, 14b–15a) begins with Ruth – probably because of the Davidic genealogy – and isolates Esther from the other Megilloth. The relation of Job to Proverbs fluctuates among the various Jewish traditions, as does also Daniel's relation to Esther. The book of Chronicles usually follows Ezra-Nehemiah, concluding the list, except in the Masoretic and Spanish orders in which Chronicles begins the sequence by also preceding the Psalter. The Greek orders are even more fluid because of the variation in the positioning of the apocryphal books (cf. Swete, *Introduction*, [2]1914, 201ff.; Sundberg, 58f.). Neither the Hebrew nor the Greek orders show a consistent chronological or material order.

The major theological implications to be drawn from this evidence is that the collection of material into a third division, which supplemented the Law and the Prophets, performed a significant canonical role for Judaism. The canonical process left its impact in fixing the scope of the section and in the shaping of the individual books. However, the sequence of the books within the canonical division had little significance and no normative order was ever established by the synagogue.

XXXIII

THE PSALMS

Commentaries

E. Hengstenberg, [2]1849–52
J. Olshausen, KeH, 1853
H. Hupfeld, 1855–62
W. M. L. de Wette, [5]1856
F. Delitzsch, BC, 1871
J. J. S. Perowne, [7]1890
J. Wellhausen, [3]1898
A. F. Kirkpatrick, CB, 1891–1901
C. A. Briggs, ICC, 1906–7
B. Duhm, KHC, [2]1922
H. Gunkel, HKAT, [4]1926
R. Kittel, KAT, [5-6]1929
E. W. Barnes, WC, 1931

H. Schmidt, HAT, 1934
W. O. E. Oesterley, 1939
A. Cohen, SonB, [2]1950
H. Lamparter, BAT, 1958
A. Weiser, ET, OTL, 1962
E. J. Kissane, [2]1964
A. Deissler, 1965
M. J. Dahood, AB, 1966–70
H.-J. Kraus, BK, [4]1972
A. A. Anderson, NCeB, 1972
D. Kidner. TOTC, 1975
J. W. Rogerson, J. W. McKay, CNEB, 1977

Bibliographical Surveys

The amount of secondary literature on the Psalms is so immense that the reader is referred to the following modern bibliographical surveys: M. **Haller**, 'Ein Jahrzehnt Psalmenforschung', *ThR* NF 1, 1929, 377–402; A. R. **Johnson**, 'The Psalms', *The Old Testament and Modern Study*, ed. H. H. Rowley, Oxford and New York 1951, 162–209; J. J. **Stamm**, 'Ein Vierteljahrhundert Psalmenforschung', *ThR* NF 26, 1955, 1–68; J. **Coppens**, 'Études Récentes sur le Psautier', *Le Psautier*, ed. R. de Langhe, Louvain 1962, 1–91; É. **Lipiński**, 'Les psaumes de la royauté de Yahwé dans l'exégèse moderne', ibid., 133–272; A. S. **Kapelrud**, 'Scandinavian Research in the Psalms after Mowinckel', *ASTI* 4, 1965, 148–62; J. **Schildenberger**, 'Die Psalmen. Eine Übersicht über einige Psalmenwerke der Gegenwart', *BiLe* 8, 1967, 220–31; D. J. A. **Clines**, 'Psalm Research since 1955: I. The Psalms and the Cult. II. The Literary Genres', *Tyndale*

Bulletin 18, London 1967, 103–25; 20, 1969, 105–25; L. **Sabourin**, *The Psalms, Their Origin and Meaning*, II, Staten Island, N.Y. 1969, 337–67; P.-É. **Langevin**, *Bibliographie Biblique 1930–1970*, Quebec 1972, 147ff.; E. **Gerstenberger**, 'Literatur zu den Psalmen', *VF* 17, 1972, 82–99; É. **Beauchamp**, *DBS* 9, 1973, 127ff., 167ff., 188ff.; E. **Gerstenberger**, 'Psalms', *Old Testament Form Criticism*, ed. J. H. Hayes, San Antonio, Texas 1974, 220–21; O. **Kaiser**, *Introduction to the Old Testament*, ET Oxford and Minneapolis 1975, 337ff.; B. S. **Childs**, 'Reflections on the Modern Study of the Psalms', *The Mighty Acts of God. In Memoriam G. E. Wright*, ed. F. M. Cross, Garden City, N.Y. 1976, 377–88.

Selected Bibliography

G. W. **Ahlström**, *Psalm 89. Eine Liturgie aus dem Ritual des leidenden Königs*, Lund 1959; W. F. **Albright**, 'A Catalogue of Early Hebrew Lyric Poems: Psalm 68', *HUCA* 23, 1950, 1–39; L. **Alonso Schökel**, 'Poësie Hébraïque', *DBS* 8, 47–90; A. **Arens**, 'Hat der Psalter seinen "Sitz im Leben" in der synagogalen Leseordnung des Pentateuch?', *Le Psautier*, ed. R. de Langhe, Louvain 1962, 107–31; *Die Psalmen im Gottesdienst des Alten Bundes*, Trier² 1968; E. **Balla**, *Das Ich des Psalmen*, FRLANT 16, 1912; C. **Barth**, *Die Errettung vom Tode in den individuellen Klag- und Dankliedern des Alten Testament*, Zürich 1947; *Introduction to the Psalms*, ET Oxford and New York 1966; É. **Beauchamp** and I. **Saint-Arnaud**, 'Psaumes. II, Le psautier', *DBS* 9, 125–214; J. **Becker**, *Israel deutet seine Psalmen*, Stuttgart 1966; *Wege der Psalmenexegese*, Stuttgart 1975; J. **Begrich**, 'Das priesterliche Heilsorakel', *ZAW* 52, 1934, 81–92; A. **Bentzen**, *King and Messiah*, ET London and Naperville, Ill. 1955; K.-H. **Bernhardt**, *Das Problem der altorientalischen Königsideologie im Alten Testament*, SVT 8, 1961; W. **Beyerlin**, 'Die *tôdā* der Heilsvergegenwärtigung in den Klageliedern des Einzelnen', *ZAW* 79, 1967, 208–24; *Die Rettung der Bedrängten in den Feindpsalmen der Einzelnen auf institutionelle Zusammenhang untersucht*, FRLANT 99, 1970; H. **Birkeland**, *Die Feinde des Individuums in der israelitischen Psalmenliteratur*, Oslo 1933; *The Evildoers in the Book of Psalms*, ANVAO II, 1955, No. 2; W. **Bloemendaal**, *The Headings of the Psalms in the East Syrian Church*, Leiden 1960; R. G. **Boling**, 'Synonymous Parallelism in the Psalms', *JSS* 5, 1960, 221–55; D. **Bonhoeffer**, *The Psalms as the Prayer Book of the Church*, ET Philadelphia 1970 (*Gesammelte Schriften* IV, Munich 1961, 544ff.); H. A. **Brongers**, 'Die Rache- und Fluchpsalmen im Alten Testament', *OTS* 13, 1963, 21–42; F. F. **Bruce**, 'The Earliest Old Testament Interpretation', *OTS* 17, 1972, 44–52; M. **Buss**, 'The Psalms of Asaph and Korah', *JBL* 82, 1963, 387–92.

H. **Cazelles**, 'La question du *lamed auctoris*', *RB* 56, 1949, 93–101; B. S. **Childs**, 'Psalm Titles and Midrashic Exegesis', *JSS* 16, 1971, 137–50; K. R. **Crim**, *The Royal Psalms*, Richmond, Va. 1962; F. M. **Cross**, 'The Divine Warrior in Israel's Early Cult', 1966; reprinted in *Canaanite Myth* and Hebrew Epic, Cambridge, Mass. 1973, 91–111; F. M. **Cross** and D. N. **Freedman**, 'A Royal Song of Thanksgiving: II Sam 22=Ps.18', *JBL* 72, 1953, 15–34; F. **Crüsemann**, *Studien zur Formgeschichte von Hymnus und Danklied in Israel*, WMANT 32, 1969; R. C. **Culley**, *Oral Formulaic Language in the Biblical Psalms*, Toronto 1967; A. **Deissler**, *Psalm 119(118) und seine Theologie. Ein Beitrag zur Erforschung der anthologischen Stilgattung im Alten Testament*, Munich 1955; L. **Delekat**, 'Probleme der Psalmenüberschriften', *ZAW* 76, 1964, 280–97; *Asylie und Schutzorakel an Zionheiligtum*, Leiden 1967; H. **Donner**, 'Ugaritismen in der Psalmenforschung', *ZAW* 79, 1967, 322–50; P. **Drijvers**, *The Psalms, Their Structure and Meaning*, ET New York and London 1965; J. H. **Eaton**, *Kingship and the Psalms*, SBT II.32, 1976; I. **Engnell**, *Studies in Divine Kingship in the Ancient Near East*, Oxford[2] 1967; 'The Book of Psalms', ET in *A Rigid Scrutiny*, Nashville 1969 (=*Critical Essays on the Old Testament*, London 1970), 68–122; J. **Fichtner**, 'Ist das Beten aller Psalmen der christlichen Gemeinde möglich und heilsam?', *WuD* NF 3, 1952, 38–60=*Gottes Weisheit*, Stuttgart 1965, 67–87; L. **Finkelstein**, 'The Origin of the Hallel (Pss.113–118)', *HUCA* 23, 1950/1, 319–37; J. **de Fraine**, *L'aspect religieux de la royauté israélite*, Rome 1954; N. **Füglister**, *Das Psalmengebet*, Munich 1965.

A. **Gelin**, 'La question des "relectures" bibliques à l'intérieur d'une tradition vivante', *Sacra Pagina* I, Louvain 1959, 203–15; *La Prière des Psaumes*, Paris 1961; E. **Gerstenberger**, 'Der klagende Mensch', *Probleme biblischer Theologie, FS G. von Rad*, Munich 1971, 64–72; H. **Gese**, 'Zur Geschichte der Kultsänger am zweiten Tempel', *Abraham unser Vater, FS O. Michel*, London and Cologne 1963, 222–34; reprinted *Vom Sinai zum Zion*, Munich 1974, 147–58; 'Die Entstehung der Büchereinteilung des Psalters', *Wort, Lied und Gottespruch, FS J. Ziegler*, Würzburg 1972, 57–64; reprinted *Vom Sinai zum Zion*, 159–67; M. **Gevaryahu**, 'Biblical Colophons: A Source for the "Biography" of Authors, Texts and Books', *SVT* 28, 1975, 42–59; J. J. **Glueck**, 'Some Remarks on the Introductory Notes of the Psalms', *Studies on the Psalms*, Potchefstroom 1963, 30–39; M. **Goshen-Gottstein**, 'The Psalms Scroll(11QPs[a]). A Problem of Canon and Text', *Textus* 5, Jerusalem 1960, 22–33; M. D. **Goulder**, 'The Fourth Book of the Psalter', *JTS* 26, 1975, 269–89; G. B. **Gray**, *Forms of Hebrew Poetry*, London and New York 1915; H. **Gunkel**, 'Psalmen', *RGG*[1] 4, 1913, 1927ff.; *Ausgewählte Psalmen*, Göttingen [4]1917; 'Psalmen', *RGG*[2] 4, 1609ff.: ET *The Psalms*, ed. J. Muilenburg, Philadelphia 1967; H. **Gunkel** and J. **Begrich**, *Einleitung in die Psalmen*, Göttingen 1933; W. W. **Hallo**, 'Individual Prayer in Sumerian. The Continuity of a Tradition', *Essays in Memory of E. A. Speiser*, New Haven 1968, 71–89; H.-J. **Hermisson**, *Sprache und Ritus im altisraelitischen Kult. Zur 'Spiritualisierung' der Kultbegriffe im Alten Israel*, WMANT 7 19, 1965; S. **Holm-Nielsen**, 'The Importance of Late Jewish Psalmody for the Understanding of Old Testament Psalmodic Tradition', *StTh* 14, 1960, 1–53; *Hodayot. Psalms from Qumran*, Aarhus 1960.

S. H. **Hooke**, ed., *Myth and Ritual*, London and New York 1933; H. Luden **Jansen**, *Die spätjüdische Psalmendichtung. Ihr Entstehungskreis und ihr 'Sitz im Leben'*, Oslo 1937; A. R. **Johnson**, *Sacral Kingship in Ancient Israel*, Cardiff [2]1967; H.-J. **Kraus**, *Die Königsherrschaft Gottes im Alten Testament*, Tübingen 1951; R. **de Langhe**, ed., *Le Psautier, ses origines, ses problèmes littéraires, son influence*, Louvain 1962; A. **Lauha**, *Die Geschichtsmotive in den alttestamentlichen Psalmen*, Helsinki 1945; É. **Lipiński**, 'Yahweh mâlâk', *Bibl* 44, 1963, 405–60; *La royauté de Yahwé dans la poésie et le culte de l'ancien Israël*, Brussels 1965; 'Psaumes: Formes et genre littéraires', *DBS* 9, 1–125; J. L. **McKenzie**, 'Royal Messianism', *CBQ* 19, 1957, 25–52; D. **Michel**, 'Studien zu den sogenannten Thronbesteigungspsalmen', *VT* 6, 1956, 40–68; S. **Mowinckel**, *Psalmenstudien*, I. *Awän und die individuellen Klagepsalmen*: II. *Das Thronbesteigungsfest Jahwäs und der Ursprung der Eschatologie*; III. *Kultprophetie und prophetische Psalmen*; IV. *Die technischen Termini in den Psalmenüberschriften*; V. *Segen und Fluch in Israels Kult und Psalmendichtung*; VI. *Die Psalmendichter*, SNVAO, 1921–1924; *The Psalms in Israel's Worship*, ET Oxford 1962; P. A. **Munch**, 'Die jüdischen "Weisheitspsalmen" und ihr Platz im Leben', *AcOr* 15, 1936, 112–40; R. **Murphy**, 'A Consideration of the Classification "Wisdom Psalms"', *SVT* 9, 1962, 156–67; C. T. **Niemeyer**, *Het Problem van de Rangschikking der Psalmen*, Leiden 1950; J. H. **Patton**, *Canaanite Parallels to the Book of Psalms*, Baltimore 1944; J. P. M. **van der Ploeg**, 'Réflexions sur les genres littéraires des Psaumes', *Studia Biblica et Semitica T. C. Vriezen dedicata*, Wageningen 1966, 265–77; R. **Press**, 'Die eschatologische Ausrichtung des 51. Psalms', *TZ* 11, 1955, 241–49; 'Der zeitgeschichtliche Hintergrund der Wallfahrts-Psalmen', *TZ* 14, 1958, 401–15.

C. **Quell**, *Das kultische Problem der Psalmen*, BWANT II.11(=36), 1926; G. **von Rad**, 'Erwägungen zu den Königspsalmen', *ZAW* 58, 1940/1, 216–22; N. H. **Ridderbos**, *Die Psalmen*, BZAW 117, 1972; A. **Robert**, 'Le Psaume CXIX et les Sapientaux', *RB* 48, 1939, 5–20; 'L'exégèse des Psaumes selon les méthodes de la "Formgeschichte". Exposé et critique', *Miscellanea Biblica B. Ubach*, ed. R. Díaz, Montserrat 1953, 211–25; J. A. **Sanders**, *The Psalms Scroll of Qumran Cave 11*, Oxford 1965; 'Cave 11 Surprises and the Question of Canon', *New Directions in Biblical Archaeology*, ed. D. N. Freedman and J. C. Greenfield, New York 1971, 113–30; N. M. **Sarna**, 'The Psalm for the Sabbath Day (Ps. 92)', *JBL* 81, 1962, 155–68; 'Psalm 89: A Study of Inner Biblical Exegesis', *Biblical and Other Studies*, ed. A. Altmann, Cambridge, Mass. and London 1963, 29–46; 'Prolegomenon', *The Psalms Chronologically Treated*, by M. Buttenweiser, New York 1969; 'Psalms and the Cult', *EJ* 13, 1315–7; H. **Schmidt**, *Das Gebet der Angeklagten im Alten Testament*, BZAW 49, 1928; H. **Schneider**, 'Die Psalmen im Gottesdienst des Alten Bundes', *ThRev* 58, 1962, 225–34; R. **Smend**, 'Uber das Ich der Psalmen', *ZAW* 8, 1888, 49–147; J. A. **Soggin**, 'Zum ersten Psalm', *TZ* 23, 1967, 81–96; 'Zum zweiten Psalm', *Wort – Gebot – Glaube. FS W. Eichrodt*, Zürich 1970, 191–207; A. **Szörényi**,

'Quibus criteriis dignosci possit, qui Psalmi ad usum liturgicum compositi sunt', *Bibl* 23, 1942, 333–68.
R. **Tournay**, 'Les psaumes complexes', *RB* 54, 1947, 521–42; 56, 1949, 37–60; M. **Tsevat**, *A Study of the Language of the Biblical Psalms*, *JBL* Monograph Series 9, 1955; G. **Wanke**, *Die Zionstheologie der Korachiten in ihrem traditionsgeschichtlichen Zusammenhang*, BZAW 97, 1966; W. R. **Watters**, *Formula Criticism and the Poetry of the Old Testament*, BZAW 138, 1976; A. **Weiser**, 'Zur Frage nach den Beziehungen der Psalmen zum Kult', *FS A. Bertholet*, Tübingen 1950, 513–37; M. **Weiss**, 'Wege der neuen Dichtungswissenschaft in ihrer Anwendung auf die Psalmenforschung', *Bibl* 42, 1961, 255–302; A. S. **Welch**, *The Psalter in Life, Worship and History*, Oxford and New York 1926; C. **Westermann**, 'Struktur und Geschichte der Klage im Alten Testament', *ZAW* 66, 1954, 44–80; 'Zur Sammlung des Psalters', *Forschung am Alten Testament*, Munich 1964, 336–43; 'Vergegenwärtigung der Geschichte in den Psalmen', *Forschung am Alten Testament*, 253–80; *The Praise of God in the Psalms*, ET Richmond, Va. 1965; J. W. **Wevers**, 'A Study in the Form Criticism of Individual Complaint Psalms', *VT* 6, 1956, 80–96; G. **Widengren**, *The Accadian and Hebrew Psalms of Lamentations as Religious Documents*, Stockholm 1937; H. W. **Wolff**, 'Psalm 1', *EvTh* 9, 1949/50, 385–94; W. **Zimmerli**, 'Zwillingspsalmen', *Wort, Lied und Gottesspruch. FS J. Ziegler*, Würzburg 1972, 105–113; H. **Zirker**, *Die kultische Vergegenwärtigung der Vergangenheit in den Psalmen*, BBB 20, 1964.

1. The Impact of the Critical Approach on the Psalter

The importance of the Psalter for both Judaism and Christianity can hardly be exaggerated. Jewish religious life, both corporate and private, has been shaped from the beginning by the biblical psalms. In the prayer book, the midrashim, and the rituals of the synagogue the all-encompassing presence of the Hebrew Psalter is visible. Similarly for the Christian church, the New Testament is saturated with citations from the Psalter and such hymns as the 'Magnificat' reflect an unbroken continuity with the praises of Israel. The Psalter provided the decisive impetus in shaping Christian liturgy in all the branches of Christendom both in the early, medieval, and Reformation periods. Even today many of the most enduring hymns of the church are based on Old Testament psalms.

Yet it is also true that critical biblical scholarship has effected a sharper rupture with the traditional interpretation of the Psalter than with almost any other book. Since the history of Psalms research has been rehearsed many times and is readily available (cf. bibliography), there is no need for a detailed recapitulation. A brief summary will suffice to sketch some of the main lines of the modern development.

By the middle of the nineteenth century the Psalm titles, which had been thought to provide the key to psalm interpretation, had been almost universally abandoned as late, inauthentic, and insignificant. The last major scholarly commentary to defend completely the traditional stance was that of Hengstenberg in 1842, and it already appeared anachronistic to the new world of biblical criticism. During the last half of the nineteenth century biblical scholars first sought to establish a genuine historical setting for the psalms by reconstructing specific historical events, often in the Maccabean period (cf. Duhm), which had allegedly evoked each of the psalms. But this move was basically unsuccessful. As if one could write the history of England on the basis of the Methodist hymn book! Nor did the attempt to focus solely on the psalms as a mirror of piety appear illuminating.

The crucial historical critical discovery came with the form-critical work of H. Gunkel who established conclusively that the historical settings of the psalms were not to be sought in particular historical events, but in the cultic life of the community. The psalms could be divided into different literary genres each of which had been shaped by its peculiar function within the cult. Gunkel's younger contemporary, S. Mowinckel, pursued the cultic setting even further. He criticized Gunkel's interpretation that only the traditional forms had a cultic setting and that the now extant psalms were only spiritualized imitations of the cult. Mowinckel sought to relate each concrete psalm to a cultic *Sitz im Leben* and so to expand the categories of genre into cultic, historical ones (cf. Mowinckel, *Psalms in Israel's Worship* I, 29ff.).

In the subsequent period Gunkel's programme for the study of the psalms has been developed along two different lines in particular, that of literary genre and sociological function (cf. the review by Lipiński, *DBS*). First, there have been several major attempts to refine or alter Gunkel's literary classification. From such work there have emerged some new insights into the literary problems and several vulnerable points within Gunkel's classification have been pointed out (cf. Westermann, *Praise*). However, in general the main lines of Gunkel's form-critical analysis have been sustained.

Secondly, the influence of Mowinckel has continued to be strong in the search for an exact cultic setting for the various psalms, although criticism against his own theory of a coronation festival has grown. For a short period the 'myth and ritual school' of Hooke, and the 'patternism' of Engnell attracted wide attention, but increasingly these interpretations came under attack and have been discarded as being ill-founded or excessively tendentious. In sum, even though important critical work has gone on being done, few of the proposals which have suggested a radical change in the model for doing psalm research have been able to convince a wide audience in the manner in which Gunkel succeeded.

Indeed the breadth of the modern consensus which has formed around the general outlines of Gunkel's programme remains impressive. There is a wide agreement which is both international and interconfessional that Gunkel succeeded in bringing a new order into the study of this literature. Nevertheless, the theological problems raised by the historical critical study of the psalms have not been dispelled by Gunkel's approach. Rather, the more sharply the lines of the original sociological context emerged within ancient Israel, the sharper became the rupture with the traditional Jewish-Christian understanding of the Psalter. The traditional messianic psalms (2, 44, 72, 110, etc.) were now seen to be hymns of adoration, which were directed, not to the future, but to an existing, reigning monarch and patterned, both in form and content, after royal hymns of Egypt and Babylon where the form had originated in the setting of ancient Near Eastern divine kingship. The Davidic songs of Book I (3–41) emerged as mainly individual complaint psalms which were anchored in the cult and which reflected a variety of different circumstances including incubation rites, prayers for rain, and the exorcising of demons. Hitherto unknown festivals such as the enthronement of the king were thought to have provided a major force in the formation of the hymns. In the light of this development, it is hardly surprising that the traditional use of the Psalter by the synagogue and church appeared highly arbitrary and far removed from the original function within ancient Israel. With one stroke Gunkel appeared to have rendered all pre-critical exegesis of the Psalter invalid.

Of course, the theological implications of Gunkel's methodology were seen by many scholars, and one of the characteristic features of biblical scholarship during the last forty years has been the effort of Christian theologians to bridge the gap between critical exegesis and the actual faith of the church. (Jewish scholars handled the problem in a somewhat different manner, but also sought to defend a meaningful relationship between the critical and the traditional interpretations.) A steady stream of books appeared which sought to affirm that the psalms could still be understood as Christian prayers and used both corporately and privately within the church. Most of these books – Drijvers, Gelin, Barth – share the method of first accepting Gunkel's approach, perhaps with some slight adjustment, and then adding to it a theological interpretation. At times the attempt to recover a modern theological dimension has been fairly successful (cf. Barth). At other times one has the impression that the real exegetical and hermeneutical problems raised by the historical critical method have been glossed over. At least the suggestion is not too helpful that one seek to discover the spiritual meaning which is 'buried under the surface meaning of the text' (Drijvers, 12). In my judgment, the theological response to the challenge raised by Gunkel and his followers must be offered in a far more rigorous manner. It must be pursued from a very different vantage point, rather than seeking an easy compromise. Again it is my thesis that the modern interpretation of the Psalter suffers from not dealing seriously with the role of the canon as it has shaped this religious literature.

2. The Canonical Shape of the Psalter

It has long been recognized that the present shape of the Psalter reflects a long history of development in both its oral and literary stages. The presence of early collections of psalms throughout the Psalter is evident, as for example, in the pilgrimage songs of Pss. 120–134, and in the collections of Asaph and Korah (cf. Westermann and Gese). The colophon-like conclusion of Ps. 72: 'the prayers of David, the son of Jesse, are ended', also appears to mark an earlier collection because other psalms are attributed to David in the books which follow. It is also clear that the psalms have undergone a complex history of literary redaction such as is visible in the Elohistic editing of Pss. 43–83.

At times it is possible to trace quite easily some of the stages in the development. Book I of the Psalter appears to be one of the

earliest collections and made up almost entirely of psalms attributed to David. Books II and III seem to have been formed about
two Levitical collections (42–49; 73–83) which were then combined
with Book I along with other psalms. The complexity of the history
is revealed from the note in 72.20. Psalm 119 stands apart and may
have once closed an early form of the Psalter (so Westermann). At
least the later collections (120–134; 138–145) show signs of subsequent editorial inclusion. Gese has demonstrated convincingly that
the present Psalter divisions have arisen from a long and complex
process of growth and are not simply the result of liturgical influence.
Yet it is also evident that much of the history of the development
remains obscure. Nor is it possible to determine with certainty the
intention, if any, of the editors. One simply does not know why Ps.
50 was isolated from the major collection of the Asaph psalms
(73–83), or why the last books of the Psalter lack musical references, or why the historical superscriptions to David's life are clus-
tered so thickly about Pss. 50–60.

However, in spite of the uncertainty regarding the historical
development of much of the Psalter – Gese's attempt to connect the
history of the temple singers with the growth of the Psalter remains
tentative at best – certain features in the present shape are clear.
The Hebrew Psalter in its Masoretic text consists of five separate
divisions or books. The first four conclude with a separate doxology; the last psalm consists of a doxology in its entirety. Psalm 1
serves as a introduction to the whole Psalter. An appropriate conclusion is provided by the last five psalms which all begin with the
phrase 'halleluya'. Most of the Hebrew psalms – there are 34
exceptions – are supplied with superscriptions of different sorts.
Some of the titles consist in musical instructions ('with stringed
instruments') and are directed apparently to the choirmaster.
Other elements of the titles distinguish between different categories
of psalms. Some 73 psalms are ascribed to David, whether in terms
of authorship or of collection is debatable (cf. Mowinckel, *Worship*
I, 77). Other psalms are attributed to Moses, Solomon, Asaph, the
Sons of Korah, and others. In some 13 instances specific historical
events in the life of David are connected with the composition of the
psalm. Occasionally a psalm is related to the dedication of the
temple (Ps. 30), or the sabbath (Ps. 90).

What significance can be attributed to these elements of the
present form of the Psalter? In what way does the final editing of

the Psalter testify as to how the collectors understood the canonical material to function for the community of faith?

The introduction

Psalm 1 is generally classified as a 'Torah Psalm' and is akin to Pss. 19b and 119 in its praise of the law. The psalmist pronounces a blessing on the godly man who occupies himself day and night with the divine commandments. The parallels with Deut. 30 and Josh. 1 reveal clearly that the commandments of Moses constitute the divine law on which the godly reflect. It is highly significant that the psalmist understands Israel's prayer as a response to God's prior speaking. Israel's prayers are not simply spontaneous musings or uncontrolled aspirations, but rather an answer to God's word which continues to address Israel in his Torah.

The present editing of this original Torah psalm has provided the psalm with a new function as the introduction to the whole Psalter. Westermann may be right in seeing Pss. 1 and 119 as forming the framework for an earlier collection of psalms. Certainly in its final stage of development, Ps. 1 has assumed a highly significant function as a preface to the psalms which are to be read, studied, and meditated upon. The Torah of God which is the living word of God is mediated through its written form as sacred scripture. With the written word Israel is challenged to meditate day and night in seeking the will of God. Indeed, as a heading to the whole Psalter the blessing now includes the faithful meditation on the sacred writings which follow. The introduction points to these prayers as the medium through which Israel now responds to the divine word. Because Israel continues to hear God's word through the voice of the psalmist's response, these prayers now function as the divine word itself. The original cultic role of the psalms has been subsumed under a larger category of the canon. In an analogy to Israel's wisdom collection the study of the Psalter serves as a guidebook along the path of blessing.

Dietrich Bonhoeffer once reflected on the question of how the psalms which were the words of men to God could ever be considered God's word to men. The redactional position of Ps. 1 testifies that this hermeneutical shift did actually take place within Israel. The prayers of Israel directed to God have themselves become identified with God's word to his people. Israel reflects on the psalms, not merely to find an illustration of how godly men prayed to God in the past, but to learn the 'way of righteousness' which comes from obeying the divine law and is now communicated through the prayers of Israel.)

The Psalter bears the title in the Hebrew Bible of *t'hillîm*, songs of praise. This is not a literary classification and does not accurately describe the various genres of prayer, songs and liturgies which the Psalter contains, but it does accurately reflect the theology of Israel. The psalms have to do with the praise of God. The title correctly bears witness to the conviction that the voice is that of Israel, but it is only an echo of the divine voice which called his people into being.)The introduction to the Psalter testifies to a new theocentric understanding of the psalms in the continuing life of the people of God. The introduction is, therefore, the first hint that the original setting has been subordinated to a new theological function for the future generations of worshipping Israel.

The anthological style

There is another indication within the Psalter that the traditional prayers of Israel have assumed a new role as sacred scripture of the community. It has long been noticed that certain psalms are actually only compilations of other psalms. Thus, for example, Ps. 108 consists of two parts made up by joining Pss. 57 and 60. In other psalms such as Ps. 86 almost every line has picked up a phrase from another portion of scripture and fashioned it into a poem. Although this feature had been already described by Mowinckel as characteristic of the late 'learned psalm' (*Worship* II, 104ff.), and often judged as a sign of the loss of spontaneous piety, the real credit for understanding the significance of this development goes to the French scholars associated with the school of Robert and Gelin. They used the term 'relecture' or 'anthological style' to describe the process by which a later biblical writer made use of an earlier writing in order to produce a new form with its own individual integrity.

The interesting thing to note is that already in the book of Chronicles we are given an insight into this use of the Psalter. I Chron. 16 describes the bringing of the ark into Jerusalem and David's appointing Asaph and his choir to render thanksgiving to God. The liturgical nature of the service is made clear by the concluding Amen response of the people (v. 36). The actual hymn which is then cited as constituting the service of thanksgiving is made up of a catena of psalms, namely, portions from 105, 96, and 106. Likewise in II Chron. 6 and 7, Solomon includes in his prayer a citation from Ps. 132, and the people respond with the refrain from Ps. 136.

The point to be stressed is that within Israel the psalms have been loosened from a given cultic context and the words assigned a significance in themselves as sacred scripture. These words of promise could be used in a variety of new contexts. They could be reworked and rearranged in a different situation without losing their meaning.

The growing tendency of later Israel – the *Hodayot* of Qumran provide an excellent example – to re-use the older language grew out of an increasing awareness of the role of a body of authoritative and sacred writings. Far from being a sign of a loss of piety or an attachment to the past, this move testified to Israel's desire to articulate new praise to God through the mediation of older forms.

The royal psalms

Historical critical research has made out a strong case for believing that the royal psalms arose in a specific cultic historical setting which shared many features of the ancient Near Eastern royal ideology (cf. Gunkel, Begrich, *Einleitung*, 140ff.). The psalm honoured a reigning king, often in terms akin to deification, and sought his blessing as a channel for divine blessing. 'May he live while the sun endures . . . may he be like rain that falls on the mown grass . . . in his days may righteousness flourish and peace abound' (Ps. 72). The original occasion for such royal psalms was clearly different from that of the messianic hope of the prophets. The majority of modern scholars are fully in accord with Gunkel and Mowinckel in rejecting the traditional interpretation of messianic psalms.

In my judgment, the usual critical approach, in spite of its many valid observations, has failed to reckon either with the alterations which the canonical shaping has given to the royal psalms or the new function which these psalms perform within the collection of the Psalter. In the first place, it is interesting to notice that no ancient groupings of royal psalms have been preserved. Whereas

other psalms such as community complaint psalms, songs of pilgrimage, and collections of individual complaint psalms have been
transmitted within a collection, the royal psalms have been
thoroughly scattered throughout the Psalter. Could this be a first
indication of a new understanding of these psalms?

The peculiar features of Ps. 2 have long attracted attention. The
psalm is set off from the rest of the poems within Book I by not
having a title and by not being part of the early collection of
Davidic complaints. Indeed the Western Text of Acts 13.33 cites
from the psalm as from 'the first psalm' (cf. Berakoth 9b). The
older commentators debated at length whether to see Ps. 2 as part
of the introduction to the whole Psalter. Some saw the 'Law' in Ps.
1 balanced by the 'Prophets' of Ps. 2. Although the content of Pss. 1
and 2 differ greatly, there are some signs that the redactor sought to
link the two psalms together. Ps. 1 appears to reflect in historical
terms a model provided by the didactic pattern of Ps. 2. Moreover,
Ps. 1 begins with the blessing formula; Ps. 2 ends with the same
formula. Perhaps one should leave open the question of whether or
not Ps. 2 was conceived of as a formal part of the introduction. The
evidence is not sufficient to press the point. Still one wonders why
this psalm was placed in such a prominent place unless it was to
emphasize the kingship of God as a major theme of the whole
Psalter. Certainly the original mythopoetic setting of the older
adoption formula in v. 7, 'you are my son, today I have begotten
you', has long since been forgotten (cf. von Rad). Rather, the
weight of the psalm falls on God's claim of the whole earth as his
possession, and the warning of his coming wrath against the pre-
sumption of earthly rulers. In other words, the psalm has been
given an eschatological ring, both by its position in the Psalter and
by the attachment of new meaning to the older vocabulary through
the influence of the prophetic message (cf. Jer. 23.5; Ezek. 34.23).
Indeed, at the time of the final redaction, when the institution of
kingship had long since been destroyed, what earthly king would
have come to mind other than God's Messiah? (cf. Westermann,
'Sammlung', 342.)

Psalm 72 now bears the superscription: 'a psalm le (to or for)
Solomon'. Because the psalm closes with the sentence, 'the prayers
of David are ended', it seems natural to assume that the redactor
understood the psalm to be 'for' Solomon and offered by David. By
means of this title the editor indicated to the reader that the psalm

was to be understood in the context of the biblical story found in Kings and Chronicles. The promise of divine blessing in I Kings 8 is connected with the oracles of Nathan (II Sam. 7) and is predicated on the obedience of God's commands. When read in this context, Ps. 72 no longer functions as an example of ancient Near Eastern royal ideology, but as a prayer of David that Solomon rule as a righteous king who faithfully executes the kingship of God according to the divine promise. The extravagant language is possible in Israel because the rule of God is the ultimate object being praised. The eschatological dimension of the royal psalms emerges in even clearer form in Pss. 89 and 132 where the prophetic promise to Nathan is actually cited. To be sure, the psalmist has developed this tradition along different lines from the prophet, but increasingly the prophetic model poured its content into the idiom of the psalmist.

In sum, although the royal psalms arose originally in a peculiar historical setting of ancient Israel which had received its form from a common mythopoetic milieu, they were treasured in the Psalter for a different reason, namely as a witness to the messianic hope which looked for the consummation of God's kingship through his Anointed One.

New eschatological interpretation

Modern psalm interpretation is characterized by its emphasis on the cult. There is a wide consensus in seeing the force of a stereotyped practice of worship giving shape to the various literary genres of the Psalter. The cult seems to be totally alien to eschatology. Thus Mowinckel could contrast sharply the eschatological scanning of the future with the cultic role of transporting the believer *hic et nunc* into primordial time. In his well-known hypothesis, he sought to derive Israel's eschatology from a disillusionment with the cultic expectation of royal ideology which was projected into the future during the post-exilic period.

However, one of the striking features of the Psalter in its canonical form is the large number of psalms which sound dominant eschatological notes. 'I wait for Yahweh more than the watchman for the morning' (Ps. 130.5, EVV 6). 'Yahweh will build Zion, he will appear in his glory' (Ps. 102.15, EVV 16; cf. Pss. 69.34, EVV 35; 126.4ff. etc.). Many of these psalms exhibit all the stereotyped characteristics of the individual complaint psalms so carefully analysed by Gunkel. The psalmist fluctuates between complaints in his present plight, pleas for help, and outbursts of confidence in God. Although it is true that many psalms in this category end on the same note of complaint with which the psalm began (cf. Ps. 88, etc.), in many of these psalms the psalmist comforts himself, not by reflecting on events in the past, but by his hope in some future action of God which will be different in kind from that of the past.

Commentators have long noted that often the eschatological part of a psalm has been juxtaposed to the characteristic features of the complaint psalm without a logical bridge. Thus, within Ps. 102, vv. 2–12 and 24–25a (EVV 1–11, 23–24a) exhibit all the marks of the complaint, but intertwined within these sections is an entirely different sort of material. Here the focus is directed to the 'generation yet to come' and to 'the children who shall dwell secure'. At times the individual complaint psalm is suddenly cut off and continued in what seems to be a psalm of thanksgiving. Psalm 22. 2–22 (EVV 1–21) exhibits all the marks of a complaint, whereas from vv. 23ff. (EVV 22ff.) the psalmist turns his attention completely to the future with words which remind of the prophetic hope.

Of course, commentators have attempted to explain the change in tone within a complaint psalm in a variety of ways, especially in terms of an oracle of forgiveness or absolution (Begrich). One cannot rule out this possibility in its original setting. Other scholars prefer a literary critical solution and see the early psalm having been reworked in the post-exilic period which accounts for its eschatological reinterpretation (J. Becker). However one explains it, the final form of the Psalter is highly eschatological in nature. It looks toward to the future and passionately yearns for its arrival. Even when the psalmist turns briefly to reflect on the past in praise of the 'great things which Yahweh has done', invariably the movement shifts and again the hope of salvation is projected into the future (Ps. 126.6). The perspective of Israel's worship in the Psalter is eschatologically oriented. As a result, the Psalter in its canonical form, far from being different in kind from the prophetic message, joins with the prophets in announcing God's coming kingship. When the New Testament heard in the psalms eschatological notes, its writers were standing in the context of the Jewish canon in which the community of faith worshipped and waited.

The corporate reference

Gunkel described the individual complaint psalm as forming the actual backbone of the Psalter (*Einleitung*, 173). This genre of psalm clearly dominates the collection and is found widely represented outside the Psalter as well. In the later part of the nineteenth century the question was widely debated as to whether the reference to the recurring 'I' of the Psalter was an individual or a corporate person. However, by the first part of the twentieth century a consensus was again reached, chiefly on the basis of the excellent monograph of Gunkel's student Balla, who argued that the 'I' must be interpreted individually. Balla's chief evidence for this conclusion rested on ancient Near Eastern parallels, the concrete life situations of the psalmist's original setting, and the clearly contrasting style and content of the few genuine communal complaints. Balla concluded his study by triumphantly rejecting the older collective interpretation of R. Smend as an 'allegorical vestige'.

In my judgment, there is little doubt but that Balla got the better of the argument with Smend in the debate which focused on the original meaning of the 'I' of the Psalter. But the issue takes on a different face when the question is raised in respect to the final form of the Psalter. Is it so obvious that the 'I' retains its strictly individual referent? Several factors would immediately suggest that much more is involved. First of all, the title to Ps. 30, 'A Song at the Dedication of the Temple', is an obvious example, although of a later period, of a communal interpretation of an original individual psalm of thanksgiving. The psalmist originally described his own desperate plight and how God brought up his soul from Sheol in deliverance. He then called on the faithful to give praise to God. However, at a later date the same psalm expressed the community's praise in providing the words for its joy at the dedication of the second temple.

Moreover, there are numerous psalms in which the psalmist moves directly from speaking as an individual to representing the community with no apparent difficulty (cf. Becker, *Israel deutet* ... , 41ff.). Thus in Ps. 130 one notices the clear shift: 'Out of the depths I cry to thee; I wait for Yahweh ... O Israel, hope in Yahweh ... He will redeem Israel from all his iniquities.' Likewise, the individual complaints of Pss. 14, 25, 51, 61, etc. end on the theme: 'Redeem Israel out of all his troubles.' Whether one wants to explain this movement by an appeal to H. Wheeler Robinson's hypothesis of 'collective personality' remains a moot question, but certainly there is evidence to suggest that the individual psalms were often understood collectively by the later generation of worshippers. Of course, this is hardly a surprising development and one which seems entirely natural even to modern liturgy. However, it is significant in again showing a new function which ancient psalms had already acquired within ancient Israel, and it calls into question an exegesis which fails to deal seriously with the final shape within the canonical collection.

Psalm titles

Finally, and surely the most far-reaching alteration with which the collector shaped the canonical Psalter, was in his use of superscriptions. Little interest has been paid to these titles in recent years. The reason for this lack of interest is clear. A wide consensus has been reached among critical scholars for over a hundred years that the titles are secondary additions which can afford no reliable information toward establishing the genuine historical setting of the psalms. Yet, although the titles are a relatively late addition, they represent an important reflection of how the psalms as a collection of sacred literature were understood and how this secondary setting became authoritative for the canonical tradition (cf. Childs, 'Psalm Titles').

The titles are of a wide variety of kinds and reflect many different functions. Some are of a liturgical nature and designate the manner in which the psalm was to be rendered by the choirmaster. Many of these technical terms can no longer be understood and appear unintelligible even to the early Greek translators. But most significant in the titles is the close connection established with David. The Masoretic Text assigns 73 psalms to David. The LXX increased the number and later rabbinic tradition ascribed all of the Psalter in a sense to Davidic inspiration. Clearly, David came to be regarded as the source of Israel's psalms as Moses was for the law, and Solomon was for wisdom.

Perhaps the key to understanding this Davidic tradition regarding the psalms is to be found in the thirteen examples in which a specific incident in David's life is described as the occasion for the writing of the psalm. Thus Ps. 51 is connected with David's sin with Bathsheba, and Ps. 56 with his being seized by the Philistines in Gath. Now the interesting thing to note is that the psalms are related to historical incidents recorded elsewhere in scripture, specifically in Samuel. Moreover, the process by which the relationship was established derived from an exegesis of the psalms themselves which sought to establish the setting from the content of the psalm (cf. Childs). In other words, the titles are not independent historical traditions. How are we to understand this move?

Psalms which once functioned within a cultic context were historicized by placing them within the history of David. Moreover, the incidents chosen as evoking the psalms were not royal occasions or representative of the kingly office. Rather, David is pictured simply as a man, indeed chosen by God for the sake of Israel, but who displays all the strengths and weaknesses of all human beings. He emerges as a person who experiences the full range of human emotions, from fear and despair to courage and love, from complaint and plea to praise and thanksgiving. Moreover, by attaching a psalm to a historical event the emphasis is made to fall on the inner life of the psalmist. An access is now provided into his emotional life. One now knows how his faith relates to the subjective side of his life.

The effect of this new context has wide hermeneutical implications. The psalms are transmitted as the sacred psalms of David, but they testify to all the common troubles and joys of ordinary human life in which all persons participate. These psalms do not need to be cultically actualized to serve later generations. They are made immediately accessible to the faithful. Through the mouth of David, the man, they become a personal word from God in each individual situation. In the case of the titles the effect has been exactly the opposite from what one might have expected. Far from tying these hymns to the ancient past, they have been contemporized and individualized for every generation of suffering and persecuted Israel.

To summarize: The attempt has been made to outline the canonical shape of the Psalter and to describe the elements within the final redaction. Several important alterations have been detected which have pointed to a different function in the final collection from its original role in ancient Israel. There was a growing consciousness of the Psalter as sacred scripture reflected in the intro-

THE WRITINGS

duction and in the anthological style. There was a reinterpretation which sought to understand the promise to David and Israel's salvation as an eschatological event. At times there was a move within the Psalter to broaden an original individual reference to incorporate the collective community, whereas at other times, the move toward universalizing the psalm was achieved by relating it to the history of David as a representative man.

Above all, one senses the variety within the canonical process. Although the psalms were often greatly refashioned for use by the later community, no one doctrinaire theology was allowed to dominate. Then the question arises, did the later refashioning do violence to the original meaning? One's answer depends largely on how one construes 'doing violence'. Certainly the elements of continuity between the earlier and later interpretations are evident. Nevertheless, the original meaning is no longer an adequate norm by which to test the new.

3. Theological and Hermeneutical Implications

(a) The most characteristic feature of the canonical shaping of the Psalter is the variety of different hermeneutical moves which were incorporated within the final form of the collection. Although the psalms were often greatly refashioned for use by the later generations, no one doctrinaire position received a normative role. The material was far too rich and its established use far too diverse ever to allow a single function to subordinate all others. The psalms were collected to be used for liturgy and for study, both by a corporate body and by individuals, to remind of the great redemptive acts of the past as well as to anticipate the hopes of the future. Yet in spite of the openness of the canonical editing to these various roles, the collecting process did establish very clear and fixed parameters. The presence of other psalms at Qumran and in the LXX, which were not received within the Hebrew canon, testifies to the equally significant role of the canon in establishing boundaries. However, far from being a stultifying influence, the sharp distinction between text and targum served to ensure Israel's freedom in the use of its hymnic tradition.

(b) The canonical shape of the Psalter offers the modern interpreter a warrant for breaking out of the single, narrowly conceived mode of exegesis which is represented by most modern critical commentaries. Thus, for example, a liturgical hearing of the Psalter works with a different semantic unit from that needed for grammatical analysis of a prose sentence. Similarly, the juxtaposition of a psalm with another portion of scripture creates a new context for a communal response which is different in kind from free association.

One of the major reasons for working seriously in the history of biblical exegesis is to be made aware of many different models of interpretation which have all too frequently been disparaged through ignorance. With all due respect to Gunkel, the truly great expositors for probing to the theological heart of the Psalter remain Augustine, Kimchi, Luther, Calvin, the long forgotten Puritans buried in Spurgeon's *Treasury*, the haunting sermons of Donne, and the learned and pious reflections of de Muis, Francke and Geier. Admittedly these commentators run the risk, which is common to all interpretation, of obscuring rather than illuminating the biblical text, but because they stand firmly within the canonical context, one can learn from them how to speak anew the language of faith.

(c) John Calvin, in the preface to his commentary, described the Psalter as ... 'the anatomy of all the parts of the soul, for not an affection will anyone find in himself whose image is not reflected in this mirror. All the griefs, sorrows, fears, misgivings, hopes, cares, anxieties, in short all the disquieting emotions with which the minds of men are wont to be agitated, the Holy Spirit hath here pictured exactly.' The canonical shape of the Psalter assured the future generations of Israelites that this book spoke a word of God to each of them in their need. It was not only a record of the past, but a living voice speaking to the present human suffering. By taking seriously the canonical shape the reader is given an invaluable resource for the care of souls, as the synagogue and church have always understood the Psalter to be.

History of Exegesis

Carpzov III, 141–153; *DBS* 9, 188–90 (Qumran Psalms); **Höpfl**, *Introd. VT*, ⁵1946, 311–14; *RGG*³ 5, 684–6.

A. **Allgeier**, 'Les commentaires de Cajétan sur les Psaumes', *Revue Thomiste* 39, Bruges 1934, 410–43; J. **Baker** and E. W. **Nicholson**, 'Introduction', *The Commentary of Rabbi David Kimḥi on Psalms CXX-CL*, Cambridge and New York 1973, xi-xxxii; P. **Blanchard**, 'Le Psautier dans la liturgie', *Richesses et déficiences des anciens Psautiers latins*, Collectanea Biblica Latina XIII, Rome 1959, 231–48; W. G. **Braude**, 'Introduction', *The Midrash on Psalms*, I, New Haven 1959, xi-xxxvi; A. **Büchler**, 'Zur Geschichte der Tempelmusik und der Tempelpsalmen', *ZAW* 19, 1899, 96–133, 329–44; 20, 1900, 97–135; E. **Cardine**, 'Psautiers anciens et chant grégorien', *Richesses et déficiences*, 249–58; J. **Daniélou**, 'Le psaume 22 dans l'exégèse patristique', *Richesses et déficiences*, 189–211; G. **Ebeling**, 'Luthers Psalterdruck vom Jahre 1513', *ZTK* 50, 1953, 43–99; 'Luthers Auslegung des 14.(15.) Psalms in der ersten Psalmenvorlesung im Vergleich mit der exegetischen Tradition', *ZTK* 50, 1953, 280–339; I. **Elbogen**, *Der jüdische Gottesdienst in seiner geschichtlichen Entwicklung*, Berlin 1913; D. **van den Eynde**, 'Literary Notes on the Earliest Scholastic Commentarii in Psalmos', *Franciscan Studies* 14, New York 1954, 121–54.

B. **Fischer**, *Das Psalmen Verständnis der alten Kirche bis zu Origenes*, Kath. Habil. Schrift, Bonn 1944; 'Christliches Psalmenverständnis im 2. Jahrhundert', *BiLe* 3, 1962, 111–19; A. **George**, 'Jésus et les psaumes', *A la recontre de Dieu, Mémorial A. Gelin*, 1961, 297–308; H. **Gese**, 'Psalm 22 und das Neue Testament', *ZTK* 65, 1968, 1–22; M. **Harl**, *La Chaîne Palestinienne sur le Psaume 118* (*Origène, Eusèbe, Didyme, Apollinaire, Athanase, Théodoret*) I, SC 189, 1972, 17–179; S. **Holm-Nielsen**, *Hodayot. Psalms from Qumran*, Aarhus 1960; E. **Kähler**, *Studien zum Te Deum und zur Geschichte des 24. Psalms in der Alten Kirche*, Göttingen 1958; H. C. **Knuth**, *Zur Auslegungsgeschichte von Psalm 6*, BGBE 11, 1971; H.-J. **Kraus**, 'Vom Leben und Tod in den Psalmen. Eine Studie zu Calvins Psalmen Kommentar', *Leben angesichts des Todes, FS H. Thielicke*, 1968, 27–46; J. A. **Lamb**, *The Psalms in Christian Worship*, London 1962; J. **Leclercq**, 'Les Psaumes 20–25 chez les commentateurs du Haut Moyen Âge', *Richesses et déficiences*, 213–29; O. **Linton**, 'Interpretation of the Psalms in the Early Church', *Studia Patristica* IV, TU 79, 1961, 143–56; R. **Loewe**, 'Herbert of Bosham's Commentary on Jerome's Hebrew Psalter', *Bibl* 34, 1953, 44–77, 159–92, 275–98.

J. **Mann**, *The Bible as Read and Preached in the Old Synagogue*, 2 vols., Cincinnati 1940, 1966; J. M. **Neale** and R. F. **Littledale**, *A Commentary on the Psalms from Primitive and Mediaeval Writers*, 4 vols. London 1860–1874; A. **Neubauer**, 'The Authorship and Titles of the Psalms according to the Early Jewish Authorities', *Studia biblica et ecclesiastica* II, Oxford 1890, 1–57; L. J. **Rabinowitz**, 'The Psalms in Jewish Liturgy', *Historia Judaica* 6, New York 1944, 109–22; S. **Raeder**, *Die Benutzung des masoretischen Textes bei Luther in der Zeit zwischen der ersten und zweiten Psalmenvorlesung (1515–1518)*, BHT 38, 1967; M.-J. **Rondeau**, 'Le "Commentaire des Psaumes" de Diodore de Tarse et l'exégèse antique du Psaume 109/110', *RHR* 176, 1969, 153–88; S. H. **Russell**, 'Calvin and the Messianic Interpretation of the Psalms', *SJT* 21, 1968, 37–47; I. **Saint-Arnaud**, 'Les Psaumes dans la tradition chrétienne', *DBS* 9, 206–14; J. A. **Sanders**, *The Psalms Scroll of Qumran Cave 11 (11QPsᵃ). Discoveries in the Judaean Desert IV*, Oxford 1965; T.

Süss, 'Über Luthers sieben Busspsalmen', *450 Jahre lutherische Reformation*, *FS Franz Lau*, Berlin 1967, 367–83; E. **Werner**, 'Preliminary Notes for a Comparative Study of Catholic and Jewish Musical Punctuation', *HUCA* 15, 1940, 335–60.

XXXIV

JOB

Commentaries

G. H. A. Ewald, ²1854
E. W. Hengstenberg, 1870–75
F. Delitzsch, BC, ²1872
O. Zöckler, ET, LCHS, 1875
A. B. Davidson, CB, 1884
J. Knabenbauer, CSS, 1886
A. Dillmann, KeH, ³1891
B. Duhm, KHC, 1897
A. S. Peake, CeB, 1905
K. Budde, HKAT, ²1913
S. R. Driver, G.B. Gray, ICC, 1921
N. Peters, EH, 1928
E. J. Kissane, 1939

V. E. Reichert, SonB, 1946
H. Lamparter, BAT, 1951
G. Hölscher, HAT, ²1952
N. H. Tur-Sinai, 1957
A. Weiser, ATD, ³1959
S. Terrien, CAT, 1963
G. Fohrer, KAT², 1963
E. Dhorme, (1926) ET 1967
F. Horst, BK, I, 1968
H. H. Rowley, NCeB, 1970
M. H. Pope, AB, ³1974
F. I. Anderson, TOTC, 1976
R. Gordis, 1978

Bibliography

A. **Alt**, 'Zur Vorgeschichte des Buches Hiob', *ZAW* 55, 1937, 265–8; J. **Barr**, 'The Book of Job and its Modern Interpreters', *BJRL* 54, 1971–2, 28–46; K. **Barth**, *Hiob*, ed. H. Gollwitzer, BSt 49, 1966; G. A. **Barton**, 'The Composition of Job 24–30', *JBL* 30, 1911, 66–77; L. W. **Batten**, 'The Epilogue to the Book of Job', *AThR* 15, 1933, 125–8; F. **Baumgärtel**, *Der Hiobdialog*, BWANT IV.9 (=61), 1933; N. P. **Bratsiotis**, 'Der Monolog im Alten Testament', *ZAW* 73, 1961, 30–70; K. **Budde**, *Beiträge zur Kritik des Buches Hiob*, Bonn 1876; M. **Burrows**, 'The Voice from the Whirlwind', *JBL* 47, 1928, 117–32; R. **Cartensen**, 'The Persistence of the "Elihu" Tradition in Later Jewish Writings', *Lexington Theological Quarterly*. 2, Lexington, Ky. 1967, 37–46; T. K. **Cheyne**, *Job and Solomon*, London 1887; M. B. **Crook**, *The Cruel God, Job's Search for the Meaning of Suffering*, Boston 1959; M. **Dahood**, 'Northwest Semitic Philology and

Job', *The Bible in Current Catholic Thought*, ed. J. L. McKenzie, New York 1962, 55–74; L. **Dennefeld**, 'Les discours d'Elihou (Job 32–37)', *RB* 48, 1939, 163–80; G. R. **Driver**, 'Problems in the Hebrew Text of Job', *VT* 3, 1955, 72–93; H. **Duesberg**, *Les scribes inspirés* II, Paris 1939, 53–157, Maredsous ²1966; J. **Fichtner**, 'Hiob in der Verkündigung unserer Zeit', *Gottes Weisheit*, Stuttgart 1965, 52ff.; G. **Fohrer**, 'Zur Vorgeschichte und Komposition des Buches Hiob', *VT* 6, 1956, 248–67; *Studien zum Buch Hiob*, Gütersloh 1963; D. N. **Freedman**, 'The Elihu Speeches in the Book of Job', *HTR* 61, 1968, 51–9; K. **Fullerton**, 'The Original Conclusion to the Book of Job', *ZAW* 42, 1924, 116–35; 'Job, chapters 9 and 10', *AJSL* 55, 1938, 225–69.

B. **Gemser**, 'The Rîb- or Controversy Pattern in Hebrew Mentality', *Wisdom in Israel*, FS H. H. *Rowley*, ed. M. Noth and D. W. Thomas, *SVT* 3, 1955, 120–37; H. **Gese**, *Lehre und Wirklichkeit in der alten Weisheit. Studien zu den Sprüchen Salomos und zu dem Buche Hiob*, Tübingen 1958; H. L. **Ginsberg**, ''Job the Patient and Job the Impatient', *Conservative Judaism* 21, New York 1966/7, 12–28; N. H. **Glatzer**, *The Dimensions of Job*, New York 1969; E. M. **Good**, *Irony in the Old Testament*, Philadelphia 1965, 196–240; 'Job and the Literary Task: A Response (to David Robertson)', *Soundings* 56, New Haven 1973, 470–84; R. **Gordis**, *The Book of God and Man. A Study of Job*, Chicago and London 1965; W. H. **Green**, *The Argument of the Book of Job Unfolded*, New York 1873; 'The Dramatic Character and Integrity of the Book of Job', *Presbyterian and Reformed Review* 8, New York 1897, 683–701; H. **Gunkel**, 'Hiobbuch', *RGG*², 3, 1924–30; J. **Hempel**, 'Das theologische Problem des Hiob', *Zeitschrift für Systematische Theologie* 6, Berlin 1929, 621–89= *Apoxysmata*, BZAW 81, 1961, 114–174; J. G. **von Herder**, *Vom Geist der ebrischen Poesie*, Leipzig 1825, Vol. I, 107–21; ET, *The Spirit of Hebrew Poetry*, Burlington, Vt. 1833, Vol. I, 99–121; W. H. **Hertzberg**, 'Der Aufbau des Buches Hiob', *FS A. Bertholet*, Tübingen 1950, 233–58; P. **Humbert**, 'Le modernisme de Job', *SVT* 3, 1955, 150–61.

W. A. **Irwin**, 'The First Speech of Bildad', *ZAW* 51, 1933, 205–16; 'The Elihu Speeches in the Criticism of the Book of Job', *JR* 17, 1937, 37–47; A. **Jepsen**, *Das Buch Hiob und seine Deutung*, Berlin 1963; C. G. **Jung**, *Answer to Job*, ET London 1954; K. **Kautzsch**, *Das sogenannte Volksbuch von Hiob*, Tübingen, Freiburg, Leipzig 1900; E. G. H. **Kraeling**, 'Man and his God. A Sumerian Variation on the "Job" Motive', *SVT* 3, 1955, 170–82; C. **Kuhl**, 'Neuere Literarkritik des Buches Hiob', *ThR* 21, 1953, 163–205, 257–317; 'Vom Hiobbuche und seinen Problemen', *ThR* 22, 1954, 261–316; R. **Laurin**, 'The Theological Structures of Job', *ZAW* 84, 1972, 86–92; J. **Lévêque**, *Job et son Dieu*, 2 vols, Paris 1970 (exhaustive bibliography); R. A. F. **McKenzie**, 'The Purpose of the Yahweh Speeches in the Book of Job', *Bibl* 40, 1959, 435–45; J. J. **Owens**, 'The Prologue and the Epilogue', *Review and Expositor* 68, Louisville, Ky. 1971, 457–67; R. H. **Pfeiffer**, 'Edomitic Wisdom', *ZAW* 44, 1926, 13–25; R. M. **Polzin**, 'An Attempt at Structural Analysis: The Book of Job', *Biblical Structuralism*,

Missoula and Philadelphia 1977, 54–125; G. **von Rad**, 'Hiob XXXVIII und die altägyptische Weisheit', *SVT* 3, 1955, 293–301 = *GSAT* Munich 1958, 262–71; ET in *Studies in Ancient Israelite Wisdom*, ed. J. Crenshaw, New York 1976, 267–77; *Wisdom in Israel*, ET London and Nashville 1972, 207–26; G. **Richter**, 'Erwägungen zum Hiobproblem', *EvTh* 18, 1958, 302–24; *Studien zu Hiob*, Berlin 1958; David **Robertson**, 'The Book of Job: A Literary Study', *Soundings* 56, 1973, 446–69; reprinted in slightly different form in *The Old Testament and the Literary Critic*, Philadelphia 1977, 33–54; H. W. **Robinson**, *The Cross of Job*, London ²1938; T. H. **Robinson**, *Job and his Friends*, London and Toronto 1954; H. H. **Rowley**, 'The Book of Job and its Meaning', *BJRL* 41, 1958, 167–207 = *From Moses to Qumran*, London and New York 1963, 139–83.

J. A. **Sanders**, *Suffering as Divine Discipline in the Old Testament and Post-Biblical Judaism*, Rochester 1955; N. M. **Sarna**, 'Epic Substratum in the Prose of Job', *JBL* 76, 1957, 13–25; H. H. **Schmid**, *Wesen und Geschichte der Weisheit*, BZAW 101, 1966, 173ff.; P. W. **Skehan**, 'Job's Final Plea (Job 29–31) and the Lord's Reply (Job 38–41)', *Bibl* 45, 1964, 51–62; N. H. **Snaith**, *The Book of Job. Its Origin and Purpose*, SBT II.11, 1968; W. B. **Stevenson**, *The Poem of Job*, London and New York 1947; S. T. **Terrien**, *Job: Poet of Existence*, Indianapolis 1957; 'Quelques remarques sur les affinités de Job avec le Deutéro-Isaïe', *SVT* 15, 1965, 295–310; M. **Tsevat**, 'The Meaning of the Book of Job', *HUCA* 37, 1966, 73–106; W. **Vischer**, *Hiob. Ein Zeuge Jesu Christ*, Zürich ⁶1947; C. **Westermann**, *Der Aufbau des Buches Hiob*, BHT 23, 1956; H. **Wildberger**, 'Das Hiobproblem und seine neueste Deutung', *Reformatio* 3, Zürich 1954, 355–63, 439–48; E. **Würthwein**, 'Gott und Mensch in Dialog und Gottesreden des Buches Hiob', 1938, in *Wort und Existenz*, Göttingen 1970, 217–95.

1. The Present Impasse in the Study of Job

Few books in the Old Testament present such a wide range of critical problems as does the book of Job. The difficulty of its interpretation was not first discovered in the modern period, but a full range of problems had already been seen in the early Jewish and Christian medieval commentaries. The problems of the book involve, on the one hand, a series of detailed issues which have continued to evoke controversy, and, on the other hand, problems concerning the overarching issues of the purpose of the whole composition. We turn first to the special problems, and then to the general.

Special problems

The first critical issue turns on determining the relation of the prologue-epilogue (1.1–2.13; 42.7–17), which is written in prose, to the poetic dialogue comprising the remainder of the book (3.1–42.6). At a very early date commentators sensed a tension between the prose and poetic material. How could God commend Job in the prose epilogue and yet rebuke him for his ignorance in the poetic section? The mood between the 'patient Job' of chs. 1–2 and the defiant Job of the dialogues seemed hard to reconcile (cf. Ginsberg). Or again, other scholars have argued that the 'happy ending' of the prose undercuts the whole force of Job's attack on the doctrine of retribution found in the dialogue.

Beyond this initial issue of the conceptual integrity of these two parts of the book, critical scholars have sought to establish the historical relationship of these two sections. An early hypothesis that the prologue-epilogue were subsequently added to the poetic dialogue has generally been replaced with the opposite theory that an original folktale has been expanded to include the dialogue. In spite of a wide range of variations within this last position (cf. the discussion in Kuhl and Fohrer) no real consensus has developed in regard to the history of the composition, authorship, or ultimate purpose.

A second set of special problems focuses on the role of the divine speech in 38.1–40.34. In spite of a few dissenting voices (Hölscher), there is general agreement that this section forms an integral part of the original poetic composition. Still it remains a puzzlement why there are two distinct divine speeches which vary considerably in literary quality. Again, how does the intervention of God fit in with the rules established by the prologue in the contest between God and the Tempter? Finally, does not the appearance of God in a theophany serve to bully Job into submission just in the manner which Job had sarcastically predicted would happen, thus leaving a real solution to the poem unresolved?

A third set of issues turns on the highly controversial Elihu speeches (32.1–37.24). Among the majority of critical scholars – Budde was an exception – there has emerged a wide consensus that these speeches are secondary and disruptive of the original composition. Several reasons have been adduced to support this judgment. Elihu is never addressed in any response either by God in the epilogue or by Job within the dialogue. Again, the Elihu speeches appear to interrupt Job's plea for God to answer him (ch. 31) and the divine response (ch. 38ff.). Then again, there are several stylistic features of the Elihu speeches which set them apart from the other dialogues in a striking way (cf. Dhorme). The most important element is that these speeches appear to be working from a written text of the previous dialogues. The Elihu speeches cite, often verbatim, Job's accusations and then refute them. Finally, many scholars question whether Elihu's solution to Job's problem adds anything substantially new to the book.

A fourth set of issues focuses on various alleged dislocations and additions. The literary problems become acute especially in chs. 25–28. In the present form of the book Bildad's third cycle of speeches is extremely short, and Zophar does not appear at all. Moreover, what follows in chs. 26–27 as a reply of Job seems to reflect a line of argument wholly inconsistent with Job and far more akin to the content of the friends. As a result, much energy has been expended in reconstructing the last cycle of the dialogue and assigning large portions to Zophar's missing speech (cf. a list of the attempts in R. H. Pfeiffer, *Introduction*, 671ff.). No one reconstruction has won out as yet, although most commentators agree on the high probability of serious dislocation. In addition, there is almost universal agreement that the chapter on wisdom (ch. 28) is a secondary interpolation into the book. The motivation behind this later move is not fully explained among competing theories.

There is a final set of complex issues which involves the dating of the book of Job and establishing its form and historical background. This group of issues has been discussed from the beginning of the critical study of Job and is reviewed in every modern commentary. The most significant result is that no consensus whatever has arisen regarding the dating of the book, except possibly to rule out the most extreme options, which would be the Mosaic age, on the far right, and the Maccabean period on the far left. In a similar way, the innumerable attempts to describe the form of the book have reached no solid consensus, other than to re-emphasize the unique shape of the present composition. Certainly there are literary parallels – both from within and from without the Hebrew Bible – to the different parts of the book, but the whole defies any close analogy. Finally, there seems little value in rehearsing the many speculations regarding the historical background of the author since the evidence used in support of each of the theories is extremely meagre (cf. Pfeiffer's *Introduction* for details).

General problems

In the light of these many special problems, it is not surprising to find much disagreement respecting the over-all purpose of the book. The traditional view, still supported in part by some modern scholars, that the book describes Job as 'a type of the suffering godly Israelite' (Driver, *Introduction*[8], 411), has generally been rejected as inadequate because it does justice to such a small portion of the book. Nor has a variant of this theory been able to sustain itself that Job is a type of the Hebrew nation in suffering (Ewald).

Another major alternative for assessing the purpose of the book sees its principal aim to be a negative one. The book sought to contest the theory that suffering is a sign of divine punishment and presupposes sin on the part of the sufferer. Although there is general agreement that a negative function is certainly involved, it is far from clear that this is the major purpose of the book, nor does it adequately assess the role of the prose material. Occasionally a scholar (e.g. Hengstenberg) has defended the view that the Elihu speeches actually describe the author's real intention, namely that suffering serves as a divine discipline. To the large majority the difficulties with this interpretation appear insurmountable.

Quite a different stance to the purpose of the book has been taken by those scholars, who, despairing of any literary or theological purpose, seek to find the key to the book in the religious experience of Job. According to Rowley (*Job*, NCeB, 19) the point of the book is to assert: 'It is in the sphere of religion rather than in theology that the meaning of the book is to be found.' But this sharp contrast between religion and theology reflects a modern post-Kantian category far more than it does a genuine biblical polarity. This attempt to resolve the problem does not touch the real issues at stake.

Finally, because of the complexity of the issues and the inability of any one theory to win consent, some of the more recent commentators have abandoned hope of finding any one purpose. Some feel that the book has at least two irreconcilable purposes in mind (so Fullerton, 'Original Conclusion') or contains two irresolvable con-

cepts of Job (Ginsberg). Occasionally the view has been expressed
that the lack of a clear purpose is itself the answer of the book. The
response of Job is simply to submit in resignation since there is no
rationale behind this suffering. One can hardly expect this option of
despair to be regarded with much satisfaction.

Major approaches to the book

In the history of exegesis a variety of different approaches to the
book have emerged which are related to the above set of questions,
but are nevertheless distinct. First, there is the approach which
would try to attribute an integrity to the composition as a whole by
emphasizing one or two themes to the exclusion of others. Thus,
Vischer's controversial interpretation sees the major issue of the
entire book turning on the clause within the prologue: 'Does Job
serve God for naught?' More frequent is the effort to focus entirely
on the theme of human suffering, or theodicy. Rarely in modern
times has the focus been on immortality, which was a popular
pre-critical interpretation. Nevertheless, these different approaches
have in common a tendency to emphasize one certain feature and
eliminate others in an effort to synthesize the parts into a whole.

A more widespread approach which is a hallmark of the modern
period seeks to achieve a unified reading by various literary critical
moves. This method can involve a realignment of the different
parts, but usually it argues for a critical elimination of 'secondary'
material, such as the Elihu speeches, the prologue, or the figure of
Satan. An obvious extension of the strictly literary method is to
introduce a theory of historical development, both on the oral and
written levels, by means of which the parts can be aligned along a
sequence of growth. Most modern commentators would recognize
in principle the validity of seeking this depth dimension, but few
would agree on how to reconstruct the alleged history.

Finally, there are those approaches which supplement the above
methods with any number of psychological categories and seek in
this way to bring a unity into their interpretation. F. Delitzsch (*Job*
I, 81) sought to reconcile an inner tension by speaking of a 'subjective and objective' criterion of truth. Fullerton proposed a theory in
which the author purposely concealed his true intention by means
of two levels of discourse one directed to the pious, and one to the
sceptical among his hearers. Perhaps the most consistently

psychological solution is that used by C. G. Jung in *Answer to Job*, which uses the biblical text merely as a springboard from which to engage a whole set of larger religious issues.

To summarize: A review of the problems arising from the exegesis of the book of Job confirms the impression that Old Testament scholarship has reached an impasse. One might even suspect that every possible variation has already been explored. Nevertheless, with full recognition of the range of issues involved, we would like to propose a fresh study of the book from a canonical perspective.

2. The Canonical Shape of the Book of Job

The diversity of canonical function

To approach the book of Job in terms of its canonical function is to suggest at the outset a different understanding of the nature of scripture. The goal of the interpreter is not to seek to discern one conceptual unity within the book, or to reconstruct one consistent line of theological discourse throughout the dialogue, but rather to see how this literature was designed to function as a normative guide within a continuing community of faith, which acknowledged its authority. To speak of canonical function is to view the book from the perspective of a community whose religious needs and theological confessions are being addressed by a divine word. The immediate implication of this move is to allow the book to perform a variety of different roles within the one community whose unity is not threatened by the presence of tension.

Yet to defend seeing the book's canonical function in relation to a concrete religious community is not to suggest that variety of function is synonymous with arbitrary or undisciplined usage. It is our thesis, rather, that the diversity of function has been carefully structured within the book in order to establish guidelines for its authoritative role within the community. Therefore, it remains the chief task of the exegete who takes seriously the canonical function to seek to discern and to interpret this shaping.

An initial warrant for supporting the hypothesis that the book of Job in its canonical form performs a variety of functions is supplied by the prose framework of the prologue-epilogue which now encloses the poetic dialogue. At the outset the reader is given information which is never provided to Job himself. The reader knows of a celestial contest between God and Satan. Therefore he knows why Job is suffering and that he is innocent. But the Job of the dialogue does not know why he is suffering nor why God appears to be angry with him. As a result, the book of Job poses two sets of questions, one for the reader who views the ensuing dialogue from the perspective of the framework, the other for the reader who chooses to share Job's stance of ignorance of the divine will in order to pursue his probing questions. Both sets of questions, whether viewed from the perspective of the celestial contest or of the ignorant Job, address the continuing community with basic issues of faith. In my judgment, it is a serious misunderstanding of the diversity of the book's canonical role when someone, such as Rowley (NCeB, 13), sets these two perspectives in irreconcilable conflict and eliminates one. Because the reader is told in the prologue why Job is suffering, the truth of another solution is not ruled out which arises from the perspective of an ignorance of God's purpose in which the Job of the dialogue has been placed.

A similar diversity of function in the differing appraisals of Job's behaviour is reflected in the divine speeches (ch. 38.1ff.) and in the epilogue (42.7). Pope claims that the tension is incomprehensible, that Yahweh first rebuffs him and later commends him over against the three friends. However, this interpretation again fails to reckon with the different perspectives explicitly established for the book. In the context of the framework Job could be commended rather than his friends, whereas in the context of the dialogues Job was rebuked for his ignorant reaction.

It is now the task to describe more fully this diversity of canonical function.

The dialogue between Job and the three friends

One of the most difficult aspects of the entire book of Job is in determining the place of the dialogue (3–31). Von Rad posed the issue sharply when he wrote: 'The hermeneutical question as to how the poet himself wished the dialogues to be read and understood has never been clearly answered' (*Wisdom in Israel*, 217). Yet can we at least establish how the canonical editors wished the dialogue to function?

The dialogues begin in ch. 3 with a soliloquy of Job who cursed the day of his birth which brought him into such a world of trouble. The point is that Job began his questions before the friends spoke. His outcry was not simply a rebuttal to them. The implication of this observation lies in assigning an integrity to Job's questions apart from the friends' attempted explanations. Job's experience of desolation, confusion, suffering and sorrow are registered as real, and not denied. The close similarity both in form and content with the complaints of the Psalter would further establish the reaction as genuine and representative. None of the special content from the contrived setting of the prologue is carried over, but rather Job's suffering is typical of every human being, but in an extreme form.

However, the dialogue performs a different function for the reader from that of the complaints of the Psalter. In the psalms the reader identifies with the representative sufferer in his struggle with God. He shares with the Psalmist both his despair and hope, whether he uses the psalm in its continuing liturgical function or in a later private adaptation. In Job's dialogues the reader shares with him his typical human suffering, but is not asked by the story at the outset to identify with Job in his debate with the friends. Rather, the reader overhears a dialogue among Israel's sages who debate the common problem within traditional wisdom.

The context of a wisdom dialogue does not establish the truth of everything which Job says nor the falsity of the friends' arguments. There is no touchstone offered. Rather extreme positions, *ad hominem* arguments, and visceral reactions are all recorded in the debate. The reader is only informed of the results of the dialogue. The friends were not able to sustain their case against Job and in the end failed to come forward. Because truth is not measured in the Old Testament by its correspondence to a theoretical norm but by its ability to achieve its goal, the friends demonstrate, by their failure to continue the debate, the falsity of their position against Job. Job is revealed to be right in so far as he negated the friends' appeal to traditional wisdom.

This negative function of the dialogue is further enhanced by the writer's device of carefully differentiating among the three friends, who appear individually in a set cycle. Each friend is allowed to develop an aspect of traditional wisdom's response to Job's suffering, to which at times Job responds, and at other times does not. Thus the failure of the friends provides a negative judgment which encompasses a wide variety of possible sapiential learning.

The primary effect of the concluded dialogue is to register the failure of human wisdom in its ability to penetrate into the mystery of human suffering. Yet the dialogue does not offer an absolute value judgment on the wisdom concept proffered by the friends or on the responses of Job apart from that specific context. That there is often a similarity between the traditional wisdom of Ps. 73 and the position of one of the friends does not imply a judgment on any concept *per se*. Calvin (*Sermons on Job*) may well be right in his observation that the dialogues contain a mixture of true and false statements. However, Calvin's method is surely in error when he subordinates the major negative function which the canon assigns the debate, and seeks to abstract true and false statements of the participants according to some overarching principle.

Job argues from his personal conviction of his innocence which refused to be coerced by deductions from an application of traditional wisdom. Yet his own experience also fails to penetrate the darkness. At the same time, much after the fashion of the Psalmist, he intensifies his struggle with the God whom he experienced in judgment and yet one on whose ultimate vindication he relies. The climax in his struggle is reached when he calls upon God to appear (31.35ff.). The effect of this movement within the dialogue is to force the reader out of his stance of overhearing a debate on wisdom, and increasingly to identify with Job's struggle with God himself very much after the manner of the Psalter. The movement of the dialogue thus assigns a positive note to Job's struggle to meet God, while not endorsing Job's accusations against the deity any more than it had the 'wise' arguments of the friends.

The function of the prologue-epilogue

The first feature of the prologue-epilogue to be observed is that the narrative setting has both a beginning and an ending. On a particular day a celestial contest was begun which initiated Job's sufferings. The epilogue brings this episode to a conclusion and returns Job to his former state. The setting does not establish any permanent relationships or seek to legitimate aetiologically a structure of reality. The contrast between the functions (say) of Genesis 1–3 and these chapters of Job is striking. The Job framework serves to establish a particular context from which certain basic religious questions arise.

What is the effect of reading the poetic dialogue from the perspective of the prologue-epilogue? How does the framework reinterpret the dialogue? As we have seen, the dialogue wrestled with the question of the incomprehensibility of human suffering, particularly innocent human suffering. The dialogue demonstrated the inability of traditional wisdom to resolve the issue regardless of whether it was Job's search through his own experience or the friends' application of wisdom teaching. Job was forced out of the arena of human wisdom to God himself. Yet the prose framework provides a radically new perspective and raises a completely different set of questions. The reader stands within the celestial court. He knows of the heavenly wager. He knows more than Job; indeed, he understands why Job is suffering. He has been told that this is only a test. His question is no longer: Why do the righteous suffer? What then is the question of the framework?

The basic issue of the prologue is posed by the Accuser. When God said to Satan: 'Have you considered my servant Job, that there is none like him on the earth, a blameless and upright man who fears God?', he answered: 'Does Job fear God for naught?' The basic theological issue at stake in the prologue concerns the integrity of God. As Vischer correctly discerned, the reader is allowed to share God's perspective. God's honour is at stake. Can a human being love God for his own sake?

Thus the contest begins. Clearly God wins round one. Job said, 'Yahweh gave and Yahweh has taken away; blessed be the name of Yahweh' (1.21). But Satan is not impressed. 'Skin for skin! All that a man has he will give for his life. Touch his bone and his flesh and he will curse thee to thy face.' Then Satan went forth and afflicted Job with sores and Job sat among the ashes. When his wife said: 'Curse God and die', Job replied: 'Shall we receive good at the hand of God and shall we not receive evil?' The narrator then summarizes the test: 'In all this Job did not sin with his lips' (2.10).

So God wins round two as well. This is the last one hears of Satan in the book of Job. He has played his role, which was to raise the theological issue, and he now retires from the stage. God has been vindicated. The issue has been finally settled! Or has it? By attaching the dialogues (3–31) to the prologue a whole new dimension of the theological question has been opened up. Job, the patient, turns into Job, the impatient, and all the ambivalence of Job's reaction in the dialogue is made to cast a new light on the Accuser's question.

Indeed Job rejects his friends' advice to 'buy God off' by confessing an unknown sin in order to regain his former prosperity. Job now seeks to justify himself rather than God. He makes his own integrity the criterion for divine justice. He views God as his enemy because he cannot understand him. Then God reveals himself in chs. 38ff., and Job confesses that he spoke of things which he did not understand.

What about the theological question raised by the prologue? Does Job fear God for naught? Can a man love God for his own sake? Indeed the contest ended in ch. 2, but the real theological problem was not solved, as the dialogue shows. God is forced to vindicate himself.

What then is the purpose of the epilogue? It is not to conclude the heavenly contest. Satan is no longer present while the three friends of the dialogue are. Rather, the story of Job is brought to an end. Job is commended whereas the three friends are condemned. Their solution is surely wrong. Their understanding of wisdom does not do justice to God himself. Moreover Job is rewarded and his fortunes restored in spite of his ambivalence, in spite of his being sharply rebuked by God from the whirlwind, and in spite of the theological question of the prologue not being answered.

Finally, it is significant to raise the question regarding the historical setting which the framework uses. Although no absolute dates are offered within the book, a background akin to that of the patriarchs has often been suggested. The speakers use the divine names peculiar to patriarchal times. Job is portrayed as rich in cattle and flocks like the ancient forefathers of Israel, and he also functions like the family priest. The fact that the age assigned to Job within the narrative and the probable age of the book itself differ widely would seem to indicate a canonical intentionality. A similar tension lies between the portrayal of Job from the land of Uz (probably Edom) who debates with his Arabic friends, and the book's authoritative role within Israel.

These strange features of the prologue, however, are fully consistent with the book's place within Israel's wisdom tradition. Wisdom is not confined to the chosen people. Nor are the issues being addressed by the book tied to Israel's peculiar national history, as if Job were only a type of the suffering Jew of the exile. The setting

assures Job's proper place within Israel's canon, namely, as wisdom literature which addresses theological issues basic to all
human beings.

The divine response

The divine response called for by Job in ch. 31 comes in chs. 38ff.
and passes over in silence any notice of Elihu. The response is now
divided into two separate speeches, each one introduced with a
similar introduction: 'Then Yahweh/God answered Job out of the
whirlwind.' At the conclusion of each speech Job repents of his folly
in speaking of things he did not understand (40.3–5; 42.1–6).

Whatever the historical reasons lying behind the double form of
the speech – the question has not been satisfactorily resolved – the
effect of the repetition is to heighten the rebuke. In the first speech
the imagery focuses on the immensity of God's creative power; in
the second, it focuses on the divine power in constructing the fear-
some Behemoth and Leviathan. Both descriptions are laced with
biting sarcasm which is designed to deflate Job's pretence of wisdom (cf. 38.4; 40.15).

The dialogue between Job and the three friends ended with their
defeat. They failed to come forward, thus admitting failure to sustain their case against Job. If Job had succeeded in supplying a
negative check on the traditional wisdom of his friends, his own
case is subjected to a far more devastating attack. The divine
response does not deign to address any of Job's complaints nor to
enter into the discussion of why the innocent suffer. Instead, the
one point is made over and over again that Job cannot possibly
comprehend what God is doing. The sharpest possible limitations
are set on human wisdom, personified in Job's appeal to his own
experience, to comprehend the divine.

Does the divine response also address the theological question
posed in the prologue, namely, the possibility of loving God for
himself? There is no further mention of the celestial wager. The
prose context is completely disregarded. However, it cannot be
forgotten by the reader of the whole book. Indeed in his response to
Job God shows the futility of human wisdom. He vindicates his own
purpose and power in creation. He annihilates Job who then
'despises himself and repents in dust and ashes' (42.6). But to
despise oneself is not to love God for himself. When viewed from the

context of the whole book, the divine response only serves to heighten the feeling that no answer to the theological question has emerged. This issue has not been settled.

Moreover, a host of problems remain unanswered by the divine reply. Does not God's appearance actually defy the rules set down in the celestial contest? Why are not Job's questions addressed, and has he not been bullied into silence just as he feared? Why is there no reference to Elihu's speech? At the outset of our treatment we tried to establish some order within the present book of Job in the face of such perennial questions by suggesting a variety of functions within the canonical form for the community of faith who used the book authoritatively. We argued that the dialogue form was gradually discarded by Job as he increasingly assumed the role of the suffering 'I' of the Psalter in his struggle with God himself.

What is now apparent in the light of the divine response is that the distinct perspectives with their separate sets of questions have been collapsed into the one basic theological issue, namely, the nature of God. Thus the divine response does not address Job's questions as to why he is suffering, and the pretext of a celestial contest found in the prologue is completely disregarded. The divine response serves to direct the attention of the reader – regardless of the context in which he now stands – back to the person of God himself whose wisdom is of a different order from all human knowledge. The divine response thus provides the ultimate critical judgment on wisdom.

The Elihu speeches

The literary and conceptual difficulties of understanding the Elihu speeches have already been mentioned and are reviewed in detail in every critical commentary. What role does this section play within the context of the canonical book of Job? The suggestion that the inclusion of this section is a secondary literary development may well be correct, but it is not particularly helpful in assessing its canonical role. Several features of the Elihu speeches have to be taken into consideration in reaching a judgment. First, it has long been observed that the Elihu speeches presuppose a knowledge of the entire poetic dialogue and Job's retorts are cited almost verbatim at numerous places (cf. 33.9–11 // 13.24, 27; 34.5–6 // 27.2; 35.6–7 // 22.2–4, etc.). Secondly, the Elihu speeches are directed at Job and not to the three friends since Elihu begins with the admission that Job has thwarted them. Thirdly, the Elihu speeches are structured in such a way as to provide a transition to the divine response. This feature is especially apparent in the final peroration of God in ch. 37. Finally, the Elihu speeches make no reference to the context provided by the prologue, nor in turn does the epilogue take any note of Elihu's presence.

The implication to be drawn from these features is that the Elihu speeches have no independent role within the book. There is no indication, for example, that Elihu's reply actually reflects the perspective of the final author. Rather, these speeches now function as a supplement and commentary to the divine response. They seek to spell out the implications of God's exclusive claim of ultimate wisdom revealed in his appearance. Whereas the divine response did not deign to address Job's questions at all, but simply redirected his focus to God himself, the Elihu speeches now seek to perform the very task of answering Job from the perspective of a sapiential tradition which does recognize the limitations set by God on human understanding. The Elihu speeches serve to refute the frequent claim that the only purpose of the book of Job ‚was a negative one in demolishing any claims from the side of wisdom. These speeches attempt to show the positive role of wisdom within the critical limitations which have emerged both in the dialogue and in the divine response. For this reason, the canonical book of Job cannot be characterized in its final form as 'anti-wisdom', but remains a true expression of Israel's wisdom in virtue of its critical stance over against the tradition.

The Elihu speeches function hermeneutically to shape the reader's hearing of the divine speeches. They shift the theological attention from Job's questions of justice to divine omnipotence and thus offer a substantive perspective on suffering, creation, and the nature of wisdom itself. Elihu uses the theme of divine discipline in an attempt to force Job out of the theological dilemma of assuming that, if God does not recognize his innocence, God is either lacking in justice or power. Elihu reasserts the integral relationship between wisdom and creation by re-emphasizing the sustaining work of creation. The concluding hymn of ch. 37 provides the climactic hermeneutical link between the speeches and the divine response.

Dislocations within the book

In no part of the book of Job does the usual historical critical judgment stand in greater need of correction than in the treatment of the alleged dislocations within the dialogues. The failure to assign any value to the final form of the book, but rather to assume that a proper interpretation is fully dependent on a critical reconstruction of an original level, has resulted in widespread confusion. The possibility of an accidental dislocation of a passage and of an injury to the original sequence of the third cycle is not to be dismisssed out of hand. Yet even the presence of arbitrary disarray does not relieve the interpreter of the task of exploring the effect of the present shape of the text on the reader. Nevertheless in this case, there are enough indications to suggest that a theory of unintentional corruption is inadequate to describe the present literary shape of the book.

First of all, the introduction to the Elihu speeches which marks the conclusion of the dialogue with the three friends (32.1ff.) suggests that the dialogue was broken off as unsuccessful. The friends had failed to dislodge Job. The present abrupt ending with Bildad's shortened third speech and the total absence of a response by Zophar dramatizes the extent of the failure. In other words, whatever the cause of a disruption – whether intentional or not – the effect on the final shaping of the text is to reinforce a major theme of the book.

In the second place, 27.11ff. serves now to introduce the great wisdom poem of ch. 28 as a speech of Job. There is a clear sign of intentional design in the shaping of ch. 27. The effect of placing chs. 27–28 in the mouth of Job is to reinstate him as a sage. Job has refuted the false application of sapiential tradition to explain his suffering, but the present role of these chapters rules out the theory that Job is therefore rejecting Israel's wisdom *per se*. This is far from the truth. Job can even describe the certain fate of the ungodly in terms reminiscent of the friends' arguments (27.7).

The effect of assigning ch. 28 to Job is to support the move, which was already found in the Elihu speeches, that Job also recognizes the divine limitations set on human wisdom. Only God knows the way to wisdom. The inclusion of the rubric as a summary of the chapter, 'Behold the fear of Yahweh, that is wisdom', offers an explicit canonical directive on how the critical stance to wisdom found in the book of Job relates to the wider wisdom corpus. Even Job can affirm a positive role for wisdom within the restrictions which the dialogues have established. Moreover, the effect of ch. 28 is to provide a link between the portrayal of the 'patient Job' of ch. 2 and the 'impatient Job' of the dialogue. The canonical shaping of these chapters suggests that these are not two irreconcilable portrayals, but a calculated tension marking the proper limits of wisdom for the community of faith.

In sum, this interpretation of the alleged dislocations does not imply that the final shape is without its tensions and even reflects elements of striking disharmony and conflict. Nevertheless, the present form shows signs of intentional shaping for the purpose of instructing the reader in the true role of wisdom.

3. Theological and Hermeneutical Implications

(a) An interpretation which seeks to defend the theological integrity of the final form of the biblical text does not depend on being able to establish a book devoid of all tension. Canonical integrity is not synonymous with literary unity. Rather, the issue at stake is whether or not the reader who stands within the community of faith is given sufficient guidelines from the book to obtain a clear witness for a variety of different issues of faith. In my judgment, the present shape of the book seeks to address a wide range of different questions about wisdom which vary in accordance with the battle being fought. The contours of both the outer and inner limits of wisdom are carefully drawn, and any attempt to cut the tension is to sacrifice the specific canonical role of this remarkable book.

(b) The interaction between the various parts of the book of Job indicates that a dynamic movement between the individual parts and a holistic reading of the book continues to inform the canonical reader. It is therefore possible and fully legitimate to use only a portion of the book of Job for sapiential instruction, such as the prologue and epilogue, or even the Elihu speeches. Nevertheless, such a reading must never be divorced from a critical hearing of the total effect of the book. That this interaction within the present book defies a simplistic scheme of literary development serves as a warrant for preserving this vital dynamic within the community which strives for a faithful hearing.

(c) The book of Job serves an important canonical function in respect to the larger canon. Above all, it supplies a critical corrective to the reading of the other wisdom books, especially Proverbs and Ecclesiastes. Conversely, its proper interpretation depends on seeing Job in the perspective, not only of wisdom tradition, but also of Israel's liturgy and historical traditions. The Hebrew canon functions to preserve the integrity of its authoritative traditions by a restrictive outer boundary, yet it also encourages a creative exchange among its multiple parts.

History of Exegesis

Carpzov II, 80–87; *DThC* 8, 1484–6; *EB* 1, 256; J. **Lévêque**, *Job*, II, 705ff.; *RGG*³ 3, 360f.

W. **Bacher**, 'Das Targum zu Hiob', *MGWJ* 20, 1871, 208–23; G. **Bardy**, 'Commentaires patristiques de la Bible', *DBS* 2, 73ff.; J. **Daniélou**, *Les saint 'païens' de l'Ancien Testament*, Paris 1956, 109–28; E. **Dhorme**, *A Commentary on the Book of Job*, ET London 1967, ccxxi–ccxxiv; L. **Dieu**, 'Le commentaire de S. Jean Chrysostome sur Job', *RHE* 13, 1912, 640–58; R. **Draguet**, 'Un commentaire grec arien sur Job', *RHE* 20, 1924, 38–65; R. **Gillet**, 'Introduction', *Grégoire le Grand. Morales sur Job*, SC 32, 1950, 7–113; N. N. **Glatzer**, *The Dimensions of Job*, New York 1969; R. P. C. **Hanson**, 'St Paul's Quotations of the Book of Job', *Theology* 53, London 1950, 250–53; C. **Kannengiesser**, 'Job. II. Commentaires patristiques', *DS* 8.2, 1974, 1218–25; M. **Lewin**, *Targum und Midrasch zum Buche Hiob*, Bern 1895; J. P. M. van der **Ploeg** and A. S. **van der Woude**, *Le Targum de Job de la Grotte XI de Qumrân*, Leiden 1971; H. M. **Schulweis**, 'Karl Barth's Job', *JQR* 65, 1975, 156–67; M. **Seligsohn**, 'Job in Rabbinical Literature', *JE* 7, 193–5; R. **Wasselynck**, *L'influence des Moralia in Job de S. Grégoire le Grand sur la théologie morale entre le 7ᵉ et le 12ᵉ siècle*, Diss. Lille 1956; 'L'influence de l'exégèse de S. Grégoire le Grand sur les commentaires bibliques médiévaux', *Recherches de théologie ancienne et médiévale* 32, Louvain 1965, 157–204; I. **Wiernikowski**, *Das Buch Hiob nach der rabbinischen Agada*, Frankfurt 1893; *Das Buch Hiob nach der Auffassung der rabbinischen Literatur in der ersten fünf nachchristlichen Jahrhunderten* I, Breslau 1902.

XXXV

PROVERBS

Commentaries

O. Zöckler, ET, LCHS, 1870
F. Delitzsch, BC, 1873
G. Wildeboer, KHC, 1897
C. H. Toy, ICC, 1899
J. Knabenbauer, CSS, 1910
T. T. Perowne, CB, 1916
W. O. E. Oesterley, WC, 1929
H. Renard, SB, 1949
A. Cohen, SonB, ²1952
J. van der Ploeg, BOuT, 1952

C. T. Fritsch, IB, 1955
H. Lamparter, BAT, ²1959
B. Gemser, HAT, ²1963
A. Barucq, SoBi, 1964
D. Kidner, TOTC, 1964
R. B. Y. Scott, AB, 1965
H. Ringgren, ATD, ²1967
W. McKane, OTL, 1970
R. N. Whybray, CNEB, 1972

Bibliography

W. F. **Albright**, 'Some Canaanite-Phoenician Sources of Hebrew Wisdom', SVT 3, 1955, 1–15; A. **Barucq**, 'Proverbes (Livre des)', DBS 8, 1972, 1395–476; E. G. **Bauckmann**, 'Die Proverbien und die Sprüche des Jesus Sirach', ZAW 72, 1960, 33–63; W. **Baumgartner**, Israelische und altorientalische Weisheit Tübingen 1933; J. **Becker**, Gottesfurcht im Alten Testament, AnBib 25, 1965; G. **Boström**, Proverbiastudien: Die Weisheit und das fremde Weib in Spr. 1–9, Lund 1935; G. E. **Bryce**, 'Another Wisdom "Book" in Proverbs', JBL 91, 1972, 145–57; W. **Bühlmann**, Vom rechten Reden und Schweigen, Göttingen 1976; J. **Conrad**, 'Die innere Gliederung der Proverbien', ZAW 79, 1967, 67–76; B. **Couroyer**, 'L'origine égyptienne de la Sagesse d'Aménémopé', RB 70, 1963, 208–24; J. **Crenshaw**, 'Wisdom', Old Testament Form Criticism, ed. J. H. Hayes, San Antonio, Texas 1974, 225–64; ed., Studies in Ancient Israelite Wisdom, New York 1976; M. J. **Dahood**, Proverbs and North-west Semitic Philology, Rome 1963; E. **Drioton**, 'Sur la Sagesse d'Aménémopé', Mélanges bibliques rédigés en l'honneur de A. Robert, Paris 1956, 254–80; A. **Drubbel**, 'Le conflit entre la Sagesse profane et la Sagesse religieuse', Bibl 17, 1936, 45–70, 407–28;

A. M. **Dubarle**, 'Où en est l'étude de la littérature sapientielle?', *ETL* 44, 1968, 407–19; H. **Duesberg** and J. **Fransen**, *Les scribes inspirés*, Maredsous ²1966, 177ff.

O. **Eissfeldt**, *Der Maschal im Alten Testament*, BZAW 24, 1913; A. **Erman**, 'Eine ägyptische Quelle der Sprüche Salomos', *Sitzungsberichte der Deutschen (Preussischen) Akademie der Wissenschaften zu Berlin*, 1924 (XV), 86–93; J. **Fichtner**, *Die altorientalische Weisheit in ihrer israelitisch-jüdischen Ausprägung, eine Studie zur Nationalisierung der Weisheit in Israel*, BZAW 62, 1933; B. **Gemser**, 'The Instructions of 'Onchsheshonqy and Biblical Wisdom Literature', *SVT* 7, 1960, 102–8; E. **Gerstenberger**, *Wesen und Herkunft des 'Apodiktischen Rechts'*, WMANT 20, 1965; H. **Gese**, *Lehre und Wirklichkeit in der alten Weisheit*, Tübingen 1958; R. **Gordis**, 'The Social Background of Wisdom Literature', *HUCA* 18, 1943/4, 77–118; H. **Gressmann**, 'Die neugefundene Lehre des Amen-em-ope und die vorexilische Spruchdichtung Israels', *ZAW* 42, 1924, 272–96; J. **Harvey**, 'Wisdom Literature and Biblical Theology', *BTB* 1, 1971, 308–19; H.-J. **Hermisson**, *Studien zur israelitischen Spruchweisheit*, WMANT 28, 1968; 'Weisheit und Geschichte', *Probleme biblischer Theologie, FS G. von Rad*, Munich 1971, 136–54; P, **Humbert**, *Recherches sur les sources égyptiennes de la littérature sapientale d'Israel*, Neuchâtel 1929; C. **Kayatz**, *Studien zu Proverbien 1–9*, WMANT 22, 1966; K. **Koch**, 'Gibt es ein Vergeltungsdogma im Alten Testament?', *ZTK* 52, 1955, 1–42; B. W. **Kovacs**, 'Is there a Class-Ethic in Proverbs?', *Essays in Old Testament Ethics, J. P. Hyatt in memoriam*, New York 1974, 171–89; B. **Lang**, *Die weisheitliche Lehrrede. Eine Untersuchung von Sprüche 1–7*, SBS 54, 1972; G. **Kuhn**, *Beiträge zur Erklärung des salomonischen Spruchbuches*, BWANT III. 16 (=57), 1931.

W. **McKane**, *Prophets and Wise Men*, SBT I. 44, 1965; J. L. **McKenzie**, 'Reflections on Wisdom', *JBL* 86, 1967, 1–9; R. E. **Murphy**, 'The Kerygma of the Book of Proverbs', *Interp* 20, 1966, 3–14; 'Assumptions and Problems in Old Testament Wisdom Research', *CBQ* 29, 1967, 407–18; 'The Interpretation of Old Testament Wisdom Literature', *Interp* 23, 1969, 289–301; W. O. E. **Oesterley**, 'The "Teaching of Amen-em-ope" and the Old Testament', *ZAW* 45, 1927, 9–24; R. H. **Pfeiffer**, 'Edomitic Wisdom', *ZAW* 44, 1926, 13–25; O. **Plöger**, 'Zur Auslegung der Sentenzensammlungen des Proverbienbuches', *Probleme biblischer Theologie, FS G. von Rad*, Munich 1971, 402–16; H. D. **Preuss**, 'Das Gottesbild der älteren Weisheit Israels', *SVT* 23, 1972, 117–45; G. **von Rad**, *Wisdom in Israel*, ET London and Nashville 1972; 'Sprüchebuch', *RGG*³ 6, 287; O. S. **Rankin**, *Israel's Wisdom Literature*, Edinburgh ²1954; W. **Richter**, *Recht und Ethos. Versuch einer Ortung des weisheitlichen Mahnspruches*, Munich 1966; H. **Ringgren**, *Word and Wisdom: Studies in the Hypostatization of Divine Qualities and Functions in the Ancient Near East*, Uppsala 1947; A. **Robert**, 'Les attaches littéraires bibliques de Prov. I–XI', *RB* 43, 1934, 42–68, 374–84; 44, 1935, 344–65, 502–25; J. C. **Rylaarsdam**, *Revelation in Jewish Wisdom Literature*, Chicago 1946.

G. **Sauer**, *Die Sprüche Agurs*, BWANT V. 4 (=84), 1963; H. H. **Schmid**, *Wesen und Geschichte der Weisheit*, BZAW 101, 1961; R. B. Y. **Scott**, 'Solomon and the Beginnings of Wisdom in Israel', *SVT* 3, 1955, 262–279; reprinted Crenshaw, *Studies*, 84–101; 'Wisdom in Creation: The 'Amôn of Proverbs VIII 30', *VT* 10, 1960, 213–23; 'The Study of the Wisdom Literature', *Interp* 24, 1970, 20–45; 'Wise and Foolish, Righteous and Wicked', *SVT* 23, 1972, 146–65; P. W. **Skehan**, 'The Seven Columns of Wisdom's House in Proverbs 1–9', *CBQ* 9, 1947, 190–8; 'A Single Editor for the Whole Book of Proverbs', *CBQ* 10, 1948, 115–30; reprinted Crenshaw, *Studies*, 329–40; U. **Skladny**, *Die ältesten Spruchsammlungen in Israel*, Göttingen 1962; C. I. K. **Story**, 'The Book of Proverbs and Northwest Semitic Literature', *JBL* 64, 1945, 319–37; J. M. **Thompson**, *The Form and Function of Proverbs in Ancient Israel*, The Hague 1974; W. **Vischer**, 'Der Hymnus der Weisheit in den Sprüchen Salomos, 8,22–31', *EvTh* 22, 1962, 309–26; G. **Wallis**, 'Zu den Spruchsammlungen Prov. 10,1–22,16 und 25–29', *TLZ* 85, 1960, 147f.; M. **Weinfeld**, *Deuteronomy and the Deuteronomic School*, Oxford 1972, 261ff.; C. **Westermann**, 'Weisheit im Sprichwort', *Schalom*, *FS A. Jepsen*, Berlin 1971, 73–85; R. N. **Whybray**, *Wisdom in Proverbs. The Concept of Wisdom in Proverbs 1–9*, SBT I.45, 1965; 'Proverbs VIII 22–31 and its Supposed Prototypes', *VT* 15, 1965, 504–514; 'Some Literary Problems in Proverbs I–IX', *VT* 16, 1966, 482–96; A. **Wright**, 'Wisdom', *Jerome Biblical Commentary* I, Englewood Cliffs, N.J. 1969, 556–68; W. **Zimmerli**, 'Zur Struktur der alttestamentlichen Weisheit', *ZAW* 51, 1933, 174–204; ET Crenshaw, *Studies*, 175–207.

1. Historical Critical Problems in Proverbs

The recent flood of books and articles on the book of Proverbs is indicative of the general rebirth of interest in the wisdom literature of the Old Testament. Clearly the book of Proverbs remains the basic source for the study of biblical wisdom to which Job and Ecclesiastes are secondarily related.

There are certain features respecting the composition of this book on which a wide scholarly consensus has been reached. First, it has been agreed for a long time that the present form of the book is made up of various smaller collections, many of which carry a separate superscription (chs. 1–9; 10.1–22.16; 25–29; 30.1–33; 31.1–9; 31.10–31). However, attempts to refine these divisions further, such as that suggested by Skladny, continue to be hotly contested. The ascription of sections to various people (Agur, Lemuel) indicates that the initial superscription to Solomon was

understood loosely even in the biblical period. Partial and full duplication of proverbs both within a collection and between collections has been observed, but no one convincing explanation as to its
cause has emerged. Secondly, there is a growing tendency to date
much of the material of Proverbs in the pre-exilic period while
recognizing that the process of collection could have extended well
into the post-exilic period. Often the collection 10.1–22.16 was
thought to be considerably older than 1–9, but recently this view
has been challenged (by Kayatz), and a difference in form rather
than age has been emphasized. Finally, the close relationship between the form and content of the book of Proverbs with the international literature of the ancient Near East, especially Egypt, has
been reinforced through recent study. Erman's classic study which
sought to demonstrate a dependence of 22.17–23.11 on the Instruction of Amenemopet has been, by and large, sustained against
sporadic efforts to reverse the relationship (Drioton). Of course, the
uniquely Hebrew stamp which Israel gave its borrowed material
has not been denied. To what extent parallels to Israel's sapiential
literature existed also in Canaanite culture remains obscure at present because of the lack of evidence (cf. Albright's summary).

Beyond this broad consensus recent scholarship has focused its
attention on a variety of other areas. At times there has been a fresh
and illuminating penetration into the meaning of the biblical text;
at other times the issues remain unresolved and contested.

Form criticism

The early pioneer studies of wisdom forms done by O. Eissfeldt
and W. Baumgartner have been vigorously pursued and the various forms of the proverb have been carefully analysed (cf. the
review by Crenshaw, 'Wisdom'). Gerstenberger and Richter,
among others, have examined the form of the prohibitive. McKane
(*Proverbs*, 1ff.) has contrasted the form of instruction with the wisdom sentence. Particularly fruitful has been the form-critical study
of Prov. 1–9 in the light of Egyptian literature by Kayatz. Other
comparative work has been carried on successfully by Boström, von
Rad, and Gese, to name but a few. Unquestionably such critical
work has aided in recovering the original function in the prehistory
of this literature as well as bringing into sharper focus the particular nuances of the present Hebrew text of Proverbs. It is also clear

that this formal study is closely related to other larger problems of content and historical setting which often affect the significance which is assigned to the form-critical analysis.

Traditio-history of Proverbs

Much interest has concentrated on exploring the original prove-nance of wisdom within the life of ancient Israel. Opinions have widely varied. Gerstenberger has sought to locate wisdom's original place in the larger family (*Sippenethos*). Hermisson, disputing Eiss-feldt's theory of the popular folk proverb, derived the parable from the learned activity of the scribal school which was directed toward the education of a privileged class. McKane described the original function of wisdom as 'primarily a disciplined empiricism engaged with the problems of government and administration' (*Prophets and Wise Men*, 33). Others, such as Gese and von Rad, stressed the analogy to the Egyptian concept of *maat* in criticizing the emphasis on the pragmatic side of wisdom. They accentuated the general religious and intellectual search for an understanding of a divine order which encompasses human experience. Finally, Skladny assigned different original settings to the various collections and spoke of a 'farmer's manual' or a 'ruler's guide'. In sum, in spite of many illuminating suggestions, no one setting has emerged as offer-ing an exclusive *Sitz im Leben*, nor is one likely. Scott's suggestion (*Interp* 1970, 29) may be the wisest when he lists six sources for wisdom tradition without allowing any one the dominant place.

History of redaction

Several interesting studies have been attempted which sought to trace the present shaping of the book of Proverbs through a com-plex history of growth. Perhaps the most controversial issue in this area is that posed by McKane (*Proverbs*) and sustained by Scott (*SVT* 1972). McKane has argued that in their original form the proverbs were fully secular and pragmatically oriented. Only at a later period did a pious circle within Israel add a theological level – McKane calls it 'God-language' – to the original. McKane tries to support his theory with some philological evidence claiming that a change in the meaning of certain key words can be observed. Yet ultimately his theory rests heavily upon the author's concept of the earliest level of wisdom. McKane's theory has been strongly opposed by von Rad and others who reject the sharp polarity in old wisdom between the secular and the sacred which the theory of McKane assumes.

The theology of wisdom

A discussion of theology ordinarily does not belong in an Old Testament Introduction. Nevertheless, in the history of recent scholarship on wisdom the theological issues are closely intertwined with those of composition. Clearly how one reads the critical evidence is strongly affected by one's overall concept of wisdom. Much of the recent study of wisdom has focused on 'old wisdom'. Since this stage requires reconstruction, opinions respecting its theology vary greatly. Perhaps it will be helpful simply to enumerate some of the basic issues at stake:

(a) To what extent is the search for divine order a basic element in the 'old wisdom' of Israel? Its importance is greatly stressed by Gese and von Rad, but contested by McKane, Murphy (*Interp* 1969) and others.

(b) Is there a concept of divine retribution in wisdom or should one rather speak of an intrinsic act-sequence relationship? The discussion of Koch and his critics is relevant.

(c) What is the concept of wisdom, often termed hypostatization, which is found in chapters such as Prov. 8, Job 28, and Sir. 26? Does this concept represent a different stage in the development of wisdom and how does it relate to 'old wisdom'? Are there important extra-biblical roots to this development? Important contributions have been made by Ringgren, Scott, Rylaarsdam, and most recently, by von Rad (*Wisdom*) to this set of problems.

(d) Finally, how does one relate Israel's wisdom literature to the rest of the Old Testament within the discipline of Old Testament theology? As is well known, many of the standard works of the previous generation on Old Testament theology had little positive place for wisdom (Eichrodt, G. E. Wright). Several important attempts have been made to correct this omission (von Rad, Zimmerli), but the issue is far from settled.

To summarize: This brief survey has indicated the multi-faceted dimensions of the contemporary study of wisdom. Moreover, it is also clear that the problems of literary, form, and redactional criticism, along with that of theology, are all closely interrelated and mutually influence each other.

My major criticism to the approach of modern historical criticism does not lie in the complexity of the discussion, nor in the ability to resolve many of these difficult problems. The tentative quality of much research is constitutive of the discipline. Rather, my criticism arises from the hermeneutical assumptions which seem to dominate, often uncritically, much of modern biblical study. Specifically in terms of wisdom, one is left in the end without a clear description of how the canonical book of Proverbs functioned as sacred scripture within the community of faith which caused the book to be treasured. Because this central problem is not addressed rigorously, the many excellent insights gained from a study of the book's prehistory do not always contribute to a more profound understanding of the present text, as one would hope.

2. The Canonical Shape of Proverbs

What then can one say about the present shape of the book of Proverbs? How was the material heard by the community of faith and how did it function as sacred scripture for Israel?

The superscriptions

The book of Proverbs is introduced with the superscription, 'The Proverbs of Solomon, son of David, king of Israel'. This title obviously serves as an introduction to the entire book. The fact is significant since several other titles are included within the book which attribute sections to others beside Solomon. The implication is that the ascription of the authorship of Proverbs to Solomon was a far broader concept than our modern understanding. The proverbs were assigned to Solomon who was the traditional source of Israel's sapiential learning (as Moses was of Torah and David of psalmody), but later sections collected by the men of Hezekiah (25.1) were added, as well as sections by known and unknown authors (30.1; 31.1; 22.17; 31.10ff.).

There are several effects on the interpretation of the book which derive from this title. First, Solomon is introduced as the author of the proverbs in a historical sequence. He is the 'son of David, king of Israel'. Solomon is thereby identified with his position within the total Hebrew tradition in the light of which he is understood to be interpreted. The title thus establishes an obvious connection with the 'official' record of Solomon's place within Israel. If one turns to I Kings 3ff. the connection of Solomon with wisdom, indeed with this authorship of proverbs and songs, is made explicit (5.9–15; EVV 4.29–34). The book of Kings links Solomon with international wisdom, with examples of his wisdom and renown, rather than with the sacred historical tradition of Israel. The superscription of Proverbs which connects with I Kings 3 thus serves a different function from the psalm titles which establish a link between David's psalmody and Israel's historical tradition. The title of Proverbs does not seek to provide a secondary context on the basis of the Law and the Prophets from which to interpret the proverbs, but forms a connection only with the sapiential material within Kings. The superscription thus guards against forcing the proverbs into a context foreign to wisdom such as the decalogue, which is a traditional theological move most recently used by Lamparter. The title serves canonically to preserve the uniqueness of the sapiential witness against the attempts to merge it with more dominant biblical themes.

Secondly, the superscription which assigns the proverbs to Solomon serves an important canonical function in establishing the relative age of wisdom within Israel. This sapiential witness arises at the beginning of the monarchy and continues through Hezekiah's reign and beyond. The superscription ties the proverbs to the period of the early monarchy and thus opposes the attempt to derive them only from the late post-exilic period. For the canonical editors wisdom was a portion of Israel's sacred writing which extended from the nation's early history even though its running parallel to the historical traditions of Torah and Prophets was without an explicit internal connection. It is highly significant that in both the subsequent titles (30.1; 31.1) as well as in I Kings 3 the connection of proverbs with international wisdom was maintained. The titles thus offer a canonical warrant for comparison with extra-biblical material which is unusual for the biblical tradition.

Chapters 1–9 as a framework

A far more basic form of the shaping of the tradition by the canon is found in the role which chs. 1–9 play in respect to the whole book. Zimmerli (189) spoke of these chapters providing the 'hermeneutical guide' for understanding the rest of the book. Although chs. 10ff. are usually regarded as the clearest example of Israel's 'old wisdom' and historically the earliest, in its present order this earliest level is now read through the prism of chs. 1–9. The effect is far-reaching.

The book begins with a prologue which sets out the purpose of collecting the proverbs: 'that men may know wisdom . . . receive instruction in wise dealings . . . ' Kayatz has pointed out convincingly that the presence of such a prologue is a feature common to Egyptian wisdom as well. Furthermore, to the traditional wisdom prologue the biblical editor has added his programmatic statement (v. 7): 'The fear of Yahweh is the beginning of knowledge.' Without entering into a detailed discussion of the precise meaning of the phrase 'fear of Yahweh' which has occupied much recent attention (cf. Becker), the general thrust of the verse is clear enough. Commitment to Yahweh – the issue is not legal adherence – is inextricably linked to the search for human knowledge.

Indeed, it provides the proper starting place for the acquiring of wisdom. The biblical editor thus joins into a unity intellectual, experiential activity, and religious behaviour. Scholars have argued over the role which religion played in Israel's 'old wisdom'. Was it originally purely secular (McKane), or was there always a religious dimension which established limits to experience (von Rad)? However one may decide what historically was the case originally, the biblical writer goes beyond both of these alternatives in programmatically establishing a religious perspective from which he intended the rest of the book to be understood. As sacred scripture the book was not to be read according to a history of development in the concept of wisdom, rather from a fully developed confessional standpoint. In my judgment von Rad's interpretation is far closer to the mark than McKane's regarding the original understanding of wisdom. The later biblical editor, therefore, did not transform the tradition in kind, but developed programmatically a religious understanding of wisdom which was at first only implicit.

There is a second sign of editorial shaping which chs. 1–9 reflect. Although scholars will continue to debate about the original sociological setting of sapiential knowledge within Israel – royal, folk, scribal – the editor of the final form has made fully clear the present didactic role of wisdom. The father addresses his son; the older generation instructs the younger; the experienced sage advises the inexperienced novice. The dominant form is the imperative. The wise man not only describes the way of the wise, but he commends it with great persuasion. If originally certain sections of the proverbs were addressed to some specialized group within the nation, the effect of the present ordering is to blur the original intent. When older commentators such as O. Zöckler sought to understand the proverbs as the ethics of the Old Testament – Proverbs addressed the subjective side whereas the Law offered the objective imperative – they could at least find a certain warrant in chs. 1–9. The appeal is didactic and directed towards right conduct. Yet the concerns of these chapters are far broader than ethics, and the motivation for wise behaviour is not grounded in the Mosaic law.

There is a third effect which derives from the new role assigned to chs. 1–9. Recent scholarship has worked out very clearly the sharply different understanding of wisdom which one finds in the earlier period from that of the later. In chs. 10ff. wisdom is a human, indeed rational process of intellectual activity, which sought to discern patterns of truth within experience circumscribed by God. But in the later period wisdom is, above all, a gift of God (2.3). Moreover, in its personified form it is pictured as an aggressive woman actively calling and urging the simple to embrace wisdom (1.20ff.). When chs. 1–9 are read as an introduction to chs. 10ff., the effect is that the search for wisdom emerges in a dialectic between its being a gift of God which is given and an acquisition which one actively pursues.

Perhaps the most striking development of the 'self-revelation' of wisdom appears in Prov. 8 (cf. Job 28; Sir. 24). A full discussion of the meaning of this passage lies beyond the scope of an Introduction, but its hermeneutical effect for interpreting the whole book is worth exploring. Proverbs 3.19 speaks of 'Yahweh founding the earth by wisdom'. Chapter 8 goes far beyond the connecting of wisdom to creation in describing wisdom as a personified entity who was itself created before the world and assisted God in his creative work. If it had not previously been fully clear in chs. 10ff. as to the exact nature of the divine order which prevailed in human society – can one really speak of a Hebrew counterpart to Egyptian *maat*? – the canonical ordering of chs. 1–9 provided a theological context of wisdom in creation from which the whole book was to be read. However, it is also important to add that the creation of chs. 1–9 is conceived of as a cosmic event of God, but not explicitly as the first historical event in a series, that is, as part of a *Heilsgeschichte*. In sum, the world order of chs. 10ff. is brought firmly within the order of divine creation, but not that tradition of creation found in Genesis 1–3.

Chapters 10–29

In describing the canonical shaping of the book of Proverbs it is equally significant to register the lack of serious alteration in the original form of a collection. As we have suggested, chs. 1–9 serve as a hermeneutical guide for reading what follows. Yet it is of importance to note that the older collection of chs. 10ff. has been left largely in an unedited stage, that is to say, there has been no attempt to interject the later developments upon the earlier stage. No comprehensive perspective has been imposed on the whole collection. The reasons for this conservative treatment of chs. 10ff. can be debated. Some would argue that the force of tradition preserved it intact against innovators, others that there was no need felt for change once the framework provided a developed theological perspective. Regardless of how one adjudicates this issue, the effect on the final form is clear enough. An earlier stage in the history of Israelite wisdom has been left virtually unchanged and confirmed in this state as canonical literature. Apart from the broad guidelines offered by the introductory position of chs. 1–9, the reader is given no overarching principle by which to interpret these chapters. Rather, the reader is left freedom to follow the many different leads found in the original collection.

A few characteristics of these chapters can be summarized. There is no significant ordering of the individual proverbs into larger groups. Occasionally single proverbs are linked in a loosely connected group either by word association or by general similarity of content. Characteristic stylistic features such as antithetic parallelism have been retained consistently in some sections. Again, the original polarities in concept and vocabulary between the righteous and the wicked, the wise and the foolish have been maintained without any major attempt to link them internally (cf. Scott, *SVT* 1972). In my judgment, McKane's attempt to relegate the proverbs with religious content to a later redaction is unjustified. Rather, the 'religious' proverbs are preserved along with the so-called secular ones without any particular order. Occasionally paralleled formulations are reflected (13.14 // 14.27), but there is no adequate reason to speak of a 'religious substitution' (McKane, *Proverbs*, 18). Indeed, the present canonical shape of these chapters strongly opposes the attempt to separate into modern categories of 'religious' and 'secular'. Finally, although the indicative form dominates, there are some examples of the imperative as well which show that no absolute distinction would hold even at an early stage and that a strong didactic element was already present in the earliest collection.

Proverbs 30.5–6

There is one final sign of canonical shaping in one of the concluding appendices to the book. In an exceedingly difficult passage an inquirer seeks after God, the Creator of the world. He confesses his ignorance and failure to acquire wisdom. He inquires after God's name, but despairs of learning because of God's hidden nature.

Verses 5 and 6 offers an answer to this oracle – whether original or redactional is irrelevant in terms of the effect. The reply comes in the form of two citations from the Old Testament: v. 5 is a slight variation of II Sam. 22.31 (Ps. 18.31) and v. 6a of Deut. 4.2. In his commentary, C. H. Toy argues that the pattern of citation reflects the threefold division of the Jewish canon, but the evidence for this opinion is not clear. Nevertheless, reference to an authoritative body of scripture is clearly implied. As an answer to the inquirer's despair at finding wisdom and the knowledge of God, the answer offered is that God has already made himself known truthfully in his written word. His self-revelation must be obeyed and not falsified by additions.

Most commentators would agree that this passage exhibits one of the latest stages in the composition of the book of Proverbs, but the passage is highly significant from a canonical point of view. It registers the point that the proverbs which originally derived from man's reflection on human experience of the world and society had become understood as divine words to man which functioned as sacred scripture along with the rest of Israel's received traditions. If one recalls that in chs. 1–9 wisdom had already been seen as a self-revelatory gift of God to man, then the canonical formulation represented only a logical extension of a fully developed theology of wisdom.

3. Theological and Hermeneutical Implications

(a) One of the more striking features which has emerged respecting the canonical shaping of the book of Proverbs is the manner in which various stages within the development of Israel's wisdom tradition have been carefully structured to produce the final form. Yet this theological ordering has occurred without recourse to the historical traditions of the Law and the Prophets. Even at the comparatively late historical period in which the final editing process of Proverbs took place, there was no attempt to legitimize wisdom from the side of the law. Rather, canonical shaping took place, by and large, through debate within the wisdom tradition which sought to interpret and supplement the early stages of wisdom in the light of a fuller understanding of the divine ordering of the world and human experience. The major theological implication from this canonical process is the support which the canon lends to the full integrity of the wisdom literature. It is not a 'foreign body' nor an original secular philosophy which achieved religious status for Israel by being brought within the orbit of *Heilsgeschichte*. Nor can its role be accounted for by a process of nationalization. It is an independent witness to God's revelation which functions like the Law and the Prophets as sacred scripture for the people of God.

(b) The canonical ordering of chs. 10ff. has not attempted to arrange the proverbs into any clearly discernible topical or historical order. Indeed, it has retained the sharp polarities, even flat contradictions, in successive proverbs which derived from the earliest collections. One hermeneutical implication to be drawn from this shaping is that the proverbs continue to function within scripture in their original dialogical role. The significance of the proverb does not lie in its formulation of timeless truths, but in the ability of the wise man to use the proverb in discerning the proper context by which to illuminate the human situation.

(c) The point has been repeatedly made that the didactic function of the book of Proverbs which was highlighted by the editor's using chs. 1–9 as a framework for the whole composition served a far broader role than what is implied by the modern use of the term 'ethics'. When the wisdom teacher challenged his pupil to pursue wisdom, it involved not only moral decision in respect to right behaviour, but was an intellectual and highly pragmatic activity as well which sought to encompass the totality of experience. There is a certain analogy in the covenant theology of the Torah which likewise involved a relationship far broader than the term ethics.

Nevertheless, it is striking that the patterns of human behaviour which the Proverbs inculcate overlap to a large extent with that set of ethical standards prescribed in the Pentateuch for the covenant people. In spite of the radically different starting points, both sets of Hebrew traditions converge on a basically unified expression of the good and obedient life. Both the Proverbs and the Law call for a commitment to God and his divine order. Both parts of the canon call for man to love justice and honesty, to care for the poor and the needy, and to accept life as a cherished gift from God. Obviously there are areas in which the correspondence ends. Clearly the witnesses are not to be identified. Rather the major point is that in spite of striking variety in theological perspective, the canon has rightly recognized the profound unity between these witnesses and used them both without the need for adjustment in order to instruct and guide God's people in the way of righteousness.

(d) The particular shaping process of Proverbs raises a series of extremely difficult questions regarding the canon. If the editor of Proverbs sought to read earlier wisdom through the eyes of its later and fuller developed form, should not then the book of Proverbs also be read through the prism of Sirach and the Wisdom of Solomon? (cf. R. E. Murphy's posing of the question, *Interp* 23, 1969, 295ff.). The issue of the limits and authority of the Hebrew canon is a complex issue which involves many historical and theological problems lying beyond the scope of this chapter (cf. chs. II, III and XLIV). Nevertheless, there is an urgent modern challenge to re-examine theologically the substance of the canon rather than to decide the issue along traditional, denominational lines.

There is at least one important factor arising from the study of the redaction of Proverbs which should be considered in conjunction with the other issues of the canon. The theological relationship between the different layers within Proverbs is a very different one from that obtaining between Proverbs and the non-canonical books of the Jewish canon, Sirach and Wisdom of Solomon, in spite of the elements of historical continuity. Whereas Proverbs reflects a debate within wisdom without an attempt to relate wisdom to Law, Sirach offers a striking change of approach. Wisdom is nationalized in Sirach (ch. 24). It sought a resting place and found it in Zion (vv. 7, 10).

This move within Sirach is not a simple, logical development within wisdom, but it assumes an important new historical element, namely, the development of the Hebrew canon. Sirach 44ff. confirms the author's acquaintance with the three parts of the Hebrew canon. The theological issue at stake is whether the manner by which Sirach related the law and wisdom for the first time in the light of the whole canon reflects an adequate theological understanding of the whole. Apparently Judaism did not feel that it did, or at least remained uncertain. One of the issues which the modern biblical theologian must face in reaching a decision would be the extent to which Sirach (and Wisdom) reflect the canonical checks to wisdom found in the Prophets and in the other wisdom books of Job and Ecclesiastes. A study of the New Testament would indicate that quite a different approach to wisdom could be reached which also claimed a canonical warrant from the Old Testament.

History of Exegesis

Carpzov II, 195–9; *DBS* 8, 1472f.; *DThC*, 13, 932–35; *EB*, 1, 256; *RGG*³ 6, 288f.

E. G. **Bauckmann**, 'Die Proverbien und die Sprüche des Jesus Sirach', *ZAW* 72, 1960, 33–63; W. **Baumgartner**, 'Die literarischen Gattungen in der Weisheit des Jesus-Sirach, *ZAW* 34, 1914, 161–98; A. **Barucq**, 'Proverbes, VI. Le Livre dans l'Église', *DBS* 8, 1469; C. H. **Gordon**, 'Rabbinic Exegesis in the Vulgate of Proverbs', *JBL* 49, 1930, 384–416; J. **Marbock**, *Weisheit in Israel. Untersuchungen zur Weisheitstheologie bei Ben Sira*, Rome 1971; J. **Obersteiner**, 'Die Erklärung von Prov 31, 10–31 durch Beda den Ehrwürdigen und Bruno von Asti', *Theologisch-praktische Quartalsschrift* 102, Linz 1954, 1–12; C. **Roth**, 'Ecclesiasticus in the Synagogue Service', *JBL* 71, 1952, 171–8; S. **Schechter**, 'The Quotations of Ecclesiasticus in Rabbinic Literature', *JQR* 3, 1891, 682–706; B. **Smalley**, 'Some Latin Commentators on the Sapiential Books in the Late Thirteenth and Early Fourteenth Centuries', *Archives d'Histoire Doctrinale et Littéraire du Moyen Âge* 18, Paris 1950, 103–28; 'Some Thirteenth-Century Commentaries on the Sapiential Books', *Dominican Studies* 2, Oxford 1949, 318–55; 3, 1950, 41–47, 236–74; W. **Völker**, 'Die Verwertung der Weisheits Literatur bei den christlichen Alexandrinern', *Zeitschrift für Kirchengeschichte* 64, Stuttgart 1952/3, 1–33.

XXXVI

RUTH

Commentaries

P. Cassel, ET, LCHS, 1865
C. F. Keil, BC, 1868
E. Bertheau, KeH, ²1883
G. A. Cooke, CB, 1913
H. Gressmann, *SAT*, ²1922
W. Rudolph, KAT, 1939
M. Haller, HAT, 1940
I. W. Slotki, SonB, ²1952
P. Joüon, ²1953

G. A. F. Knight, TB, ²1956
J. de Fraine, BOuT, 1956
H. Lamparter, BAT, 1962
W. Rudolph, KAT², 1962
G. Gerleman, BK, 1965
J. Gray, NCeB, 1967
E. Würthwein, HAT², 1969
E. F. Campbell, AB, 1975
W. J. Fuerst, CNEB, 1975

Bibliography

D. R. Ap-**Thomas**, 'The Book of Ruth', *ExpT* 79, 1967–8, 369–73; S. **Bertman**, 'Symmetrical Design in the Book of Ruth', *JBL* 84, 1965, 165–8; M. **Burrows**, 'The Marriage of Boaz and Ruth', *JBL* 59, 1940, 445–54; 'The Ancient Oriental Background of Hebrew Levirate Marriage', *BASOR* 77, 1940, 2–15; W. W. **Cannon**, 'The Book of Ruth', *Theology* 15, London 1928, 310–19; M. B. **Crook**, 'The Book of Ruth. A New Solution', *JBL* 16, 1948, 155–60; M. **David**, 'The Date of the Book of Ruth', *OTS* 1, 1942, 55–63; O. **Eissfeldt**, 'Wahrheit und Dichtung in der Ruth-Erzählung', *Sitzungsberichte der Sächsischen Akademie der Wissenschaften zu Leipzig* 110, 4, 1965, 23ff.; J. **Fichtner**, 'Ruthbuch', *RGG*³ 5, 1961, 1252–4; A. **Geiger**, 'Die Leviratsehe, ihre Entstehung und Entwicklung', *Jüdische Zeitschrift* 1, Breslau 1862, 19ff.; G. S. **Glanzman**, 'The Origin and Date of the Book of Ruth', *CBQ* 21, 1959, 201–7; R. **Gordis**, 'Love, Marriage and Business in the Book of Ruth: A Chapter in Hebrew Customary Law', *A Light unto My Path, FS J. M. Myers*, Gettysburg 1974, 241–64; H. **Gunkel**, 'Ruth', *Reden und Aufsätze*, Göttingen 1913, 65–92; 'Ruthbuch', *RGG*² 4, 1930, 2180–82; H. **Hajek**, *Heimkehr nach Israel. Eine Auslegung des Buches Ruth*, BSt 33, 1962; R. M. **Hals**, *The Theology of the Book of Ruth*, Philadelphia 1969; 'Ruth, Book of', *IDB Suppl* 758f.; P. **Humbert**, 'Art et leçon de l'histoire de Ruth', *RThPh* 26, 1938, 257–86=*Opuscules d'un Hébraïsant*, Neuchâtel 1958, 83–110; A. **Jepsen**, 'Das Buch Ruth', *ThStKr* 108, 1937–8, 416–28; L. **Koehler**, 'Die Adoptionsform von Ruth 4.16', *ZAW* 29, 1909, 312–14; 'Justice in the Gate', in *Hebrew Man*, ET London 1956, 149–75.

D. A. **Leggett**, *The Levirate and Goel Institutions in the Old Testament with special attention to the Book of Ruth*, Cherry Hill, N.J. 1974; L. **Levy**, 'Die Schuhsymbolik im jüdischen Ritus', *MGWJ* 62, 1918, 178–85; É. **Lipiński**, 'Le Mariage de Ruth', *VT* 26, 1976, 124–7; O. **Loretz**, 'The Theme of the Ruth Story', *CBQ* 22, 1960, 391–9; 'Das Verhältnis zwischen Rut-Story and David-Genealogie in Rut-Buch', *ZAW* 89, 1977, 124–26; J. M. **Myers**, *The Linguistic and Literary Form of the Book of Ruth*, Leiden 1955; J. **Nacht**, 'The Symbolism of the Shoe with Special Reference to Jewish Sources', *JQR* NS 6, 1915/6, 1–22; G. **von Rad**, 'Predigt über Ruth 1', *EvTh* 12, 1952/3, 1–6; O. F. **Rauber**, 'Literary Values in the Bible: The Book of Ruth', *JBL* 89, 1970, 27–37; E. **Robertson**, 'The Plot of the Book of Ruth', *BJRL* 32, 1950, 207–28; H. H. **Rowley**, 'The Marriage of Ruth', *The Servant of the Lord and Other Essays in the Old Testament*, London ²1965, 169–94; J. **Schildenberger**, 'Das Buch Ruth als literarischer Kunstwerk und als religiöse Botschaft', *Bibel und Kirche* 18, Stuttgart 1963, 102–8; W. E. **Staples**, 'The Book of Ruth', *AJSL* 53, 1936–7, 145–57; T. and D. **Thompson**, 'Some Legal Problems in the Book of Ruth', *VT* 18, 1968, 79–99; P. **Trible**, 'Two Women in a Man's World: A Reading of the Book of Ruth', *Soundings* 59, New Haven 1976, 251–79; J. L. **Vesco**, 'La date du livre de Ruth', *RB* 74, 1967, 235–47; H. H. **Witzenrath**, *Das Buch Rut*, Munich 1975; L. B. **Wolfenson**, 'The Character, Contents and Date of Ruth', *AJSL* 27 1910/11, 285–300; 'Implications of the Place of the Book of Ruth in Editions, Manuscripts and Canon of the Old Testament', *HUCA* 1, 1924, 151–78.

1. Historical Critical Problems

The contents of the book are familiar and do not require a lengthy summary. In the days of the judges of Israel, Elimelech, a native of Bethlehem, went with his wife, Naomi, and two sons to Moab because of a famine. He died and his two sons married Moabite women. In time, both sons died and Naomi returned to Bethlehem with one daughter-in-law, Ruth, who refused to be separated from her. The main portion of the narrative describes the relation of Ruth to Boaz, a distant kinsman, and how, after some intrigue from Naomi, Boaz married Ruth whose offspring became the grandfather of David.

The simplicity of the narrative has not hidden a large number of problems with which critical scholarship has been engaged.

The form of the book

There has been general agreement ever since Gunkel's illuminating essay that the form of the book is that of a *novella*, which is to say, the book consists of a highly artistic story which develops a plot through various scenes before reaching a climax. The characters of the story are carefully sketched and closely integrated within the literary composition. The form of the *novella* is to be contrasted with a collection of originally independent sagas which still maintain a strong traditional connection and lack the literary creation of an author. Gunkel saw a kinship between Ruth and the Joseph cycle and contrasted the form with the collection of tradition in the Abraham and Jacob cycles. Although Gunkel discounted any historical elements in Ruth, many of his successors have accepted his form-critical category, but have also argued for a historical dimension (cf. Fichtner, Campbell). Nevertheless, it is generally conceded that the historical concerns have been pushed into the background by the dominant literary interests of the author.

Considerable attention has been directed to analysing the literary techniques of the author in constructing his story (cf. Bertman, Campbell) and even to its poetic substructure (Myers). Generally Goethe's high esteem for the book's literary quality has been enthusiastically sustained.

Age of the book

Although the Talmud established the dating of the book by assigning its authorship to Samuel (Baba Bathra 14b), modern critical study has had great difficulty in establishing a widely accepted date. Wellhausen and his school argued for a post-exilic date on the evidence of the book's location in the Hagiographa, its distance from the customs reported, its relation to Deuteronomic formulae (1.1), and alleged Aramaic influence on the language (cf. Eissfeldt). The philological arguments in particular have suffered considerable erosion. In recent times there has been a strong voice contesting this evidence and arguing for a dating in the early monarchial period (Hals, Campbell), but also here there is an undeniable flavour of special pleading often involved. Hals' use of von Rad's concept of a 'Solomonic Enlightenment' no longer carries the weight it once did. The many suggested dates in between the two extremes would seem to confirm that the issue has not been resolved. Within the recent discussion Gerleman's attempt to relate the concept of David in the book of Ruth to that of the Chronicler has opened up a largely unexplored avenue. His observation serves mainly to challenge the extremely early dating without being able to establish conclusively the theory of late dating.

Integrity and purpose of the book

The issue of how one evaluates the purpose of the book turns to some extent on how one evaluates the role of the concluding verses. There is a widespread consensus that the genealogy in 4.18–22 is a late, secondary addition to the book which has been taken from I Chron. 2.9–15. More controversial is the role of 4.17b. Gunkel, followed by Eissfeldt and others, first pointed out the lack of the traditional aetiological naming pattern in v. 17b in which the child's name reflected a word play on the preceding exclamation. He argued that the original name of the child had been subsequently altered to that of Obed and that the story of Ruth originally had nothing to do with David. Although Gunkel's historical conclusion can be contested, his form-critical observations are acute and significant.

Long before Gunkel's essay there had been many attempts to explain the purpose of the book of Ruth as a simple story cloaking a deeper ideological concern of its author. A. Geiger, followed by Weiser (*Introduction*) and Rost (*Einleitung*), saw the book's origin as a protest against the strict marriage laws of Ezra and Nehemiah. Others argued that the book sought to inculcate the duty of levirate marriage (Driver), or to glorify David's pious ancestors. Gerleman proposed that the book sought to legitimate David's ancestors by transforming Ruth Moabitess from a foreigner into a fully Jewish heroine.

In a reaction against this tendency to politicize the book, other scholars saw its purpose as religious in nature. Gunkel described the book as a portrayal of the heroism of faith demonstrated by the loyalty of the young wife. Humbert in particular, followed by Hertzberg and Hals, have stressed the theological intention as cen-

tral, which would describe God as the controlling agent behind the
events of the story.

Canonical order

Considerable attention has been paid to the contrasting position
of the book within the Hebrew and Greek Bibles (cf. Rudolph,
Campbell, etc.). The Hebrew Bible has assigned the book to the
Writings to be read at the Feast of Weeks, but this is admittedly a
very late development. Its place within the third division of the
canon is, however, old. The Greek Bible, followed by the Latin,
placed the book in the Former Prophets after Judges. Josephus
supports the Greek order; II Esdras 14.44–46 the Masoretic.

Campbell (34f.) has recently argued that the Greek order must
be secondary since he finds it difficult to imagine moving a book out
of the Prophets into the Writings, whereas the reverse is easily
understood. In my opinion, there are far too many unverified
assumptions with such an argument to rest much weight on it. A far
more fruitful avenue of investigation would be to explore the effect
of a canonical ordering on the reading of the book and the differing
theologies involved in the canonical arrangements of the Hebrew
and Greek Bibles.

2. The Canonical Shape of the Book of Ruth

The nature of the story

The canonical shape of the book of Ruth has retained the original
story as the vehicle for its message in its role as scripture. All the
features of the narrative – artistry, plot, characters, movement –
have been transmitted without change. The story was not made
into a simple lesson nor shortened for didactic reasons as was
Jonah. Nor were there any typological or allegorical moves made.
Therefore, those interpretations which emphasize the symbolic
nature of some of the names – Naomi, Mahlon, Chilion – run the
risk of replacing the major narrative form with a minor feature.

The canonical process did not have to transform a secular story
into a religious one because the original story was already highly
theological. Indeed, the major purpose of the narrative, as has been

correctly described by several recent scholars (Humbert, Hertz-berg, Hals) was to show the ways of God in the life of one family. The original story was structured around a theological issue, as is evident from Naomi's discourse (1.21f.): 'I went away full and Yahweh has brought me back empty ... the Almighty has brought calamity upon me!' The mysterious ways of God form the major thread of the plot in chs. 2 and 3 (2.12, 20; 3.10, 13), and culminate in the blessing in 4.14. All the features which make up the qualities of a good story bear witness to God at work. Ruth came to glean in Boaz's field 'by accident'. Boaz 'happened' to be a kinsman. Naomi schemed to force Boaz into marriage. The canoni-cal editors accept the story in its totality as a witness and make no attempt to moralize or justify the events. Any theological interpre-tation which threatens the narrative itself is surely wrong, such as Hajek's (86) strained exegesis of 4.14 to make God the *goēl*.

Part of the difficulty of interpreting the book lies in the manner in which some of the story's features have been blurred and rendered confusing to the reader. For example, it is not clear why Ruth would glean as a pauper when Naomi still owns property. Nor is the application of the levirate law to Boaz, who is not a brother-in-law, immediately obvious. Again, one wonders why the *goēl* of ch. 4 did not have the same information as did Boaz respecting the oblig-ation of marrying Ruth, if he desired the land. Finally, the announcement of a son to Naomi (4.17) rather than to Mahlon comes as somewhat of a puzzlement.

However, none of this confusion seems to reflect a canonical intention, but derives from other sources. Certain of the problems of the narrative stem from the modern reader's lack of information which was assumed by the story. We do not know enough about the nature and scope of levirate marriage in Israel at this period to follow the exact sequence, but there is no evidence that the narrator himself was uninformed respecting the custom. Then again, some of the features which have puzzled scholars can be attributed to the freedom of the storyteller in emphasizing certain elements and de-emphasizing others. Thus, atttributing the son to Naomi rather than Mahlon (4.17) climaxes a major theological theme, even though it runs counter to parts of the levirate law which formed the background of the story.

The book's conclusion

The most important sign of canonical shaping of the original narrative comes in the last chapter of the book, in vv. 17b and 18–22. Both additions appear to have been secondary to the original story. This observation says nothing about the historicity of the tradition which connects Ruth to David, but only that its literary form indicates a later expansion of the primary narrative. The effect of the addition of v. 17b is to provide the material with a new theological role. The verse now extends the original point of the narrative beyond showing the ways of God in the life of one family to include the entire nations of Israel. The ways of God are set in the broader context of a *Heilsgeschichte*. Not only is a son born to Naomi, but the history of God's rule under David has begun. The addition of the genealogy in vv. 18–22 only serves to formalize the same history which v. 17b sets forth.

However, it is important to recognize that the canonical shaping simply extended the theological point which had already been made by the original story. The addition did not itself form the basis of the book. To suggest that the concern with David actually initiated the narrative is to misread the literary evidence and to misunderstand the theological significance of the book by a politicizing ploy.

The canonical setting of Ruth

Finally, there are several minor features which reflect familiar canonical shaping. The story is set 'in days when the judges ruled'. Regardless of its place within the Old Testament canon, this clause establishes both a historical and a literary context in which the book is to be understood. Its historical setting is pre-monarchial, which offers a canonical check against reading the book as a concealed political tract directed against Ezra and Nehemiah. Again, its literary context is provided by the book of Judges. This observation is not offered as a defence of the Greek order, but simply indicates that the book of Ruth is to be interpreted in the context of the larger corpus of scripture.

There are two other moves to set the book of Ruth within the larger collection of scripture. In 4.11f. the people bear witness to

Boaz's assumption of the duties of levirate marriage by invoking upon him the blessings of Perez. This reference back to the story of Tamar (Gen. 38) places Ruth's action in gaining a husband in analogy to this earlier example of extreme loyalty in preserving the name of a deceased husband. This canonical perspective thus rules out a variety of modern interpretations which would attribute other motivations to Ruth's behaviour (cf. Gerleman).

Finally, the genealogical supplement in 4.18–22 reinforces the point of 4.17b by drawing on material from I Chron. 2 in order to confirm the testimony. Consequently the book of Ruth is firmly anchored to the record of Israel's early and late histories. When Rudolph and Würthwein claim that the addition of the genealogy destroys the force of the story, they fail to distinguish adequately between literary style and canonical function.

3. Theological and Hermeneutical Implications

(a) The canonical shaping guards the integrity of the original literary form of the story against various attempts to shift the emphasis away from the narrative. The theological witness of Ruth cannot, therefore, be separated from its form, either by extracting a moral or deriving a lesson apart from the context of these particular events. The canon has thus retained unimpaired the realistic language of the original story, and provides a warrant for serious attention to the literary features which constitute its witness.

(b) Although the characters within the story have been pictured in language fully commensurate with its historical period and share in the cultural milieu of its time, certain of them – particularly Ruth and Boaz – emerge as models of the faithful religious life of Israel. The commendation is not provided by direct commentary on the part of the author, but is offered by the movement of the whole story. The figures are not dehistoricized to become stereotyped vehicles of virtue, but evidence signs of genuine character in the midst of historically conditioned circumstances, such as the ancient legal fiction of levirate marriage.

(c) The story has been actualized by highlighting its role in the larger divine economy. However,the connection between ordinary history and redemptive history (*Heilsgeschichte*) is not a sharply separated one. Rather, the two flow easily together when viewed from the theological perspective of a God from whom all causality ultimately derives.

History of Exegesis

Carpzov I, 206–210; *DThC* 14, 382; *EB* 6, 343; *RGG*³ 5, 1254.

J. B. **Bauer**, 'Das Buch Ruth in der jüdischen und christlichen Über-lieferung', *Bibel und Kirche* 18, Stuttgart 1963, 116–19; D. R. G. **Beattie**, *Jewish Exegesis of the Book of Ruth*, JSOT Suppl 2, 1977; E. F. **Campbell**, Jr., *Ruth*, AB, 1975, 32ff.; B. **Grossfeld**, *The Targums to the Five Megilloth*, New York 1973, 3–19; D. **Hartmann**, *Das Buch Ruth in der Midrasch–Literatur*, Leipzig 1901; L. B. **Wolfenson**, 'Implication of the Place of the Book of Ruth in Editions, Manuscripts, and Canons of the Old Testament', *HUCA* 1, 1924, 151–78.

XXXVII

SONG OF SONGS

Commentaries

E. W. Hengstenberg, 1853
F. Hitzig, KeH, 1855
C. D. Ginsburg, 1857
O. Zöckler, ET, LCHS, 1873
F. Delitzsch, BC, 1875
K. Budde, KHC, 1898
A. Harper, CB, 1907
P. Joüon, 1909
K. Budde, *HSAT*, ⁴1923
M. Haller, HAT, 1940
S. M. Lehrman, SonB, ²1952
D. Buzy, SB, ³1953

G. A. F. Knight, TB, 1955
T. J. Meek, *IB*, 1956
H. Ringgren, ATD, ²1962
W. Rudolph, KAT², 1962
H. Lamparter, BAT, 1962
A. Robert, R. Tournay, A. Feuillet, ÉB, 1963
G. Gerleman, BK, 1965
R. Gordis, ³1968
E. Würthwein, HAT², 1969
M. H. Pope, AB, 1977

Bibliography

J. **Angénieux**, 'Structure du Cantique des Cantiques,' *ETL* 41, 1965, 96–142; 'Le Cantique des Cantiques en huits chants à refrains alternants', *ETL* 44, 1968, 87–140; J.-P. **Audet**, 'Le sens du Cantique des Cantiques', *RB* 62, 1955, 197–221; A. **Bentzen**, 'Remarks on the Canonization of the Song of Solomon', *Studia orientalia I. Pedersen dicata*, Copenhagen 1953, 41–7; K. **Budde**, 'Was ist das Hohelied?', *Palästinajahrbuch* 78, Berlin 1894, 92–117; D. **Buzy**, 'La composition littéraire du Cantique des Cantiques', *RB* 49, 1940, 169–94; 'L'allégorie matrimoniale de Jahvé et d'Israël et le Cantique des Cantiques', *RB* 52, 1945, 77–90; Albert **Cook**, *The Root of the Thing. A Study of Job and the Song of Songs*, Bloomington, Ind. 1968; S. R. **Driver**, 'Appendix to Song of Songs', *Introduction to the Old Testament*, Edinburgh and New York ⁸1909, 451ff.; R. B. **Dubarle**, 'L'amour humain dans le Cantique des Cantiques', *RB* 61, 1954, 67–86; 'Le Cantique des Cantiques', *RSPhTh* 38, 1954, 92–102; J. Cheryl **Exum**, 'A Literary and Structural Analysis of the Song of Songs', *ZAW* 85, 1973, 47–79; A. **Feuil-**

let, 'Le Cantique des Cantiques et la tradition biblique', *Nouvelle Revue Théologique* 74, Louvain 1952, 706–33; *Le Cantique des Cantiques*, Paris 1953; R. **Gordis**, 'A Wedding Song for Solomon', *JBL* 63, 1944, 263–70; S. **Grill**, *Die Symbolsprache des Hohenliedes*, Heiligenkreuz ²1970; P. **Haupt**, 'The Book of Canticles', *AJSL* 18, 1901–2, 193–245; 19, 1902–3, 1–32; J. G. **von Herder**, *Lieder der Lieben, die ältesten und schönsten aus dem Morgenlande*, Leipzig 1778; A. **Hermann**, *Altägyptische Liebesdichtung*, Wiesbaden 1959; F. **Horst**, 'Die Formen des althebraischen Liebesliedes', *FS E. Littmann*, Leiden 1935, 43–54=*Gottes Recht*, Munich 1961, 176–87; S. N. **Kramer**, 'Sumerian Sacred Marriage Songs and the Biblical "Song of Songs"', *Mitteilungen des Instituts für Orientforschung* 15, Berlin 1969, 262–74; C. **Kuhl**, 'Das Hohelied und seine Bedeutung', *ThR* NF 9, 1937, 137–67. A. **Lacocque**, 'L'insertion du Cantique des Cantiques dans le Canon', *RHPhR* 42, 1962, 38–44; O. **Loretz**, 'Zum Problem des Eros im Hohenlied', *BZ* NF 8, 1964, 191–216; *Studien zur althebräischen Poesie* I. *Das althebräische Liebeslied*, Neukirchen-Vluyn 1971; M. L. **Margolis**, 'How the Song of Songs Entered the Canon', in W. H. Schoff, ed., *The Song of Songs: A Symposium*, Philadelphia 1924, 9–17; T. J. **Meek**, 'Canticles and the Tammuz Cult', *AJSL* 39, 1922/3, 1–14; R. E. **Murphy**, 'The Structure of the Canticle of Canticles', *CBQ* 11, 1949, 381–91; 'Recent Literature on the Canticle of Canticles', *CBQ* 16, 1954, 1–11; 'Form-Critical Studies in the Song of Songs', *Interp* 27, 1973, 413–22; 'Song of Songs', *IDB Suppl*, 831–8; 'Towards a Commentary on the Song of Songs', *CBQ* 39, 1977, 482–96; G. **von Rad**, *Wisdom in Israel*, ET London and Nashville 1972, 166–76; A. **Robert**, 'Le genre littéraire du Cantique des Cantiques', *RB* 52, 1945, 192–213; 'La déscription de L'Époux et de l'Épouse dans Cant. 5,11–15 et 7,2–6', *Mélanges E. Podechard*, Paris 1945, 211–23; 'Les Appendices du Cantique des Cantiques (8, 8–14)', *RB* 55, 1948, 161–83; H. H. **Rowley**, 'The Interpretation of the Song of Songs,' *The Servant of the Lord*, London ²1965, 195–245; W. **Rudolph**, 'Das Hohe Lied im Kanon', *ZAW* 59, 1942/3, 189–99; N. **Schmidt**, 'Is Canticles an Adonis Litany?', *JAOS* 46, 1926, 154–70; H. **Schmökel**, 'Zur kultischen Deutung des Hohenliedes', *ZAW* 64, 1952, 148–55; —, *Heilige Hochzeit und Hoheslied*, Wiesbaden 1956; S. **Schott**, *Altägyptische Liebeslieder*, Zürich ²1950; M. H. **Segal**, 'The Song of Songs', *VT* 12, 1962, 470–90; R. **Tournay**, 'Abraham et le Cantique des Cantiques', *VT* 25, 1975, 544–52; J. G. **Wetzstein**, 'Die syrische Dreschtafel', *Zeitschrift für Ethnologie* 5, Braunschweis 1873, 270–302; W. **Wittekindt**, *Das Hohe Lied und seine Beziehungen zum Ištarkult*, Hanover 1927; E. **Würthwein**, 'Zum Verständnis des Hohenliedes', *ThR* NF 32, 1967, 177–212.

1. Historical Critical Problems

Few books of the Old Testament exhibit such a wide range of differing opinions on the part of interpreters as does the Song of Songs. It is the usual practice of Introductions to trace the history of exegesis and to document with great ease the confusion which has often reigned. But the simple recounting of this history, such as that offered of the older period by Ginsburg and of the later period by H. H. Rowley, has failed to make clear the exact nature of the hermeneutical problems at stake. The issue turns on determining the particular context from which the interpreter seeks to understand this ancient writing. Because no consensus has emerged, it follows almost automatically that the resulting exegesis will differ widely. This thesis can be illustrated from a brief review of the history of exegesis.

(a) Hellenistic Judaism and early Christianity sought to interpret the Song of Songs allegorically; that is, although the text seemed to be speaking about one subject, its real meaning was thought to be different from the verbal sense. This hidden meaning was unlocked by an allegorical key. For the Jews the book spoke of the mystical love of God for his people, Israel; for the Christians the love was between Christ and his church. The theological reasoning behind the allegorical interpretations was not obscure. The Song of Songs formed part of the canon of sacred scripture, indeed, in the Jewish tradition it was read as part of the passover liturgy. Did it not then follow that the book must have a sacred meaning if it had been incorporated into this sacred context? Moreover, the fact that Akiba could object strenuously to Jews using the Song of Songs in the local tavern (Tos. Sanhedrin 12.10) seemed to confirm its non-secular function within the synagogue.

(b) In the modern period the allegorical method has been largely abandoned and regarded by critical scholarship as arbitrary and apologetic. However, there has emerged, particularly in France, a newer form of the method which has sought to defend a modified form of allegory with the tools of critical scholarship. A. Robert and A. Feuillet have defended the thesis that the Song of Songs is actually a type of post-exilic midrash which was constructed from a mosaic of biblical motifs and was intended to be read as a prophetic allegory of Yahweh's love for his people. Of course, many other scholars (cf. Audet, Dubarle, Murphy) remain highly critical even of this new form of allegory. They have raised the issues of imposing a false set of categories on the text, of failure to come to grips with the particular genre of the Song, and ultimately of returning to an apologetic stance for traditional allegory.

(c) One of the most popular theories which emerged in the late eighteenth century and came to dominate nineteenth-century interpretation for a while was the dramatic theory (Ewald, Delitzsch, Driver, etc.). In its most developed form the Song was thought to contain three principal characters – the earlier form found only two voices – a beautiful maiden, her shepherd lover, and King Solomon. In a form roughly analogous to a play, the king sought to entice the girl by his extravagant offers of luxury, but in the end the young village lovers were reunited through their unswerving love for each other. Two principal criticisms have been levelled against this interpretation. First, this kind of drama does not appear elsewhere in the Bible or in the literature of the ancient Near East, and it is doubtful whether such a form of composition was actually used. Secondly, the sorting out of the speeches of the alleged participants remains highly arbitrary and often goes against a more obvious reading of the text (cf. the critique of Gordis).

(d) Probably the dominant contemporary theory is one which sees in the Song of Songs a collection of secular love songs (Rowley, Gordis, Gerleman, etc.). This theory has undergone a variety of different forms. During the latter part of the nineteenth century, on the basis of Wetzstein's description of the Syrian wedding ceremony, the analogy to these songs of praise (*wasf*) was developed at great length by Budde and others. However, since the analogy breaks down in part, the more recent commentators have described the book as a collection of secular love songs or lyrics, which developed over a long period of time in the folk practice of the nation. The approach finds no clear structure or movement in the collection, but rather a variety of songs built about the celebration of human love. A variation of the love song theory has been offered by D. Buzy, who argued that the songs were intended to be understood metaphorically, and that the praise was to divine love.

(e) Finally, the so-called cult theory has been proposed in different forms by scholars such as T. J. Meek, W. Wittekindt, and M. H. Pope. The theory holds that the original function of the Song was ritual or cultic in close analogy to the Babylonian Tammuz festival or the Baal cycles of Canaanite myth. This interpretation has been criticized on various points. The mythical motif of a dying and rising god which is constitutive for the extra-biblical parallels is missing from the Song of Songs. Again, it is not clear how such a piece entered the canon, if this were its original function. Finally, the subtle use of erotic imagery in the biblical poem is far removed from the crass 'explanations' of the book's alleged original meaning.

In sum, the disagreement among the various theories is extreme and results in radically differing understandings of almost every passage. Lying at the basis of the disagreement is the confusion regarding proper context. Are we to bring a symbolic context to bear on the text, or separate the text into a variety of different voices, or seek to recover an original historical function behind the present form of the biblical book?

2. The Canonical Shape of the Song of Songs

The history of exegesis, in my judgment, illustrates the failure from both the right and left to take seriously the canonical shape of the book. What then is the particular stamp which the collectors of Israel's scripture left as a key for its interpretation within the community of faith?

The superscription and wisdom

Certainly the place to begin is with the book's superscription: 'The most excellent song of Solomon'. The title ascribes the poem to Solomon in a Hebrew idiom which conveys the sense of the superlative. Usually this ascription has been treated within a narrow historical framework. How much, if any, of the book stemmed from the authorship of Solomon? Because the language and content of the book reflect a later age than that of Solomon (cf. Delitzsch's characterization), the superscription has generally been dismissed as worthless. Yet there are many indications within the book itself – not to speak of the rest of the Old Testament – which would suggest that the title performs a different and far broader role from that of establishing authorship in the modern sense of the concept. Audet (205f.) has pointed out with great insight the differing approach of the ancient world to authorship. Whereas the modern reader considers a book to be the property of its individual author, the Old Testament viewed a book as traditional, communal, and developing. By ascribing the Song to Solomon the collector did not rule out other later voices adding to the poem, as is evident from 8.11f. in which Solomon is himself the addressee. Nevertheless, some important claims are being made by the title which determine the context from which the book is to be interpreted.

The book, along with the book of Proverbs and Ecclesiastes, is ascribed to Solomon as the source of Israel's wisdom literature. As Moses is the source of the Law, and David of the Psalms, so is Solomon the father of sapiential writing. Solomon's role as Israel's wise man *par excellence* is further reflected in the prose tradition of Kings (I Kings 3.1ff.; 5.1ff., EVV 4.29ff.). The ascription of the Song of Songs to Solomon by the Hebrew canon sets these writings within the context of wisdom literature. Indeed this song is the 'pearl' of the collection. The effect of this classification has some immediate implications for the reading of the book, both in terms of its form and content.

The Song is to be understood as wisdom literature. What does this involve? Wisdom literature derived from Israel's sages and extended throughout Israel's entire history from its earliest to latest period. As a minimal statement of a complex and varied phenomenon, wisdom sought to understand through reflection the nature of the world of human experience in relation to divine reality. The function of wisdom within Israel was essentially didactic and not philosophical. By ordering the Song within wisdom literature certain other alternative contexts for interpreting it are ruled out. Thus, for example, the Song is not to be understood simply as secular songs which have only superficially been offered a sacred meaning. Rowley's naturalistic interpretation badly misses the point. The polarity of 'secular versus sacred' is alien from the start to the categories of Hebrew wisdom. Rather, reflection on human experience without resort to the religious language of Israel's traditional institutions of law, cult, and prophecy is characteristic of wisdom, and is by no means a sign of secular origin.

Again, recognition of the Song of Songs as wisdom runs counter to allegorical interpretation (cf. especially Audet). This traditional method seeks to transfer the Song into a different genre of biblical literature. By interpreting the Song's imagery primarily within the framework of prophetic literature, the book is made to symbolize the prophetic themes of God's love for his people, of the new exodus, etc. But these are precisely the themes which are missing in the wisdom corpus. Robert's attempt to designate the Song as a type of midrash is again a disregarding of the canon's wisdom category. It transfers the canonical text into a product of a learned reflection akin to Chronicles. Only after the Old Testament period did wisdom and midrash come together in this way, as for example in Ben Sira and early rabbinic literature. Similarly, to seek to understand the Song of Songs as cultic moves the book from its place within wisdom into the context of ancient Near Eastern mythology and disregards the function which the canon has assigned it.

The designation of the Song as a wisdom book of Solomon also affects how one describes its content. The role of Solomon is extended into the Song itself. 3.11 pictures the arrival of Solomon's royal entourage for 'the day of his wedding' (cf. Ps. 45.12ff.). The 'king' is introduced as the lover (1.4, 12; 7.5) who seeks his 'bride' (4.8). The Song is wisdom's reflection on the joyful and mysterious nature of love between a man and a woman within the institution of marriage. The frequent assertion that the Song is a celebration of human love *per se* fails utterly to reckon with the canonical context (cf. Audet, 214ff.). Nowhere is human love in itself celebrated in wisdom literature, nor in the whole Old Testament for that matter. Wisdom, not love, is divine, yet love between a man and his wife is an inextinguishable force within human experience, 'strong as death', which the sage seeks to understand (cf. Prov. 5.15ff.). The writer simply assumes the Hebrew order of the family as a part of the given order of his society, and seeks to explore and unravel its mysteries from within.

Wisdom and erotic language

It has long been observed that the wisdom books have made much use of erotic language (Prov. 7.6ff.; 9.1ff.; Sirach 51.13ff.; Wisd. 8.2). Wisdom is pictured as a woman of the streets enticing and cajoling those who pass by. Scholars have debated whether this application within Israel's wisdom circles was a conscious attempt to oppose the inroads of the Canaanite goddess of love by portraying wisdom as the only true partner who calls men to choose life.

Von Rad (*Wisdom*, 168) has reflected on whether Israel read the Song of Songs as an allegory on the search for wisdom. According to this understanding, Israel did not simply sapientialize the Song. Rather, on the basis of an earlier symbolic relationship between aggressive human love and wisdom which had been used elsewhere in wisdom circles, the sages changed the semantic level of the Song to that of metaphor. The Song was thus brought into line with other biblical imagery which interpreted erotic yearning as a search for true wisdom.

Quite clearly the allegorical interpretation of the Song of Songs which soon emerged in Judaism and Christianity actually made the hermeneutical shift which von Rad has outlined. Yet the question is crucial whether the canonical process had already shaped the material in this direction. In my judgment, there is no evidence within the biblical text itself to support this interpretation. The wisdom context never functioned to shift the semantic level of human love to become a metaphor, but rather it sought to probe the mystery of human love within the creative order.

Structure and tension

Commentators continue to debate the issue of the structure of the book, but without great success. The fact that no structure is clearly indicated in its canonical form speaks against the dramatic theory of interpretation which rests everything upon the reader's ability to reconstruct the variety of different actors and a plot. The two voices of the male and female lover are introduced, sometimes in dialogue, often in monologue. There is considerable repetition of lines (2.17; 8.14) and a refrain (1.7; 3.5; 5.8), but there does not seem to be any clear movement and certainly not a plot. Rather, the one topic of sexual love is dealt with from a variety of perspectives, particularly the longing before union and the satisfaction of mutual surrender. Various parts of the book can be distinguished, but they all tend to circle around the one subject. In a loose sense one can speak of a unity of composition. The two lovers and the daughters of Jerusalem run through the whole. But the unity is lyrical and has made use of traditional wedding songs without achieving a rigid uniformity of style. Nowhere has the editor imposed upon his material a uniform redactional pattern, which also speaks against an allegorical interpretation.

It has been suggested that the present form of the Song incorporates two different recensions, one of a royal figure from Jerusalem, the other of a rustic lover from the north. Indeed, it is easy to recognize two sets of distinct imagery which have not been fused within the book. Nowhere, for example, is there the combination of a rustic shepherd king. This unresolved tension in the book's imagery undoubtedly reflects some phase within the development of the material. However, from a canonical perspective the major exegetical task arising from this observation turns on determining the effect of the tension on the final form of the book.

The two sets of imagery have not been given equal status, but the shepherd figure has been subordinated to that of the royal figure of King Solomon. The poems are firmly tied to the royal wedding, yet the effect of the shepherd imagery is greatly to broaden the context. The experiences described throughout most of the Song are no longer confined to a royal ceremony, but extend to include general human emotions of love. The lover comes not as a king (2.8), but as an ordinary man awakening to a season of love like the rebirth of nature about him, calling his beloved into fields and gardens. The various descriptions which the lovers offer of their partners (4.1ff; 6.4ff.; 7.1ff.) bear a traditional stamp of ancient Near Eastern love poetry (cf. Schmökel, Schott), but are also not exclusively royal. The effect is to portray the lovers in idealized form when seen through the eyes of the other. It is possible that the wide geographical references which cover the entire country work toward the same purpose of extending the scope beyond the royal city.

Conclusion

There is another important sign that the initial context of being wisdom literature from Solomon has been significantly broadened in its final canonical form. In 8.11f. Solomon is no longer the speaker of the love poetry, but rather the addressee. Another voice is introduced which is explicitly set over against that of the king. In contrast to the great wealth of Solomon, which is portrayed in staggering proportions, another voice evaluates his own exclusive possession of a beloved one as of even greater value: 'my vineyard, my very own, for myself!' If there had been any doubt up to now that the love being described extended beyond the king's to every man, this explicit contrast indicates the effort to incorporate even the poorest of Israel within the same reality of human love. A voice within the community disputes Solomon's exclusive claim. Significantly, the canon's assigning of the Song to Solomon (1.1) does not rule out other voices, indeed even one which appears to use Solomon as a foil.

Finally, there is a clear sign of editorial activity in the passage 8.6–7. These verses are unique in the book because they represent a clear example of reflective generalization, which is characteristic of wisdom literature. Elsewhere in the Song assertions are grounded by a *kî* clause of motivation (1.2), but in 8.6 a characterization of love apart from that of the two lovers is offered. Not 'your love', but simply generic love is portrayed as 'strong as death' and a 'most vehement flame'. The passage functions to summarize the message of the entire book and to abstract its teaching beyond the historical instance afforded by Solomon.

3. Theological and Hermeneutical Implications

(*a*) It has become a commonplace for Old Testament Introductions to assert that the Song of Songs entered the canon because it had already been allegorized. In the light of the evidence of its canonical shaping, this statement appears highly questionable. There is no sign that the canonical shape of the book ever received an allegorical shaping. Rather, its place within wisdom literature resisted attempts to replace its message with prophetic themes. Nor did the Song of Songs enter the canon as a 'secular' love poem in need of being made sacred. Instead, the Song entered the canon in essentially the same role as it had played in Israel's institutional life. It celebrated the mysteries of human love expressed in the marriage festival.

(*b*) It is also clear that the Song of Songs did not arise originally from within the same wisdom circles as did, for example, the book of Proverbs. Rather, it was secondarily drawn within this orbit of wisdom to function canonically as a theological construct which established a particular context for the book's reading. The Song of Songs was to be heard along with other portions of Israel's scripture as a guide to wisdom. The canonical concerns were highly theological, but expressed in such a way that the profane and sacred dimensions of life were never separated. The wisdom framework served to maintain the Song's integrity as a phenomenon of human experience reflecting the divine order which the community of faith continued to enjoy.

(*c*) The actualization of the message of the Song was accomplished by a subtle broadening of the historical context beyond that of Solomon to include the phenomenon itself as universal experience. The historical references to Solomon serve primarily to classify the material within its genre but do not tie the material irrevocably to the past.

History of Exegesis

Carpzov II, 270–78; *DThC* 2, 1679; *EB* 6, 653–5; *RGG*³ 3, 430f.

B. W. **Ball**, 'The Apocalyptic Significance of the Song of Solomon', *Great Expectation: Eschatological Thought in English Protestantism to 1600*, Leiden 1975, 239–42; J. **Beumer**, 'Die marianische Deutung des Hohen Liedes in der Frühscholastik', *Zeitschrift für katholische Theologie* 76, Innsbruck 1945, 411–39; J. **Bonsirven**, 'Exégèse allégorique chez les rabbins Tannaites', *RSR* 24, 1934, 35–46; F. **Cavallera**, A. **Cabassut** and M. **Olphe-Galliard**, 'Cantique des Cantiques: II. Histoire de L'intérpretation spirituelle', *DS* 2. 1, 1949, 93–109; G. **Chappuzeau**, 'Die Exegese von Hohelied 1, 2a und 7 bei den Kirchenvätern von Hippolyt bis Bernard', *Jahrbuch für Antike und Christentum* 18, Münster 1975, 90ff.; J.-M. **Déchanet**, 'Introduction', *Guillaume de Saint-Thierry, Exposé sur le Cantique des Cantiques*, SC 82, 1962, 7–69; C. D. **Ginsburg**, *Song of Songs*, London 1857; B. **Grossfeld**, *The Targums to the Five Megilloth*, New York 1973, 171–251; H. **Höpfl**, *Introductio Specialis in Vetus Testamentum*, Rome ⁵1946, 339–58; J. **Kirchmeyer**, Origène, Commentaire sur le Cantique, prol.', *Studia Patristica et Liturgica* 4, Regensburg 1970, 230–35; D. **Lerch**, 'Zur Geschichte der Auslegung des Hohenliedes', *ZTK* 54, 1957, 257–77; R. **Loewe**, 'Apologetic Motifs in the Targum to the Song of Songs', *The Lown Institute for Judaistic Studies* 3, Cambridge, Mass. 1966, 159–96; F. **Ohly**, *Hohelied-Studien, Grundzüge einer Geschichte der Hoheliedauslegung des Abendlandes bis um 1200*, Wiesbaden 1958; M. H. **Pope**, *Song of Songs*, AB, 1977; O. **Rousseau**, 'Introduction', *Origène. Homélies sur le Cantique des Cantiques*, SC 37, 1966, 7–57; S. **Salfeld**, *Das Hohelied Salomons bei den jüdischen Erklärern des Mittelalters*, Berlin 1879; G. G. **Scholem**, *Jewish Gnosticism, Merkabah Mysticism and Talmudic Tradition*, New York 1960, 38–40; E. E. **Urbach**, 'The Homiletical Interpretations of the Sages and the Exposition of Origen on Canticles and the Jewish-Christian Disputations', *Scripta Hierosolymitana* 22, Jerusalem 1971, 247–75; P. **Vulliaud**, *Le Cantique des Cantiques d'après la tradition Juive*, Paris 1925.

XXXVIII

ECCLESIASTES

Commentaries

E. W. Hengstenberg, 1860
C. D. Ginsburg, 1861
F. Delitzsch, BC, 1877
E. H. Plumptre, CB, 1881
K. Siegfried, HKAT, 1898
G. Wildeboer, KHC, 1898
G. A. Barton, ICC, 1908
E. Podechard, ÉB, 1912
A. L. Williams, CB², 1922
K. Budde, *HSAT*, ⁴1922
A. Allgeier, HS, 1925
H. W. Hertzberg, KAT, 1932

K. Galling, HAT, 1940
D. Buzy, SB, 1946
G. C. Aalders, COuT, 1948
V. E. Reichert, SonB, ²1952
H. L. Ginsberg, 1961
W. Zimmerli, ATD, 1962
H. W. Hertzberg, KAT², 1963
R. B. Y. Scott, AB, 1965
K. Galling, HAT², 1969
W. J. Fuerst, CNEB, 1975
A. Lauha, BK, 1978

Bibliography

W. **Baumgartner**, 'The Wisdom Literature. IV. Ecclesiastes', *The Old Testament and Modern Study*, ed. H. H. Rowley, Oxford and New York 1951, 221–7; A. **Bea**, *Liber Ecclesiastae qui ab Hebraeis appellatur Qohelet*, Scripta Pontificii Instituti Biblici 100, Rome 1950; E. **Bickerman**, 'Koheleth', *Four Strange Books of the Bible*, New York 1967; R. **Braun**, *Kohelet und die frühhellenistische Popularphilosophie*, BZAW 130, 1973; D. **Buzy**, 'La notion du bonheur dans l'Ecclésiaste', *RB* 43, 1934, 494–511; G. R. **Castellino**, 'Qohelet and his Wisdom', *CBQ* 30, 1968, 15–28; M. J. **Dahood**, 'Canaanite-Phoenician Influence in Qoheleth', *Bibl* 33, 1952, 30–52; 'Qoheleth and Recent Discoveries', *Bibl* 39, 1958, 302–18; F. **Ellermeier**, *Qohelet*, Herzberg² 1970; K. **Galling**, 'Kohelet-Studien', *ZAW* 50, 1932, 276–93; 'Stand und Aufgabe der Kohelet-Forschung', *ThR* NF 6, 1934, 355–73; 'Das Rätsel der Zeit im Urteil Kohelets (Koh. 3, 1–5)', *ZTK* 58, 1961, 1–15; H. **Gese**, 'Die Krisis der Weisheit bei Koheleth', *Les sagesses du Proche-Orient Ancien*, Paris 1963, 139ff.; H. L. **Ginsberg**, *Studies in Koheleth*,

New York 1950; 'Supplementary Studies in Koheleth', *PAAJR* 21, 1952, 35–62; 'The Structure and Contents of the Book of Kohelet', *SVT* 3, 1955, 138–49; R. **Gordis**, *Koheleth. The Man and His World*, New York ²1955; 'Qoheleth and Qumran – A Study of Style', *Bibl* 41, 1960, 395–410; H. **Graetz**, *Kohelet*, Leipzig 1871; M. **Hengel**, *Judaism and Hellenism*, ET London and Philadelphia 1974, I, 115–30; A. S. **Kamenetzky**, 'Das Koheleth-Rätsel', *ZAW* 29, 1909, 63–9; 'Der Rätselname Koheleth', *ZAW* 34, 1914, 225–8; P. **Kleinert**, 'Sind im Buche Koheleth ausserhebräische Einflüsse anzuerkennen?', *ThStKr* 56, 1883, 761–82; 'Zur religions- und kulturgeschichtlichen Stellung des Buches Koheleth', *ThStKr* 82, 1909, 493–529; M. A. **Klopfenstein**, 'Die Skepsis des Qohelet', *TZ* 28, 1972, 97–109.

O. **Loretz**, *Qohelet und der Alte Orient. Untersuchungen zu Stil und theologischer Thematik des Buches Qohelet*, Freiburg 1964; A. **Miller**, 'Aufbau und Grundprobleme des Predigers', in *Miscellanea Biblica edita a Pontificio Instituto Biblico* II, Rome 1934, 104–22; J. **Pedersen**, 'Scepticisme israélite', *RHPhR* 10, 1930, 317–70; R. H. **Pfeiffer**, 'The Peculiar Skepticism of Ecclesiastes', *JBL* 53, 1934, 100–09; T. **Polk**, 'The Wisdom of Irony: A Study of *Hebel* and its Relation to Joy and the Fear of God in Ecclesiastes', *Studia Biblica et Theologica* 6, Pasedena, Calif. 1971, 3–17; G. **von Rad**, *Wisdom in Israel*, London and Nashville 1972, 226–37; H. **Ranston**, *Ecclesiastes and the Early Greek Wisdom Literature*, London 1925; H. H. **Rowley**, 'The Problems of Ecclesiastes', *JQR* 42, 1951/2, 87–90; R. B. **Salters**, 'Qoheleth and the Canon', *ExpT* 86, 1975, 339–42; H. H. **Schmid**, *Wesen und Geschichte der Weisheit*, BZAW 101, 1966, 186ff.; G. T. **Sheppard**, 'The Epilogue to Qoheleth as Theological Commentary', *CBQ* 39, 1977, 182–9; W. **Vischer**, L'Ecclésiaste, Témoin de Jésus Christ', *Valeur de l'Ancien Testament*, Geneva 1965, 101–21; J. G. **Williams**, 'What Does it Profit a Man?: The Wisdom of Koheleth', *Judaism* 20, New York 1971, 179–93, reprinted J. L. Crenshaw, ed., *Studies in Ancient Israelite Wisdom*, New York 1976, 375–89; A. G. **Wright**, 'The Riddle of the Sphinx: The Structure of the Book of Qoheleth', *CBQ* 30, 1968, 313–34, reprinted Crenshaw, *Studies*, 245–66; J. S. **Wright**, 'The Interpretation of Ecclesiastes', *EvQu* 18, 1946, 18–34; W. **Zimmerli**, 'Zur Struktur der alttestamentlichen Weisheit', *ZAW* 51, 1933, 177–204; *Die Weisheit des Predigers Salomo*, Berlin 1936; 'Das Buch Kohelet – Traktat oder Sentenzensammlung?', *VT* 24, 1974, 221–30.

1. Historical Critical Problems

There are a variety of difficult problems in the book of Ecclesiastes which have engaged the attention of critical scholars in each successive generation. It is helpful to sketch the broad lines of this research both in respect to areas of agreement and of disagreement before raising the canonical question.

(a) There is an almost universal consensus, shared by extremely conservative scholars, that Solomon was not the author of the book. This agreement is significant because it runs counter to the traditional ascription to Solomon by both Jews and Christians. Several considerations have led to this consensus. The name of Solomon is nowhere explicitly mentioned as the author. Again, the language of the book consistently reflects signs of late Hebrew and offers the closest parallels to Mishnaic Hebrew in the Old Testament. However, there is no agreement as to the implications of this non-explicit reference to Solomon. Was the book issued as an intentional pseudepigraph or was the implicit reference to Solomon a literary device?

(b) The book is generally dated between 300–200 BC, chiefly on the basis of language, but further reasons have been sought on conceptual grounds. The Qumran fragments support this period, at least against assigning it a much later *terminus ad quem*. Neither the repeated efforts to date certain concepts of Koheleth as necessarily late, nor to trace the influence of Greek philosophical streams, have been successful.

(c) Increasingly, modern scholars have returned to the position of seeing the book as basically a unified composition of one author. The earlier theories of multiple authorship or of extensive interpolation have not been sustained. However, some editorial work is generally recognized in the prologue and epilogue.

(d) In regard to the structure of Koheleth no consensus has emerged. Scholars are usually grouped into two camps. On the one hand, there are those who find no unified order or sequence of thought. A leading advocate of this approach is K. Galling ('Kohelet-Studien'), who describes the book as consisting of independent aphoristic units (so also Ellermeier). On the other hand, scholars such as A. Bea and A. G. Wright see an overarching unity in the work with some progression of thought which can be outlined. In my judgment, the truth lies between these two extremes. Zimmerli's carefully argued mediating position (*VT* 1974) agrees with Galling in deriving the basic form of the book from a collection of individual wisdom sayings which has no clearly defined outline of the whole. However, the present form of the book reflects far more inner coherence than the advocates of the collection theory admit. The sayings have been formed around certain topics and a progression of thought is often discernible.

(e) Scholars remain divided in their estimate of the theological contribution of the book as a whole. A considerable number tend to view the book in largely negative terms as an example of growing scepticism within a segment of Israelite society which effected a breakdown of religious tradition (von Rad). However, others have sought a more positive evaluation in terms of a corrective within the school of wisdom (Zimmerli), even though the exact nature of the religious crisis remains contested (cf. Gese).

(f) Finally, there is a broad hermeneutical conviction shared by the majority of scholars, which S. R. Driver expresses forcefully: 'If the Book of Ecclesiastes is to be properly estimated, it must be read in the light of the age in which it was written, and the temper of the author' (*Introduction* [8]1909, 470). In other words, the key to the book's interpretation lies in discerning the historical and psychological influences on the writer. In my judgment, this assumption often results in an approach which fails to deal seriously with the canonical role of the book as sacred scripture of a continuing community of faith.

2. The Canonical Shape of Ecclesiastes

The superscription

The book of Ecclesiastes is introduced by a superscription: 'The words of Koheleth, the son of David, king in Jerusalem.' The name *qōhelet* presents an initial problem because it is unique to this one book of the Old Testament. The word is a feminine singular qal participle of the root *qhl*, which has the meaning of 'assembling or gathering together the community'. The closest Hebrew parallels to the formation occur in such names as *hassōperet* (office of scribe, Ezra 2.55) and *pōkeret haṣṣ'bāyim* (office of those tending gazelles, Ezra 2.57). The occurrence of the name Koheleth with the article in 7.27 and 12.8 confirms the interpretation of the name as an office of some kind. Thus, the various traditional attempts at a translation have tried to capture this connotation: e.g. LXX = Ἐκκλησιαστής; Vulg = Ecclesiastes; Luther = Prediger.

Commentators have made much of the superscription's belonging to a final redactional stage and being dependent upon 1.12.

From a canonical perspective this literary, historical observation –
whether true or not – is of secondary importance because in the
final form of the composition the superscription does play a
significant role. Nevertheless, if Galling's theory (*ZAW* 1934) that
the editorial framework was based on a misunderstanding were
correct, it would have implications for the canonical interpretation.
Up to now he has received little support. Still the more difficult
question, and of primary importance, is to determine the function
of the title. Why is the author identified with Koheleth, and yet
immediately described in a way which is only appropriate to Solomon? He is 'the son of David', 'king in Jerusalem', 'surpassing
in wisdom all in Jerusalem' (1.16), and one who 'built houses,
vineyards, etc.' (2.4ff.). The traditional biblical profile of Solomon
is clearly reflected which is portrayed in such passages as I Kings
5.26ff. (EVV 4.29ff.); 10.23ff.; II Chron. 1.7ff.; and Song of Songs
8.12ff. To suggest that the book is actually pseudepigraphic and
that an attempt was made to acquire an authoritative status by
ascribing it to Solomon runs into a variety of problems. First, the
name of Solomon is never used, which is without parallel if a claim
for authorship were intended. Secondly, the fiction of Koheleth as a
pseudonym for Solomon is clearly abandoned within the book itself
(8.2ff.; 10.16f.; 12.9ff.).

It seems much more likely, therefore, to suppose that the picture
of Koheleth as Solomon served another purpose. In its canonical
form the identification assures the reader that the attack on wisdom
which Ecclesiastes contains is not to be regarded as the personal
idiosyncrasy of a nameless teacher. Rather, by his speaking in the
guise of Solomon, whose own history now formed part of the community's common memory, his attack on wisdom was assigned an
authoritative role as the final reflections of Solomon. As the source
of Israel's wisdom, his words serve as an official corrective from
within the wisdom tradition itself. Once this point was made, the
literary fiction of Solomon was dropped.

The epilogue

The most obvious sign of canonical shaping appears in the
epilogue. Critical commentators debate at length its unity and
authorship. Some scholars have ascribed the epilogue to a pupil of
Koheleth since Koheleth is addressed in the third person much in

the manner of the book's superscription. Others (e.g. Zimmerli) follow Podechard in seeing two distinct redactors at work in vv. 9–11 and 12–14, and note the repeated introduction in vv. 9 and 12. From the canonical perspective the crucial issue focuses on determining the effect of the epilogue on the interpretation of the book regardless of whether the addition derives from one or two editorial layers. What guidelines are established for the community which now uses the book of Koheleth as authoritative scripture? Few passages in the Old Testament reflect a more overt consciousness of the canon than does this epilogue (cf. Sheppard).

The first exegetical problem turns on determining the scope of the epilogue, specifically the position of v. 8. The older commentaries (Hengstenberg) generally saw it as part of the epilogue. The newer commentaries, with the exception of Galling, assign it to the preceding section as a conclusion. An argument for assigning it to the preceding verses lies in seeing the motto as a framework for the book (1.1 and 12.8) to which an epilogue has subsequently been added. The verse also serves as an appropriate summary of the final poem on old age (12.1–7).

What then is the perspective on reading Koheleth which the epilogue offers? Verse 9 first characterizes Koheleth as 'wise'. His sayings are not just pessimistic emotions, but designated as part of Israel's wisdom. Moreover, his words are put into the larger context of his teaching ministry. He had an office or at least a function within the community. His use of wisdom was not just a private affair, hence the name Koheleth. Further, the nature of his role is described as a critical one: weighing, studying, and ordering. The emphasis does not fall on his writing activity, although this is included, but on his critical judgment in the collection of wisdom. Moreover, his literary critical role is explicitly characterized as 'truthful'. The phrase 'pleasing words' (v. 10) is not an aesthetic description, but rather portrays his writings as 'fitting' and 'appropriate'.

In v. 11 the epilogue sets Koheleth's work into the larger context of other wisdom teachers. The sayings of the $h^a k \bar{a} m \hat{\imath} m$ (sages) are parallel to their 'collective sayings'. The role of wisdom collections is then succinctly characterized: they act as 'goads' to stimulate with a sting, and together they function as 'firmly fixed nails', points of reference which stake out an area in which wisdom is found. Nevertheless, in spite of this variety of functions the source

of all wisdom is from God, 'the one Shepherd'. This characterization thus legitimates Ecclesiastes as divine wisdom and rules out
any merely private interpretation. In addition, there is a warning
against other books which the writer explicitly excludes from the
community as a distraction from the canonical collection.

Verse 13 offers a final summary. The major points have been
made regarding Koheleth and need only to be briefly rehearsed.
The imperative to 'fear God and keep his commandments' is
offered as the epitome of man's duty. The biblical idiom of fearing
God and keeping his commandments could only have been heard in
the broadest context of the Jewish faith which included the Mosaic
legislation. Clearly no sharp distinction between wisdom and law
was being suggested by the epilogue.

In addition to the imperative addressing man's whole duty, the
epilogue offers an overarching theological rubric under which all
human behaviour was to be viewed, namely, the judgment of God.
God's hidden wisdom penetrates the secret things of this world and
thus relativizes all human strivings by his final act of distinguishing
the good from the evil. In the present form of the book this
eschatological motif finds its confirmation in such verses as 3.17,
8.11f., and 11.9.

The theory was first put forward by Krochmal (cf. Graetz, 47ff.)
that the last three verses of the epilogue do not refer just to
Koheleth, but function as a conclusion to the whole Hagiographa.
The suggestion has not received much support (cf. Barton, Gordis).
Yet is it possible that the reference to the 'words of the wise' could
extend beyond Koheleth and give the canonical key to the book of
Proverbs as well? As is well known, Koheleth immediately followed
Proverbs in the order of the Talmud (Baba Bathra 14b) and there
are some parallels in language with Proverbs 1. In my judgment,
the interpretation is unlikely. The evidence is not strong enough for
relating the 'sayings of the wise' specifically to the book of Proverbs.
The phrase simply establishes the larger literary category of which
Koheleth is an example. A more serious objection to Krochmal's
theory is that it removes vv. 11ff. from a specific reference to
Koheleth and thus greatly weakens the critical impact of the
epilogue on the reading of the book.

The main body of the book

In his often quoted conclusion F. Delitzsch ruled out the possibility of ever finding any consistent literary movement within the book (188). This observation provides an important guideline to how the main body of the book was to be understood. The book is a collection of sayings which have an integrity within smaller units, but which do not intend to comprise a unified reflection on God and society. As K. Galling later discovered (*ZAW* 1932), Koheleth's sayings arose in reaction to an assumed body of wisdom tradition. Therefore, almost every topic within the traditional teachings of the sages is touched upon in Ecclesiastes: God rewards the righteous and punishes the wicked; an act and its consequence is inextricably linked; life is the highest gift of God and death is a threat; diligence brings its reward and slothfulness its toll. At times Koheleth flatly rejects the tradition, while at other times he modifies or even affirms it. That there are contradictions within the book arises from the shifting contexts to which he speaks and from his critical judgment against traditional wisdom which would lay claim to greater human understanding than Koheleth would grant. To attempt to eliminate the tension within the book either by a theory of different literary sources (Siegfried), or by suggesting different voices in a dialogue is to seek to circumvent the context established by the editors.

However, this analysis would be inadequate if it implies that there was no effort on the part of the canonical process to tie together the various sayings in some fashion. Zimmerli's commentary has made out a strong case for recognizing certain unifying tendencies which are reflected in the final form of the book. For example, the poetic introduction (1.3–11) seeks to raise the basic question of the value of human achievement which sets the critical tone of the entire book. By understanding this initial poem as establishing a proper critical stance rather than summarizing a worldview, the reader is led to see, in the variety of critical judgments of the book, examples to support this basic evaluation of all human activity.

3. Theological and Hermeneutical Implications

(a) The canonical shaping both of the body of the book and also the epilogue makes it clear that Koheleth is to be used as scripture along with other books in the collection. Its authoritative role lies in its function within a larger context. The editorial shaping of the book did not consist of a heavy-handed reworking of the original sayings of Koheleth. His words are left basically in their original form without being blurred or softened. Instead, a new and larger context is provided in which the book is to be interpreted. To what extent the particular views of Koheleth arose from his personal disposition is left unanswered. What is significant in a canonical sense is rather the judgment that his sayings serve as a critical sapiential guide for the community when placed with other authoritative writings. The point of using the literary fiction of Solomon, the eponymic father of Hebrew wisdom, is specifically to guard the normative status of this message against ascribing it to the individual quirks of its author. The hermeneutical implication of this move is to call into question interpretations which would derive Koheleth's views from his changing moods or pessimistic disposition rather than to see them as playing a critical role within Israel's corpus of wisdom literature. Indeed, Koheleth's sayings do not have an independent status, but function as a critical corrective, much as the book of James serves in the New Testament as an essential corrective to misunderstanding the Pauline letters.

(b) Secondly we shall not achieve the proper interpretation of the book of Koheleth for the community of faith by seeking to uncover unusual historical or psychological influences on the author. This statement is not to deny that such influences were present, as is obvious for any historical writing. But in its particularity the canonical process assigned to each part of scripture a new role for a different context. The message of Koheleth is heard and interpreted from a 'rule of faith' which is far broader than even the wisdom corpus (12.13). By being set in the eschatological framework of a coming divine judgment, Koheleth's message is not only limited to present human activity, but sharply relativized in the light of the new and fuller dimension of divine wisdom. When later Jews and Christians contrasted the wisdom of this world (I Cor. 1.20) with the wisdom of God, they were interpreting the Hebrew scriptures according to their canonical shaping.

(c) It is often claimed that the epilogue of Ecclesiastes robs the book of its original vitriolic force. Is it not the goal of the historical critical method to make the modern reader experience the same jolt as was felt by Koheleth's first addressees? This commonly held theory of actualization of a biblical text stems from a romantic understanding of history (deriving from Herder). However, from a theological perspective it is far from obvious. Indeed, the purpose of a canon of sacred writings is to propose a very different understanding of actualization. The authority of the biblical text does not rest on a capacity to match original experiences, rather on the claim which the canonical text makes on every subsequent generation of hearers.

History of Exegesis

Carpzov II, 235–9; *DThC* 4, 2053; *RGG*³ 5, 514.

R. **Braun**, *Koheleth und die frühhellenistische Popularphilosophie*, Berlin 1973; G. **Calandra**, *De historica Andreae Victorini expositione in Ecclesiasten*, Palermo 1948; B. **Grossfeld**, *The Targums to the Five Megilloth*, New York 1973, 67–85; S. **Holm-Nielsen**, 'The Book of Ecclesiastes and the Interpretation of it in Jewish and Christian Theology', *ASTI* 10, 1976, 38–96; J. **Muilenburg**, 'A Qoheleth Scroll from Qumran', *BASOR* 135, 1954, 20–28; A. **Palm**, *Die Qohelet-Literatur. Ein Beitrag zur Exegese des Alten Testamentes*, Mannheim 1886; S. **Schiffer**, *Das Buch Kohelet. Nach der Auffassung der Weisen des Talmud und Midrasch und der jüdischen Erklärer des Mittelalters*, Leipzig 1884; S. **Vajda**, *Deux commentaires Karaïtes sur l'Ecclésiaste*, Leiden 1971; E. **Wölfel**, *Luther und die Skepsis. Eine Studie zur Kohelet-Exegese Luthers*, Forschungen zur Geschichte und Lehre des Protestantismus X. 12, Munich 1958.

XXXIX

LAMENTATIONS

Commentaries

O. Thenius, KeH, 1855
H. Ewald, [3]1866
C. F. Keil, BC, 1880
J. Knabenbauer, CSS, 1891
K. Budde, KHC, 1898
A. W. Streane, CB, 1899
M. Löhr, HKAT, [2]1906
A. S. Peake, CB, 1911
M. Löhr, *HSAT*, [4]1923
W. Rudolph, KAT, 1939
M. Haller, HAT, 1940

S. Goldman, SonB, [2]1952
G. A. F. Knight, TB, 1955
T. J. Meek, *IB*, 1956
A. Weiser, ATD, 1958
H. Lamparter, BAT, 1962
W. Rudolph, KAT[2], 1962
H.-J. Kraus, BK, [3]1968
O. Plöger, HAT[2], 1969
D. R. Hillers, AB, 1972
W. J. Fuerst, CNEB, 1975

Bibliography

B. **Albrektson**, *Studies in the Text and Theology of the Book of Lamentations*, Lund 1963; G. **Beer**, *Individual- und Gemeindepsalmen*, Marburg 1894; G. **Brunet**, *Les lamentations contre Jérémie. Réinterprétation des quatre premières lamentations*, Paris 1968; K. **Budde**, 'Das hebräische Klagelied', ZAW 2, 1882, 1–52; 3, 1883, 299–306; W. W. **Cannon**, 'The Authorship of Lamentations', *Bibliotheca Sacra* 81, Dallas, Texas 1924, 42–58; A. **Gelin**, 'Lamentations (Livre des)', *DBS* 5, 237–51; R. **Gordis**, 'A Commentary on the Text of Lamentations', *The Seventy-Fifth Anniversary Volume of the JRQ*, ed. A. A. Neuman and S. Zeitlin, Philadelphia 1967, 267–86; 'Commentary on the Text of Lamentations (Part Two)', *JQR* NS 58, 1967–68, 14–33; 'The Conclusion of the Book of Lamentations', *JBL* 93, 1974, 289–93; N. K. **Gottwald**, *Studies in the Book of Lamentations*, SBT I.14, 1954; H. **Gunkel**, 'Klagelieder Jeremiae', *RGG*[2], 3, 1049–52; H. **Jahnow**, *Das hebräische Leichenlied im Rahmen der Völkerdichtung*, BZAW 36, 1923; E. **Janssen**, *Juda in der Exilzeit*, FRLANT 69, 1956, 9–12.
W. F. **Lanahan**, 'The Speaking Voice in the Book of Lamentation', *JBL*

93, 1974, 41–49; M. **Löhr**, 'Der Sprachgebrauch des Buches der Klageliedes', *ZAW* 14, 1894, 31–50; 'Threni III und die jeremianische Autorschaft des Buches der Klagelieder', *ZAW* 24, 1904, 1–16; 'Alphabetische und alphabetisierende Lieder im Alten Testament', *ZAW* 25, 1905, 173–98; T. F. **McDaniel**, 'The Alleged Sumerian Influence upon Lamentations', *VT* 18, 1968, 198–209; 'Philological Studies in Lamentations, I-II', *Bibl* 49, 1968, 27–53, 199–220; P. A. **Munch**, 'Die alphabetische Akrostichie in der jüdischen Psalmendichtung', *ZDMG* 90, 1936, 703–10; M. **Noth**, 'Die Katastrophe von Jerusalem im Jahre 587 v. Chr und ihre Bedeutung für Israel', *GSAT*, Munich ²1960, 346–71; W. **Rudolph**, 'Der Text der Klagelieder', *ZAW* 56, 1938, 101–22; S. **Segert**, 'Zur literarischen Form und Funktion der fünf Megilloth', *ArOr* 33, 1965, 451–62; R. **Smend**, 'Über das Ich der Psalmen', *ZAW* 8, 1888, 49–147; H. **Wiesmann**, 'Der planmässige Aufbau der Klagelieder des Jeremias', *Bibl* 7, 1926, 146–61; 'Der Zweck der Klagelieder des Jeremias', *Bibl* 7, 1926, 412–28; 'Der geschichtliche Hintergrund des Büchleins der Klagelieder', *BZ* 23, 1935/6, 20–43; 'Der Verfasser der Klagelieder ein Augenzeuge?', *Bibl* 17, 1936, 71–84.

1. Historical Critical Problems

The clarity of the structure of the book of Lamentations has led to an initial unanimity of scholarly opinion which is rare for Old Testament studies. The book consists of four acrostic poems which are coterminous with the chapter divisions, and a fifth poem which is non-acrostic, but shows the influence of the form in its length of 22 lines. The Hebrew text also exhibits fewer problems than most poetic sections.

The form-critical discussions regarding the literary genre have produced areas of disagreement as one would expect, but even here the differences between the alternative theories are less than with most biblical books. The content of the book is dominated by the theme of complaint. Within this broad rubric further distinctions can be made. Gunkel, building on the work of his student Jahnow, described chs. 1, 2 and 4 as political dirges, ch. 5 as a communal complaint psalm, and ch. 3 as a mixed form of an individual complaint. However, Gunkel was quick to add that these forms have all undergone modification and are far removed from a pristine form. The tendency of many contemporary scholars is to go much further than Gunkel in seeing the dissolution of oral forms and argue that the present chapters represent free composition with only vestiges from the older, stereotyped patterns. The exegetical significance of the handling of the prehistory of these poems can best be studied by comparing the analysis of ch. 3 by Plöger and Hillers. Both commentators reckon with the element of free composition, but Plöger takes far more seriously the influence of older patterns on the present form of the biblical poems.

The one recent form-critical attempt to move in a strikingly different direction was made by H. -J. Kraus. Taking his lead from cuneiform parallels offered by A. Falkenstein and W. von Soden, Kraus argued for the presence of a particular genre which he entitled 'Lament over the Ruined Sanctuary'. Moreover, Kraus saw in this genre the reflection of an actual cultic ceremony rather than simply a literary imitation. By and large, Kraus' theory has not been well received and appears to many to raise more problems than it solves (cf. McDaniel).

The most controversial chapter in the book is clearly ch. 3. The initial problem turns on how to interpret the figure who is introduced in the first person. The issue is made more complex by the shift to the plural form in vv. 40ff., and a return to the first person again in vv. 48ff. Moreover, the mixture of different genres within the song has greatly increased the puzzlement (cf. Plöger). Elements of individual complaint (vv. 1ff.), wisdom instruction (25f.), credal formulations (22f.), and thanksgiving psalms (52ff.) are all present. During the early part of this century there was considerable discussion as to whether the first person figure in ch. 3 was to be interpreted in a collective sense as Zion (Smend, Beer) or as an individual (Budde, Löhr). Increasingly the form-critical weight fell on the side of the latter interpretation.

However, another exegetical option has continued to find support. As is well known, there is a strong tradition found in the LXX, Vulgate, and Targums that Jeremiah was also the author of the book of Lamentations. Beginning in the eighteenth century the identification was attacked as historically inauthentic (Hardt, 1712). It was generally assumed that the reference in II Chron. 35.23 to Jeremiah's laments over Josiah, which were written in a book, was mistakenly connected to the book of Lamentations. Indeed, most modern critical commentators spend only a few paragraphs showing the inappropriateness of several passages in Lamentations to Jeremiah's message. However, because of the many parallels between the two books (cf. S. R. Driver), conservative scholars such as Keil and Wiesmann continued to support it. In a somewhat different form, Rudolph has argued that the author sought to use the figure of Jeremiah as a paradigm of suffering and forgiveness. By and large, the majority opinion favours seeing the figure in ch. 3 as a representative figure without a connection with Jeremiah.

The discussion of the metre of the Hebrew poetry of the book has been carefully rehearsed recently by Hillers and need not be repeated. In sum, Budde's initial discovery of the *qinah* verse has been considerably modified over the years, especially by Sievers, and the fact of mixed metre within Lamentations has been generally accepted.

There is also a general consensus on the historical background of the book. The period immediately following the destruction of Jerusalem in 586 is reflected. There have been attempts to make the dating of the chapters more precise. Rudolph in particular has sought to assign ch. 1 to the period of the first capture of the city in 597 and chs. 3 and 5 to a period somewhat later than chs. 2 and 4, but the evidence for the theory is inconclusive.

Within recent years two scholars particularly have sought to analyse the major theological thought of the book within its historical context. N. Gottwald described the key to understanding the book's theology to lie in the tension between the Deuteronomic faith in a doctrine of retribution and reward, and the historical reality of adversity. However, most scholars doubt whether this is the tension of the book, particularly since the writer acknowledges that the judgment of the city was deserved. B. Albrektson saw the tension to lie between specific religious concepts, such as the inviolability of Jerusalem, and the historical realities of Jerusalem's destruction. Although Albrektson has made a good case for the presence of the Zion tradition, the issue is not resolved to what extent such an alleged tension actually lay at the centre of the book's concern. The case for a different interpretation of the theology of Lamentations will be made below.

2. The Canonical Shape of Lamentations

There is no literary evidence to indicate that the book of Lamentations was edited in a way which differed extensively from its original form. Indications of how the book was understood must, there-fore, lie in the form and function of its various parts in relation to the whole.

The relation between the various chapters does not appear to establish any progression of thought. Indeed, it is striking how many of the same themes appear in all five chapters. All deal with the misery of the siege and the sorrow of the survivors. Yet beyond the broad similarity of subject matter, detailed parallels are found in the themes of the desecration of the temple (1.10; 2.6, 7, 20; 5.18), Zion's sin (1.8, 20; 3.39, 42; 4.6; 5.16), the horrors of famine (2.11, 12, 19; 4.4, 9, 10), and the hope for retribution against the enemy (1.22; 3.64, 66; 4.21). The effect of the repetition of these common themes is to focus on the national sorrow from every poss-ible angle. The influence from the literary genre of the dirge is felt especially in chs. 1, 2 and 4 in creating an atmosphere of death, finality, and resignation which is picked up in a slightly different form by the communal lament in ch. 5.

Chapter 3 stands apart from the other chapters, both in form and content, but it plays a crucial role in interpreting the whole book. The chapter begins with the lament of an individual which reflects the stereotyped features of this genre similar to that of the Psalter (Pss. 6, 88, etc.). The psalmist describes his trouble (vv. 1–18) and appeals to God for relief (19–21). In vv. 22–24 the psalmist confes-ses his faith in God's mercy in a formulation which makes free association with Israel's traditional 'creeds' (Ex. 34. 6f.; Num. 14.18; Ps. 86. 15). There follows in vv. 25–30 another confessional statement more akin to the wisdom saying of Ps. 37. Again the theme of God's mercy is picked up in the form of instruction not uncommon to the lament and concludes with a series of rhetorical questions (vv. 37–39).

The influence from Israel's liturgical service is everywhere strong; the older forms, however, have been blurred together in a free composition. What is of particular significance is the change of perspective which ch. 3 now brings to bear on the book. A shift has been effected from the communal focus to an individual, and from the events of 587 to an individual's personal history. This is not to suggest that the writer has moved from historical concerns into a timeless area – the historical quality of the lament is dominant – but rather that he has incorporated history within liturgical lan-guage. The suffering of one representative man is described in the language of worship which transcends any one fixed moment in history. The effect is that historical suffering is now understood metaphorically as in the Psalter, but its actuality is in no way diminished.

In vv. 40–47 the writer shifts to the plural form and, identifying with the nations, he appeals for a return to God with confession of sin (v. 40). What then follow are elements from communal complaint psalms (vv. 43–47). The confessing community raises its lament to God in the traditional terminology of the liturgy. In vv. 48ff. the song again shifts to the first person, but there are now some striking differences in the figure of this suffering individual from that of the initial verses in the chapter. The form of the traditional thanksgiving psalm dominates. The psalmist recounts his plight (52ff.) and the wonderful rescue by the hand of God (55ff.). God is now seen as his ally (v. 58), supporting him against the enemy (61ff.) whereas earlier he had been the source of his affliction (v. 1).

The effect of the second half of the song is again to incorporate the history of the nation in its moment of greatest humiliation and despair within a liturgical context. The community is summoned to return to faith in God, but at the same time to lift up its devastation and destruction in corporate prayer. The dirge has been replaced by Israel's true form of supplication. The psalm concludes with a confession of thanksgiving. It is not put in the mouth of the community, but of an individual. Again a representative figure can confess that God has answered his plight and spoken a word of comfort.

To summarize, the function of ch. 3 is to translate Israel's historically conditioned plight into the language of faith and by the use of traditional forms to appeal to the whole nation to experience that dimension of faith testified to by a representative figure. The promises of God to Israel have not come to an end, but there are still grounds for hope (3.22ff.).

Chapter 5 concludes the book with a communal complaint psalm. The community is still in dire straits and all the horrors of her condition are recounted with the same vividness as before. At the same time Israel confesses to the kingship of God whose 'throne endures to all generations', and continues to implore divine rescue. The canonical shaping of the material has not supplied a 'happy ending', but it has moved the problem into its proper confessional context from which the community of faith must continue to struggle with its own history before God, as it always has in the past.

3. Theological and Hermeneutical Implications

(a) The effect of the canonical process on the book of Lamentations
was not one of dehistoricizing the fully time-conditioned response of
the survivors of the destruction of Jerusalem. Rather, the response
was brought into relationship with a dimension of faith which provided a religious context from which to seek meaning in suffering.
One of the results of incorporating the events of the city's destruction into Israel's traditional terminology of worship was to establish
a semantic bridge between the historical situation of the early sixth
century and the language of faith which struggles with divine
judgment. For this reason the book of Lamentations serves every
successive generation of the suffering faithful for whom history has
become unbearable.

(b) The various scholarly attempts to find the key to the theological problem of the book in a tension between different theological
positions found in the Old Testament has proved to be inadequate
mainly on literary historical grounds. By failure to take seriously
the canonical shape of the book, the actual historical response to the
destruction by those who treasured Lamentations as scripture has
been overlooked. The major theological issue at stake in the canonical book is the conflict between those who thought that the destruction of Jerusalem had rendered the truth of Israel's traditional
faith in God's promise meaningless, and those who confessed that
in spite of the enormous rupture caused by Israel's sin, the avenue
of God's renewed mercy, even if withdrawn momentarily, was still
open to the faithful as it had been in the past.

(c) The debate over the role of Jeremiah in ch. 3 has been pursued as a literary and historical problem, but seldom have its hermeneutical implications been raised. We have argued elsewhere
that the canonical function of the superscriptions of certain psalms
served to historicize traditional prayers and thus actualize the
psalms for subsequent generations. In the case of Lamentations the
hermeneutical issue at stake is very different from that of the Psalter. The introduction of the traditional language in ch. 3 functions
to typify the historical particularities of the community and thus to
give them meaning by means of liturgical categories. If, however,

the figure of ch. 3 is interpreted as Jeremiah, the exegetical move to typify Israel's experience is greatly confused. Thus the book's canonical shape adds another reason against an identification. The broader hermeneutical implication to be drawn is the need for caution in generalizing about the canonical process, lest the full variety by which the biblical tradition was rendered into scripture be jeopardized.

History of Exegesis

Carpzov III, 193–7; *DThC* 8, 2531–37; *EB* 1, 262; *RGG*[3] 3, 1629.

H. I. **Caro**, *Beiträge zur ältesten Exegese des Buches Threni mit besonderer Berücksichtigung des Midrasch und Targum*, Berlin 1893; E. **Cothenet**, 'Lamentations (Livre des)', *DS* 9.1, 1976, 160–5; B. **Grossfeld**, *The Targums to the Five Megilloth*, New York 1973, 21–65; J. M. **Schonfelder**, *Die Klagelieder des Jeremias nach rabbinischer Auslegung*, Munich 1887; H. **Wiesmann**, 'Der Kommentar des hl. Thomas von Aquin zu den Klageliedern des Jeremias', *Scholastik* 4, Freiburg 1929, 78–91.

XL

ESTHER

Commentaries

C. F. Keil, BC, 1870
E. Bertheau, R. Ryssel, KeH, ²1887
P. Cassel, 1888
G. Wildeboer, KHC, 1898
K. Siegfried, HKAT, 1901
A. W. Streane, CB, 1907
L. B. Paton, ICC, 1908
C. Steuernagel, *HSAT*, ⁴1923
M. Haller, *SAT*, ²1925
M. Haller, HAT, 1940

J. Schildenberger, HS, 1941
L. Sourigon, SB, 1949
S. Goldman, SonB, ²1952
B. W. Anderson, *IB*, 1954
H. Ringgren, ATD, 1958
A. Barucq, JB, ²1959
H. Bardtke, KAT², 1963
E. Würthwein, HAT², 1969
C. A. Moore, AB, 1971
G. Gerleman, BK, 1973

Bibliography

B. W. **Anderson**, 'The Place of the Book of Esther in the Christian Bible', *JR* 30, 1950, 32–43; Hans **Bardtke**, 'Neuere Arbeiten um Estherbuch. Eine kritische Würdigung', *Ex Oriente Lux* 19, Leiden 1965–66, 519–49; A. **Bea**, 'De origine vocis *pûr*', *Bibl* 21, 1940, 198f.; E. J. **Bickerman**, 'The Colophon of the Greek Book of Esther', *JBL* 63, 1944, 339–62; 'Notes on the Greek Book of Esther', *PAAJR* 20, 1950, 101–23; *Four Strange Books of the Bible*, New York 1967; G. J. **Botterweck**, 'Die Gattung des Buches Esther in Spektrum neuerer Publikation', *BiLe* 5, 1964, 274–92; H. **Cazelles**, 'Note sur la composition du rouleau d'Esther', *Lex tua veritas*, FS H. *Junker*, ed. H. Gross and F. Mussner, Trier 1961, 17–29; V. **Christian**, 'Zur Herkunft des Purim-Festes', *FS F. Nötscher*, BBB 1, 1950, 33–37; J. L. **Crenshaw**, 'Method in Determining Wisdom Influence upon "Historical" Literature', *JBL* 88, 1969, 129–42; D. **Daube**, 'The Last Chapter of Esther', *JQR* 37, 1946–7, 139–47; W. **Dommershausen**, *Die Estherrolle. Stil und Ziel einer alttestamentlichen Schrift*, Stuttgart 1968; W. **Erbt**, *Die Purimsage in der Bibel*, Berlin 1900; T. H. **Gaster**, *Purim and Hanukkah in Custom and Tradition*, New York 1950; H. S. **Gehman**, 'Notes on the Persian Words in the Book of Esther', *JBL* 43, 1924, 321–8; G. **Gerleman**, *Studien zu Esther. Stoff-Struktur-Stil-Sinn*, BSt 48, 1966; R. **Gordis**, 'Studies in the Esther Narrative', *JBL* 95, 1976, 43–58; *Megillat Esther*, New York 1974; H. **Gunkel**, *Esther*, Tübingen 1916; 'Das Königschloss von Susa und das Buch Esther', *TLZ* 44, 1919, 2–4; P. **Haupt**, 'Critical Notes on Esther', *AJSL* 24, 1907–8, 97–186; W. L. **Humphreys**, 'A Life-Style for Diaspora: A Study of the Tales of Esther and Daniel', *JBL* 92, 1973, 211–23; 'Esther, Book of, *IDB Suppl*, 279–81.

B. **Jacob**, 'Das Buch Esther bei den LXX', *ZAW* 10, 1890, 241–98; G. **Jahn**, *Das Buch Esther nach der Septuaginta hergestellt, übersetzt, und kritisch erklärt*, Leiden 1901; P. **Jensen**, 'Elamitische Eigennamen', *Wiener Zeitschrift für die Kunde des Morgenlandes* 6, Vienna 1892, 47–70, 209–26; J. C. H. **Lebram**, 'Purimfest und Estherbuch', *VT* 22, 1972, 208–22; J. **Lewy**, 'The Feast of the 14th Day of Adar', *HUCA* 14, 1939, 127–51; 'Old Assyrian *puru'um* and *pūrum*', *Revue Hittite et Asianique* 5, Paris 1939, 117–24; C. A. **Moore**, 'A Greek Witness to a Different Hebrew Text of Esther', *ZAW* 79, 1967, 351–8; 'On the Origins of the LXX Additions to the Book of Esther', *JBL* 92, 1973, 383–93; *Daniel, Esther, and Jeremiah: The Additions*, AB, 1977; L. B. **Paton**, 'A Text-Critical Apparatus to the Book of Esther', *Old Testament and Semitic Studies in Memory of W. R. Harper* II, Chicago 1911, 1–52; H. **Ringgren**, 'Esther and Purim', *SEA* 20, 1956, 5–24; L. A. **Rosenthal**, 'Die Josephgeschichte, mit den Büchern Ester und Daniel verglichen', *ZAW* 15, 1895, 278–84; D. **Schötz**, 'Das hebräische Buch Esther', *BZ* 21, 1933, 255–76; A. **Striedl**, 'Untersuchung zur Syntax und Stilistik des hebräischen Buches Esther', *ZAW* 55, 1937, 73–108; S. **Talmon**, 'Wisdom in the Book of Esther', *VT* 13, 1963, 419–55; C. C. **Torrey**, 'The Older Book of Esther', *HTR* 37, 1944, 1–40; W. **Vischer**, *Esther*, TheolEx 48, 1937; H. **Winckler**, Esther', *Altorientalische Forschung* 3, Amsterdam 1902, 1–66; H. **Zimmern**, 'Zur Frage nach dem Ursprünge des Purimfestes', *ZAW* 11, 1891, 157–69.

1. Historical Critical Problems

There is general agreement that the major purpose of the book of Esther is to provide the historical grounds for the celebration of the feast of Purim. However, the questions of the nature of this festival and its possible historical antecedents have caused much discussion.

The festival is named Purim after the term *pûr* which in 3.7 is explained as meaning 'lot'. By casting the lot Haman determined the day suitable for the destruction of the Jews. However, the connection between this use of the term and the festival itself is never clearly made, which has led many to suppose that the word for the festival is older than its interpretation. At first, attempts were made to probe into the etymology of the word as a possible avenue into the festival's prehistory. Etymologies from Hebrew, Greek, Old Persian, and Babylonian were put forward, but within recent years a wide consensus has accepted J. Lewy's derivation of the Hebrew from the Akkadian *pūru* which indeed means 'lot' (cf. A. Bea, 198f.; V. Christian, 33ff.). Although this agreement has brought to a successful resolution one aspect of the problem, the determining of the etymology has not solved the major issue of the source of the festival.

The majority of scholars have regarded the festival as having originally been of pagan origin and only later appropriated and adapted by the Jews for their own purposes. At the height of the 'Pan-Babylonian' period, Zimmern, Jensen, and Winckler sought to derive the festival from a Babylonian festival – both the New Year's festival and the Sakaia festival were suggested – and they linked the major figures to a mythical background (Mordecai = Marduk; Esther = Ishtar). Later, Gunkel argued for a Persian festival as the prototype which was occasioned by the murder of the Magi according to the report of Herodotus (III, 68–79). Again, Lewy, building on the earlier suggestion of Lagarde, proposed a link with the Persian *Farvardīgān*, the feast of the dead. Numerous other variations on these theories which are associated with Gaster and Ringgren, need not be reviewed in detail. In sum, although the assumption of a non-Jewish origin of Purim has much to commend it, the evidence for its reconstruction has been insufficient. The same judgment must also be made respecting the minority opinion, such as Gerleman's which defends the indigenous roots of Purim.

The discussions of the literary and historical features of the book have been more fruitful. Again there is widespread agreement that the literary skill of the narrative is of high quality. Scholars such as Gunkel and Dommershausen have pointed out features which have greatly enhanced the story's effectiveness. Much attention has also been given to analysing earlier stages in the book's literary composition and in distinguishing different forms of the story. For example, Bickerman has proposed seeing the present book as a combination of two major stories with two heroes and two plots which were fused in the Hellenistic period. Bardtke suggests seeing three unrelated tales. Perhaps the most ambitious attempt of this kind has been undertaken by Lebram. Taking his lead from the reference to Purim in II Macc. 15.36 as the 'day of Mordecai', he argued for constructing two different forms of the story, the one celebrated by Palestinian Jews on the fourteenth of Adar, and the other by the eastern Diaspora, centred in Susa, on the fifteenth. Although the evidence is not fully convincing, the essay is fresh and stimulating.

A very different literary analysis has been proposed by Gerleman, who attributed the main impetus in forming the story to the re-use of the themes and motifs of the exodus tradition. In those places in which the stories diverge sharply, Gerleman has argued for an intentional polemic against the older tradition. Gerleman's analysis has not been generally accepted in spite of some interesting observations. Finally, a very different analysis of the literary features has been offered by S. Talmon. He stressed the stereotyped quality of the narrative with its close parallels to the Joseph narrative and proposed seeing the narrative as a historicized genre of wisdom literature. Talmon's interesting analysis suffers from the growing uncertainty which surrounds the whole debate over 'wisdom influences' on narrative material (cf. J. L. Crenshaw).

Any discussion of the literary features of the book of Esther must take into account the six major additions to the Hebrew text which are found in the Greek. In one sense, these additions belong to the later midrashic tendency, found in the two targums, of expanding the religious elements. However, Bickerman has made a good case for seeing the expansions as part of a Hellenistic culture which had developed new interest in the citing of documents and in the exposition of dreams (cf. C. A. Moore on *The Additions*).

In regard to the issue of the historicity of the book of Esther one can discern a growing consensus forming around a compromise position which shares neither the traditional position of the book's complete historicity (Keil), nor the theory of its whole fabrication (Semler). It is generally acknowledged that the writer shows a genuine historical knowledge of the Persian court, of the king's palace, and of several details of the administrative system of the country. (It is not yet clear whether the recently discovered personal name *mrdk* in an Aramaic letter of the fifth century can be directly identified with Mordecai as Gordis has recently proposed.) Conversely, certain features of the narrative conflict directly with generally accepted historical evidence, such as the age of Mordecai, the name of Ahasuerus' queen in the period of his reign, and the hereditary qualifications for a Persian queen. Other elements in the story have also been judged to be highly improbable, such as the grounds for Vashti's dismissal, the preparation of the concubines (2.12), and the slaying of 75,000 enemies (9.16).

There remains considerable disagreement regarding the dating of the book. Arguments for an early dating have been found in the style of the book which is certainly earlier than that of Qumran. There are also no Greek words according to Moore and Gordis. Conversely, other scholars have argued for a later date from the omission of Esther in Ben Sira, its apparent absence from the Qumran community, and the remoteness in which the events of Xerxes' reign are treated (Pfeiffer, *Introduction*; Striedl). Probably a date towards the end of the Persian period for the main part of the book would find the greatest support, but the possibility of some minor Hellenistic reworking would not be excluded.

Finally, an evaluation of the book's religious significance continues to play a significant role in the critical discussion. Several recent commentators find support in Luther's assessment for a very negative judgment. Eissfeldt (*Introduction*) and Paton object to the elements of nationalism, its secularity of tone, and an ethnic rather than religious understanding of Judaism. Conversely, most Jewish scholars defend the book as a heroic example of Jewish self-preservation against the evils of anti-Semitism (cf. Gordis). The most vigorous modern defence of the book's place within the Christian canon comes from W. Vischer. Although many have admired the bold timing of this essay (Munich 1937!), few have accepted his christological interpretation (cf. Gerleman's typical reaction). A more characteristic Christian formulation is offered by the carefully balanced essay of B. W. Anderson, who weighs the book's strengths and weaknesses on the scales provided by the Biblical Theology movement of the 50s. To the extent that Esther portrays a *Heilsgeschichte*, its message can be sustained; the remaining elements must be tested by the fuller Christian revelation. The reasons for my dissatisfaction with these positions will appear in the ensuing analysis.

2. The Canonical Shape of the Book of Esther

The function of 9.20–32

A major key to the canonical shaping of the book is to be found in ch. 9. 20–32. The reasons for most critical scholars' seeing this section as a secondary, redactional level have been briefly reviewed above. However, the canonical significance of this appendix has not been recognized, nor has its function for the book as a whole been properly evaluated.

The first nine chapters of the book recount the story of the rescue of the Jews from destruction by Mordecai and Esther which provided the grounds for the celebration of the festival of Purim. However, the section beginning at 9.20ff. provides the authoritative institutionalizing of the festival which was to be celebrated by every future generation of Jews. The directives are given in the form of two letters from the two major protagonists, Mordecai and Esther. Although festivities of celebration for the historical deliverance from Haman's plot were already under way (9.17ff., 23), the new directives from the letters set the standard for the festival of Purim, which in several significant places altered the form of the original celebration.

First of all, 9.20ff. establishes the cultic significance of Purim. It is a festival which is 'binding' – note the piel of *qûm* in vv. 21, 27, 29, 31, 32 – for every successive generation. The perpetuity of the festival and its comprehensiveness is stressed; 'their descendants', 'kept throughout every generation', 'in every family, province, and city', 'never fall into disuse', 'never cease among their descendants'.

Secondly, the proper time of the festival is set: 'enjoining them that they should keep the fourteenth day of the month of Adar and also the fifteenth day of the same, year by year' (9.21). Esther's second letter confirmed these 'appointed seasons' (v. 31). The original events of the celebration had also taken place on the fourteenth and fifteenth, but for different reasons. The Jews in the provinces had defended themselves on the thirteenth and celebrated on the fourteenth. But the Jews in the capital, Susa, were allowed an additional day for slaughtering their enemies (9.13) and, therefore, celebrated on the next day, the fifteenth. Mordecai's directive obliterates the original historical distinction of different local practices, and combines the two dates in a normative season for all Jews to celebrate Purim.

Thirdly, the letters of Mordecai and Esther establish the exact manner in which the festival is to be correctly celebrated. The days are to be hailed by 'feasting and gladness' to commemorate the turning from sorrow into gladness. The festival celebrates the days of rest when the Jews got relief from their enemies (v. 22). It is, therefore, not to be understood as a victory celebration, but a rejoicing over the relief from persecution, a celebration of rest. This same tone of reconciliation is sounded in describing Esther's letter as 'words of peace and truth'. Again, there is an additional stipulation for the festival's correct observance. To send choice portions to one another was already part of the original observance (v. 19). To this is added the requirement that gifts were also to be sent to the poor (v. 22). Furthermore, Esther's letter specifies that the days of Purim at their appointed seasons be observed in relationship to 'their fasts and their lamentations' (v. 3.). Mourning on the days of the celebration of gladness is inconsonant with Purim and is forbidden, but the traditional fasting and lamentations serve to remind Israel of the background of Purim and provide the proper context for the season of joy.

Finally, the emphasis in both letters is upon fixing the order of Purim in writing (vv. 26, 27, 32). Verse 27 enjoins that the celebration should be kept 'according to what was written'. The antecedent is the letter of the king (v. 26) and not the whole book of Esther. Nevertheless, the point of the injunction is that the festival be regulated by the carefully recorded events of the oppression and deliverance. The authoritative letter of Esther which fixed the shape of the festival was also recorded in writing (v. 32). That later Jewish tradition understood the festival to be regulated by the reading of the whole book of Esther is a step not far removed from the intent of ch. 9.

What is the canonical effect on the book of Esther which this appendix in 9. 20–32 provides? The original story of the persecution and rescue of the Jews is retained as normative scripture along with its intrigue, brutality, nationalism, and secularity, but the story has been given a new theological interpretation within the worship of Israel. The celebration is set in the framework of fasting and mourning, the full religious meaning of which has been carefully defined throughout the rest of Israel's sacred tradition. The manner of the celebration in all its original 'secularity' is unchanged, but the object of the hilarity is redefined. All Israel shares in the joy of rest and relief which is dramatized by the giving of gifts, especially to the poor. It is a time to remember by hearing again the story of Purim. The effect of the reshaping of the festival is not to make a secular festival into a religious one, but to interpret the meaning of Purim in all its secularity in the context of Israel's existence, which is religious. The very language by which the festival is now regulated as the 'appointed seasons', 'gifts to the poor', 'rest from enemies', 'remembrance throughout every generation ... for ever', draws Purim within the orbit of Israel's religious traditions. The canonical shape does not attempt to eliminate offensive elements in the original story (e.g. 9.13), but it does carefully define what the effect of the story is to be on successive generations.

The typifying of the characters

There is a second aspect of the canonical shaping which is clearly subordinate to the previous one, but is significant for understanding the function of the book. Haman, the enemy of the Jews, is portrayed as the son of Hammedatha, the Agagite (3.1). He is thus linked to Agag, the king of the Amalekites (I Sam. 15.32), and to the long tradition of enmity with this tribe (Ex. 17.8ff.; Deut. 25.17ff.; I Sam. 15.17ff.). Conversely, Mordecai is described as a descendant of Kish, the father of Saul. The effect of the introduction of these genealogies is, of course, to typify the characters, a move which the later midrashim exploited to the fullest. One sees other minor features which have the same tendency. Haman is the enemy of the Jews *par excellence* whose vengeance seeks to incorporate all the people. The narrative makes the transition from a personal grudge to a Jewish pogrom by means of Haman's speech to the king in 3.8ff., which is a bit strained, but generally successful. Finally, some of the typifying tendency has been increased both by use of exodus motifs which Gerleman observed, and by wisdom themes which Talmon recognized. Yet in both instances the typifying move functions on a secondary and subordinate level of the narrative.

It is very important to see the limitations which the canonical shaping has put on the impetus to typify. There is no attempt made to extend the representative reading of the story in order to embrace the whole narrative, nor is the semantic level of the story systematically raised to a level different from that of the literal sense. Rather, only certain features are generalized and thus extended more readily into the future for subsequent generations to appropriate.

3. Theological and Hermeneutical Implications

(a) The canonical appropriation of the book of Esther opens up a theological understanding of the book very different from that usually suggested by commentators. First of all, the canonical approach does not attempt to moralize the story, either by defending the morals or its characters as 'heroic', or disparaging them as 'sub-Christian'. Again, the canonical approach does not allow the book to be polarized into 'secular' and 'religious' elements, but incorporates both within a profound interpretation of the nation's total life which has both a past and a future. Thirdly, there is a critical dimension in the canonical process which has lifted up certain elements as normative and continuing, but has subordinated others by tying them forever in past history as unrepeatable. Haman's ten sons are not hung on each Purim, but gifts are given to the poor to share the joy of Israel's deliverance.

(b) W. Vischer saw the theological significance of Esther to lie in the manner in which it posed the 'Jewish question'. E. Bickerman denied that there ever was such an issue in the book. Perhaps the basic theological issue at stake in this disagreement has been more clearly formulated by R. Gordis: 'It is fundamental to the Jewish world-outlook that the preservation of the Jewish people is itself a religious obligation of the first magnitude' (*Megillat*, 13). In my judgment, Gordis' assertion holds true for Christian theology if kept within the critical guidelines which have been fixed by the canonical context of Esther.

On the one hand, the book of Esther provides the strongest canonical warrant in the whole Old Testament for the religious significance of the Jewish people in an ethnic sense. The inclusion of Esther within the Christian canon serves as a check against all attempts to spiritualize the concept of Israel – usually by misinterpreting Paul – and thus removing the ultimate scandal of biblical particularity. On the other hand, the canonical shape of Esther has built into the fabric of the book a theological criticism of all forms of Jewish nationalism which occurs whenever 'Jewishness' is divorced from the sacred traditions which constitute the grounds of Israel's existence under God.

History of Exegesis

Carpzov I, 364–6; *DThC* 5, 870f.; *EB* 1, 492; *RGG*³ 2, 707f.

M. **Baumgarten**, 'Esther', *Real-Encyclopädie*, ed. J. J. Herzog, vol. 4, 1855, 177–85; H. **Bardtke**, 'Zur Auslegungsgeschichte des Buches Esther', *Das Buch Esther*, KAT², 1963, 255–65; *Luther und das Buch Esther*, Tübingen 1964; T. H. **Gaster**, *Purim and Hanukkah in Custom and Tradition*, New York 1950; B. **Grossfeld**, *The Targums to the Five Megilloth*, New York 1973, 87–170; B. **Jacob**, 'Das Buch Esther bei den LXX', *ZAW* 10, 1890, 241–98; L. B. **Paton**, *Esther*, ICC, 1908, 97ff.; F. W. **Schultz**, 'Introduction', *The Book of Esther*, ET, LCHS, 1876, 1–28.

XLI

DANIEL

Commentaries

L. Bertholdt, 1806–1808
H. A. C. Hävernick, 1832
C. von Lengerke, 1835
F. Hitzig, KeH, 1850
O. Zöckler, ET, LCHS, 1871
C. F. Keil, BC, 1872
J. Meinhold, *SZ*, 1889
A. A. Bevan, 1892
F. W. Farrar, ExB, 1895
S. R. Driver, CB, 1900
K. Marti, KHC, 1901
J. Knabenbauer, CSS, ²1907
J. Goettsberger, HS, 1928
R. H. Charles, 1929
L. Dennefeld, SB, 1946

J. A. Montgomery, ICC, ²1949
E. J. Young, 1949
J. J. Slotki, SonB, 1951
A. Bentzen, HAT, ²1952
E. W. Heaton, TB, 1956
J. Barr, Peake rev., 1962
O. Plöger, KAT², 1965
N. W. Porteous, OTL, 1965, (²1979)
M. Delcor, SoBi, 1971
A. Lacocque, CAT, 1976
L. F. Hartman, A. A. Di Lella, AB, 1978
J. G. Baldwin, TOTC, 1978

Bibliography

P. R. **Ackroyd**, *Exile and Restoration*, OTL, 1968, 242f.; C. A. **Auberlen**, *The Prophecies of Daniel and the Revelation of St John*, ET Edinburgh 1856; James **Barr**, 'Jewish Apocalyptic in Recent Scholarly Study', *BJRL* 58, 1975, 9–35; G. A. **Barton**, 'The Composition of the Book of Daniel', *JBL* 17, 1898, 62–86; W. **Baumgartner**, *Das Buch Daniel*, Giessen 1926; 'Das Aramäische im Buche Daniel', *ZAW* 45, 1927, 81–133; 'Ein Vierteljahrhundert Danielforschung', *ThR* NS 11, 1939, 59–83, 125–44, 201–28; M. A. **Beek**, *Das Daniel-Buch. Sein historischer Hintergrund und seine literarische Entwicklung*, Leiden 1935; 'Zeit, Zeiten und eine halbe Zeit', *Studia Biblica et Semitica T.C. Vriezen dedicata*, Wageningen 1966, 19–24; A. **Bertholet**, *Daniel und die griechische Gefahr*, Tübingen 1907; E. **Bickerman**, *Four Strange Books of the Bible*, New York 1967; C. **Boutflower**, *In and Around the Book of*

Daniel, London and New York 1923; C. H. W. **Brekelmans**, 'The Saints of the Most High and Their Kingdom (Dan. 7, 26.27)', *OTS* 14, 1965, 305–29; F. F. **Bruce**, 'Josephus and Daniel', *ASTI* 4, 1965, 148–62; 'The Book of Daniel and the Qumran Community', *Neotestamentica et Semitica*; *FS M. Black*, ed. E. E. Ellis and M. Wilcox, Edinburgh 1969, 221–35; 'The Earliest Old Testament Interpretation', *OTS* 17, 1972, 37–52; H. **Burgmann**, 'Die vier Endzeittermine in Danielbuch', *ZAW* 86, 1974, 542ff.; J. J. **Collins**, 'The Court-Tales in Daniel and the Development of Apocalyptic', *JBL* 94, 1975, 218–34; *The Apocalyptic Vision of the Book of Daniel*, Missoula 1977; J. **Coppens**, 'Le fils d'homme daniélique et les relectures de Dan 7, 13', *ETL* 37, 1961, 5–51; 'Le chapitre VII de Daniel', *ETL* 39, 1963, 87–113.

M. **Delcor**, 'Les sources du chapitre VII de Daniel', *VT* 18, 1968, 290–312; L. **Dequeker**, 'Daniel VII et les saints de Très-Haut', *ETL* 36, 1960, 353–92; F. **Dexinger**, *Das Buch Daniel und seine Probleme*, Stuttgart 1969; W. **Dommershausen**, *Nabonid im Buche Daniel*, Mainz 1964; A.-M. **Dubarle**, 'Daniel', *DBS* 8, 736–58; O. **Eissfeldt**, 'Die Menetekel-Inschrift und ihre Deutung', *ZAW* 63, 1951, 105–14=*KS* III, 1966, 210ff.; A. **Feuillet**, 'Le fils de l'homme de Daniel et la tradition biblique', *RB* 60, 1953, 170–202, 321–46; A. **Finkel**, 'The Pesher of Dreams and Scriptures', *RQ* 4, 1963/4, 357–70; D. **Flusser**, 'The Four Empires in the 4 Sibyl and the Book of Daniel', *Israel Oriental Studies* 2, Tel Aviv 1972, 148–75; D. N. **Freedman**, 'The Prayer of Nabonidus', *BASOR* 145, 1957, 31f.; 'The Flowering of Apocalyptic', *Journal of Theology and the Church* 6, New York 1969, 166–74; A. **von Gall**, *Die Einheitlichkeit des Buches Daniel*, Giessen 1895; K. **Galling**, 'Die 62 Jahre des Meders Darius in Dan 6, 1', *ZAW* 66, 1954, 152; J. G. **Gammie**, 'The Classification, Stages of Growth, and Changing Intentions in the Book of Daniel', *JBL* 95, 1976, 191–204; M. **Gertner**, 'Terms of Scriptural Interpretation: A Study in Hebrew Semantics', *Bulletin of the School of Oriental and African Studies* 25, London 1962, 1–27; H. L. **Ginsberg**, *Studies on the Book of Daniel*, New York 1948; 'The Oldest Interpretation of the Suffering Servant', *VT* 3, 1953, 400–4; 'The Composition of the Book of Daniel', *VT* 4, 1954, 246–75; P. **Grelot**, 'Les versions grecques de Daniel', *Bibl* 47, 1966, 381–402; E. **Gross**, 'Weltreich und Gottesvolk', *EvTh* 16, 1956, 241–51; H. **Gunkel**, *Schöpfung und Chaos in Urzeit und Endzeit*, Göttingen 1895; R. A. **Hall**, *Post-Exilic Theological Streams and the Book of Daniel* Diss. Yale University 1974; R. **Hanhart**, 'Die Heiligen des Höchsten', *SVT* 16, 1967, 90–101; 'Kriterien geschichtlicher Wahrheit in der Makkabäerzeit. Zur geschichtlichen Bedeutung der danielischen Weltzeitlehre', *TheolEx* 140, 1967, 7–22; P. D. **Hanson**, 'Jewish Apocalyptic Against its Near Eastern Environment', *RB* 78, 1971, 31–58; *The Dawn of Apocalyptic*, Philadelphia 1975; J. F. **Hasel**, 'The Identity of the "Saints of the Most High" in Daniel 7', *Bibl* 56, 1975, 173–92; 'The First and Third Year of Belshazzar (Dan 7:1; 8:1)', *Andrews University Seminary Studies* 15, 1977, 153–68; M. **Hengel**, *Judaism and Hel-*

lenism. Studies in their Encounter in Palestine during the Early Hellenistic Period, ET London and Philadelphia 1974; E. W. **Hengstenberg**, *Dissertations on the Genuineness of Daniel*, ET Edinburgh and New York 1848; G. **Hölscher**, 'Die Entstehung des Buches Daniel', *ThStKr* 92, 1919, 113–38; A. **Jepsen**, 'Bemerkungen zum Danielbuch', *VT* 11, 1961, 386–91; B. W. **Jones**, 'The Prayer in Daniel IX', *VT* 18, 1968, 488–93; C. **Julius**, *Die griechischen Danielzusätze und ihre kanonische Geltung*, Freiburg 1901; H. **Junker**, *Untersuchungen über literarischen und exegetische Probleme des Buches Daniel*, Rome 1932; K. A. **Kitchen**, D. J. **Wiseman**, et al., *Notes on some Problems in the Book of Daniel*, London 1965; K. **Koch**, 'Spätisraelitisches Geschichtsdenken am Beispiel des Buches Daniel', *Historische Zeitschrift* 193, Munich 1961, 1–32; *The Rediscovery of Apocalyptic*, ET, SBT II. 22, 1972; E. G. **Kraeling**, 'The Handwriting on the Wall', *JBL* 63, 1944, 11–18; C. **Kuhl**, *Die drei Manner im Feuer (Daniel Kapitel 3 und seine Zusätze)*, BZAW 55, 1930.

M.-J. **Lagrange**, 'La prophétie des soixante-dix semaines de Daniel (Dan. IX, 24–27)', *RB* 39, 1930, 179–98; J. C. H. **Lebram**, 'Perspektiven der gegenwärtigen Danielforschung', *Journal of the Study of Judaism*, 5, Leiden, 1974, 1–33; 'König Antiochus im Buch Daniel', *VT* 25, 1975, 737–72; A. **Lenglet**, 'La structure littéraire de Daniel 2–7', *Bibl* 53, 1972, 169–90; A. **Mertens**, *Das Buch Daniel im Lichte der Texte vom Toten Meer*, Würzburg 1971; G. W. E. **Nickelsburg**, *Resurrection, Immortality and Eternal Life in Intertestamental Judaism*, Cambridge, Mass. 1972, 11–27; M. **Noth**, 'Zur Komposition des Buches Daniel', *ThStKr* 98/99, 1926, 143–63 = *GSAT* II, 1969, 11ff.; 'Noah, Daniel und Hiob in Ezekiel XIV', *VT* 1, 1951, 251–60; 'The Understanding of History in Old Testament Apocalyptic', ET, *The Laws in the Pentateuch*, Edinburgh 1966, Philadelphia 1967, 194; 'The Holy Ones of the Most High', *ibid.*, 215–28; E. **Osswald**, 'Zum Problem der vaticinia ex eventu', *ZAW* 75, 1963, 27–44; O. **Plöger**, 'Siebzig Jahre', *Aus der Spätzeit des Alten Testament*, Göttingen 1970, 67–73; E. B. **Pusey**, *Daniel the Prophet*, Oxford 1865; G. **von Rad**, *Old Testament Theology* II, ET Edinburgh and New York 1965, 301–15; H. H. **Rowley**, 'The Bilingual Problem of Daniel', *ZAW* 50, 1932, 256–68; 'The Unity of the Book of Daniel', reprinted *The Servant of the Lord and Other Essays*, Oxford ²1965, 247–80; 'The Composition of the Book of Daniel', *VT* 5, 1955, 272–6; *Darius the Mede and the Four World Empires in the Book of Daniel*, Cardiff ²1959; 'The Meaning of Daniel for Today', *Interp* 15, 1961, 387–97; D. S. **Russell**, *The Method and Message of Jewish Apocalyptic*, OTL, 1964; H. **Schmid**, 'Daniel der Menschensohn', *Jud* 27, 1971, 192–220; J. M. **Schmidt**, *Die jüdische Apokalyptik*, Neukirchen-Vluyn 1967; J. **Schreiner**, *Alttestamentliche-jüdische Apokalyptik*, Munich 1969; M. **Smith**, *Palestinian Parties and Politics that Shaped the Old Testament*, New York and London 1971; O. H. **Steck**, 'Das Problem theologischer Strömmungen in nachexilischer Zeit', *EvTh* 28, 1961, 445–54; J. W. **Swain**, 'The Theory of the Four Monarchies: Opposition History under the Roman Empire', *Classical*

DANIEL 611

Philology 35, Chicago 1940, 1–21; A. **Szörényi**, 'Das Buch Daniel, eine kanonisierter Pescher?', *SVT* 15, 1966, 278–94; W. S. **Towner**, 'The Poetic Passages of Daniel 1–6,' *CBQ* 31, 1969, 317–26; B. **Vawter**, 'Apocalyptic. Its Relation to Prophecy', *CBQ* 22, 1960, 33–46; A. C. **Welch**, *Visions of the End*, London and Boston 1922; J. C. **Whitcomb**, *Darius the Mede: A Study in Historical Identification*, Grand Rapids, Mich. 1959; R. D. **Wilson**, *Studies in the Book of Daniel*, 2 vols., New York 1917, 1938; Z. **Zevit**, 'The Structure and Individual Elements of Daniel 7', *ZAW* 80, 1968, 385–96.

1. Historical Critical Problems

The critical study of the book of Daniel has gone through various stages during the last two hundred years which has resulted in a radically different approach to the book from that held by Jewish and Christian tradition up to the nineteenth century. The force of this new critical approach caused the older controversy over the Greek additions to the book to pale into virtual insignificance.

The first period, which was decisive, focused on the problems of authorship, dating, and character of the book. Beginning in the eighteenth century, in the writings of the English deist, Anthony Collins, and in Corrodi and Michaelis, the ancient arguments of Porphyry were revived and put forward with new and impressive evidence. Shortly thereafter, in the massive German commentaries of Bertholdt and von Lengerke the detailed case against the traditional sixth-century dating of the book appeared. These scholars argued on the basis of language, history, theology, and logic that the book was a pseudepigraphical tractate written in the Maccabean age to encourage the Jews in their resistance against the persecution of Antiochus IV Epiphanes. The prophecies of Daniel were *vaticinia ex eventu*, prophecies-after-the-event, and were used as a device by which to ensure authority for an apocalyptic message.

Of course, this challenge to the traditional interpretation did not go unheeded from the side of the conservatives. For a time in the nineteenth century the book of Daniel was considered by many to be the major battle line of church's defence against which the assault of modern criticism was being hurled. In Germany in the middle of the nineteenth century scholars of considerable learning such as Hengstenberg, Hävernick, and Keil rose to the defence of the traditional view. In England the major champion of the older orthodox position was Pusey, whose lectures on Daniel contained both impressive erudition and savage apologetic. Pusey was willing to rest the validity of the whole Christian faith upon the sixth-century dating of Daniel, and he rejoiced that this issue established a clear battle line between faith and unbelief: 'It admits of no half-measures. It is either Divine or an imposture . . . The writer, were he not Daniel, must have lied on a most frightful scale . . . '(75). In America the last great defender of Daniel's traditional authorship was R. D. Wilson of Princeton, who continued the Pusey tradition of combining great learning with heated polemics.

This brief review of the first stage in the history of scholarship is not to suggest that there are no defenders of the traditional position – one has only to recall the names of E. J. Young or K. A. Kitchen – but it does imply that the authorship of Daniel ceased to be considered a major battle front by most Christians, and by Jews as well. By the end of the nineteenth century an amazing consensus had formed which accepted unequivocally the Maccabean dating of the book. In England F. W. Farrar, the well-known Archdeacon of Westminster (soon to be Dean of Canterbury), effectively popularized the German critical position to his Victorian audience in his contribution to the *Expositor's Bible* (1895). Above all, it was S. R. Driver's commentary of 1900 which broke the back of the conservative opposition. In his lucid style and meticulous scholarship Driver mounted the case for Maccabean authorship in a way which appeared to most Englishmen not only to have successfully salvaged the book's religious value, but to have established definitively the critical position. Among Roman Catholics the shift away from the traditional position to various critical alternatives has been carefully documented by A.-M. Dubarle.

The periods which followed in the history of biblical scholarship have built upon the critical foundations laid in the nineteenth century (cf. Eissfeldt, *Introduction*, for a careful review). A second phase perhaps begun by Hölscher's important essay in 1919, focused on such problems as the language, the inner structure, and the literary integrity of the book. This period included such representative studies as those of Baumgartner and Noth, and the vigorous controversy between Rowley and Ginsberg in the 50s. Although no clear-cut consensus emerged, a new appreciation of the complexity of the book's literary history resulted. Strong arguments were mounted from the side of form-criticism and traditio-criticism for seeing a long development lying behind the narrative, at least within the first seven chapters. However, the final redactional stamp on the entire book was almost universally regarded as Hellenistic.

Only recently a third phase of research has begun associated with the names of Plöger, Steck, Koch, M. Smith, Hanson and others. Certainly some of the impetus for the new questions derived from von Rad's controversial theory of wisdom as the source of apocalyptic literature. However, these scholars have sought to move beyond the literary and form-critical questions and to explore the place of Daniel within the larger sociological milieu of developing apocalpytic traditions. The emphasis has fallen on sketching the profiles of the diverse and conflicting ideologies of post-exilic Judaism, and in determining the relation between religious beliefs and the political struggles of the period.

Although I do not contest for a moment the genuine insights which have emerged from this history of critical research – the destruction of the rationalism implicit in the older orthodox position was a major contribution – it remains a perplexing phenomenon that the theological insights into the book of Daniel have not increased proportionately. One could almost wonder whether there is a reverse ratio. Driver, at least, thought that the book was a 'noble testimony of faith', even if erroneous in judgment. More recently, the book has been judged to reflect a 'loss of nerve', or to be a breakdown in the 'creative tension' of genuine prophecy which held together cosmic and mundane reality. Could it be that an important dimension of the book has been overlooked?

2. The Canonical Shape of the Book of Daniel

In an attempt to reassess the book from a canonical perspective, a somewhat different set of questions will be pursued from those which have occupied the centre of attention up to now. I am interested in exploring how the book of Daniel was heard by Jews in the post-Maccabean period. How was it possible that a writing which apparently predicted the end of the world with the death of Antiochus IV Epiphanes could have been canonized in a period after the Greek danger had passed? Again, how was it possible that the New Testament, some two hundred and fifty years later, could interpret the visions of Daniel as foretelling events which still lay in the future?

The study of the canonical shape of Daniel will focus on two sets of issues. First, how did the book of Daniel originally function in its Maccabean context, and secondly, how was this original function altered by its new canonical role? In this treatment the problem of the prehistory of the tradition before the Maccabean period is being consciously left aside because this complex set of issues has been amply handled in other Introductions (cf. especially Eissfeldt).

The form and function of the book in the Maccabean age

The peculiar features of the book of Daniel which set it apart from the prophetic books of the Old Testament, such as Isaiah and Ezekiel, have long been noticed. In terms of its structure the book falls into two clearly distinct parts. The first six chapters present stories about Daniel and his friends in a style in which the third person narrative dominates. In the last six chapters the visions of Daniel are offered, chiefly in a first person style. Yet these two parts of the book are clearly related to each other. The stories about Daniel in the first part of the book describe him as one granted 'understanding in all visions and dreams' (1.17), which are then recounted in the second part of the book. Again, the challenge of the visions of the last chapters which call for endurance to hardship as faithful servants of God is illustrated, above all, in the example of Daniel and his companions.

Of even greater significance is the perspective of the book. Never once does Daniel address his hearers in the traditional idiom of the prophet: 'hear the Word of Yahweh'. Rather, he interprets dreams and has visions. Often he is told that the visions 'pertain to many days hence' (8.26). They are to be sealed for a time which has been fixed in the distant future. Moreover, Daniel is pictured often as not understanding, and of being confused or unconscious (8.27). The contrast with the direct historical confrontation of an Amos or Isaiah is striking.

Daniel's relation to the nations is also unusual. C. A. Auberlen characterized it succinctly: 'The subject of revelation is no longer Israel in its relation to the powers of the world, but the powers of the world in their relation to Israel' (21). The prophets usually had a message for the nations which surrounded Israel – Amos, Isaiah,

Jeremiah – but Daniel did not view the nations from the perspective of within Israel. He was himself an exile, dwelling in a foreign land which was far removed from Jerusalem. He dealt with the powers of the world in their own history as they related to one another and Israel entered the picture only at the periphery with the coming of the kingship of God. The reason for this peculiar concentration on the history of the nations is made clear from within the book of Daniel itself. The book describes the period of Israel's 'indignation' (8.19) which marked the destruction of the nation, and her sojourn in exile among the nations of the world. Therefore, the book begins with the destruction of Judah under Nebuchadnezzar. It ends with the entrance of the kingdom of God when the last of the nations is cut off and Israel's period of shame brought to a close (8.19, 25). Between the beginning and the end of Israel's time of trial lay the history of the world powers envisioned by Daniel as a sequence which accelerated towards the end.

How are we to suppose that the book of Daniel functioned in its original historical setting? As previously suggested, historical critical scholars have made out a convincing case for believing that the visions of chs. 7–12 were written about the year 165 BC, shortly before the death of Antiochus (163) at the moment of intense persecution. (To what extent the material had a history prior to its second-century composition is not a present concern.) The Maccabean author described the last great convulsion of the nations before the end of the age in the form of Daniel's visions. Moreover, he focused on the final indignation of the fourth kingdom and described its development leading up to its destruction by tracing the detailed history of the Persian and Greek eras step by step. There seems little doubt that the writer in ch. 11 understood Antiochus IV Epiphanes to be the last 'contemptible person' who would desecrate the temple, take away the burnt offerings, and commit the final blasphemy before the moment in which God cut him down in order to usher in the end (11.36). The visions called the community of faith to obedience and challenged it to hold on because the end of time which Daniel foresaw would shortly come. Because it was written in the form of a *vaticinium ex eventu*, the effect of this message would have been electrifying. Daniel had prophesied about the rise and fall of the earlier three kingdoms and these events had occurred. Now his vision of the last days was being fulfilled before their very eyes. The 'little horn' had appeared; the

persecution had reached its height; the end was imminent. Therefore 'blessed is he who waits'. The visions of chs. 7–12 were probably accompanied by the stories of Daniel and his friends to illustrate obedience under a similar persecution for the sake of one's
faith.

Yet how was it possible that a later Maccabean author could
have cloaked his own words in the mantle of the sixth-century
writer of the exile? Does not this device call into question the validity of the message which depends at best on a literary technique,
and at worst on a ruse? In spite of the efforts of several generations
of critical biblical scholars to dispel this objection, the issue continues to trouble the average lay reader of the Bible who has not
been initiated into the critical approach.

In my judgment, the solution to this problem lies within the book
itself. There are many signs to indicate that the author of chs. 7–12
understood his role as one of filling in the details of the early visions
of Daniel through the study of scripture and thus confirming
Daniel's prophecies in the light of the events of contemporary history. The later author was neither creating new prophecies on his
own, nor consciously employing a clever literary ploy. Rather, he
was confirming and elucidating the visions of Daniel in ch. 2 for the
benefit of his Maccabean audience on the basis of further revelation
of scripture.

The evidence for this interpretation is apparent both from the
structure and content of the book. The vision in ch. 7 which bears a
clear Hellenistic stamp is an elaboration and confirmation of
Daniel's vision in ch. 2 The Maccabean author had received the
ancient prophecy of Daniel which spoke of the rise and fall of the
four world empires before the end. The author of ch. 7 attests to the
truth of this vision. Indeed, 'the dream is certain and its interpretation is sure' (2.45). Three kingdoms will arise and the fourth will be
far worse. He quickly passes over the first three which were then
past history and concentrates on that which still lay ahead. Chapter
2 had spoken vaguely of the toes of the great image – surely there
were ten – consisting partly of iron, partly of clay. Chapter 7 picks
up this motif and spells out in greater detail the last great empire.
The fourth beast had ten horns, but there emerged from among
them the 'little horn' with a mouth which spoke great things. 2.21
had praised God as the one who 'changes times and seasons'. Now
in ch. 8 this evil one who blasphemes God would even try to

'change the times and the law' and the saints would be delivered over to him for a season (7.25).

Again, the vision of Daniel in ch. 2 had spoken of the coming kingdom, but had made no mention of the people of God. Yet precisely here the need was felt most acutely for a prophetic word. 2.37 had described God's giving to Nebuchadnezzar 'the kingdom, the power, the might and the glory'. Chapter 7 now transfers this promise to 'the people of the saints of the Most High'. To them is given 'the dominion, the glory, and kingdom' (7.27). Indeed, their kingdom will be eternal (7.27) as 2.44 had announced.

The same exegetical move – call it midrashic – can be seen in the remaining visions within the second half of the book of Daniel. Thus, the visions of ch. 8 continue to elaborate and confirm elements in both chs. 2 and 7. Chapter 8 picks up the central theme of the rise and fall of the four world kingdoms from ch. 2, but focuses only on the last two within the original vision. Chapter 8 then confirms the vision of Daniel by affirming that the final kingdom would be 'broken without a human hand' (8.25, citing 2.45). But the main emphasis of ch. 8 falls on explicating the prophetic themes of ch. 7 in even greater detail. In speaking of 'the little horn' (8.9; cf. 7.24), of the 'people of the saints' (8.24; cf. 7.27), and the arrogance of the evil one (8.11; cf. 7.25), the writer continues to explain what Daniel really meant by recounting the persecution of Antiochus in historical detail.

Then again, in ch. 9 Daniel is pictured reflecting on the ancient prophecy of Jeremiah that Israel would suffer exile for seventy years. In his prayer Daniel combines the prophecy of Jeremiah with the punishment of disobedience which the law of Moses (Dan. 9.11) had threatened. The land would lie fallow to make up for the sabbaths which had been disregarded. Then the writer is made to understand that the exile was only a foreshadowing of the final period of indignation. Not seventy years, but seventy weeks of years were intended. The point of this reinterpretation is not that Jeremiah was mistaken in his prophecy, but that which he correctly envisioned was further clarified by a fresh illumination of scripture through the spirit.

Finally, the last vision in chs. 10–11 with an epilogue in ch. 12 once again explicitly develops the themes of ch. 2 along with the interpretation of chs. 7–9. Reference is made to the arrogance of the evil one, to his persecution of the saints, his removal of the burnt

sacrifices, to his setting up of the 'abomination which makes desolate', and the time of 'indignation'. 13.7 cites the mysterious reference of 7.25 to 'a time, two times, and a half' in explaining the
coming end of the age.

To summarize, chs. 7–12 extend the vision of ch. 2 into the
period contemporary with its Maccabean author for the purpose of
testifying to the truth of the prophecy and encouraging the faithful
within Israel. Although the modern historical critical scholar can
characterize the description in ch. 7 as a prophecy-after-the-event,
the biblical writer came to his material from a totally different
perspective. The introduction of the Maccabean history, far from
being a device to generate credence to an early prophecy, served to
confirm the earlier prophecy which he fully believed. He was firmly
convinced that what he now saw was intended by the original
vision. By studying the sacred writings he was able to clarify the
divine message. The writer did not view his own role as independent of the visions of Daniel. He had no new prophetic word
directly from God. Rather, he understood the sacred writings of the
past as the medium through which God continued to make contemporary his divine revelation. His own identity had no theological significance and therefore he concealed it. It is basically to
misunderstand the work of the Maccabean author to characterize it
as a ruse by which to gain authority for himself, nor was it a
conscious literary device. Rather, it arose from a profoundly
theological sense of the function of prophecy which was continually
illuminated through the continuing reinterpretation of scripture.
The Maccabean dating of the book does not undercut the validity
of its witness when it is properly understood.

The canonical reinterpretation of Daniel

Up to this point we have sought to determine how the prophecies
and visions of Daniel originally functioned as a divine message to
the Israelite community in the Maccabean period. However, several crucial issues remain to be examined. How was this message
understood later and what shape was it given in its canonical form?
How was a message to serve future generations which appeared to
be so securely anchored to the Maccabean age?

First of all, the form in which the message originally functioned in the Maccabean crisis and the form within its canonical context appear to be essentially the same. All the historical particularity of chs. 8, 9 and 11 have been left unchanged. The canonical text still speaks of Media, Persia, and Greece, of the cutting off of an anointed one after sixty-two weeks and the cessation of burnt offerings. Here the contrast with the editing process of other biblical books is striking especially when one recalls how the canonical process almost totally eradicated the original setting of such a book as 'Second Isaiah'.

However, there is strong evidence to suggest that the interpretation of the book of Daniel has been sharply altered by those who edited it. Although the original author of the visions appeared to have identified the fourth kingdom with the tyranny of Antiochus, this interpretation was no longer held. Thus, II Esdras 12.10ff. is very well aware that his interpretation differs from that originally understood by Daniel when Esdras identifies the fourth beast with Rome. Similarly, the writers of the New Testament gospels, who also lived in the Roman period and portrayed the Christian church as suffering under the persecution of the fourth kingdom (Matt. 24; Mark 13, etc.), provide additional evidence that the book of Daniel was still being understood eschatologically by a later generation. In sum, Daniel continued to be read as scripture in the post-Maccabean age, as a true witness to the end of the age, which still lay in the future.

It is important to notice how the book was reinterpreted. The belief in the coming new age, which would be ushered in by God, was not separated from the end of the fourth kingdom and then projected into the future, as one might have expected. Rather, the original sequence of the destruction of the last world power and the immediate entrance of the kingdom of God was retained unaltered. Then both the period of the fourth kingdom and the coming of God's kingdom were projected into the future to mark the end of the age. Obviously a major hermeneutical move in respect to the biblical text had been effected. The description of the 'period of indignation' which reflected the policy of Antiochus against the Jews was now understood typologically. Antiochus had become a representative of the ultimate enemy, but he himself was not the fulfilment of the vision (cf. Lebram, *VT* 1975, for the prehistory of the typology). For the reader of the canonical book Daniel still spoke prophetically of the end of the age. He still called upon Israel 'to discern the times' and to endure trial for the sake of the coming kingdom.

How was this move possible for the canon, especially since it would appear that the original writer actually had identified Antiochus IV Ephiphanes with the coming of the fourth kingdom? First of all, it should be remembered that nowhere did the original author actually identify Antiochus by name with the evil one. The Maccabean author continued to work within the framework of Daniel's prophetic visions and carried on the same idiom. The vision was a mystery, hidden from the human mind, which only God could reveal. Therefore, the biblical writer used symbolic language, and spoke of 'times and seasons', of the 'contemptible one', of the 'transgression that makes desolate', and of the 'little help'. Regardless of how sure the interpretation of these figures may have seemed to the wise, nevertheless, they always required a translation. The vision itself remained veiled.

Secondly, and more basic, the object of Daniel's visions was a prophetic description of the beginning and end of Israel's 'indignation' among the nations. The Maccabean author of the visions at no time was simply cloaking a political commentary with religious language. Such an approach to Daniel reflects a fundamental misunderstanding which is all too prevalent among modern commentators. Rather, he was interpreting history in the light of prophecy and not prophecy in the light of history. Therefore, if Antiochus did not prove to be the Old Testament Antichrist and the kingdom of God was not ushered in with his death, then for the canonical editors it was not the prophecy which was at fault, but the earlier identification with those specific historical events. For the community of Israel the book of Daniel continued to point faithfully to the last great struggle. The inspired visions were intended for the 'wise who understood' (12.10) and who would wait for the time appointed in God's calendar.

There is one final issue to be discussed. Particularly in ch. 12, along with the mysterious language of the apocalyptic calendar, there are two specific periods of time mentioned. Verse 11 speaks of 1290 days from the time the burnt offerings were removed. Verse 12 uses the figure 1335. In respect to the literary evidence it is generally held by most critical scholars that both vv. 11 and 12 are later glosses which sought to supplement the negative response of v. 9 to the question of 'how long'. In respect to the numbers themselves scholars are much divided on their historical significance and their role within the book. Plöger's explanation (*Das Buch Daniel*, 143) is a typical response: a later writer tried to extend the terminus as the expected arrival of the end was delayed.

However, in my judgment, the recent interpretation of Burgmann points in a direction which is far more consistent with the rest of the book. The numbers in ch. 12 represent attempts by a later hand to make more precise the nature of the three-and-a-half year period which played such a central role within the apocalyptic scheme of Daniel (7.25; 9.27; 12.7). The numbers offer modifications of this traditional unit of time based on different calendar systems and reflect a variety of different intentions. Once again a type of midrashic exegesis is at work which seeks to illuminate the received biblical text.

From a canonical perspective these calculations in ch. 12 do not play a significant role for understanding the book as a whole. In the final shaping of the book, the numbers were allowed to stand uninterpreted without a clear indication of their significance. They have been inserted with the final message of Daniel which spoke of 'words . . . shut up and sealed' (v. 9) and the expectancy of the end (v. 13). Chapter 12 offers a good illustration of redactional elements which entered into the literature subsequent to the major canonical shaping and function in a subordinate role even though they were part of the final literary process.

3. Theological and Hermeneutical Implications

(*a*) The book of Daniel serves as scripture for the faithful in 'discerning the times'. It testifies to the divine purpose of God for Israel to languish for a time among the powers of the world. It speaks of the beginning and the end of Israel's sufferings and encourages the people of God to be faithful. Above all, the witness of the book is theocentric. Neither the faith of Daniel nor that of a Maccabean author can be made the object of the biblical witness when divorced from the hope which evoked the obedient response. It is theologically inadmissible to undercut the seriousness of the biblical witness by characterizing it as an example of a 'late Jewish loss of nerve', or as a typical sociological reaction of Hellenistic minority groups under persecution. From the perspective of the tradition itself – and this is what canon means – the book continues truthfully to instruct and to admonish the people of God in the crisis of faith.

(b) The danger of misunderstanding the apocalyptic vision has been present from the beginning. The curious human mind has often sought to know 'when shall these things be' (12.6; cf. Matt. 24.3) in terms of a human timetable. However, the biblical writers pointed to the end of the world in order to call forth a faithful testimony from the people of God. They sought to evoke a commitment 'even unto death'. The manner in which the book was shaped in the canonical process provides a critical check against the perennial danger of politicizing and trivializing its message. Unfortunately, the history of exegesis – both Jewish and Christian – offers a sobering record of the frequency with which the prophetic vision has been transformed into a mathematical game, or the call of faith converted into an esoteric mysticism which repudiated the agony accompanying the birth of God's kingdom.

(c) The apocalyptic visions of Daniel offer a witness distinct from the classic prophets of the Old Testament. This theological tension remains regardless of whether or not the book is assigned a position in the canon among the Prophets or the Writings. Daniel's radical stance calls into question all human endeavours of 'bringing in the kingdom' or of 'humanizing the structures of society'. Rather, this biblical witness challenges the faithful to be awake and ready for the unexpected intervention of God in wrapping up all of human history. The stories of Daniel and his friends picture men who bear eloquent testimony in both word and deed to an unswerving hope in God's rule. As a consequence, they were made free to hang loosely on the world because they knew their hope rested elsewhere.

History of Exegesis

Carpzov III, 263–9; *DBS* 2, 1277ff.; *DThC* 4, 75ff.; *EB* 2, 696f.; *RGG*³ 2, 31; **Rosenmüller**, *Scholia in VT* X, 1832, 40–51.

O. **Albrecht**, 'Luthers Arbeiten an der Übersetzung und Auslegung des Propheten Daniel 1530 und 1541', *Archiv für Reformationsgeschichte* 23, Berlin 1926, 1–50; G. **Bardy**, 'Introduction', *Hippolyte. Commentaire sur Daniel*, SC 14, 1947, 7–66; K. **Berger**, *Die griechische Daniel-Diegese*, Studia Post-Biblica 27, Leiden 1976; E. **Bickerman**, *Four Strange Books of the Bible*, New York 1967; N. **Bonwetsch**, *Studien zu den Kommentaren Hippolyts zum Buche Daniel und Hohenliede*, TU 16.2, 1897; F. F. **Bruce**, 'Josephus and

Daniel', *ASTI* 4, 1965, 148–62; P. M. **Casey**, 'Porphyry and the Origin of the Book of Daniel', *JTS* NS 27, 1976, 15–33; N. **Cohn**, *The Pursuit of the Millennium*, London 1957, 18ff., 256ff.; J. **Daniélou**, 'Daniel', *RAC* III, 575–85; Leon **Festinger**, H. W. **Riecken**, et al., *When Prophecy Fails*, Minneapolis 1956; F. **Fraidl**, *Die Exegese der Siebzig Wochen Daniels in der alten und mittleren Zeit*, Graz 1883; A.-F. **Gallé**, *Daniel avec commentaires de R. Saadia, Aben-Ezra, Raschi*, Paris 1900; L. **Hartman**, *Prophecy Interpreted*, Lund 1966, 172ff.; C. **Julius**, *Die griechischen Danielzüsatze und ihre kanonische Geltung*, Biblische Studien 6. 3–4, Freiburg 1901; W. **Käser**, 'Die Monarchie im Spiegel von Calvins Daniel-Kommentar', *EvTh* 11, 1951/2, 112–37; C. **Kuhl**, *Die drei Männer im Feuer*, BZAW 55, 1930; J. **Leclercq**, 'Daniel', *DACL* 4, 221–48; I. **Levi**, 'L'histoire de "Suzanne et les deux vieillards" dans la littérature juive', *REJ* 95, 1933, 157–71; J. T. **Milik**, '"Priere de Nabonide" et autres éscrits d'un cycle de Daniel', *RB* 63, 1956, 407–15; J. **Montgomery**, *The Book of Daniel*, ICC, ²1949, 105ff., 185ff., 390ff., 468ff.; C. A. **Moore**, *Daniel, Esther, and Jeremiah: The Additions*, AB, 1977; H. H. **Rowley**, *Darius the Mede and the Four World Empires in the Book of Daniel*, Cardiff ²1959; H. **Volz**, 'Beiträge zu Melanchthons und Calvins Auslegungen des Propheten Daniel', *ZKG* 67, 1955/6, 93–118.

XLII

EZRA AND NEHEMIAH

Commentaries

E. Bertheau, V. Ryssel, KeH,
²1887
C. F. Keil, BC, 1888
H. E. Ryle, CB, 1893
L. W. Batten, ICC, 1913
G. Hölscher, *HSAT*, ⁴1923
M. Haller, *SAT*, ²1925
W. Rudolph, HAT, 1949

J. J. Slotki, SonB, 1951
K. Galling, ATD, 1954
A. Gelin, JB, ²1960
J. de Fraine, BOuT, 1961
J. M. Myers, AB, 1965
F. Michaeli, CAT, 1967
P. R. Ackroyd, TB, 1973
R. J. Coggins, CNEB, 1976

Bibliography

P. R. **Ackroyd**, *Exile and Restoration*, OTL, 1968; 'God and People in the Chronicler's Presentation of Ezra', *La notion biblique de Dieu*, ed. J. Coppens, BETL 41, 1976, 145–62; F. **Ahlemann**, 'Zur Esra-Quelle', *ZAW* 59, 1942/43, 77–98; W. F. **Albright**, *The Biblical Period from Abraham to Ezra*, Pittsburg 1955, reissued New York 1963; A. L. **Allrik**, 'The Lists of Zerubbabel (Neh. 7 and Ezra 2) and the Hebrew Numeral Notation', *BASOR* 136, 1954, 21–7; E. **Bayer**, *Das dritte Buch Esdras und sein Verhältnis zu den Büchern Esra-Nehemia*, Biblische Studien 16.1, Freiburg 1911; A. **Bentzen**, 'Priesterschrift und Laien in der jüdischen Gemeinde des fünften Jahrhunderts', *AfO* 6, 1930/31, 280–6; E. **Bickerman(n)**, 'The Edict of Cyrus in Ezra 1', *JBL* 65, 1946, 249–75; J. **Bright**, 'The Date of Ezra's Mission to Jerusalem', *Y. Kaufmann Jubilee Volume*, Jerusalem 1960, 70–87; M. **Burrows**, 'The Topography of Nehemiah 12, 31–43', *JBL* 54, 1935, 29–39; H. **Cazelles**, 'La mission d'Esdras', *VT* 4, 1954, 113–40; F. M. **Cross**, Jr., 'Aspects of Samaritan and Jewish History in Late Persian and Hellenistic Times', *HTR* 59, 1966, 201–11; 'A Reconstruction of the Judean Restoration', *JBL* 94, 1975, 4–18; T. **Denter**, *Die Stellung der Bücher Esdras im Kanon des Alten Testaments*, Diss. Fribourg 1962; J. A. **Emerton**, 'Did Ezra go to Jerusalem in 428 BC?', *JTS* NS 17, 1966, 1–19; review of U.

Kellermann's *Nehemia* in *JTS* NS 23, 1972, 171–85.

K. **Galling**, 'Der Tempelschatz nach Berichten und Urkunden im Buche Esra', *ZDPV* 60, 1937, 177–83; 'The "Gōlā-List" according to Ezra 2/ Nehemiah 7', *JBL* 70, 1951, 149–58; *Studien zur Geschichte Israels im persischen Zeitalter*, Tübingen 1964; J. **Goettsberger**, 'Über das III Kapitel des Ezrabuches', *Journal of the Society of Oriental Research* 10, Toronto 1926, 270–28; P. **Höffken**, 'Warum schweigt Jesus Sirach über Esra 7?', *ZAW* 87, 1975, 184–201; A. **van Hoonacker**, 'Zorobabel et le second temple. Étude sur la chronologie des six premiers chapitres du livre d'Esdras', *Le Muséon* 10, Louvain 1891, 72–96, 232–60, 379–97, 489–515, 634–44; 'La succession chronologique Néhémie–Esdras', *RB* 32, 1923, 481–94; 33, 1924, 33–64; S. **Japhet**, 'The Supposed Common Authorship of Chronicles and Ezra-Nehemiah Investigated Anew', *VT* 18, 1968, 330–71; A. **Jepsen**, 'Nehemia 10', *ZAW* 66, 1954, 87–106; A. **Kapelrud**, *The Question of Authorship in the Ezra-Narrative*, Oslo 1944; U. **Kellermann**, 'Die Listen in Nehemia 11, eine Dokumentation aus den letzten Jahren des Reiches Juda?', *ZDPV* 82, 1966, 209–27; *Nehemia. Quellen, Überlieferung und Geschichte*, BZAW 102, 1967; 'Erwägungen zum Problem der Esradatierung', *ZAW* 80, 1968, 55–87; 'Erwägungen zum Esragesetz', *ZAW* 80, 1968, 373–85; R. W. **Klein**, 'Old Readings in I Esdras: The List of Returnees from Babylon (Ezra//Nehemiah 7)', *HTR* 62, 1969, 99–107; 'Ezra and Nehemiah in Recent Studies', *The Mighty Acts of God. In Memoriam G. E. Wright*, ed. F. M. Cross, Garden City, N.Y. 1976, 361–76; K. **Koch**, 'Ezra and the Origins of Judaism', *JSS* 19, 1974, 173–97; W. M. **Kosters**, *Die Wiederherstellung Israels in der persischen Period*, Heidelberg 1895.

A. **Lefèvre**, 'Néhémie et Esdras', *DBS* 6, 393–424; E. **Meyer**, *Die Entstehung des Judenthums*, Halle 1896; S. **Mowinckel**, 'Die vorderasiatischen Königs- und Fürsteninschriften', *Eucharisterion* I, *FS H. Gunkel*, FRLANT 36, 1923, 278–322; ' "Ich" and "Er" in der Esrageschichte', *Verbannung und Heimkehr, FS W. Rudolph*, Tübingen 1961, 211–33; *Studien zu dem Buche Ezra-Nehemia. I. Die Nachchronische Redaktion der Buches. Die Listen.* SNVAO II. NS 3, 1964; II. *Die Nehemia-Denkschrift*, SNVAO II. NS 5, 1964; III. *Die Ezrageschichte und das Gesetz Moses*, SNVAO II. NS 7, 1965; R. **North**, 'Civil Authority in Ezra', *Studi in onore di Edoardo Volterra*, Milan 1971, 377–404; M. **Noth**, *Überlieferungsgeschichtliche Studien* I, Halle 1943, 110–79; A. **Pavlovský**, 'Die Chronologie der Tätigkeit Esdras–Versuch einer neuen Lösung?', *Bibl* 38, 1957, 273–305, 428–56; K. F. **Pohlmann**, *Studien zum dritten Esra*, FRLANT 104, 1970; J. R. **Porter**, 'Son or Grandson (Ezra X 6)?', *JTS* NS 17, 1966, 54–67; G. **von Rad**, 'Die Nehemia-Denkschrift', *ZAW* 76, 1964, 176–87; L. **Rost**, 'Erwägungen zum Kyroserlass – Esra 1', *Verbannung und Heimkehr, FS W. Rudolph*, Tübingen 1961, 301–07; H. H. **Rowley**, 'The Chronological Order of Ezra and Nehemiah', *The Servant of the Lord*, Oxford [2]1965, 135–68; 'Nehemiah's Mission and its Background', *BJRL* 37, 1954, 528–61=*Men of God*, London and New York 1963, 211–45; 'Sanballat and the Samaritan Tem-

ple', *BJRL* 38, 1955/6, 166–98=*Men of God*, 246–76.
H. H. **Schaeder**, *Esra der Schreiber*, BHT 5, 1930; W. **Schottroff**, *'Geden-ken' im Alten Orient und im Alten Testament*, WMANT 15, ²1967; M. H. **Segal**, 'The Books of Ezra-Nehemiah' (Hebrew), *Tarbiz* 14, Jerusalem 1943, 81–103; R. **Smend**, *Die Listen der Bücher Esra und Nehemia*, Basel 1881; Morton **Smith**, *Palestinian Parties and Politics that Shaped the Old Testament*, New York and London 1971, 119–47; W. T. **in der Smitten**, 'Die Gründe für die Aufnahme der Nehemiaschrift in das chronistische Ges-chichtswerk', *BZ* NF 16, 1972, 207–21; 'Zur Pagenerzählung in 3 Ezra (3 Ezra III 1–V 6)', *VT* 22, 1972, 492–5; *Ezra*, Studia Semitica Neerlandica 15, Assen 1973; S. **Talmon**, 'Ezra and Nehemiah, Books and Message', *IDB Suppl*, 317–28; C. C. **Torrey**, *The Composition and Historical Value of Ezra-Nehemia*, BZAW 2, 1896; *Ezra Studies*, Chicago 1910; R. **de Vaux**, 'The Decrees of Cyrus and Darius on the Rebuilding of the Temple', *The Bible and the Ancient Near East, FS W. F. Albright*, ed. G. E. Wright, Garden City, N.Y. 1961, 63–96; W. **Vischer**, 'Nehemia, der Sonderbeauftragte und Statthalter des Königs', *Probleme biblischer Theologie, FS G. Von Rad*, Munich 1971, 603–10; H. C. M. **Vogt**, *Studie zur nachexilischen Gemeinde in Esra-Nehemia*, Werl 1966; A. **Welch**, 'The Source of Nehemiah IX', *ZAW* 47, 1929, 130–37; *Post-exilic Judaism*, London 1935; J. **Wellhausen**, 'Die Rückkehr der Juden aus dem babylonischen Exil', *Nachrichten von der könig-lichen Gesellschaft der Wissenschaften zu Göttingen* 1895, 166–86; J. S. **Wright**, *The Date of Ezra's Coming to Jerusalem*, London ²1958.

1. Historical Critical Problems

The books of Ezra and Nehemiah formed a single book in the Hebrew canon and preceded Chronicles in the order established for the Writings. The separation into two books was a relatively late development – it did not appear in the Hebew Bible until the fifteenth century – and apparently arose in Christian circles, first attested in Origen, through the influence of a development within the LXX. (Cf. the fuller treatment by Talmon, 317f.) In spite of the great veneration in which Ezra was held in Jewish tradition, mod-ern critical scholarship has tended to disparage his importance, often on the basis of an implicitly negative judgment on post-exilic Judaism (cf. Wellhausen). Beyond this, the discovery of a larger number of difficult literary and historical problems associated with the writings of Ezra and Nehemiah has caused many scholars to regard the present canonical shape of these books as confused and distorted. They have usually concluded that a proper understanding of these writings entails an extensive reconstruction of the present form of this collection (cf. the detailed reviews of current theories by Klein and Talmon).

In terms of literary problems the relation between the editorial work of the final author and the sources which he used is not at all clear. Did the author have access to separate 'memoirs' of both Ezra and Nehemiah along with other Aramaic documents which he formed into a continous narrative? How is one to explain the abrupt alterations in the narrative between the first and third persons along with the shift from Hebrew to Aramaic? To what extent did the author of Chronicles shape the present form of Ezra and Nehemiah, and can the age of the composition be established? Particularly, how is one to explain the large number of apparent anomalies in the structure of the two books? For example, Ezra arrives in Jerusalem in Ezra 8 with a mandate to teach his statutes and ordinances in Israel, but after a brief mission seems to disappear until he reappears abruptly some twelve years later in Neh. 8. Has there been a literary displacement? Again, Neh. 7 introduces the topic of enrolment of the populus for the settlement of Jerusalem, but the execution of the project is delayed until ch. 11. Finally, the parallel genealogies in Ezra 2 and Neh. 7 and the similarity between the introductions in Ezra 3.1 and Neh. 7.73 are difficult to understand.

In recent years attention to the literary problems has focused especially on the form-critical issues. What are the genres represented in the literature and what implications can be drawn from such an analysis? The marked similarity between Nehemiah's 'memorial book' and the biographical inscriptions of the ancient Near East was first thoroughly investigated by Mowinckel (*FS Gunkel*), and subsequently pursued by von Rad who sought to limit the parallelism to Egyptian sources.

Mowinckel argued that the variation between the first and third person narratives did not arise because of earlier sources, but was a stylistic feature of a *Denkschrift*. The use of the first person was a device for self-glorification. More recently Kellermann (*Nehemia*) has criticized Mowinckel's failure to recognize the distinctive content of the Nehemiah material which had nothing to do with self-aggrandisement. Rather he sought to relate the first person address to the psalmic genre of 'a prayer of an accused person' which had first been described by Hans Schmidt (cf. ch. XXXIII). Most recently, Koch has argued that the remembrance formula offers the key to understanding the original function of the book, both as a memorial of political self-justification and a prayer for divine vindication. However, in spite of the variety of different genres which appear in Ezra-Nehemiah, it remains a debatable issue to determine on what level of the literature these forms functioned. Thus Ackroyd would argue that such form-critical diversity does not in itself call into question the decisive role of a school of the Chronicler.

The historical problems of the books are no less acute than the literary. The most difficult issue arises from the impression that the historical content of the books does not match the historical framework into which the material has been put. Thus the historical sequence of Ezra's preceding Nehemiah is not easy to reconcile with the overall historical background of the period (cf. especially van Hoonacker and Rowley). Then again, a number of specific historical references are very perplexing such as the relationship between the figures of Eliashib and Johanan in Neh. 12.22 (23) and in Ezra 10.6 (contrast the analysis of Klein, 372, with Kaiser, *Introduction*, 184). Moreover, the lack of any close historical relation between the activity of the two men raises the question of the historical accuracy of the presentation. Finally, the problem of assessing the historical value of the sources used, over and above the issue of the Chronicler's role, remains a perennial crux.

In response to these literary and historical problems modern critical scholarship has offered a variety of solutions which can be briefly summarized.

(*a*) First, several theories have been proposed to explain the relation between the editor and his sources. A large number of scholars would assign the present shape of Ezra-Nehemiah to the editorial work of the Chronicler, who used sources such as letters, royal decrees, lists, and genealogies to continue the history which had begun in Chronicles. There would, however, be considerable disagreement as to the nature of the Chronicler's own contribution and the extent of his reworking of his sources. Noth, Kellermann, and in der Smitten assigned the Chronicler a very large role and considered him the actual author rather than editor of sources. Likewise Torrey assigned much of these books to the creative imagination of the Chronicler. Ackroyd speaks more cautiously of the 'school of the Chronicler' in order to allow more flexibility on the question of authorship. Other scholars such as Mowinckel and Pohlmann argue on the basis of III Esdras that the Chronicler's original work did not include Nehemiah, and that the final form of the book derives from a post-Chronicler addition. Finally, there are those who envision two or more editions of the Chronicler's work (Galling, Cross), or an accidental disarrangement of the original order of the Chronicler at a later period (Rudolph). Although philological studies have attempted to establish grammatical and syntactical criteria for the different literary levels (cf. Japhet), the dating of Ezra-Nehemiah continues to depend largely on one's theory of the Chronicler's participation.

(*b*) Secondly, there is a widespread agreement among critical scholars on restoring a different order from that represented in the canonical books. Usually the reconstruction rests on reasoning from a combination of factors including literary, historical and logical evidence. The major alteration suggested, on which critical scholars reflect wide agreement, is to shift the account of Ezra's reading of the law (Neh. 7–8) into close proximity with Ezra's initial arrival (Ezra 8). There remains some disagreement as to where it belongs exactly, either after ch. 8 or after ch. 10 (cf. Mowinckel, *Studien* III, 1ff. for the various suggestions). The effect of the move is to disconnect the activity of Ezra fully from that of Nehemiah and to assign the verses which explicitly intertwine their activity to secondary glosses (Neh. 8.9; 12.36). Then again, by removing these chapters from Neh. 8 the theme of Jerusalem's repopulation, which was introduced in 7.1–5, is brought into closer connection with 11.1–2.

(*c*) Thirdly, the majority of scholars feel the need critically to reconstruct the historical events which surround the work of Ezra and Nehemiah within the Persian period. Immediately the problem of the chronological order of their activity arises and no consensus has emerged. The evidence from the Elephantine papyri has confirmed Nehemiah's place in the period of Artaxerxes I. However, the hypothesis which would place Ezra after Nehemiah – whether 438, 428, or 398 is contested – continues to have the widest support (Albright, Noth, Cazelles, Rowley), even though this position has recently been described by Talmon as decreasing in popularity. Those who defend the traditional date of 458 frequently resort to historical theories of 'Ezra's failure' (in der Smitten; cf.

4.23f.) to account for his period of silence, but the explanations go beyond a plain reading of the canonical text.

To summarize, the great majority of scholars – whether liberal or conservative is only a matter of degree – approach the interpretation of Ezra-Nehemiah with the assumption that its proper interpretation depends on establishing an accurate historical sequence of events to which these writings must obviously be correlated. Because of the difficulty of accomplishing this task and the radical reconstructions of the literature involved, the interpretation remains unusually tentative and vulnerable to excessive speculation. In addition, an implicit judgment is rendered on the canonical text that it is fragmentary, tendentious, and in much need of improvement.

2. The Canonical Shape of Ezra-Nehemiah

The attempt to describe the canonical shaping of these books must be careful to avoid two pitfalls. The one approach – call it modern midrashic – would rule out *a priori* the possibility of any accidental factors at work and would evaluate the present composition consistently on the same level of intentionality throughout. The weakness of this approach is its inability to deal with the historical dimensions of the canonical process which established a scale of intentionality in the actual use of the literature as authoritative scripture. The other extreme in the spectrum, which is characteristic of the dominant historical critical method, seeks to establish a historical sequence as normative and thus disregards any theological intent which would override the concerns of the modern historian. Keeping the methodological issue in mind, we turn to an analysis of the canonical shape of Ezra-Nehemiah.

Ezra-Nehemiah and the Chronicler

There are some features present in the books of Ezra and Nehemiah which we would describe at the outset as belonging to the characteristic editing of the Chronicler. Thus, for example, we find a highly selective use of the source material, the paraphrasing of earlier scripture, the arranging of passages in typological patterns (Ezra 3.12; 6.22; Neh. 8.17; 12.43), the paradigmatic use of prayer and an application of the prophecy-fulfilment schema. There seems to be little doubt that the Chronicler played a significant role in giving these books a structure.

However, in my judgment, it is a mistake to overestimate the role of the Chronicler, either by attempting to restore the books in a form even more similar to that of Chronicles (Rudolph), or to minimize the present differences between the writings of Ezra-Nehemiah and Chronicles. The essential point is not so much to account for the present differences between these books as to recognize that discontinuities exist. Thus, one could argue for the importance of a post-Chronicler redaction in setting the peculiar shape of the present composition, or one could attribute the uniqueness of the witness of Ezra-Nehemiah to the content of the sources which the Chronicler used. What is crucial is that the unique effect of a shaping be accurately described, however it came about, and this descriptive analysis be not blurred because of a theory of authorship. The point is to maintain the integrity of the witness of Ezra and Nehemiah apart from the book of Chronicles. In my judgment, the features which Ezra-Nehemiah share with the Chronicler lie at an earlier level than the final shaping of the book which points to a post-Chronicles redaction.

Chronological sequence

The present structure of the books of Ezra-Nehemiah shows a clear mark of intentionality which an author or editor established by means of a chronological sequence. The book of Ezra begins with a date formula (538) and continues with a series of dates to the completion of the temple in 516. Ezra's arrival is set in ch. 7 ('the seventh year ... , ... the first day of the fifth month'), and carefully carried through to the execution of Ezra's reform in 10.17. Again, the book of Nehemiah follows a clear chronological schema from the twentieth year of Artaxerxes (2.1) to his thirty-second year (13.6). The only major disruption in the scheme occurs in Ezra 4.6–23. This section is enclosed within references to the reign of Darius, and is clearly a use of a topical order to illustrate the nature of the continual resistance against the Jews. In sum, the present arrangements of the chapters are not simply accidental, but reflect a purposeful chronological pattern.

Of course, one could argue that the shifting of Neh. 8 to a position after Ezra 8 would not disturb this general chronological sequence and would rather restore the original historical order. Because the date formula in Neh. 8 has only included the month and the day ('the first day of the seventh month'), this event could be fitted in between the dates given in Ezra 7.9 and 10.9. Why should a later pattern of redaction be more normative than an earlier chronological sequence? However, there are several objections to this move from the perspective of a canonical analysis. First, the suggested reconstruction is based on a logical deduction from a historical pattern, but there is no sign that it ever so functioned within the Jewish community. Secondly, the theory of dislocation rests on an unproved assumption that the shift of Neh. 8 is made easier because the year is missing in the chapter's date formula and increases the likelihood of a simple interpolation between the months in Ezra 8–10. However, Neh. 8 is firmly anchored to the twentieth year of Artaxerxes by its larger setting within the book and the radical nature of the literary rearrangement in respect to its present structure is not decreased by the literary critical hypothesis. Finally, other elements within an intentional pattern of the final editor are seriously affected by the theory of dislocation, such as the sequence of Neh. 8 to the dedication of the wall in ch. 12. Therefore, even if the original historical sequence is not represented in the present position of Neh. 8, one must be aware of the possibility of a new dynamic having been established within the chapters which has disregarded the earlier chronological sequence.

Formal and material periodization

Another indication of canonical shaping lies in the historical periodization within the two books. Although the historical events dealt with in the tradition are highly selected with many long gaps of total silence, the writer's theological witness is inextricably tied to the nation's history. The repetition of the last verses of Chronicles in the introduction of Ezra, regardless of the original order of the books within the Hagiographa, interprets the Ezra story as a continuation of Israel's history. The author focuses only on certain events as theologically significant. Chapters 1–6 progress from the release under Cyrus to the reconstruction of the temple. Chapters 7–10 treat the arrival of Ezra and his initial reform. Nehemiah 1–6 records the building of the walls and Neh. 7–13 handle the re-ordering of the community's life. Moreover, the particular structuring of these events reveal the writer's perspective. Ezra 1–6, 7–10 along with Neh. 1–6 are only preparation for the climax of this sacred history which occurs in the combined activity of Ezra and Nehemiah in chs. 7–13. Likewise, the last chapter (13.4ff.) is subordinated to this section and not given an independent significance (note 13.4).

In addition to the formal structuring of his material into historical periods according to varying degrees of theological significance, the author has also employed a variety of themes by which further to explicate his theological intent. The theme of God's use of foreign rulers for Israel's sake begins with Cyrus' edict (Ezra 1.2ff.) and is picked up in Darius' decree (Ezra 6) with the explicit commentary in 6.22: 'the Lord . . . turned the heart of the king of Assyria to them so that he aided them in the work'. Again, Artaxerxes' letter to Ezra (Ezra 7.11ff.) develops the same theme and concludes with the prayer: 'Blessed be Yahweh . . . who put such a thing into the heart of the king' (v. 24). Finally, the same theme is developed at length throughout Neh. 1–6 (cf. 1.11, etc.).

A contrasting theme which is intertwined with the above motif describes the continuing bitter opposition from the people of the land. The theme is first introduced in Ezra 3.3: 'fear was upon them because of the people of the land'. When the adversaries hear of the building of the temple and are rebuffed (4.1ff.), 'the people of the land . . . made them afraid to build'. The theme of opposition is then illustrated throughout the rest of Ezra 4 with examples from the reign of Ahasuerus and Artaxerxes. In ch. 5 the writer picks up the historical sequence of his account, returning to the second year of Darius, and again speaks of the opposition. In the book of Nehemiah, the opposition to the rebuilding of the walls by Sanballat and the other enemies becomes one of the major themes of the first six chapters. Continually Nehemiah overcomes the physical threats and the attempts to create fear (6.9, 14). In the final chapter, even after the restoration, the theme is once again dealt with in ch. 13.29.

There is one more theme which plays such a major role in both books that it has often been thought to sound the dominant note of the entire composition. The theme is the separation of Israel from foreigners of the land in order to reflect the purity of the people of

God (*contra* Koch). Ezra 2 initiates the theme by describing the function of the genealogies as a means of protecting the purity of the priesthood. The theme recurs in Ezra 4 in the refusal to accept help in the rebuilding of the temple. Again, in 6.21 only those who have 'separated themselves from the population of the people of the land' can keep the passover. The note of separation dominates Ezra's prayer in ch. 9, which paraphrases the early legal prohibitions, and culminates in the abolition of mixed marriages (ch. 10). The theme continues in an unbroken manner throughout the book of Nehemiah. Foreigners 'have no portion or right or memorial in Jerusalem' (2.20). In ch. 5 Nehemiah appeals to the unity of the people of God in their task, and the book culminates in the restoration of the community which excludes foreigners (10.28ff; 13.1ff.). In a real sense, the building of the wall signifies not only physical protection, but also the separation of the people of God from foreign intercourse. As a result, Nehemiah can close the gate and exclude those who profane the sabbath (3.15ff.).

Of course, it can be argued that the use of themes as evidence in a literary analysis is a highly subjective enterprise. This objection must be taken seriously. One test of its validity is the application of negative controls. For example, in my judgment, the evidence is insufficient to claim that the theme of a 'second exodus' is present in Ezra-Nehemiah, or to project a cultic procession from Babylon (*contra* Koch). In contrast, the exodus theme does have an important typological function in Chronicles. Koch's characterization of Ezra 1.4 and 6 as a typical use of the theme 'spoiling of the Egyptians' is unconvincing because the identity rests on a change in the semantic level on which Ezra is read and is a move without a warrant from the literature itself. If one keeps the lines of a theme closely drawn without recourse to a shift in the level of abstraction, then a clear profile can often be sketched.

To summarize, the use of themes throughout the books of Ezra and Nehemiah reveals a consistent perspective from which the material has been selected and interpreted. These themes set the message of these two books apart from the Chronicles in which different themes play a dominant role.

The relation of Ezra and Nehemiah

The final indication of canonical shaping lies in the particular manner by which the activities of Ezra and Nehemiah are related. As we have seen, this is the area which has called forth the major historical reconstructions from critical scholarship. Nevertheless, it is also the area in which the special shaping of the tradition by the biblical authors can be most clearly discerned. The issue turns on how one understands the sequence of Ezra's reform in 7–10, followed by Nehemiah's activity in Neh. 1–7, and concluding with their joint programme in Neh. 8–12. In my judgment, the usual critical move which disregards the present form of the tradition and seeks to reconstruct a more historical sequence on the basis of literary and historical criteria runs the risk of failing to understand the theological concerns which are reflected through the canonical process. It seems obvious that an accurate historical report of the Persian period according to the canons of modern historical writing is not being offered, but that the biblical material has been shaped and transmitted toward another end.

First, it is an essential feature of the canonical shaping of the material that the activities of Ezra and Nehemiah have been linked together. The initial work of Ezra (7–10) as well as the building of the wall by Nehemiah (Neh. 1–6) receive their significance only in the light of the religious re-ordering of the community of faith in Neh. 8–12. The explicit intent of the author is to describe this event as one shared by both Ezra and Nehemiah. Thus, Nehemiah participates with Ezra in the instruction of the people, and conversely Ezra shares in the dedication of the wall built by Nehemiah (12.27). Clearly the author envisions the political and religious work of the two men as functioning together in the reconstitution of the community. In spite of the literary problems that the linkage of the persons is limited to chs. 8–12 of Nehemiah, and in spite of the historical problems of seeing them as contemporaries, the canonical shaping explicitly joined them together. Significantly, no attempt was made otherwise to alter the sources which dealt with each man individually.

The community under the law

There is another important theological concern expressed in the canonical ordering of the sequence of Neh. 8–12 which has been overlooked in all the theories of literary dislocation. Undoubtedly the present order exhibits a variety of anomalies and leaves unexplained what Ezra was doing during the twelve years prior to his

appearance in Neh. 8. No connection is made between Ezra's earlier action against mixed marriages and the new reform programme
begun in Neh. 8ff. Nevertheless, the present structuring of the tradition appears to be addressing the basic theological issue of how one
understands the restored community under God's law. In ch. 7
Ezra arrives in Jerusalem empowered with a royal edict 'to make
inquiries about Judah and Jerusalem according to the law of your
God' (v. 14). In ch. 9 Ezra intervenes to abolish mixed marriages;
moreover, he instigates a reform following his prayer of confession
and fasting by calling an assembly. In response to his homily the
people respond favourably to his rebuke. It has struck commentators as odd that Ezra did not read from the book of the law at that
time, but rather postponed it until thirteen years later in Neh. 8.
Particularly during the hegemony of the Wellhausen school, it was
widely assumed that Ezra's major purpose was to impose a new law
– the P code – upon the post-exilic community. However, this
hypothesis regarding the new law runs counter to the expressed
intention of this biblical witness. Ezra encourages repentance from
the people, not by introducing a new, more exclusive legal system,
but by recalling the ancient Mosaic laws preached by the prophets
(9.11ff.), which forbade intermarriage. In this context the law functioned indirectly through Ezra's prayer and homily to call forth
repentance.

However, this situation is not to be confused with that portrayed
in Neh. 8–12. Ezra does not read the law in order to reform Israel
into becoming the people of God. Rather, the reverse move obtains.
It is the reformed people to whom the law is read. The reading of
the law does not function to evoke a confession of guilt. Indeed,
when the people weep, the Levites admonish them to put away
sorrow and to be joyful. The observation to be made is that the
reading of the law in Neh. 8 is a part of the liturgical celebration by
the people of God. The attempt to shift the reading of the law to
Ezra 8 derives from a typical Protestant misunderstanding of Old
Testament law. Far from being a legalistic system which seeks to
dictate religious behaviour by rules, the tradition assigned the law a
liturgical function which had been reserved for the restored and
forgiven community.

The reading of the law has been assigned to this section of
Nehemiah because it was only after the completion of the wall and
the settlement of the people (7.5ff.) that the conditions for the full

restoration of the community were met. Separation unto God was internal as well as external. For this reason, Ezra's early reform and Nehemiah's building programme only served to foreshadow the full restoration. It has been reserved for the Nehemiah chapters to describe the formation of the ideal community of faith. This task required a combining of the sacred with the secular in a divine theocracy, and thus called forth the participation of both Ezra and Nehemiah as representatives of these two different offices. The paradigmatic purposes of these chapters in describing the ideal, faithful community is made further apparent in the two summaries at the conclusion of the assembly. 'On that day' (12.44; 13.1) both the service of worship and the purity of the people were established.

To summarize, the books of Ezra-Nehemiah offer an extreme example of a canonical process which has disregarded a strictly literary or historical sequence in order to describe the restoration as a theological model for the obedient and holy people of God.

3. Theological and Hermeneutical Implications

(a) Close attention to the canonical shape offers a guide in the reading of the tradition which resists the historical critical assumption that the biblical text can only function as a referent to identifiable historical events. To bring the historical background of a passage into sharper focus does not necessarily illuminate the biblical text, nor should such a correlation be confused with the genuinely historical task of understanding the canonical process.

(b) There are times in which historical and literary questions can be left unresolved without jeopardizing the hearing of the biblical message. For example, the exact relation between Sheshbazzar and Zerubbabel is not definitely established by the tradition (cf. above on Haggai and Zechariah), nor is Ezra's relationship to Nehemiah always clear. Indeed, the canonical process can even make use of a faulty historical record when measured by modern critical standards, as a vehicle through which a faithful and truthful theological testimony is made. Thus, it is at least possible that Nehemiah did precede Ezra – the evidence is still inconclusive (cf. Kellermann, 'Ezradatierung') – but this better historical information, even if established, would not necessarily provide a key to the theological testimony of the canonical scriptures.

(c) The liturgical force at work in the shaping of the book does not function canonically as a warrant for imitation. The description of the ideal, restored community does not issue in an imperative analogous to the message of Deuteronomy, but rather it serves as an indicative statement. Such is the nature of the faithful community which God has established as a sacred reality within the secular world.

History of Exegesis

Carpzov I, 333–5, 349–50; *DThC* 5, 551f.; *EB* 6, 151; *RGG*³ 2, 697.

J. **Fürst**, *Der Kanon des Alten Testaments*, Leipzig 1868, 112–19; A. **Kuenen**, 'Über die Männer der grossen Synagoge' (1876), in *Gesammelte Abhandlungen zur biblischen Wissenschaft von Dr Abraham Kuenen*, Freiburg 1894, 125–60; L. J. **Liebreich**, 'The Impact of Nehemiah 9.5–37 on the Liturgy of the Synagogue', *HUCA* 32, 1961, 227–37; M. **Munk**, *Esra der Schriftgelehrte nach Talmud und Midrasch*, Phil. Diss. Würzburg 1931; W. **Schneemacher**, 'Esra', *RAC* 6, 595–612.

XLIII

CHRONICLES

Commentaries

C. F. Keil, BC, 1872
E. Bertheau, KeH, ²1873
O. Zöckler, LCHS, 1879
I. Benzinger, KHC, 1901
R. Kittel, HKAT, 1902
F. de Hummelauer, CSS, 1905
E. L. Curtis and A. A. Madsen,
    ICC, 1910
W. A. L. Elmslie, CB, 1916
J. W. Rothstein, *HSAT*, ⁴1923
J. W. Rothstein, J. Hänel, KAT, (I
    Chron.) 1927

A. Noordtzij, KV, 1937–38
J. Goettsberger, HS, 1939
L. Marchal, SB, 1949
I. W. Slotki, SonB, 1951
K. Galling, ATD, 1954
W. Rudolph, HAT, 1955
H. Cazelles, JB, ³1961
J. M. Myers, AB, 1965
F. Michaeli, CAT, 1967
K. Roubos, POuT, 1969–72
P. R. Ackroyd, TB, 1973
R. J. Coggins, CNEB, 1976

Bibliography

P. R. **Ackroyd**, 'History and Theology in the Writings of the Chronicler', *CTM* 38, 1967, 501–15; *Exile and Restoration*, OTL, 1968; 'Historians and Prophets', *SEA* 33, 1968, 18–54; 'The Theology of the Chronicler', *Lexington Theological Quarterly* 8, Lexington, Ky. 1973, 101–16; 'The Chronicler as Exegete', *JSOT* 2, 1977, 2–32; W. F. **Albright**, 'The Date and Personality of the Chronicler', *JBL* 40, 1921, 104–24; 'The Judicial Reform of Jehoshaphat', *Alexander Marx Jubilee Volume*, New York 1950, 61–82; L. C. **Allen**, *The Greek Chronicles. The Relation of the Septuagint of I and II Chronicles in the Massoretic Text*, 2 vols., Leiden 1974; A. **Alt**, 'Die Rolle Samarias bei der Entstehung des Judentums', *FS O. Procksch*, Leipzig 1934, 5–28=*KS* II, 1953, 316–37; J. P. **Asmussen**, 'Priestercodex und Chronik in ihrem Verhältnis zueinander', *ThStKr* 79, 1906, 165–79; E. W. **Barnes**, 'The Midrashic Element in Chronicles', *Expositor* V.4, London 1896, 426–39; A. **Bea**, 'Neuere Arbeiten zum Problem der biblischen Chronikbücher', *Bibl* 22, 1941, 46–58; G. J. **Botterweck**, 'Zur Eigenart der chronistischen Davidsgeschichte', *ThQ* 136, 1956, 402–34; R. **Braun**, 'The Message of Chronicles: Rally Round the Temple', *CTM* 42, 1971, 502–13; 'Solomonic Apologetic in Chronicles', *JBL* 92, 1973, 503–16; 'A Reconsideration of the Chronicler's Attitude toward the North', *JBL* 96, 1977, 59–62; A.-M. **Brunet**, 'Le Chroniste et ses sources', *RB* 60, 1953, 481–508; 61, 1954, 349–86; 'La théologie du Chroniste, théocratie et messianisme', *ETL* 12, 1959, 384–97; 'Paralipomènes (Livre des), *DBS* 6, 1220–61; K. **Budde**, 'Vermutungen zum "Midrasch des Buches der Könige" ', *ZAW* 12, 1892, 37–51.

F. M. **Cross**, 'A Reconstruction of the Judean Restoration', *JBL* 94, 1975, 4–18; J. G. **Dahler**, *De librorum Paralipomenon auctoritate atque fide historica disputatio*, Strasbourg 1819; D. N. **Freedman**, 'The Chronicler's Purpose', *CBQ* 23, 1961, 436–42; K. **Galling**, *Studien zur Geschichte Israels im persischen Zeitalter*, Tübingen 1964; H. **Gese**, 'Zur Geschichte der Kultsänger am zweiten Tempel', *Abraham unser Vater, FS O. Michel*, Leiden and Cologne 1963, 222–34=*Vom Sinai zum Zion*, Munich 1974 147–59; J. **Goldingay**, 'The Chronicler as a Theologian', *BTB* 5, 1975, 99–126; E. **Janssen**, *Juda in der Exilszeit*, FRLANT 69, 1956; S. **Japhet**, 'The Supposed Common Authorship of Chronicles and Ezra-Nehemiah Investigated Anew', *VT* 18, 1968, 330–71; *The Ideology of the Book of Chronicles and its Place in Biblical Thought*, Diss. Hebrew University, Jerusalem 1973; R. W. **Klein**, *Studies in the Greek Texts of the Chronicler*, Diss. Harvard University 1966; K. **Koch**, 'Das Verhältnis von Exegese und Verkündigung anhand eines Chroniktextes', *TZ* 90, 1965, 659–70; A. **Kropat**, *Die Syntax des Autors der Chronik verglichen mit der seiner Quellen*, BZAW 16, 1909; W. E. **Lemke**, 'The Synoptic Problem in the Chronicler's History', *HTR* 58, 1965, 349–63; F. L. **Moriarty**, 'The Chronicler's Account of Hezekiah's Reform', *CBQ* 27, 1965, 399–406; R. **Mosis**, *Untersuchungen zur Theologie des chronistischen Geschichtswerkes*, Freiburg 1973; F. C. **Movers**, *Kritische Untersuchungen über die biblische Chronik*, Bonn 1834; S. **Mowinckel**, 'Erwägungen zum chronistischen Geschichtswerk', *TLZ* 75, 1960, 1–8; J. M. **Myers**, 'The Kerygma of the Chronicler', *Interp* 20, 1966, 259–73; E. **Nestle**, 'Zur Frage nach der ursprünglichen Einheit der Bücher Chronik, Esra und Nehemia,' *ThStKr* 52, 1879, 517–21.

J. D. **Newsome**, Jr., 'Toward a New Understanding of the Chronicler and his Purposes', *JBL* 94, 1975, 201–17; A. **Noordtzij**, 'Les intentions du Chroniste', *RB* 49, 1940, 161–68; R. **North**, 'Theology of the Chronicler', *JBL* 82, 1963, 369–81; M. **Noth**, *Überlieferungsgeschichtliche Studien* I, Halle 1943; O. **Plöger**, 'Reden und Gebete im deuteronomistischen und chronistischen Geschichtswerk', *FS G. Dehn*, Neukirchen 1957, 35–49=*Aus der Spätzeit des Alten Testaments*, Göttingen 1971, 50–66; *Theocracy and Eschatology*, ET Oxford and Philadelphia 1968; E. **Podechard**, 'Le premier chapitre des Paralipomènes', *RB* 13, 1916, 363–86; K.-F. **Pohlmann**, *Studien zum dritten Ezra*, FRLANT 104, 1970; G. **von Rad**, *Das Geschichtsbild des chronistischen Werkes*, BWANT IV.3 (=54), 1930; 'The

Levitical Sermon in I and II Chronicles' (1934), ET *The Problem of the Hexateuch*, London and New York 1966, 267–80; M. **Rehm**, *Textkritische Untersuchungen zu den Parallelstellen der Samuel-Königsbücher und der Chronik*, Münster 1937; G. **Richter**, 'Untersuchungen zu den Geschlechtsregistern der Chronik', *ZAW* 34, 1914, 107–41; 49, 1931, 260–70; 50, 1932, 130–41; G. **Rinaldi**, 'Quelques remarques sur la politique d'Azarias (Ozias) de Juda en Philistie (2 Chron XXVI 6ss.)', *SVT* 9, 1963, 225–36; W. **Rudolph**, 'Problems of the Books of Chronicles', *VT* 4, 1954, 401–9. J. D. **Shenkel**, 'A Comparative Study of the Synoptic Parallels in I Paraleipomena and I-II Reigns', *HTR* 62, 1969, 63–85; W. T. **in der Smitten**, 'Die Gründe für die Aufnahme der Nehemiasschrift in das chronistische Geschichtswerk', *BZ* NF 16, 1972, 207–21; O. H. **Steck**, 'Das Problem theologischer Strömungen in nachexilischer Zeit', *EvTh* 28, 1968, 445–58; C. C. **Torrey**, 'The Chronicler as Editor and as Independent Narrator', *AJSL* 25, 1908–9, 157–73, 188–217; *The Chronicler's History of Israel. Chronicles–Ezra–Nehemiah Restored to its Original Form*, New Haven 1954, London 1955; P. **Vannutelli**, *Libri Synoptici Veteris Testamenti seu Librorum Regum et Chronicorum loci paralleli*, 2 vols., Rome 1931–34; A. C. **Welch**, *The Work of the Chronicler*, London 1939, New York 1940; J. **Wellhausen**, *De gentibus et familiis Judaeis*, Göttingen 1870; *Prolegomena to the History of Israel*, ET Edinburgh 1885; P. **Welten**, *Geschichte und Geschichtsdarstellung in den Chronikbüchern*, WMANT 42, 1973; W. M. L. **de Wette**, *Beiträge zur Einleitung in das Alten Testament*, 2 vols., Halle 1806–7, reprinted Hildesheim 1971; G. **Widengren**, 'The Persian Period', *Israelite and Judaean History*, ed. J. H. Hayes and J. M. Miller, OTL, 1977, 489–538; T. **Willi**, *Die Chronik als Auslegung*, FRLANT 106, 1972; H. G. M. **Williamson**, 'The Accession of Solomon in the Books of Chronicles', *VT* 26, 1976, 351–61; *Israel in the Book of Chronicles*, Cambridge and New York 1977; R. R. **Wilson**, *Genealogy and History in the Biblical World*, New Haven 1977; A. **Zeitlin**, 'Midrash: A Historical Study', *JQR* 44, 1953, 21–36; L. **Zunz**, *Die gottesdienstlichen Vorträge der Juden*, Frankfurt ²1892.

1. Historical Critical Problems

The traditional Christian – and to some extent Jewish – understanding of Chronicles is reflected in the Greek title given the books, Παραλειπόμενα, which was retained in the Latin Paraleipomena, meaning additions. The repetition of the earlier material from Samuel and Kings by the author of Chronicles was interpreted as a supplementation. In spite of a few obvious exceptions (e.g. Jerome), the books did not receive much attention during most of the Christian era. The same generalization does not hold true for the Jews who used readings from Chronicles on the Day of Atonement. Still the interest in the book by medieval Jewish commentators was not high. The rise of the historical critical method in the seventeenth century brought a striking change to this approach. Cappellus found much of his evidence for textual corruption of the Hebrew text by a careful collation of the parallel passages. However, the major credit for breaking open the exegetical problems of Chronicles in its most radical and challenging form goes to de Wette in his *Beiträge* (1807). De Wette argued that the writer had 'reworked, altered, and falsified' his earlier sources in the interest of a tendentious dogmatic frame of reference so as to render it useless as a historical source. In spite of a steady stream of conservative responses to de Wette (Dahler, Keil, Movers), this basically negative assessment of Chronicles continued to gain ascendancy throughout the nineteenth century, and culminated in the harsh judgment of Wellhausen.

In the period following World War I signs of a more positive evaluation began to appear. C. C. Torrey's estimate of the historical worth of the book was strictly in line with Wellhausen's, but at least Torrey attributed to the author considerable literary creativity and imagination which had previously been denied him. Beginning in the early 20s, W. F. Albright began to defend the historical accuracy of some of the Chronicler's separate traditions. The monographs of von Rad and A. C. Welch began to awaken new interest in the theology of the Chronicler. Especially von Rad's form-critical study of the Levitical preaching in 1934 did much to open a new vista. By 1955 in the impressive commentary of Rudolph one had a good indicator of the distance which had been travelled since de Wette and Wellhausen. To be sure, there remained a considerable number of negative judgments, but a start towards recovering the contribution of the book had been begun. In the last decade an impressive list of monographs and articles have appeared which have made great strides in offering a positive, fresh evaluation of these books (cf. especially the writings of Ackroyd, Willi, Mosis, among others). It remains without saying that much research still needs to be done in this area.

2. The Canonical Shape of Chronicles

Distinctive features

The issue of determining the canonical shaping of Chronicles involves certain features which are different from many of the earlier books. In the study of the prophetic books a tension was often observed between the original activity of the prophet and the redactional shaping of his words. Again, in the study of the earlier histories, critical focus has fallen on investigating the original historical event in relation to its literary form in the biblical text. The hermeneutical issue is not principally different for the Chronicler, but the process of canonical shaping does vary significantly. First of all, the major critical tension is not between the original event and its biblical record, but between the earlier tradition in the text of Samuel-Kings and the Chronicler's reshaped composition. Secondly, the historical process leading up to the final stage of redaction has not extended over such a lengthy period through the numerous stages of oral and literary transmission which one finds in the Pentateuch or in the books of Samuel. Rather, the Chronicler's own intention is basically identical with the canonical shape of the book of Chronicles. The probability of some development later than that of the Chronicler has not seriously altered the decisive shaping by the Chronicler himself. To put the issue in another way, it was the Chronicler himself who was raising the canonical question of how Israel's sacred historical traditions functioned authoritatively for the continuing life of the people of God.

The aim of the Chronicler

Scholars remain in considerable disagreement as to the purpose of the Chronicler's writing his history. Much of the disagreement stems from a critical assumption that the author has cloaked his real intentions behind some tendentious handling of his sources. Thus, his purpose was really to polemicize against the Samaritans, or to offer 'the first apology for Judaism' (Pfeiffer, *Introduction*), or to legitimate certain post-exilic institutions such as the Levitical priesthood (Freedman). However, if one takes the statements of the author of Chronicles at face value, his purpose in writing seems entirely straightforward. The author was attempting to interpret to the restored community in Jerusalem the history of Israel as an eternal covenant between God and David which demanded an obedient response to the divine law. On the basis of past history he sought repeatedly to draw the lesson that Israel prospered when obedient but courted God's wrath and the destruction of the nation through disobedience. In spite of continual warnings from the prophets, Israel abandoned God's law and suffered the consequences (II Chron. 36.15f.). However, after the judgment, God once again restored his people who continue to stand under the same divine imperatives. The author assumes that the will of God has been made known through revelation. It does not need to be actualized or reinterpreted for a new era. Rather, both the judgments which the writer cites upon disobedience in the past (I Chron. 10.13f; II Chron. 12.2; II Chron. 36.15f.) as well as the promises proffered for a faithful response remain authoritative for every generation (II Chron. 6.1ff.; 7.11ff.; 21.7). Significantly, the term Israel retains for the Chronicler its basically religious connotation of the people of God and does not become simply a political designation (cf. Williamson).

Another aspect of this same methodological problem in the study of Chronicles can be illustrated by comparing the approaches of two recent monographs, that of T. Willi and R. Mosis. Willi argues that the task of the modern exegete is to illuminate the work of the Chronicler by understanding the writer's exegetical techniques in interpreting the authoritative texts of Samuel-Kings (53ff.). However, Willi rejects the attempt to discover the influence of the writer's own history upon his composition as a misleading endeavour which seeks to get behind the text (cf. 55, 66, 193). Conversely, Mosis often finds the key to the meaning of a text in Chronicles to lie in the writer's portrayal of his own post-exilic situation which differs from the narrative context of the story itself (80, 124, 202, etc.). According to Mosis, the Chronicler reflects his own historical situation sometimes intentionally, and sometimes unintentionally. P. R. Ackroyd (JSOT, 23) supports Mosis' position that it is exegetically important to discover the Chronicler's real historical context even if it has been buried below the surface of the text.

The disagreement centres on one's hermeneutical concept of the exegetical task. It is clear that historical information can often be extracted from a biblical text by means of an oblique reading or probing below the surface. The crucial exegetical issue turns on how one uses such information. In my judgment, a canonical reading of the Old Testament seeks to describe how the shape of the biblical text determined a perspective from which the historic Jewish community encountered its scripture. Any information which can aid in understanding the canonical function of the material is welcomed. However, information which works from a context foreign to the intentionality of the text itself, whether of a historical or psychological nature, falls outside the descriptive task of exegesis within the context of the canon. Therefore, Willi's approach to the interpretation of Chronicles is closer, at least in theory, to the descriptive goals of canonical exegesis than is Mosis, although the analysis which follows differs from both in some crucial respects.

The Chronicler's use of sources

The recognition that the author of the book of Chronicles is using a selection of material from a wide variety of sources may at first appear obvious because of his frequent and explicit reference to sources (I Chron. 29.29f.; II Chron. 9.29ff.; 13.22, etc.). However the issue of the Chronicler's use of sources is more complex than one might at first suppose and has continued to evoke debate among the commentators. It is generally agreed that the majority of the historical sources which are cited under different names are variations of the same work ('Book of the Kings of Judah and Israel', II. 16.11; II 25.26; 'Book of the Kings of Israel and Judah'. II 27.7; II 35.27; 'Histories of the Kings of Israel', II 33.18). However, the real issue at stake is the relation of the Chronicler's sources to the canonical books of Samuel-Kings. The intensive study of the close relationship between these books in recent years would seem to rule out the older view which sought to explain the parallelism as stemming from a common source, whether oral or literary. Rather, most modern commentators have little doubt that the Chronicler made use of the books of Samuel and Kings. It is also true that a textual history is involved and the Chronicler's text of Samuel-Kings seems to have been of a different text type from the Masoretic (cf. Lemke). At the same time there are enough important additions in the Chronicles account over and above that of Samuel-Kings which cannot be satisfactorily explained, if one limited the Chronicler to this one source. A majority of scholars have also rejected the theory of de Wette and Wellhausen which relegated all these latter additions to the creative imagination of the Chronicler. As a result, scholars remain divided on whether to explain the additions as separate new sources, independent oral tradition, or an expanded edition of a canonical form of Samuel-Kings.

A similar problem arises from the frequent citation of written sources which are attributed to various prophets, both known and unknown from the canonical books. In several places (II 20.34; II 32.32) the citation implies that the prophetic writing has already been incorporated within a larger historical source. The inclusion of prophetic writings within the earlier canonical historical collections is evident (Isa. 36–39//II Kings 18–19).

It is probably fair to say that the historical critical problem of the Chronicler's use of sources has not been solved and may never be completely. Nevertheless, such research as Albright's, on the one hand, has performed a valuable service in keeping open the question of the historical value of the Chronicler's separate sources. On the other hand, research such as that of Willi, Mosis and Ackroyd has done much to illuminate the extent to which the author exerted his freedom over against the canonical sources. In sum, although the question of sources has not been fully resolved, the two extreme positions, represented on the left by de Wette and on the right by Keil, have not been sustained.

There is still another side to the problem of the Chronicler's use of sources which needs exploring and is not identical with the historical critical form of the question which has been pursued above. What can one say about the author's own understanding of his sources? First of all, it is clear that the Chronicler is making a selection of material from a much larger source which is available to him. Thus, for example, he passes over in silence the whole history of the Northern Kingdom after the division of the nation and only uses it when it has a direct bearing on Judah (II Chron. 18). However, it is a basic error of interpretation to infer from this method of selection that the Chronicler's purpose lies in suppressing or replacing the earlier tradition with his own account. Two reasons speak directly against this assumption. First, the Chronicler often assumes a knowledge of the whole tradition on the part of his readers to such an extent that his account is virtually incomprehensible without the implied relationship with the other accounts (cf. I Chron. 12.19ff.; II Chron. 32.24–33). Secondly, even when he omits a story in his selection he often makes explicit reference to it by his use of sources. For example, the Chronicler omits reference to Jeroboam's divine election (I Kings 11), but his explicit reference to the prophecy of Ahijah (II Chron. 9.29) rules out a theory of conscious suppression. Then again, the Chronicler's frequent method of repeating large sections of earlier material to which he supplies a theological explanation of its causes indicates that the author views his work, not simply as a supplement, but as a necessary explication of the tradition.

The method in which the Chronicler cites his historical sources is also of significance for revealing the author's perspective. He does not make reference to one canonical source, even in the sections which parallel closely the Samuel-Kings material, which would indicate a period of great flexibility prior to its formation into one canonical source with a specific nomenclature. Nevertheless, the author is drawing on authoritative writings whose authority lies in the nature of the material rather than in an official status.

Of particular interest is the frequent citation of prophetic writings. The Chronicler makes much of the literary activity of the prophets whose writings are cited, rather than those whose oracles are heard. Even Elijah, the prophet, communicates his message through a letter (II Chron. 21.12). The close relation between the histories and the prophetic writings indicates the author's belief that prophetic inspiration lay at the source of all his material. One can detect already at this time the beginning of the later tradition which identified the historical writings of Israel as Former and Latter Prophets.

Exegesis of authoritative scripture

Perhaps the crucial discovery of the modern study of Chronicles is the extent to which the Chronicler sought to interpret Israel's history in relation to a body of authoritative scripture. Although it is obvious that the Chronicler did not at any point articulate his concept of canon, he made use of the earlier writings in such a way as to indicate how strongly the consciousness of a body of authoritative writings affected him. When the Chronicler in II. 6.16 alters the text of I Kings 8.25 from 'walk before me' to 'walk in my Torah', Willi (125) characterizes this move as stemming from a theology of sacred scripture. Indeed, most of the crucial exegetical moves which comprise the Chronicler's method derive directly from his concept of authoritative writings through which the will of God is revealed to every generation of Israel.

(a) Harmonization

A characteristic feature of the Chronicler's method arising from his concept of scripture is his reading of its various parts as a unity. He views his sources all on the same plane with no regard for historical development which would attempt to distinguish between older and younger elements. The effect of this method is to harmonize the various parts into an inner unity which reconciles differences, resolves tensions, and establishes links between disparate parts. At times the process of harmonization is quite unconscious and appears as almost a reflex from a concept of canon. However, most often the process of harmonization within Chronicles reveals a serious exegetical activity on the part of the author. Thus, in the Chronicler's account of the bringing of the ark to Jerusalem (I Chron. 15.1ff.) the Levites are explicitly assigned the task of transporting the ark, which is a feature missing in II Samuel 6. Indeed, David justifies his demand for the Levites' role in accordance with the prescription in Deut. 10.8. The particular role of the Levites appears again in the story of Jehoiada's revolt (II Kings 11.4ff. // II Chron. 23.1ff.). According to the earlier account the revolt is staged by Jehoiada in co-operation with the captains of the guard. However, a problem arises for the Chronicler because the story in Kings might imply that someone other than a priest or a Levite entered the temple (II. 23.6). Therefore, his account focuses on the Levites in the revolt who guard the temple and surround the king.

It is important to notice in the process of harmonization that the Chronicler did not for a moment feel himself at liberty to change his text at will, as commentators have tended to imply. In fact, such an assumption is totally foreign to a sense of canon. Rather, on the basis of a close study of the tradition the Chronicler sought to explore the outer limits which the text allowed in order to reconcile the differences. His method permitted him great creativity only within certain boundaries which he could justify from the received tradition. It is precisely this tension, indigenous to the Chronicler's method, which explains his oscillation between freedom and constraint. In the above mentioned case of Jehoiada's revolt (II Kings 11) there were enough indications of Levitical participation to allow the Chronicler margin for this harmonization. The later author would have considered it unthinkable that Jehoida, the high priest, would not have used the clergy in his support as well as the army. Moreover, the priest who, according to the account in Kings, delivered to the captains the spears and shields of David, according to the later traditions reflected in I Chron. 26 could only have been a Levite. Therefore, the Chronicler could reinterpret the story according to his tradition which did not contradict the earlier account of Kings, but simply provided the other side of the fuller picture.

Often the process of harmonization by the Chronicler reflects the influence of other authoritative texts upon the Samuel-Kings tradition. For example, when the Chronicler supplements David's sacrifice with 'wheat for a cereal offering' (I Chron. 21.23), one can detect the influence of such priestly material from Num. 15.1ff. or Ex. 29.38ff. Or again, the shift in the calendar between the account of I Kings 8.66 and II Chron. 7.9f. seems to have arisen when the Chronicler adjusted the story to the festival prescription of Lev. 23.34ff.

The process of harmonization often involved the Chronicler's attempt to make sense of an apparently poor Hebrew text, which may have provided a means of reconciling the various traditions regarding the slaying of Goliath (II Sam. 21.19 // I Chron. 20.5) and the death of Saul (I Sam. 31.1ff. // II Sam. 1.1ff. // I Chron. 10.1ff.). The treatment of Willi is particularly interesting on the problem of the use of different texts (69ff.). In I Chron. 15.27 David is described as wearing a 'robe of fine linen' which would be consonant with his role as priest, but this possibility of interpretation may have arisen from a textual confusion between *mkrkr* and *mkrbl* (cf. the commentators). At other times, the Chronicler attempts to clarify geographical localities in the light of his fuller knowledge, or he substitutes an easier word for an obscure reference (cf. II Chron. 23.7).

(b) Supplementation

Closely akin to the Chronicler's aim to establish an inner harmony of all his sources through harmonization is his concern to supplement the earlier accounts with the full range of prophetic revelation in an outer harmony. The Chronicler had at his disposal other authoritative texts which he used to bring out the full dimension of divine revelation. The issue is not that of his combining written scripture with oral tradition because he cites the prophets according to their writings, and views all sources as a living testimony instead of a dead letter. Rather, it is a canonical concern that the full extent of the normative tradition be represented. Although some stories could be omitted with impunity in a selection, it was thought necessary that other prophetic messages must be supplied over and above the account in Kings to round out the tradition. For example, it is not by accident that the Chronicler elaborates at length on Hezekiah's celebration of the passover which had been omitted in the earlier source, while he greatly condenses the story of Sennacherib's invasion. Likewise, the Chronicler considers David's ordering of the liturgical service of normative value and deals with it at length (I Chron. 15.16ff.). By means of the Levitical sermon the Chronicler brings in lengthy homilies by which to instruct in the significance of the given event in God's economy. Usually it is a mistaken interpretation to regard an expansion of the Chronicler as only a 'natural' embellishment to be explained from general laws of literary accretion and glossing. Rather, these expansions reflect a critical, theological process in which the Chronicler supplemented the earlier record with material considered to be normative for Israel.

(c) Typology

Another aspect of the Chronicler's method which arises directly from his attempt to unify a variety of traditions is his typological exegesis. The approach is basically a non-historical ordering of material according to patterns which arise from a similarity of content. It is a device by which the Chronicler can express his value judgments as to what is normative, enduring, and representative within the multiplicity of varying historical situations. The method thus emphasizes that which is deemed essential while omitting and curtailing elements which obscure the lines of continuity. For example, by a small addition of the phrase 'the house was full of a cloud' (II. 5.13b) the Chronicler describes the dedication of the temple in language which parallels the dedication of the tabernacle in Ex. 40.34f., and thus records the selfsame divine reality at work. Again, the description of the joy of the people and the abundance of freewill offerings in Josiah's rebuilding of the temple (II. 24.1ff.) parallels the people's response to Moses' earlier activity (Ex. 35.20ff.) and prefigures the ideal time of Neh. 12.44 (cf. Mosis, 163). Again, the form of prayer offered by Abijah, Asa, Jehoshaphat, and Hezekiah, which were all made under similarly threatening conditions, displays such a continuity of expression as to portray a clear representation of the 'obedient king'.

This typological method is particularly compatible to the canonical process since it makes use of lead words and stereotyped expressions by which to call to the reader's consciousness other examples of the same pattern within the whole range of authoritative scripture. Thus, when David charges Solomon in I Chron. 22, he uses exactly the same series of phrases as those with which Moses challenged Joshua: 'Be strong and of good courage. Fear not, be not dismayed ... Yahweh is with you' (Josh. 1.9). Von Rad has pointed out the extent to which the Chronicler has later figures actually citing earlier biblical passages, such as Jehoshaphat's use of a word from Isaiah (II. 20.20). Although it is clear that later rabbinic Judaism developed this technique of the interchanging of words into a formal hermeneutical principle (*gezērā šāwā*), it is important to observe the restrictions under which the method is held in Chronicles (*contra* Willi, 135ff.). The Chronicler used the method to draw out elements of ontological continuity within Israel's history, but it never became a formal interchange of words divorced from the context of the narrative.

A logical extension of the typological method can also be seen in the Chronicler's tendency to schematize his material into fixed patterns. In II Chronicles he aligns his kings in patterns of faithfulness followed by unfaithfulness. At times the same king is both faithful and faithless, such as Asa and Uzziah; at other times a good king is followed immediately by an evil one. Because the kings are judged by fixed categories, they emerge as recurring types of good and evil. Similarly the prophets speak basically the same vocabulary in Chronicles and represent a consistent voice of divine warning which usually lacks traits of individuality.

(d) The Coherence of Action and Effect

One of the most controversial features of the Chronicler's method is often characterized as his rigid doctrine of retribution which he is alleged to have forced upon all his material. For example, Saul's death is caused by his consulting a medium (I Chron. 10.13), Uzziah's leprosy stemmed from his cultic transgression (II. 26.16ff.), and Josiah's débâcle is attributed to his disobedience to a prophetic oracle (II. 35.22). Yet to see this feature apart from the Chronicler's larger concept of scripture is to distort its significance.

Actually the Chronicler's use of the motif of retribution is another aspect of his analogical historical thinking which is grounded in authoritative writings and is not different in kind from his use of typology. Whereas in typology, the author sought to draw patterns from history of the analogous workings of the selfsame divine reality, in his use of retribution he attempts to illustrate the continuity in God's economy between human action and its inevitable effect. Far from imposing a strange doctrine upon his material, the Chronicler was attempting to illustrate in specific events an understanding of God's ways with Israel which comprised the heart of the covenant: 'If you seek him, he will be found by you, but if you forsake him, he will forsake you' (II Chron. 15.2). By emphasizing the verifiable consequences of disobedience, the Chronicler simply drew forth the truth of a lesson which history itself had confirmed.

Willi (209) has made the important point that the Chronicler made use of this historical device when he sensed a gap in the tradition of pre-exilic Israel which he had inherited. Indeed, the infrequency of its use in the books of Ezra and Nehemiah stands in striking contrast to its use in I and II Chronicles. Often the Chronicler spelled out in detail what was already partially implied in his source. For example, a suggestion of a connection between Rehoboam's unfaithfulness and a divine judgment was implied in Kings by a juxtaposing of the two traditions in I Kings 14.22–24 and 14.25–28. The Chronicler made the connection explicit. Again, in the Chronicler's interpretation of the death of Josiah (II Chron. 35.22) it is uncertain to what extent he was drawing on an historical source independent of the account in Kings. Nevertheless, it seems clear that the Chronicler reached the conclusion that Josiah's death must have arisen from an act of disobedience analogous to that of an earlier king in Israel. Therefore, he patterned Josiah's death typologically upon Ahab's (II Chron. 18).

There is one final aspect of the problem to be considered. The Chronicler did not conceive of his own work as prophetic. Rather, he envisioned his work as a commentary on the writings of the prophets. Israel had experienced disaster because it had failed to 'believe in Yahweh and in his prophets' (II Chron. 20.20). Therefore, it was an important concern of the Chronicler to demonstrate the truth of the prophetic word. He did this by pointing out the coherence between the prophetic word and the inevitable effect of its disobedience.

Nevertheless, the Chronicler's understanding of the role of prophecy and fulfilment is strikingly different from that of the 'Deuteronomistic historian' who edited the early historical books. For the Dtr. historian, history was the process of the prophetic word fulfilling itself in history. Therefore, he was at pains to establish the exact correspondence between the spoken prophecy and its fulfilment (cf. ch. XV above). When Elijah's prophecy concerning the death of Ahab (I Kings 21.19) was fulfilled (22.37), the Dtr. historian records its fulfilment exactly 'according to the word spoken'. Interestingly enough, in the Chronicler's parallel account the proof of fulfilment is omitted. The reason for this omission lies in a different understanding of the prophetic word. The Chronicler has broadened his understanding of the prophetic word to include no longer just the spoken oracle, but to encompass the entire corpus of prophetic writing. His history is written to validate the truth of the entire prophetic history, and he does so by linking human action with its historical effect. In a real sense the Chronicler's use of retribution runs parallel to the Dtr. historian's argument of prophecy and fulfilment.

The concept of the prophetic word has been broadened to encompass the whole of divine revelation. Saul is destroyed on Mount Gilboa because he failed to heed the Word of God, but instead turned to a medium (I Chron. 10). Jehoram died of an incurable disease as had been prophesied in Elijah's letter (II Chron. 21). Uzziah disregarded the warnings of God's priests who cited to him the laws of Leviticus (II Chron. 26), and was therefore punished. The story was recorded by Isaiah the prophet (II Chron. 21.21) and verified by the Chronicler.

In sum, the Chronicler's attempt to document the correspondence between action and effect is an essential part of his concept of God's revelation through his prophets which is contained in a body of authoritative scripture.

3. Theological and Hermeneutical Implications

Our study has sought to demonstrate that the Chronicler in the process of giving his material its canonical shape has made use of a variety of exegetical methods many of which are akin to later Jewish midrash and all of which are looked upon with askance by modern historical critical methodology. This includes the techniques of harmonization, typology, and historical schematization. Of course, it is obvious even to the hard-nosed historian that these various exegetical moves by the Chronicler have at least to be correctly analysed in a descriptive enterprise, if the author is to be understood. However, the constructive task of theology requires the theologian to go much beyond the point of mere description. Indeed, we would argue that it is a theological desideratum to take this particular canonical shape with which the Chronicler has fashioned his tradition with utmost seriousness. What is involved in this affirmation?

(a) First of all, the Chronicler's use of midrashic method does not provide the modern theologian with a warrant for the continuing use of midrash. Various biblical authors employed a whole range of hermeneutical techniques in shaping their material, but these have no theological validity apart from the material which bears their stamp. However, the midrashic method did provide the exegetical tools by which the Chronicler gave his material its definitive, canonical shape. Moreover, it is this historically conditioned shape which both church and synagogue acknowledged as authoritative scripture. To speak of its normative role within the canon is not to absolutize an arbitrary pattern of historical conditioning, but to acknowledge as unique and authoritative this witness in its received form.

What then are the theological implications of the peculiar shape of Chronicles? The Chronicler bears witness to the unity of God's will for his people which has often been lost in the modern concern for history. The author relativizes all issues of historical change and development, and deals with God's will for his people as eternal and unchanging. The Word of God addressed ancient patriarchs, pre-exilic kings, and exiles from the Babylonian captivity with the same imperatives and accompanied them with the same promise. In other words, the Chronicler speaks to the ontological question and faithfully testifies to the unchanging reality of the One God.

(b) Secondly, the Chronicler bears witness to the continuity of the obedient response within the history of Israel. Because God did not change his will, demanding one thing of his people earlier and something different later, there emerged a common profile of the faithful within Israel. There is a family resemblance in their praise and thanksgiving, in prayers and laments which extends throughout all ages. The Chronicler shaped his material to highlight the continuity within the community of faith.

(c) Thirdly, the book of Chronicles testifies to the fundamental correspondence between an action and its outcome. 'Whatsoever a man soweth, that shall he also reap.' Of course, this conviction is grounded in the author's belief in the justice and power of God over his creation. To be sure, other witnesses would be needed to explore the full dimensions of God's providence – both in terms of mystery and eschatology. Nevertheless, the Chronicler's witness remains a foundation on which the others stood.

(d) Finally, the book of Chronicles bears witness to the role of sacred scripture as providing the rule of faith by which the community lives. Far from being a dead hand of the past, the writings of the prophets offer both a chart and a compass for the boldest possible exploration of the inner and outer structure of faith within the world and without. The fact that the book of Chronicles does not replace Samuel and Kings, but stands along side the earlier traditions, illustrates the function of the canon as a means of enrichment of the biblical traditions in the process of critical reflection.

The History of Exegesis

Carpzov I, 298–302; *DThC* 11, 1994; *EB* 2, 606; *RGG*[3] 1, 1806.

E. L. **Curtis**, A. A. **Madsen**, *The Book of Chronicles*, ICC, 1910, 44ff.; E. G. **Hirsch**, 'Chronicles – in Rabbinical Literature', *JE* 4, 60; A. **Klostermann**, 'Chronik, die Bücher der', *RE*[3] 4, 84f.

PART SIX

CONCLUSION

XLIV

THE HEBREW SCRIPTURES AND THE CHRISTIAN BIBLE

Bibliography

A. **Amsler**, *L'Ancien Testament dans l'Église*, Neuchâtel 1960; D. L. **Baker**, *Two Testaments – One Bible*, Leicester and Downers Grove, Ill. 1976; J. **Barr**, *Judaism – Its Continuity with the Bible* (The Seventh Montefiore Memorial Lecture), Southampton 1968; 'Le Judaïsme postbiblique et le théologie de l'Ancien Testament', *RThPh* 18, 1968, 209–17; O. **Betz**, *Offenbarung und Schriftforschung in der Qumransekte*, Tübingen 1960; F. **Blank**, 'Erwägungen zum Schriftverständnis des Paulus', *Rechtfertigung*, *FS E. Käsemann*, Tübingen 1976, 37ff.; F. **Bleek**, 'Über die Stellung der Apocryphen des Alten Testaments im christlichen Kanon', *ThStKr* 26, 1853, 268–354; J. **Bloch**, *On the Apocalyptic in Judaism*, JQR Monograph Series 2, Philadelphia 1952; 'Outside Books', *Mordecai Kaplan Jubilee Volume*, English Section, New York 1955, 87–108; H. **Bornkamm**, *Luther and the Old Testament*, ET Philadelphia 1969; F. F. **Bruce**, *Tradition Old and New*, Exeter 1970; F. F. **Bruce** and E. G. **Rupp**, eds., *Holy Book and Holy Tradition*, Manchester 1968; R. **Bultmann**, *Primitive Christianity in its Contemporary Setting*, ET New York and London 1956; J. **Calvin**, *Institutes of the Christian Religion*, Book II, chs. 10–11, Library of Christian Classics 20, London and Philadelphia 1961, 428–64; H. **von Campenhausen**, *The Formation of the Christian Bible*, ET London and Philadelphia 1972; J. G. **Carpzov**, *Introductio ad libros canonicos bibliorum Veteris Testamenti omnes*, Leipzig 1721, 20–37; B. S. **Childs**, 'The Old Testament as Scripture of the Church', *CTM* 43, 1972, 709–22.

B. **Gerhardsson**, *Memory and Manuscript*, Lund and Copenhagen 1961; H. **Gese**, 'Erwägungen zur Einheit der Biblischen Theologie', *Vom Sinai zum Zion*, Munich 1974, 11–30; 'Das biblische Schriftverständnis', *Zur biblischen Theologie*, Munich 1977, 9–30; L. **Ginzberg**, 'Some Observations on the Attitude of the Synagogue towards the Apocalyptic-Eschatological Writings', *JBL* 41, 1922, 115–36; A. H. J. **Gunneweg**, *Understanding the Old Testament*, ET, OTL, 1978, ch. II; V. E. **Hasler**, *Gesetz und Evangelium in der Alten Kirche bis Origenes*, Zürich 1953; M. **Hengel**, *Judaism and Hellen-*

ism, ET London and Philadelphia 1974, 107ff.; F. **Hesse**, *Das Alte Testament als Buch der Kirche*, Gütersloh 1966; E. **Hirsch**, *Das Alte Testament und die Predigt des Evangeliums*, Tübingen 1936; G. **Hoelscher**, *Kanonisch und Apokryph*, Leipzig 1905; H. **Höpfl** and L. **Leloir**, *Introductio generalis in S. Scripturam*, Rome ⁶1958; R. **Hummel**, *Die Auseinandersetzung zwischen Kirche und Judentum in Matthäusevangelium*, Munich ²1966; P. **Katz**, 'The Old Testament Canon in Palestine and Alexandria', *ZNW* 47, 1956, 190–217; J. L. **Koole**, *De Overname van het Oude Testament door de christelijke Kerk*, Hilversum 1938; H.-J. **Kraus**, *Die Biblische Theologie. Ihre Geschichte und Problematik*, Neukirchen-Vluyn 1970; 'Theologie als Traditionsbildung?', *Biblisch-theologische Studien*, Neukirchen-Vluyn 1977, 61–73; C. **Larcher**, *L'Actualité Chrétienne de l'Ancien Testament, d'après le Nouveau Testament*, Paris 1962; J. C. H. **Lebram**, 'Aspekte der alttestamentlichen Kanonbildung', *VT* 18, 1968, 173–89; R. C. **Leonard**, *The Origin of Canonicity in the Old Testament*, Diss. Boston University 1972; M. **Limbeck**, *Die Ordnung des Heils. Untersuchungen zum Gesetzesverständnis des Frühjudentums*, Düsseldorf 1971; B. **Lindárs**, *New Testament Apologetic*, London and Philadelphia 1961.

C. G. **Montefiore**, *The Old Testament and After*, London and New York 1923; G. F. **Moore**, 'The Definition of the Jewish Canon and the Repudiation of Christian Scriptures', 1911, reprinted in S. Leiman, ed., *The Canon and Masorah of the Hebrew Bible*, New York 1974, 115–41; *Judaism in the First Centuries of the Christian Era*, I, Cambridge, Mass. 1927, 125–216; G. **von Rad**, *Old Testament Theology* II, ET London and New York 1965, 319ff.; D. **Roessler**, *Gesetz und Geschichte in der spätjüdischen Apokalyptik*, WMANT 3, ²1962; A. A. **van Ruler**, *The Christian Church and the Old Testament*, ET Grand Rapids 1971; J. F. A. **Sawyer**, *From Moses to Patmos*, London 1977; M. **Smith**, *Palestinian Parties and Politics*, New York and London 1971; A. C. **Sundberg**, *The Old Testament of the Early Church*, Cambridge, Mass. and London 1964; 'The Protestant Old Testament Canon: Should it be Reexamined?', *CBQ* 28, 1966, 194–203; 'The "Old Testament": A Christian Canon', *CBQ* 30, 1968, 143–55; 'The Bible Canon and the Christian Doctrine of Inspiration', *Interp* 29, 1975, 352–71; W. C. **van Unnik**, 'ἡ καινὴ διαθήκη – A Problem in the early History of the Canon', *Studia Patristica* 4, TU 79, 1961, 212–27; C. **Westermann**, *The Old Testament and Jesus Christ*, ET Minneapolis 1970; H. H. **Wolf**, *Die Einheit des Bundes. Das Verhältnis von Altem und Neuem Testament bei Calvin*, Neukirchen 1958; L. B. **Wolfenson**, 'Implications of the Place of the Book of Ruth. .', *HUCA* 1, 1924, 177f.; W. **Zimmerli**, *The Law and the Prophets*, Oxford and Richmond, Va. 1965.

The major concern of this Introduction has been to describe the canonical shape of each of the Old Testament books within the context of Hebrew scriptures. In contrast to the usual historical critical approach I have sought to analyse the growth of the biblical literature in relation to its function as religious literature within a community faith and practice. The emphasis has fallen on the effect which the use of the material as scripture has left on the final form of the tradition.

However, a crucial issue still remains to be discussed. To speak of scripture is to raise the question regarding the religious community for whom this literature performs this function. Does the Hebrew Bible have the role of scripture for Jews alone or also for Christians? The issue emerges immediately even in the terminology used. Throughout this analysis I have followed the traditional Christian practice of employing the term 'Old Testament' when in fact I have been studying the Hebrew scriptures. Although I think that this less precise usage can be defended because of its long history in Western civilization – there is no good substitute in common parlance – the terminology does raise a basic theological issue which cannot be ignored. In what sense is the Hebrew Bible also the scripture of the Christian church?

<h1 style="text-align:center">I</h1>

Several strong arguments have been mounted in recent years by Christian scholars for sharply distinguishing between the Hebrew scriptures of Judaism and the Old Testament of Christianity. Although the issue has been given a new formulation by scholars such as A. C. Sundberg and H. Gese, the basic problem is one with which the Christian Church has wrestled since its inception without ever having reached a clear consensus.

The arguments for sharply distinguishing the Christian Old Testament from the Jewish scriptures can be conveniently treated under two aspects, the formal and the substantive, although there is considerable overlap between the two. First, from the formal side, it is argued that the Christian Old Testament differs markedly from the Hebrew Bible in terms of its text, its scope, and its order. In respect to the text, Christians have favoured Greek and Latin, rather than Hebrew; in respect to the scope, much of the church has included additional books beyond those of the Jewish canon; in respect to the order, the church has employed a form dependent on the arrangement of the Septuagint rather than the tripartite division of the Hebrew canon.

Secondly, from the substantive side the case is mounted that these formal features are only indicative of a far-reaching historical process which effected a fundamental rift between the two faiths. Thus, both Sundberg and Gese have argued that the present Hebrew Bible of the synagogue has been shaped by features peculiar to rabbinic Judaism (*Spätjudentum!*). The decisive forces which gave rise to Pharisaic Judaism arose in part from the political crises of the Roman rule which culminated in the destruction of Jerusalem, and in part from the inner socio-religious struggles among the conflicting ideologies of Graeco-Roman culture represented by such groups as the Samaritans, Essenes, apocalpytic sects, and Christians (cf. M. Smith). The effect of establishing Judaism in terms of halachic and haggadic traditions left its characteristic stamp also on the form of the Hebrew Bible. The Torah was given the dominant role, which subordinated the other parts of the Bible. The gift of prophecy was thought to have ended in the Persian period. The apocalpytic writings were largely excluded from the canon with the exception of Daniel which was subordinated by its position in the Hagiographa. The Masoretic tradition was assigned sole hegemony and rival textual traditions were suppressed.

In the light of this evidence Sundberg has argued impressively that the difference between the Jewish Bible and the Christian Old Testament arose not because the church added books or used a larger Alexandrian canon unknown in Palestine, but because of the narrowing process of rabbinic Judaism which eliminated from its canon a large body of previously authoritative writings. Similarly, Gese concludes categorically: 'Christian theology can never accept the Masoretic canon' ('Erwägungen', 16f.).

There is another line of argument which has been developed by Gese against identifying the Christian Old Testament with the Hebrew canon. He contends that the Christian Old Testament has its integrity only in reference to the New Testament. The formation of the New Testament brought the Old Testament to its historical conclusion and to its theological fulfilment. He envisions a unified process of tradition-building which extends from the Old Testament to the New Testament and stands in discontinuity with the Hebrew canon and Judaism.

Finally, there are a large number of traditional Christian arguments which have, in one way or another, stressed the discontinuity between the Christian faith and the Hebrew scriptures. For example, a contrast is made between the 'letter' of the Old Testament and the 'spirit' of the New, or between the 'tradition of the elders' and the authority of the 'living Christ', or between the historical orientation of the Old with the eschatological perspective of the New. Although basic theological issues are clearly involved, it lies beyond the scope of this chapter to address all these traditional problems (cf. D. L. Baker). Rather, the present discussion will focus on the more narrowly formulated problem of the Hebrew scriptures and the Christian Bible.

II

Before attempting to address the issues which have been raised by those who stress the discontinuity between the Christian Old Testament and the Hebrew Bible, it is significant to point out the implications which the canonical analysis of each Old Testament book in this Introduction has on the theological issues at stake. The historical and literary analysis of the various books of the Hebrew canon has sought to give evidence for a long and complex process of canonical shaping in which the role of the Hebrew tradents in collecting, transmitting, and ordering of the tradition played a decisive role. The experience of the Jewish community was in no way limited to an external and passive role, but was incorporated into scripture itself. It must again be emphasized that the community did not create scripture from its own experience. Neither ancient Israel nor later Judaism ever made such a claim. Rather, its response was to the authority of the divine Word which became incorporated into the message itself, testifying to the continuing divine initiative within the tradition.

Now the point to be emphasized is that the Christian Old Testament has taken over as its scripture Hebrew tradition which is largely in the same form which the shaping process of the Hebrew canon gave it. When one recalls both the length of the development in its oral and written stages, as well as the extent of the shaping process, then the full nature of the continuity between the Jewish and Christian Bibles becomes clear. The canonical book of Genesis was appropriated, not the book of Jubilees. The figure of Moses, the giver of the law, was received in an unchanged form from the book of Exodus. Even Esther found its place within the Christian Old Testament. Moreover, nowhere in the New Testament is the shape of the canonical scriptures of the synagogue repudiated or altered. The controversy of the Christian church with the Jewish synagogue turned on the *interpretation* of a common scripture. When viewed in the light of the entire canonical process, the formal differences between the two Bibles – text, scope, order – appear as minor variations within the one unified body of sacred tradition. The heart of the argument on the authority of the Hebrew scripture for the church does not turn on the occasionally controversial relationship between Jews and Christians in the first century AD, or on the exact date of the canon's closure, or even on the extent of the canonical boundaries, but on the decisive shape which the synagogue gave to the Hebrew scriptures during an extended period of growth. The crucial fact that the revelation was mediated through this historical community is the issue which is not called into question by a slightly differing form of its appropriation and subsequent ordering of the books.

Nevertheless, it is important to address the arguments in more detail which have been raised in order to stress the discontinuity between the Hebrew scriptures and the Old Testament. We begin with the formal and conclude with the substantive.

(a) Text

The argument that the Christian church is not restricted by or committed to the Hebrew text of the Masoretic tradition uses as its evidence the New Testament's use of the Septuagint which practice was continued by the church fathers. In addition, the final fixing of the Hebrew text in a stabilized form occurred in the period after the rise of Christianity, and is therefore hardly authoritative for Christians.

In the chapter on 'Text and Canon' (ch. IV), I have sought to deal with this issue from a canonical perspective. The major point to be made is that the early Christian church did not make any claims of having a better text than the Jews, as did for example the Samaritans. Rather, the early Christians who were themselves Jews, sought to establish the claims of Jesus Christ on the basis of the Jewish scriptures in whatever form was currently available. Obviously within a Hellenistic culture Greek was the *lingua franca*, but the recensional history of the Septuagint confirms its dependence upon a normative Hebrew text. It is a false biblicism to argue that because ancient Christians often used a Greek text, a warrant is thereby provided for dispensing with the Hebrew text. Rather, the theological issue at stake is the maintenance of a common scripture, between church and synagogue as witness to Jesus Christ, which is threatened if the Hebrew text is abandoned as the normative Old Testament text by the church.

(b) Scope

The argument that the scope of the Christian Old Testament should not be limited to the books of the Hebrew canon has traditionally been supported within the Roman church, and most recently by the new historical case made by Sundberg. The division within the Christian church on this issue only confirms the complexity of the problem. At least two major issues are involved.

The first issue again turns on the role of the Jews as bearers of the sacred tradition of Israel. The canonical process of selecting some books as authoritative from among a larger number has a parallel in the narrowing process involved in the establishing of the Masoretic text. The criteria for the selection remain largely obscure. However, literary and aesthetic judgments regarding the literature played little part, as is made plain by the retention of Obadiah and the exclusion of Ben Sira. It is also clear that the political, social, and religious factors, particularly the inner conflicts within the various circles of Judaism, left an impact on the canonical process. Obviously the entire canonical process reflects historical influences, not just the final period. Moreover, as I have sought to show in a previous chapter on the canon (ch. II), the closing of the Hebrew canon had been largely effected before the rise of Christianity. The 'Council' of Jamnia in the first century AD had nothing to do with its closing, but it rather confirmed the prior decisions of canonicity by the very nature of the debates as a scholastic exercise. Therefore, I do not agree with Sundberg's reconstruction of this history or his formulation of the theological problem. To take the canon seriously is also to take seriously the judgments which circumscribed the scope of the Hebrew canon. In no sense is a claim to the infallibility of the canonical process being defended, but rather the argument turns on Christian identification with the Jewish scriptures.

There is a second issue respecting the scope of the Hebrew canon as normative for the Christian Old Testament. Both Jews and Christians bring to the sacred scriptures of the Hebrew canon another set of normative religious traditions by which to interpret Israel's ancient tradition. For Judaism it was the tradition of the synagogue fathers now codified in the midrashim, Mishnah, and Talmuds; for Christianity the gospel of Jesus Christ found in the New Testament. Christians confess to understand the Old Testament from the perspective of the New, but the New serves to fulfil the Old, not to replace or destroy it. The expansion of the Christian Bible to include both an Old Testament and a New separates the Christian faith from the Jewish, but does not sever the common link with the scriptures of Israel.

In order to maintain a common scripture with Judaism I have argued that the scope of the Hebrew canon has also a normative role for the Christian Old Testament. However, it would perhaps be possible to argue for the inclusion of a larger canon, such as the Apocrypha, on the grounds that these books, like the New Testament, testify to the promise of the New without destroying the common link with the Old. Although I personally agree with the tradition of Jerome in supporting the Christian use of the Hebrew canon, I would not disparage the claims of those Christians who follow Augustine in supporting a larger canon. However, the basic theological issue for its inclusion turns on the ability to maintain the crucial canonical relationship between Christian and Jew. Up to now at least I have not seen this canonical argument for the inclusion of a larger canon adequately developed.

(c) Order

The problem of the arrangement of the books of the Hebrew canon into an order presents a somewhat different issue from that of text and scope. Although the tripartite division of the canon had been established at least by the second century BC, and is testified to by the New Testament (Luke 24.44), the order of books within the second and third divisions of the Hebrew canon varied greatly. In fact, an exact order of these sections was never settled, as a perusal of the orders in the various Jewish lists makes immediately clear (cf. Ryle, *Canon*, 280; Swete, *Introduction*, 200). In other words, the order within the Hebrew canon never achieved the same canonical status within Judaism as did the text and the scope.

I would argue for the priority of the Jewish tripartite division –

normative is now too strong a word – when dealing with the Hebrew Bible for the same theological reasons which have been outlined before, namely to confirm the role of the Jews as tradents of the canonical tradition. However, it should also be stressed that the Jewish order is, in no sense, a 'better' or 'original' order. Katz and Lebram have clearly demonstrated that other orders, such as those reflected in the Septuagint, were equally as old and were long rivals in Palestine of the tripartite division. Indeed, the tradition of twenty-two books with its implication for the original position of Ruth and Lamentations, is older than the Talmudic tradition of twenty-four books.

However, the question of the order of the books takes on a different face entirely when one speaks of the Christian Old Testament. The order of the Hebrew canon has no historical or theological claims for the Christian Bible. The order of the Christian Old Testament varies considerably within the church (cf. the lists in Sundberg, *Old Testament*, 58f.), but shares in common both a dependence on the Septuagint and a disregard for the tripartite division of the Hebrew canon. The chief point to be made is that Christians did not create a new order for their Old Testament, but chose an order from among the variety of options which best supported the Christian claim of a different understanding of the Old in terms of the New. Clearly a different theological interpretation was offered by the Christians assigning the book of Daniel to the prophets, and regrouping the tripartite division into a new sequence of legal, historical, poetical (or wisdom), and prophetical (cf. Leonard).

III

In addition to the arguments against the continuity of the Christian Old Testament with the Hebrew canon which are based on the formal differences, a case has been mounted for sharply distinguishing between the Christian and Jewish Bibles by some modern scholars who have buttressed the formal differences with further substantive reasons.

Sundberg has argued in several articles that the present shape of the Hebrew canon reflects the concerns of Pharisaic Judaism of the first century AD. In reacting to various historical forces of the period, Judaism narrowed the scope of the Hebrew traditions which were elsewhere represented in the late Hellenistic age in an effort to establish its own religious hegemony. Consequently, Christianity has been misled in holding to the narrow Hebrew canon of Judaism, but should embrace unreservedly the larger canon which includes the Apocryphal books. In my judgment, there are several important objections to Sundberg's arguments.

First of all, the 'Jewish quality' of the Old Testament, that is to say, those elements of closest continuity with rabbinic Judaism, are deeply embedded in the Old Testament and cannot be restricted to a late rabbinic redaction. One only has to recall the books of the Psalms, Ezra, Nehemiah, and Esther as well as the entire Priestly legislation of the Pentateuch to drive home this point. That elements within these books have often raised problems for the Christian church cannot be denied, but the issue is a theological one and cannot be resolved historically. The notion that the 'real' Old Testament is purely 'Hebrew' in character and was later distorted by Judaism is a legacy of Wellhausen which cannot be sustained either from a historical or theological perspective.

Secondly, the eschatological and apocalyptic emphasis of Christian theology which distinguishes it from rabbinic Judaism in certain decisive points is derived in the New Testament from Old Testament books which are within the present Hebrew canon (Isaiah, Ezekiel, Daniel, Joel, Zechariah). In spite of a passing reference in the New Testament to Enoch (Jude 14f.), the substance of Christian theology, especially when it differs from rabbinic Judaism, cannot be attributed to its dependence on material outside the Hebrew canon. Indeed, the remarkable lack of citations from the books of the Apocrypha within the New Testament speaks against Sundberg's thesis of the theological need for a larger canon.

Thirdly, the polemical statements of the New Testament which disparage aspects of rabbinic Judaism as merely 'tradition of the elders' rather than divine revelation (e.g. Matt. 15.1ff.) are never attached to the books of the Hebrew canon as such. The controversy turns always on the interpretation of a commonly held sacred scripture (e.g. Matt. 9.10ff.; 15.1ff.; 19.3ff., 16ff.; 22.41ff.). Moreover, the New Testament writers have so identified with the Jewish canon that they can often adopt post-biblical midrashic traditions which extend far beyond the form of the Hebrew canon itself (I Cor. 10.1ff.; II Cor. 3.12ff.). In sum, although Sundberg has made a major contribution in his destruction of the thesis of an Alexandrian canon, his application of this evidence to stress the discontinuity of the Christian Old Testament with the Jewish canon cannot be deemed a success.

A very different case, which is based largely on literary and theological grounds, has been mounted by H. Gese to demonstrate that the Christian church cannot accept the Hebrew canon as normative scripture. He argues that the Old Testament and the New Testament form a unity on the basis of a tradition-building process which has been independent of the development of the Hebrew canon. Indeed, essential elements of the Christian Old Testament are threatened unless the sharp distinction between its form and that of the Jewish Bible is maintained. In my judgment, Gese's position cannot be sustained either historically or theologically.

In the first place, recent New Testament research has increasingly confirmed the observation that the early Christians read the Old Testament as a book of sacred writings, and shared in this respect the hermeneutical axioms of both Qumran and rabbinic Judaism. In other words, the New Testament writers received the Hebrew tradition in its canonical form and did not stand outside the Jewish community in a new tradition-building process. Indeed, a major problem with von Rad's *Old Testament Theology* is that he has failed to deal with the canonical forces at work in the formation of the traditions into a collection of scripture during the post-exilic period, but rather set up the New Testament's relation to the Old in an analogy to his description of the pre-exilic growth of Hebrew tradition. Gese's thesis not only builds on this fundamental weakness of von Rad, but even extends the concept of tradition in such a way as to exacerbate the problem to an extreme. As a result, the canonical process is completely disregarded in his theological construction and replaced by a phenomenology of tradition which is neither historically or theologically defensible (cf. Blank, and H.-J. Kraus, *Bibl.-theol. Studien*).

IV

There is another aspect to the problem of relating the Hebrew Bible to the Christian Old Testament which arises from the side of Judaism and which has been forcefully presented by L. B. Wolfenson.

He distinguishes between two different senses of the term 'canon'. The first sense denotes a traditional or classic collection of religious writings and is synonymous in Judaism with the term Bible. The second sense denotes a norm of recognized regulations for faith and practice. Wolfenson denies that the whole Hebrew canon ever had such a normative role for Judaism in this second sense of canon. Only the Torah was considered normative, that is to say, legally and morally binding, and by the term Torah was included the interpretation of the Mishnah and Gemara as well.

There are at least two distinct issues involved in Wolfenson's argument, a historical and a theological. From the historical perspective it can be contested whether his assertion regarding the authoritative role of the whole Hebrew canon is correct for early Judaism. Although it is obvious that the primary authority rested with the Torah, the history of the canonization of the Hebrew Bible testifies to some form of authority accorded to the whole Bible which was far more important for Judaism than Wolfenson acknowledged. In this regard Leiman's analysis of the historical process of canonization appears to be closer to the mark (cf. ch. II).

However, regarding the theological problem, if Wolfenson's description of the Jewish attitude towards the canon is correct even for later, post-Talmudic Judaism then he has indeed focused on a basic theological difference toward the use of the Bible which distinguishes Judaism from Christianity. The issue at stake turns on the extent to which the later theological developments of both Judaism and Christianity acquire priority over the canonical witness of the Hebrew scriptures. However, to deal seriously with this set of problems is a major task for Jewish and Christian theology which exceeds the scope of this chapter. Wolfenson's point does appear to lend support to those who stress the elements of discontinuity between the two faiths.

V

To conclude, the problem for Christian theology in delineating the relation of its Bible to the Hebrew canon can perhaps best be summarized in terms of a delicate balance between the elements of continuity and discontinuity, which both unite and separate. The point is not to defend a mediating position between extremes, but to establish the proper theological dialectic between the Old and the New.

The threat which is posed by overemphasizing the discontinuity between the Christian Bible and the Hebrew scripture is that of severing the ontological relationship between Christianity and Judaism. The Old Testament becomes simply background material for the New and must be either ignored or christianized if it is to remain in the Christian Bible. As a result, not only is the theological integrity of the Old Testament sacrificed, but also the New Testament is rendered unintelligible and vulnerable to heresy.

The threat which is posed by overemphasizing the continuity between the Old Testament and the Hebrew scriptures is that of destroying the integrity of the Christian Bible. The Christian church confesses to find a witness to Jesus Christ in both the Old Testament and the New. Its Bible does not consist of the Hebrew scriptures plus an appendix called the New Testament. Rather, the form of the Christian Bible as an Old and New Testament lays claim upon the whole scripture as the authoritative witness to God's purpose in Jesus Christ for the church and the world. By reading the Old Testament along with the New as Christian scripture a new theological context is formed for understanding both parts which differs from hearing each Testament in isolation. The Old Testament is interpreted by the New, and the New is understood through the Old, but the unity of its witness is grounded in the One Lord.

INDEX OF AUTHORS